PRINTED IN THE UNITED STATES OF AMERICA
THE CORDAY & GROSS COMPANY, CLEVELAND, OHIO

The House of
GOODYEAR

FIFTY YEARS OF MEN AND INDUSTRY

1949
By Hugh Allen

P. W. LITCHFIELD
Chairman of The Board
The Goodyear Tire and Rubber Company

VI

Dedication

. . . A New England Yankee, with a technical training and a heritage of adventure (the latter reaching back to the Clipper ships and the Mayflower)—who started in as superintendent of a very small plant in 1900, saw it grow to world-wide size—whose industrial career saw the whole automotive age emerge—and the aeronautic age—and with them, far-reaching changes in transportation, commerce, agriculture, warfare and in all human relations—who has seen new relationships grow up in industry between management and men, new opportunities created for men of talent and energy and character, and higher standards of living for all his countrymen, as a result of these various factors—and who himself has made some contribution during the 48 years to these results. The story of Litchfield and Goodyear is fairly representative of the opportunities for men and society in the free economic system, under which America has moved to the forefront of the nations of the world. The story is written as the Goodyear Company reaches its 50th anniversary in 1948.

Contents

BOOK 1. Building a World-Wide Company.

BOOK 2. Goodyear in World War II.

BOOK 3. Postwar Developments.

BOOK

1

1898-1940

Building A World-Wide Organization

The Biography of a Business House

House of Goodyear

Introduction

THE recent world war was a challenge to the Private Enterprise system and to the Mass Production program which it had developed in America in the past fifty years.

This was a war of supply, to a greater degree than in any previous war. Millions of men fighting on the five continents had to have food, clothing, housing, air fields, radio and radar installations, harbors, bases, shipping and all the equipment of modern warfare. It was a war of machines, fast-moving, hard-hitting, intricate and complicated machines, taking long to build.

These our enemies had, and we did not, except in token measure. Calculating the odds, they had collected supplies and weapons well in advance and in such volume as to make victory swift and certain, assure dominance for a thousand years—a goal they came closer to realizing than it is comfortable even yet to contemplate.

To a very considerable extent it was American industry which upset these calculations. The war was won in the factory as well as on the battle front.

Our enemies underrated the American people, thought we had grown soft and sluggish with prosperity and easy living, that isolationism was merely a mask for a people not too proud to fight, but who did not want to fight, had lost the militant qualities of earlier years.

They did not dream that America could turn out 10,000,000 of the finest fighting men in the world.

But raw courage is not enough in mechanized war. And the history of the world would have been far different if Germany and Japan had remotely visioned the possibility that United States, starting from be-

I

hind scratch, would be able so quickly to overtake them, to match machine with machine, produce ships and guns, planes and tanks which would outrange and outslug theirs, and in such overwhelming volume as to win control of the air and the sea, and to send its land forces smashing like a juggernaut across half the continent of Europe.

And not only be able to supply its own vast armies, but produce enough more to help England and Russia stay in the war, and to maintain our home economy, with hardly a trace of an austerity regime.

Production was America's real surprise weapon in this war. It is perhaps not too strong a statement to say that it was Supply which turned the balance toward final victory—with all the implications which victory in that struggle involve.

Into that effort our great industries poured every ounce of power, used every production trick learned in the years of peace. Steel was in it, Petroleum, Automotive, Rubber, Chemicals, Textiles and a hundred more; ship builders, plane builders, engine builders; transportation by tankers and tank cars, by freight cars and trucks carrying freight-car loads, by cargo planes and merchant ships loaded to the gunwales; into it, too, went mechanized mining, logging, and agriculture.

America has never been a scientific-minded nation like Germany. It did not have the patience. It had never been a trading nation, like England. It had huge home markets, closer at hand. But it had large natural resources. It had great practical gifts, the knack of taking an idea and making it work. It had mechanical gifts, widely diffused. Farm-born enlisted men who knew all about tractors and diesel engines, and city-bred ones who knew cars and radios and motor boats, contributed much to the nation's industrial power in peace time, and in the war were able to put a plane or tank back in service with a pair of pliers and a wrench, or keep a damaged submarine moving forward to its rendezvous, something not apt to happen in other armies.

But beyond all that America "invented," if one may use the word, a system of large-scale, low-cost production, something distinctively American, the technique which made it possible for the individual to increase his productive capacity with less effort, and so for United States in time of war to out produce as well as out fight enemies bent on world conquest.

This is not a brief for industry, or for this industry. It is the story of a business house which started on a shoe string fifty years ago and grew to large size. It is a factual report with only an occasional nudge of the elbow toward principles and policies, written primarily for an internal audience, the 75,000 men and women in this country and abroad who have worked together over the years under the Goodyear flag.

If the story is properly written, however, it may throw light on the significant half century in which it grew up. That period saw America change from an agricultural nation to the most powerful industrial country in the world. It saw the evolution of Big Business, with whatever advantages and disadvantages went with that. It saw the development of the Piecework System, under which men were paid not for the time they put in but for the products they turned out. It saw the creation of the Mass Production System, which utilized machinery, scientific layout and methods, expedited transportation, including conveyors, to increase output and drive back-breaking hand labor out of the factory, the device by which the industrial miracle was achieved that America could pay the world's highest wages and yet match costs with low wage nations.

The period too saw business come into a more enlightened attitude towards its employees and their wages. Industry came to realize that it could make more money not by holding wages down, but by giving men the incentive of high wages to turn out better goods and more of them. Wages in such industries had gone up by the middle 1930's voluntarily, without pressure from government or agitation by employees, from a dollar a day to a dollar an hour.

Business came into new viewpoint toward the customer. It concluded that rather than charge the customer as much as the traffic would bear, it would make more money by taking a small profit on a larger volume of business, placing its products within the reach of more people, actually sharing the wealth it was creating.

It made the revolutionary discovery that the employee was also a customer, for its own and other men's goods.

Industry reached the conclusion that no business house could afford to make too much money, because that would invite competition to spilt up the market. Better to turn profits back to the public in the form of lower prices. Low production costs and good wages expanded markets which in turn created still more jobs in beneficient cycle.

The period brought increased national wealth and rising standards of living and Americans owned more automobiles, telephones, radios, washing machines and electric refrigerators, took out more insurance, sent more boys to college than any other nation. American workmen were better paid, lived better, had greater opportunities than any others.

However through the years we came to think of good times as automatic, that Business would always have jobs at good wages for everyone wanting them. The brief but violent 1920 depression came on to remind us of the facts of economic life, but it was not till the more protracted one of the 1930's that these were really brought home, with repercussions to be discussed later in this narrative.

Our first impulse was resentment. Business had let us down. The Private Enterprise system, which had made America the envy of the world, was through. Government must take over, men cried. That was a curious and critical period in our history.

That men within the government should advance doctrines of government control is not surprising. Ambitious and strong-willed men have appeared many times in history seeking to persuade or compel the people to accept their rule. That is no new phenomenon. The amazing thing is that so many people in a nation having a history of freedom like ours, should be so ready to accept such a doctrine, be willing to turn the ordering of their lives over to anyone.

Business of course is far from perfect, nor will be as long as men are free to order their lives as they choose. There are strong men in business, as are in government, ambitious men, ruthless men, men who make mistakes. Society must be on the alert in the future as in the past to safeguard against abuses, to root out evils, to keep competition free and keep it fair.

But government regulation must be based on an understanding of what business is, and what forces govern it, things confused during that period of distress and conflict.

In any society where competition is free, a business house can grow large or even remain in the field only as it serves society, and to the extent that it does so. The consumer must be served, or he will go elsewhere.

Private enterprise does not provide jobs at all times for everyone willing to work. We had a shortage of men one year, a shortage of jobs in another, and the number of men affected grew larger as the industrial system grew more complex, and due to better communication we were more conscious of them. But the system has worked out over the long run for the greatest good to the greatest number.

The system emphasized opportunity, rather than the stability characteristics of older and more static nations. It did not guarantee that a man could work at a given job all his life, it offered him something better, gave him a chance to start in at the bottom and drive through to the top.

The system did not provide that a man's sons would take his place in the shop when he grew too old to work; it offered him a chance to send his boy to M.I.T., or Michigan, get a technical training which would enable him to go farther, make more out of his life.

The system took seniority and service into consideration, but did not let age slow down the eager pace of youth and ability. It did not guarantee that a man could hold his job as long as he had seniority over his fellows, but it promised that a man who could do a superior job would almost never be out of work.

We tried to legislate Security into a system based on Opportunity. Security and Opportunity may not be found in the same package. A nation constituted as America was preferred opportunity, which was largely the secret of the nation's growth to world leadership.

We tried in that period to protect people against themselves, but in doing so we put the brakes on an open-handed nation which did not too much mind taking a chance and losing, as long as there was a chance of hitting the jackpot. We pegged our losses, but we pegged our gains as well.

Economics in the final analysis is simply a man getting hungry and doing something about it. Every man must be fed, clothed, sheltered. Meeting those needs is primarily his own responsibility. The world owes no one a living merely because he was born into it. His ways of achieving that result are also largely of his own choosing.

The oncoming generation should understand the essential Capital-Labor-Consumer relationship on which a sound economy in a democracy rests—for it will have to apply these fundamentals under changing world conditions.

There is a parallel on the surface between the situation in America after World War I and World War II—an eager demand for consumer goods, rising wages and prices. But the parallel does not continue through.

The productivity of the individual worker went up after the first war, went up faster than wages and so created new capital to meet the increasing need for more and better production tools—buildings, machines, transportation, research equipment.

But productivity trended down rather than up after the second war, created no such surplus capital; public debt went up beyond anything previously dreamed of, took its tithe out of every dollar value created; and the production of additional tools is handicapped by rising prices. A factory which cost $100,000 in 1940 might cost $300,000 in 1948.

Increasing demands for goods must have capital to provide facilities of production. That is not being created as before, and the people who have capital grow reluctant to invest it in industry, because of the declining rate of return, and the growing belief promoted by groups seeking disunity that capital is not entitled to a return anyway.

A second factor: America came out of the first war without an enemy in the world. It went through the second war as a united nation, with little subversive activities to prevent maximum output.

But the outlook for continued peace is not as good in 1948 as it was in 1918 and, due to the cracks in the wall of national unity, we may not be able to do a proportionately good job of war production in World War III, if that comes, as we did in War II.

These are immediate problems for the men who will head America's industries tomorrow and for the next 50 years, but they are problems as well for every citizen. Our continued growth as a nation rests on the public's understanding of the necessity of maintaining a balance between capital, labor and the consumer.

The story of Goodyear or of any large-size business house, may throw light on these things.

1. The Running Story

The Beginning Days (1898-1908)

IN THE spring of 1898 a young man in his late 30's, farm-born, with a gift for business, had a chance to pick up a vacant factory in Akron, Ohio, at a bargain price. He was broke and in debt, but he borrowed enough money to make a $3500 down payment, gave notes running four years for the $10,000 balance, and in the next 20 years ran this into a hundred million dollar business, the largest tire company in America—and then lost it—for such are the hazards of business.

Another young man, who came to Akron in the summer of 1900, a New Englander in his early 20's, took the helm in 1926, carried the company on to world dimensions with plants in 12 foreign countries, still holding first place in the industry up to the present day, and able to deliver upwards of a billion dollars a year in imperative war materiel during World War II.

In the story of Frank Seiberling, Paul W. Litchfield and the 50 years of the Goodyear company can be traced all of the business forces which during that period have made America a great industrial nation.

The last thing in Frank Seiberling's mind, when he set out on a business trip to Chicago 50 years ago, was to buy any more property. He went there to try to liquidate some he already had.

Starting with mowers and reapers the Seiberlings had built up a big business, expanded into cereal mills, strawboard, banking, had street railways in Akron, Cleveland and Zanesville, one of the first interurban lines in the country between Cleveland and Akron.

They had their ups and downs but always came back. Frank Seiberling, the older son, had had to leave Heidelberg College and his brother, Charles, to leave Oberlin in one of the down periods of the family fortunes.

The depression of 1893, however, had dealt a heavy blow to the Seiberling empire, and they lost control of one after another of their various enterprises. It was in this connection that Frank Seiberling was in Chicago. He met a business acquaintance on the street, talked a minute.

"By the way, Frank," said the other man, "keep your eyes open for someone who will take that old strawboard plant in Akron off our hands. It has been idle for five years, is eating its head off in taxes."

Seiberling knew the property. It was out in East Akron, back of the Seiberling's former cereal mill, two rundown buildings facing each other across the Little Cuyahoga River, with a small power plant and seven acres of land.

"What are you asking for it?" he inquired.

"We have $140,000 invested in it," the man replied, "but we'd take $50,000 for it."

"You'll be lucky to get half that," said Seiberling.

The man thought a moment. "We might even sell it for $25,000," he said.

A bell rang in Seiberling's fast-thinking mind. The depression was passing, he was 38 years old, there was still money to be made in the world. This might be it.

"Cut that in two and I'll buy it myself," he said.

The man hesitated, but only briefly. "Add another thousand dollars and it is yours," he said.

That is how the Goodyear Tire and Rubber Company started, and why the original property was purchased for the odd sum of $13,500.

Seiberling went back to Akron that night, owning a property he had never intended to buy. He did not know what he would do with it, or how he was going to pay for it.

However, he roused Lucius Miles, his brother-in-law, out of bed the next morning, borrowed the $3500 to close the deal, and in a few days had decided what business he would go into, picked a name, a trade mark and was selling stock.

The business would be rubber.

That industry had grown slowly in the first 50 years after Charles Goodyear's discovery of vulcanization in 1839, footwear, raincoats, belting, hose and molded goods being manufactured mostly in small plants in New England—though Dr. Goodrich had started a factory in Akron in 1870.

The bicycle boom of the 1890's, however, had given new life to the industry, particularly in the now awakening manufacturing area of the middle west. Goodrich got on its feet, soon had three competitors in Akron, Barber, the "match king," next door, the Pfeiffer brothers, druggists, making rubber gloves and other sundries and Kelly-Springfield, who moved up from down state. The business looked good, and Akron had workmen who knew how to run mills and calenders.

Seiberling named his company after Charles Goodyear, honoring the founder of the industry, who had died broke in 1860. None of the Goodyear family were in the rubber business or connected with the new company.

For a trade mark he recalled a statuette of the wing-footed Mercury on the banister of the stairway of his home. It seemed to him a symbol of speed. The company was incorporated on August 29, 1898.

Looking around for capital he noted that the sewer pipe industry had survived the depression better than other Akron companies, and he had a connection there through another brother-in-law, Henry Manton, large stockholder in Robinson Clay Products, the biggest company. Manton put some money in the business, and served as a director almost continuously until his death in 1941. David E. Hill, head of the rival clay company was persuaded to put in some money on the argument that another factory in East Akron would increase the value of his real estate holdings. He bought $20,000 of stock and later $10,000 for his son and became the first president of the company.

Goodyear started with a capital stock of $100,000, of which $43,500 worth was paid in.

Two men were hired in July to put the building in shape, Hippensteal, a machinist, and Swartz, a carpenter, Goodyear's first employees. The plant had been idle for several years, floors had rotted, machinery had rusted and most of the windows had been broken, since the window of any empty building was an irresistible target then as now to a boy with a stone.

Seiberling picked up some second-hand mills to mix the rubber on, and calenders to spread it on fabric, found a couple of old boilers in the scrap heap of the street car company he had formerly operated, got a few orders for bicycle and carriage tires, and late in November was ready to start. To open the company under good auspices, he brought his young daughter out to turn on the steam, start the mills turning.

It is sometimes thought that business is somehow automatic, that if you put in so much money, materials, machinery, manpower, there will be a market waiting for your merchandise, a market big enough to pay all expenses. However, thousands of enterprises, better financed than Goodyear have been launched since 1898 and have gone on the rocks.

Seiberling started from scratch. As a shrewd buyer he might get his machinery on long-term payments, but his raw materials would come in C.O.D. for several years, and for a long time Hills, the company dray-man, could unload from the box cars in the yards only as much rubber as the company could manage to pay for. Workmen had to be paid in cash every Saturday night, and there were hundreds of weeks in the first Goodyear decade when Seiberling or someone had to scurry around half a day or half a week, getting together enough money to meet the payroll.

Nor was there any assurance that goods once fabricated could be sold for enough money to recover what had gone into them in wages and materials—or be sold at all. No one was clamoring for its merchandise. There were plenty of other companies making as good or better goods. Goodyear would have to fight even for a toehold, and its entry into various fields would be resented by others already established there. And even though it was able to find customers, the money from those sales would get back to Akron long after the wages and material bills that went into that merchandise had been paid out.

In the gamble of business the workman was fairly safe. He could not lose more than a week's wages at the worst. The suppliers of materials were protected as long as they shipped C.O.D. But the men who put their money into the company, whether by normal advances of credit, taking the company's notes or buying stock, realized fully the hazard that attended the venture.

For several years Seiberling was continually borrowing money and trying to sell stock to meet payrolls and pay for materials. There were times when anyone could have bought the entire business for a song— in fact, the story was that Seiberling often carried a bill of sale around with him on the chance that he might find someone to take the company off his hands.

Years later some of the people who refused to accept stock and demanded notes would take a melancholy pleasure figuring their might-have-beens. For an investment in Goodyear then was a hundred-to-one shot. A $100 share of stock in 1900 would be worth $9600 20 years later and averaged over the years would have paid cash dividends of $143 each year.

Outside of being underfinanced, there were other factors.

As a location for rubber manufacturing, Akron, then a town of 42,000, was both good and bad. Part of the Western Reserve, it had been settled by Yankees from Connecticut who brought their manufacturing traditions with them. Other like-minded settlers had come in, thrifty Pennsylvania Dutch, and home-seekers from England and Ireland and, after Carl Shurtz' rebellion, freedom loving refugees from Germany.

In the exciting years after the Civil War, men had started half a dozen industries on a shoe string, built them to national stature. Important companies like Diamond Match, Quaker Oats, International Harvester, American Tin Plate, American Sewer Pipe—and some of the railroads—had a part or all of their roots in this little community.

It was the era of the entrepreneur, and Frank Seiberling early caught the idea that a young man getting out of school should not look for a job working for someone else, but start something of his own. The whole business community had turned out to help Dr. Goodrich get started.

But if the atmosphere of Akron was sympathetic to industry, physical factors were adverse. Its geography was against it. Rubber had to be shipped in from Brazil and Africa, the best grade of cotton came from the Sea Islands off the Georgia coast or the Nile Valley of Egypt, and Akron was an inland town, with no water transportation and below average rail transportation. Moreover, rubber processing requires a large amount of water for cooling purposes, and Akron lay on the divide between the St. Lawrence and Mississippi River systems, and in later years the city would have to build a ring of dams around its borders to conserve what water there was.

The timing, however, was good. If the bicycle had given stimulus to rubber manufacture, the automobile would create a demand greater than anyone dreamed of. The horseless carriage might not amount to much for another ten years, but after that the industry would grow as none had done in the history of the world. Goodyear, starting with the automobile, would grow with it.

The narrative divides itself into three phases: the years 1898-1908 when the company was fighting for a place in the sun; 1908-1920 when matching the amazing stride of the automobile industry, it staged a drive for leadership which, through sustained power and an enthusiasm, could almost be called devotion, reached its objective in eight years—only to come a cropper at the end; then the period of 1921 to date, when less spectacularly but solidly the financial structure was rebuilt, the gains made in production and sales were consolidated, and the foundation laid for the long future which must always be planned for, if a corporation is to continue permanently after death or circumstance has removed the genius of its founders.

We might now introduce the individuals who built the house of Goodyear. Frank and Charles Seiberling have been out of the Goodyear picture now for many years, but any history which failed to take their contributions into account would be not only incomplete, but unintelligent.

Seiberling had inherited mechanical gifts from his father, was ingenious in getting out of tight places, had great talents of persuasion, courage that flamed high when things were at their worst and, above all, was quick to recognize an opportunity and act on it.

Perhaps the single thing most responsible for Goodyear's rapid growth was that as Litchfield came up with a better product, Seiberling would stake everything on it, shoot double or nothing. It was perhaps fortunate that it was rubber he decided to go into. He might conceivably have tired of a business with more limited capabilities. Rubber would give full scope to his gifts in finance, tax even the daring of his imagination.

Seiberling contributed another idea important to his business, and to modern business generally. Up to that time most American business houses had been one-man companies, with a single forceful personality dominating it. Few men are so well balanced that they can be equally outstanding in production, engineering, sales and finance.

Seiberling realized he would have his hands full providing the finances to keep the company's head above water, looked around for men who could handle other phases of the business. He found two such men shortly—Litchfield in manufacturing, in 1900, and G. M. Stadelman in sales in 1902. Both were in striking contrast to the dynamic Seiberling.

Litchfield, a graduate (1896) from Massachusetts Institute of Technology, was one of the first technically trained men to go into the business. In his senior year at college he had spent his week ends visiting various New England factories, had selected the rubber industry deliberately, as his life pursuit. The factories were about the least attractive

.A.SEIBERLING, (1859-   )
Dynamic, fast thinking

C. W. SEIBERLING, (1861-1946)
Left imprint of humanity

P. W. LITCHFIELD, (1875-   )
Joined company in formative years

.M.STADELMAN, (1872-1926)
/rote sales policy for industry

Wm. STEPHENS, (1877-1932)
Demanded–and gave–fair play

W. C. STATE, (1871-1933)
Built machines and factories

he visited, dirty, smelly, not too prosperous, little touched by research
and experiment. He made his decision, not because rubber was a successful industry, but because it was a backward one, with much needing
to be done.

Planning his career carefully, he worked for three different eastern companies in the next four years, starting as a compounder, then fore-man, to get the feel of production. During this period he had built some automobile tires for the Locomobile car and the Waltham Orient, also for Richard Croker's 5th Avenue bus line. That is how Seiberling heard about him.

Litchfield was a man of strong convictions, with a passion for improvement, and quality was almost a religion to him.

Just as Litchfield was to earn the name of one of the great production leaders of the United States, Stadelman came to be rated as one of its great sales managers. Though Stadelman would be almost the last man one would pick out as a salesman. He was intellectual, kindly, under-standing, shy, almost gentle. In his 20 years in charge of Goodyear sales he never made a speech. He avoided crowds. He had, however, foresight, the gift of analysis, integrity, a high sense of honor, and personal qualities which won for him the support of his men and the confidence of the industry.

C. W. Seiberling's imprint may not be found as clearly anywhere in sales, production or administration, but it was everywhere pervasive, knitting the organization together, keeping it a unified group which worked and played together. Charley Seiberling knew every man in the organization by his first name, could always manage to find time to visit the sick and injured, was a moving spirit in every employee picnic or baseball game, danced alike with 16-year-olds and grandmothers, was never too busy to listen to anybody's troubles or to congratulate him on his new baby. The family spirit that came to characterize the organization largely reflected the contagious humanity of C. W. Seiberling.

Goodyear's thinking in the early period was directed by men who, as one looks back on it, seem ideally suited to take maximum advantage of the situation at the turn of the century. Seiberling, Litchfield and Stadelman were different in temperament, but the convictions of each comple-mented those of the others.

All were deeply interested in the development of the automobile. If their approach to the subject was different, they agreed exactly as to what Goodyear should do about it. Seiberling was the business man, quick to see an opportunity, and saw this as an opportunity. Stadelman was a student, an analyst of markets. Litchfield was a man of vision, could see well beyond the end of his nose, saw the automobile as something much larger than a successor to the horse-drawn carriage, with possibilities limited to the number of horses it would replace. If the automobile could be made practical and popular, it would revolutionize transporta-tion, bring plenty of demand for rubber tires. How practical the automobile might become depended to an extent at least on the tires it would ride on. It could go no faster nor farther than its shoes could carry it.

Litchfield held the basic conviction too that a company's job was not merely to turn out goods for which there was a current demand. He believed it should build only those goods which were definitely useful to society, for demand in that case would follow automatically. If this new system of transportation could be brought into existence, it would bring wealth and power to his company.

Seiberling had decided on three main lines of rubber products— bicycle tires, a booming business, carriage tires, just getting under way but having great promise, and the new field of automobile tires which might prove the most important of all. The company also made rubber bands, horseshoe pads, druggist sundries and smaller items, to furnish some revenue as business was built up on the major products.

The bicycle was an important discovery in the 1890's, particularly when pneumatic tires came in. It would carry men faster and farther than a horse could. Bicycling was good exercise, exhilarating, took people out of doors. It was a social vehicle. A party of people could start off together, stop where they chose, make up their route as they went along. The bicycle needed no oats or hay or gasoline, made powerful appeal to people who had travelled previously only by train or boat, or horse and wagon. There were cycle clubs in every town. The young men wore visored caps and pants guards, the more daring of the young ladies went about in flowing bloomers. As Litchfield rode out to the plant that first day he might have heard someone playing on the piano a popular song of the day:

> "And you would look sweet
> Upon the seat
> Of a bicycle
> Built for two."

Everybody was riding bicycles and its vogue promised to continue indefinitely. So bicycle tires looked like a good business, and there were accessories, such as handle bar grips, pedals, rubber plugs that you stuck into a puncture, repair material, and even a luggage carrier which you could carry your dinner bucket on, or if a female, your shawl.

The second item was carriage tires. After centuries of jolting people along on steel rims the carriage manufacturers had discovered rubber, and to take the young lady of your choice, or even your second choice, out riding on a Sunday afternoon in a rubber-tired buggy, was the 1900 idea of a good time. Carriage manufacture was a growing business, even though it used solid rubber tires rather than pneumatic in large measure.

What the automobile might amount to no one could guess. But it could travel faster than a horse and buggy, took less effort than a bicycle, and people might take to it.

All these profitable lines of business had been discovered by other companies and their manufacture was in strong hands. Competition would be severe.

However, the company soon encountered a more formidable obstacle, one which might prevent it from going into any of these lines at all. This was patents.

The most successful type of bicycle tires were built under the Tillinghast patent owned by Hartford Rubber, the best carriage tire under the Grant patent owned by Kelly-Springfield. In automobile tires, the patent owners and licensees of the standard type, the clincher, had formed an association, a common procedure at that time, which could say who might enter the field and how many tires he might build.

Manufacturing rights were granted to other companies, but the patent owners were under no obligation to grant a license to anyone who asked for it. Kelly-Springfield refused Goodyear a license. The Tillinghast patent owners issued a license but revoked it when the company began to get too much business. The Clincher Tire Association granted a license, but with the stipulation that Goodyear could have only 1¾ per cent of the nation's tire business.

This period when Goodyear started was a critical one in the nation's industrial history. It was the era of trusts, combines and the beginnings of Big Business. Human nature being what it is, it was natural that companies in a given field would resent competitors coming in to split up the market and try to keep them out. Modern industry was at the crossroads. Whether it would prove a useful tool in making the United States a great nation, or whether competition would be throttled lay in the balance.

America would have to decide, and did decide, under the fighting leadership of Theodore Roosevelt, whether it would hold to the principles of free competition.

Goodyear, a fighting company, refused to be barred from any field it wanted to enter, or to be content with crumbs of business begrudgingly granted. It chose to fight. That decision may have some significance as showing the effect of liberty on a country. Perhaps in an older nation where there was less individual freedom, men would have accepted the situation and quit. But Americans do not like to be told that they cannot do something they have set their heart on. The rest of the automobile industry would meet a similar situation soon in the Selden patent.

The decision to break through the patent blockade was important to the company as well. It made Goodyear. To succeed it would have to fall back on its fullest resourcefulness, and devise products which did not conflict with the patent—and the new product would have to be better, or the public would have none of it.

These difficulties started almost before the company opened its doors. Seiberling did not know that any patents were involved in carriage tires until he read an article in the newspaper on Christmas day, 1898, that the Grant patent had been declared valid. The next morning Kelly-Springfield came in with notification that he could continue to manufacture carriage tires only under its license. Seiberling applied for a license but, after some delay, it was refused, on the advice of other licensees who knew Seiberling's mettle, thought he might be a dangerous competitor. Seiberling got mad, decided to go ahead anyhow.

Kelly filed an infringement suit, and a desist order was upheld by the courts. Goodyear appealed. The court ordered it to put up a bond of $1,000,000. Seiberling got this reduced to $250,000 and persuaded another brother-in-law, R. C. Penfield of Willoughby, Ohio, to post the bond for him.

Then he called in Joe Burroughs, head of carriage tire sales, figured manufacturing costs down to the lowest possible point, sent him out after business. It was a declaration of war.

Burroughs came back with contracts from three of the largest carriage manufacturers in the country. The business was taken, however, with a Damocles sword over the heads of the young company. All of its profits from carriage tire sales must be held in escrow until the higher courts ruled on the Goodyear appeal. If Goodyear lost, it might be wiped out. But the little company had the courage of its convictions, went ahead as if there was no impediment.

Despite these difficulties the little company did a $500,000 business, with a profit of $35,000, in its first full year, and started work on a new office building on Market Street in the winter of 1900.

This last was a characteristic Seiberling gesture. Charles Dick, congressman from the Akron district, was chairman of the Republican National Committee, directing McKinley's campaign for re-election under the "full dinner pail" slogan. He was also a Goodyear director, having been a partner of L. C. Miles, Seiberling's brother-in-law, in the feed business. The long depression of 1893 was passing, and Dick painted a bright picture of rising prosperity if the Republicans won.

Seiberling caught it up.

"I offer a motion," he said. "If McKinley wins, we will build a new office building."

A handsome two-story structure, still part of the present General Office building, went up immediately after the election.

Litchfield, 25, but looking younger and wearing a high choker collar and derby hat, joined the company in July of that year.

Al Cunnington, head of the shipping room, looked up curiously as he saw the stranger going around the plant, asked Ed Viers, carriage tire builder, who he was.

"Hadn't you heard?" said Viers. "He's the new super. Name is Litchfield."

"That kid!" Cunnington exclaimed.

Probably Litchfield too was not too much impressed by the Goodyear he found, a little group of frame buildings lying in the creek valley off the highway, with a dirt road leading down to it, vacant land and cow pastures around. There was a red barn on Market Street, where Ohio C. Barber, another of Akron's early entrepreneurs had worked with his father after the Civil War, dipping pieces of wood into sulphur, then peddling them around the neighborhood, the beginnings of the Diamond Match Company.

Barber had built a new plant, and Goodyear was using the old barn to house its horses and wagons. There were just 176 people on the payroll, factory and everybody—of whom only Cunnington, Viers and George Swartz, the first foreman, were still around 50 years later, Goodyear's Old Guard.

Litchfield had an offer from another Akron company in his pocket, a better-financed company, had to weigh the issue of security vs. opportunity. Goodyear might go broke in a year—or it might go far. But if the surroundings were unpromising, he liked the fighting spirit he found. The challenge of the patents appealed to him. He took off his coat and went to work.

His office was a small room down the hill, with barely space enough for a drawing board alongside his desk. In addition to running the factory he was to do the hiring, be the compounder, tire designer and company doctor. There was a medicine chest on the wall, with a little first-aid kit and a bottle of whiskey in case anyone became ill at work—though he soon substituted spirits of ammonia, which seemed to work just as well and cut down the number of calls.

Litchfield picked Ned Topping, a promising salesman with a gift in handling men, as his assistant, looked around for other men. A strike in the solid tire department in October brought in the first important re-

Tires were built almost entirely by hand in the early years, the plies being stretched into position manually. Development of machinery, a continuing process over the years, improved quality and uniformity, cut costs, opened the use of tires to universal market—and increased wages.

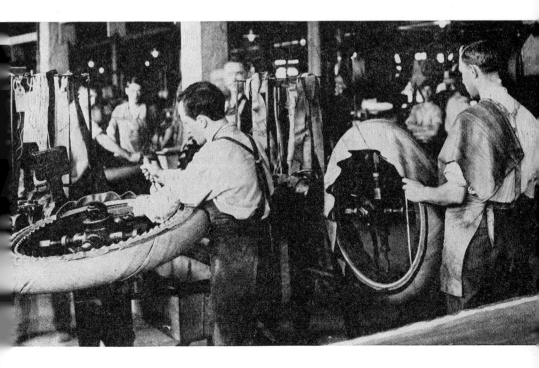

cruit. This was not so much a strike as it was a test of the mettle of the new superintendent. The solid tire department was the most profitable in Goodyear, the big money maker. A tie-up of any length would be serious. Litchfield reasoned with the men, but they refused to give in. All of them walked out, except George Spaulding, one of the "Old Guard" who was running the tubing machine.

Tim Marshall, the paymaster, suggested that Ed Koken over at Goodrich would be a good man to take charge of the department if they could get him.

Koken, later to be superintendent in Canada, was one of the many practical shop men of Goodyear's early history. Born in Columbus, he got into the rubber business at 18 through helping a friend work out an idea for a bicycle tire. He joined Goodrich in 1895, became a foreman.

Litchfield called him, and the two men met at the post office downtown, walked the length of Market Street to the factory and back, talking things over. Koken took the job, and in two weeks the department was running as smoothly as ever.

William Stephens, one of the colorful figures in Goodyear's early history, the boy from across the tracks who became in time Litchfield's right-hand man, signed up the following January.

Stephens was a natural athlete, the leader of all the town's activities in sports. He had the kick of an army mule in his right arm, the hint of a Scotch accent on his tongue and a soft spot for the underdog in his heart. He was 24 when he came to Goodyear. He had heard they were getting up a baseball team.

Steve could get a job anywhere, but men knew he would not stay long. He got restless when spring came. He was so full of energy and high spirits that it was hard for him to stay at a machine if someone suggested a fishing trip, or there was a ball game on. There were plenty of times in the first years when Litchfield was ready to let him go. Instead he made him a foreman.

He recognized that Stephens was a natural leader, felt that if he could harness his great energy and humanity into the sober field of business, he would go far—and attract other men of like temperament —and Goodyear needed fighters. Stephens carried the spirit of the athletic field into the factory, built a team spirit, whipped men into shape, coached ordinary men into champions, brought out their full usefulness—and fought their battles, when necessary, with the management.

Up until 1900 Stephens had not held any job more than a few months. He stayed with Goodyear more than 30 years, became production superintendent, left the mark of his spirit on the company.

It took Litchfield several years, however, to get him to wear a shirt and tie. He liked sweaters better.

Good men attract good men. Gillen and Red Phillips came in. Fred Colley, a great quarterback, and the three Huguelet brothers were already there. A difficulty in the carriage tire department brought in W. C. State as chief engineer in May, 1901.

Carriage tires were built in lengths and rolled up on reels like garden hose. The manufacturer had to supply channel iron to be shrunk onto the wheels and wires to go through the tires, and must braze the ends of the wire together. The Grant patent owners also controlled the tire-mounting machinery, and other manufacturers had to send their tires to Kelly to be mounted. Goodyear, the upstart in the industry, was getting too much business. Why should Kelly mount its tires? It stopped doing so.

State dropped in about that time. A mechanical engineer from Springfield, Ohio, who had done some promising work on automobiles, and was on his way to join the Winton company in Cleveland, he stopped off at Akron to visit a friend in Goodyear. He was promptly dragged into Seiberling's office.

"Here's the man we're looking for," he said.

Mr. Seiberling talked to him a few minutes, sized up his man.

"All right, State, you're hired, right now," he announced.

State was surprised and half indignant. He was not looking for a job. Seiberling pulled his trump card. He outlined the difficulty the company was facing. That was something different. That was a problem which interested him. Already as State listened he was thinking of ways and means. A tough nut to crack was a challenge to a man of his temperament. He hung up his hat, picked out a corner of the shop, went to work. He was back before long with a process of his own, so simple that brazing compound, blow torch and the mounting device could be sold to dealers with a stock of tires. Any blacksmith, or the dealer himself could mount them.

The company had trouble in bicycle tires in its first years. It had taken out a license, but older companies—Morgan & Wright, Hartford and G. & J. (who would all later be part of the U. S. Rubber Company), Dunlop and a Boston house making a tire called Vim had the bicycle manufacturers' business well sewed up. It was hard for a young company without reputation or finances to break in. The only opening seemed to be through jobbers who sold tires for replacement. This business was largely done on price, the jobbers pitting one company against another. They demanded still lower prices in 1901. The sales manager of the department recommended acceptance.

"Price is king," he said. "When price gets up to talk, everybody else sits down."

It was hard for the young organization, already beset by litigation and financial troubles to turn down business, but Litchfield objected, held out for quality. Seiberling agreed and an important decision was reached. It was:

"We'll build the best product we can, then go out and sell it aggressively as a quality product. We must make the name of Goodyear mean something."

Goodyear had secured an excellent volume of business, however, with its price tires, too much in fact. Shortly before Litchfield came, the company got a big order challenging the mettle of the Goodyear spirit and on a peak day had built 4500 bicycle tires—and blew a whistle and hoisted a flag in celebration.

Perhaps they should have kept the achievement quiet, for the Tillinghast patent owners moved in and revoked the license, practically closed down that department. It was a stunning blow. But the little group was resourceful. They had already been thinking of ways to improve the tires, and in this emergency evolved a two-ply tire with a strip of muslin in between to keep the plies separate until vulcanized. This proved expensive so they substituted tissue paper, which worked just as well. Sued for infringement, they went ahead selling tires anyhow, built up a production of 4000 tires a day, and finally the patent owners, doubtful of sustaining their case in court, withdrew their suit.

With the Grant patent litigation still under way, the factory devised a carriage tire of its own, too, the Wing tire, applied for a patent. It had side flanges to keep the sand from working in between tire and rim, so prolonging the life of the tire. They felt this was not only a departure from the Grant patent but an improvement on it.

During all this time Litchfield was devoting his major energies to automobile tires, the company's main chance. Primarily he wanted to get away from the clincher type. Goodyear could have no important place in the industry as long as it could have but 2 per cent of the country's tire business under the Clincher Association rules. In any case the tire itself was not right. Something better must be found.

Two things, he felt, were holding back the nation's acceptance of the automobile: The engines were always stopping and the tires going flat. Cartoonists of that day always show the car-owner on his back under the car tinkering with the motor, or blowing up a tire with a hand pump. Tires must be stronger, and must be easier to change.

Since the Straight-Side tire which came out of his studies was important to the company and the whole automobile industry, we should understand the principles involved.

The old Clincher (left) had to be stretched over the rim. The Straight-Side (right) was easy to mount and remove.

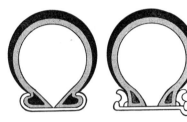

Development of the Straight-Side tire, which could be locked on—and unlocked—was a milestone in the industry.

A pneumatic tire in cross section has a horseshoe shape. Hang this "horse shoe" up and the two prongs correspond with the sidewalls and beads of the tire, the bead being the part which holds it on the rim. In the clincher this bead was made of rubber, could be stretched over the rim in mounting and demounting the tire—with a crowbar, patience and a bit of profanity. The clincher had worked out fairly well for the bicycle, but was giving trouble with the automobile—particularly as tires grew larger and had to be changed often, usually out on the highway after a puncture.

If the clincher gave this much trouble with the small tires of that day, what would happen as cars were built in larger sizes?

So Litchfield was looking for a tire with a bead strong enough to be locked on, instead of stretched over, and be easily unlocked, be readily detachable. He had worked out various devices, none too satisfactory, when Nip Scott came up from Cadiz, Ohio, in the coal mining country, in 1900, with the first clue.

Scott was an inventor, a curious character who had sold Goodyear several of his ideas. Wearing his usual corduroys this day, with a red bandana handkerchief hanging out of his hip pocket, he dumped a gunny sack on Seiberling's desk. He had devised a machine to braid wire, tried it on bed springs, found it too expensive, thought it might be used on tires. Seiberling called Litchfield over.

"What do you think?" he asked.

"It's just what we're looking for," said Litchfield. "A tire can be locked securely on the rim only if the bead cannot stretch and work off. With this braided wire cured into the bead, the tire will lock tightly, yet have the flexibility required on the road."

Now all he needed was a pair of flanges for the tire to ride in. Bolts through flange and wheel would hold the tire in place.

The sides of the tire could run straight down now, since they did not have to curve in to lock over the rim, which suggested the name "Straight Side" although the name was not given the tire immediately. The new tire had 10 per cent more air space than the clincher, would ride more easily on that account. Litchfield built it as strong as he knew how.

It looked as if this was the tire which would release Goodyear from the grip of the clincher monopoly, put it on the highway to success. The company ran its first advertisement in the Saturday Evening Post, a small ad in 1901, got out booklets with pictures of the tire and the story of the principle, used the slogan—

"The Best All Roll
They All Roll Best
On GOODYEAR Tires."

The tire caught on. The Winton company ordered ten sets in 34 x 4 sizes, Goodyear's first original equipment tires. Davis and Allen, exporters, took the agency for the tires in England where they made a big hit. The Prince of Wales, Sir Thomas Lipton, Lord Salisbury and other dignitaries ordered Goodyear tires.

Newspapers printed a story of how Lord Salisbury, while riding at Brighton (on Goodyear tires), had a puncture, and his chauffeur stuffed hay into the casing and drove on, but soon got an imperious demand from his Lordship in the back seat to stop the car. The friction generated in the hay had set fire to it. People have tried for many years to find something better than compressed air for tires. The Salisbury experiment showed that new-mown hay was not the answer.

Goodyear tires were entered in a 2500 mile race in England in 1902 with Lord Northcliffe, leading British publisher, putting up the prize money. England and France had been more aggressive in the development of automobiles than this country and Litchfield wanted to study developments, asked for a month's vacation. Kavenagh, who had come with him from his last job at Chelsea, Massachusetts, went along.

There were no expense accounts then. The men travelled on a cattle boat, this being before refrigeration when cattle were shipped on the hoof and men got a free trip to Europe for feeding and looking after the cattle. Litchfield and Kavenagh, by paying a bit, were relieved of any duties with the steers, went on to watch the race.

The Goodyear tires were picked to win but, as a matter of fact, fared rather badly. Both Dunlop and Michelin, European manufacturers, showed much better performance. The race was a big disappointment and Litchfield came back with his teeth clenched.

Things had not gone well in Akron while he was away. Goodyear had done fairly well financially in 1901, but in 1902 it was losing money. Also it had lost its two key men in the important carriage tire division. Ed Koken had been hired away by another company who offered him more money, urged him to quit a sinking ship, and Burroughs of Sales had had to go west for his health.

Koken's job could be filled, but Burroughs was hard to replace. He knew everyone in the carriage tire field. C. W. Seiberling had a suggestion. He had met a man named Stadelman shortly before at the carriage manufacturers' convention in Cincinnati, a big fellow with a good mind, and fine character. Everyone seemed to respect him. He was Morgan & Wright's best salesman. Seiberling turned to Burroughs.

"Do you know this man?"

"I know this much about him," Burroughs replied. "He is the hardest competition I have, and the squarest shooter in the industry."

That seemed sufficient, and Stadelman came on.

His decision called for plenty of faith on his part. Goodyear's application for a patent on its Wing tire had been thrown out and its appeal was before the courts. Its profits in escrow, the company was harder up than it had ever been, still had difficulty getting enough cash in to meet its payrolls. The company traded a set of tools on one occasion for a bale of rubber it did not have the money to pay for.

Another time, Al Cunnington, in the receiving room, opened up an incoming freight car, found it full of bicycles, reported to the office thinking it was a mistake, but found that a bicycle manufacturer, still harder up than Goodyear, had turned them in for payment of its tire bill. The bicycles were sold to employees at $10 apiece and every boy in East Akron presently had a new bicycle, and Goodyear had a little more money in the cash drawer.

This was perhaps the darkest hour in the company's history. But the little organization which had battled so courageously was entitled to get a break eventually. Toward the end of the year 1902, it came.

Word came that the court would announce its decision the following day on the Grant patent. All that day men walked around apprehensive. If the most profitable department was closed down by court order, and its hard-earned profits snatched away, it did not seem possible that the company could survive, or that any of them would have a job on the morrow. The company was small and no one could fail to understand the significance of the situation. The fighting spirit which grew up in the shop came out of such emergencies. Stephens, Gillen, Phillips, the Huguelets, Ed Koken, Colley, all waited tense for the decision. Finally it came—in Goodyear's favor. The money in escrow would come pour· ing back into the treasury.

So great was the sense of relief that everyone stopped work, the whistles blew, and men climbed to the roof to nail a crisp new broom to the top of the flag staff, a new broom to sweep clean, a new start for Goodyear.

Heartened by the decision, the company went ahead and by 1905 became the leader in the carriage tire field. The irony of the situation was that just as it was winning this first major victory, the carriage tire business, like the bicycle tire field, was beginning to waver.

Litchfield had gone back to his drafting board immediately on his return from Europe. He thought he knew why his tires had not performed better in the Northcliffe race. It had nothing to do with the Straight Side principle. The tires had not failed because they were too weak, but because they were too strong.

Litchfield came from a long line of seafaring ancestors, ship captains and ship builders, had spent many hours as a boy around the shipyards of Bath, Maine, was to carry through life a deep interest in things nautical. During his European trip he had watched the ships riding at anchor, noted how firmly they were held to the snubbing blocks on the wharf by hempen ropes, despite the tugging of wind and waves, against jerks that would have parted a steel cable of much higher strength. He recalled watching fishermen hauling in their nets with tons of fish, a weight that would have broken stronger materials. An idea came to him. Flexibility was the answer, in ship lines or automobile tires. It was not to build a tire strong enough to *resist* the shocks of the roadway, but flexible enough to *absorb* them. He would never forget this.

Construction methods were quickly altered to make the Straight Side more flexible, but the principle stuck in the company's tire design thinking from then on, was reflected in the later balloon tires and the Airwheel. The 50 pounds of air pressure carried in the smallest three-inch tires of that day would be cut in half in the modern tires, even those of much greater size.

However Litchfield was still not satisfied with the way the tire was attached to the rim. There must be a simpler method. He and Scott and Seiberling worked long over that, finally hit on the solution. That was to use a metal locking ring whose ends did not quite meet, so that it could be snapped into a groove in the rim to hold the flange in place. When you wanted to remove the tire it was an easy matter to pry off the ring, release the flange and the tire would slide off.

No such rims were in existence, and arrangements had to be made with a Cleveland company to manufacture them. Moreover, rims of that day were built for clincher tires, and car manufacturers would hesitate to change their rims over to fit an untried type of tire, nor car owners go to that expense. Seiberling made a suggestion.

"If you changed the contour of the outboard flange just a little," he said, "you could reverse them, turn them in instead of out and they'll fit clinchers as well as Straight Sides."

Litchfield himself wrote the first specifications for the "Quick Detachable," as it was called, in December, 1903. But he was not through improving it. For one thing tread and carcass were apt to separate as tires were driven faster, and it was a common thing for racing drivers to "throw a tread." A breaker strip had been introduced, a ply of square-woven fabric placed between the two to give better adhesion, but was not too satisfactory.

Perhaps a more open-weave fabric would do it. Then the rubber could flow through, anchor tread and carcass together like a series of rivets. There was no such fabric on the market, and until the textile mills could be persuaded to produce it, men and girls pulled out the cross threads by hand.

The "rivet fabric," as it was called, quickly became standard in all Goodyear tires, and marked an important step forward, for it not only stopped tread separation, but also distributed the jarring of the highway around the tire instead of concentrating it at the point of impact.

With all these things it was not until 1905 that the company was satisfied and ready to put the tire on the market full scale.

Its introduction was spectacular. The company put every dollar it could scrape together into sales and advertising, bought full-page space in the Saturday Evening Post and other magazines. Never before in America had a new tire been introduced in such fashion.

The big tire companies were all skeptical. It would not be easy to convince the public that one of the smallest companies in the industry was right and everyone else wrong. Goodyear might well have played safe, gone slowly until it was entirely sure. But it staked everything on the Straight Side, would win big or go under. There was no middle ground.

The first big test of the tire came in England. A five-day endurance race had been organized, a long one, all the way from London up into Scotland and back, designed to see what the horseless carriages could really do. Two American companies, Buick and Reo, were trying to break into the British market, entered cars. The tire was a vulnerable part of the car. They studied the new Straight Side carefully, adopted it for this important test.

Litchfield and Stephens went over to England to witness it. They got ample revenge for the defeat of four years earlier. The American cars made an excellent showing, but more important to the Goodyear men, the Reos went through the entire race without a single puncture, something almost unheard of then and the Buicks fared almost as well. Perhaps Goodyear *had* something in its new tire.

The matter was pretty well cinched when Stephens on his return persuaded Louis Chevrolet to use Straight Sides in the 500 mile Indianapolis Speedway race.

The battle was long and hard-fought, but presently the tide began to turn. Other car manufacturers called for Straight Sides and in the end the companies who had ridiculed them began putting in equipment to build them—but would have to do considerable experimental work before they could produce them satisfactorily—and Goodyear had a long head start. Production increased, went from 90 tires a day in 1905 to ten times that number in three years, and the company had to expand the plant to keep up.

The victory not only took Goodyear over the hump financially, but made it one of the half dozen leaders in the industry.

Ironically the clincher tire monopoly, which had forced Goodyear to build a different and better tire, was broken up during this period, though for a different reason. Theodore Roosevelt's convictions as to free competition in business were gaining general acceptance, and he had the long arm of the law to fall back on in case any single company proved recalcitrant. Seeing the handwriting on the wall, the Clincher Tire Manufacturers' Association folded up in 1906.

The Straight Side type quickly came into universal use on all but the smaller sized cars. European tire manufacturers were the last to give up, and it was some years later that the largest company, and the one most outspoken in its opposition, surprised the industry by swinging in line overnight—after building up a stock so that it could immediately supply the market. Smaller European manufacturers who had been following that lead were unprepared for the switch and caught flat-footed.

Other things happened during Goodyear's first decade. Seiberling became president of the company in 1906, having been general manager up to then. Hill, the first president, had resigned in 1899, feeling

Seiberling's ambitious ideas too much at variance with the conservative practices of his own industry, and Seiberling had to find someone to take over his stock. He turned to his family.

The Seiberlings were a large family, and if the community was a little skeptical of his ventures, the family at least believed in him. Five different brothers-in-law took a prominent part in the company. Penfield of Willoughby, who took up part of Hill's stock and threw out a financial life preserver during the patent difficulties, became the second president, was followed in 1903 by Miles, who had furnished the money for the original $3500 down payment in 1898. A third brother-in-law, Manton, was a large stockholder; a fourth, Sam Miller, the first superintendent. Charles Seiberling was vice president and purchasing agent, and his brother-in-law, Frank Carnahan, manager of flooring sales and sundries.

By 1906, with things in better shape, Seiberling would rely more on men who were active in the company, made Litchfield and Stadelman directors.

Goodyear stationery of that year pointed out with a touch of pride that the company had its own long distance telephone line, Akron 12, and that Western Union and Postal Telegraph wires ran directly into the office.

State had been working with Seiberling on a tire building machine, which would take some of the hard manual labor out of the job, give a more uniform tire. In the first days the workman placed one foot against the roller and stretched each ply of fabric into place. State got his machine into operation in 1908. It was so successful that other companies sought licenses to use it. Seiberling set up a demonstration, sold licenses to Morgan & Wright, Fisk, G. & J., Hartford and 50 other companies. However, the patent was thrown out by the United States Circuit Court of Appeals in Cincinnati in 1920, in a memorable lawsuit, as tending to create a monopoly.

Litchfield had set up his own factory accounting system in 1907. Costs were important in a competitive industry and he had trouble getting all the information he wanted from the Accounting Department, which was busy on sales and general expense. He wanted all the costs that went into the tire broken down so that each could be studied separately, the beginning of modern cost accounting. Howard Hoskin, who had come in in the early days, but had left, was called back to set up such a system.

Bourne came on in 1908 as chief chemist, also looking after crude rubber buying under Litchfield's direction—and took charge of Litchfield's first aid kit until Dr. W. S. Chase, another brother-in-law of the Seiberlings, was employed to look after plant accidents and hygiene. Kavenagh took charge of compounding.

Other men joined the company in the next few years—Brooks in 1909 in Purchasing, Steele in Production, Carroll in Traffic and Zieske in Engineering in 1910, Slusser whom we shall meet later in 1911, Blandin in Crude Rubber in 1912.

Koken came back as assistant superintendent in 1907 after Topping left to join his father's manufacturing business at Ashland. Al Huguelet had the tire room, Gillen the stock room and solid tires, Stephens the tube room and golf balls, Colley crude rubber, Cunnington the store room, Falor and Brunswick had motorcycle and bicycle tires.

Carl Klingenhagen, one of the original "Old Guard" became night superintendent with the starting of a night shift in 1907. The night shift worked 13 hours, the day shift 11.

Tire builders carried the iron cores around on their shoulders, even two at a time. A core weighed as high as 250 pounds. There was one core for 36 x 5 tires that weighed 350 pounds and Swede Halberg, the strongest man in the department, could pick this up with ease. In later years with turrets and conveyors and collapsible cores and other inventions designed to take the fatigue out of factory work, the old timers who had seen the factory a quarter of a century earlier would grow a little scornful at times about the easier days, much like retired sea captains, recalling the days of wooden ships and iron men.

The hiring-in rate in 1908 was 16 cents an hour. Supervision got a maximum of 27½ cents, but a good tire builder, working piecework, might make as high as 30 cents an hour. There were 850 employees now. The plant occupied five and a half acres of floor space.

In the sales department Stadelman was building up his staff. Osterloh was one of the first, joining up in 1903 at Chicago; Hazlett came on in 1906, was soon to be manager at Pittsburgh, then take charge of all eastern sales and later go to England. Jackson came in 1907 as Detroit manager, but was soon heading up sales to auto manufacturers. Rockhill started modestly in the repair department in 1907, was destined to go far. Jasper Blake came in 1906, went to Boston. Already branches were scattered across the country in strategic centers.

W. D. Shilts came in 1905. He had gone to Mount Union College in nearby Alliance and taken one year of law in Cleveland when his funds ran short and he answered an ad for a stenographer at Akron. He never got back to finish his law studies, and soon became an important factor in administrative work where his strong character, vigorous mind, and gift for detail made him useful.

Shilts' account of the Akron he found in 1905 throws some light on the company's position at that time.

"The plant was still down in the valley, with a small office on Market Street, Krumeich's saloon and a few houses stood where the general office is now. Goodyear Avenue and Goodyear Heights were farm land. People walked to work, went home for lunch. There were several teams and delivery wagons to bring the rubber up from the railroad station and carry tires back. F. A. Seiberling owned the only automobile in the company, a one-cylinder Cadillac, though a Thomas flyer was purchased that year.

"Al Cunnington was getting $75 a month as manager of the receiving room, Hank Gillen $65, as manager of the shipping room, Clara Bingham, C. W. Seiberling's secretary and assistant in purchasing, drew $70, Billy Wilson $23 as office boy. Goodyear had a total of 300 employees, the Sales Department having 28, though that included 18 girls who constituted the Advertising Department, whose duties were chiefly to mail out folders, our principle method of advertising at that time."

By reason of its victory in the Straight Side tire battle, Goodyear was well established by 1908, ready to enter the amazing next period.

The Driving Years (1908-1920)

With its finances on a fairly sound basis, the Goodyear company set off in 1908 to write an exciting narrative, one seldom matched in the history of business.

Following up its victory in the Straight Side tire battle, the company brought out a Cord tire in 1913, which was just as revolutionary an advance and gave rise to an industry battle no less hard fought—and one which carried it in 1916 into first place in the industry, a position it has held ever since.

The same year in which it hit top rank saw Goodyear, again in the face of industry skepticism, come out with the pneumatic truck tire which changed the whole course of transportation in America.

Matching the seven-league-boot stride of the dynamic automobile industry, tire production went from 35,000 in 1908 to seven million in 1920, and sales from $2 millions to almost $200 millions in the twelve years.

It became imperative in 1908 to provide room to build tires in the volume needed. The old strawboard plant was all but bursting at the seams. There was money enough in the till to expand. Floor space grew from 40,000 feet in 1908 to 5,000,000 in 1920. The young company had to move fast to keep abreast of increasing demand for tires. Litchfield later characterized this period in this way:

"The automotive industry was more than receptive to goods which would popularize travel by car; the public was eager to get tires which would run longer, give greater safety, greater freedom from the interruptions and annoyance of road failures. With an improved tire in our hands, the need for saving time became imperative. We could have the market to ourselves for a short time only. If we could not produce the tires fast enough with existing buildings and machines we must build new buildings, buy or design more and better machines. I have no hesitation in saying that in such a situation we paid more money for buildings and machinery than we would have done had we been willing to wait. Time literally was money to us and the extra money we spent was spent deliberately and with our eyes open, knowing that we were buying precious days and weeks and months which were worth much more than they had cost us. For those were the driving days of a driving industry."

A clock tower was included in the first factory building erected on Market Street in 1915. It was not a decoration but a subtle reminder to everyone of the importance of time. A clock tower went up too at Plant II, and after that in Goodyear plants over the country.

There were plenty of difficulties in Goodyear's second decade.

A pool in Brazilian rubber in 1910 ran the price of rubber up to $3 a pound, bringing difficulties in financing materials. The first big advertising campaign was organized that year, the Labor Department was started, and an aeronautical department created.

The year 1912 was notable in Akron for the merger of Goodrich and Diamond, the starting of Goodyear Heights, the beginning of the manufacture of mechanical goods and the construction of a large addition to the General Office on Market Street.

The year 1913 was eventful. It brought a flood, a rubber strike, the starting of textile manufacture in New England, the winning of the International Balloon Race in Paris, and the starting of the Flying Squadron. The flood which had disastrous effects around Dayton struck many sections of Ohio and Indiana. Goodyear came to work one morning to find the Little Cuyahoga a roaring torrent, the mill room and calenders flooded, the fires dead in the boiler room, houses and sheds floating down the railroad tracks, and crude rubber drifting down town to Howard Street. The disaster made a sharp call on the resourcefulness of en-

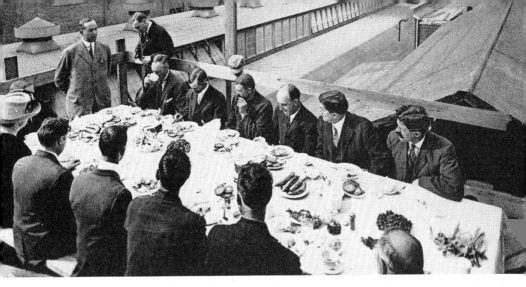

On temporary platform built on foundation of new smoke stack, the "Old Guard" celebrated significant step in expansion of factory in 1910.

The growing plant filled up the valley off Market Street, then moved upstream in a phalanx of factory buildings for more than a mile.

gineering and production men, brought to the attention of management an aggressive young clerk in the superintendent's office named Slusser.

Expansion did not stop in Akron. The company got into the export field with an office in London and a factory in Canada—and had to erect a second one four times as large within a few years, took over a cotton mill in New England, began growing its own rubber on 20,000 acres of jungle in the Dutch East Indies, and its own cotton in Arizona, with holdings half as large again, and mining its own coal in southern Ohio.

This period saw the starting of the Experimental or Development Department, as the first application of scientific principles to rubber, leading to a long series of improvements in design, processing, compounding and machinery—and the birth of the famous diamond tread.

Tire manufacture is an assembly job, the bringing together of half a dozen separate parts, made up in as many different departments. A complex system of Production Control was started in 1916, as a major division of manufacturing, under which the foreman no longer had to chase his own stock, but had it brought to him as fast as he was ready for it, and in the exact amounts needed.

Few business houses in America were carrying on so many and divergent activities. Profit and loss were involved in each one, demanded trained management if it was to aid and not hamper the company's progress—and in the doing provide opportunities for men with a wide range of latent talents and ability.

It is fairly difficult to relate these different activities in any consecutive sequence, since so many things were going on at the same time, so we might go down the hill to the factory, as the phrase was then, look at the Cord tire and other products which carried the company so fast and so far on the highway of success, saving other phases for more detailed examination later.

The automobile was a rather bizarre looking contraption in 1908, as a trip through any industrial museum will reveal.

It had to be cranked to start, it made a lot of racket, it squeaked and rattled and jolted. If anyone drove at night he mounted a tank of fuel on the running board, connected it up through rubber tubes to the head lamps, struck a match to light the lamps.

People jacked up their cars in the winter and waited for spring. They generally confined their driving to the city or nearby country. There was plenty of dust in either case, as hard surface roads were confined to the cities. They wore a linen duster to protect their clothes, and ladies wore veils as well. Everyone wore gauntlets.

Barney Oldfield might drive at a mile a minute, but the rest of the populace held to a modest 15 or 20 miles per hour. They usually stopped when a horse and buggy approached, pulled off to the side of the road while the driver led his horse past. Even so there were plenty of runaways.

Bankers and conservative business men, indeed most men past 50, shook their heads at the automobile in 1908, laughed at the prediction that eventually a million cars would be rolling over the highways of the nation.

Actually, however, the industry was just beginning to hit its stride. Car registration had already gone from 77,000 in 1905, to 105,000 to 140,000, and reached almost 200,000 by 1908. The experimental period was past. The horseless carriage was finding itself, and ownership would not be limited much longer to the rich.

Durant organized General Motors in 1908, taking in Buick and Oldsmobile, two of the most aggressive young companies, would add Cadillac and Oakland the following year. Ford brought out his Model T that year, Packard was well under way, after moving up from Warren, Ohio. The Fisher Body Company was organized that year, and Chevrolet was to come into existence three years later. The situation presented an opportunity for a manufacturer of tires.

Two things had to be done if Goodyear was to capitalize fully on that opportunity. First it must build better tires than anyone else. The Straight Side was the best tire men knew how to make in 1908, but it still had a long way to go.

It was still the spindly offspring of the bicycle tire. Tires for the small-sized cars were three inches in cross section, as compared to 6¼ to 6¾ inches for cars of that type today.

It was far from strong, would wear out after 2500 miles.

It was drum-taut and rode hard. The three-inch tire had 50 pounds of air pressure and the largest tires 120 pounds, as compared to the 24 pounds pressure of the resilient, smooth-riding tires of today.

It had a smooth tread, which was all right for horse and buggy speeds and loads, but on an automobile was apt to slide on wet paving, to spin helplessly in snow and mud.

Finally, it cost too much. If a set of tires for a Packard cost $500, the automobile would remain a luxury which only the rich could afford.

It was time for someone to make a painstaking, scientific study of the pneumatic tire, part by part, go into compounding, materials, tire design, machine design, do on an organized scale what up to now a few men—Litchfield, State, Seiberling, Nall and the others—had struggled with single-handed. How would they go about it?

There were no geniuses around to be hired. There were not even any tire engineers. The field was too new. The company would have to find men and train them. So it set up a drafting room, a small laboratory, picked promising young men from the technical universities, told them to find out everything about each part of the tire, master it. Everything yields to concentration. Something might come out of it.

And something did.

In the next several years the Experimental Department, later called Development, brought out the S-V solid tire for the slow-moving trucks, the All-Weather Tread, a motorcycle tire and an airplane tire, each the best in its field, tackled mechanical goods, but from the outset, spent most of its time on automobile tires, the company's main chance.

It got its first big challenge in 1912 when an aggressive competitor brought out a tire which threatened to sweep the market.

To understand this we must remember the important part cotton plays in the industry. Automobile tires, as most people know, are not made of pure rubber but are built up around a carcass composed of successive plies of rubberized fabric. It is the cotton, not the rubber, which gives body and strength to a tire, at least so long as the rubber protects it from chafing and abrasion, and from the deteriorating effects of moisture.

The cotton used in automobile tires was square woven "duck" with warp and woof of the same size and strength. It was strong and durable, its defect being that the sawing action of cord against cord while the tire was flexing under contact with the highway, created friction, built up an internal heat which burned the life out of the fabric, shortened the life of the tire to a few thousand miles.

There was another type of tire fabric called "cord" fabric. In this fabric the threads all ran one way, with only a light cross thread or woof, to hold them together, light enough to be broken in course of vulcanization. The result was that the sawing action characteristic of the square woven "duck," was greatly lessened. Goodyear had become interested in "cord" fabric through building tires for "electrics." These vehicles had to have their batteries charged at frequent intervals, in fact every night if driven much during the day. And Goodyear engineers had noted the curious fact that while the electrics must have their batteries charged after six or seven hours of driving on "fabric" tires, they would start more easily, run more smoothly, use less power, give 30 or 40 per cent more mileage on "cords."

It was interesting, but not important, since electrics were going off the market, and the cord fabric was not strong enough to take the strain required by gasoline-driven cars.

But about that time an English tire company brought out the Palmer Cord tire. The Diamond Rubber Company across town got wind of it, sent J. D. Tew, later Goodrich president, over to buy the American rights. Goodrich, at that time a next door neighbor to Diamond and its bitter rival, was building a Palmer tire, so Diamond called its new tire Silvertown, after the village where the English factory was located. It was not the Silvertown cord tire of today. The name was to outlast the tire.

The English tire was built around two plies of rather large cords, somewhat larger than the thickness of a pencil lead. They were impregnated with rubber and laid down from bead to bead, with a cushion of rubber between. They cost two or three times as much as other tires but they had resiliency far beyond that of the fabric tires, and they got away largely from the sawing motion of the fabric and so did not heat up as much.

The new tire created a veritable sensation. It was real competition even at a higher price.

However, Goodyear was not stampeded, set to work and emerged with a cord fabric of its own. It was quite different from the English type. Litchfield had gone back to the resilient, but not overstrong, cord fabric of the electrics. Instead of using two plies of the whipcord Silvertown, he built a tire of multiple plies of a thread-like cord fabric, using a 1/32″ diameter cord, one-fourth as large as his competitor. Each ply was insulated by a cushion of rubber.

But there was still one extremely important obstacle. Cord fabric was so flexible that even in bicycles and electrics it was apt to chafe against the metal rim and wear out prematurely, or be broken and the tire ruined if it struck a sharp obstruction which, if only for an instant pressed it against the metal. How could the engineers preserve the flexibility of the tire, which was its great virtue, and still keep it strong enough to withstand wear and impact? Somehow they must taper off that extreme flexibility in the inch or so of space before it reached the inflexible rim.

Finally they resorted to the unorthodox scheme of combining cord and fabric, building the tire of cord and protecting it at the base with a "boot" of tough cross-woven fabric called the "flipper." The early Goodyear cords, indeed, were called "No-Rim-Cuts" to emphasize this feature, and this was an important sales point since many competitive tires failed prematurely from this cause.

Then the tire was put on the market. And what a furore it caused. It was the story of the Straight Side versus clinchers all over again. Diamond championing the English cord, and Goodyear the American, locked horns in the testing field, in the newspapers, in the advertising columns, in the final test of public use. This is not a genuine cord tire at all, said one. It is a thread tire. "What is a cord and what is a thread?" asked the other. The rest of the industry watched, waited, uncertain which way to move.

The courage of its convictions. Again one of Goodyear's supreme characteristics. The young company staked everything on its new tire, drove ahead. Goodyear went again to the racing drivers, proposed the gruelling test of the 500 mile Indianapolis race for its new tires. Ralph de Palma, long-time believer in Goodyear tires, was the first to try them out over that course. They stood the gaff. The other drivers were impressed and in the following year all of them called for cords. Litchfield urged the tires strongly on Col. J. G. Vincent, chief engineer at Packard, but found him skeptical. To prove that Litchfield was wrong Vincent mounted a set on his own car and started out from Detroit, with the intention of driving until he wore the tires out. He kept going, finally reached Indianapolis. The tires were still all right. So he started around the speedway, made many laps without wearing them out. He convinced himself finally that they had merit. The English cord in the meantime was developing defects. It would rim-cut, stone-bruise, it was subject to separation between cords and between plies. Many car owners tested the Goodyear tires out, found that they increased the mileage from 2500 to 7500. The tire industry wavered. Again the automobile manufacturers, alert to utilize everything that would improve their product, experimented—gave the Goodyear cord their OK. The death blow to the English type tire came when the government barred it from its specification for military purposes during the war.

The square-woven fabric continued to be used for many years in the smaller-sized tires because of its lower price, but while the industry was changing over to cords on the larger sizes, Goodyear went into the lead.

United States Rubber, Goodrich and Diamond were neck and neck in 1912, with Goodyear a good fourth. Then came the merger of Goodrich and Diamond, which gave Goodrich the use of the English cord, and put it well ahead of its rivals. But Goodyear was not to be headed. Within four years it had overtaken the merged company and definitely took the lead in the tire industry. The United States Rubber Company, producing a varied list of rubber products—perhaps 60 per cent of its business being in clothing, footwear, mechanical goods, and the like

—held the lead in total rubber goods until 1926 when Goodyear passed it also.

From 1916 on the statement could be made that "More People Ride on Goodyear Tires Than on Any Other Kind."

The company got another slogan in 1915, an internal one: "Protect Our Good Name."

Theodore F. McManus, pioneer Detroit advertising man, was working with Goodyear's agency, Erwin Wasey of Chicago, on some automotive accounts. He wrote an advertisement pointing out that the public judged every company by what it was and what it did, the quality of its goods and the character behind them.

Those things built good will, a priceless asset, he said. Every company should be jealous of its good name. And in that result everyone in the company had a stake, the men in the laboratory who specified highest quality materials, the men in the factory content only with highest workmanship—and for that matter everyone else in Akron and the field. The company's good name was in their hands.

Seiberling and Litchfield were so much impressed with this thinking, which fitted in so exactly with their own, that they had it printed on Nov. 6, 1915 as a full-page advertisement in the Saturday Evening Post, and in newspapers over the country—then had signs made up carrying the phrase, "Protect Our Good Name," ordered them placed throughout the factory and in every branch office. A third of a century later those signs were still up.

The development department continued its efforts throughout this period to improve the solid truck tire. The rubber-tired truck was some improvement on the horse-driven dray, but it was slow moving, 10 or 12 miles an hour, 15 at the best, was used principally in city hauling of coal, or gravel, machinery. Goodyear's SV solid tire came out in 1912-13, widened this field. The factory had developed a hard rubber compound with excellent adhesion to metal, used a sawtooth surface on the rim to improve that adhesion, used with a softer layer of rubber which bonded the tire to the base. The tire had bands pressed on the wheel rather than being held in place by bolts and lugs. And when it was on, it stayed on, gave long wear.

Tests were run with competitors' tires mounted on the same truck as the SV. The new tire outwore all the rest.

But the factory had something else up its sleeve than merely a better soled tire. That was to adapt the resilient cord tire to the truck, put it on pneumatics.

Again everyone thought this was entirely impractical. Up to that time the fragile cord fabric had been barely strong enough for a bicycle or electric, and although used now on passenger cars, would never work with a truck, whose heavy loads would always be carried on solid tires.

However, some pretty fundamental things compelled Goodyear to try. If it was successful the truck could supplement the work of the railroads, reaching into sections where the railroads did not penetrate, opening up sections where none would ever be built. The railroad demands a fixed track and comparatively easy grades. A pneumatic tired truck required no such smooth roadway. Its cushion of compressed air would absorb the unevenness of the topography. Its traction and nonskid properties would enable it to be driven up steep inclines and down abrupt grades.

The truck could go anywhere on pneumatic tires! And doing so would give tremendous impetus to the exchange of commodities, which is commerce; could extend and increase the field of the older carrier, the railroad. And if this were done, trucks would come into a usefulness far beyond that of the solid-tired trucks, many more trucks would be built and so the market for tires would grow proportionately.

This was always Goodyear's major sales psychology—not to be satisfied with handing over the counter goods that the public came in to buy, but to create demand by developing goods which society needed, whether it realized that need or not.

The light, tough cord fabric now sweeping the passenger car market, could be used on trucks, by building in additional plies till it had the necessary strength, with no loss of resiliency. The tire was brought out in 1916, tested thoroughly, worked.

But it was a tire no one wanted. Again the public was skeptical. So much so that Goodyear had to demonstrate them itself before anyone would try them.

The company organized the Wingfoot Express line, making the 750 mile run from Akron to Boston with finished tires to the branch there, bringing back tire fabric from the New England mills. The first trip took 24 days. The caravan spent from 8 a.m. till midnight covering the three mile unpaved stretch between Ravenna and Edinboro in the adjoining county. The cargo was principally spare tires—and they were needed. The trucks, too, to tell the truth, were not geared at that time to cross-country driving. A stop had to be made at Greensburg, Pennsylvania, while the men sent back for a new engine. The bearings had burned out.

Major defects were soon ironed out, however, and by the end of the summer the trucks were making the trip in five and one-half days, and

To show the possibilities of pneumatic-tired transport, Goodyear trucks blazed a trail across the prairie to the Coast in 1918.

While the earlier Boston Express of 1916 proved that bridges must be strengthened to meet the requirements of the Automotive Age.

people were beginning to open their eyes.

City and cross country buses, as well, grew out of these experiments.

Goodyear Heights, a residential section built for employees, lay a quarter mile from the plant at its nearest point, a mile and a half away at the farthest. In paving the main streets leading into it, the company had left an ungraded strip in the center for street car tracks. But the street car company did not feel there was enough business to justify putting in a line.

"All right," said Litchfield, "we'll start a bus line of our own. That will furnish information on operating costs, and maybe someone else will pick up the idea, build other lines, create more tire business."

The Goodyear Heights line, one of the first in the country, except the Fifth Avenue line in New York City, went into service, demonstrated that passengers could be carried on this relatively short haul for two cents a ride.

These experiments attracted the attention of street car operators, and though they crossed their fingers when Litchfield predicted that eventually city and interurban passengers would be carried on rubber instead of steel, they did become interested, car builders got busy designing buses, and in another decade workmen started ripping up street car tracks all over America.

The company was compelled to move fast with each new product, before competitors caught up with it. The new tires were not patented and any competitor could cut one up, and figure out fairly accurately how it was made.

In tires, as in automobiles, America was getting away from the European idea of secrecy. One company would get an idea which would suggest a variation to someone else, a third would add another improvement and the whole industry moved ahead—which may be one of the reasons why the American automotive industry in this period so far outstripped that of Europe.

Litchfield once said, "The manufacturer who closes his doors to the world is apt to shut out more than he shuts in."

Nip Scott had patented his braiding process in 1899 and had four separate hidden locks guarding his factory at Cadiz when he was making bead wire for the company, and Goodyear would braid its own wire at Akron after his death in a special-pass department. Still competitors were able to match it fairly closely, and in time the steel wire manufacturers got into the business and it was open to everyone.

The campaign to put over the pneumatic truck tire got unexpected help early in World War I from the United States government. The army was needing horses, but that was not the main point. The big thing was that there were 2,000,000 work horses in Illinois, Iowa, Wisconsin and the Dakotas alone, and it took two acres of farmland to raise enough feed for each horse. Part of that land should be used for food-stuffs for the Army. Could the farmers be persuaded to switch over to trucks, and plant wheat and corn on that land, Washington wondered.

"Maybe the Goodyear people could help on that," someone suggested.

Goodyear could and would. There were 16 companies now making trucks and several of the tire companies were making pneumatics. So a tour was organized, of trucks from 3/4 ton size to five tons, all on rubber.

It was a colorful caravan that rolled down Michigan Boulevard, Chicago, that summer in 1917, headed by a 20 piece band. In the next two months it covered the main county seat towns over the five states. Luncheons were staged by chambers of commerce, and in the afternoon the trucks went out into the field, hauled wheat and other crops, did in four to six hours work that would have taken horse-drawn vehicles from dawn to dark to do, showed that pneumatic tired trucks could travel faster, get through muddy and rutted roads which would have been all but impassible to traverse otherwise. The demonstration gave a big impetus to the use of trucks on the farm.

Goodyear staged a demonstration of its own the following year. The good roads movement was under way, and Frank Seiberling had been elected as the first president of the Lincoln Highway Association. Goodyear started two trucks off from Boston in the summer of 1918 bound for San Francisco. Though this was only 30 years ago, it was the first time anyone had ever attempted to cross the entire country by truck.

It took three weeks to make the trip and turned out to be quite an adventure. In crossing Wyoming the trucks broke through 36 of the 56 crude bridges they met, propped them up and went on.

They met Seiberling at Salt Lake City on the way back, took part in the ceremony dedicating a section of road as part of the Lincoln Highway, continued on through Kansas and Missouri, where the rich black soil all but blocked travel in wet weather, got into Boston on Armistice Day.

The factory was working all this time trying to improve processes as well as products, looking for machines, compounds and methods which would make tires cost less so that more people could own automobiles. State's tire building machine was an important step but other improvements were sought. An opportunity arose in the mill room.

One of the laborious and time-consuming operations was mixing the rubber with the various compounds. Chunks of rubber were fed into two large steel rolls moving in opposite directions and at different speeds, which broke it down into an endless sheet. Then the compounds were added.

It was one of the most colorful operations in the plant, the rubber twisting, writhing and crackling like a live thing, taking on strange patterns like watermarks on paper as the yellow sulphur and other compounds were worked in. Cold water was forced into the interior of the rolls as they grew hot during the battle.

But though the mill room was an interesting place, it was hot and dirty. The mills took up a lot of room with rolls six, seven and eight feet long, and it took around 25 minutes to mix a batch of rubber into an integral mass and sheet it out. Then slabs were cut out, dusted with soapstone to keep them from sticking, and piled in metal batch boxes to be trucked away.

F. H. Banbury, a young engineer on the staff of the Birmingham Iron Foundry in Connecticut, which made mixing mills and other machinery for the rubber industry, had been working on an automatic machine where the rubber and compounds could be dumped into a container and mixed by rotating blades like a churn. State dropped in to see him one day in 1916.

"When are you going to have one of these internal mixers ready, do away with those damn two-roll mills you've been selling us?" he demanded.

"We're making headway," said Banbury. "In fact, we're making up parts for the first one right now. Here are the blue prints."

State scanned the prints, sniffed.

"Let's see it," he said.

They went out into the shop and looked it over. State asked a couple of questions, went back to the office, called the railroad on the telephone.

"I want you to have a car on the Birmingham Foundry siding Thursday morning to ship a ten ton machine to Akron, Ohio," he said.

Banbury protested.

"Wait a minute, Bill," he said, "That's two days off. We've just started on this machine. We have to test it out. There are always a lot of adjustments to be made in any new machine."

"Well," said State, "you can finish it in three days, four at the most. Then you come to Akron for two or three months, and we'll run the tests there, try it out with every compound we use, work out the bugs, make the necessary changes, put the machine into operation.

"Save time," he concluded.

Few companies were more conscious of the importance of time than Goodyear, particularly then, when the factory was furiously busy. If the machine worked, Goodyear would save a few months by running the test at Akron, be ready to go.

It was an opportunity for Banbury, too, to get a quick check through full scale operations on what changes might be needed. He put on an extra crew of men, offered bonuses for early delivery, had a cot set up in his office, checked progress every two hours night and day, shipped the machine out within the four-day deadline which State had, let us say, suggested.

The testing program at Akron also ran day and night, with everyone helping, the compounders, production men, time study men, cost men, tabulators, inspectors, and the mill room men who would actually run the machine. If it was too late when they finished for Banbury to go back to the Portage Hotel and go to bed, or if he was too tired to make the effort, he would take a nap on a cot in the first-aid room.

To prevent complaints from his other customers, Banbury ordered a duplicate machine built at the Birmingham shop, invited men from other rubber companies in to study it and make their own tests, but Goodyear, more time-conscious than the others, again got off in the lead on an extremely important improvement in tire manufacture. State ordered ten of them once he was satisfied.

The first Banbury could handle only 250 pounds of stock at a time, as compared to 1000 pounds in the largest of the old fashioned mills, but later models would step this up to 750 pounds, and the rubber could be mixed in the Banbury in two minutes as against 25 minutes the old way. The Banbury mixer, which like other machines was improved over the years, became a standard part of the equipment of all later factories except one or two of the smaller plants like Java.

It took one of the disagreeable operations out of the factory, the old type mills being used in later years only to warm up stock, and it saved a large amount of floor space. Goodyear production today would need literally acres of floor space if the old type mills were still in use.

This narrative of necessity runs ahead of its chronological order. Other events were in the making.

The company took over 20,000 acres of jungle land in Sumatra in 1916, set out a rubber plantation, began to produce its own rubber. This grew to a $17,500.00 investment, but never overtook the increasing requirements of the factory. In 1941 with 52,000 acres in full bearing, the plantation furnished only enough rubber to keep the Akron factory going for two and one half months out of the year, or one month's supply for Goodyear world wide.

The same year, with war conditions placing an embargo on shipping in Egyptian cotton, the company bought 36,000 acres of desert land in Arizona, re-established the long staple cotton industry in America, securing as strong and as long a staple as the best grades from the valley of the Nile.

A second factory was built in Canada in 1917, at Toronto, the original Canadian factory at Bowmanville being used thereafter for mechanical goods and solid tires. Plant Two in Akron went up in 1916, almost as large as Plant One, constructed especially for smaller sized tires and mechanical goods.

Goodyear had long generated its own power and in that year took over a coal mine property in Southern Ohio and thereafter mined its own coal.

Then came America's entry into the world war, which was profoundly to affect all human endeavor. Born during the Spanish-American war, Goodyear was a strapping 19-year-old when war again touched this country—and subject to draft.

Its manufacturing experience would be useful to the country. It had the best solid tire on the market (at least the majority of American truck manufacturers had adopted it as standard equipment), and this could be used on trucks and gun carriages in the world's first motorized war; it had a highly promising, though less fully proved, pneumatic tire for trucks; it was the only company which had ever designed a tire especially for the airplane; it had had no experience in making the unearthly-looking gas masks which came in during the war, but had men and machines and could learn; finally, it was the only company in America which knew anything about the spectacular new field of lighter-than-air. This was strategically important. The lighter-than-air Zeppelin was one of Germany's two surprise weapons during that war. The other, the submarine, was one weapon which blimps might challenge.

Solid tires was the first department to feel the impact of war. The Army established a big truck depot between Nevers and Dijon, well back of the fighting line (although the enemy got within 30 miles of it in the break-through at Chateau Thierry), recruited auto mechanics, battery specialists and tire repair men, including some Goodyear men, started trucks rolling out over the old Roman roads.

These roads had been built in three layers, large rocks or aggregate at the bottom, then a layer of medium-sized rocks, then crushed stone hammered into place by heavy rolls as a bonding agent. Under the stress of war many of these roads developed holes through one or even two layers, a foot or so wide, not a gradual wearing down but a sharp break, which was hard on the pneumatics of that day. Consequently, these were used principally on staff cars, motorcycles and bicycles. On one occasion Filson telephoned in excitedly from Chicago to report a big order from the Signal Corps, 9000 38 x 7's for the rear wheels, and 25,000 35 x 5's for the front. Light GMC, Nash and White trucks and half-ton Fords, most of which were just a stake body covered with tarpaulin, used some pneumatics to carry ammunition and supplies, but, for the most part the Army used solid tires.

Goodyear had built a total of 2000 pneumatic truck tires in 1916 against 125,000 solids, and while pneumatics in the peak year, 1918, reached the 40,000 mark, solids had mushroomed to more than half a million. Solid tire production went from 250 a day to 4000 by the end of the war, and the Quartermaster's Department bought hundreds of presses for mounting and demounting them in depots in this country and abroad. Allied commissions also ordered them in large numbers.

When the Army did get into using pneumatic truck tires, orders were allocated on the basis of normal supply and a number of companies put in molds to get into the business, but lacking Goodyear's step-by-step experience, did not have too satisfactory results, and the pneumatic truck tire got something of a black eye with the public, which would delay its general acceptance until the 1920's.

The tiny airplane tire department grew to large size, more than justified the research done in that field, and turned out a large percentage of the tires used on the 11,000 planes built during the war. Goodyear found itself called on for still larger tires as the one-ton bombers at the outset grew to a size of 15 tons by the time of the Armistice.

The manufacture of gas masks started early in the war, and thousands were shipped to France to protect the lives of American soldiers. One interesting story came out of that. Several rubber companies given orders for gas masks were asked to pool their compounding secrets so that everyone would have access to the fullest information. Goodyear masks, however, proved superior to others and suspicion arose that it was withholding information. The complaining companies were invited to send their men to Goodyear, stay as long as they wanted, ask all the questions that occurred to them. In the end it developed that the processes and compounding were identical, that the difference in results grew out of superior workmanship and more scrupulous observance of specifications as to precisioned temperatures and pressures which had been drilled into Goodyear workmen. Almost right is not enough with rubber.

The company's most spectacular war activity, however, was in lighter-than-air. Both the Allies and their enemy used large numbers of observation or kite balloons to direct artillery fire and to observe enemy movements, and hundreds of these went up back of the fighting lines half way across Europe, swaying at the end of 2000 feet of cable. Also the French and British had found the smaller airship, or blimp, an effective weapon against the submarine, since it could fly low and slowly, see deep under the water, hover over suspect areas.

A tract of 720 acres was acquired at nearby Wingfoot Lake as a landing field and a hangar 400 feet x 100 x 100 erected, along with cantonment buildings, work shops and a hydrogen plant. Cadet officers from Army and Navy, in olive drab and forest green, poured into Akron from primary training schools at Cornell and M.I.T. to take flight instruction at the lake, with Goodyear men as instructors. The balloon room was expanded to 2000 men and girls, and by the time of the Armistice, Goodyear had built a thousand balloons and upwards of a hundred airships. A large number of the balloons were shipped to Europe, and the blimps took up defense stations along the American coast.

Goodyear grew to a $100,000,000 company during the war, reached $168,000,000 sales by the end.

The war brought problems in trying to fill the places of 6200 Goodyear men who flocked to the colors. More than 100 Goodyear men gave up their lives, and a great bronze plaque bearing their names was later mounted in Goodyear Hall. One man, reported dead, came back to Akron after a long siege in a French hospital—and had the unique satisfaction of watching a workman chisel his name off the tablet.

With the signing of the Armistice thousands of Goodyear men came back to find their old jobs waiting for them. Business picked up fast, with a shortage of goods of many kinds. The post-war boom got under way.

•   •   •

Then came 1920, a year of bonanza and disaster.

Depression Strikes (1920-1921)

The year 1920 started more auspiciously than any in the company's history. Signed up and on the books were contracts to supply tires for half of America's new automobiles, 60 per cent of its pneumatic-tired trucks, 35 per cent of its solid-tired trucks, half of its motorcycles and 60 per cent of its remaining carriages and buggies.

Moving fast after the war the company built a six-story engineering building, was completing Goodyear Hall, and a new California factory which would add 5000 tires a day production, was working on plans for a plant in Brazil, bought a huge abandoned pottery east of the factory from the Robinson Clay Products Company for warehousing and storage. Floor space went from nine acres to more than 100. Stock was selling at over $400 a share, and the company had more than 30,000 employees.

The Canadian factory, of which the company owned 76 per cent, was going strong. The Arizona plantation was turning in a million dollar profit a year. The trees on the Sumatra rubber plantation were just coming into bearing. Export trade had reached $8,000,000 in 1919 and would double that during 1920, 15,000 new service stations had been signed up to handle Goodyear tires, twice the prewar total. Total sales had reached $168,000,000 in 1919 and orders were on the books for 1920 indicating a volume of $1,000,000 for each working day.

Goodyear was sitting on the top of the world.

The end of the year would find it on the verge of bankruptcy. Such are the hazards of business.

The story of the 1920 depression and its effect on the company is not a pleasant one, but one which must be told as a part of the story of business.

Depressions in America have usually come about a generation apart, with the result that the generation which had gone through one, and learned caution from it, is likely to be no longer in control when the next one comes—or its counsels are discounted by a driving, confident, unscarred new generation. So there may be some value in setting down the circumstances of this one.

On the face of it, there was no need for caution. The automotive industry, of which rubber was a part, had had a growth comparable to nothing in previous history. It had given stimulus on one hand to all

industry, steel, glass, rubber, leather, and to the nation's transportation
on the other. It had used new and unorthodox methods, had financed
itself on prospects and expectations, had carried the burdens of huge
working capital with income from current sales, and while conservative
bankers and business men shook their heads dolefully, the automobile
companies went out and justified the wildest expectations of their
backers.

They had struck gold! And in all ages there is no fever that quickens
the pulses and energizes the efforts and intoxicates the judgment like
that of gold.

Leadership in the industry was aggressive, and bold to the point of
daring. The companies which fell by the wayside were not those which
overestimated the market, but those who were too cautious. The men
who had the imagination to visualize the possibilities, and the ability to
develop engineering research and production efficiency, who dramatized
advertising and selling, had succeeded in bringing a product as expensive as the automobile within the reach of the majority of the people of
America in 20 years. They had visualized the market, created it, and had
met its clamorous requirements.

Goodyear sales by years furnishes an example of the terrific growth
of the industry:

YEAR	SALES
1907-08	$ 2,189,749
1908-09	4,277,067
1909-10	9,560,144
1910-11	13,262,265
1911-12	25,232,207
1912-13	32,998,827
1913-14	31,056,129
1914-15	36,490,651
1915-16	63,950,399
1916-17	111,450,643
1917-18	131,347,258
1918-19	168,914,982

Earnings on common stock, including stock dividends, had averaged
better than 50 per cent per year for the 12-year period up to 1920.

The post-war boom brought hundreds of men into the factory—from
the farms of Ohio and Pennsylvania, and from all the southern states,
creating a new housing shortage. They were buying automobiles and
silk shirts, but were sleeping two shifts to a bed. During the spring

C. H. CARLISLE, 1910
Built Canadian Company

E. G. WILMER, 1921
President and Chairman

L. C. ROCKHILL, 1907*
Built Dealer Organization

H. T. GILLEN, 1901
Early Production Leader

E. H. KOKEN, 1902
Strong Man of Canada

W. G. KITHER, 1916*
Built Australian Company

J. B. INGLE, 1915
Natural, Synthetic Rubber

H. E. BLYTHE, 1915
Sales and Production

W. C. WININGS, 1915*
Mechanical Goods Sales

ased.

of 1920 the car manufacturers warned Goodyear again and again to be ready for unprecedented business. "Buy rubber," "Buy fabric," these words rang through the purchasing offices. Fabric especially was the bottleneck. There were 3,000,000 cotton spindles in America and they were all humming, but it still seemed impossible to get enough fabric ahead in the warehouses to feel safe. At one time the situation was so acute that Goodyear was within two and a half hours of shutdown.

The war had interrupted normal production and the shortage of manpower and government restrictions had left the nation's supply of many commodities out of balance, invited speculation which soon got under way.

For a time it did not matter what men bought, they could always sell it for more. Prices were going up and up and showed no signs of abating. Corners were started in various commodities. Sugar was one of the favorites. In New England it was tire fabrics. Prices went from 30 cents to 50, to $1, to $1.25 a pound. New mills were built and existing ones bid up to unheard of prices. Dunlop, the English company, wanted to build a mill in the United States, but the contractor reported that the machinery manufacturers were far behind on their orders, could not make delivery until 1922.

The rubber companies had to contract for commitments over a long period ahead to get fabric at all, had to buy not merely their requirements for the next few months, but for a year, or two years or three years ahead before the mill owners felt justified in putting in additional plants and machinery to fill their orders.

If certain storm clouds were faintly visible on the horizon at the half year point, few men in America heeded the warning.

Goodyear's position seemed impregnable. But there is no such thing in business. Hazards wait with each year end. A business is successful only as men drive forward at full speed when conditions are favorable, draw tight the reins as they turn adverse. But when they will turn adverse, and when is the time to stop and dig in, constitutes the greatest of the gambles of business.

It is not to be expected, perhaps, that the spirit of adventure and of caution will be found in the same individual. Frank Seiberling had won throughout his Goodyear career by virtue of a daring that was almost audacity. He had won big because he had taken chances, because he had seen the automotive industry as one having almost limitless possibilities. A more conservative imagination would have played safe, but would have had to content itself with slower progress. At each turn in the road which Litchfield's developments in the factory offered, Frank

Seiberling plunged, staked everything on success. Each time he had won. But this time, unaware, the little Napoleon of the industry was riding full tilt toward the plains of Waterloo.

Depression, unseen, was moving in to upset the equation. It started that summer in a sudden slowing up of sales, cancellation of orders; grew to cataclysmic proportions in the succeeding months. Buying dried up. People quit buying tires, patched up their old ones and made them do.

Perhaps we should stop a minute to restate one of the principles of business which is often misunderstood or misinterpreted. Basically it is simple. A manufacturer buys materials, pays wages, creates floor space for the making of goods. It will take several months before the money comes back through the sale of products. If the price of materials drops during that interval, he may find himself forced to sell his goods for less than the money he put into them. That is the risk of business.

There is nothing he can do about material prices and little he can do about his own selling price, for the public fixes that through the law of demand and supply. A transaction which promised a million dollar profit in the spring may show a million dollar loss by fall after the goods are sold.

In this case material prices did fall, not a few cents a pound, but with staggering swiftness and force.

Specifically, Goodyear was using 8,000,000 pounds of rubber a month at the beginning of the year. At the then market price of 55 cents a pound, a month's supply cost $4,500,000. Since rubber takes two to four months for delivery from the Middle East, the company must have that much supply on hand or en route at all times. Another month would elapse between the time the rubber reached the receiving room and the date it emerged from the shipping room ready to sell. As we shall see, Goodyear's inventory of crude rubber dropped in value for a total of 50 million dollars in the single twelve months starting in May, 1920.

The interval between buying rubber and getting the money back is longer than in some industries, around six months. The company must be able to finance a six month supply. The same thing applies to fabrics and, to a less extent, to compounds and to other supplies. For tire fabric takes almost as long going from the plantation through the intricate process of the cotton mill till it reaches the calenders at Akron.

The company was using 3,000,000 pounds of fabric per month at the start of 1920, costing on the average of perhaps $1.50 a pound, or another $4,500,000, currently invested in a month's supply, and that figure must be multiplied several times to get the company's total investment in cotton inventory.

The wages and salaries which went into factory product ran around $1,000,000 a week, and many weeks of wages were invested in the finished tires for which there was a rapidly diminishing sale.

People sometimes have the idea that a large company need not worry about such things. But size is no protection. It only magnifies the difficulties. The fistic philosopher who said "the bigger they are, the harder they fall" spoke more truth than he realized. Goodyear as the largest and fastest growing company in the industry was hit harder than any of its competitors.

The Arizona plantation, which had been contributing handsomely to the company's business, now added to its difficulties, as raw cotton crashed from a dollar a pound to 20 cents, between planting time and harvest. And there were commitments running up to 60 cents a pound for still more cotton which no one wanted.

The original capitalization of Goodyear was $100,000 authorized, of which only half was actually issued and $43,500 paid in when the plant opened. In the 1908-9 year it had net earnings of $651,000 and the market value of the stock had risen to unwieldy proportions. The company had pursued a rather frugal policy with regard to cash dividends. There is continual need for working capital in a growing company, so earnings were largely plowed back in, the stockholders retaining their proportionate share in the ownership of a company that much larger. The stock dividends, in this case two shares for one, was the usual way to keep the value of the shares at a level where people could easily trade in them. Similar stock dividends were declared in 1910 and 1912, a 20 per cent dividend in 1914, a 100 per cent one in 1916; and in the early part of 1920, with the stock selling at more than $400 a share in the market, a stock dividend of 150 per cent. New money came in with the issuance of more stock—$17,500,000 in 1916 to help finance the building program, $10,872,000 in 1917, as the war brought new demands, $15 millions in 1918, $69 millions in 1919 and 1920. In the latter year the capital stock stood at $126 millions, almost equally divided between common and preferred, and plant investment at $55 millions.

But there were no large reserves against the rainy day. Cash reserves were rather narrow as against the large working capital required, and Goodyear even in normal times had difficulty in financing its current needs.

And when sub-normal times came, Goodyear had no strong banking affiliations to turn to. That is, no one banking group which felt Goodyear as its responsibility. It had no "financial godfather." And rubber brokers, fabric mills and machinery men began swarming into Goodyear's doors demanding their money. The banks were calling loans rather than making new ones. Three months of nightmare ensued. Dividends on the common were passed, of course, for the first time since the early days.

Temporary refinancing to the extent of $18,000,000 effected through Goldman, Sachs and Company, a New York banking house, proved inadequate. The indebtedness continued to mount and a receivership was recommended, just before Christmas.

During this hectic period Seiberling, in New York trying to raise money, met Harvey Firestone on the street.

"Harvey," cried the unsinkable Seiberling, "you take the other side of the street. I am working this side."

On New Year's Eve, members of the "old Guard," the men who had joined the company up to the year 1900, gathered as had been their custom each year in an upper room of the company offices for a friendly dinner. This time, the spontaneous gaiety of past years was absent, officers and workmen hid their feelings, talked of old days, exchanged reminiscenses of the time when Goodyear was young, and without a care.

Suddenly from the clock tower beyond the windows began the slow count of midnight. Every man was on his feet, each wondering what the new year held for them all. The last note sounded. Frank Seiberling looked up quickly. "Well, Charley, there goes 1920," he said.

"I am damn glad to see it go," said Charley Seiberling.

But more difficulties were to come with 1921. A receivership would entail heavy losses to merchandise creditors, send them to the wall, like ten pins toppling against each other. Banking groups, including the house of Morgan, sought to prevent this catastrophe.

Early in January, 1921, Paul D. Cravath, New York lawyer, acting for Goodyear, called a conference of creditors and bank representatives, pointed out the gravity of the situation. Several of the banks said they would help if someone would take the load and be responsible for the financing. That brought Dillon, Read & Company into the picture.

The hazards of business had turned with incredible suddenness against one of the most successful business houses in America, and control was to pass into new hands. That Goodyear would be able to carry the staggering load of indebtedness incurred and to bring control back to its stockholders within six years was striking proof that basic soundness had been built into the structure.

The 1921 re-financing was on a large scale, and the story is complicated. Its main outlines can be made clear. The company needed money to take up its loans at the bank, needed money to pay off its merchandise creditors, needed working capital beyond that. It was not possible in the panicky market of that time to go to the banks and borrow the large sums which would be necessary. But perhaps the same result could be reached by creating new securities and putting them out instead of the cash. The stock would have to be made exceptionally attractive to get people to accept it. The stock that would be good only if Goodyear, with this help, pulled through. The men who formulated the plan banked on the sound manufacturing organization built up behind Litchfield, the aggressive sales organization behind Stadelman, and the prestige of Goodyear tires with the public to carry the company through, once its emergency money troubles were solved.

The plan as finally adopted provided for the issuance of $27,500,000 in debenture bonds, half of it to pay off bank loans, the rest to provide working capital, $30,000,000 in prior preference stock to pay off the merchandise creditors, and $30,000,000 in bonds for additional working capital. Dillon, Read & Company agreed to take the bonds if the bank creditors' committee and the merchandise creditors' committee could dispose of the other two issues.

Beyond that the plan provided for the issuance of $10,000 in management stock to be issued to three men selected by the three groups who were to be given control of the company through the power to name a majority of the board of directors, the control to continue until the bonds were paid off. A large amount of money was being put at Goodyear's disposal. The men furnishing the capital would get their money back only if the company was successful. Good management was essential. So the men who put their money in insisted on the right to select the men who were to run the company.

The bonds were to be issued at 90, callable at 120, would run for 20 years, would pay 8 per cent interest. The debentures were put out at 90, callable at 110, were to pay 8 per cent interest, would run 10 years. As added incentive each $1000 debenture was to carry 10 shares of common stock—275,000 shares of additional common thus being created.

That settlement that Dillon effected has been variously criticized and later was attacked in court on the ground that the terms were too onerous, that too hard a bargain had been driven with a company in desperate need. The defense was that the terms arrived at were the best that could be made with the creditors in the then condition of the money market. As it was, it took three months' hard work to get the debentures and prior preference stock accepted. In the case of the debentures, the whole plan was all but upset at the last hour. The bank creditors' committee, after weeks of work, had $20,500,000 of the $27,500,000 debentures subscribed, but that seemed to be the last dollar that could be found. Dillon, Read would take the bonds only if all the debentures were underwritten. Almost all was not enough.

The merchandise creditors were canvassed. Some of them were so deeply involved that if the Goodyear deal did not go through, they themselves would be forced into bankruptcy. Two of them finally decided to take $2,500,000 between them, crediting it against later deliveries of tire fabric. That left $4,500,000 to go. Two New York investment houses, Blair & Company, Inc., and Hallgarten & Company, agreed to take one-third of this apiece if the committee would find someone to take the rest. Two other merchandise creditors agreed to divide up the last million and a half. That was on May 12, 1921. The plan was to be consummated the following day. Receivership had been averted on assurances from the bank creditors' committee that the plan would be completed. Tomorrow was the last day of grace.

But that night John Sherwin, chairman of the bank creditors' committee, sent out a hurried call for a meeting. A hitch had come up. The two creditors who were to take up the final $1,500,000 of debentures had withdrawn. The situation was deadlocked for lack of the last million and a half.

The committee went vigorously to work. Long distance calls were put in across the country. Members of the committee urged and argued with distant creditors and banking houses. All without effect. The depression was then in full swing. Everyone insisted he had gone as far as he could. The session lasted until midnight, went on. Daylight began to stream in through the windows. No progress had been made. The last source had been exhausted. Sherwin's bank was already a heavy subscriber for the debentures since Goodyear owed Union Trust better than a million dollars.

"Well," his gruff voice boomed out, "we have to put this over somehow. We cannot let an $85,000,000 deal peter out for the lack of a million and a half."

Suddenly he turned to R. C. Shaffner, head of A. G. Becker & Company, Chicago banking house, who was to render valuable service to Goodyear for years as a member of its board of directors.

"How is your nerve, Shaffner," he said, "we will take half of that if you will take the other half."

Shaffner considered a moment. The great room grew tense and still.

"All right," Shaffner said quietly, "you're on."

"Well, it's licked," said Sherwin, rising, "let's have breakfast."

The new securities would all rank ahead of the old common and preferred stock, and the common at that time would be actually less than nothing. Approval of stockholders was necessary but, apparently feeling that this was the best settlement they could get, they approved the plan and the immediate danger of collapse was over.

The "management stock" was issued to Clarence Dillon, representing the bondholders, Sherwin for the bank creditors, and Owen D. Young, General Electric chairman, representing the merchandise creditors.

The reorganization brought the retirement of the two Seiberlings and of W. E. Palmer, treasurer. There was one dramatic moment in the final meeting of the old board of directors. The main purpose of the meeting was to accept the resignation of the outgoing men, as a legal necessity, prior to the new board taking hold.

F. A. Seiberling presided as chairman, stated the purpose of the meeting, waited for a motion to accept the resignations.

There was a moment's pause. Business is business. But after all, here was the retirement of the two men who had founded the company and led it to the heights. There was a second of hesitation about offering the formal motion.

But the Seiberlings could take it. C. W. Seiberling, sensing the situation, arose.

"Mr. Chairman," he said, "I move these resignations before us be accepted."

There was undistinguishable seconding of the motion. Unhurried, Frank Seiberling declared the motion passed and retired from the meeting and from further participation in Goodyear management.

Edward G. Wilmer, 38, Milwaukee lawyer and financier, had been selected as Seiberling's successor. With him came a dozen men of varied business backgrounds, though none with experience in rubber.

Six months after Wilmer took office he said in a speech to some two hundred executives and department heads:

"Frankly, we expected to have to make a lot of changes. But we have studied the organization with extreme care, and I am amazed and delighted at the strength and judgment you have gathered together.

"There have been some changes, but they were compelled by the exigency of the situation, would have been made whoever was president. However, that job is done. Any man who is let out from now on may be sure that it is because he has not measured up. Each of you knows whether he is swinging his job or not. It is up to you from here on."

With the money provided by the reorganization, Goodyear paid off its obligations, was able again to discount its bills, had money for research and advertising and would use these to build back up, as we shall see in the next section, retain leadership of the industry.

In the years following 1921 a number of the Wilmer group left, including Wilmer himself, to become head of Dodge when that was taken over by Dillon Read in 1926, Espenhain to try to resuscitate Fisk, and Stone to go into public utilities, though remaining on the board. Others passed away during the years, leaving only Brook still on the job in 1948.

It may fairly be said of the Wilmer men that they served the company with loyalty, judgment, even with distinction.

Forces in Recovery (1921-1929)

Looking over the half century of Goodyear history, there seems to be action and drama in each period, more than might be expected in the sober story of business. The 1920 decade, however, is outstanding—and perhaps throws more light on the nature of business than others.

Here was a company which had gone to the top and plunged over the precipice; which after the books were balanced found its common stock worth $44 a share less than nothing; whose stockholders had lost control of their company to creditor and banking groups; which had to borrow some $80 millions in cash and credits to pay off its bills and start up again—but which came back so fast and so strongly that within five years the stockholders were back in control, and the company had not only held its leadership in tires, but had gone on to become the world's largest manufacturer of rubber goods.

That is not all. In this same decade which started so badly the company was able to build a new factory in the south, second in size only to Akron, start up four cotton mills, north and south, build factories in England, Australia and Argentina, and treble its holdings in rubber plantation in the Netherlands Indies; it launched a drive for foreign trade so successful that its export business grew to be larger than the total business of most rubber companies; it took leadership in mechanical goods and soles and heels, as well as tires, and found its pioneering efforts in lighter-than-air pay off in the biggest single peacetime contract ever awarded in that field.

These things did not come out of the returning prosperity of the Coolidge administration. The rubber industry as a whole got little good out of that. Many companies found themselves in difficulties instead, and some long-established ones closed their doors.

Nor did Goodyear's recovery result from any action by government. New economic theories have been advanced in recent years. And many people have come to believe that government itself can create prosperity through laws and regulations—forgetting that it is individuals, not government, who create wealth.

It is significant, perhaps, that the credit extended to the company in 1921 was private capital, not government money. Private capital does not send good money after bad. It must be sure it will get its money back. Government does not necessarily have to do this. If it makes a loan to business or to another nation and the loan is defaulted, the government would not go broke, as a private individual might. Government does not have to earn its way. It gets its money from the taxpayers, and there is always more where that came from. Consequently, the fact that money borrowed from a bank must be paid back is more of a prod to effort and resourcefulness than if it came from a rich government, which if things went bad, could write it off and forget it.

Goodyear's recovery came from its own efforts, and in two different ways. One grew out of its old formula, new products so useful to society that men would somehow find the money to buy them. The pneumatic truck tire which Goodyear had developed, and had tried not too successfully to put over before, now came through in striking fashion, as tires were further improved, and trucks and buses came to take over an increasingly larger part of the transportation of men and goods in every city, and in cross-country lines spanning the continent. The balloon tire came in for the passenger car, and toward the end of the period an airplane tire which would not only help aeronautics realize its potentialities, but lead into exceedingly important new fields.

Except for products like these—which Goodyear had a leading part in developing—the tire industry might well have reached the saturation point in the 1920's, and grow after that only as more people drove automobiles—with some recessions indeed since the better tires of the 1920's lasted longer, and people bought fewer of them. The pneumatic truck tire, the farm tire and the off-the-road tire created new markets for rubber, at least comparable in size to the passenger tire market—and with the truck tire market even larger in many foreign countries where fewer people could afford an automobile.

The second reason for Goodyear's recovery was new processing methods devised out of extremity which would lower costs. This is top strategy in depression.

All the forces of engineering, production, compounding, machine design, tire design and industrial engineering were thrown into the job of simplifying all of the processes in the manufacturing cycle, a program in which whole departments disappeared and others were changed beyond recognition—and every worker got more money for less physical effort.

The point might be made here, too, without too much emphasis, that the financial reorganization in 1921, costly as it was, did provide the working capital to enable the company to drive ahead hard and fast into research, development, machinery, advertising and sales effort, and into export, while competitors were still groggy—and that management after 1920 fully realized that this new money was not to be hoarded, but put back to work if the purpose of the refinancing was to be accomplished and money earned to pay off the loan.

The 1920 decade saw two complete economic cycles, from prosperity to depression to prosperity and depression again. Four different men served as president during this period, for it saw the retirement of Seiberling and Wilmer, the death of Stadelman and the election of Litchfield, who would serve longer at the helm than anyone had done.

Operating expenses had already been reduced to match shrinking income when the reorganization was effected in May, 1921. The payroll had been cut from 33,000 people to 5000, with every department holding onto its best men. Factory, sales, office had had a complete house cleaning. Every unnecessary step in operating the business had been routed out.

Wilmer, the new president, then 38, a young man who had made a reputation in finance and administration, brought a small group in with him, mostly in the operating end, including Stone as counsel, Stillman as secretary, Hart in finance, Brook as controller, Weberg as assistant controller for export—also Espenhain in charge of foreign sales, and a few others who did not stay very long. One of them was a traffic manager, whose leaving gave Carroll, hard-headed Goodyearite born in the shadow of a Colorado roundhouse, his chance.

Litchfield and Stadelman remained in charge of manufacturing and sales respectively, and Seiberling could have stayed on as general manager if he had been willing to step back into second place, but instead started a new company of his own at the age of 64, carved out a new fortune.

Leroy became assistant treasurer, Shilts assistant secretary, Hoskins assistant controller. Some further reorganization became necessary shortly, when the two top men in Development and several people in

Sales, including Bailey, head of mechanical goods, went over to the new Seiberling company. However Burr, Bailey's assistant, was ready to take over his work, and Litchfield reached out to California for Darrow in tire design and Dinsmore in compounding, starting the latter on the road to a vice presidency, called Steere in from the Los Angeles cotton mill a little later as difficulties arose in that field, and 1923 brought Slusser back to take charge of all staff work, Engineering, Development and Personnel, leaving Stephens free to concentrate on manufacturing.

Things got under way fast. Brook put in a modern budget system to give a better control of finance, and Wilmer got busy clearing up the financial obligations in California and Arizona, as well as the parent company, Canada handling its own. These obligations offered no great difficulties except in the case of the commitments to buy tire fabric at prices as high as $1.50 a pound and enough of it to last two or three years at the then rate of production. With fabric selling at half that in the open market, this would throw Goodyear's manufacturing costs out of balance, put it at a competitive disadvantage when recovery depended on its meeting competition in price as well as quality.

This was eventually cleared up by an unusual device. Two mills holding the heaviest commitments, both largely controlled by Myron C. Taylor, later ambassador to the Vatican, were bought outright, one at New Bedford, Massachusetts, in 1924 and another at Passaic, New Jersey, in 1926. After that the company would owe the money to itself— and find itself in the cotton milling business.

Primary responsibility for recovery, however, rested with the factory.

Goods must be sold, aggressively. It takes too long for the public to find out about the better mousetrap, or the better tire, and beat a path to anyone's door.

Books must be kept, else a company is walking blindfold, and finances must be carefully handled if a company is to have money at hand to pay bills when due, including wages, and a reserve against the contingencies of the morrow. All departments indeed are important, and a company is fortunate when each of them feels its work is the most important of all, and each individual feels his job is essential. Modern business must be competently manned through the entire range of its operations, for one weak link may be costly.

However, industry has only one way to make money. That is to produce something the public likes well enough to spend its money to buy. That is its only way of getting the money for wages, salaries, material bills, interest, dividends and the rest. The only thing it has to sell is product.

Consequently Production, with its useful departments of Engineering, Development, Personnel, Purchasing, Scheduling, Warehousing, Shipping, may well determine whether a company in the end makes money or loses it.

So Goodyear went back to the machine shop and the laboratory, and applied the painstaking process of research to earn the money to pay off its debts.

Slusser threw in a potent suggestion from California. The plant there had been cut back comparably to Akron as business fell off. Division foremen moved back into the factory to be closer to their dwindling group of men, the technical men went back to the laboratory, the sales staff was cut back to Osterloh, Hough in tire sales and Coe in aeronautics. Slusser, at one end and Osterloh at the other, were now almost a block apart, with only vacant rooms between them.

The situation was one particularly to irk Slusser, a driving personality who, for the first time in his life, did not have enough to do. One afternoon the situation had him completely down. He had to get out. He thought of a man he had met a few days before, the superintendent of the Swift packing plant who had invited him to come over some time and see his factory. On an impulse Slusser called up and drove over.

It was an important call. Slusser watched the quarters of beef moving down the line, each workman doing his special job on it as it passed, got an idea. Goodyear had put in conveyors when Plant II was built, particularly in the vulcanizing department to carry the heavy cores and molds around the curing cycle, had done something with inner tubes.

But in an industry like tires, where so many parts were manufactured separately in different places, and brought together for final assembly, conveyors could be used much more widely than they were, would bring costs down, put the company in a better competitive position.

He wrote a long letter to Litchfield that night.

"You've laid out a new job for yourself," Litchfield wrote back. "Come on into Akron."

Having rebuilt his team, Litchfield directed a planned drive to reduce manufacturing costs.

This would not be accomplished by cutting salaries and wages. That had already been done in the dark days, though with the Industrial Assembly working closely with management to put the company into a solvent position, wages were back at their previous level by 1923, moved ahead after that.

Nor would costs be cut by driving men harder, trying to get more work out of them. On the contrary Litchfield, Slusser, State and the rest sought to take all the hard back-breaking jobs out of the factory. This was not altruism but dollars and cents. Fatigue costs money, reduces output, compels too much rework of parts that will not pass the inspectors.

Every process was studied looking for places where machines, conveyors or layout changes would step up production with less manual effort. From the receiving platform to the shipping room the drive carried through each department.

We might start with the rubber itself. That had been sent through rolls at the plantation, sheeted out and folded into 200 pound bales. These sheets often stuck together, and by the time the bales reached the factory the workmen had to tear them apart with hook-like tools before they could be fed into the mixing mill.

So the "merry-go-round" came first, with the bales being carried past knives which sliced them like bread, a later device being the "pie cutter," where a hydraulic-propelled ram divided them into segments, easy to handle.

Some wild rubber was still coming in, and the African rubber particularly was often in bad shape, had to be broken down on mills, then sent through dripping washer rolls to clean out the dirt, sticks and stones, then hung up to dry. The washers went out when the company changed over completely to plantation rubber.

The Banbury mills closed up the old mill room in time and eliminated more bad working conditions. The calender, which spread the rubber on fabric, saw little change, for calenders never wear out, and some of them in use in the industry after 60 years still flaunt their Doric pillars and elaborate ornamentation.

The bias cutters, where calendered fabric was carried past the "guillotine" which cut it to length, were replaced by a vertical machine with a razor-like knife which slit it, let it slide down on a conveyor belt. Carbon black which is really soot formed by burned gas, came in in sacks in the early years, a powder so light that the air would carry it throughout a building, so it had to be mixed with other compounds in a separate department away from the rest. Carbon black began to arrive in pellet form during this era (although this was a development by the carbon black people themselves) and could be carried by gravity into the bins and from there to the Banbury.

Tire building had got away from the early method of stretching the plies over a core by hand, but was still a two-part process, and midway in it the tire builder would call the tire finisher and the two of them would lift the 60 pound core off the building stand, put it on the fin-

ishing stand. It was estimated that a tire builder lifted more than a ton
of metal a day. So collapsible cores came in, which did not have to be
moved, and building and finishing could be done on the same machine.
And the first steps were taken in the long series of improvements on
State's tire building machine which would make it all but automatic.

Goodyear developed a single-cure process in the 1920's as we shall
see later, which eliminated the old "mud room," the most disagreeable
department in the plant. The flat-built tire came in 1922, under license
from another company, was shaped by a vacuum or metal expanders.

The circular tables, turned by stomach power, where the beads were
built, were replaced by machines which braided the wire, covered it with
rubber then fabric, after which it was fed by a deft-fingered girl into a
machine which cut it to length, formed it into a hoop, while she merely
covered the ends, hung it up on the conveyor alongside.

In the vulcanizing process, as many as 30 tires, each encased in a metal
mold, were placed one on top of the other, and lowered into a pit where
heat and pressure were applied. When the cure was complete, the heavy
lids of each mold were removed with hoists, and the tire taken out with
crowbars and compressed air. This department called for the strongest
men in the plant.

In building Plant Two conveyors were installed to carry the tire to
and from curing pots, but much manual effort was still required. The
first steps were taken in the 1920's toward the watchcase mold, which
cured one tire at a time, with the lids opening automatically at the end
of the curing cycle, so that the workmen merely took out the cured tire,
hung it on a conveyor, took an uncured tire from the adjoining conveyor,
put it in place.

Because of the need for almost continuous checking back and forth
between the factory and the companies which built the machines rubber
needed, a half dozen big machine shops grew up in Akron, and gradually took over much of this business from New England—another effect
of the growth of one industry on those around it.

Anyone familiar with the tire-making process in 1920 would hardly
have recognized the Goodyear factory at the end of the decade. But
to a large extent it was the unseen, unheralded things such as these
which brought costs down and played an important part in the company's financial recovery, justified the faith in its resourcefulness that
creditors and bankers counted on.

Goodyear held its place as the leader of the industry, got its full
share of business as business picked up, and in 1925 passed its prewar
peak with a sales volume of $200 million.

With things in good running order, Wilmer had already moved up in 1923 to be chairman of the board, and G. M. Stadelman became Goodyear's sixth president—and made his first speech to the organization two years later. A meeting of some 200 men from sales and manufacturing had been called to review developments and make plans for the coming year. Wilmer thought the new president should make a talk. Stadelman was taken aback.

"Why should I?" he demanded. "I've never made a speech in my life."

The younger man smiled.

"I won't be here permanently," he said. "You're going to be head of this company. It's time for the organization to know you better. Everyone has great respect for you, but you're the man nobody knows.

"You have no difficulty expressing yourself around a conference table," he continued. "You write a better letter than anyone I know. Men work better when they feel that they know their leader."

Stadelman smiled wryly. "I agree with you thoroughly," he said. "It is something I should do and, frankly, it is something I would very much like to be able to do. But I realize that once I got up in front of an audience I would forget everything I planned to say. I can't make a fool of myself before men who should respect me. I know my limitations. I can't play the violin, I can't write poetry, I can't make a speech. I'd really like to."

Wilmer dropped the matter, but he had an idea in the back of his mind. Litchfield was away, Rockhill and Slusser were to give the principal talks, and Stadelman would merely take a bow as he had done for 20 years. However, instead of giving a conventional introduction, Wilmer made a brief talk on the character and principles of George Stadelman, and the guidance he had given the industry. He was an able speaker and many in the audience got their first picture of the real Stadelman. So when he got up to acknowledge the introduction every man in the room sprang to his feet to cheer—and kept on cheering. It was an ovation.

This action was so spontaneous and so sincere that no one could merely say "thank you" and sit down. Stadelman started to do this, to tell them what their friendship and support had meant to him, and before he realized it he had talked 15 minutes—and had made a very effective speech. The spell was broken. He walked over afterwards to Wilmer and shook hands.

"It wasn't hard to do at all," he exclaimed. "Let's set up some more meetings, I feel closer to the organization now than I ever have."

He did make several speeches after that, and his death the following year was a real loss to the organization. Litchfield came into the presidency in 1926, Slusser succeeding him as vice president of manufac-turing.

William Stephens had the first call on the vice presidency but turned it down.

"Slusser is your man," he said. "I'm a production man. Cliff has had staff experience as well as production, has had contact with engineering, personnel, efficiency—and the cotton mills. He's younger than I am, has a lot of drive that you will need. Give him the job. I'll give him the same support that I've given you."

So Slusser, who had started in as Stephens' clerk, became a vice president before he was 40.

There are not many men big enough to put the interests of the company ahead of their own.

The House of Goodyear grew fast and went far under Litchfield's leadership, with himself as the most tireless traveller of all, proceeding by train, boat, plane and car to New York, to Los Angeles, to Detroit, to Washington, to Europe, to South America, the Far East, to every part of the vast industrial development, meeting men, watching progress.

Throughout his presidency Mr. Litchfield brought home to the widening organization his deep-rooted conviction that personnel was of primary importance; that men of promise must be found, must be trained, must be given the chance to prove themselves; that competent men must be on hand for each new plant, for each new job, for each new industrial opportunity; that replacements of man-power must be available and ready for every job in Goodyear—including his own. Perhaps he even kept in mind his successor's successor, another quarter century or so ahead, for he continued to scrutinize promising new men as they came in, moved them around from place to place trying to bring out their full potentialities.

His accession to the presidency came after a quarter century of preparation. His administration saw the expansion of manufacturing facilities abroad in response to new nationalistic impulses; the dispersion of domestic manufacturing, amounting almost to decentralization; the impact of a new depression, more far-reaching and longer lasting than that of 1920; broad changes in the social and industrial structure; labor trouble on a wide scale; further government regulation of business; further amendment of the company's financial structure; increasing diversion of company earnings into taxes; saw world war again make new demands on the company.

The first thing he got into, however, after becoming president was the company's financial situation.

Goodyear's comeback was the talk of the financial world. Starting from the cellar it had earned $12 millions before interest and charges in 1923, $17 millions in 1924, and nearly $26 millions in 1925. But the early redemption requirements of the 1921 securities and high interest charges still kept it poor. From 1921 to 1925 the company spent nearly $30 millions in redeeming stocks, bonds and debentures, paid out $26 millions on top of that in interest and dividends on the prior preference stock.

Preferred stock was back on a dividend basis by 1926, but common stockholders had seen no dividends for six years and did not seem likely to see any.

Before taking up the Litchfield settlement, let us take a brief look at the corporate structure.

Reduced to simple terms we may regard the common stockholders as the virtual owners of the company. They put their money in the business, with the expectation that if profits were made, these would be divided up proportionately to their investment. The common stockholders were partners in the business, even though there were thousands of them.

But the company came to need additional money in large sums, due to its rapid growth, for buildings, machinery, rubber, cotton, more money than the partners could well supply.

Banks loan money, but a bank's capital must be kept reasonably liquid. When it loans money, it expects to get it back within a specified and rather short time, not be tied up for long periods. Goodyear's requirements for buildings, machinery and the like could not be paid back quickly. That was no job for banks.

So preferred stock came in, early in the company's history, was sold to people seeking a more or less permanent investment of their funds. Goodyear preferred was to pay 7 per cent and be cumulative, that is, if dividends could not be paid in any one year, they would accumulate and have to be paid before common stockholders could get any return.

Preferred stockholders were not partners in the sense that common stockholders were, could never get more than seven per cent no matter how much a company might earn, but they would get dividends ahead of the common stockholder. The stock had preference. In Goodyear's case dividends on preferred were 25 per cent in arrears by 1926.

The bonds issued in 1921 were to run 20 years, 5 per cent of them to be called in and paid off each year. The debentures were to run ten years, with one-tenth of them called in each year. It was good business also to redeem the Prior Preference stock as fast as finances permitted, since that paid 8 per cent dividends.

So in six years the company had reduced the outstanding bonds from $30,000,000 to $21,750,000; the $27,500,000 in debentures to $17,-227,000; and the prior preference stock from $30,000,000 to half that figure. But it had taken more than $33,000,000 out of earnings to get these off the books.

Litchfield, Leroy and his financial advisors on the board of directors worked out a plan. Longer terms securities at easier rates of interest could now be issued. Consequently, new bonds in the amount of $60,-000,000, to run for 30 years and pay 5 per cent interest, were substituted for all the 1921 securities.

To pay off the 25 per cent accumulated dividends on preferred and so open the way for the common stockholders to get a return, it was proposed to increase the amount of preferred stock by 25 per cent and give the preferred stockholders additional stock in place of the cash.

The program was approved by stockholders in July, 1927, and all the old 1921 securities were called in, the management stock was retired and the company was back in the control of the stockholders. Mr. Litchfield was reelected for a three-year term, to give him full opportunity to put the new program into effect, the motion being made by Newton D. Baker, former Secretary of War, who was a member of the Goodyear board of directors at that time.

The several interested banking groups continued to be represented on the directorate, but Goodyear men came into fuller representation in succeeding years through the election to the board of Slusser and his successor, De Young in manufacturing, Wilson of sales, Leroy of finance, Cameron of export, Hyde, legal, and of course President Thomas. Stone from the Wilmer group remained on the board through the years.

Many leading business men and public figures have served on the Goodyear directorate since and usually someone from the community of Akron, Manton and Francis Seiberling for many years, and B. A. Polsky, Akron merchant going on the board in 1946.

The financial story has been told in some detail to indicate that a company must be continuously alert for signs of trouble, be ready to trim sails quickly to meet the stresses of bad years, and must maintain adequate reserves. Having learned this lesson through bitter experience the company went into the 1929 depression in much better shape, was put to no extraordinary measures to maintain its equilibrium.

Edwin J. Thomas, born in the shadow of the plant, started as a
stenographer in 1916, became president of the company in 1940.

R. S. Wilson, Vice President (Sales)
Started in Service department 1912

P. E. H. Leroy, Vice President (Finance)
Came into Treasury Department in 1919

Russell DeYoung, Vice President, (Manufacturing) joined Squadron in 1927

J. M. Linforth, Vice President (Manufacturers Sales) came in from Navy 1922

R. P. Dinsmore, Vice President (Research) came in from Boston Tech in 1914

Fred W. Climer, Vice President (Industrial Relations) started in personnel work 1917

A. G. Cameron, Vice President Export, Started in as salesman in 1914

Howard L. Hyde, Legal Counsel, Came in from law practice 1940

Clifton Slusser, Vice President,
Started in factory in 1912
Deceased March, 1949

C. H. Brook, Comptroller, came
in with 1921 reorganization

W. D. Shilts, Secretary, joined the
company as a stenographer, 1905

Z. C. Oseland, Treasurer, joined
Treasury Department in 1929

The Strenuous Thirties (1929-1939)

The 1930 decade was crowded with action.

It saw a depression which cut deep and lasted long, intensive competition in the industry as companies fought for survival, company sales shrinking at the rate of $50 millions a year for three years in a row—but saw Goodyear ride through the storm, retain its leadership.

The decade saw new theories of Planned Government Economy tried out as a way to end depression—as against the proved methods of a free nation in the past—a movement which, whatever else it accomplished, hampered rather than helped recovery—and set afoot a flood of unionism throughout industry, including Goodyear—and the company's first serious labor trouble.

Despite all this however, the difficult 1930 period was notable for the extension of rubber into new fields, with widespread consequences to industry and agriculture. Pneumatic tires were carried to the farm, throughout the whole range of its operations, into mining, logging, road building, dam building, often carrying freight-car loads—fields which pneumatic tires might penetrate only as they paid for themselves by doing work which could not have been done as well or at all otherwise.

There were other important developments, too, in passenger tires, truck tires, rayon tires, airplane tires, and the Life Guard, the most important single contribution to driving safety yet brought out by the industry.

Mechanical goods had just as spectacular an expansion of use, particularly conveyor belts used as rubber railroads on huge construction projects in the west, literally moving mountains.

The research men came out of the laboratory during this decade with striking new products, Pliofilm, Airfoam, synthetic rubber.

Goodyear had to enlarge its production facilities with new plants at Jackson, St. Mary's and Cumberland in this country, and in distant fields like Java, Brazil and Sweden. Rubber seedlings were flown across the Pacific from the Philippines to Central America to start rubber growing on this hemisphere.

Finally the 1930's saw the company's long efforts in lighter-than-air culminate in the building of the great Akron and Macon for the Navy, and the accumulation of expeditionary experience with its blimp fleet which would be highly useful to the nation in World War II, which now had begun to throw its long shadows across our coasts.

. . .

The 1930 decade was one of the most extraordinary periods in America's economic history.

For in that decade we tried to substitute Government Planning for Individual Initiative as a way out of depression, sought to put men back to work by passing laws and issuing directives. It was a well-meant effort but as futile as King Canute's commanding the tide to turn back.

"Employers are laying off men," politicians shouted. "It is high time for the government to step in. The Private Enterprise System has failed."

And government did step in, spent as much money in eight years trying to cure the depression as it had to win a world war—with as many men out of work at the end as when it started. It took another world war to put men back to work.

The great mistake we made was to overlook the recuperative forces within our own people, and expect government to do a job which only the people themselves could do.

It was not the first depression America had seen, nor would it be the last. We had had depressions every twenty years, and each time had worked our way out of them. To a resourceful people every depression contains the seeds of its own recovery, and in each case we emerged hard and lean and sobered, drove ahead more strongly than before.

As a matter of fact recovery from the depression which had started in 1929 was already under way by the summer of 1932. The administration then in office had taken vigorous steps to meet the situation. It sought to stabilize credits with the Reconstruction Finance Corporation and Home Loan Banks. To take up unemployment slack, it had set up a public works program, like Hoover Dam, on a scale greater than all public construction done in the previous 36 years—including the Panama Canal. The stock market was going up and business moving forward.

The reasons why the curve of recovery did not continue upward after November, 1932, are clearer now than they were then. It goes back to the nature of business.

Recovery starts when an employer starts hiring men. He will do that just as fast as he thinks he can find a market for their output. If Venture Capital is not fairly sure, it will hesitate to take the risk.

And as business hesitates, men scheduled for jobs do not get them, and the machinery and materials they would use are not made or grown, transportation units lie idle, more men fail to land jobs, more potential customers decide to wait a while, and the depression goes on.

In the summer of 1932 there were storm clouds gathering which made men hesitate. Every national election creates uncertainty in the business world, but this one to a greater degree than most. If the then administration was unseated, it would be followed by one not so much unfriendly to business as having untried theories to put into effect. A prudent employer had better wait and see what happened before he hired more men, bought materials, expanded his plant.

What happened when the New Deal came in was nothing to encourage him to take the risk. America, a warm-hearted nation, deeply stirred by the spectacle of millions of men out of work, wanted to do something about it, could see no reason why the employer should not find jobs for these men. Jobs mean sales, Washington cried.

We thought all we had to do was to crack the whip and make Business put men to work. It was the scapegoat for all the nation's ills. It had failed to find jobs for men who needed them, so off with its head. The government would take charge.

The National Industrial Recovery Act of 1933 was the first step. It started with the premise that if every manufacturer and merchant got a fair price for his goods, all would be well. Neither would have excuse then for cutting wages. The Blue Eagle flew from every business house as a reminder that prices and wages must remain unchanged.

The program took care of two of the three partners, Capital and Labor, but forgot the third, the Consumer, who was the most important of all, since he paid all wages and all dividends. The consumer was hard up, could not afford to buy on a scale which would maintain wages and prices at their then levels in adequate volume.

No three-legged stool will stand on two legs. NIRA, which the public significantly shortened to NRA, fell of its own weight well before the Supreme Court knocked it in the head. It was the first and last attempt on the part of the new administration to help business. However, Washington still attempted to maintain wage levels. The principle written into Section 7A of NRA, giving men the right to bargain with their employers, was reenacted in the Wagner Act, bringing unions into the field on a wide scale. Strong unions might prevent wage cuts.

In all previous depressions, we had recognized the Consumer as the key to recovery. Get him back into the market by whatever devices resourceful men could, get him buying again, and gradually employment and purchasing power would feel that impulse. But this time we made the employee the key man. We thought that if we looked after his wages he would spend us back into prosperity. What we forgot was that it was the consumer, not the employer, who really pays wages. And that the consumer was extremely hard up.

If we had left wages free to find their own level, prices would have come down and demand have gone up. We had seen that formula work in the previous depression, only a decade before—and might well have taken a lesson in Government Planning from the effects of the Stevenson Act on the rubber plantations.

Among all employers, actual or potential, the one in best position actually to create jobs and put men to work was the manufacturer. He took the materials which others turned out, the raw products of the mill, the mine, the quarry, the woods, the farm, transformed them into consumer goods which people could buy. So he created jobs not only in his own plant, but among all his long line of suppliers.

Every community realizes the value of factories, and will go to great lengths to get them, provide sites, money, low taxes, favorable rates for gas, power, water. A city does this because it realizes that whatever it puts out it will get back many times over, in increased population, buying power, tax values and community wealth.

We might expect that the nation in a time of depression would follow this formula, give the manufacturer every assistance in putting men to work. We did not do so. We harried the faithful milch cow of Industry all over the pasture to force it to produce more jobs. Any farm boy would know better than that.

Every past depression has seen new industries come into existence, as men forced to new resourcefulness, saw in lower wage levels and dwindling inventories of goods the chance to bring out new goods and new services. The Goodyear company itself grew out of just such a situation in the 1890's, providing jobs and opportunities for thousands of men, for foremen and dispatchers and superintendents; for men expert in materials, in the expediting of traffic, in the design of machinery; for master mechanics, electrical engineers, construction engineers, power engineers, hydraulic engineers, industrial engineers; for buyers, accountants, sales executives, men expert in foreign exchange; for chemists and research men, for advertising men and artists, so far reaching are the ramifications of modern business.

Few new industries came into existence during the ten-year depression which started in 1929. Getting a new business under way is no easy task at the best. We made it more difficult this time for men even to start.

Relief and made jobs would be necessary in 1933 as in the past to tide over people placed at a special disadvantage, and perhaps to a greater extent, because of the increased complexity of our business system. But these were palliatives, not a remedy. And we should do nothing to weaken the most precious of all our national qualities, the independence and self-reliance of the individual. We should give no one reason to think that he should look to government for support rather than to his own efforts.

Men grow strong as they work their way out of difficulty. And strong individuals make a strong nation.

The New Deal was not so much an integrated program as it was a set of impulses pointing in the same general direction, and personified by a magnetic leader whose very assurance and confidence offered hope to frightened men. Behind that banner marched men with a wide range of opinions, from the economic liberals in the universities to the crackpots on the soap boxes, most of whom had in a strict sense never been either employee or employer, had not had to face the simple fact that when business puts a man to work it must be reasonably sure that it will get back from a consumer somewhere the money he paid out in wages, machinery, materials and floor space.

Undoubtedly, too, in the whole movement, unseen and unsuspected, was the leaven of Communism, of scheming men who realized that distress could be used to create confusion, division, internal strife and class hatred, out of which would come chaos, and perhaps Revolution.

Also there were shrewd men around who realized that all this was good politics in an election year.

Whatever else the New Deal accomplished it did not solve the depression nor, on the other hand, reach the objective of complete government control. Private Enterprise might be reviled and crucified, but in the end men would have to come back to it if they were to eat—unless they wanted to give up their individual freedom, turn everything over to the government, as was happening in Russia, Germany and Italy. Men can run their own lives, or let the government run them for them.

• • •

Two changes in Goodyear's financial setup were effected in the 1930's. The first one sought to improve the position of the common stockholders, the owners of the business.

Common had just come into a dividend-paying basis when the 1929 depression started, and dividends on both common and the $7 preferred were continued through the first quarter of 1932, as some contribution toward business recovery which seemed to be under way. After that, however, dividends were passed on the common and could not be paid fully on the preferred, with the result that the latter was $8.25 in arrears by February, 1936, and common stockholders could hope for no return until those back dividends were cleared up.

Company sales had slumped to a low of around $100 million in 1932 and 1933, as against the $256 million peak of 1929, but were picking up, reached $185 millions in 1936.

So the company went to its preferred stockholders on September 26, 1936, with this proposal: Since it was difficult to maintain dividends on the $7 preferred, it would exchange for each share of that stock one share of new $5 preferred, with dividends beginning as of February 23, 1936, plus a third of a share of common stock.

Goodyear had more than 25,000 preferred stockholders, living in all the 48 states of the Union and many foreign countries, but by November 16th, less than two months after the proposal went out, it had been accepted by more than three-quarters of the old preferred stock.

A second call went out in January, 1937, to the remaining holders of the old preferred and by the middle of March 98½ per cent of it had been exchanged. The remaining 1½ per cent was called in for redemption, dividends for arrears having been paid as of March 25, 1937.

This opened the way for common stockholders to participate in company earnings, and common stock continued thereafter on a dividend basis, though getting only 25 cents a share in 1938 and a maximum of $2 a share during the war.

The other change in the financial structure was effected in 1938, when taking advantage of cheaper money, the $60,000,000 five per cent bonds of 1927, already reduced by $7,500,000, were replaced by $40,-000,000 in 3½ per cent bonds, plus $10,000,000 in short term notes, at 1½ and 2½ per cent interest. The load of debt carried out of the 1921 depression had then been adjusted to the point that it was no longer burdensome.

Goodyear also found itself in the banking business during the 1930's. In building Goodyear Hall quarters were provided in the flatiron intersection of Market Street and Goodyear Avenue for a bank to serve employees and East Akron people, who otherwise would have had to travel two miles downtown. The Ohio Savings and Trust Company was organized, with some Goodyear stockholders.

However, in the hectic days following the bank holiday in 1933, the Ohio Bank merged with others downtown, and when the merged bank closed its doors, East Akron was left for two months without any banking facilities. So the company organized a new bank, The Goodyear State Bank, with Tom McEldowny, a practical bank man, as president, the current directors including Litchfield, Thomas, Leroy, Oseland and Hyde.

Mr. Litchfield relinquished the presidency of Goodyear in 1940 to become chairman of the board but retaining chief executive authority. E. J. Thomas, who had started as a stenographer in the laboratory in 1916, just before he graduated from high school, became the eighth president of the company.

Mr. Litchfield thought that he would be able to turn more and more work over to President Thomas, leave himself free for counsel and planning. But events ruled differently. There was a huge new job ahead more urgent than any up to now.

This chapter completes the main outline of the company's history up to World War II. Many of the activities referred to had wide ramifications, some would make a book in themselves. Before starting the war story, we should look at these in some detail, since they help explain the war job accomplished, and contributed to making that result possible.

2. Raw Materials

The Story of Rubber

NO NATURAL resource used by man has a stranger history than rubber, none has a wider range of useful characteristics, and no raw material which we do not ourselves produce, is more essential to our economy—as we found out in the Second World War.

In normal times we spend more money for rubber than for any other single thing we import from abroad.

What are the characteristics of rubber that make it useful to mankind?

One, rubber is plastic. Heat up a batch of it and put it into a steel mold under pressure, and it will take any shape desired, and after vulcanization —which was Charles Goodyear's discovery—it will hold that shape permanently. However, bear in mind that rubber is also incompressible, always occupies the same amount of space. Every mold must have pinholes through which even a cubic centimeter of surplus rubber may escape. For steel molds or hydraulic rams will break before rubber gives way.

Two, rubber is flexible. It will give and return to its original position all but indefinitely without breaking down.

Three, put a little rubber between the metal parts of any structure and the rubber will seal it, make it air-tight, water-tight, gas-tight, steam-tight—and rubber dissolved and spread over fabric will do the same thing.

It took the world, however, a long time to get any good out of rubber. It was a mysterious material.

Discovered at the time America was discovered, it defied practical use for nearly three and a half centuries—when the secret was revealed capriciously to a harassed inventor trying to avoid a curtain lecture from his wife.

And for almost a hundred years after vulcanization was discovered, scientists were not quite sure what had happened during that process. The rubber had changed, was thereafter fixed, set, indifferent to heat and cold, but just what had gone on within the material itself was long a matter of dispute. The chemical symbol for rubber was $(C_5H_8)X$, meaning it was five parts carbon, eight parts hydrogen, multiplied by "X", the unknown quantity.

The fact that research chemists were finally able, just before World War II, to produce, synthetically, something which had most of the characteristics of rubber, was a tremendous technical achievement—and perhaps saved civilization as we know it. The story of synthetic rubber will be told in a later chapter.

The physical properties of rubber seem somehow related to its other characteristics. Its price movements have been as erratic and resilient as the material itself, and the fortunes of any rubber manufacturer depended in no small degree on the shrewdness of his purchases in the changing markets of London, Singapore and Amsterdam.

The Goodyear company, a large user of rubber, has seen times when a change of a cent a pound meant a million and a half dollars difference in its inventory.

In May, 1920, the company had a larger stock of rubber than usual and still larger commitments in fabric, but with orders for tires coming in at the rate of a million dollars a day it could not risk running short.

However, because of a drastic change in business conditions, that was the last rubber it purchased for a whole year. Bought on a rising price market, this rubber inventory was worth, in May, 1920, $20,000,000 more than the company had paid for it, but in May, 1921, was worth $30,000,000 less than it had cost, a change in value of $50,000,000 in twelve months.

There is hazard in every business venture. But rubber, with its wide range of price changes, presents more hazards than most.

Rubber can be grown only within ten degrees of the equator. Twirl the globe and trace the world's rubber belt for yourselves. Rubber has been fought over by nations and continents, with famous names appearing in the story.

Every nation which sought to take an undue profit out of rubber has presently found that control has slipped through its fingers. The Belgian Congo was once an important source of world supply. But stories got out as to how that rubber was obtained, of slave drivers' whips, forced marches through the jungle, black men dying like flies. When the facts were exposed the abuses were stopped, but the Congo fell far behind in the process, was no longer a competitor to the Amazon.

European speculators formed pools in Brazilian rubber in 1906 and again in 1910, ran the price up to exorbitant figures. Rubber yields but bounces back. Control slipped from the Amazon to British plantations in the Middle East.

Then British control in turn was challenged by Dutch and native growers in the middle 1920's because it exacted from the world too large a price for its rubber under the Stevenson Act.

Had the Philippine Islands accepted the opportunity to get into this field in the early 1900's, the whole history of the Middle East might have been different.

And this was the business on which the young Goodyear company decided in 1898, knowing little about the material or the risks involved, to found a business enterprise.

HISTORY OF RUBBER

There is not time here to relate the whole history of rubber, but we should review the situation as it existed in 1916 when Goodyear decided to produce rubber itself. A few dates will help.

1496—Christopher Columbus found natives in the West Indies playing a strange game using large bouncing balls, something no one had seen before.

1770—Priestly gave it the name rubber, because it would rub out pencil marks. The Indians had called it caoutchouc.

1839—Charles Goodyear's discovery of the principle of vulcanization made it possible to use rubber commercially.

1876—Henry Wickham, an English botanist, smuggled 30,000 seeds of hevea (rubber) trees from Brazil, set them out in Kew Gardens, London, trans-shipped 2700 slips to Ceylon and the Straits Settlements, and in the doing gave a new industry to British colonies.

1906—Brazil, controlling 90% of the world's supply, made handsome profits, as speculators ran the price up to $1 a pound matching the $1.10 per pound rubber of 1897, but this time high prices started the planting industry in the Middle East.

1910—Second Brazilian pool which ran the price up to $3.06 gave tremendous stimulus to the planting program with the Dutch taking part as well.

1915—Plantation rubber goes ahead of wild rubber.

1916—Goodyear starts its first plantation.

Wickham did not foresee the billion-dollar industry which was to develop, but he felt he was making an important contribution to the resources of the Empire. As the dates indicate, however, his enthusiasm found few converts for 30 years. As late as 1905 the total export of rubber from the Middle East was only 174 tons, as against a world consumption of almost 40,000. Hard-headed owners of British estates were more interested in other things, coffee for example.

But when the speculators ran the price up from 61 cents to a dollar in 1906, they did more to stimulate the planting of rubber trees in the East than the exhortations of Wickham and colonial governers could in a century. Capital will go in without the urging when large profits are to be had. That is Lesson One in economics. Law Two is that supply and demand are likely to defeat monopoly, no matter how carefully planned or powerfully backed.

The speculators reaped a harvest, but they were sounding the doom of Brazilian rubber. And after a second coup in 1910 rubber moved out from the Amazon, bag and baggage, and took up its habitation in the East.

Brazil drew a strange compensation for its loss of rubber. The coffee plantations in the East had had successive bad years. Rubber offered larger profits, and planters abandoned coffee to set out rubber trees. Brazil switched to coffee. The Rio-Mocha-and-Java of the Victorian nineties was to be largely Rio thereafter, an exchange of basic commodities between continents without parallel in economic history.

If there is any comfort in the fact, Brazil could not have supplied enough rubber anyhow. For the automobile was coming in, with ravenous demands for rubber and more rubber, which demands Brazil could not have met, and in that case the amazing growth of the automotive industry would have been held back. The difficulties were inherent. Brazilian rubber came from the jungle from trees growing in nature's haphazard pattern. There might be a stand of half a dozen close together, or the tapper might have to walk a mile between trees. The average in the Amazon valley is about one or two trees to the acre.

Rubber gathering was a toilsome, dangerous and solitary trade, and none too profitable to the tapper. He had to make two trips through the jungle each morning, the first time to tap the trees and put his cup in position, and a second trip to collect the latex. Then he took the latex back to camp, coagulated it into large balls, by pouring it over a stick which he turned slowly over a low fire—and he was still a long way from the market, would have to carry his rubber on his back or by canoe to some point where a river boat could pick it up.

The best rubber growing areas lay 2000 to 2500 miles from the Atlantic. There were two important collection depots, Manaos in Brazil, 1000 miles up the Amazon, and Iquitos in Peru, 1300 miles still further away, on one of the river's numerous tributaries. Transportation charges cut into the tapper's revenue.

Brazil in its biggest year, 1912, produced 41,619 tons of rubber, but another ten years would see world consumption grow to half a million tons, with the automotive industry demanding four out of every five pounds grown.

Not by any stretch of the imagination would it have been possible for Brazil to expand its production to anything like that total.

PLANTATION RUBBER

The economics, too, were all in favor of the Middle East. If rubber trees grew only one or two to the acre in the Amazon, they could be planted on plantations as thickly as 100 to an acre, and a brisk native could tap 400 trees between daylight and ten in the morning. Middle East rubber lay close to the ocean, simplifying the matter of shipping. Labor was scarce in the Amazon valley, plentiful in the East—and commanded a relatively low wage.

And yet speculators, twice in four years, gave British planters on the other side of the globe the supreme incentive of exorbitant prices to meet the world's need for rubber, at the very time when those needs were mounting to undreamed of volume.

And what an incentive dollar rubber was to the setting out of plantations. It became the most popular of British "specs". From duke to coster-monger, everyone who could afford it hurried down to Mincing Lane, invested his pounds and shillings in these newly discovered mines of plastic gold. All you had to do was to plant the seeds, wait seven years for the trees to grow up, and be rich. The lucky holders of plantation shares sent their dividends back for reinvestment.

It is no small undertaking to clear and plant 1000 acres of land. But the Brazilian rubber corner set the British planting at the rate of 300,000 to 400,000 acres a year. By 1915 there were 3,000,000 acres under cultivation in the East, and already plantation rubber had taken the lead in world consumption. One decade saw 95 per cent of the world's rubber produced in Brazil and 5 per cent in the Eastern plantations. The next decade saw those figures exactly reversed.

Wickham was knighted, listed among the Empire builders.

Brazil continued to produce rubber but in declining volume. Manaos had had one of the great theatres of the continent in the boom years, brought in great operatic and dramatic stars from Europe. Now the strong-necked jungle growth began to make its way between the planks of the floor, and boring insects honey-combed the walls.

The plantations grew with the automotive industry, but did not quite catch up. Prices continued to permit generous profits. Some of the tire manufacturers, now large consumers of rubber, began setting out their own plantations—The U. S. Rubber Company in Sumatra and Malaya; Dunlop, the British company, in Malaya; Michelin, the French tire maker, in Indo-China; Goodyear in Sumatra. Each planted considerable acreages, but so fast had the industry grown that these were all but negligible in the great range of the East. The total production from estates owned by tire manufacturers in 1940 was a little more

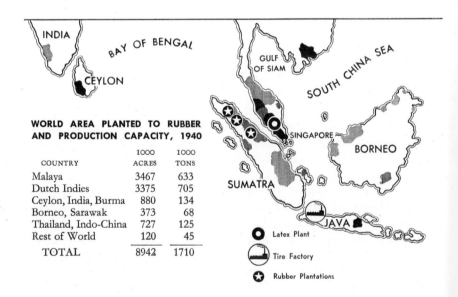

WORLD AREA PLANTED TO RUBBER AND PRODUCTION CAPACITY, 1940

COUNTRY	1000 ACRES	1000 TONS
Malaya	3467	633
Dutch Indies	3375	705
Ceylon, India, Burma	880	134
Borneo, Sarawak	373	68
Thailand, Indo-China	727	125
Rest of World	120	45
TOTAL	8942	1710

than five per cent of the total. The total investment in rubber estates in 1920 was around $800,000,000, mostly British capital.

But dire events were in the making. The plantation industry crashed with the 1920 depression. Rubber fell from 55 cents a pound to 10 cents. Paper fortunes, made in rubber, faded again into paper. The industry faced ruin. Production costs on the plantations were higher than New York selling prices. And since the great majority of plantation shareholders were British, the distress in England was acute and far-reaching.

THE STEVENSON ACT

Winston Churchill, then Colonial Secretary, moved into the situation, named a commission to see what could be done. It was headed by Sir James Stevenson, a successful business man (Johnny Walker whiskey), the other members being rubber planters. The Commission recommended restricting shipments of rubber from the plantations until the price rose to a fair level, which was set at 30 cents a pound, later raised to 36 cents. Scarcity of rubber would force the price up.

The Dutch were also raising rubber in the East and were invited to join in the plan, but when they refused, Britain, which controlled 85 per cent of the growing areas of the world, decided to go ahead on its own.

The Stevenson Act passed in November, 1922, limited shipments immediately to 60 per cent of standard production, provided for review at three-month intervals at which time more rubber might be released, or further reductions made.

The United States, which used more than half of the rubber grown in the world, showed some concern over the passage of this Act, but was given assurances that Britain planned only to stabilize the price of rubber, and that the law was flexible enough to prevent prices from getting out of hand.

American uneasiness over the Stevenson Act gradually abated as a year passed, with the 1920 surplus still undigested, and rubber selling well below 30 cents. Two years after the law took effect, the quarterly price survey resulted in restricting shipments to 50 per cent. Only half of British rubber was going to market.

But in that same quarter year the tide turned, and rubber, depressed too long, bounced back. The low point in restriction coincided almost exactly with the low point of world supply and the beginning of business recovery. The automobile business began booming again; the tire business kept apace with it; European rubber consumption was increasing; the balloon tire, which used more rubber than the old high pressures, had come in and was sweeping the market. Rubber began a sensational march upward. It passed the stabilizing figure of 30 cents a pound, and kept going, to 50 cents, to 75 cents, to a dollar, hit a peak of $1.23.

Then things began to happen on both sides of the Atlantic. Churchill and Stevenson might have congratulated themselves in 1925 when they saw millions of dollars pouring into British banks as a result of the restriction act, but they felt genuine concern when they realized that the Stevenson Act had ruffled Anglo-American relations as nothing had done since the Venezuela episode in Grover Cleveland's day. Restriction was denounced in the United States as a device to make the American car owner pay the British war debt. Rubber became Page One news in New York, in London, in Washington, in The Hague, in Singapore, became the subject of debate in the House of Congress and the House of Parliament.

Parliament could have stepped in and changed the law, but did not do so. So much feeling had been stirred up as to make it impossible politically. Additional rubber was released only in three-month intervals and it was not until February of 1926 that the planters were free to send all their rubber to market.

Apparently the Stevenson Act had been a success, saved the day for the plantations. But two and a half years later, in November, 1928, the Act was repealed, and the price of rubber, then standing at 40 cents, dropped immediately to 30 cents—and kept on going down.

The story of restriction deserves review as an example of the working out of economic laws. From the day the Stevenson Act was passed, economic laws began making themselves felt. Nature, if she abhors a vacuum, seems equally to abhor a monopoly. If one man corners a commodity and seeks to force other men to pay him an unreasonable price, he lays a challenge to the world to defeat him. He may build a great wall around his goods, but no matter how high or how strong it is, the ingenuity of other men is instantly stimulated to try to find a hole in it or a way around or over or under it, or for that matter to find some other way of getting in.

In this case men began to use less rubber. As tire prices went up people drove their tires harder, patched them up and kept going rather than buy new ones. Reclaiming picked up amazingly. *But the big factor was that the high prices brought thousands of new rubber growers in to the field.* Even America studied this possibility. Congress ordered Secretary of Commerce Herbert Hoover to make a search for rubber growing areas anywhere in the world which this country might go into.

The Stevenson Act offered the Philippines a second opportunity to get a foothold in the industry, but the insular laws stood in the way.

This grew out of the Spanish-American War, and the acquisition of the islands. Led by William Jennings Bryan, the "anti-imperialists" raised a great hue and cry in Congress about any exploitation of new possessions—and were joined by ambitious politicos in Manila, who feared that if American capital made any large investment in the islands, any chance of eventual independence would go glimmering.

The Philippine legislature asked William Howard Taft, first governor general, to draw up legislation to protect the interests of the island, keep out foreign capital. This might be done by barring immigration and limiting landholding by an individual to 2500 acres.

Taft was a good lawyer and the code he drew up was so iron-clad that no one was ever able to get around it—except the Japanese, to some extent in pre-war years, by registering tracts under dummy names in far away parts of the southern islands. Planters could not import Malay and Chinese labor as the Dutch had done in Sumatra, and land-holders were limited under the Taft law to 2500 acres. This did it.

Efficient management might have been able to use Philippino labor despite the lower wages paid elsewhere, but the limitation of land holding made any large-scale development impracticable. In this business 2500 acres is only a drop in the bucket. At an annual production of 400 pounds to the acre, it could produce only 500 tons a year.

Any European colonial administration would not have hesitated to step in where the national advantage was so clearly indicated. But an attempt by the American Congress to change the laws of the islands would stir up a hornet's nest, perhaps bring on a revolution. Bryan was dead but there were plenty of statesmen ready to take up the gauge if so drastic a change were proposed. A more liberal policy might have been good business for the Philippines economically. It was bad business politically. The Philippines were out.

THE DUTCH PLANTATIONS

The Dutch were under no such handicap and would find a way. It would cost uncounted millions to match British rubber investment if Holland went into it as England had done. The British had developed its great plantations chiefly with money from home. The average cost of acquiring, clearing and planting rubber was around $400 per acre. It would not cost Holland that much.

British and Dutch held different theories as to colonial administration. English colonies have been largely developed by British money, with the government alert to protect and forward them. The Dutch were more inclined to let the native develop the territory himself—and to take their return second-hand. If the native prospered, The Hague would benefit through increased tax returns. The Dutch program from 1922 on called for relatively small investment of thrifty Holland guilders.

The European planter had to build towns, hospitals, highways, warehouses; must pay stipulated wages, plus so many pounds of rice a day. If he imported natives from the densely populated Dutch islands he had to send them home at the end of the period. All these things build up plantation costs.

But when a native went out to plant rubber, he was on his own. His tastes were simple. Dutch field agents gave him selected seeds, told him where to plant trees. He could live comfortably on rice and fish while his trees were growing up. He would plant only as much land as he and his family could tap, the average being around 10 acres, though some of the more enterprising natives planted as high as 100 acres, tapping the balance on shares.

There are many Dutch-owned estates in Sumatra, in fact Queen Wilhelmina was a considerable stockholder in two of the biggest. But the native had always been an important factor. He became more so from 1922 on when the Dutch sent him out to fight the battle of rubber. So quiet was this movement that it attracted little attention for a few years. The migration of Javanese into undeveloped Sumatra went slowly until the price of rubber began to skyrocket. Then it took on boom proportions. The Javanese needed no suggestion from the government after that. Chinese traders, plying their sailing boats up every navigable bit of water and along 2000 miles of coast line, encouraged the movement. And back into the jungles and rich uplands of Sumatra moved a veritable army of brown-skinned Johnnie Appleseeds, planting rubber broadcast, settling down along highways and streams, building their little villages, upsetting the plans of the Secretary of State for the Colonies, forcing the final repeal of the Stevenson Act, setting up a real challenge to the white man for the future.

A few figures will indicate the magnitude of the movement. In 1921, just before the Stevenson Act was passed, native planters sent 6000 tons of rubber to the market. In 1927 they marketed 95,000 tons. Of the estimated 8,000,000 acres of rubber in the world, more than 3,000,000 acres were planted after 1922. To a large extent this additional acreage was Dutch-native ownership. In a decade British control fell from 85

An army of natives was needed to clear the thousands of jungle acres before planting could begin. The latex from the tree is coagulated (below), sheeted out between steel rolls, hung up to dry, then packed for shipping.

per cent to not a great deal more than 50 per cent. Ownership and planting costs had been spread among hundreds of thousands of Javanese. The additional acreage had cost the Dutch practically nothing.

It was the little brown man who in the end broke the British monopoly. He had no town sites to keep up, no payrolls to maintain, no managing directors, no Scotch-and-soda chits, no sons to be educated in Europe, no daughters to be presented at court. Give him his holiday festivals and enough to eat and he was content. He was not a business man, had no ambition to build an industrial empire. His challenge was that of numbers, of the vast areas of trees that he held.

Output from the Dutch possessions came up by the 1930's almost even with the British, and between them they controlled 90 per cent of the world supply.

However, the new planting which high prices brought about gave the world more rubber than it could use, and the depression sent the price careening down anew, reaching the ruinous low mark of $2\frac{7}{8}$ cents in 1932. For 18 months the price hung around the five cent level, well below production costs, even on the most efficient plantations. This brought in a new restriction plan in 1934. Holland and French Indo-China joined the British this time, but it was not until 1938 that prices moved up to a profitable level, ranging that year from 11 cents a pound up to 25 cents.

After that came the Japanese, and on their heels American synthetic rubber.

The Importance of Cotton

The story of cotton has less drama, but cotton is just as essential in this industry as rubber. No pneumatic tires are made entirely of rubber. An all-rubber tire would swell up as air was pumped in until it filled the fender well.

The inner tube could be made of rubber alone, since it merely clung the more tightly to the inside of the tire under pressure, but the pneumatic casing needed a stout harness of fabric to hold it in shape. So the casing is made up of plies of fabric, which are impregnated and coated with rubber to protect them from moisture, with the rubber treads and sidewalls to protect it from abrasion.

Stronger fabric came in with the years, but shortly before World War II, huge cross-country trucks began to make demands greater than cotton could meet. The tire industry had to find something else, which brought in new fabrics like nylon and rayon—but that is another story, which will be told later on.

For nearly 40 years the tire industry depended on cotton alone, and to a major extent still does in 1948.

What makes cotton important in the rubber industry? The answer lies in the nature of the material.

Cotton growing in the field consists of slender fibres rising from a cotton seed, so slender that if magnified to an inch in diameter, they would be more than 100 feet long, so light that it would take from 10,000 to 20,000 of them to weigh one grain. If one pound of these fibres were placed end to end they would extend 2200 miles.

These fibres have one strangely useful property. Under the microscope they are seen to be minute hollow tubes, which as the cotton dries in the sun, begin to twist around, hook on to neighboring fibres, with as high as 100 to 300 of these convolutions to an inch of length. It is this characteristic, absent in fibres like milkweed and thistledown, which enables cotton to be spun and woven into cloth, gives basis for a billion-dollar industry.

What curious naturalist first observed this, and what ingenious inventor found a way to utilize it, goes back centuries beyond any written record. Cotton weaving existed in India 15 centuries before the Christian era, spread from there to China, Japan, Egypt. Even primitive people picked up the secret. Columbus found natives of the West Indies wearing clothing of a crudely woven cotton. Vasco de Gama observed a similar phenomenon when he first touched the Cape of Good Hope.

Spinning and weaving were household arts until the Industrial Revolution in England took the looms and spinning wheels out of the home, established them in factories, and through lowering costs gave England a firm grip on the textile industry.

The American colonists brought their spinning wheels with them to this country, and early in our history cotton mills went up in New England, with British-born weavers as the backbone of the industry, and Massachusetts began to run second to Lancastershire in the manufacture of cotton fabric.

New England, however, was largely an industrial extension of Old England, and even when many cotton mills moved to the south after 1900, to the Carolinas, Georgia and Alabama, in order to be closer to the raw materials, and get the benefit of low labor and power costs, they took their customs, traditions, and mill villages with them.

Consequently, when rubber and cotton met in the early years of the

The spinning of cotton is an all but endless process of drawing, twisting and doubling until the delicate fibres have been transformed into stout cords.

In the weaving room cords from thousands of spindles are drawn onto the loom where bobbins flashing back and forth weave it into fabric.

automobile, it was a meeting of one of the youngest industries with one of the oldest, and there were contrasting and conflicting viewpoints growing out of their different backgrounds. The cotton industry was old, solid, conservative, almost to the point of being set in its ways, held to ideas and even nomenclature reading well back in the history of the industry.

Even today the textile mills speak of slubbers and doffers, of cards, combs and drawing frames, of bobbins, spools and reels. The foremen are still "overseers," and the employees are still "hands," and the industry retained up to fairly modern times a paternalistic atmosphere unduplicated in American industrial life—except to a small degree in the coal mining industry, which was also imported from England.

The automotive industry by contrast was fast moving, experimental minded, daring almost to the point of recklessness, a Middle West industry which broke away from the New England tradition, pioneered a new industrial thinking. More than a bit of adjustment of viewpoint would be necessary between the two industries, and those difficulties would in time lead Goodyear to acquire its own textile mill.

The tire industry was not satisfied to use the standard cotton from Georgia and Alabama, which was good enough for almost everyone else. It wanted long staple cotton from the Sea Islands off the Georgia-Carolina coast, or from the Nile Valley in Egypt—which was used in this country chiefly in making thread.

Tensile strength is not particularly important in a cotton dress or a handkerchief, but it is extremely so in tires, hose and belting. Georgia cotton had a staple length of seven-eighths inch, Egyptian was one and one-quarter inches. The extra length gave that many more tiny handholds of fibre with fibre to make a stronger thread. Technological improvements in later years would make it possible for the rubber industry to use the medium length Peeler cotton of the Mississippi Delta, but in 1908 long staple cotton was necessary to good tires and the industry would use nothing else.

Tire fabric was a small item in the textile industry, hardly worth the mills bothering with, particularly if they had to change over machines and processes to turn it out in such small volume. Even today, despite the tremendous growth of the automotive industry, tires consume only about 5 per cent of the nation's cotton.

This was the general picture when the automotive industry began to grow. With such a background it is easy to understand that the textile industry felt somewhat distrustful of the automobile and the things accessory to it. The automotive industry was too new, too extravagant, too reckless, too confident. Its financing was built, not on accumulated earnings, but on fantastic expectations. And though the new industry won vast gambles, justified investments running into the millions, paid handsome dividends on huge borrowings, whether from the banks or stockholders, the older industry still shook its head.

The automotive industry was wasteful, scrapping machines after a few years which had years of life in them; it paid absurdly high wages; it paid out money extravagantly to get a job done today which could be done better and more cheaply if it had been willing to wait until next week. It was restless, never satisfied, always changing, always wanting things done differently—asking for new weaves, for greater strength, tried to tell the textile industry its own business. These western customers from Detroit and Akron paid their bills and would even offer a thrifty bonus for expedited delivery, but the hard-headed Yankee mill owners thought they were a confounded nuisance.

The Need for Compounds

If rubber needed cotton for some products, it would need compounds in all of them. Rubber alone has practically no commercial usefulness. It would melt and run in hot weather, congeal and crack in cold. Society got scant good out of rubber in the 350 years between Christopher Columbus and Charles Goodyear, because it did not know what to do with it. The discovery of vulcanization in 1839 had the extremely important result that, once vulcanized, rubber became indifferent to heat and cold.

So Charles Goodyear (1800-1860), a Yankee from Connecticut, made a billion dollar industry possible. Goodyear was not a scientist. He was a prosperous hardware merchant in Philadelphia at the time he became interested in rubber, through seeing its shortcomings, decided there must be some way to turn it to the use of man, and once he started on that search would not quit until he found the answer.

He knew little of the chemical properties of the various substances he mixed with rubber. With almost incredible patience he tried everything he could think of, alone and in various combinations, and under various conditions, was almost literally looking for the needle in the haystack. When he did succeed after six years of unremitting effort, he did not know what had happened to the rubber—though that is not

In his humble kitchen at Woburn, Mass., Charles Goodyear, one of the world's
great figures, finds secret of vulcanization of rubber after many vicissitudes.

strange, for scientific men were still arguing that point 50 years after he was dead.

The thing that marked Goodyear for greatness, apart from the importance of his discovery, was his courage and determination. He met not merely the setbacks which are part of all experimentation, but the greater disappointments which come when failure stalks in at the very instant of seeming success. More than once Goodyear thought he had found the secret and drove ahead to put it to work, only to find it had again eluded him. But he had courage to pick up the pieces and start in again. Despite failure and ridicule, poverty, distress and evil-smelling jail cells, he held to his search with a persistence that has few counterparts. The most perverse fortune must respect such fortitude.

Let us repeat the legend of the discovery. Goodyear had been working for six years on the enigma of rubber. It had cost him his hardware business and all the money he had or could borrow. He had a large family that suffered with his reverses. His wife was a patient, courageous person, but in the end even she begged him to give it up, find work which would at least provide food and clothing for their children.

He was moved by her distress, but men of Goodyear's temperament cannot really quit a quest they have set out on. Rubber was an obsession to him. Men said he was crazy. He could not get the thing out of his mind. He reviewed past failures, thought of other possibilities. Sulphur had always seemed promising, and he was kneading some into a batch of rubber one day in the kitchen when he heard his wife's step at the door. She had gone to market and he had expected to have half an hour by himself, but there she was. He did not want to hurt her feelings and threw the batch hastily into the stove. However he did not forget about it. He had to take a surreptitious look at it later. It was a historic moment. For something had happened to the rubber. He subjected it to heat, nailed it up outdoors in freezing weather. Neither heat nor cold changed it. It was still flexible. Sulphur, plus heat, was the answer. His long search was over.

This legend lacks complete historical verification, but deserves full belief as a symbol of human progress. Other great discoveries have come by seeming accident, and it would seem that when men have gone to the full extent of their powers, a kindly Providence sometimes jogs their elbow, points out the solution they would otherwise have missed.

Goodyear called his discovery vulcanization, after the Greek god Vulcan, the deity of blacksmiths and of metals.

Rubber goods manufacture got under way at once, but did not make too much progress in the next half century. It was the period of the practical shop man, of secret processes and rule of thumb. Ingenious men experimented, trying a little of this, a little of that, observed results. They tried with some success to make rubber easier to work with, and to reduce the curing time, which took three or four hours at 285 degrees temperature.

Rubber manufacture was largely confined to New England (though the bicycle brought in Middle West companies), and frequently was a one-family business, making footwear, rubberized clothing, fire hose, mill hose, molded goods like valves, belting to compete with leather.

That was what drew P. W. Litchfield into the industry, namely that it was such a backward one. It was unexplored territory, with large unmapped and unknown areas.

Each compounder guarded his secrets jealously, kept his formulas in a little book in his pocket, or in his head. He alone knew what was mixed with rubber as it went on the mill rolls. Often he was the superintendent as well.

One of the legends of the period illustrates the importance of the compounder. Dr. Goodrich, head of the Goodrich Company, had an argument with Tew, his brother-in-law, who was the superintendent, and Tew walked off the job—carrying his compound book with him. The company had almost to close down until the doctor could make his peace with his brother-in-law.

Early experimenters found that the materials they used with rubber did not always act uniformly. Some acted quite differently when used alone than in combination with others. Someone noticed that antimony sulphide, a coloring agency, was useful also as a sulphur carrier, helped incorporate the sulphur into the rubber.

One difficulty was that wild rubber of that era was itself not uniform in quality or characteristics. Compounding difficulties were summarized by James C. Lawrence in his book, "The World's Struggle With Rubber":

"Charles Goodyear founded the rubber industry on five variables:

"(1) Rubber, which could vary with every tree, with every Indian who prepared it for shipment, with methods of packing, shipping and storage, and with methods of preliminary handling in the factory;

"(2) Sulphur, the quantity of which included in every given batch could range from one per cent to 50 per cent of the weight of rubber;

"(3) Compounding ingredients and activating agents now so numerous as to offer infinite possibilities for varying the character of rubber mixtures;

"(4) Temperature of vulcanization, which varies from that of superheated steam down to the temperature of the room in which work is carried on;

"(5) Time of vulcanization, which may be measured in minutes or in hours."

By 1900 four groups of compounds were in general use, fillers, softeners, accelerators and coloring agents. The fillers, rather inert chemically, diluted the rubber, made it go farther. The softeners made it easier to work with, less sticky, the principal ones being whiting, barytes, china clay, Fuller's earth and talc. Accelerators were found which speeded up the curing process, included litharge, lime, magnesium oxide and white lead. Coloring agents, used in clothing, footwear and drug sundries, were chiefly ochre, ultramarine blue, mercuric sulphide and antimony sulphide.

However, the advent of the automobile started a new era in compounding. Raincoats, overshoes, garden hose, could get along without such characteristics as resistance to abrasion. A tire could not.

It was high time for the chemists to get busy and find out more about rubber and its reactions. And to this problem, Litchfield at Goodyear, who had started as a compounder and knew the practical end of the business, Marks and Oenslager at Diamond, Geer at Goodrich and others set themselves.

The most important early finding was the use of organic materials by Oenslager in 1906. To put the matter in simple terms of fundamental chemistry, all the materials compounded with rubber previously were inorganic substances, such as lime, litharge, metal, rock. The number of these is limited. To form organic substances, however, carbon, hydrogen, oxygen and sometimes nitrogen and sulphur combine in almost endless variation, form such widely different things as coal, gases, dye stuffs, petroleum. Organic compounds offered limitless possibilities to the rubber chemist. Oenslager discovered that aniline oil, and later thio-carbanilide, had an accelerating effect, and in addition to speeding up the cure, made the product more uniform, gave it better physical properties. His findings were kept secret for some time, patents not being issued until 1912 and then through a foreign company.

But with the hint that Oenslager's discovery furnished, the chemists set off in intensive researches into organic accelerators and wrote a brilliant chapter in the history of the industry.

When Goodyear set up its own Development Department in 1908, one of its two major functions was compounding, technically trained men being brought in to study the matter of increasing the usefulness of rubber in its present fields, and of opening up new fields, in both cases through compounding with it various materials that would give it a wider range of characteristics, reach fuller potentialities to society.

Two products of the Goodyear laboratory were so successful that they were widely sold throughout the industry. One was Captax, an organic accelerator, brought out in 1922, which could be used with any kind of stock and permit vulcanization over a wide range of temperatures. Accelerators were important in reduced manufacturing costs, since more products could be cured from the same presses.

The other, developed in 1923, was an anti-oxidant. Rubber is organic material and like all such materials is subject to deterioration, a problem from the earliest days, especially under bright sunlight. It aged too rapidly, might soften up or grow brittle and crack. The Goodyear anti-oxidant retarded oxidation, gave the tires longer life.

In setting up a compounding department, however, the company did not throw away any of the information accumulated by practical men in the past, used both types of personnel. This was particularly the case in mechanical goods, an older industry than tires, which had grown up in the trial and error period of the industry. William Metzler, first production head, who had started in the business in 1886, and Hal Campbell, who succeeded him later, had come out of the old school, combined their practical experience with the technical findings, helped carry mechanical goods on to the important place it occupies in the industrial world today.

There were many occasions when things did not work out as anticipated, and it was the practical experience of the two men and some of the old-time foremen which brought the answer.

The necessity of getting increased strength and resistance to abrasion and wear came up early in the tire industry, particularly for the tread. One of the pigments or powders used as fillers from the early days had the property of giving additional strength. That was zinc oxide, which became extremely important to the industry—and incidentally gave the country the white sidewall tire.

World War I brought a shortage of zinc oxide and the chemists had to work fast to find a substitute. They found in carbon black an exceedingly important one. That, as everyone in the rubber business knows, is practically pure carbon or soot, generated by the burning of gas.

Coming in as a substitute, carbon black added something of its own. It bound the tiny rubber particles more tightly together, making a tougher, better-wearing stock, better able to resist the abrasive effect of rocky highways.

White tread tires, however, went out with carbon black, and some car owners were not too happy about that. Zinc oxide continues to be widely used in the tire industry, is the second most important pigment used by the compounders, carbon black being first, and highly important in the later synthetic rubber as well. Today more than 40 per cent of the weight of the tread is carbon black, and nearly a quarter of the weight of the sidewalls.

The rubber chemists were beginning by now to know more about rubber. Under the microscope it was seen to be composed of almost countless small pear-shaped globules. In the latex as it comes from the rubber tree, each of these globules had a covering around it, a protein substance which the chemists call a protective colloid. This cover is broken sufficiently when acetic acid is added to the latex that the particles of rubber come together to form a solid substance. These globules are very small, from 1/50,000 to 1/80,000 of an inch in diameter; if one were to lay all of these individual globules from a single gallon of latex end to end, they would extend 372 miles.

So early experimenters had made a shrewd guess when they selected fine powders or pigments to mix with rubber. The clay, lithopone, magnesium carbonate, barytes and whiting of early days are all fine, mix easily with the minute rubber globules. The particles in zinc oxide are still smaller, about 1/250,000 of an inch in size.

These pigments do not combine with rubber in a chemical sense. Mix two parts of hydrogen and one part of oxygen and you have something which is neither oxygen nor hydrogen, but water. They combine in exact proportions, any excess oxygen or hydrogen remaining as a free gas.

Zinc oxide mixed with rubber in the mill room becomes a fairly homogeneous mixture, but the zinc oxide has not combined with the rubber. One has merely a mixture of the two. Separate them and they have the same properties as before. But while there is no chemical change, there are profound changes in the resulting physical properties.

Carbon black became useful because its particles are even finer than zinc oxide, having a diameter of 1/500,000 of an inch. In fact, carbon black is so light that the least breeze will set it scattering through a room. The particles of carbon are so fine that they had never been seen separately, until the electron microscope came in, in recent years, and it was possible to photograph them.

An ingredient so light that it floated in the air, blackened faces and clothing no matter how carefully guarded, brought problems to the factory. For years it was mixed with small batches of rubber in an isolated building, confining the damage to one spot rather than dispersing it over the entire plant. The men in the department quickly got accustomed to it, took a shower and put on clean clothes before leaving, and the department had lower turnover than others where working conditions were more favorable. In later years carbon black manufacturers found a way to process it into pellets, which could be carried by suction from freight cars directly into tanks which feed into the Banbury mixers.

The chemists were certain by 1920 that the size of the particles had some bearing on the reinforcing properties of any pigment, so others were added. The most important pigments today are gas black, zinc oxide, clay, magnesium carbonate and the soft or thermal blacks.

Compounds, then, are an essential part of the rubber business, sometimes creating serious bottlenecks as war or other emergencies result in a shortage, with satisfactory substitutes difficult to obtain. But the compounds had to be found and their reactions known. Much of this has been done since 1900.

The Pneumatic Tire Itself

Before we get back into the narrative, we should also take a look at the tire, this thing of rubber and fabric on which Goodyear had based its business destiny.

Litchfield once said that a business house was on sound ground as long as it produced something men needed at a price they could pay.

The pneumatic tire was something men needed, even though they did not realize it, for it could greatly serve transportation.

The automobile would have more effect on transportation than any vehicle since the dawn of history. It would widen every individual's range of contacts, broaden the markets for whatever he raised or made. It would carry box car loads of cargo at express train speed anywhere where there was a highway, would enable America's Mass Production System to expand its tonnage enormously by making the assembly of parts produced in other plants in a 500 mile radius almost as simple as from departments under its own roof.

But the automobile could not do this job without pneumatic tires. The tire was an indispensable part of the Automotive Age. Within the few inches of space between the inflexible concrete highway and the inflexible steel wheel, it must absorb the million jolts of high speed travel. The automobile rode on air, and only rubber, of all materials, was flexible enough to act as the container. To realize the importance of the pneumatic tire, watch a car rattling down the street on the rim.

The rubber tire started a little more than a century ago, in 1846, seven years after the discovery of vulcanization. In that year Robert W. Thomson (1822-1873), a 23-year-old civil engineer in Scotland, using a leather tread to protect the rubber, demonstrated that a pneumatic tire would reduce skidding and noise, and that a horse-drawn cart would have 60 per cent more traction over good roads and 300 per cent more over rough ones with pneumatics. He patented his idea, tried to develop self-propelled vehicles on which to use his tires. He was handicapped, however, by the Red Flag Act of 1865, which provided that a man carrying a red flag must walk ahead of any vehicle travelling faster than four miles per hour. Thomson died at 51, and apparently the pneumatic tire died with him.

The bicycle came in in 1818, two wheels with the seat low enough that the rider could keep both feet on the ground and propel it forward. McMillen, in 1839, thinking a rider might learn to balance himself, evolved a bicycle with a front wheel drive. Since a large wheel could travel faster, the front wheels grew as high as eight feet by 1870, though the average was about five. The low-wheeled "safety" bicycle, with a gear drive on the rear wheel, came in in 1885, and the two types battled for public favor until the pneumatic tire came along to tip the scale in favor of the safety, since it was hard to build pneumatic tires for the high wheels.

That brings in another Scotchman, Dr. John Boyd Dunlop (1840-1922), a veterinary practicing in Ireland, who learning that he had been born two months prematurely, thought of himself as an invalid, avoided all possible exertion—though he died at 82 after the first serious illness he had ever had. Worrying that his 10-year-old-son, presumably also delicate, might ruin his health by riding his safety bicycle over the cobblestones of Dublin's streets, Dr. Dunlop contrived a rubber tubing, with a one way valve, covered it with canvas, cemented it to the wheel.

The device was successful and he applied for a patent in 1889, started a company and was just well launched in pneumatic tire manufacture when the long forgotten Thomson patent came to light and the tire business was thrown open to everyone.

3. First Expansion Period

Growth at Akron

FROM 1908, when the automotive industry hit its stride, to 1920, when business took a holiday, one of Goodyear's biggest jobs was to build enough tires to keep up with the mounting demand for its product.

It was an exciting period. Building succeeded building in an almost continuous construction program. Factory additions filled the creek valley where the company started, moved up to Market Street, cleared out the scattered stores and homes there to create an unbroken façade of factory buildings, then moved upstream to create the huge Plant II, almost as large as the main factory. Hard-driving Bill State, chief engineer, was in his element in these years. By 1920, factories parallel street and creek bed for almost a mile, and Goodyear had the largest tire capacity of any plant in the world.

It was high time in 1908 for Goodyear to expand. Tire production had gone from a total of 4476 tires in 1902 to 28,000 in 1907, must now be stepped up from the 90 tires to 6500 tires a day by 1914 when the World War broke out.

To take full advantage of the sales opportunity the Straight Side tire furnished, would compel an increase in manufacturing space from the original one acre to nine.

Other buildings went up in 1912 in the valley and a large receiving and storage room on Market, where great grain elevators eight stories high had long been a conspicuous part of the East Akron skyline.

This had been another Seiberling enterprise of the 1880's, with a brother-in-law, L. C. Miles, and Barber, the match king, associated with it. A merger in 1890 had passed control to the Great Western Cereal Company, which in turn sold out in 1911 to Quaker Oats, who closed it down, already having one factory in Akron. Goodyear took over the property and dismantled the building.

The clamorous needs for floor space called for ingenuity as well as speed. For example, in 1912 the factory wanted three additional floors built on top of Building 13, but the wooden supporting columns would not carry the load. There was no time to tear the building down and rebuild it, so the engineers simply reinforced the foundations, built lattice work columns of steel around the wooden pillars, ran these to the roof and constructed the additional floors on them without any interruption of production.

A river got lost in this period. A dam had been thrown across the Little Cuyahoga upstream from the factory to create a small lake, with sluice gates controlling the amount of water which came into the plant. Now the river was covered over by factory buildings, flowed unseen in culverts after that. Old timers watched its passing with regret, for in the peaceful early days they had done a bit of fishing there during the noon period and, if the truth were told, occasionally during working hours, if no one was looking.

The Little Cuyahoga, however, took its revenge in the 1913 flood when it over-flowed its banks, closed down the factory for several days.

By the end of 1912 floor space which had started with 44,000 square feet reached almost the million mark.

From that time on plant capacity was a continuous problem. Buildings went up at record speed. One day saw the steam shovels start tearing great holes in the ground. Before one knew it the foundations were in and the floors being laid. The next time one looked, the upper floors were being built and machinery was moving in. In an incredibly short time, the building had been roofed over and men were going to work.

To make the construction men's tasks harder, the manufacture of tires calls for a set sequence, from crude rubber to mills, calenders, compounding and so on, and it was all but impossible to maintain anything like a straight assembly line in an industry growing so fast—and changing so fast.

As new factory buildings moved up the hill on Market Street and were connected up with the old ones in the lower levels of the valley, the anomaly resulted that the third floor of one building became the fifth floor of another and, the fourth floor of the factory office was on the street level.

Constructors grew still busier in 1915-17. The war in Europe gave additional stimulus to an industry already booming, and tire production at Goodyear grew from two and a half million tires to almost six million. Litchfield drew up a comprehensive building program, one which would give the factory a breathing spell.

The program included a seven story building for the storage and processing of crude rubber on the far side of the B. & O. tracks with overhead crossovers connecting with the main plant, a huge receiving room for incoming materials and supplies, a garage for company and employee cars, an addition to the general office with a new Factory Office alongside. It also included an entirely new plant to be devoted to what were then called Ford-size tires and mechanical goods.

Plant II, as the new factory was named, gave Litchfield the opportunity to build a plant laid out to permit a more efficient movement of materials in process. Plant I, like Topsy, had "just growed", would always be something of a makeshift. Conveyors were installed for the first time. The tire division would concentrate on the production of smaller tires, 30 x 3 and 30 x 3½, chiefly for Ford and Chevrolet, to get the fullest benefit of quantity production.

However, while Plant II was the last word in tire factories at the time it was built it was not to remain so. Changes came in, eliminating entire departments; tires were built in larger sizes, in shorter curing time and always increasing volume. As later factories came to be built at California, at Gadsden, and abroad, each showed many divergencies from the plant which preceded it, marking the several stages in the evolution of the industry.

It was typical of the company's interest in new things that it went into radio transmission in 1916, perhaps the first industrial use of radio. A wireless tower was erected on top of the old general office building to talk to Detroit, and a second one at Bowmanville to keep contact with Toronto. Radio had not developed far at that time, and the installations were not too satisfactory. Both were taken down at the suggestion

Plant II, built in 1916 for industrial rubber goods and small tires, grew to huge size. The lighter areas are basins where the water is cooled and used over.

A coal mine in southern Ohio, acquired in 1917, was modernized and mechanized by company engineers, still furnishes power for the Akron plants.

of the government after this country got into the first World War.

Goodyear was the city's largest consumer of power by 1917 and in that year purchased a coal mine down state near the town of Adena.

Although the mine was acquired merely to furnish power for the Akron plant, the restless Goodyear mind could not resist the temptation to seek improvements. Engineer State started early to utilize machinery wherever possible to reduce costs, improve working conditions, relieve some of the back-breaking work of the mine. Machinery was adapted to drill and cut the coal, and power-driven motors installed on the cars to carry the coal out, and by 1924 the last of the patient mine mules was turned out to graze.

The Adena mine became one of the pioneers in mechanized mining, work being continued after State's death in 1933. Electric drills mounted on tripods were used to drill holes for the powder blasts; machines undercut the mine, curious looking machines with nine-foot long snouts, somewhat resembling a sword fish, which would lean down, under-cut the ledge, back up, cut a vertical swath down the middle, lumber on into the next room.

The loading machine followed. It had crab-like claws which alternately, with one claw then the other, raked the coal aboard the car where a chain drive carried it back and dumped it into a waiting shuttle car. The shuttle car was equipped with rubber tires, needed no railroad tracks, gave more headroom. The car would haul the coal out and dump it aboard a conveyor belt which carried it to the dispatching station, loaded it on the outbound cars. Pick and shovel work was limited to the minor cleanup operations, and the Goodyear mine became one of the most modern in the country.

Goodyear Hall was started in 1917 to house the company's educational work, but construction was interrupted by the war, and only the high-ceilinged gymnasium was completed, to be used for the assembly and inspection of the great kite balloons.

End of the war brought the post-war business boom, called for still more production capacity, but except for a small addition to Plant II for mechanical goods, this expansion had to go elsewhere because of the shortage of water for cooling purposes, even though using the water over and over, and California got the benefit of the needed expansion. Goodyear Hall was completed to its full six story height, an abandoned pottery of the Robinson Clay Products Company beyond Plant II was acquired for storage, and work was started on a six-story engineering building.

The post-war boom, however, was short-lived, and Goodyear found itself for the first time with more floor space than it needed. Work was stopped on the new engineering building and the warehouse, and the steel skeletons were cited by armchair critics as mistakes in corporation judgment.

However, that would not last long. The factory that was too large in 1920 was too small again within five years. Improved machinery had made it possible to turn out more goods in less floor space, but the water situation still stood as a deterrent to large-scale expansion in Akron. New construction was largely for activities not as thirsty as rubber. Completion of the engineering building made its former space available for manufacturing, three wings were added to Plant II for mechanical goods, and the reclaiming plant enlarged to a capacity of a ton a day as the runaway prices brought by the Stevenson Act brought a wider use of reclaimed rubber.

In 1927 two more wings were added at Plant II for mechanical goods, the Rim Plant was built on the Robinson pottery site, and a 600,000 sq. ft. building for warehousing went up alongside it, the largest single unit yet built by the company, marking the beginning of Plant III.

Further expansion, the big Airship Dock, the Synthetic Rubber Plant in the 1930's, and the huge war and post-war developments, all but doubling the capacity of the Akron works will be told elsewhere.

As expansion continued after 1920 outside of Akron, Goodyear engineers, because of the specialized nature of the industry and the demands for speed were sent out to direct construction, men expert in electrical, mechanical, steam and ventilating phases, in layout and planning.

Some of the men travelled far. LaDue who helped build Plant II, made the preliminary studies in England, built factories in Sweden, Java, Cedartown, Jackson, St. Marys, Arizona Aircraft, the Houston synthetic plant and Topeka. He also made the advance surveys for Argentina, Brazil, Peru and Mexico, and spent more time in the 32 years outside of Akron than in.

It will be appropriate to stop here and see why engineering needed a six-story building providing seven acres of floor space.

The machine shop was an important part of the company's work from the first days, not only for maintenance and repair, but as a production factory for the cores on which the tires were built and the molds in which they were cured. Goodyear built these itself, largely because they could not be bought in the open market, since they were intimately related with the tire industry and its changing developments, and to tell the truth, because specifications were not to be had.

In the early molds it was largely a matter of cut and try, build a mold, cure a tire in it, see where it was wrong, trim the mold again, and still again until it would produce a perfect tire. It was not until 1911 that Elmer Clark, later master mechanic, developed master templates from which other templates were made, so a workman did not saw the template off along with the metal he was cutting to fit.

There were a dozen men in the department on the day shift and three or four on the night shift in 1908 when Boigegrain, the longest service man in the department, came in as a boy in his teens after learning the die-setting trade from his father. There were no technically trained engineers in the group. The men would have chased any white-collared people out. These men had learned their trade under apprenticeship to older machinists. Many of them were Englishmen like Ed Nall, who left traditions of sound workmanship.

The machine shop grew rapidly after 1908 particularly as new types and sizes of tires were developed, calling for a tremendous job of recutting molds and building new ones. In the end the company had to farm out a lot of this work and Akron developed a sizable machine shop industry serving the rubber companies.

A staff department of considerable size grew up as well, with Machine Design becoming a separate department, maintenance, which must always be carried on, and a growing number of men from the engineering schools, specialists in steam engineering, hydraulic, electrical, conveyorization, ventilating and equipment engineers.

Next to production itself, engineering, in all its phases became the largest department in the company, had some 1200 people on its payroll.

Manufacturing in Canada

The year 1910 saw Goodyear's first expansion outside of the country. Canada was becoming an important market itself, and with export duties coming in, would be a convenient stepping stone to British Empire markets.

The development of the automotive industry in Canada was largely Canadian-American. European manufacturers never gained a foothold, due in part to the proximity of American manufacturers, and in part to road conditions in a new country which required more rugged cars than were used abroad. A smaller influence may have been the fact that English cars used the right-hand drive which Canada in the main rejected, or in the case of the city of Victoria and the Maritime Provinces, later discarded.

Ford started manufacturing across the river at Windsor as early as 1904. Buick concluded an arrangement in 1907 with the McLaughlin people, famous carriage makers at Oshawa, to manufacture McLaughlin-Buicks, the beginning of General Motors in Canada. Other American companies came in shortly: Studebaker, Packard, Hupp and Chrysler at Windsor; Hudson at Tilbury; Reo at Toronto; also the truck manufacturers, White, International Harvester, Mack.

Seiberling had been watching the situation, and when Toronto in 1909 announced the first automobile show in Canada, he sent C. H. Carlisle over to size things up.

A thrifty Scotch Irishman with marked gifts in finance and merchandising, Carlisle had spent seven years with the M. O'Neil Company, Akron department store, was at that time its credit manager. The O'Neil Company was selling Goodyear quite a bit of fabric, and Carlisle went out personally to see Seiberling about a disputed bill. He not only collected the bill but left Seiberling so well impressed with the way he handled the matter that he offered him a job on the spot. Canada was his first important assignment.

Carlisle did not rest with visiting the auto show. He did a lot of window shopping, appraising the kind of goods Canadians bought, spent half a day riding the street cars, changing every few blocks to another car to size up the population. He came back well impressed with the substantial character of the Canadian people and of Canada as a market for automotive goods. So he got the job of setting up a branch at Toronto.

Proposing to live within the company's means, he started in on a modest scale, rented a small 30 x 80 foot building, helped the workmen put up shelving, brought in carpenters' horses and plain boards for counters. This was in March, 1910.

Shortly afterward Canada set a 35 per cent import duty on tires. It was clear that the company must manufacture tires in Canada if it wanted to sell any there. However, the cautious Carlisle did not recommend building a plant. He looked around to see if he could not avoid that large an investment. The Durham Rubber Company was making mechanical goods at Bowmanville, 50 miles east and not doing too well, so shortly after the first of the year Durham agreed to put up a two story addition, and to compound enough rubber and calender enough fabric to permit production of 200 Goodyear tires a day in the new building.

Bowmanville was a pleasant little town of brick houses surrounded

The huge tire plant at Toronto, which grew with the years, was further expanded in World War II. Head offices of Goodyear-Canada are in Toronto.

Bowmanville, making mechanical goods (above), is three times as large as the original 1910 plant. Textile mill (below) at picturesque St. Hyacinthe, Quebec.

by rich farming country. The Bowmanville Rubber Company had started there in 1887 to make fire hose, garden hose, packing, bicycle tires, had been succeeded in 1898 by the Durham Rubber Company, which had had its ups and downs, had tried several times to sell out.

In fact whenever the head of the company was able to persuade someone to come out to look at his plant, he would send the hackman to the depot with instructions to drive like the wind so the visitor would not realize how far the factory was from the railroad. The Goodyear deal was a windfall, he felt.

However, the rubber industry in 1910 was ready to drive forward in Canada as well as in the United States, though its progress would be in tires rather than mechanical goods.

The company did not start off with a seasoned organization acquainted with Goodyear methods. Carlisle, who became secretary-treasurer, was a newcomer with the company, as was Van Bever who went over as sales manager. Moriarty with manufacturing experience in the Dominion became superintendent and P. D. Saylor, a Canadian whom we shall meet later in England, became assistant sales manager in charge of mechanical goods.

The company got off to a good start. McLaughlin-Buick at Oshawa, eight miles away, was Goodyear's first big customer—and quickly calling for more and more tires. The Durham branches at Toronto, Montreal and Winnipeg, which had been taken over, began to increase their orders. With the preferential Canadian duties, export business picked up. Carlisle had new desks and benches installed in the sales room at Toronto. Bookkeepers and clerks crowded each other.

The tire ticket of 200 a day was raised to 250, to 300, and by fall had reached 400 tires a day. Durham, its placid existence thrown into confusion by the avalanche of business, threw up its hands. Unable to finance the purchase of new mills and calenders and its increasing needs in rubber and fabric which the tire builders next door were calling for, it sold out. In October of that year, Goodyear took over the plant, paying $100,000 in cash, the balance in stock.

Durham mechanical goods had a good reputation for quality, so manufacture was continued under Hardy as superintendent, and the 100 Durham employees went on the Goodyear payroll. The tire division had 50 men, but with business growing had to start hiring at once.

Export sales by now looked so promising that Van Bever went to London to open the company's first export branch, Saylor succeeding him at Toronto.

The first full year brought a profit of $72,000 and 1912 saw it reach

$164,000. The head office in Toronto was completely outgrown and a five-story office building went up in 1913.

Then came product trouble, something new to Goodyear.

No one expected long mileage from his tires in those days. If a man said he had driven from Toronto to Hamilton and back, 80 miles, without puncture or blow-out, his veracity was questioned. But Goodyear tires began to fall below even the minimum expectations of those days. The adjustment department was kept busy. Tires came back by the carload. Akron specifications had been disregarded. The situation became so critical that Litchfield sent his right-hand man, Ed Koken, over to take charge.

Koken moved to Canada, corrected the difficulties, made sure that Goodyear specifications were followed to the letter. The company again began to move ahead. Carlisle became general manager, Saylor went to London, succeeding Van Bever. Akron sent a few experienced men over to strengthen the organization, Barrett and Allman in production, Dinsmore, as chief chemist, Brown on tire design, Shumaker in personnel.

Goodyear was the first American rubber company to locate in Canada, though Dunlop, the English company, had a factory in Toronto and U. S. Rubber took over a plant at Kitchener, changing the name to Dominion Rubber Company, and other American companies entered the field later.

Canada was also the first Goodyear plant to be operated outside of Akron, and an incident shortly after Koken's arrival brought home the need for close contact.

Every workman likes to keep the best tools, so as Canada called for new equipment, it was apt to get whatever Akron did not want. Koken took Litchfield out in the plant one day, showed him some machinery just in from Akron. Litchfield called Slusser, the trouble shooter, in on his return.

"Canada must not be treated like an orphan," he said. "See that it gets first class equipment."

For a while Slusser followed all Canadian shipments through personally clear to the railroad cars to make sure no one switched anything. Then he set up a new department to act virtually as Canada's representative in Akron. This was the beginning of the Interplant Relations department which grew to large proportions as outside plants multiplied.

With the stimulus of World War I, fast increasing export business, and growing car registration in the Dominion, paralleling that across the border, Goodyear became the largest tire manufacturer in Canada by 1917, outgrowing its facilities. Production reached 65,000 casings in 1914, doubled in 1915, and more than doubled the 1915 total in 1917. Courts were covered over and used as manufacturing space. Total floor space grew from 44,000 square feet to 118,000. Employees were brought in from Toronto by train, sent back at night. Fifty houses were built on what was called Carlisle Avenue, and even the town hotel was taken over to house employees. But it was not enough.

Goodyear could increase its factory facilities but it could not build a town. Bowmanville might have been another Oshawa if it had seized the opportunity which the situation presented; but since it did not, a move was imperative.

Toronto had ample water supply, plenty of labor, was an excellent shipping point. A site of 23 acres was purchased in New Toronto, 10 miles west of the city proper, and here a modern factory went up in 1917. The tire department moved in that fall, mechanical goods and solid tires remaining at Bowmanville with 218 employees out of the total of 900.

Hardy stayed there in charge. A native of the town, who had hired in at Durham in 1899, making bicycle tires, he had long experience in mechanical goods, becoming foreman of the hose department, then of belting, and was general foreman when Goodyear took over.

After the tire departments moved out it was suggested that the empty buildings at Bowmanville be torn down. But mechanical goods too was growing, and in a few years filled the vacant floor space, called for more room twice the original size, with further additions built later, and Bowmanville became the largest mechanical goods plant in Canada. Its great conveyor and transmission belts were widely used in Canadian factories and mines, and it found a growing market for V belts, hose, soles and heels and molded goods.

The move to Toronto gave opportunity to build a model plant, as Bowmanville had been largely a makeshift. There would be plenty of room, capacity of 2000 tires a day, ten times the estimate under which manufacturing had been started in Canada seven years before. Plant capacity, it was thought in 1917, would be ample for years to come. But the Canadian factory was just starting, would have to increase its capacity 300 fold in the next dozen years as demand grew from 2000 tires a day to 10,500.

Carlisle who had gone out to Goodyear in 1909 to collect a bill, had become one of the acknowledged leaders of Canadian industry and president of one of its biggest banks. Both he and Koken became Canadian citizens.

The Move to California

The post-war business boom was on in 1919, and the water situation made expansion difficult at Akron. The company turned to the Pacific coast. A new plant there would serve the western market, and the rubber could be shipped by water almost to its door.

Two studies, independent of each other, concurred in recommending Los Angeles, then a city of 575,000 people, a little larger than Buffalo. A site was picked, part of the old Teague ranch, which dated back to the covered wagon days. It lay pretty far from town, and there was some criticism of the selection for that reason, but the land could be bought on the acreage basis, and there was plenty of it. The property was half a mile wide, two miles long. The old Ascot race track lay at the end nearest town, and beyond it were walnut groves and acres of cauliflower farms—and someone called the company the Goodyear Tire and Cauliflower Company.

Mr. Litchfield directed the studies as to the site, laid out the manufacturing program. F. A. Seiberling undertook to set up the financial structure.

He went out, talked to two men, explained that Goodyear was not merely building a branch factory, but starting a California company, manned by California employees, drawing on the west as far as possible for materials, and built in part by California money, so that the west would have a stake in the enterprise.

He proposed to issue $8,000,000 par value of preferred stock, $4,000,000 common. Goodyear would turn over to the new company full selling rights for the west, contribute its manufacturing and technical experience, and put in $4,000,000 in cash, taking up all the common stock.

The preferred, 7 per cent cumulative, would have equal voting rights share for share with the common, and have preference in dividends. That is, if not enough was earned to pay dividends on both common and preferred, the preferred would have prior claim and if dividends could not be paid in any year, they would accumulate and have to be cleared up before Goodyear, as the one common stockholder, could get any return from its investment.

Goodyear proposed also, he explained, to build a textile mill alongside, so as to manufacture its tire fabric in Los Angeles, rather than ship it in from the East, already short of productive capacity. This would be a separate corporation, $2,000,000 preferred stock and $1,-000,000 common, Goodyear again subscribing for the common stock.

The men to whom Seiberling talked asked him to leave the matter with them for 24 hours. It was a large order. But Los Angeles had already become used to thinking in large terms, and the possibility of raising $10,000,000 did not dismay them. They were alert enough to see in the situation what they thought was an opportunity for Los Angeles.

The city was a commercial city, had few industries, though motion pictures promised to be important. The back country was given over to farm and orchard products. But Los Angeles was ambitious. It had obtained adequate water supply by a daring engineering feat, bringing the water in from 300 miles away, tunneling through the mountains. It had built a harbor at San Pedro, nearby, though tonnage was still comparatively light. More and more tourists were coming out for a visit—and staying. The men to whom Seiberling talked felt that an industrial development was the one thing the city needed to drive it forward to be a great city. If Goodyear came out, others would follow.

The following evening, Seiberling was invited to a meeting where he found 20 of the business leaders of the city gathered. He talked for 30 minutes, told the story of Goodyear, of the rubber and automotive industry, of the company's plans. His talk made electric appeal to his listeners. One man after another arose to assure him of support and by the end of the hour the entire issue had been subscribed. Someone asked how long it would take to get the factory under way.

"We'll be building tires one year from tonight," Seiberling promised. The meeting had been enthusiastic, everyone was excited about the project, but most of the audience discounted this statement. One year! That was hardly possible.

But Bill State went out, and in 30 days a dynamic engineering job was under way. The grandstand was partitioned into drafting rooms and store rooms for materials. Gang plows ripped up the race track, steel, concrete and machinery roared into the premises and the huge E-shaped building, 1000 feet long and three stories high, took shape so quickly that on June 14, 1920, a little over 11 months after Seiberling's talk, the first Goodyear California tire was built. A number of the original subscribers were present.

Among the spectators, too, was a slender youngster, just turned 21, making his first trip for the company. This was Eddie Thomas, Litchfield's secretary—who would succeed him as president of the company twenty years later.

Los Angeles factory, one of the most attractive of all Goodyear plants, was a forerunner to important industrial developments on the west coast.

This air picture shows the size of California plant. Airplane markings are on roof of original textile mill. Blimp hangar is at far left.

Personnel for the new plant was studied carefully. Canada had gotten off to a bad start because of product trouble, till Koken went up. California had to be a success. Osterloh, crack salesman, by now secretary of the company, was selected as general manager.

"I suppose you'll send Bill Stephens out as superintendent," Seiberling said.

"No, I'm sending Slusser," said Litchfield.

"Steve is your top production man," Seiberling reminded him.

"I'll gamble on Cliff," said Litchfield. "I think he's ready."

Seiberling was still a little dubious. "But it's your responsibility," he said. "You're in charge of manufacturing."

Personnel plays an important part in business. Clifton Slusser, who would succeed Litchfield as vice president in charge of all Goodyear production before he was 40, was typical of the fighting spirit of the early days.

He was not born with a silver spoon in his mouth, had no college degree. What he did have, however, was the faculty of getting things done, regardless. Every time a tough job came along it seemed to land in his lap, and he had handled it, and learned by the doing.

Born in the nearby coal mining town of Massillon, he had had to work hard for everything he got. He had left school early, worked at the various jobs a small town offers, came to Akron to take a job at Goodrich, noticed in the minor depression of 1906 that more laboring men were out of work than office men, so set out to educate himself, went to business school at night after working twelve hours in the factory, studied bookkeeping and shorthand, got a job as bookkeeper in a coal company and was promoted to cashier. On that job, however, he had to be bonded, and he was under 21.

So he quit and took a job at Goodyear in the service department, checking tires that came in for adjustments, writing customer letters. This was in 1911. His energy caught the attention of William Stephens, who asked him to come to work for him as his secretary. Stephens did not want someone to take dictation. He did not write many letters, would rather talk to men personally. But the factory was growing and he needed a follow-up man to go out in the plant to see that things were going as he wanted. That was no easy job, but Slusser was tough enough to take it. One day work was being held up because some castings had not been delivered.

"Go over to Ed Nall's office and ask him when in the hell we're going to get those castings," Steve called to Slusser. Nall, the master mechanic, was the czar of his department and people watched their step in talking to him. But Slusser delivered Steve's inquiry verbatim. Nall was taken aback. People did not talk to him like that. He started for Slusser to throw him out of the office. Slusser met him half way. Suddenly Nall stopped and grinned.

"You little devil, I believe you would fight," he said.

"Well, how about those castings?" said Slusser.

"You and I'll get along all right, kid," said Nall. "Tell Steve they'll be ready at one o'clock."

When the flood of 1913 hit the factory Slusser was the first office man to volunteer. Water and debris poured through the factory. The flood waters had killed the fires under the boilers and the whole plant was at a standstill until things could be cleaned up. It meant climbing down into storm sewers, wading knee-deep and hip-deep clearing out refuse that had the water trapped. Slusser worked 18 hours a day, won his spurs.

Consequently, when it was decided to form a Flying Squadron he was given the job of organizing it. The Efficiency Department job came next, then the organization of the Personnel Department. Nine years after Slusser came to work for Goodyear as a clerk, he was general superintendent in California.

Key men were picked to head up Development, Tech Service, Engineering, Personnel, Purchasing, most of them from Akron, although Dinsmore came from the Canadian plant, and Steere, the cotton mill superintendent, was hired in New England—and took 30 picked men out with him, since he could not expect to find experienced men on the west coast.

Slusser took 107 men from the Squadron to start production and break in new men, many of whom stayed on to become foremen and supervisors. Osterloh selected men to head up the sale of passenger and truck tires, mechanical goods, aeronautical goods. Accounting and credit departments were represented. California was another Akron on a smaller scale.

Slusser set up a factory council to keep each department informed about what went on elsewhere and he and Osterloh compared notes daily on larger problems. An industrial relations program was set up, hospital, restaurant, Wingfoot Clan, Efficiency Department, Flying Squadron, an athletic program.

The Pony Blimp was shipped out as part of the aeronautical program and a small hangar built at one end of the property. The Ascot grandstand was partly dismantled and the rest of it used as a garage. The city cut streets through, started paving them. A streetcar line extended to the property. The plant was on its way.

Between the spring of 1919 when the plant was decided on, and the summer of 1920 when it got into production, business remained good. Depression hit just as it was getting under way. Then sales fell off almost to the vanishing point, the working force was cut back almost to the original Akron group, and some of them left. Dividends were passed, of course, and there was some talk among California stockholders of taking over control of the company. Some rubber companies lost their subsidiaries under similar circumstances during this period. President Wilmer sent John K. Mapel out as his representative. Well-versed in finance, he proved a steadying influence, restored confidence among the stockholders.

The depression, though severe, did not last long, and as business picked up California got back on its feet, and by 1924 current and back dividends had been paid up. The textile mill came back even more quickly since it had but one customer, the tire mill alongside who was always needing fabric. Blythe succeeded Slusser as superintendent.

The surplus land the company did not need was sold, for more than the entire tract had cost originally, proved a good real estate deal. The property can be visualized as four pieces of land, each half a mile square. Goodyear built on Section Two, sold Section One, which was closer to town, and Three and Four beyond. Later the company sold the back half of its own section, retaining a property half a mile long and a quarter mile deep, still plenty of room so that it would not be hemmed in, and ample space for an athletic field on one side of the plant and the landing field for the larger blimp, Volunteer, which went out in 1929.

The property disposed of was used almost entirely for industrial and commercial purposes until the entire section was built up with factories and warehouses, with residential sections alongside, and within seven years the factory, which at the outset was out in the country, was completely surrounded and the city extended for several miles beyond.

The soundness of the decision to build on the coast was indicated in the next ten years as the other members of rubber's Big Four followed Goodyear west, and Los Angeles became the second largest rubber manufacturing center in the country.

Goodyear-California did well enough financially from 1924 to 1930 as to show an average profit of a million dollars a year for the ten year period, while the city's belief that the advent of a big company like Goodyear would start other eastern houses thinking along the same line, was verified in a large-scale industrial development. *That Los Angeles*

grew from half a million people to a million and a half in ten years is
due to a number of factors, but certainly the industrial stimulus was one.

Its coming to California had affected other industries as well. The
company drew on the west for materials and supplies as far as possible.
Though the rubber came from Sumatra, Arizona and California cotton
was used. It got its sulphur from Texas through plants located in California, the useful material soapstone, which keeps rubber from sticking
during manufacturing processes, comes from California, carbon black
from Texas, Wyoming and Montana.

Mineral rubber was developed from California petroleum. Paul
Shoaff, a chemical engineer who would go far in the company, first
attracted Akron's attention by working this out with the oil companies.
California mineral rubber was later exported to Goodyear Australia.

Other compounds used less extensively in rubber manufacture, including whiting, limerock, mica and Gilsonite, came in from the adjoining mountain states. The factory also led to the development of machine shops and machinery manufacture in Southern California.

Progress slowed down with the 1929 depression. There were three
other large tire companies now in Los Angeles to divide up a dwindling
amount of business. Stockholders began to murmur again. Some felt
that the parent company should make up the California losses, pay
dividends. So a plan was worked out in 1934, by which California preferred stock could be exchanged, share for share, with that of the parent
company. Coast stockholders were then put in a more secure position,
since adverse conditions in one section of the world might be offset by
more favorable ones elsewhere. The 16,000 shares of the textile company were called in also.

The California plant was built for a capacity of 5000 tires a day but
various improvements in the manufacturing processes developed in
Akron were installed in the new plant and by 1930 it was possible to
turn out 7500 tires a day in the same floor space, though with adverse
business conditions in the following decade, actual production ran from
3000 to 5000.

There were other things, however, contributed by California which
were even more useful to the over all corporation.

This was the first effort to apply the Akron program full-scale in a
new plant, make what adjustments were necessary due to size or environment, arrive at a program which could be used anywhere, in case
further expansion proved necessary.

Canada had been started earlier before the program was fully developed.

The policy was laid down that while ideas from the outside as to improvements in products, processes and machines were highly welcome, Akron would install the laboratories and experimental shops and take responsibility for development, not duplicate facilities in each factory. Another rubber company kept each of its outside plants as independent units, made them compete with each other. Something can be said for both plans.

The Goodyear system, however, made an immediate and complete exchange of information necessary between the parent plant and those outside. The Interplant Relations Department, headed for years by Hurley, became more important.

Akron had many departments. Any question which came up from outside should find someone at Akron who had had a similar problem, and an experience that would help solve it. It was not easy, however, for someone in England or Argentina to know what man to write to, so Interplant took the responsibility of handling all inquiries, running down information and getting it back. It went a little farther than that. Its men took the position that they were virtually the Akron representatives of the outside plants to look after their interests at the home office.

To an unusual degree California became a training ground for men. It was far enough away to put men on their own, yet close enough for Akron to see how they handled themselves. New capabilities came to light and men moved ahead.

Slusser and Dinsmore became vice presidents, Darrow head of Development. Blythe, vice president of tire sales, then headed the vast Aircraft plant during World War II. Urquhart became superintendent in Australia, Denny in Canada, Tomkinson in Akron, Warden at Kelly-Springfield, Steele in Gadsden, England, then back to the coast, Sheahan in Australia and Jackson. From California came three managing directors for the English factory, Thomas, Hough and Hazlett. The three men Steere took out to start the California cotton mill all became superintendents, the last of them, Beggs, being in Brazil in 1948. Steere himself became top man in fabric development and production at Akron. Pope, Langdon, Ball, Mick, Yoak, Cleaves in personnel, Sullivan in finance, and Young in the comptroller's division, Sanford, Coe, Harper, Miles in sales—the list of California alumni is a long one.

Two of these might be cited in more detail. Fleming, the fifth superintendent, exemplified the working out of a long-held Litchfield idea. Fleming who hired in in 1911 after two years at what was then Buchtel College (later Akron University) was talking one day to Wolfe and Kilborn, graduates of Massachusetts Institute of Technology.

Finding him anxious to get a technical education, they told Litchfield about him. The factory manager helped him get a scholarship. After graduation Litchfield asked him what he would like to do, was glad to hear that production was the one job he really liked. Stephens, who had come through the practical school of industry, was skeptical, urged him to pick a staff department.

"You won't last six months in the factory," said Steve.

There were no college men in the plant at that time, very few in the ranks of industry. But Litchfield had the idea that a few technical men would balance up the production organization as they had in Development, that men sympathetic to experiment and research would be useful in complementing the practical man of the shop. Fleming and Steele from Case School, who succeeded Fleming later in California, were the first engineering men to go directly into production.

Fleming was assistant superintendent at Plant II in the bleak year of 1922, when he got the major assignment of a thorough housecleaning and a revamping of inventory. If time could be saved between the arrival of crude rubber, cotton and other materials, and its shipment out as finished products, inventories running into millions of dollars could be reduced.

He instituted studies into minimum and maximum quantities of all materials and supplies, set up definite rules for purchasing and storerooms as a check against overbuying and deterioration. The factory would need so many days' supply of rubber, so many of fabric, so much of this and that compound, through a long list. That was all it got. He found other economies in standardizing sizes and types of a wide range of supplies used by Engineering and other departments, created reservoirs from which all departments could draw, cut down the total amount of supplies.

While he was at it, he had a survey made of every piece of equipment that was out of use through damage, obsolescence, change of process or other cause, had a decision made as to whether it could be of any further use and if not, had it scrapped and disposed of. A lot of things no longer needed accumulate in a factory as in a house over a few years.

Fleming cleaned house. After that he went back into production. But since no experience a man has had is ever wasted, he would find a bigger job waiting when he returned from California in 1939, to take charge of the warehousing and shipping of the products of all of Goodyear's American factories.

The most outstanding case, however, is that of E. J. Thomas, who found the California superintendency a stepping stone to the presidency.

A native of Akron, born almost in the shadow of the factory, Thomas' career was to be perhaps the most striking of all the men who studied the principles of industry under Litchfield. He had left high school two months before graduation in 1917 to take a typing and clerical job at Goodyear when he was 18, became Mr. Litchfield's secretary two years later.

It was Litchfield's custom, on his trips to the outside plants, to take one or two promising younger men along, give them a broader picture of the business. Thomas went out to the opening of the California plant in 1920. On the trip he impressed his chief with his energy and interest, and was given full access afterward to all the matters clearing through the Factory Manager's office. Few men utilized such a training experience more fully. In a short time he had become more than a secretary, was an assistant without title. He made it a point to understand everything which passed through the office, was soon surprising department managers by his familiarity with their problems.

Litchfield had a full calendar in the years following the reorganization. Staff work was being revamped by the energetic Slusser; Stephens was driving ahead at increasing speed to keep abreast of the demands for production; research and improvement were being stressed; conveyors were going in.

No matter how much Mr. Litchfield desired to keep his door open to the men in the plant, the growing complexity of his position made it impossible for him to give immediate audience to everyone who wanted guidance or a decision. Thomas stepped into that breach. He conceived it his job not to keep his chief from interruption by department heads, but rather to extend the usefulness of the factory manager's office as far as possible throughout the shop. He was not so much working for Litchfield as he was for the men who came to consult him.

Litchfield might be busy, not available for some time. At first Thomas' answer might be, "I don't know, but I will find out and get the word back to you as quickly as possible." And nothing was ever forgotten or delayed one minute longer than was necessary. After a bit Thomas was saying, "I'm not sure, but I think Mr. Litchfield would rule this way—I'll get confirmation and let you know." Then it was, "I'm sure he would want you to do it this way. I'll take the responsibility of saying go ahead," or "I don't think he would want it done that way, but if you do it this other way, I know he'll okay it. Shoot."

And so using his contact with Litchfield to check and review his own conclusions, Thomas built up his own store of knowledge—and as well won the confidence of the rest of the organization.

Eddie Thomas got his first break in 1926. He was more ready for it than people imagined. He was still merely Litchfield's secretary, but Pierce, who had succeeded Blythe as personnel manager, was leaving to go to Standard Oil. The two ranking men in Personnel were Sherry in Efficiency and Climer in Labor. There was a question in Litchfield's mind which one to move ahead, so as a temporary measure, he had both of them report to himself, with Thomas as the clearing house. So well did Thomas utilize this opportunity that it was no surprise to the organization when he formally took the title of Personnel Manager the next year, nor that two years later, in 1929, the former stenographer became general superintendent of Goodyear-California.

The California experience was to be just the thing Thomas needed to round out his Goodyear education. The nation was in a period of great prosperity. Thomas caught the exact crest of that wave. The organization which Slusser and Blythe had built up at Los Angeles he drove forward with new dash and spirit. He had the unusual faculty of going ahead without arousing the jealousy of other men. He had a rare gift for friendship. No superintendent of Goodyear-California had been so universally liked. The company was hiring men, wages were increasing, the sales department could sell all the tires the factory could turn out, happy days were here again, and Thomas, tireless, enjoying every minute of the day, was in and out of every department, was out in the sales field, out in the branches, taking the deepest interest in every phase of Goodyear's activities, quickening the pace of every man he met. He played on the Goodyear baseball team, took part in all employees' activities, knew every man and his dog.

He would go from there to England, to vice president at Akron, then the top. California was his proving ground.

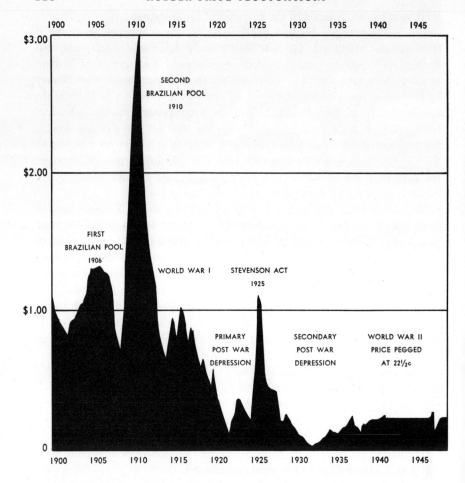

CRUDE RUBBER PRICES (in cents per pound), 1900-1948

A much larger chart would be needed to show the actual fluctuations of a material whose price in times of stress often varies widely from one month to another, and even from one day to the next.

The effect of longer-range movements like the pools in Brazilian rubber which gave rise to the planting of rubber in the Far East, the distress status of the rubber growers during two depressions and the sharp, though fairly brief, skyrocketing of price under the Stevenson Act are in marked contrast to the table-level status during World War II, when the price was controlled —and still more significantly through the stabilizing effect given by synthetic rubber after the war ended.

4. Rubber and Cotton

The Sumatra Plantations

IN THE spring of 1916, with World War I under way, two Hollanders
called at the Goodyear offices at Akron. They had two tracts of land
in the distant island of Sumatra totalling between 40,000 and 50,000
acres they wanted to sell.

"We've come to you first as one of the progressive American companies," they said. "The price is right. We can give you an option for a
reasonable time but we should tell you that this tract will not be on the
market long. It's what you Yankees call a bargain."

Goodyear had for some time been studying the matter of growing a
part, at least, of its requirements in rubber.

Back in 1910 indeed when prices were sky-rocketing, Frank Seiberling
made a trip to Brazil to investigate the possibility of buying perhaps
50,000 acres of jungle land so that Goodyear could grow its own rubber,
be independent of the speculators.

He landed at Para (now Belem), the shipping center on the Atlantic, took a boat up to Manaos, went up some of the tributaries. What he saw as to the difficulties of getting the rubber out made him give up the idea, but only for the time being.

The automotive industry was growing fast in 1916. The need for materials, particularly rubber, seemed insatiable. The preferencing of war needs and the uncertainties of shipping added to the difficulties.

And though the Brazilian pool of six years before had furnished impetus for a veritable flood of rubber planting in the Far East, rubber was often scarce and hard to get, and the price varied erratically with scarcity. The company paid all the way from 51 cents to a dollar for its rubber that year. In those fluctuations lay profit and loss.

The company had its own buying office in Singapore to try to keep abreast of its requirements, but more than once as inventories dwindled, a sharp cablegram from Akron would remind the distant buyers that the company was depending on them to keep the factory going. Three of the company's competitors, U. S. Rubber, British Dunlop and French Michelin had started their own plantations.

Purely from a business standpoint the investment in rubber looked attractive to the Goodyear men. The company was long out of the red now, was making good profits, would by the end of the year become the leader of the tire industry.

A gamble in rubber land, even 15,000 miles distant, was the sort of risk the dynamic young company was accustomed to take—and win.

Litchfield, conservative New England superintendent, agreed with his associates that they should go ahead.

"Let's find out more about raising rubber," he said. "What it should cost, how it can best be processed and handled for the special needs of the tire industry. Rubber supply is the most important factor in our business."

There is a twelve-hour difference in time between Akron and Singapore. Early the next morning, John J. Blandin, Annapolis-trained engineer, who was Goodyear's buyer in the East, got a cablegram saying in effect:

"Company has taken option at X dollars per acre on tract of land at Dolok Merangir, Sumatra, said to be favorable for rubber growing. Proceed there immediately and report recommendations earliest possible."

During the next three weeks Blandin and a native party traversed the entire area, usually on foot, often cutting a trail through with machetes, fording streams, paddling their way up others, visited jungle country which few white men had ever seen. Blandin made inquiries as to land values, concluded that the price asked was reasonable and so cabled Akron.

Odell, then manager of crude rubber at Akron, and Carlisle, who built the Canadian Goodyear company, took the next boat for Holland to close the deal. But the exigencies of wartime, waiting for convoys, the threat of submarine attack, the preference necessarily given to military travel over business trips delayed their arrival in Amsterdam until after the option had expired.

Their Dutch hosts gave them cordial greeting.

"However," they said, "another syndicate has been waiting to buy the property in case you did not take up your option. We have just sold the larger of the two tracts. The smaller tract is still for sale and you may purchase it, if you choose, at the acre price quoted you before."

The Americans completed the deal for the remaining 20,000 acres and Akron instructed Blandin to start preliminary plans immediately to develop the property. Odell hurried out from Holland to join him. This is what the men found:

With the wave of speculation in plantation stocks in England, Holland and elsewhere, companies had been organized to develop rubber properties for absentee owners. Any one of them would take the job of clearing the jungle and setting out trees for specified fees and percentages, but with the stipulation that they should have complete control, and would be given the management of any further properties the owners might decide to buy. In no case would they agree to clear and plant more than 2500 acres in any one year.

The Americans reported the terms to Akron. The reply flashed back by cable, via London and Suez to Singapore. "Develop it yourselves."

The two men were well acquainted with grades of rubber, sources of supply, inspection and shipping; they had acquired the seventh sense that a rubber buyer has to have, the feeling of influences which will force the unstable price up or down.

But neither of them knew anything about clearing a jungle or operating a plantation once the land was cleared. However, their orders were explicit and they could only apply their ingenuity to the task and do the best they could. Blandin took on the job.

Since Goodyear would be a part of business life of the Netherlands Indies for the next 30 years, we might stop a moment to look over the country, particularly the two islands of Sumatra and Java. Sumatra is the big one, a narrow, 1100-mile long island which the equator exactly bisects.

The straggling antenna of the Malaya Peninsula all but touches

Sumatra, separated only by the Straits of Malacca. Neighboring islands acted as stepping stones to Asia, offered secret hiding places to pirate craft in an earlier day, furnished a base in World War I for the German raider Emden to ambush Allied merchantmen, saw grimmer battle in World War II. From Singapore headlands on a clear day you can see across to the coastal islands of Sumatra.

Java is the smaller, blockier island, lying to the south and east, 36 hours by steamer from Singapore. Java is little more than one-fourth the size of Sumatra but has six times as many people, is one of the most densely populated areas in the world. Its people had been forced by necessity to cultivate the soil intensively. The Sumatrans, with vast areas to hunt and fish over, were rather disdainful of farming, not interested in working on a plantation.

So Sumatra was largely to be developed by the Javanese, and it was to Java that the Americans turned to recruit the 7000 workmen needed to clear the jungle and develop the property.

Both islands were Dutch colonies, and the Dutch, traditionally good colonizers, had rigid rules to protect natives moved from one island to another. They went under a contract which provided that they might return if they chose at the company's expense at the end of three years. The company must furnish housing, free medical and hospital treatment, and 45 pounds of rice per month for each native, at a price not to exceed two and a half cents per pound. It must pay stipulated wages, which ran from 17 to 20 cents (U.S.) a day.

Experienced Hollanders were picked as key men, Chinese coolies brought in to do the heavy work, and the little group plunged in with such equipment as they had or could use in that area.

In the absence of roads, bullock carts worked out better than tractors. A railroad ran into the property from Medan, 62 miles away, but they would largely depend on supplies brought in on a five-day haul by the patient bullock carts, hurrying down the highway at 14 miles a day.

The larger trees had to be felled at a height of 12 feet and the stumps pulled out with hand stump-pullers, with natives pulling back and forth on a ratchet, increasing the tension until the stump came out.

Thousands of dollars worth of valuable timber had to be burned because the market was too far away and there were no facilities to transport it.

And so through the three years the coolies marched ahead clearing the way, while the Javanese followed, building roads and villages and planting trees. The speed with which the Americans cleared and planted

Slips from high-yielding rubber trees are being grafted onto the young trees at left. Right is women tapper in Malaya near Goodyear's postwar latex factory.

Typical modern field station on Sumatra plantations. Native tappers bring in the latex to be coagulated, sheeted, dried and made ready for shipment.

Dolok Merangir was a small sensation in the East. By the time the last trees were planted, the first ones were beginning to produce latex.

Blandin cleared and planted 5000 acres the first year and by 1920 he was growing rubber on virtually the entire 20,000 acres. The plantation kept its native name, Dolok Merangir.

Ironically enough the first rubber produced was worth less in the market than the cost of raising it. The depression had sent the price careening down from the profitable 55-cent level to 10 cents a pound. Not since Charles Goodyear had paid a few cents a pound for rubber brought in as ballast in the holds of tramp steamers, more than three-quarters of a century earlier, had rubber been held so cheaply.

But depressions pass, the investment was sound and would return a good profit to the company when conditions became normal.

EXPERIMENTS IN SUMATRA

The company bought a second tract, trebling its acreage in 1927, but in the interim the plantation men had been working on a program to bring costs down through increasing the output per tree, a horticultural job which had spectacular results.

It was just as well that Goodyear had not turned the management over to agents, as many absentee estate owners did. Its men had free hand to experiment, and were responsible only to Akron.

The average yearly output throughout the East was between 380 and 400 pounds per acre in 1916. The Goodyear plantations saw this mount to 1000, 1500 and even higher.

This increase in output was important to Goodyear, but it was also important to everyone else. Low prices opened up new uses for rubber, created jobs, conveniences and wealth to the nations using it, on the highway, in the factory and on the farm.

As part of the 1921 reorganization, Blandin was called back to Akron to head up the entire crude rubber division. Bogardus from the Singapore buying office, who had worked on the first plantation, came in also, in immediate charge of purchasing. Goodyear would always buy more rubber than it grew, even though the plantations expanded to vast size. If Dolok Merangir's 20,000 acres averaged 650 pounds of rubber per acre by 1929, that would still be only 6000 long tons, and Goodyear would be using more than 120,000 tons of rubber by then.

With rubber so large a factor in the company's whole program, it remained throughout the years responsible directly to Litchfield.

Departure of Blandin and Bogardus brought in Ingle as plantation manager, one of the first technically-trained men to go into this field. A Californian, with degrees from the state university and Massachusetts Tech, Ingle had gone to the East in 1915 with Blandin, had shared the headaches of cultivating and planting, was a good administrator, had a good business head. He plunged into the new assignment with enthusiasm and good judgment.

No one anywhere knew too much about raising rubber. Up to a dozen years before practically all the world's rubber had come from the jungle, which no one had planted. Blandin made many inquiries, studied existing practices, but found that planting theories varied with each planter. The business was too new for anyone even to say how many trees one should plant to the acre. Practices varied all the way from 40 to 400. He had to use his best judgment, make corrections as experience proved new methods sound. It would take years to arrive at the conclusion that the best results could be had by planting trees 150 to 250 to the acre, depending on topography, drainage, and other factors, then trim out to 125 or so.

It was perhaps fortunate that the Goodyear plantation was located in Dutch rather than in English territory. The British had started the business, controlled most of it, and the easy large profits made up to 1920 had offered little incentive to improvement. The Dutch were in a different position. They were the contenders, had started in fairly late in the day, could not pick up labor in the neighborhood, as the British had in Malaya, put on extra men in good times, lay them off in slack. The Dutch had to work harder to make a place for themselves. Fortunately, they were good horticulturists. They had to be, to make a living from the soil in the limited territory of the homeland. The Dutch government had put in experimental stations in Sumatra and Java, was glad to work with a progressive American firm, exchanging ideas, experiences and seedlings, since the islands would benefit from any improvements found.

One change in planting practices came out of the depression itself. Up to then it had been the practice to clear the space between the trees as clean as a baseball diamond, so that the trees would get all of the benefit of the fertility of the soil and fiercely growing jungle growth not choke it out. But many remote areas over the island had gone uncultivated when the price dropped, since the planters could not afford to have that done.

But a surprising thing had come to light, namely that the areas which had gone uncultivated got along just as well as those which were. The shade from the broad leaves of the mature rubber tree prevented jungle growth from making headway harmful to the trees. Apparently a rubber tree once it got its growth, could fend for itself. After all, they did all right in the jungles of Brazil. The planting men made a note of this, one expense which could be cut out.

There were other questions for the Goodyear men to answer. How soon could a rubber tree be tapped, and how long would it continue to produce efficiently? There were trees in Brazil estimated to be 200 years old, and some of the first trees from Wickham's day were still flourishing in Ceylon. The Goodyear men concluded that tapping might safely be started at five years under favorable growing conditions, with output increasing until the tree was 10 or 15 years old, and that the economical life of a rubber tree was around 25 to 30 years.

Tapping practices varied widely. After various experiments Dolok decided to tap the trees every other day, at a 30 degree angle, halfway around the tree. The tappers would start the cut 40 inches above the ground, work down until they got within six inches of the ground, then start in on the other side. This cycle took six to seven years, giving the bark ample time to reform after the tapping process.

Loss of output through the erosion created by the tropical rains was checked by the thousand-year-old device of native tea planters, terracing the hillsides.

The largest possibility for improvement however lay in increasing the output per tree. It took no more time to tap a high-yielding tree than a low-yielder, no longer to handle a full cup of latex than one in which the bottom was scarcely wet. Records were kept on some four million trees in the estate, just as a dairy farmer keeps track of how much milk each of his cows is giving. It was found that 30 per cent of the trees were producing 70 per cent of the latex, and the other 70 per cent were slackers, to be gradually weeded out.

From there Ingle and his staff went into a large-scale horticultural program, sought through cross-breeding to find promising variants, then to concentrate on them. The cycle was not a single season, for it took five to seven years to get the first check on each experiment. This called for painstaking, tedious and unbelievably patient effort on the part of the scientists.

A search was made for trees which were really outstanding, with yields double or triple those of run-of-mine trees. There might be half a dozen such trees in a million. And no one could tell offhand whether that high yield was due to a specially favorable environment, or to remote hereditary factors, throwbacks perhaps to some lusty great grandfather tree sent over to Ceylon by Sir Henry Wickham in 1876. It would take time to find out.

Again seeds from high-yielding trees could not be depended on to produce high-yielding offspring, though bud grafts from superior trees would do so. So new trees were planted from good seeds, but as they reached a diameter of about one inch, slips or buds from known high yielders were grafted on them, and when the graft was well started the original stalk was cut off, so it was really the graft which grew up. This was called "bud-grafting" and represented an extremely important step forward.

Some 35 such grafts were started from each of the high yielding trees, and they were watched carefully during their growth to maturity. Results were as expected. Many of the grafted families grew up to be indifferent yielders, high, low, medium, proving that the productiveness of the parent was the result of accident, a specially rich soil, favorable drainage, or sunlight or other factor.

But in a few cases—one or two out of a hundred—a grafted tree grew up straight, tall and full latexed, reproducing exactly the yield and other characteristics of its parent. This discovery was important, and each "mother tree" became the starting point of a new clone or family. From them unlimited numbers of trees could be developed with identical characteristics by grafting their buds on the root stock of ordinary seedlings. This process provided the first generation of high yielding trees.

The second step was to select a pair of "mother trees" which had the high yields and other desired characteristics, and using them as parents, cross-pollenize their blossoms in the hope of securing seeds, and trees therefrom, some of which might be superior to either of their parents.

Those mother trees presented a curious appearance during the "mating season." High platforms were built around them, and cheese-cloth bags placed around each cluster of blossoms, and the powder-fine pollen from the male blossom of one tree was brushed by hand over the pollen of a female blossom from the other tree, with a bit of cotton placed as additional protection against accidental pollenization from unpedigreed and philandering neighbors.

These trees might not mate with any Tom, Dick or Harry of a tree whose pollen the wind or an insect might present, could mate only with their peers.

The seeds of these unions ripened in time and were planted, and again the scientists must wait through the five-year cycle to see what happened. It could be certain that the offspring would still be mixed, representing many strains in Nature's curious demonstration of Mendel's law, but with the chance that out of the thousands, one or two

variants would appear, throwing back this time perhaps to remoter ancestry in the Brazilian forest, variants with yield and other characteristics
superior to their parents. These then became the founders of new clones,
the second generation. This took so long that it was not until 1941
that the third generation came in.

These experiments were only well started when the high prices
brought by the Stevenson Act set afoot a new planting boom throughout the East. Dolok Merangir was turning in a handsome profit, and it
might be well to plow part of that back into additional acreage.

True, the high prices were probably temporary, unlikely to last until
any new planting came into bearing, but even if the prices slumped
again, the plantations looked good as a long term investment. Increasing yields indicated that Ingle's men were on the right track, Dolok
Merangir could still make money at the Stevenson "bogie" figure of
16 cents a pound.

THE SECOND PLANTATION (1927)

So Ingle looked around, located a large tract back in the interior,
twice as big as Dolok, one which a Japanese syndicate was offering for
sale, having done practically nothing with it. The land was not bought
outright, but leased for 75 years, as the custom was. Negotiations were
completed in 1927, and Wingfoot Plantation came in, a chance for
Ingle's men to apply all the experience they had accumulated, create the
best rubber plantation in the world. It is harder to change over an existing plantation than to start a new one right. For one thing, Wingfoot
would be completely bud-grafted, the first in the East.

To give a quick picture of Goodyear's entire rubber-growing program, here are the sizes of the various tracts, then and thereafter:

Dolok Merangir	1916	20,000	acres
Wingfoot	1927	40,000	,,
Philippines	1928	2,500	,,
Lepan, Sumatra	1931	33,000	,,
Panama *	1935	2,850	,,
Costa Rica	1936	2,500	,,

* Now operated by the government.

Every man who has built a house has looked back afterward and seen
things he would have done differently if he had it to do over again.
Ingle's men had this opportunity, not only laid out the new plantation
on scientific lines, but provided a system of transport and collection
depots new to the business.

Tapping started at daybreak, must be finished by 9:30, before the sun got too high and dried up the flow of latex. With yields increasing and loads growing heavier a tapper might have to make two trips. At Dolok bicycles and small carts had been utilized, as some of the tappers had to walk more than a mile to the collection station. It would be better if the plantation could be laid out so that no one would have to walk more than a third of a mile.

So the 64 square miles in the new plantation were divided up into 16 divisions of 2000 to 3000 acres, depending upon the topography. Each division was to be a self-contained unit, with a native village, housing for the Dutch overseers, and a small factory, where the latex could be coagulated, sheeted out and smoked, ready for shipment. Modern trucks and Diesel-motored trains, which had long replaced the faithful bullocks and water buffalos, would pick up the processed rubber, carry it into the Head Emplacement or main office, ready for inspection and packing, then to be shipped to Akron or other Goodyear plant.

The vast clearing job was planned as carefully as if the Army's Corps of Engineers, or the Navy's SeeBee's had laid it out. Supplies had to be brought in through the jungle, clearing equipment, engines, coagulating tanks, and food for an army of 16,000 people. Look at the map. Dolok lies 65 miles south of Medan, chief supply center for Sumatra, a city of 120,000 people near the harbor of Belawan. The new plantation lay 120 miles farther inland. There was a paved road from the harbor as far as Dolok, but from there on the highway dwindled to a dirt road, little wider than a path at times and practically impassable in the rainy season.

There were five rivers to cross, and even in the dry season, heavy equipment, machinery, food and supplies for the 16,000 workers, and even automobiles, had to be carried across on ferries or men's backs. However, there was a harbor closer at hand at the village of Laboean Bilik, and supplies could be taken 40 miles up the Bila River on lighters, to a narrow gauge railroad which led into the estate. The railroad was so old that only pushcars could be used on it, so the first job of the Goodyear staff was to rebuild it completely, use it for incoming and outgoing shipments.

The Dutch government, realizing that the new plantation would help develop the island, gave excellent cooperation, built bridges and extended the main road into the new plantation and across one end of it.

While surveys and plans were being made, a force of 16,000 men was being recruited in Java. Three crews of natives with Hollanders as section leaders moved across the plantation simultaneously, with a keen rivalry as to which would reach its objective first.

The scouts went ahead—tough, hardy Chinese coolies, used to heavy work. They located the division centers marked on the map, cleared openings for the villages, put in railroads, highways, built houses. As the main wave of the jungle armies reached these points they could move in and continue clearing without delay.

There was no stump-pulling equipment at Wingfoot. As the trees were cut down, the stumps were left to rot and so further enrich the soil. Quick-growing vines were planted around them to quicken the process, a trick they had picked up at Dolok.

Nurseries covering hundreds of acres were laid out, from which eventually 7,500,000 trees were transplanted into the field, thinned out as they grew up, only the best ones being kept. Each one was bud-grafted and Wingfoot became the largest estate in the world to be completely bud-grafted from high-yielding stock.

The clearing job beat the record made previously at Dolok. The Goodyear army planted the 40,000 acres at an average of 8000 acres a year, reached 10,000 acres one year. By 1933 they were shipping rubber into Akron, a record for virgin jungle never before approached in rubber growing.

Like Dolok Merangir, the Wingfoot Plantation came into bearing just as rubber prices were at their lowest level. But again this was not too important. The price pendulum would swing back, and the Goodyear plantations could tighten their belt and live on a price level of five cents a pound if they had to, thanks to the improvements found.

The long experimental program was completely justified. Wingfoot reached an average of 1000 pounds per acre by 1941 and was still increasing, with an average of 1200 and even higher in prospect as the trees grew older. Dolok's average was increasing also, and in some sections reached as high a percentage as Wingfoot, but the replanting program, as low yielders were replaced, was necessarily a slow process, and the new trees would be five years coming to maturity and their output lost in the interim.

Dolok Merangir turned in 8,000,000 pounds of rubber in the critical year 1941, while the new plantation at Wingfoot produced 30,000,000.

In all the years in the Netherlands Indies Goodyear men had worked closely with the Dutch government in labor relations as well as in research.

Goodyear tried to make living and working conditions such that the natives would want to stay on at the end of the three year contract term.

Attractive homes for field supervisors were built at strategic points at Good-year-Sumatra, with native villages and collection stations nearby. Godowns, or warehouses, dotted the harbors. Rubber was first loaded into lighters.

The American and Dutch staff studied housing as one factor. Left to himself, the Javanese would build curious thatched roof houses around a hollow square, the houses being mounted on stilts and reached by a ladder. The center was available for dances, ceremonials, pageants and native games. The native villages were called Kampongs.

The Wingfoot plantations preserved the hollow square at first, erected long barrack-like buildings called "pondoks" around the sides, 20 to 40 families to a unit—just a series of rooms, 10 feet by 10, each room housing a family. A later improvement was detached houses, or rather duplex houses, with two rooms, a porch in front, outdoor kitchen in back, on a lot 120 feet by 300, big enough for a garden. The natives were skeptical at first but soon decided they liked the new houses better. The villages were built along the streams. Larger "pondoks" were built as bachelor quarters.

With good living conditions, fewer and fewer employees availed themselves of the privilege of going home after three years—and many of them went back only for the trip, or to visit relatives, then returned.

An interesting community life had sprung up among the American colony, not dissimilar to that on an isolated army post. A dozen or so families lived in the attractive homes surrounded by luxuriant gardens in the plantation townsite located toward the center of the estates. The children attended a Dutch school in the mountains when they were little, might be sent back to the States as they grew older, just as the children of British and Dutch residents went to European schools.

The weather was not too hot but that the men could get in a little golf and tennis. The company maintained a lodge at Brastagi, a resort 100 miles up in the mountains where it was always cool and made an ideal vacation spot.

The two plantations were not too far away from each other for visits to be exchanged. Wingfoot built a club house, and there were parties from time to time on holidays, or to greet visitors or neighboring Europeans from the other plantations. Occasionally the Governor General or other dignitary paid the colony a visit, and once in a while a native potentate arrived in state.

The temperature in lowland Sumatra stays fairly uniform at 80 to 90 degrees during the day throughout the year and 70 degrees at night, with the rainy season starting in October and lasting until February, and a "little rainy season" in May. The rain interfered with the work on the estate only if it fell during the tapping hours of the early morning.

Like other Goodyearites overseas the plantation men made vacation trips back to the States every third year.

Housework was simple. For $50 a month you could have a cook and a second boy, a gardener and perhaps a nurse for the children. On one occasion a new bride came out to the plantation and a dozen of her husband's friends went down to meet the boat. As they sat around at the hotel after lunch the husband suggested that everyone join them for dinner that night. The bride was horrified. She had not even seen her new home, had no idea what was in the larder, knew it was impossible to arrange a dinner party on that short notice, thought her husband must be joking.

But the husband had merely telephoned his Chinese cook who passed the word along, and neighbors' servants responded with their mistress' china, silver and whatever food was at hand. It was the custom of the country. The bride was still startled at times, until she got used to it, to recognize her own china and silver on the dinner table at a neighbor's home.

Another thing which disturbed her was to find tiny lizards crawling around the walls and ceilings, but it was explained that they brought good luck and were not to be disturbed. They were called tjitjaks, a word resembling the cheerful chirping noise they made. The expansion of American business abroad calls for adjustments.

The company acquired a third huge tract of 33,000 acres in 1933, bringing its Sumatra holdings up to 93,000 acres. Lepan, as the new plantation was called, was not developed immediately but held as a reserve. In any case new rubber restrictions set up in 1934 forbade any new planting for the time being.

So when World War II broke out an army of natives was tapping more than three million trees and Wingfoot and Dolok between daylight and 9:30 every morning, processing the latex and the rubber bales and shipping it out to Goodyear factories in America, England, Australia and Argentina—a large-scale job and one typical of American enterprise.

RUBBER IN LATEX FORM

Before we leave the Dutch islands another development should be noted. In 1929 Litchfield called in Paul Shoaff, head of the reclaim plant. Shoaff had joined the company seven years earlier at Los Angeles after graduating from the University of Southern California, had helped develop a process of making "mineral rubber" from petroleum, had come into Akron to take charge of the Chemical plant. Now he was to go to Sumatra.

His experience was entirely foreign to rubber growing, and probably

Litchfield himself could not have told Shoaff just what was expected of him in the East, but he would at least approach the matter of rubber growing from a fresh viewpoint, and if he found only minor improvements, these multiplied by millions of pounds of rubber would easily cover his expenses out and back. Litchfield expected a man to use his initiative, not wait for detailed instructions. If he were the right type of man he might well find things which no one would have thought to tell him to look for. Shoaff made his survey and came back. He had had an interesting experience. But before Litchfield had finished reading his report, it was settled in his own mind that Shoaff was to go back. So by 1933 he was second man to Ingle—and succeeded him as manager of the plantations in 1937—and the two of them had gone intensively into the matter of getting out rubber in latex form to be used in the new "sponge rubber", Airfoam, which promised to become important.

The latex as it drops into the tapper's cup is about 65 per cent water, which is largely removed in coagulating and drying. To ship the pure latex to the States cost more because of the water carried over the ocean, so processing plants were built at the plantation and the latex was treated with ammonia to prevent coagulation, then put through high speed centrifugals to reduce the water content. The latex remained in liquid form but after treatment the latex was a little more than 60 per cent rubber.

Storage tanks for the processed latex were set up in the harbor town of Belawan, from which it was pumped into special tanks aboard ship, carried across the ocean through the Panama Canal to Baltimore where it was pumped into specially designed receiving tanks on the pier.

From there it was transferred by gravity to railroad tank cars, which hauled it into switch tracks alongside the Airfoam plant at Akron. Latex rubber was a substantial part of the company's operations when the war broke out.

The Philippine Plantation

In the meantime Goodyear started a plantation in the Philippine Islands in 1928. Remember that the Philippine laws limited land holdings to 2500 acres, which deterred the setting up of large plantations.

An attempt was made in 1927 to open up the situation. A Texas oil operator, visiting the country, was impressed with the opportunity offered to increase the exports from the islands, then limited to sugar, hemp, copra and tobacco. He talked to Riveire, Goodyear sales manager at Manila, had studies made. Then he went to see various government officials, told them that if the laws were liberalized he could find American capital willing to invest as high as $12,000,000 in rubber plantations, estimated that once the industry got started the Philippines should ship half a million dollars' worth of rubber a day.

Henry L. Stimson, then governor general, and Manuel Quezon, president of the Philippine Assembly, were impressed with the proposal, thought it might be possible to change the law. But legislative obstacles proved too great, and nothing came of it.

Goodyear, however, moved into the Philippines the following year. Export restrictions had been removed with the repeal of the Stevenson Act and high yield seeds and budded stock could be shipped out for the first time. The door would not stay open long, and the company had to move fast.

Goodyear bought as much land as the law allowed, 2500 acres, located on the southern island of Mindanao outside the typhoon zone, set out an experimental plantation. It had two purposes in mind. Its technicians would find out something about growing and climatic conditions in the islands in case restrictions on rubber cultivation were removed. Also they wanted to see whether bud-grafted stock could be transplanted there successfully, and whether in that case by utilizing the scientific findings made at Sumatra, they could offset the wage handicap. Obviously the Philippine Islands would be able to raise rubber only if they were able to get their costs down comparable to those in the British and Dutch possessions. Since labor could not be brought in the only possibility was to try to get other costs down.

Goodyear staked its case on bud-grafted trees of high yield. The new tract, the largest in the Philippines, was planted with seedlings already grafted with budded stock.

"Bud-wood," a little branch with buds on it, was generally used in transplanting operations in Sumatra, but would dry out if transported any great distance, so "budded-stumps" were used instead. These were seedlings which had been bud-grafted and the original stock cut off after the graft was well started. In going to the Philippines, these were taken out of the ground, roots and all, packed up and treated so that they would lie dormant for a few weeks, long enough to be transplanted to their new home.

The experiment succeeded, the trees thrived, costs were satisfactory, and the plantation provided a stepping stone later from the Far East to Latin America.

Rubber in Central America

The opening of rubber plantations in Panama in 1935 and in Costa Rica the following year were initial steps in a long-range experiment to see whether it was practical to grow rubber on plantations on this hemisphere.

In the narrative is the story of conferences in Washington, in Rio, Lima, and the capitals of the Central American republics, of precious planting stock carried across the Pacific on Clipper ships, then down the coast on Army bombers; and the story, little known, of how an American company was able in emergency, to supply to a dozen foreign governments under the sponsorship of its own, the only high yielding rubber plants available in the world.

The project attracted little attention in 1935. This country could get all the rubber it needed from the Far East. Rubber cultivation was controlled by friendly nations—England, Holland, France.

However, American manufacturers were not very happy over having to go half way around the world for their raw materials. It took 45 to 51 days to make the 11,000 mile trip from Singapore to New York by way of the Suez Canal. The larger companies had to carry a four months supply of rubber, in this country or enroute, which tied up a large amount of working capital. Latin America would be much more convenient as a source of supply, and trade relations would be stimulated if it had millions of dollars worth of rubber to exchange for American-made goods.

Could the economies of scientific production found in Sumatra and confirmed in the Philippines be applied in Latin America not on large-scale plantations, but by individual small land holders, as the natives had done in Sumatra under Dutch leadership? That was the question.

The Goodyear plantations were small, 2850 acres in Panama, 2500 in Costa Rica, and were experimental. The Goodyear staff must find out what adjustments must be made in methods and techniques, what difficulties must be overcome. They knew of one, a leaf blight, long a menace to rubber growing in Latin America.

The disease had not bothered wild rubber trees in the jungle, scattered as they were over vast areas, but it ran like an epidemic through stands of trees planted close together. Plantations started in Trinidad, in Dutch and British Guiana and elsewhere, had been ravaged by the disease and abandoned. Spraying might check its spread, but only at prohibitive cost.

From here on the narrative will deal only with the Costa Rica plantation, since the Panama holdings were disposed of in 1940, when the demand for labor to build military installations around the Canal sent wages to too high a level to make a fair test. The Panama tract was taken over by the Inter-American Institute of Agricultural Sciences, and is still operated as an experimental station.

Costa Rica is one of the smaller countries of Central America, with plateaus and mountain ranges at 3000 to 10,000 feet elevation, sloping fairly abruptly to the Caribbean and the Pacific. The eastern slope gets a heavy rainfall, creates growing conditions for rubber comparable to the Middle East.

The country had a stable government, a population largely of European descent. Land ownership was widely distributed, most of it being in fairly small farms.

The area selected was one which the leaf blight had recently ravaged. The original tract of 1000 acres was an abandoned banana plantation which the United Fruit Company had planted partly to rubber in 1923 as an experiment, but had given up in 1932, because of the low price rubber brought on the market during the depression years. The blight had struck later, and when Goodyear took over, the 35,000 trees set out had been reduced to one-tenth that number. However, the fact that any of them had survived was interesting. It might indicate that they had inherent resistance to the leaf disease, in which case they would furnish a starting point, to be cross-bred with high-yield stock from the Philippines.

Two men, well acquainted with rubber growing, were assigned to the job. Klippert, in charge, a six-foot-three former footballer from Mt. Union, had gone to Sumatra from the Squadron. Bangham, director of plant research for the company, would concentrate on the scientific phases. Hernan Echeverri, with practical planting experience in Costa Rica, signed on as resident manager, glad to have part in something potentially important to his country.

A nursery was laid out, native seeds planted, and as the seedlings grew to proper size, budded stock from the Philippines was grafted on. A search was started for other trees over Central America which had indicated resistance to the blight, and buddings from these were established as new families. Each tree was marked, and "case records" kept.

Goodyear even got some plants from Brazil in 1938, the first time any had been shipped out since Wickham's day. They had something to trade now, high-yield stock. Brazil was fully co-operative.

Then war broke out in Europe and other people all over the hemisphere became concerned about the supply of rubber in the event that that conflagration grew world-wide. Congress appropriated funds and the Department of Agriculture worked out arrangements with the various Central and South American governments for the free interchange of planting material and the pooling of scientific findings.

The Japanese drive through Malaya and the Netherlands Indies took the project out of the class of an abstract scientific experiment, made it a matter of military importance. Goodyear had the only available source of the highest-yielding new strains. The full fruits of its long experiments in the East, which had quadrupled the yield per tree, were made fully available to the Americas. Seeds and budwood, packed in Pliofilm, were rushed to this country from the Philippines, carried by plane to various South American ports.

With the spread of war to this continent, Klippert was drafted to search for stands of wild rubber trees in Central America, get out whatever rubber could be had immediately. The remaining rubber trees on the plantation continued to be tapped, but were low in yield. Bangham and Echeverri carried on. The job called for resourcefulness as well as patience. The blight struck only the tops, or crowns, of the trees, which could be sprayed, but at considerable expense. Why not graft resistant crowns to the bud-grafted trees as they grew taller, in order to give the trees resistant leaves? After all the latex came from the high-yield trunk. The "double-grafted" trees had a curious hump-backed appearance at first, where the new top had been grafted on, but this soon straightened out. Double-grafting proved a satisfactory interim practice until both high yield and high resistance could be combined into a single tree.

By the end of the war the entire plantation had been planted with the new stock, part of it already yielding rubber. The original trees would be taken out and replaced.

With the rearrangement of personnel after the war, Klippert came into Akron, and Figland, another Squadron man who had worked on the Sumatra plantations before the war and been a division superintendent at Goodyear Aircraft during the hostilities, took over at Costa Rica.

It was still too early to see whether and how soon the program could be called successful. Twelve years is a short time in this business. The scientists will not be satisfied until they have trees which are both high-yield and disease-resistant. Then a farmer can plant any kind of rubber seed, bud-graft this superior stock on, and without spraying or double grafting, sit back and wait for his latex crop to come in.

Costa Rican farmers are already becoming interested in planting rubber. The program has been laid out, even to the matter of processing equipment which any small farmer could afford. The latex can be coagulated in five-gallon gasoline cans cut in two, sheeted out with an ordinary wringer roll like the housewife uses on washday, hung up on poles in a shed to be smoked, then be ready for shipping.

Since a rubber tree does not become commercially tappable for at least five years, the program recommends that native growers plant only one-quarter to one-third of their land in rubber, growing food crops like corn, beans, rice, bananas, yuca on the rest, setting these crops out between the rubber trees as well in the early years, discontinuing this when the trees begin to shade out the intercrops. With a few cattle to add to his income, the farmer could manage through during the years the trees were growing up and thereafter have a regular income from them.

With rubber selling at 20 cents a pound, ten acres of land each producing 1000 pounds a year, which is not an unreasonable figure, would bring in $2000 a year in cash to the planter.

Using high yield stock which Goodyear and the cooperating governments would provide at a minimum charge, as well as scientific counsel when needed, it was expected that a small farmer, paying no wages, would in time be able to match costs with producers in the Far East, and with hundreds of such holdings furnish the country with a new resource of considerable value.

The United States Department of Agriculture has a large experimental farm near the Goodyear holdings, and there and at other experimental stations in Latin America, the rubber program is being watched with growing interest—and may in time have far-reaching results.

Arizona Cotton Ranch

Arizona is one of the most unusual chapters in the history of a company which has done many unusual things in its 50 years.

There is success and setback in it, and the hazards of business, but we have met these before. There is drama in it. Men going into a desert country which from the day God made the world and sent it spinning into space had produced nothing but sagebrush, cactus, Gila monsters and jackrabbits—and transforming it into a garden spot, one of the richest agricultural regions in the United States.

But thousands of people besides Goodyear had a hand in that result.

The thing that makes Arizona unique is that after it had finished the job it was set up to do, when the reasons that sent Goodyear into the desert no longer held, when the long staple cotton it grew there could not compete price-wise with that grown elsewhere, and even after Goodyear no longer had to have the extremely long staple cotton at all, the company did not pull up stakes and walk out, write Arizona off and forget about it—as many people in the Southwest fully expected—but stayed on the job, seeking, and finding, other values to justify the enterprise cost-wise to itself, and turning in unexpected returns to humanity in the doing.

Goodyear has done many things in its time which people thought unorthodox, different from those of business generally. Its liberal attitude toward labor a generation before the Wagner Act was ever dreamed of might be one, and its continuance in aeronautics during the long lean years. Taking into account particularly the events after 1920, and the methods and ingenuity utilized, the Arizona story may well rank with the things which Goodyear did differently from other companies.

It is a fairly colorful tale as well, echoing to the tramp of horses and marching men, transforming endless sandy wastes almost overnight into villages and towns, towns almost hidden in a decade by orange groves and palm trees and amazing masses of roses and flowering shrubbery.

Let us project ourselves back to the year 1916, when the company set out for the Southwest, and see what conditions made that seem advisable.

World War I was the first motorized war in the world's history. Artillery horses and mule teams could not stand the gaff. Warring nations were calling for trucks to move munitions, men, guns and supply trains, back and forth behind the pock-marked battle lines of France. Trucks and tires were called on for stern service.

In the year 1916 it was particularly important that Goodyear should have an ample supply of the strongest long staple cotton possible. Solid tires would be used chiefly, but there were big possibilities for Goodyear's new pneumatics. But success in that field was largely dependant on sturdy, flexible cotton fabric.

There were two sources of supply, Egypt and the Sea Islands off Georgia. England controlling the Nile Valley, needed her cotton for her own war purposes, still more urgently needed shipping. German submarines were sinking merchantmen by the score. Her ships could be used only for the movement of munitions and necessary war supplies, which closed the Egyptian long staple market to ordinary industrial uses in America. This country must look elsewhere.

The Sea Islands remained American territory, but the boll weevil was raising havoc there. The 100,000 bales annual output of a few years before was shrinking fast. Government experts gave the Sea Islands two years to go. If the war had laid an embargo on Egyptian cotton, the boll weevil was laying one on Sea Island.

Yet here was Goodyear with a new product which might revolutionize the tire business, as the Straight Side had done a decade earlier, with a supreme opportunity to clinch leadership in the industry—and long staple cotton was practically not to be had. There must be some way out.

An experimental station of the U. S. Department of Agriculture at Sacaton, Arizona, noting that soil and sun conditions were similar to those of Egypt, had made some experiments, and found that Egyptian cotton could be raised in the Salt River Valley as strong and long in staple as that of the Nile.

A few farmers had tried it out, not many. Maybe it would work and maybe it would not, in spite of what the professors said. They should stick to something they were sure of, like grain and cattle.

Goodyear's battle might be won in the Southwest. Litchfield hurried out. The developments of the next few years affected the economy of the entire section, so we might first visualize the topography.

Phoenix, the state capital, lay in the center of the valley, surrounded by deserts and distant mountains, the Bradshaws, the White Tanks, the Estrellas, Superstition, Camelback, the Four Peaks. But there was no snow on them to melt in the spring and form rivers. However, 150 miles further east were high mountains which did do so, creating the Salt River, and leaving jagged scars across the desert, as dry creek beds became raging torrents for a few hours or days.

The Salt River was the reason for Phoenix' existence, even though it might overflow its banks during the flood season, become a raging stream two miles wide right through town. The land immediately adjoining the river, was excellent for farming, a brush dam upstream and crude irrigation ditches widened the tillable area, and the Roosevelt Dam further extended this in 1912.

Theodore Roosevelt had preached the gospel of reclamation of America's arid wastes, and this great dam, 80 miles east of Phoenix, was one of the first major projects in that program. The water impounded there flowed down the valley for 40 miles, then was distributed by canals over an area 40 miles long and 15 miles wide, the Roosevelt Dam Project, with Phoenix in the exact center.

So Phoenix was a pleasant cattle town of around 25,000 people in

1916 when Litchfield went out. Ranchers and cattlemen with broad Stetsons and jangling spurs came in out of the sun on Saturday afternoons to sit on the broad porch of the Adams House, spin long stories of the pioneer days.

No one was too much interested when the tall easterner suggested planting their land to cotton, even though he offered to lend money for cultivating and picking, and to buy all the cotton they could raise at a guaranteed price.

One man over in Yuma, however, heard of Litchfield's visit, went to see him. At the end of their talk he agreed to lease 10,000 acres of desert land belonging to Dr. Chandler, owner of the famous San Marco Hotel, clear it, plant cotton, sell it to Goodyear at a specified price. After that he went to see his lawyer, E. F. Parker, in Pasadena, threw the contract on the table, asked him to look it over.

"I want your business opinion," he said. "Have I made a million dollars?" The lawyer read the contract carefully.

"I don't know anything about cotton," he said, finally, "but there are men around who do. There are engineering phases, clearing and leveling of land, power and irrigation problems. Where are you going to get your water, and how much is it going to cost to deliver it over those 10,000 acres? There are agricultural phases, whether this land is suitable or not. We'll have to look into the labor situation. I'll call a meeting tomorrow and start the study."

"But that might take a week," protested McDevit. "This is September already. I want to start next week. Goodyear wants its cotton quickly."

"You asked me if you were going to get rich from that contract," the lawyer reminded him.

Reluctantly he agreed to delay. They called in Quinton, Code and Hill, consulting engineers who had built the Roosevelt Dam, and laid out many irrigation systems, called in farm experts, government technicians, contractors. The study was pushed at top speed, but took two weeks to complete. At the end, Parker had to tell his client that he was not going to make a million dollars, that he might not make a dime, that he was likely to lose everything he had, including his shirt.

Litchfield returned to Akron, summed up the situation with the directors.

"He can be held to his contract but would be forced into bankruptcy," he said, "and that won't give us any cotton. The cotton shipping situation is worse than it has been any time since the war started. The price of long staple cotton is rising daily. If we are to get any cotton in

1917, for our new tire, we must raise it ourselves."

The situation was urgent. The board gave its approval.

Two tracts were purchased, Chandler's land, 8000 acres lying 27 miles southeast of Phoenix, and the Beardsley tract, which with some adjoining land, totalled 14,000 acres, lying 18 miles west of the city. The board named the latter holding the Litchfield Ranch, the other being simply called Goodyear. A third property, Marinette, of 11,000 acres, 16 miles northwest of Phoenix, was bought in May, 1920.

When it appeared that the deal would go through, wires hummed and things began to move to get cotton planted by the end of the year. Mules were hard to get. The army was buying them up. Goodyear needed a thousand. Tractors and farm machinery were shipped out.

The U. S. Labor Department permitted Goodyear to bring in Mexican and Indian labor from across the border if it would send them back when the job was finished. A colorful procession began to move across the border, hundreds of Mexicans with their wives, children and household goods headed for the desert. Hundreds of picturesque characters who had worked on difficult and dangerous construction jobs all over the west came in.

The deal with Beardsley was closed the day before Christmas. On the day after Christmas, Carillo, the general contractor, member of an old Spanish grant family, climbed into the seat of an improvised grading machine, a pair of caterpillar tractors with two steel rails lashed between them.

"Let's go," said Carillo, and the job was started. The expeditionary force included 2000 men, 1000 mules, a fleet of tractors. Before its advance the desert suddenly ceased to exist, water began flowing in cement-lined canals, seeds were sown, and by picking time 6000 acres had been cleared and thousands of bales of long staple cotton were shipped to the Goodyear factory—in time to relieve the shortage at Akron, and to get in on the rising prices.

Parker, the lawyer, was made general manager of the project. He had gone to Phoenix for a couple of days to get a client out of a bad contract, was to stay there five years.

Clearing and planting so vast an area was a huge job and costly. Most of the property lay outside the Conservation District. The company had to sink scores of wells. Fortunately there was plenty of water below ground, and though the drills had to go several hundred feet in places, the water rose close to the surface, and the maximum lift was around 100 feet. Power lines were brought in to operate the pumps, hundreds of miles of canals and ditches built. Townsites went up on each ranch, with smaller settlements for the Mexican workmen, convenient to their work. Roads were needed and 154 miles of highways were built within the boundaries of the ranches. Cotton has to be ginned and 50 gin stands went in the first year, with others following to a total of 150, not only on the company property but in half a dozen towns over the valley as other people began to raise cotton.

There were few cross country highways and these dusty, rutted and all but impassable in rainy weather. It was a day's trip from the Goodyear Ranch to Litchfield. The company even bought an airplane to carry its people back and forth over the vast area.

It was easy to figure out afterwards that if Goodyear had been content to go more slowly, to find cheaper land or wait a few years hoping for a better price, if it had built its gins and irrigation ditches with less speed, it could have done so at less expense. But it would have had to pass up the opportunity for leadership which the Cord tire presented, of producing a tire definitely superior to any on the market. Time was the essence of that situation.

A more cautious management might have played safe. Risk and hazard are inherent in business. An opportunity arises, or what seems to be one. It will cost money to find out. It may pay high stakes or exact heavy penalties. Which that will be cannot be determined in advance. The risk has to be taken. Nor is a company safe that refuses to take any risks, for galloping competitors coming up from behind will ride over it.

The Goodyear operation created plenty of excitement throughout the Salt River Valley. Cottonseed oil mills went up in Phoenix, and people came in to build new business blocks and hotels. The city almost doubled in population in a decade. The state voted $8,000,000 in bonds for good roads, the largest amount ever appropriated up to that time, began a modern highway system.

And throughout the valley and even beyond it, cotton raising boomed. Fisk, Dunlop, Firestone sent their buyers out, ran the price up. Practically everyone in the Irrigation District switched from grain to cotton, and hundreds of men went out into the desert, dug new wells, brought new land to cultivation. The company continued to lend money to ranchers to get them started, agreed to take their entire crop. This protected the company against a runaway price market, which seemed likely to come, and was an incentive as well for people to raise cotton.

But the company did not long have to urge people to do this. The land was extremely productive once water was available, produced a bale to the acre. Figure that out. A 500 pound bale at 60 cents a pound made a crop worth $300 an acre. Dangle an opportunity before people as opportunity-wise as Americans and see what happens. At the peak there were 200,000 acres planted to cotton in the Salt River Valley, and cotton raising had spread to Yuma, the Imperial Valley and the San Joaquin Valley in California. The Mexican workmen bought silk shirts and automobiles. Arizona saw itself the world center for long staple cotton.

There was another factor no one realized at the time.

Much of the snow which fell in the mountains was not caught by the Roosevelt Dam, but went underground, where it was not merely useless to agriculture, but a potential menace to the land which hid it. For if the water table, as this underground water level was called, got too close to the surface, the sun's rays would draw it up, and the evaporated water leave the alkaline minerals it carried on the surface, ruin the soil for growing purposes. At a number of places, notably near the town of Tempe, the water table was getting dangerously close to the surface in 1916.

The water could be pumped out and drained off but that would cost a great deal of money. The Goodyear wells and the hundreds which followed did this for nothing. The water table fell to safe levels—in fact, thirty years later so many wells were drawing on this subterranean supply that no one worried as to whether there was too much water underground, but whether there would be enough for the future.

Up to the fall of 1920 the Arizona ranch was a highly successful operation. It had solved the problem of an ample supply of a high quality cotton grown on American soil, free from the restraints of war and embargo, it had made money for the company, had helped put over the pneumatic truck tire, clinching the company's position as leader of the industry.

Depression moved in to upset the equation. Things happened between planting time and harvest time that year. When cotton goes from a dollar a pound and over, to 20¢ and under, in a single calendar year, it is due to forces beyond any company's control, to the fact that millions of people were willing and able to pay a large price for cotton products at one time, and at another time were unable to pay even low prices for the same goods.

The story of cotton was no different from that of rubber, steel, lumber, cattle, except that the automotive industry in 1920 was growing faster than others and its losses were commensurate to its size.

In this case the ranch found that 20¢ cotton did not even cover out-of-pocket expense of labor and materials, to say nothing of the overhead represented in land and improvements. Moreover its commitments would be exceedingly difficult. These averaged around 60¢ a pound in 1920, and as cotton went to $1 a pound, it looked like an excellent bargain. But it had a different face when the ranchers came in to demand 60¢ for cotton which could be bought on the market for 20¢. Others came in to borrow money to pick their cotton.

Eventually after the company's refinancing was effected in May, 1921, these commitments were paid in full, but a long fall and a hard winter intervened.

The valley itself came back with better times. Thousands of acres of desert land had been reclaimed, the new highways expedited the movement of farm products to the market, and an increasing army of winter visitors brought additional wealth to the state. After the depression passed, Arizona found itself definitely farther along on the economic highway than it was when all this started.

Goodyear's own situation, however, was not so simple. Built up at pressure pace and in a period when materials were high, the ranches had heavy overhead. Operating economies were effected, but could not change the fact that it cost more to raise cotton in the United States than in Egypt, where labor cost but a few cents a day and the Nile River did the irrigation inexpensively. And as long as Egypt could supply enough cotton to meet world needs American long staple could be sold only at a loss.

And to make things worse Litchfield's own development men were now bringing up the embarrassing fact that with better compounding they did not have to use the extremely long staple cotton. They could use the medium-length Peeler cotton from the Mississippi Delta. Arizona became the company's number one headache.

During the next ten years many men worked singly, or in committees, to bring the property back on a paying basis, men with a wide range of experience, trying many expedients—Hinkle, cotton expert, who later went to Boston as cotton buyer for the company; Metzler, financial man; Hudson, a successful Arizona farmer; Hastings, government man; Parsons, accounting; McMicken, farm expert who had been with the ranch from the beginning; Sherry, industrial engineer; DeBruin from the Legal Department; and finally Zieske, Gadsden engineer, in 1933.

Sending Sherry to Arizona throws light on company thinking. He was an industrial engineer with a good eye for cost control, had had production experience in World War I in operating chemical plants for Dupont, had joined Goodyear after the war. Litchfield called him in one day.

"What do you know about raising cotton?" he asked.

"I've never even seen any growing," said Sherry.

"Good," said Litchfield, "I want you to go out and take charge of the Arizona ranch."

It was a fresh look at the problem, from a new viewpoint.

The main effort was to increase income. That started with further diversification of crops. Alfalfa had always been used as an alternate crop to keep up the fertility of the soil, and now other crops were put in—wheat, maize, citrus, sorghum. Prices may be good on one crop and poor on another, but by raising several the farmer is apt to average out better.

The ranch went in the cattle business. Alfalfa did not bring much on the market, so men were sent across the border to buy lean range cattle in Mexico, fed the alfalfa to them and sold them for beef.

The ranch was further mechanized in the late 1920's.

Tractors and farm machinery had been tried out before, but bogged down in wet days, left corners that a mule team had to plow and cultivate anyhow. However, farm tractors had improved a lot in the decade and Sherry interested engineers from the International Harvester Company in using the ranch as an experimental station in the development of new machines. They made such advancements that in time all the mules were sold off, and farm costs substantially reduced.

Cotton remained in the picture, but after that in the medium staple length the tire industry needed, McMicken working with the U. S. Department of Agriculture to develop this. Arizona remained an important cotton producer, with some of the long staple Pima still being raised until World War II, when further reduction of import duties drove it out.

In laying out the property originally, the company headquarters were set up in an attractive townsite, which the directors named Litchfield Park. A company house, called the Wigwam, was built and homes for the ranch executives, all in the distinctive architecture of the Hopi Indians. Parks were laid out, and wide boulevards, flanked with palm trees, pepper trees, cottonwood and the colorful orange trees, led to the main highway.

The land was extremely fertile and in time the Wigwam was almost hidden by foliage and masses of shrubbery. More and more people were coming to the Southwest for the winter, so more houses were added and the Wigwam became a winter hotel, with riding horses, swimming pool, tennis court, golf, and desert outings.

With all these expedients the ranch was able to recover out-of-pocket expense, more than break even on operations, but still carried the heavy burden of depression losses on its back. So eventually these were written off, the value of land was reduced on the books to the going prices in the valley, and the ranch started with a clean slate.

The test fleet moved to Arizona. Long stretches of highway under the hot sun offered a quick and thorough test of new tires. If they could stand up under that they could be used anywhere.

The ranch found new usefulness, too, after 1931 when Goodyear started its revolutionary program for the use of rubber tires on the farm, for it was an ideal proving ground for adapting tires to all farm implements, plows, harrows, reapers, harvesters, balers and manure spreaders, for light vehicles to cultivate between the orange trees and take the ripe fruit straight from the pickers. At the peak 45 tractors were in use to get a quick check on results. And while the ranch played an important role in this great movement, the tractors also did most of the farm work.

Goodyear could have stopped after Arizona got out of the red. What cotton was raised was sold to brokers, might never be used in a Goodyear tire. The ranch could be sold to advantage, and as a matter of fact, the 11,000 acres at Marinette and the 8000 at Goodyear were leased and later sold, leaving only the 17,000 acre Litchfield Park holdings.

There might be some values, however, still to be found there, even if the company got no more out of it than everyone else, in improving agricultural processes so that the nation might be fed and clothed with less manual effort.

Arizona entered on a new phase.

Zieske was now in charge, with McMicken as farm manager. The latter, though born in Brooklyn, was a practical "dirt farmer," familiar with the eternal problem of guessing in the spring what crops will bring the best price in the fall, was an expert in irrigation farming, knew cotton as few men did in the Southwest, had spent some time studying Egyptian operations and been loaned to the government of Peru to counsel that nation's agricultural program.

Zieske's experience, since he was 18, was factory, simplifying processes, applying machinery to relieve arduous hand labor, expediting the movement of materials by mechanical aids, hoists, conveyors, industrial trucks. Why send a factory man to the farm?

He soon found out.

"Mechanization has been widely used in industry," Litchfield told him, "but very little has been done on the farm. See what you can do."

It was the old Litchfield principle of a fresh look at a job by men with different experience.

The assignment had interesting results, attachments and devices that would take the harvested crop straight from the combine or other farm implements, used hoists, chutes and elevators to transport it, screen it, grade it, store it until the price was right, or load it directly into freight cars, all with a minimum of labor. Storage sheds and railroad switch tracks were built, and a mill where, if the market was off, the alfalfa might be carried by conveyors, ground into poultry feed and sacked ready for shipping.

These experiments carried on in close cooperation with the farm implement manufacturers, and always with an eye to cost, covered a wide range, since operations at Litchfield Park were so highly diversified. It included in recent years a scraper plane mounted on two sets of rubber tires 50 feet apart, which could level off a large area of desert land quickly and inexpensively, bring new land into cultivation.

The individual farmer does not have the funds for such research nor would the economies secured pay on a small scale. Only a large operation could afford to concentrate specialized engineering experience to such a job. The results found cut costs at the ranch, and improvements brought to light were used by cooperative associations and individual farmers trading equipment and labor back and forth with their neighbors.

The Goodyear operations attracted wide attention, and a Farm Forum was held in Litchfield Park in 1943, which brought in not only agricultural experts from the universities and the government, but also editors of farm papers from all over America. The editors were shown every phase of modern mechanized irrigation farming, as well as colorful older ones like the roundup and branding of cattle, and their reports went to farmers all over America.

It may be human nature for any activity to seem more important to those associated with it than it actually is. Still it might happen that foodstuffs for the nation might some day be produced just a bit more economically and with less manpower, on Maryland's East Shore or the Dakota prairies, because of the things that happened in Arizona.

There was one final development, however, perhaps the most significant of all. This was the effort to find human values as well as material ones at Goodyear Farms, the Apprentice Farmer program which started in 1937.

Two separate lines of thinking came together to create this movement. Mr. Litchfield, acting as a judge in a contest of the Future Farmers of America in 1936, to select the outstanding young farmer from the various states, was impressed by the calibre of the contestants.

"How many of these boys will be able to apply this skill and enter-

Section of the village of Litchfield Park, which was all desert when Good-year went there. Business district in upper center, orange grove beyond.

Igloo houses (concrete poured over an in-flated balloon) are used for grain storage.

Headquarters of Goodyear Farms, Wing-foot Homes and airport in background.

With irrigation farming bringing thousands of acres into cultivation, Arizona remains an important producer of long staple cotton.

With the Southwest a new winter playground, guests gather at Wigwam for horseback ride over winding trails of surrounding desert.

prise they have acquired on their own farms?" he asked.

The farm officials shook their heads.

"Not many, I'm afraid," one of them said, "unless their parents have enough money to start them off with land of their own."

"You mean they'll have to go out as farm hands?" Litchfield asked.

"Many of them will," he was told.

And Goodyear still owned great stretches of irrigated land it did not need in the manufacture of tires. Instead of selling that property to one or two big operators, Litchfield wondered, men who could pay more and pay in cash, would it be possible to sell it in small tracts to boys like these, with the chance for them to earn the money to pay for it?

This idea set off a series of conferences with government and agricultural experts. Many plans of colonization had been launched in America, and most of them had failed, largely perhaps because they depended on vague, benevolent, semi-socialistic group impulses, rather than offering incentive to the individual. The Litchfield plan must be practical, hard-headed. No charity in it, but hard work, determination, planning and intelligence. If the plan offered a sizable stake in the ownership finally of 80 acres of rich, irrigated land, boys like these might be willing to work hard to achieve it.

The program was finally worked out, had four stages.

A selected group of boys with some agricultural school training would work for the first year as regular ranch employees, but with their work laid out so that they would not do the same thing over and over, would learn all the phases of irrigation and mechanized farming—just like the Flying Squadron in the factory. There were conferences after hours, too, on accounting, budgets, planning, marketing. Each boy was paid farm wages, given the use of a house and a plot of ground, and an extension of enough credit to buy a cow, giving him additional cash income beyond his wages, and further credit as he proved himself, to enlarge his herd up to eight.

The next step, for each one who measured up, was a chance to operate an 80-acre tract on shares. As the third step, he might lease that land, at a figure based not on its speculative value but minimum earning power. He could raise whatever he chose, and had the counsel of McMicken and Zieske and consultants from the state agricultural college.

Four, when an Apprentice Farmer had built up the net worth of his holdings in cattle, farm equipment or whatever, equal to one-fifth of the purchase price, he could contract to buy the 80 acres outright, and have 15 years to pay for it.

It was not to be expected that all of the eleven men in the original group and those who followed them would come through successfully. Some decided it was too hard work and gave up, some were good workmen but poor managers, the war interfered with the program, but at the end of eleven years, in 1948, two of them had taken title to their farms and seven others were well on the way.

One had specialized in pure-bred hogs, another in registered Jersey cows, another was raising feeder cattle, one went into chickens on a big scale, a number went into truck farming either as their main or minor effort, one went into cotton and had a big year in 1947, raising three bales to the acre.

The young farmers organized their own cooperative marketing association, took over the water project from the company, acquiring pumps, pipe lines and ditches, took picking contracts from other ranchers, learned to trade labor and equipment among themselves, took a pride in not asking help from the company.

They called their association the Adaman Project, Inc., meaning to "add-a-man," as he measured up. The little settlement where they lived they called Sarival, an old Goodyear trade name coming from Salt River Valley.

So the Arizona ranch, which gave the company plenty of headaches in 1920 became a colorful and important part of its overall operations. Litchfield Park had become an attractive town by 1948, with its own grade and high schools, a Catholic and Protestant church, all in the same architecture as the Wigwam, a shopping district, with stores, a restaurant, a bank, post office, doctors' offices and even a Kiwanis Club, with other ranchers in the valley sharing membership. Winter visitors, in golf clothes, bathing suits or cowboy costumes, added a colorful touch.

The Mexican settlements had changed from the brush ramadas of 30 years earlier, where the bathtubs were used for storage, the cots burned for firewood, and the cotton pickers slept on the floor by preference. Good wages brought higher living standards, and mechanized equipment required more intelligence than driving a team of mules, and the new generation made effective use of improved school facilities.

The planting program on the ranch varies from year to year with circumstances, but in 1948 3100 acres were devoted to alfalfa, 2000 to barley, 1750 to hegari, 1000 to cotton, 600 to wheat, 200 to citrus and 40 acres to sugar beets raised for seed. The ranch had 1000 head of cattle, and rented out grazing land to sheepmen who brought their herds down from the mountain valleys for the winter.

The Salt River Valley had become one of the richest in America. On 400,000 acres of irrigated land, ranchers were raising five to six crops of alfalfa a year, taking a ton to the acre in each mowing, were shipping out cantaloupe and honeydew melons by the car load. The valley raised a fifth of all the iceberg lettuce grown in the United States, growing around $1200 worth to the acre, shipped out broccoli, cauliflower, cabbage, celery, carrots, oranges, grapefruit, often by airplane, turned in a $30 million annual cotton crop.

Phoenix had become an attractive modern city, with great hotels, department stores, shops, warehouses along the railroad, and neon-lighted tourist camps surrounding the city in all directions. The population was shown at 65,000 in 1940, but in the metropolitan area was estimated at 200,000 population today, with city planners talking about a city of half a million by 1960.

Water, power, good roads, diversification of crops, mechanized farming, and the industry and resourcefulness of thousands of men had had a part in these results.

5. Personnel Factors

Industrial Relations

THE 1908-20 period in Goodyear's history which saw the company win striking victories in the laboratory and the market place, also saw the working out of a complete program of industrial relations.

The program had three phases. One was Training—finding promising men and training them to do a better job, whether at the work bench or on the lengthening list of administrative duties. Two was Industrial Engineering, the application of the piece-work plan and plant efficiency methods, integral parts of America's Mass Production System. The third was Employee Relations, which might be summed up as making Goodyear a good place to work, so that it would continue to attract and hold good men.

This third phase really started first, for it had always been part of company thinking. The Seiberlings were good men to work for. They had stayed in Akron after success came, raised their children there, felt it their permanent home, even though the industry had became world-wide in scope. There were men in the plant who had worked for them in other enterprises, and for their father before them. F. A. Seiberling was a magnetic figure, one to intrigue the imagination. Men knew that he had gone broke and was fighting an up-hill battle to come back. C. W. Seiberling was a rare personality for whom everyone felt a genuine affection. Goodyear men were not long in recognizing the human qualities of Litchfield and Stadelman. Personalities like William Stephens helped immensely, men of restless energy, high spirits and the gift of friendship. The very struggle for existence which the company had gone through had bred a loyalty unusual in business. But Goodyear grew larger.

By 1910 the company was too large for industrial relations to be handled man to man. There were 2500 people on the payroll and more coming in daily. The responsibility for meeting the situation rested primarily with the serious-minded New England superintendent. Litchfield thought long about the matter, tried to analyze what things had been done in the past to maintain good relations, to set down in his mind the things the men wanted and had a right to have and how these could be assured to them.

He set up a Labor Department to do this, made it directly responsible to himself to make sure that it worked. So this chapter becomes the narrative of what things were done to try to preserve the family spirit of the early days, and prevent a personnel situation from growing into a labor problem. There are several important dates in that story:

1914	Vacations for factory men Eight-hour day	1915	Employees' insurance Efficiency Department Factory school Service Pin Association
1909	Relief Association		
1910	Labor Department	1916	Pension Plan Americanization classes
1912	Wingfoot Clan Goodyear Hospital Factory Restaurant Goodyear Heights Seiberling Field	1919	Industrial Assembly
		1920	Goodyear Hall
1913	Flying Squadron Boy Scouts	1927	Hospital Association

The labor department was given the responsibility at the outset of hiring men, which had been previously done by foremen or superintendents. It presently added to that the responsibility of firing men, a rather significant step forward. Goodyear had 175 foremen by 1910, most of them new to the business, men who had come up from the ranks.

In taking hiring away from the foremen, the company was merely seeking greater efficiency. A good employment manager, knowing the requirements of the various jobs, could better allocate new men to departments than several foremen could, and do it in less time. But in taking away the right of discharge, Goodyear sought to protect the men against arbitrary decisions. A foreman could report a man's work or his attitude as unsatisfactory, but the labor department must get into the situation before drastic action was taken, would sometimes conclude that a man was improperly placed, that transferred to another department he could do satisfactory work. Later on the rule was laid down that a man of five year's service could not be discharged at all without the approval of the superintendent.

The department set up a record system, so that whatever preference should be based on seniority should be given. Long service at Goodyear was always important, counted toward shift preference, vacations, pensions, would be taken into consideration when lay-offs became necessary. The records also showed the quality and quantity of each man's work as factors toward promotion.

A factory restaurant was opened in 1912, a factory paper, The Wingfoot Clan, as an avenue of communication between the management and employees, and a factory hospital with six beds, a day and night nurse and a full-time doctor, the second industrial hospital started in America, International Harvester having the first.

Prior to then if an employee was hurt, he would put tobacco juice on the injury, tie it up and go back to work. With machinery coming into wider use, there were bound to be accidents, which could be treated immediately, and in the case of minor injuries the employee could go back to his job without loss of earnings. The factory became hospital-minded, accustomed to turn there immediately in case of illness, head off trouble before it became serious.

Many doctors came to be associated with Dr. Millard through the years, usually young doctors who came on for the experience, stayed on till they felt ready to strike out for themselves. Dr. Millard, a pioneer in industrial medicine, remained, made this his life work.

A Compensation Department was started with the increasing use of machinery in industry and more accidents to employees. Damage suits had begun to fill the courts. Clever lawyers specialized in bringing and defending such suits. Collection of damages was slow and uncertain. Theodore Roosevelt and others took this up as a matter of social justice, and various states began to pass laws which would provide compensation for industrial accidents without employees having to go to court. Ohio was one of the first to do this, in 1912. It set up a scale of payment for industrial injuries, and compelled all employers to contribute to a fund, based on the number of employees and hours worked, the money being used to pay for all accidents occurring at work.

The employer could however pay for his own accidents, using the same scale of payments, the state having the right to review all claims and the employee to appeal. Goodyear took the alternative, feeling it gave incentive to try to prevent accidents and the distress and pain they caused, rather than merely to pay the bills.

The story of the Relief Association may properly come in here, although it was established in 1909, before the labor department itself. It established a fund from employee contributions to take care of employees who were sick or hurt.

The principle which insurance men call averaging the risks is well known. Out of any considerable group, it is certain that some will be hurt or fall sick each year, and that when that happens the individual is not usually able to meet the expense without difficulty. It had been the custom for a company to take a dollar from each employee's pay to take care of hospital and doctor bills. Employees appreciated this protection but there was a feeling at times that the company probably took in more than it paid out, and that the plan was partially designed to avoid damage suits.

The Relief Association struck a new note. Membership was voluntary. A man could go in or stay out as he chose. The Association was not for profit, and the money was to be handled by the employees themselves through their own officers. Once an adequate surplus had been built up, the dues would be kept just high enough to take care of all claims. The plan provided not merely for accidents sustained at work or for sickness that might be attributed to employment, but covered all accidents and all sickness on the part of the members. If a man fell off a ladder at home or came down with the flu, he would still be protected.

Since this plan was primarily in the interest of employees, the Relief Association grew rapidly in membership; and even with the thousands of new people hiring in in the succeeding years, the Association always had a large percentage of employees on its lists. A new Goodyearite found an invitation at the hiring booth to join the Relief Association.

The original Relief Association included an assessment of one dollar a member when anyone died. This was abandoned in 1915 when the company took out insurance in the amount of $500 for each member of the association. Those of five years' service and over would get an additional $500 insurance. This action helped popularize the Association. Group insurance came in later with more than $100,000,000 of insurance in effect in 1948.

Similar associations were started in the first outside plants, though group insurance took over this job in later ones. The protection of the Association was also extended to office people and members of the sales department, whether at Akron, the field or export.

The Association broadened its work in 1927 to include a hospital association, one of the first in the country, and a successful experiment which was widely copied elsewhere.

The Hospital Association was started by the employees through the Industrial Assembly. Hospital costs in Akron were going up and the Assembly, studying the situation for two or three years, seriously considered building an employee hospital.

However, a better idea came in, to have employees contribute to a fund to cover hospital bills for everybody, just as the Relief Association did for sickness and accident. Akron hospitals studied the plan, agreed to it. Relief Association dues were increased from 60 cents a month to 90 cents to cover hospital expenses.

The plan helped many employees through the 1929 depression, and helped the hospitals as well, since members of the Association were sure pay, and need not wait to go to the hospital until they had accumulated the money to pay the bill. By 1948 23,500 employees and 26,500 members of their families were under the protection of the Association, which by then had 40 full-time employees, was doing a business of $1,500,000 a year.

Goodyear Heights and Seiberling Field, both started in 1912, represent a variation from other features of the company's industrial relations policy. The factory had added 1000 employees in two years, going from 2500 to 3500. North of the factory lay a tract of flat land, with Blue Pond alongside, and graceful wooded hills rising beyond. Seiberling thought of it as an ideal place to set up a community for employees. As there was some question in the minds of his directors on the subject, he bought some 100 acres of hillside himself, had the street extended through, brought on landscape artists from Boston to lay out a townsite, with the streets following the contours of the hills, brought architects in from New York who designed 19 different types of houses, inexpensively priced, had contractors bid on building 50 houses at a time.

These economies were passed on to the employees who could move in when they made their down payment and pay for their homes out of wages, on such terms that the houses would be fully paid for in 15 years. Norton Street was extended through to the Heights and renamed Goodyear Avenue. Water, sewers, and lights were put in, and the little community of Goodyear Heights, as it was called, soon filled up, and Seiberling bought a second tract beyond. Twelve acres at the foot of the hill nearest the factory was laid out as an athletic field.

Litchfield's reluctance to vote for the project as a company matter came from pretty careful reasoning. As far as his thinking on industrial relations had proceeded at that time he felt that the company should pay good wages, furnish good working conditions, establish absolute fairness beween men and management. The athletic field was probably all right, if the company could afford it; he believed thoroughly in recreation and sport, and the city had no money for such purposes. Akron was growing faster than any city in the United States, was having trouble finding money to pave streets, supply light and water and sewers. It was all right for Goodyear to help out with an athletic field which would be chiefly used by its employees.

He believed thoroughly in home ownership but he hesitated about anything savoring of paternalism. Several model towns had been built over the country, but in each case there was a question in the minds of the employees, which at times was expressed out loud, as to whether these were not paid for with money that should have gone instead into the pay envelope. Men are apt to balk at having things done for them. They would rather spend their own money as they please, spend it wastefully, extravagantly, if they want to, rather than have an all-wise and beneficent corporation take over any of the spending of it for them, attempt any regulation of their individual lives.

Litchfield had long since come to the conclusion that you can't GIVE a man anything—except an opportunity to exercise his full capabilities, grow to his full stature. Not good-will but suspicion might be generated otherwise, he felt. Whatever the employees wanted to do for themselves, the company could quite properly cooperate with, help make facilities available. But there was a finely drawn line of distinction in his mind between this philosophy and the model town idea.

As a matter of fact, however, Goodyear Heights cleared this hurdle without difficulty. The continuing growth of the plant and the shortage of homes which came a little later made this community, attractive and convenient to the factory, a real benefit. Enough homes were sold off

Goodyear Hall (1920), an "extra dividend" to employees, is the center of education and recreation work. Goodyear State Bank in foreground.

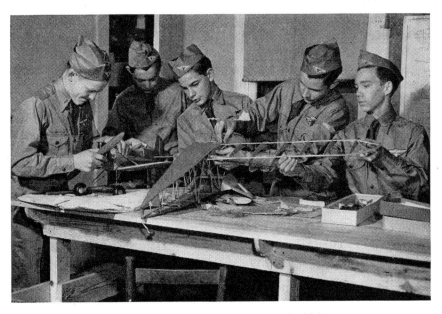

The Air Scout movement, started at Akron, spread widely over country. These boys are sons of cotton mill workers at Rockmart, Georgia.

that the company's relationship soon became largely that of any other sub-division operator, collecting payments, keeping the property up. The section was later taken into the city, operated thereafter like other sections of Akron.

Boy Scout work started at Goodyear in 1913, largely because Litchfield had become impressed with the value of scout training for the sons of Goodyearites, who by then were coming in for jobs as soon as they were old enough. Scouting developed initiative and responsibility, laid emphasis on physical fitness and clean living.

To encourage boys in the Goodyear community to take part, he built a Scout lodge on Goodyear Heights and another one at Wingfoot Lake, got foremen and staff men to volunteer as scout masters and committeemen for the five Goodyear troops which came into existence, acted as president of the Akron Scout council and later on the national executive board.

When he was trying to interest the public in pneumatic tires for trucks and buses in 1917 he sent the outstanding scouts in each troop on a long motor trip to Washington and New York. From 1918 on he provided a two-week outing at his camp at Lake Timagimi, Canada, 600 miles north of Akron, for the boys making the best record during the year, this incentive being extended later to Scouts from the tire factories at Gadsden and Jackson and the cotton mills in the South.

By this time the group included also a Sea Scout troop, and it was due to Mr. Litchfield's personal interest that the first Air Scout troop in the country was organized in 1942, to provide additional training for older scouts, growing up into a world which he foresaw would use the airplanes in increasing measure.

The full effects of any man's activities are beyond prediction. Driving past the Scout lodge on a spring day in 1916, while it was under construction, Litchfield fell into conversation with an alert youngster from East Akron, who had pedaled over on his bicycle to see how the building was coming. The boy was to finish high school in June, and ventured to ask about a job.

Litchfield told him to come in and see him when he was ready to go to work. It was his first meeting with Eddie Thomas.

An untoward set of circumstances in 1913 interrupted the industrial relations program. This was the short-lived, but serious rubber strike of that year. It started with some dissatisfaction in another rubber plant over wages. The men in the vulcanizing department were among the best paid in the shop, earning $3.50 per day, but there had been a change in process and until the men got used to it they earned less money. The dissatisfaction was seized upon by organizers, who, as it became evident later, were dispatched to Akron by the Industrial Workers of the World, a left wing radical group.

Assembly lines were snarled up as the vulcanizing department was shut down. Rioting broke out, the plants were picketed, and workers who tried to carry on were attacked and beaten. The Police Department was too small to control the situation and for a time it appeared that troops would be called in.

Dr. George P. Atwater, militant Episcopal rector, organized a citizen's committee of a 1000 men, placed them at the disposal of Sheriff Ferguson, to patrol the streets and restore order. Rioting and violence died out as quickly as it had started. Then Ferguson rounded up 50 of the leaders. None of them were Akron men, none had ever worked in the rubber factories.

"You men," said Ferguson, "are to be out of Akron by daylight." The agitators took the hint. They also took the strike funds which the workmen had contributed. In 48 hours the strike was over, and the men were returning to work.

The finale came when a legislative committee, headed by William Green, then state senator, later head of American Federation of Labor, reported that the rubber workers were getting an average of $2.60 a day, as against a $1.40 national average, and that working conditions were generally better there than elsewhere.

The strike caused some liberalization of labor policy throughout Akron. Goodyear was hiring in hundreds of new employees, unfamiliar with its industrial policies. The company realized that the doors must be opened wider, that any man who felt he wasn't fairly treated could get an audience, tell his own story, get matters adjusted if they were wrong. Additional training was probably necessary for foremen, and the personnel set-up further improved.

Litchfield concluded too after the strike and the equally disastrous flood of that year that a more flexible production system should be devised, so that interruptions in a single department would not tie up the whole plant. Out of this thinking came the Flying Squadron, to be discussed later. Probably the matter of rates too needed more definite attention. With 3500 employees working at widely differing types of jobs some plan must be set up which would keep wages fair under changing conditions. The Efficiency Department was started in the following year as a result.

The year 1914 saw another movement on the part of the company which was thought radical at the time. Office people had always had vacations. Now it was proposed to extend these to the factory. Men of five years' service and over would get a week's vacation with pay, men of 10 years' service, two weeks. A change of scene was a good thing for the man in the factory as well as for the office man. In a few years as high as 9000 factory workmen were taking vacations, with further liberalization in the 1930 decade as factory vacations became general in industry.

The eight-hour day also started in 1914. For many years men had worked 10 to 12 hours daylight and 10 to 13 hours on night shift. Now, as rapidly as matters could be worked out, there would be three eight-hour shifts. With the pressure for production and the growing difficulty of keeping enough men in the plant to meet increasing needs for tires, this could not be put into effect immediately, but by 1916 the whole factory, down to the men on the yard gang and the elevator operators, was on an eight hour day.

A pension system fitted naturally into an organization such as Goodyear was becoming. Men grow old, should not be thrown on the scrap heap when they are no longer useful. Some recognition should be had of long and faithful service. A pension system was introduced in 1916, under which older, long service employees could retire on an income based on earnings.

Service pins, to mark employee service, in multiples of five years, got under way during this period. Litchfield called a meeting of service pin holders in 1915, when he himself had completed 15 years with the company, tossed a bombshell into the gathering with the announcement that he was giving $100,000, representing his entire salary over that period, to Goodyear employees. They were not to spend the money, but could invest it as they saw fit and use the income. The Service Pin Association was organized, and built the fund up to a quarter million dollars, paying cash dividends each year. The 1920 depression cut down the principal, and after that the association put the money into awards to employees, which would serve as a stimulus to achievement.

Culmination of the whole industrial relations program came in 1919 with the Industrial Assembly, one of the first company-initiated experiments in collective bargaining in America. This will be discussed later.

The final phase, for which it is difficult to set a starting date, was Employee Activities.

These started early, with a central committee to arrange annual picnics and field days. Slusser, Stephens, C. W. Seiberling and others from management took a personal interest in them, found men like Colley, Garman, Nall, Weiss and others ready to put in long hours to make each event a success. Sports boomed with the opening of Seiberling Field, plant and inter-plant teams were organized in baseball, bowling, soccer, tennis, and rifle groups. Many employees came in from the south, were interested in hunting, fishing, outdoor things, and the company believing in healthful recreation, gave full encouragement.

Goodyear Hall, completed in 1920, gave further stimulus to employee activities, became an unique institution. A building six stories high, occupying 380 feet frontage along Market opposite the factory, it included the largest gymnasium in Ohio, a fully equipped theater, club rooms for employee groups, and classrooms for Goodyear Industrial University which was organized at the same time.

The theory behind Goodyear Hall was that it was a stock dividend to employees, comparable to the stock dividends paid to stockholders. It would stimulate education, recreation, and physical well being, and in so doing enable a man to increase his productiveness, become more useful to himself, to his company, and to society, get more out of life.

Baseball and bowling teams grew up around the Goodyear gymnasium. And in a community largely populated by newcomers and with inadequate recreation facilities, Goodyear Hall led to the formation of still more clubs, foremen's clubs, women's clubs, the Squadron, the Silents, groups putting on departmental dances, shows and musical events.

There were two big events of the year. One was the Christmas Party, with car loads of presents for employees' children, men from the office and the shop acting as Santa Claus, and as high as 25,000 children coming in from ten in the morning, passing through the gymnasium on schedule by departments, until late in the afternoon. A Christmas pageant, enacting the story of Bethlehem, became another tradition in the holiday week.

The other was the annual picnic, which also went back to the early days, and in later years would draw as many as 50,000 employees and their families, Euclid Beach on Lake Erie finally being the only park large enough to house the crowd—and with round-the-clock picnics for the different shifts during the busy war years.

Impetus to such programs was given by the shortage of man power which came with the first World War and the post-war boom which followed. There were more jobs than there were men to fill them. Employers were in competition for labor. Akron factories, pressed for production, could no longer wait for men to come in looking for jobs, but sent agents out rounding them up, from the farms, the small towns, the agricultural section of the south.

Ambitious factory workers and Squadron men continue their education before and after working hours at Goodyear Industrial University.

Scenes at Goodyear gym, the annual picnic, the Christmas party, opening of baseball season by Litchfield and Thomas and a hockey game in Canada.

Sub-division of production processes had come in to such a degree that it was no longer necessary for a man to be a highly skilled workman in order to earn good wages. If he were alert, quick, industrious, he would not be long in mastering the one or two processes entrusted to him. It was the golden age of the man of muscle. A workman might spend a few months in Dayton, spend what he made, go on to Detroit, work a while there, continue to Pittsburgh, to Akron, to Cleveland, to other industrial centers, always sure of a good job at good wages.

Men who had never worked in a factory were attracted by the wages offered. Some stayed only long enough to get a stake, and went back to the farm. Most of them however stayed as long as the boom lasted.

Labor turnover was high in every factory. In Goodyear one man in the labor department had to interview all the men who turned in their tools. Why are you leaving, he asked each one. Sometimes there were unfavorable working conditions which had not come to the management's attention, and which could be remedied. Sometimes there were personal difficulties, and the company might be of assistance. Many were leaving because housing conditions were inadequate in Akron. They could not find a house at reasonable rent to which they could bring their families, they wanted a yard and a garden, but had to live in a rooming house in Akron, perhaps share a bed with another man.

The sign "Standing Room Only," might well have been hoisted over Akron at one time. Men slept in attics and garrets, slept two shifts to a bed, one man ready to turn in as the first man got out. Goodyear Heights and Firestone Park helped, but they too were inadequate. Akron was under-housed for years.

In the draft registration of 1917, Akron registered more men than Toledo, Columbus or Cincinnati, all larger cities, sent more men to the army than any city in Ohio except Cleveland.

Akron was in competition for men with the other industrial cities of the middle west. There had to be inducements in addition to wages to get men to come to Akron, and more important to get them to stay. Most of the large industries installed industrial relations departments, fostered employee activities, sought to make their plants more desirable places to work. Goodrich inaugurated, under the far-sighted E. C. Shaw, then works manager, the most comprehensive industrial health program in the country, though arousing some suspicion that he was attempting to introduce state medicine into this country. Firestone, like Goodyear, had an employees' store, where its people could take advantage of the company's larger purchasing power, had an employee club house, though less elaborate than Goodyear Hall. All three big companies had their own factory papers.

Goodyear had 33,000 people on its payroll in 1920, but had to hire 60,000 people a year in replacements to keep the total up to that figure. It was estimated that it cost $30 to break in a new man, and if he left after a few weeks, that money was wasted. This turnover was acute in the first three months of a new employee's service, was low among older employees who had become settled in Akron, had their own homes, liked Goodyear policies. If a man stayed longer than three months there was an even chance he would be permanent. The various phases of employee relations were intended to help carry the new employee over this hump, get him through the period of acclimatization.

. . .

When the depression of late 1920 came in, many companies curtailed their industrial relations program. Goodyear, however, did not regard its plan as one merely to reduce labor turn-over, felt it integral to the job of getting and holding good men. Whether the policy actually paid dividends, as well as being a decent thing, as between management and men, was a matter to which Hoskin's figures, nor any other man's could give final answer. Goodyear believed it worthwhile, carried on, even though it was the hardest hit financially in 1920 of any of the large companies.

For while every item of expense was sharply scrutinized in 1920-21, and was reduced wherever possible, the industrial relations program survived practically intact. Only one activity, legal aid, was dropped. The rest, education and recreation, as embodied in Goodyear Hall and Seiberling Field, understanding, in company and group meetings and the factory paper, hospitals, the Squadron, restaurants, safety, all went on.

The program was accepted by the banking group which came in. President Wilmer and his associates had been put in by banking and creditor groups to safeguard a large investment and a large extension of credit to a sick company, must see that all unnecessary expense was eliminated, so that the company could meet interest and dividend charges, justify the financing.

Wilmer went over the labor program critically with Litchfield and after that appraisal expressed himself not merely satisfied but its supporter. Men, not machines, build a business, he concluded. Goodyear had been trying seriously to build an institution around men. That must not be scrapped. It was neither good morals nor good business to let that program be lost.

Efficiency

It was no accident that America should build and own more automobiles than the rest of the world combined.

Nor would it just happen that America, paying the world's highest wages could deliver better automobiles and cheaper ones to most foreign countries than those nations could build with low-priced labor.

The explanation is the Mass Production system, which America created, and which helped make this country the greatest industrial nation in the world.

American automobiles did not take world leadership because of inventive genius. As a matter of fact, many of the early improvements in cars and tires were European in origin, and American manufacturers bid against each other for manufacturing rights in this country.

We had a great internal market, selling to our own people. But China, India and Russia have large populations. Buying power as well as numbers was necessary, and this the Mass Production system created by getting costs down and wages up.

The first step in this system is to break down processes into hundreds of separate jobs, which workmen could turn out in larger quantities as they mastered simple processes, as compared to a hand-made automobile for example, completely built by a few highly skilled men.

The second step was to provide factory layouts so that a workman could turn out his part of the job in the least time and with the least effort, with his materials brought within hand reach, and machines to take out arduous manual labor. America early found that fatigue costs money, in output and quality. *The company using mass production methods must always be looking for still better methods, materials and machines, be willing ruthlessly to scrap machines which have years of life left in them if a better one comes along, must not overlook the smallest saving in time or factory cost, since these mount up fast in large scale production.*

If the reason for the constant drive to get costs down was merely to make more money for the stockholders, the system would be indeed vulnerable and justify the criticism. *But this country realized—which is the crux of the whole thing—that lower costs would widen the market, make it possible for more people to buy the product, thus make possible further economies in manufacturing in a beneficent spiral, with good wages creating more customers, further expanding the market.*

America could not have climbed to industrial leadership unless it had taken the far-sighted view that it would make more money in the long run if it shared the benefit of lower factory costs with the consumer and with labor.

This is where the piecework system came in. One fundamental of that system is that a man was not paid for the hours he put in, for the employer can not sell his time, but for the volume he turned out of salable products. The employer had to use the best machinery he could get and the best processes and layouts he could devise to increase the productivity of the individual—and must offer cash incentive for maximum production.

The greatest industrial discovery of the period was the realization that the employer would be better off paying high wages than low wages, if quantity and quality of output increased proportionately.

America is the only country where workmen are able to buy the automobiles they help build.

Efficiency work, as it is called, started in Goodyear in 1915. Up to then wages and piecework rates were set by Stephens, Koken and the foremen, based on their first-hand knowledge of the processes and their observations of the efficiency of different men.

The company hired its first industrial engineers in 1915, men from the outside, commissioned them to study the whole production system. Coming in with a fresh viewpoint they would probably see a lot of things which production men might overlook because they were accustomed to them. They studied wages as well as methods and layouts, although wage recommendations were turned over to Slusser, as a practical shop man to review, to make sure that they were fair to the men, as well as to the company.

The experts did a good job, so when they left it was decided to make such studies continuous, keep the factory operating efficiently under changing conditions. Slusser was assigned to take over from where the experts left off, organize a department and fit it into the Goodyear structure.

The department would have two functions. It would study processes and layouts with the engineers and the machine design men, seek further improvements which would lessen manufacturing costs. Its other job was wages.

In studying wages all the thousands of jobs in the plant were gone over and catalogued. Some required more skill than others. It takes a year to three years to make a good calender man, if the coating or impregnating of fabric with rubber is to be done with such precision as to give uniformly high quality to the finished product. The calender man should be better paid than the man who merely took strips of rubberized fabric off the bias cutting machines, and laid them down on the conveyor.

Processes were studied as to fatigue, length of time to learn, noise, dirt, discomfort and the like, and a sort of ladder made up, with all jobs placed on it in relation to all other jobs.

The time study men were not to be an under-cover group, peering around corners, hiding behind pillars. They worked in the open. Slusser explained to supervision and pieceworkers alike that what they were trying to get at was an accurate measurement of a fair day's accomplishment on each job by an average good man. Not the speed expert or the especially skilled man, but a good working average. Slusser had come up from the ranks himself, kept in mind the viewpoint of the pieceworker. He insisted on a full day's work, but it had to be a fair day's work as well.

While the Efficiency Department was responsible for making time studies, its conclusions must be gone over during the making and in review, with foremen and production heads on the one hand, and the men themselves on the other, through seasoned workmen familiar with conditions at the outset, and later with the Industrial Assembly, when that was organized.

That is perhaps why the Efficiency Division has remained a part of the Personnel Department. It was an integral part of the company's industrial relations program.

The piecework system was later attacked as a "speed up" plan by union organizers, used as a means to get men in the mass production industries to join a union. So it is important that the principle be understood.

The business of wages is vital in the relationship of company and men. Every person is concerned over the question of what compensation he gets for his efforts. Pay means the kind of house he lives in, the kind of clothes he wears, the make of automobile he drives, the pleasures he enjoys.

It is equally important to the corporation—the effect of wages on factory cost, of factory cost on sales prices, and of selling price on sales volume. Manufacturing and selling efficiency are determining factors in any corporation's progress, evoke the thumbs-down or thumbs-up of the buying public; they determine whether a company may sell few goods or many, and to a considerable extent, at what price it may sell them.

The Industrial Assembly

The Industrial Assembly, set up in 1919, sought to give the employees a voice in management.

The factory had grown fast and grown large. There were more than 30,000 people on the payroll. The principles embedded in the company's labor program, fair play, fair wages, good working conditions, understanding and opportunity, were being brought home to the foremen in the training classes, the Labor Department had been organized specifically to keep them functioning, but there were still chances for error in so large a group.

If a workman was dissatisfied with his pay or working conditions, he might hesitate to go to his foreman with it, or to go over the foreman's head to the Labor Department. An organization made up of pieceworkers, elected by the men in their department, and given the authority to carry disputed matters clear to the top, should be an effective check on the things the company was trying to accomplish.

A few companies, International Harvester, Bethlehem Steel and the Pennsylvania Railroad had set up shop councils, primarily to present grievances, but Goodyear wanted to go farther. A committee was set up to study the subject and bring in a concrete plan. Eight members of the committee were appointed by the company and eight men elected by the employees, two by the foremen, one by the Flying Squadron, two by the Service Pin Association, and three from the factory as a whole.

The plan they arrived at followed the lines of the American constitution, with an Assembly to legislate on all matters affecting employees —including wages. It had two houses, a Senate of 20 members, elected for two year terms, and a House of Representatives, of 40 members, each elected for a one-year term. Senators must have had fire years service in the factory, Representatives one year.

The plant was divided into 40 precincts, following factory department lines so that candidates for the Assembly should be men known personally by men in their precincts. Two precincts made up a senatorial district. Employees must be over 18, be American citizens and have six months service to be eligible to vote—although this was amended later to make new employees eligible as well.

The plan was approved by management and the directors, then submitted to employees in a factory-wide election, where 82 per cent of employees eligible to vote endorsed it.

The Industrial Assembly plan remained in effect for 16 years, through good times and bad, survived two depressions and during that time came into a first-hand contact with business problems to an extent unusual in industry. Company executives discussed the annual financial statements with the Assembly, reviewed the reasons for important moves like the building of new factories in California, Gadsden, the cotton mills, export plants and expansion of rubber plantation holdings in Sumatra and the Philippines.

While the Assembly was free to legislate on all matters affecting the workmen, it did not have final power. Legislation could be vetoed by the factory manager, and if carried over his head, by the board of directors—which was done a couple of times. The reason for reserving the veto power grew out of the fact that the company actually belonged to the stockholders, the people who had put their money into the business, the management and directors acting as agents for the owners. The Assembly could influence company policy by presenting the employee viewpoint, but could not take final action.

The veto was not often used, and where it was, contributed to understanding rather than creating resentment. One example may be given. The Assembly made continuous studies of the wage situation, got the minimum wage established early in its career, secured a blanket increase for employees in 1922 with the first lifting of the clouds of depression, and again in June, 1933, as things improved slightly in the second one. But a bill passed in February, 1926, calling for a 12½ per cent wage increase, was vetoed. As was customary management men discussed the reasons. The Assembly in passing the bill based its action on the increased cost of living and the fact that advancing tire prices had increased the company's earnings.

In supporting its veto, management showed that wages were still in line with living costs, then went into the matter of erratic rubber prices. Under the Stevenson Act rubber went to $1.25 a pound in 1925 as against a "fair price" of around 20 cents, and while restrictions were being relaxed, the company could not know how fast or how far the price would come down. The company had made money in 1925 because it was working on low-priced rubber bought earlier, which it would have to replace with higher priced rubber, consequently much of the 1925 profit would have to be held as reserve against losses a falling rubber market might bring.

When men have confidence in each other such matters can be discussed frankly. And the Assemblymen took pains to keep their constituents advised on all developments, so that the program contributed to understanding and good relations throughout the plant.

The Assembly had standing committees on wages, working conditions, safety and welfare. Hospitalization insurance, now almost universal, started with the Goodyear Industrial Assembly.

While the Assembly started as a policy-forming body, another phase of its work early became more important. That was the handling of grievances. In the early meetings the Assembly debated various subjects and took action in the form of resolutions, with the company personnel men sitting in but taking no part in the discussion. At times action was taken on incomplete information. Company and Assembly were operating at arm's length.

So in 1923 an important amendment was made to the plan. That set up committees in each senatorial district, composed of an equal number of Assemblymen and management men, to act as a clearing house for all grievances arising in the district. Foremen, personnel men, efficiency men, Tech Service, whoever was closest in touch with the work of the department made up the management group. The chairmanship alternated monthly between the two.

After that plan was installed most grievances were settled in committee, often by unanimous vote. Sometimes an airing was all that was needed. The committee could take quick action to correct unfavorable conditions. Any grievances not settled in committee would go up to a joint committee of the Assembly and topside management, and only if they could not agree would it be taken to the floor for formal discussion.

Whereas the Assembly dealt only with top management at first, by-passing the foreman, now the foreman became an integral part of it.

The Assembly made important contributions to peaceful working relations during the 16 years of its existence. The company grew stronger, wages improved, more jobs were created, the plan worked out well.

Five years after the Assembly started, a referendum was held to see if employees were satisfied, wanted to continue it. Eighty per cent of eligible employees went to the polls and 82 per cent of those voting approved it.

Many people served in the Assembly. Two women were elected to membership and three negroes. Some districts reelected the same men year after year, but in most of them the elections were hotly contested, brought new faces into the Assembly. The ballot boxes were put in the gatehouses and 90 per cent of employees took part in the voting.

While the rising tide of unionism after 1936 drove out the Assembly it would have gone anyhow under the terms of the Wagner Act. When the Assembly started, the company provided meeting rooms in Goodyear Hall, assigned a full-time secretary to the work. Assemblymen were not paid at first, but the Speaker of the House, the President of the Senate and chairmen of important committees soon found themselves putting in a considerable amount of time on Assembly business—which in a piecework industry reduced their earnings unless they did their Assembly work after hours—which was always not practical. So the Assembly passed a bill providing that members be paid at their regular factory rate for the time put in on Assembly work.

The Wagner Act outlawed collective bargaining groups to which the employer made any financial contribution.

The Flying Squadron

Personnel is a matter of first importance to a business house ambitious to go far in the world, which Goodyear from the outset was.

Picking key men was not too difficult as long as the company remained small. Litchfield needed no crystal ball to see unusual qualities in William Stephens, Gillen, Slusser, Koken. Seiberling could see in five minutes that William State was a man the company could use, and Stadelman was quick to recognize unusual qualities in Osterloh, Shilts, Hazlett and Jackson. But the company was going to need a lot of people.

It wanted the best machinists and workmen in town, was willing to pay better than the going rate to get them, sought to keep working conditions satisfactory so that they would stay.

It wanted the best foremen in the business, and though occasionally it got experienced men from other companies, for the most part it had to pick promising workmen and train them itself.

From 1908 on it needed men for the new fields where there were no experienced men—tire design, chemical, aeronautics, engineering, so it picked promising young men from the universities and trained them.

As a result few companies have been as training-conscious as this one. The training program expanded into the Flying Squadron, the Staff Training Group and Goodyear Industrial University.

Foremen training started first, and revealed intangible factors. Some men do not like responsibility. Sometimes promotion goes to a man's head, he thinks of himself as the "boss," and his job as ordering other men around. Every company has spoiled more than one good workman by promoting him. The foreman is the key man in production, the immediate contact between management and the men. He was responsible for getting out maximum production of high quality goods at an efficient factory cost. But that did not mean he was to be a driver. The company wanted leaders.

Stephens and later Slusser and others who had come up from the ranks, spent a great deal of time with the new foremen, both in the classroom and on the job. Stephens cautioned against arbitrary decisions.

"Don't ever jump on a man until you've heard his side of the story," he said again and again.

He fought favoritism, showing the foremen that if they played favorites they were only hurting themselves.

"Don't ever promote a man on the basis of friendship," he said. "You can't afford to move a man ahead unless he can pull his full share of the load. You can't afford to have a weak sister in your organization. I hold you responsible for results, and if one of your men falls down in an emergency, I blame you, not him. You either picked the wrong man, or you did not train him properly."

Stephens came early to realize that the work any one man can accomplish is limited. But the work he can accomplish by directing and energizing the work of others is beyond limitation.

"Don't be afraid that the men under you will come to know more than you do, take your job away from you. Part of your job is to find men and develop them. You'll get further ahead in this organization by bringing good men to light, than merely doing a good job personally.

"And always give credit where credit is due," he added. "If you take the credit yourself for an idea one of your men brought in, they will quit coming in. And if something goes wrong, don't pass the buck to someone under you. Be man enough to take the responsibility yourself, for it is your responsibility. And if I criticize one of your men, and I'm wrong, get in there and fight for him. Pretty soon you'll have everybody on your team, trying to develop better ways of doing a job, the company will benefit and as it grows will create more jobs, and you'll establish yourself as a real leader, the kind of man the company is looking for—and, if it goes ahead, will need."

The factory school took on another assignment during World War I, Americanization classes. The Akron rubber industry, and particularly

Goodyear, had turned to the farms and small towns for workmen, rather than hire foreign-born workmen such as many industries did. Many of the machine operations, called for something beyond mere physical strength, needed dexterity, interest in the job. There were however a few hundred foreign-born people in the shop, mostly on the mixing mills, washing machines and other less desirable jobs. They were hard-working, thrifty, loyal.

With a war on, however, Litchfield ruled that all employees must be American citizens and able to speak English. Americanization classes were set up and teachers hired and these men helped to qualify for citizenship.

Outstanding in the general training program, however, was the Flying Squadron, started in 1913, an organization which has no exact counterpart in American industry.

The Squadron did not start out as a training school for executives. It merely sought to create a group of men familiar with all manufacturing processes, who could be shifted quickly to level up inequalities in output among departments, balance production. The Mass Production system tends to create specialists, men who know the work only of their own department.

Resourceful foremen had long guarded against falling behind on their ticket by having one or two "handy men" around to take care of absenteeism, machine breakdown, accident or other interruption. But with the increasing number of departments these handy men constituted in total a force larger than the Squadron Litchfield had in mind, and their usefulness was limited to their own department. He had for some time considered throwing all of them into one group, to be drawn on as needed by all departments—to have one large reservoir rather than 20 small ones.

The difficulties of 1913 crystallized his thinking. The flood affected only a few departments directly, but it closed the entire plant. In the strike only a few men in the pit went out, and the great majority of employees were out of sympathy with the strike, but they could not continue at work because the tires were dammed up at the vulcanizing department.

A two-year course was laid out, later extended to three years and volunteers called for. The course included several hours of class work a week, not academic schooling, but close-to-the-job courses in rubber manufacturing practice, shop mechanics, blue print reading, practical mechanics and report writing.

No financial inducements were held out for men to go on the Squadron. In fact many men who signed up could make more money by continuing on piecework. They were put on salary, to be increased at six month intervals if they made good. They had a vacation schedule similar to that of the office people though this was later discontinued when the CIO came in.

A similar Squadron was started in the Engineering Department in 1915. To a considerable extent Goodyear had to design its own machinery, to fit the specialized needs of rubber manufacture, and even to build the machines because there were no standard ones on the market. As a result the company always had many mechanics and machinists on its payroll. But in the expansion years it became difficult to find men familiar with increasingly specialized needs. The Engineering Squadron grew out of this.

This course also was fixed at three years, included class work and a thorough grounding in all phases of machine shop practice. Men could select a specialty in the latter part of their course—power house practice, electrical work, toolmaking, sheet metal, machine design, pattern making, drafting, welding—or become blacksmiths or carpenters.

The third phase was the Goodyear Apprentice Machinists Class. That started informally during World War I, when with a shortage of manpower and heavy demands for war production the company had to hire boys. It was expanded in 1925, with a set course which enabled boys to continue their education and learn a trade. High school graduates, 18 to 20 years old, who had a mechanical bent, were put through a two-year shop course, spent an hour a day in the class room, studying mathematics, physics and English.

Slusser hand-picked the first Squadron men, drilled it into them that they were on trial, set up the formula that no job would be too tough for the Squadron to tackle, that the Squadron must not fall down on any assignment. Slusser himself had left school early to work in the coal mines, so used the opportunity to add to his own education, taking the school work with the class, keeping one lesson ahead of them.

A fighter himself, he picked men who had the courage of their convictions, who would not go very far out of their way to avoid trouble. It did not take long for the word to get around that a slurring remark about the Flying Squadron was apt to be answered with a punch in the jaw.

The factory was fairly skeptical of the Squadron at first. It takes time for anyone to master a new job. The Squadron men might be on half a dozen different jobs in a week, knew that foremen and fellow workers were mentally comparing their output with the department average.

This put them on their mettle, and they concentrated on each new job to pick it up fast, made it a point of pride to hit the pace of a department in the shortest possible time.

They soon won the respect of the other workmen, and their willingness to tackle any job interested the foremen, who found it a comforting thing to know that in an emergency they could always fall back on the Squadron, get a dozen men, or 20, retrieve the interruptions caused by power or machine failures.

A fire in the cement house would have closed down the plant on one occasion if the Squadron had not been on hand to back up the department and quickly build up enough stock to tide the situation.

Slusser one time called in Landefeld, Porosky and Hunter from the Engineering Squadron, had them construct a complete tire building machine and set it up in the Federal Court room in Cleveland for use in an important law suit—in two weeks.

It was not long however before the Squadron was doing more than merely balancing production, and the training values which Litchfield felt latent in it began to make themselves manifest.

Working through all departments, the Squadron men got a better picture of the relation of the departments to each other and to the business as a whole. Foremen saw supervisor material in some of the men, asked for them permanently even before they had finished their course. Many in time became foremen but, when they did, gave no preference to Squadron men assigned to them, bore down on them more heavily, expected more from them.

If Slusser had had to persuade men to sign up at first, volunteers began to come in in a few years, even men with college training, who felt the Squadron offered an unusual chance to learn the rubber business from the bottom. In time the Squadron could have filled its ranks completely with college graduates, but Litchfield and Slusser insisted that there always be room for ambitious youngsters who had not gone to college.

The size of the Squadron varied with the payroll, averaging around 5 per cent, reached a peak membership of 1582 men in the spring of 1920, when Goodyear had 33,000 men on the payroll, was trimmed down in proportion to the factory as the depression came.

New Squadron classes were formed annually and in peak periods twice a year. There was even a Squadron of deaf mutes. In 1917 Frank Andrewski applied for a position, was sent into the shipping room. Despite his handicap he made so good a record that he had no trouble getting jobs later for two of his friends. Out of this nucleus grew a colony which during World War I, numbered several hundred. The shop got to like the "silents," as they were called. They worked harder than the average, feeling the necessity to make up for their handicap; they did not talk at work, since they would have to stop work in order to do so; they became familiar figures in the restaurants around Goodyear, took an interest in sports, organized one of the best football teams in town, originated the "huddle" system of calling signals, had clubrooms in Goodyear Hall, and at basketball games carried on animated but silent conversations with friends the length of the building away.

The great silence which surrounded the "silents," helped them to concentrate, so that they learned the multitude of factory operations faster than other men.

Litchfield realized that he might be training men for other companies to hire away after all that time and money had been invested in them, but he was not too much concerned. He made a guess that a third of the men would fail to measure up, and another third drop out during or after their training, but if he got one good man out of every three who started, the company would still be ahead. Also the new graduates coming out of the Squadron every year compelled the company to have enough interesting jobs on hand to hold them.

As things turned out, Litchfield's estimate was on the conservative side. Of the 1736 men who have graduated from the Squadron since the first class in 1915, 62 per cent of the men in the Production Squadron and 71 per cent of the Engineering Squadron are still with the company, many in important positions.

While scores of them went up the line in Akron, a still larger number went to the outside plants as these were opened, taught the intricate processes of rubber manufacture to men who had never seen the inside of a tire factory.

The California plant was largely manned at the outset by Squadron men, "the 107," as the group is still called at Los Angeles. This plan worked out so well that every succeeding Goodyear factory used Squadron men to start production. And the Squad men were life savers at Goodyear Aircraft in World War II.

A number of men remained at the outside factories but in any case had a useful experience, since in a small plant it was easier to see the entire manufacturing picture—and had to develop new resourcefulness as difficulties arose which they would have to meet themselves.

DeYoung, Akron boy from the municipal university who won the Litchfield award in his year, 1933, helped start the Java plant, won the

Sloan scholarship at MIT, took his master's degree there, showed his mettle as a production man at Aircraft, became vice president and general manager, moved up to vice president in charge of production of all Goodyear factories in 1947.

Carter from Arkansas, who started as a tire builder, took the Squadron training in the class of 1925, became efficiency manager, superintendent at Brazil, director of personnel of the entire company.

The Squadron gave the company a number of plant superintendents. Among these, with the dates they graduated from the Squadron, were Hochberg, 1928, Java; Ruffner, 1921, Jackson; Shaw, 1925, Lincoln; Clayton, 1926, Sweden; Fisher, 1916, Reclaim Plant; Johnson, 1918, Rim Plant; Jacobs, 1937, Colombia; as well as four who moved out before they finished their course—Superintendents Ginaven in England, Perren in Mexico City, Cox at Windsor and Spoonamore in Cuba.

Behind these men is a long list of production and division superintendents in South America, Australia, South Africa. Some men transferred into the Sales Department, found their first-hand knowledge of the product extremely useful.

The Engineering Squadron points to Patterson, 1921, superintendent of the machine shop, and plant engineers or master mechanics in California, New Bedford, St. Marys, Argentina, Sweden, Peru, Brazil and Mexico, four general foremen at Aircraft during the war and 75 per cent of the men in supervision in Akron.

The Number Two men in mechanical goods, both production and sales, are Squadron graduates, Tidyman in the factory, 1918, whose training was interrupted by a hitch in the Marine Corps in World War I and Dupree, 1936, in sales, a graduate of Georgia Tech.

Crude rubber has largely manned its key positions with Squadron men, including Bogardus, 1921, assistant manager of the whole division, Arnold, manager in Sumatra, Huber in the Philippines, Klippert who started the Costa Rica plantation and Figland who now heads it, as well as Harrison in Singapore and Cook in Ceylon.

The Squadron has produced personnel managers for California, Gadsden, Jackson, Kelly, Windsor, Muncie, Argentina, Arizona, Java, Toronto, and Bowmanville, these two latter from Canada's own Squadron, and a dozen on the Akron staff. It has furnished efficiency managers, purchasing agents, five district sales managers in mechanical goods, provided men for machine design, technical service, wheels and brakes, mold design, specifications, production control; power plant managers, construction engineers, equipment engineers, a chief chemist for England, key men for synthetic rubber and Pliofilm.

When Litchfield turned to the universities in 1908, and picked Hall and later Kilborn, Wolfe and Morse to build the Development Department and Upson and Preston to go into aeronautics, he was one of the pioneers in a significant movement to bring technical and research thinking into the field of manufacturing, a program which helped make America a great industrial nation.

George Westinghouse at Pittsburgh had already taken steps in the same direction a little earlier, to meet difficult requirements in the young electrical industry, but practically nothing had been done in industry generally.

How far that movement has gone throughout the years is seen from the fact that today recruiting of college graduates is carried on by every important business house, and a hundred colleges and universities have had to put in full-time placement bureaus, and schedule the visits of the industry's recruiting men through the year, starting shortly after school opens in the fall.

Litchfield hand-picked the first technical men and they in turn went out personally in the next several years to select others, but in 1916 college recruiting was organized, and the Staff Training Course set up to acquaint the new men with the various phases of the business.

The personnel men who went out that year brought in Hurley from Purdue, now manager of Interplant Relations; Gagnon from M.I.T., now superintendent in Peru; Braden from Ohio State, who became superintendent of the Balloon Room; Van Orman from Case, one of the best balloon pilots in the world, who later went into Research. The next year brought in Flannery from Cornell, who served in Development, became superintendent in England, then chief engineer; Climer from Miami, who became superintendent in Argentina, personnel director of the company, then a vice president; Spransy, also from Cornell, who became district manager at Chicago. This program, held up by the 1920 depression, was resumed in 1923.

Engineering wanted specialists in mechanical, civil, electrical and structural engineering, in power plants, strength of materials, machine design, heating, ventilating and plant maintenance. Development wanted chemists, designers, research men, men to direct the testing of materials and men who could go out into the shop and put their finger on production difficulties. Other departments were needing men of specialized training.

Litchfield gave the program personal attention, saw to it that the technical men were exposed to the difficulties as well as the opportunities of business. They started in at the bottom but were not buried in routine, got a chance to show what ability they had.

The factory course, taken with the Flying Squadron, constituted the first stage of training. Men who did not like to get their hands dirty, who expected a white collar job as the reward for having gone through college, who could not take the hard work and rough work of production, these were weeded out automatically.

The men who survived were sent through staff departments in the same way, to familiarize them with Goodyear activities, to uncover special aptitudes or abilities, since anyone will do better work on a job that he likes than one he does not. All this time the men in the group were being studied without their knowing it by department managers, production foremen and Squadron foremen, who were sizing them up.

But the training must go also into other factors, intangible ones. There is no scientific way of picking future executives. Training is important, but what a man will do with it is much more so. There are no standard qualifications for executives, for men do things in different ways to arrive at the same results, and industry could make use of a wide range of temperaments and talents.

Most men will do a better job if they can do it their own way, do not want the boss leaning over their shoulder telling them to do this or that, asking them why they did that or the other thing, want to be given a job and held responsible for results. Litchfield's own practice with a promising man was to give him a certain responsibility, perhaps a little bigger than he was ready for, since the right type of man would grow with his job, then watch to see how he met his problems, now giving him a little rope, now checking him back, adding larger responsibilities as he showed the ability to carry them. Always he impressed on men their responsibiliity to train other men behind them, an idea which came to be embodied in the significant phrase:

"A man is ready for promotion only when he has his department well organized and a second man trained to take over the work."

As the years passed Litchfield came into the conviction that no organization had the seeds of permanency unless always and everywhere through it were eager young men, keen, ambitious, on their toes, moving forward, preparing themselves for larger jobs. He thought of Goodyear as democratic, rather than autocratic, recognized that no small group of men at the top could know all the conditions throughout the plant intimately enough at all times to make wise decisions, wanted men in the lower brackets who had initiative, could run their jobs with the minimum of direction.

"Management in a continuing organization is on top of its job," he

J. S. WOLFE, (1912) 1934
Factory Manager, US plants

G. K. HINSHAW, 1917
Factory Manager, Abroad

A. W. DENNY, 1928
Vice Pres't Canada,(Production)

ROY TOMKINSON, 1918
ral Superintendent, Akron

FRANK A. STEELE, 1910
Superintendent, California

H. L. GINAVAN, 1934
Superintendent, England

R. W. MANEY, 1929
perintendent, Plant II

L. E. SPENCER, 1926
(on leave in Germany)

A. L. MICHAELS, 1923
Superintendent, Gadsden

H. A. BRITTAIN, 1918
Foreign Manufacturing

L. H. COFFIN, 1927
Foreign Manufacturing

H. I. BELKNAP, 1919
Supt. Chemical Products

GEORGE SHERRY, 1919
Industrial Engineering

W. H. FLEMING, 1917
Warehousing, shipping

L. A. HURLEY, 1916
Interplant Relations

S. A. STEERE, 1919
Vice Pres't Cotton Mills

T. A. KNOWLES, 1928
Gen'l Manager, Aircraft

J. J. BLANDIN, 1912
Crude Rubber

H. S. MORSE, 1915
velopment, Mechanicals

W. W. VOGT, 1917
Development Manager

W. E. SHIVELY, 1915
Chief Tire Design

A. FLANNERY, 1916
Manager Engineering

Dr. KARL ARNSTEIN, 1924
Chief Eng'r, Aircraft

ELMER CLARK (1905) 1911
Master Mechanic

B. SEBRELL, 1922
Director Research

F. J. CARTER, 1922
Director Personnel

H. J. CARROLL, 1910
Director Traffic

said, "only when it is uncovering and developing men, each individual in the management having someone at hand ready to step in in an emergency and handle his job.

"The energy and interest and initiative of a thousand men is better in the long run than the genius of one. Men of genius are mortal and when they go, a company cannot get a new one through an advertisement in the newspaper.

"And if a corporation lacks a genius, it still will do a pretty fair job if it is calling out and utilizing the talent of a large number of men, men of energy, resolution, decision and loyalty; men who take a pride in their job because it is their job, and who know what to do in an emergency and do it without waiting for orders."

In recruiting men from the colleges the personnel men were apt to pass up the top men in the class, the Phi Beta Kappa's, looked rather for men from the upper third in scholarship who had shown themselves outstanding in other ways, shown hints of leadership and initiative. These were more apt to fit into industry. The company had always shown an interest in athletes, back to Bill Stephens' day. Athletic ability would indicate at least that a man had good health and courage, and his experience was apt to breed endurance, determination, resourcefulness and team work. There are many former football and basketball stars in the company holding important responsibilities today, applying to business the characteristics which made them outstanding on the athletic field.

THE SALES SQUADRON

Another important factor in the training program was the Sales Squadron, started in 1927, which picked out men already working for the company, who had had sales experience and shown ability, brought them into Akron for special training which might fit them to take over administrative assignments.

Litchfield was now president, and he had long wondered if the Squadron principle could not be applied to sales in the same way as it had to production. Few people were ready to agree with him. A real salesman was born, taught himself by actual selling. There were courses in salesmanship, it is true, but these were largely theoretical. A man might graduate with a perfect average but still be unable to sell goods. When the company needed a branch manager, it picked one of its top salesmen.

But Litchfield wanted to try out his idea anyhow, called Blythe in from California to organize the program. Blythe was fully familiar with the principle from his factory experience, and had himself been a salesman.

Only a few men were brought in at first to try out the plan. They were routed around through the various staff departments, exposed to a broader range of industry problems—and management had a chance to size them up, appraise their possibilities. The Sales Squadron grew in numbers, and specific training courses were organized, with the result eventually that the company could look over the list of Squadron-trained men and pick out a man to fill almost any job which came up.

LITCHFIELD AWARDS

Highly useful in the training program were the Litchfield Awards, which brought men to management attention whose capacities might otherwise have been overlooked.

Described as the Paul W. and Florence B. Litchfield Awards these were presented annually under sponsorship of the Service Pin Association to the top man in the Production and Engineering Squadrons, to the best student at Goodyear Industrial University, the employee turning in the best suggestion of the year, the best Boy Scout among the several Goodyear groups, with special medals given out as occasion warranted for unusual service beyond the line of duty. Later on the best domestic and export salesmen of the year were included, the top apprentice machinist, the best store manager, and Air and Sea Scouts.

In time a number of Award winners in the sales field had become district managers: Pound, '30, at Atlanta; Holroyd, '31, at Des Moines; Wetherbee, '38, at San Francisco; Bott, '37, at Buffalo; Humphrey, '38, at Jacksonville; Hoerster, '41, at Cincinnati; Beall, '42, at Salt Lake City; Pauley became district manager of mechanical goods; Grundy, '33, sales director in New Zealand, then Pliofilm manager on the West coast; Landefeld, '34, became manager of Pliofilm Sales; Summers, '35, of Airfoam.

Export winners included Fender, '34, who became sales director at Singapore; Harvey, '31, sales supervisor for Europe; Olbert, '41, became sales manager in Mexico. Among domestic sales winners were the veterans Blake, '39, at Boston and Lawrence, '42, the former of Footwear, the latter of Manufacturers Sales. Bell, airplane pilot and salesman, won the Medal in 1945.

The Award was given also for outstanding improvement in products, to Steere in 1922 for the development of Supertwist, to Stephens who adapted rubber belting to construction jobs like Shasta Dam, to Merrill for his work on the bullet-seal fuel tank in World War II, to Burkley for the ice-grip tire; to Shively in 1947 for the Super Cushion tire; to Kavenagh and Gates for Neolite, and Loudenslager for the cross-wind landing gear for airplanes in 1948. Kocheiser made the honor roll for developing a machine to demonstrate Supertwist, Bruney for one to test automobile batteries, and Smith of Mechanical Goods for a model showing the use of cross-country conveyor belts, which would also enable the engineers to estimate the cost of an installation.

The special award was given to Charles Brannigan, blimp pilot, and Perry Lloyd, Corsair test pilot, both posthumously, and to Wollam, balloon pilot, for gallantry in times of aviation disasters; to Cooper, the balloon builder; to Protheroe, chemist, for his courage and cool headedness at the Crile Clinic disaster in Cleveland in 1929, in which he saved several lives; to Crosier and his crew who saved a Navy blimp which caught fire in flight.

Names of all the winners were placed in bronze panels in the Memorial Lobby at Goodyear Hall.

After a period of 15 years the action of the Service Pin Association in setting up the Awards seemed amply justified by results.

OTHER TRAINING ACTIVITIES

Foremen training continued through the years, grew to large size during World War II, when the factory had to create hundreds of new supervisors and foremen. E. R. Wolfe, who had had wide production and Squadron experience, became director of training in 1937, was succeeded in 1948 by Hochberg on his return from Java. Hamlin, former blimp pilot, headed the Squadron, a position held before him by President Thomas, Vice President Blythe, and by Hochberg and Clayton, who became superintendents of outside plants.

Training both in sales and production was stepped up after the war, with hundreds of men going through intensive courses covering new postwar conditions.

6. Evolution of the Tire

The Development Program

THE principle of the wheel, that it is "easier to push something than to carry it," was man's first important upward step toward civilization. That principle came into wider use in the 20th century than in all those which had gone before, because only then did men begin to use a machine instead of a beast of burden to turn the wheel—and encased the wheels in rubber.

Riding on air actually, for rubber was only the container, and carrying its own power plant, the wheel was enabled, in this half century, to create a new major factor in transportation and to completely change over long agricultural practices; it was used on huge construction jobs in earth moving sizes—and built taller than a man it enabled a 50 ton airplane to drop 10,000 feet out of the sky and land so easily as not to cause a ripple in a glass of water in the stewardess' galley.

All these things happened within Goodyear's brief lifetime—with the company contributing its part to the result.

Long convinced that a business enterprise was on solid ground only when it was producing goods which advanced the interests of society, the Goodyear company had always been profoundly interested in transportation. Macauley once said that 90 per cent of the work of the world was involved in moving things from one place to another. Consequently, whatever expedites, simplifies or cuts the cost of the exchange of goods and services between people is highly important. Transportation gives the producer a broader market for his goods and the consumer a wider range of low-price merchandise. It creates thousands of well-paying jobs for men who build, operate, sell and repair the vehicles of transportation, puts on solid ground the fortunes of every business house which serves it effectively.

So from the first days Goodyear, transportation-minded, spent time and money it could ill afford to develop better tires for cars and trucks, went into rubber hose and conveyor belts and became greatly interested in the airplane, since these too were carriers of goods.

The rubber tire, however, was the foundation of Goodyear's business career, the thing that made it a great company, so it is time to trace that development, picking up from where we left off, with the Straight-Side tire, the Cord tire, the pneumatic truck tire—and the beginnings of the Development Department, which was started in 1908 as soon as the company could afford to do so.

With no tire engineers to be had, since the field was too new, Litchfield went back to his old school, Boston Tech as it was called then, picked E. R. Hall, outstanding member of the senior class, brought him to Akron as experimental engineer, later brought on others, Wolfe, Kilborn, C. R. Johnson, Bourne who became chief chemist, and Tuttle who long acted as technical contact with the car manufacturers.

Litchfield handed Hall a pair of gloves and overalls when he reported for work.

"What's this for?" demanded the startled young scientist.

"You'll need them out in the factory," Litchfield explained. "I want you to work through every department, learn first-hand how a tire is built."

Hall did not like the idea too well, but Litchfield had prescribed the same initiation for himself when he entered the business eight years earlier. And Hall, once he had taken the shop course, realized its value and took great delight thereafter in handing the overalls and gloves on to each new man, sent him through the same course.

Litchfield had definite ideas about the new department. He did not have in mind a group of men off by themselves in the laboratory, shel-

tered from the noise and dirt of production. They were to take off
their coats, go out in the shop, get the feel and the smell of rubber,
know how each job was done, get their hands dirty from carbon black
and soapstone, and calloused from opening up sticky bales of rubber
with a hook-shaped tool, learn the workman's viewpoint, work closely
with the engineers and production men.

The arrival of the collegians made quite a stir in the factory, where
few people had even seen the inside of a university. Stephens, Gillen,
the Huguelets were natural leaders, and State's engineers had started
in as apprentices under older men. Conflict was inevitable. The old
line production man did not like changes, which slowed things up,
created confusion, upset schedules. They wanted to settle on one plan
and go ahead, were apt to discount any ideas suggested by the white-
collared fellows from the laboratory, were sure they would not work,
might even put obstacles in their way.

Litchfield felt that industry needed both the experimental and the
practical mind, that each would act as a check on the other—and com-
plement the other.

However, he gave no help to the college men, threw them into the
factory, let them fight their own battles. The pattern was largely set in
a series of clashes between Ed Hall as experimental engineer and Ed
Nall as master mechanic. Hall was analytical, a scientist, who had to see
things on paper, evaluate them with a slide rule. Nall, a man of no
little inventive genius, who had worked with State on the tire building
machine, did not need any blue prints. He went out in the shop and
worked over a machine with his hands. They were physical opposites
as well, Hall being well above average height, Nall below it.

Both men died in 1916, Hall in his late 20's, Nall in his mid 40's.
In the eight years they had come into full respect for each other, and
Development and Production had arrived at a working program which
would be characteristic of the plant through the years. A skilled mechanic might find himself in development, and a technical man who
could get things done might end in a superintendency, as many did
over the years.

PASSENGER CAR TIRES

Looking over the assignment laid out for the Development Department, we will start with passenger car tires, although most of the principles found there could be applied to truck tires and the rest, and
usually were.

In passenger car tires we must remember that in 1908 they had smooth treads and were drum taut. Improvement was sought along two major lines, better Cushioning, which came from improving the carcass, and better Traction, which was furnished by the tread. There were times during this when one got ahead of the other. The carcass was strengthened until it outwore the tread, then the emphasis was switched to the tread to make it tougher—and presently it was outwearing the carcass. The two seesawed.

In cushioning, the job was to make the carcass more flexible, so as to increase passenger comfort and be able to carry breakable merchandise. But it must stand up under increasingly higher speeds, and give longer mileage also. Tires grew gradually larger in cross section to do this, the first big major development being the balloon tire.

Traction was not important as long as cars moved slowly, but as speed stepped up to ten and 15 miles an hour, and drivers left the few hard-surfaced roads and ventured across-country over the alternately rutted and muddy dirt roads which comprised most of the nation's highway system, smooth treads were highly unsatisfactory.

Goodyear did not, of course, invent the non-skid tire. Many people were working on that. But it did hit on a design in its first tread in 1908, the famous diamond-studded All-Weather Tread, which was mechanically better than any other, for the reason that the diamond-shaped blocks would dig in and take hold in mud and snow, resist skidding in any direction.

Other tire companies changed tread designs many times, but the All-Weather remained with minor modifications for the next 40 years, became the most distinctive of all tire treads.

Over at the rival company, Goodrich, Yale-Sheffield-trained E. C. Shaw, works manager, had come to the same conclusion, but while his company was worrying whether the public might not confuse his tread with its rival, Diamond Rubber, next door, Goodyear had put its tire on the market.

The diamond tread cannot be credited to the new Development Department, for that had just started, but the development men would have to wrestle for a dozen years with the headaches it created.

The very fact that the diamond blocks did an efficient job made their production more difficult than the simpler design of its competitors.

People unfamiliar with tire manufacture sometimes have an idea that the non-skid blocks are somehow cemented onto the tread. This is not the case. They are an integral part of it. The uncured tread has no non-skid design at all when it goes into the mold. Internal pressure, air, steam or hydraulic, forces the rubber into the mold to form the diamonds.

With the primitive compounds of that day, it was always difficult to get a uniform cure throughout any large mass of rubber, some parts being apt to be over-cured and others under-cured and soft. But in the diamond blocks the cure had to be not only as good as the rest of the tread, but better, because the diamonds had more work to do when the car was traveling over the highway.

Most companies cured carcass and tread together in one operation. If there was not quite enough rubber in the tread, the mold would be incompletely filled and the non-skid markings would be a little shallow— a fault which might not be noticed in a conventional tire, but would be in the diamond blocks of the Goodyear tread.

Also if too much rubber was used, the excess would have to move elsewhere and, since rubber is incompressible, might be squeezed out between the two halves of the molds—and carry some of the plies of the carcass along with it, or at least distort their position.

That was the risk which Goodyear, obsessed with the quality conviction, was unwilling to take. It would not give up the advantages of the diamond block merely because the tread was difficult to manufacture. Whatever time it took and whatever money it cost, the blocks must remain.

So for years, while every other company in the industry cured carcass and tread in a single process, Goodyear paid the penalty of a more expensive two-cure process in order to attain the best possible result. The uncured smooth tread was put in the mold and given a semi-cure, enough to form the diamonds, then the carcass was semi-cured separately, after which tread and carcass were brought together for the final cure.

In designing a vulcanizer to cure the treads, Hall and Nall had another of their historic quarrels. Neither could see any merit in the other's idea and Litchfield had to act as umpire. He examined both designs. Both looked all right. They would arrive at the same point, though by different routes.

"Build one under each plan," he ruled. "That's the only way we can tell which is better."

Both machines were built, and both worked. In cost and quality it was a dead heat.

The final cure involved a unique process in Department 150-D, one which all old-time Goodyear men will remember. There the semi-cured tread was put in place on the semi-cured carcass, then smeared with soapstone mud, completely covering the diamond blocks to protect them from possible distorsion. Then the tire was inflated to furnish internal pressure, and spiral-wrapped with narrow strips of wet fabric which shrank as it dried, exerted external pressure. Then it was ready to be vulcanized. When the cure was completed, these wrappings were stripped off by hand, and the thoroughly baked mud shaken loose.

Between mud and water and soapstone dust, the department was the dirtiest in the plant, except the carbon black building. The department always had a high turnover, and a new Squadron man was likely to be sent down to 150-D for a few weeks as his initiation into the factory.

The California plant had a replica of Akron's famous "mud room," and boasted a workman whose hands were so large and skill so great that he could scoop up with one hand exactly enough mud to cover a tire, leaving no channel unprotected, with no mud left in his hand at the end. This gifted individual, however, was distinctly a specialist, and when the department was abolished was unable to find any other job in the plant that he liked and eventually left the company.

For years the development men worked to get away from the two-cure process. Better accelerators and compounds helped. So did the air bag.

Tires were cured originally on a steel core which held the tire firmly as pressure was applied by the mold. But an air bag made of rubberized fabric, shaped like a tire, was introduced in 1912, did this still better because it was more flexible, and an all-rubber bag in 1920 better yet, exerting uniform pressure on the inside of the tire.

This with further improvements in compounds brought a fully satisfactory one-cure process by 1922. The mud room went out unmourned. The single-cure process became fully practical even for truck tires by 1925.

Only minor changes have been made in the All-Weather Tread over the years. When closed cars came in, the slight humming noise which the diamonds made on the road became more noticeable, and circumferential ribs were added to dampen it—and provide some additional resistance to shoulder wear.

But the question arose again in 1932, as automotive engineers sought to make cars run more quietly, and as other noises diminished, the humming noise of the diamond tread grew audible again.

A tire tread which does little work makes no noise, and the hardworking All-Weather Tread was doing too good a job. However by varying the size of the diamond blocks and staggering them, the engineers found they could break up the rhythm, so that the sound did not build up in volume. For the same reason a company of soldiers breaks step when marching across a bridge, avoids building up sway and vibration.

The balloon tire of 1923, a change from high pressure to low, was the next important step. It might be called an industry development, for everyone was conscious of the problem. Secrets are hard to keep anyhow in the tire industry, where results must be tested outdoors and three of the largest companies—and a member of alert smaller ones—are located in the same town.

Up to then passenger car tires, inflated to 50-55 pounds pressure, rode hard, and despite the non-skid treads, had a tendency to skid on curves or wet surfaces, since only an inch or so of tread surface was in contact with the highway.

Some car owners had noticed that if they let a little air out, their tires would ride more comfortably and be less apt to skid—but wore out faster.

Tires could be built larger, but they already rode too high, and automobile designers were working toward a lower center of gravity, so that cars would hold the road better on turns. What was needed was a fatter tire, not as high overall, almost doughnut-shaped, with a larger area of road contact.

The balloon tire built to meet these requirements got immediate acceptance. The public liked its greater riding comfort, and automobile engineers realized that it would cut maintenance cost by reducing the vibration which was harmful to motors and chassis.

Dodge tried them out late in 1923. The auto show of January, 1924, saw a few cars equipped with them. By the following January practically all the cars were on balloons. When Ford and Chevrolet came out with balloon tires in April, 1925, the changeover was complete. In 30 months after they were introduced, the balloon tire had swept the market.

The new tires brought a change in sizes and names. The old 30 x 3½, most widely used size, was replaced by the 4.50-21 and the 4.75-19. In the first case the figure 30 represents the height of the tire, and 3½ the cross section. The inside diameter was 30 minus seven (two times three and one-half) or 23. In the new tire a 4.50-21 size meant a four and a half inch cross section with a 21-inch inside diameter. The lower-slung characteristic of the new cars on balloon tires was still better illustrated by the 4.75-19, a four and three-quarter inch tire with an inside diameter 19 inches across as compared to 23.

The advent of the balloons, incidentally, drove the old clinchers out of the field, though Goodyear must continue to build them until the millions of Fords and Chevrolets manufactured prior to 1925 wore out. The 30 x 3½, once the mainstay of production, went off the ticket in April, 1943.

The next big step in the industry was the Airwheel, a tire brought out originally for the airplane, as will be described later, and adapted to passenger cars in 1931. It carried still further the principles of greater air volume and lower air pressure.

The Airwheel rode more easily, was harder to puncture, less apt to skid, added mileage. Its advantages and a score of others which had evolved during the 1920's were embodied in the 1932 G-3, a depression product which sought to meet fully the improved characteristics of the depression automobile which car designers had developed to get people back in the market—cars with more power, greater speed, quicker acceleration, more powerful brakes, hydraulic brakes, four-wheel brakes. The independently sprung wheel had come in. The new tire also took into account the growth of traffic, the installation of stop lights and increasing the number of stops and starts.

The testing program laid out for the G-3 was the most severe any new tire had had to undergo. The usual laboratory tests came first, though intensified. The tires were run on the "Ferris wheel," a great squirrel cage affair with its running surface dotted with irregular bumps to give the effect of driving at high speed over a rough road. They were run against grindstones made up of pulverized grit brought in from sections of the country where road surfaces were most abrasive.

A test road was built across the airport, kept flooded with water and test cars were driven over this strip at 50 miles per hour then stopped, again and again, to see the effect of hard braking on a wet track.

Test cars were sent to North Carolina and Arizona, where higher temperatures would increase the severity of the test. The drivers were instructed to speed up to 50 miles, then slam on the brakes, speed up to 50, stop again, continuing that in shifts of driving around the clock.

Brake bands suffered under this strenuous service, had to be adjusted every eight hours, replaced after 72 hours. The effect, however, was to get test results in 1500 to 2000 miles which ordinarily would require 10,000 miles. In the end the new tire showed better traction in mud and snow; 15 per cent shorter stopping distance on slippery pavement; 50 per cent reduction in uneven tread wear; and 43 per cent longer non-skid life.

The G-3 tire remained without major change until after World War II.

THE INNER TUBE

The inner tube is the vital part of the tire, since it carries the compressed air on which the automobile rides. The carcass and the tread are merely there to protect it. But tubes too had to be built stronger and tougher to meet increasing demands—and have seen many construction changes in the 50 years.

Everyone starting on a trip in the early days expected to have one or more punctures, carried a jack and tire-changing tools along, and usually a tube repair kit, ready to slap a patch on and cement it into place. A lot of work has gone into the evolution of the relatively trouble-proof tube of today.

The first tubes were made by laying lengths of rubber sheeting on a table and turning them by hand to form a cylinder, cementing the seams, then cutting to length. Then Ed Nall developed a machine to do this. Later the rubber sheeting was rolled on long pipes called mandrels, cured in that form, then stripped off with compressed air much as a girl takes off her glove. Tube stock was built up in laminated style like plywood to resist tear and reduce the likelihood of leaks.

In the modern tube, however, the compounded rubber is warmed up, then fed into a worm-driven extruding machine, something like the sausage grinder in the kitchen, with dies to give it the desired size. Cut into lengths on a conveyor as it emerges, the tubes move to the watchcase molds to be vulcanized, the molds opening automatically at the end of the cure.

The drop-center rim brought in a tube in which the lower half, which had to resist the chafing of the metal well, was compounded differently from the upper half, which needed resiliency rather than strength. Process improvements permitted the two halves to be extruded as a single unit.

Punctures have become less and less common in recent years. Better compounding helped, tougher treads and sidewalls gave better protection, better roads reduced the sharp blows of travel, and with the lower air pressures of today a tube is apt to give, when struck a sharp blow, not be injured by it.

The tire industry, however, had long sought a puncture-proof tube, the various experiments including the use of fabric with rubber, sponge rubber, and gummy compounds, each of which ideas had some disadvantages.

Goodyear brought out its Puncture-Seal inner tube in 1920 for use in the Southwest where cactus prongs were apt to puncture a tire. This used a plastic rubber which would seal up the hole. An improved type was developed in 1934, devised for taxicabs, which could not well stop on the way to a train, and for utility company vehicles apt to pick up nails and bits of metal in driving through alleys.

Early test at Akron Airport of the LifeGuard, which will not blow out—one of the most important contributions in years to driving safety.

Above are modern automatic vulcanizer and the Marsh Buggy swimming across a river, and below tractor towing company's Lodestar out of the hangar.

In an entirely different category however was the LifeGuard, developed in 1934. A puncture is annoying but not dangerous. But if a tire blows out, even at comparatively low speeds, the car may swerve into a ditch, or into the path of an approaching car.

The LifeGuard consists of a conventional inner tube, with a fabric carcass floating free inside it, the two being joined only at the base, with a small vent to permit equalization of air pressure between them. In case of a blowout, only the tube is affected, the inner carcass remaining intact, with plenty of air to support the weight of the car until it can be brought to a stop.

The LifeGuard was given the most gruelling tests before it was put on the market. A knife was fastened to the running gear, and at the driver's signal driven into the tire, opening a great gash. With a regular tube, it was hard to keep the car on the road if it was travelling as fast as 40 miles per hour, but with LifeGuards, it rode easily and safely to a stop, at speeds up to 90 miles an hour. Similar tests were made using a shotgun which blew a great hole in the tire, but left the LifeGuard carcass unaffected. Since it floated free it would give with any impact.

The LifeGuard came to be recognized as one of the great safety devices developed by the automotive industry, comparable to shatter-proof glass, steel bodies and four-wheel brakes. Soon after its introduction the LifeGuard was offered as optional equipment on new automobiles, and was used as standard equipment on some of the higher priced cars. We shall see the principle later adapted to combat planes.

Truck and Bus Tires

In the years following World War I trucks riding on pneumatic tires proceeded to demonstrate all of the possibilities suggested by the Wingfoot Express journeys between Akron and Boston, and the Goodyear Heights bus trips up and down the hill near the factory.

At first it was merely a delivery wagon, competing with the solid-tired truck and the horse-drawn dray in city hauling. It carried merchandise from the railroad to stores, lumber yards, coal yards and factories, delivered goods to people's homes. It could do this faster and more cheaply than its competitors. Department stores bought trucks, the grocer, the laundryman, the express company. Even the milk wagon found it could cover more ground in a day by using a gasoline engine—

*though there was an intermediate stage when rubber tires were put on
the wagon and the horse stayed on the job.*

But the truck would not long remain limited to city hauling. Resourceful individuals saw an opportunity to furnish an inter-city service, where
solid tires could not follow because they were too slow. The truck
could serve communities which were off the railroad. Its routes and
schedules were entirely flexible. Inter-city truck operators started on a
shoe string, but they had something to sell which business was glad to
buy. Instead of a factory having its goods hauled to a depot, loaded
aboard a freight car, hauled to another town, unloaded, and trucked to
somebody's store, a truck operator could pick them up at the factory
shipping room, unload them at the back door of the customer in another
city, cut handling expense.

Truck lines came into existence all over the country, began to take
over much of the short-haul and less-than-carload-lot transportation.
These lines early flourished in New England where industrial and
trading centers lie close together. The trucks set up depots in important
centers from which cargo could be picked up and distributed over a
widening circle of communities, or brought in for redistribution and for-
warding, working with the system and dispatch of a post office.

Trips grew longer. Long distance hauling largely started in Akron.
Men there, close to the tire industry, saw an opportunity. Starting with
short runs, to Cleveland, Detroit, or trips of 200 or 300 miles, they went
on to Baltimore, to St. Louis, to Dallas.

Goodyear saw an expanding market for tires, gave them full encouragement, had its engineers prescribe the right size and type of tires for a
given run, counseled them on rates and finances, used the trucks as a test
fleet, comparing its own tires with those of competitors, tried out new
sizes and designs, made the truck lines a travelling laboratory for better
tires.

Most of the men who started these lines were people with little money
or experience—a school teacher, a lawyer, a grocer's clerk, a second-hand
car salesman, a B. and O. telegrapher from Peninsula, a bookkeeper.

An Akron car dealer had sold some trucks to an over-enthusiastic buyer
who could not complete the payments and had to turn them back. He came
out to Goodyear to see if the company would buy them, but after talking
to Slusser and to Carroll of the Traffic Department, went back and
organized a company. He put in one of his salesmen as manager and in
five years had a three-quarter million dollar business. Roadway Express,
All-State, Bender and Louden, Motor Express, Summit Fast Freight and
other Akron lines are well-known names on the highways and at the

loading platforms across much of the United States.

Bus lines followed the same pattern of vision, small beginnings and large-scale results. A bus did not need steel rails or overhead trolleys.

During the slack season in the iron ore industry on the Mesabi Range, Carl Wickman, diamond drill operator, took on a car dealer agency and the Goodyear tire franchise at Hibbing, Minnesota. Presently he had a better idea, to use his demonstrator car to haul the miners to work, found that it paid. He bought a truck and nailed seats across the body to accommodate more passengers, went into business.

In nearby Superior, Wisconsin, Orville Caesar started a similar operation and eventually the two got together to start the great Greyhound Bus Line which ran from coast to coast.

Other lines sprang up, city and inter-city. By 1925 there were hundreds of them.

Impetus to the use of trucks in cross-country cargo carrying was given by the trailer-tractor, which started in 1928. This was two vehicles which could be used separately or together.

The rear trailer section had no power plant. It was merely a wagon, carried the load. It had no front wheels, except small steel ones which were let down while the vehicle was being loaded, pulled up out of the way when it was ready to go. Front wheels and power plant were carried on the tractor section, which was an independent unit. The two could be connected quickly by matching plates in the back of one and the front of the other.

Under this system the tractor could haul its trailer up to the loading platform, detach it, pick up a loaded trailer and be on its way, did not have to wait for a trailer to be loaded or unloaded. This principle was carried far, loads grew heavier, tires larger, with dual tires quickly coming in on the tractor section to permit it to carry larger loads.

Truck and bus operations became large-scale business. Some railroads took over competing bus lines and others took over truck lines, supplementing their own service. Independent operators merged lines and schedules, until the largest operator was covering routes five times as great as the trackage of the largest railroad system. The business grew to such size that the Interstate Commerce Commission took notice in 1935, set up regulations to cover it.

Goodyear itself was a big user of truck as well as rail transport, could send out a rush shipment of tires to Detroit at nine o'clock at night, have them at the receiving room there at seven the next morning.

There have been many times when tire fabric was short and trucks shuttling back and forth to the southern mills kept the factory from being closed down. And in emergencies like machine breakdown or material shortage, it could have new machinery or additional materials delivered by truck to any of its American factories in 48 hours, with the exception of California. And World War II found a hundred different uses for trucks, all the way from defense plants in the States to the battle front itself.

Exclusive of coal, ore, sand and gravel which is usually carried by rail, pneumatic-tired trucks were carrying a fifth of all the nation's cargo by 1948. Including such slow-moving items, truck lines were still carrying 12 per cent of the country's freight.

STAGES IN DEVELOPMENT

To secure all these results however the builders of trucks and tires must do their full part. Goodyear's first step in the case of truck tires was taken in 1918, after the war, a typically unorthodox Goodyear move, a change not in the tires, but in the trucks.

As loads grew heavier and tires larger, the truck bodies rose higher than the loading platforms. It looked as though further progress was stymied.

"Why not carry the load on six wheels instead of four?" Litchfield suggested to the truck makers. "You can use those smaller tires then, keep the height down."

However, these were boom years and everyone was busy, nobody seemed particularly concerned. So Litchfield called in McCreary, an ingenious salesman:

"I want you to go to Detroit and pick out a good practical automobile engineer," he said. "Then build a six-wheel truck with power on the four rear wheels."

McCreary blinked but went to work, and the first six-wheeler came out late in 1918, with an improved model the following year. It was demonstrated extensively, taken to the automobile shows and the idea took hold. Truck makers went into the field of multiple-wheeled vehicles, with dual wheels, then additional wheels in line to carry increasing loads. That done, Goodyear, having no intention of being a truck manufacturer, closed out the assignment.

Another obstacle arose in 1922. Tires were not standing up as they should. With good roads being built, trucks were being driven harder and farther, often overloaded and with the tires underinflated. The company could and did put out load charts, trained its dealers' service men to watch inflation, but human nature being what it was, that was not enough. The tires must be built strong enough to stand at least a reasonable amount of abuse.

The matter was extremely important to the company. There were a million trucks in service in 1922, and though the solid tires outnumbered the pneumatics ten to one, Goodyear was confident that the pneumatics would eventually drive out their slower-moving rivals. Speeds on pneumatic tires were increasing to 25 miles an hour, and at times even 35, while the solid-tired trucks poked along at ten or 15. The pneumatics cost twice as much as the solids, but were worth it because they could cover so much more ground in a day with a pay load. There was a tremendous future for pneumatics if they could be built strongly enough to meet increasingly heavier requirements.

The situation was particularly a challenge to Goodyear, for the pneumatic cord truck tire was its baby, its own development. The difficulty had to be overcome. The development department made this its main job. *To stimulate its resourcefulness was the fact that never since the difficult first years had Goodyear so desperately needed business as it did in 1922.*

Compounds were improved, and the tires redesigned, but without too much result. The development men finally reached the conclusion that the fault lay in the carcass, that the fabric was not strong enough to stand the strain. Failures came particularly at the shoulder. Sam Steere was called in from California.

A seasoned production man in textiles, with an excellent technical background, Steere went to the Goodyear mills at Killingly, Conn., to see what he could do to improve tire fabric. Relatively little research had been done in that field.

Anyone could make a stronger fabric by using a heavier cord, but tire fabric had to be flexible also. The continued flexing of a heavily loaded carcass on the road, and the sharp blows encountered as an obstruction was hit, tended gradually to weaken the fabric and finally break it down.

Litchfield's mind again went back to sea-going days: the fisherman's net and the anchor lines. Cotton fabric had plenty of strength but now called for more flexibility.

Steere, as a practical mill man, knew that by increasing the twist of his yarn, he could get more stretch into the cord. He knew, too, that a twisted cord tended to become more resilient up to a certain point, then became so tight that it was easily broken. Somewhere between the low-twist unresilient cord and the high-twist breakable cord must be one which would have a maximum of strength and resiliency. He set out painstakingly to find it, after long experiment came up with a new fabric called Supertwist which, with better compounding and design, cured the trouble and the pneumatic-tired truck resumed its drive to become a key part of the nation's transportation system.

Knowing that any new product would meet initial setbacks, Goodyear had organized a Highway Transportation division in the development department in 1919, to act as a liaison between factory and field.

Truck operators came in with a suggestion in 1922. Their costs were uneven. A number of tires might wear out one month and only a few the next. Wages, fuel, upkeep—these averaged out about the same each month. Couldn't they somehow average tire expense out too, perhaps pay so much per month for so much mileage? A plan was set up to do this, but soon brought new headaches.

A public utility in the east, whose interurban roads were meeting troublesome competition from independent bus operators, had ended by buying them out, coordinating rail and bus transportation for an entire state, became the largest bus operator in the country.

Everyone went after this company's tire business, but Goodyear, the winner, soon found that replacements were running so high that instead of making money on the contract, it stood to lose half a million dollars a year. George Sprowls, head of Highway Transportation, hurried east to see what was wrong.

He went over every piece of equipment in the fleet, located the trouble. In the hundreds of buses taken over, many had wrong sizes or types of tires, or tires improperly applied. With the company buying on the mileage basis there was less incentive for drivers to take care of their tires. Sprowls finished his study, sat down with the company's engineers, drew up a program. The bus company was interested in getting the fullest mileage out of its tires, so that future contracts could be written on the basis of the most efficient use. It was still more interested in uninterrupted service, in making as few stops for tire changes as possible.

Changes were made in tire equipment. A rigid control of air pressures was established, abuse was reduced, and in three months the average mileage went from 6000 or 7000 miles per tire to 16,000 or 17,000, and the contract had become a profitable one. The plan served as a model for other large operators around the country. The field men had a continuous job thereafter serving the expanding requirements of the truck and bus fleets which quickly formed a network over the country.

Trained technicians, these men had first-hand contact with new problems as they arose, enabled the factory to move fast to meet them.

The solid tire field had not been neglected during this period. The company not only continued to make them as long as the demand lasted, but brought out special purpose tires, high profile tires, wide bottomed ones, added the useful All-Weather Tread design, got out machines for recutting the grooves as the tread wore down. Big dealers who had bought tire-changing presses as war surplus found solid tires a profitable business.

But the limitations of the solid-tired truck were inherent. At higher speeds than 15 to 18 miles an hour the constant motion of the great mass of rubber generated so much internal heat that it eventually broke down the structure. Solid tires even suffered blow-outs in hot countries.

Compressed air carried in thin containers of rubber enabled trucks to be driven much faster safely. The truck could never have become important in the nation's transportation system, would have been limited to local and suburban hauling if it had remained on solid tires. The pneumatics took the lead in 1926, and solids were soon on their way out.

State laws would put the final quietus on them. The increasing use of automobiles had set the country off on a great road-building program, and the solid-tired truck was often blamed, sometimes unjustly, when poorly constructed or inadequately drained highways failed. Still engineers demonstrated that it was impact and not load which damaged highways—and impact was much less in the case of pneumatics. So legislatures stepped in in one state after the other, barring the solid-tired truck from main market roads, and it would be limited in recent years to industrial trucks used internally in factories.

The following table of Goodyear production of the two types of tires tells its own story.

YEAR	SOLIDS	PNEUMATICS
1916	125,841	2,141
1918	528,768	40,181
1920	201,804	121,628
1921	114,286	14,607
1925	323,471	189,334
1926	208,508	235,681
1930	75,206	779,427
1934	28,757	958,646

·   ·   ·

The balloon tire had been built for passenger cars, but as soon as it was perfected, the restless Goodyear mind began wondering about using the same principle on bus tires. There was no demand for such a tire, but Goodyear brought them out anyhow, Litchfield's old strategy, to build something people needed, whether they realized it or not.

And as the company's judgment was vindicated by results, transportation in America passed another milestone.

A company operating out of Watertown, New York, was one of the first to try the new tires. Their better riding qualities might help them meet the competition of interurban cars riding on steel. People might like them well enough to pay the extra fare.

The public did like them, but soon noticed a peculiar thing, the buses were running ahead of time. The drivers insisted they were not driving any faster. Then the explanation came to light. Maximum speeds had not been stepped up, but minimum speeds had. The drivers did not have to slow down for bumpy roads. With the better traction

The longest tire building room in the world. The 50 year program of im proving machines and methods brought costs down, put all America on wheels

furnished by balloons, they could maintain more uniform speed, could drive over rough roads at the same speed without discomfort to their passengers.

The expected effect on maintenance costs was quickly seen on the service department's books. The better cushioning of the buses on balloon tires had cut down on repairs and replacements, made the buses last longer.

With the case proved for bus balloons the development men turned to their old field—the pneumatic-tired truck, leaving the sales department to follow up the advantage with the bus operators. This was something different, and Litchfield encountered skepticism in his own organization on this idea. Eggs and fragile goods could be carried with less breakage, but what was the point of using balloon tires to carry merchandise where a little jarring more or less would make no difference. Goodyear's argument that the tire would produce economies in maintenance, make trucks last longer, went unheeded.

ith beads, plies and tread in arm's reach, men and machines quickly transform
em into finished tires, which are carried away by conveyors to be vulcanized.

If his own men had their fingers crossed on the truck-balloon tire, that skepticism was still greater outside the Goodyear gates—and forced the company into a new line of business, the manufacture of rims. The new tires called for a change in sizes, and the rim makers could not see enough demand for such a tire to justify the expense of putting in equipment to make rims for them. If Goodyear insisted on building tires nobody wanted, it would have to build the rims for them too.

All right, it would build rims. A small department was set up in 1925 in the old Robinson Clay Products building to manufacture them. Again, as in the case of wheels and brakes, a rubber company had to enter a field foreign to its other work.

The truck balloon tire was a success because it lessened vibration and cut down maintenance expense, came into universal use. So the rim shop it brought into existence, was expanded in 1931 to be the Steel Products Division, and became the main supplier of original equipment rims for trucks, tractors, farm implements and finally the big earth-movers—the company staying out of the crowded field of passenger car rims.

RAYON TRUCK TIRES

The rayon tire, introduced in 1936, is one of the most interesting in the whole series of developments in the truck tire field—and except perhaps for synthetic rubber, called for the longest, most stubborn study on the part of Goodyear research men of any product—and would play an important part in World War II.

The reason for rayon was that the pneumatic-tired truck had gone so fast and so far in half a dozen years that by 1927 it was outgrowing its shoes, threatened to outrun the physical possibilities of the materials from which it was made—particularly cotton.

Trucks carrying heavy loads were being driven across country hour after hour at speeds rivalling those of the passenger car. Under this punishment heat was being generated in the tire which cotton could not take.

Materials was a job for Research. Dr. Dinsmore, chief chemist, realized that it would not be long before a new fabric must be found to meet these extreme conditions. It might be a man-made fabric, for anything man makes he can change. Among other things he looked at rayon. That was a relatively new fibre at the time, made artificially by regenerating the cellulose from cotton linters. It had little strength, low resistance to fatigue, and probably no great resistance to heat. Its usefulness appeared to be for decorative purposes when made into cloth.

However, it was pure chemically, and presumably its physical characteristics could be changed.

He talked to the Dupont people, then the largest producers of rayon, told them what was needed.

Dupont went to work trying to develope those characteristics, with Goodyear running tests at each stage, and finally these began to appear. Goodyear started building rayon tires for test runs.

A new obstacle promptly arose, growing out of the difference between the two fabrics. Examine the cords of rayon and cotton under a microscope, and you will see that cotton cord has a myriad of tiny fibres or filaments along the sides, which helped hook the rubber firmly to the fabric during the calendering process. Rayon was smooth, had no such handholds. So the first difficulty, and one which long seemed unsurmountable, was to get rubber to adhere to rayon.

No matter how carefully built up, the plies were apt to separate under the stress of hard driving.

Research in any one field may have surprise results in other and entirely unrelated fields. The company's long work in lighter-than-air has had several such results. In this case a gelatine latex, which Sebrell had developed to replace the laboriously built and expensive gold-beater skin for the gas cells of the Navy's rigid airships, suggested the use of a similar adhesive, and a satisfactory one was developed in 1932.

Adhesion whipped, the research men looked around for the toughest truck drive in the country to try out the first rayon tires. A Greyhound run in Texas, 800 miles over blistering roads, was suggested. The tire stood the test but not with the margin of superiority expected, not enough to justify the increased cost.

They started off again. Everyone in the department had got into the act by now, Shively in design, Mallory and Handy in fabric, and Evans with his test fleet. They went back to Dupont. The rayon had to be still stronger. The search seemed endless. No visible progress was made in all 1932 and 1933. Some of the new rayon cracked in the twisting process and others came out stiff as a board after it was impregnated with rubber.

So Goodyear put in an air-conditioned laboratory to provide controlled temperature and humidity over a wide range of tests. It set up a miniature cotton mill in the laboratory, twisting the yarn, the cords, the cables, under every conceivable condition, impregnating it almost by hand over big drums, running the fabric through exhaustive fatigue tests and building test tires as fast as they found a promising fabric. They built hundreds of tires during this period, ran off thousands of laboratory experiments, used every trick they knew.

The study resulted in a complete change in the process of making rayon and this, with proper twisting, turned out in 1934 to be the key. It was the twist of the then much stronger rayon cords which gave them a spring-like quality, able to take the endless jolts of the highway and return to position, but it was highly important to know just where to place that twist. It was late that year before the research men felt reasonably sure they were on the right track.

In April 1935 they ordered 50,000 pounds of the new rayon to be delivered at the rate of 10,000 pounds a month.

The first rayon tires were sold to a few key dealers with unusual instructions. They were to sell them without telling the buyer that they were made of rayon, and if a tire did not give satisfactory mileage they were to make a liberal adjustment on it and ship it back to Akron.

The tires were sold only to operators having long, fast, hard runs. The research men waited and watched for two years before they were satisfied. The rayon truck tire was formally placed on the market in 1937, just ten years after Dinsmore started his studies.

Competitor companies bought the new Goodyear tires, cut them up for study, went to Dupont for the new rayon fabric, but had no little difficulty in reproducing the characteristics of the tire quickly, lacking Goodyear's step-by-step experience.

The rayon tire, while designed for extremely hard wear, was quickly extended to the truck tires generally, and even in premium passenger tires. The company would have cashed in more largely if World War II had not come along. The Army wanted this new rayon for its big airplane and combat tires, and as well for its bullet-sealing fuel tanks. It was stronger, lighter, less affected by altitude, did not tear but left a clean cut hole where the bullet struck it, which the rubber all but instantly sealed.

And without rayon large size tires made from synthetic rubber would not have been successful, as we shall see when we get into the war story.

Airplane Tires

Important in the Goodyear history is the development of a tire for the airplane, which radically affected all tire design.

The Airwheel, brought out in 1929, utilized a principle which the engineers called "flotation." It was so large and flexible that it would almost literally float over the ground. It would roll over ruts and broken terrain, smooth it out, climb easily out of chuck holes, take hold and pull out of mud and snow and sand where any other previous type of tire would bog down hopelessly.

The Airwheel came in just when the airplane badly needed it. After a decade of neglect, aviation had begun to move ahead. But in the still primitive airports of that era, planes were apt to get stalled in mud and sand, have to be towed out. The Airwheel permitted them to take off regardless of ground conditions. Aviation moved ahead.

This was not the company's first venture, however, in airplane tires. That had started in 1909, just six years after the Wright brothers took off at Kitty Hawk, and a year before Glenn Curtiss made his record flight down the Hudson from Albany to New York.

There were no airplane tires then, and the field was entirely too small to interest anyone in building any. There were not 50 airplanes in the whole country. The company did not need the business. The Straight Side tire was going over big and the old strawboard plant was jam-packed with production.

Still this was transportation, and potentially important. Any company that could lend a hand should do so.

The Wright brothers were using sled runners and skids, catapulting their plane off. Other flyers cemented a single-tube bicycle tire to the rim, but that was apt to rip off in landing, and was not strong enough to stand the impact of many landings. Still others used motorcycle tires, which were stronger, but pretty heavy for a 50 horse power plane. So Goodyear developed the Wing tire, which was bolted to the rim, made up rims to fit it. It was not too good, but better than anything on the market, and the early flyers all bought sets.

Litchfield made an important trip to Paris the following year to look over the whole business of aeronautics, which was further along in Europe than in this country, although the airplane was born in America.

He came back more deeply impressed than ever with the possibilities of aviation, started work on a new airplane tire, using cord fabric and the Straight Side principle, did away with the lugs, came up with a tire 18 per cent lighter than the first one, and strong enough to stand up under hard landings. The engineers set up a tire-testing machine, mounting tire and wheel on a 250 pound frame, dropped it again and again on a concrete floor from a height of 70 feet, satisfied themselves that it would meet all landing shocks.

The new tire was made in five sizes, to fit Wright, Curtiss, Martin, Farman, Bleriot, Antoinette and other pioneer planes. It was a success from the start. Rogers used them on the first transcontinental flight from Long Beach, Long Island, to Long Beach, California, a journey that took 84 days with 63 landings (without any tire trouble), in the fall of 1911. So did Ovington in the first air mail flight of September 23, 1911, and the other pioneers.

An airplane tire is different from a passenger tire. It is not called on for long mileage at slow speed, might not travel more than a few hundred miles all told. Its problem was impact, as a fast-moving plane touched the unmoving earth, and the wheels raced instantly into top speed. Principles as to the carcass and tread which would meet these stresses were worked out fully in the initial tire of 1909-10, remained virtually unchanged up to World War I and afterwards, except for the adjustments that increasing speeds and loads compelled.

The company furnished the larger part of the tires built during the first war, but no company can live on war business, and after 1918 people said there would be no more wars. Aeronautics went into the doldrums. The public, and as a consequence Congress, was peace-minded. The Army could get along with its left-over planes. Business saw no profit in commercial aviation. Aeronautics was kept alive during these years by Billy Mitchell and his disciples, men like Doolittle, Arnold, Eaker, Spaatz, by a similar group in the Navy, and barnstorming fliers making a precarious living flying passengers at a dollar a head out of cow pasture airports. Jacobs and Guinther at Goodyear, trying to sell airplane tires and brakes, and show a profit-and-loss statement not too crimson by the end of the year, knew and lived with these people.

But things began to pick up after 1927. The Lindbergh flight came as an electric shock to the public. The Graf Zeppelin crossing helped. Public interest revived. Money came in from public and government for airports, for air lines, even for research.

A man named Musselman, an inventor who had developed the safety bicycle, came into the Goodyear office in 1928 with an idea for a new airplane tire.

Development was a large department by then, with specialists in many fields. But sometimes an idea from the outside might be helpful, the door must always be kept open. If the department had to examine a thousand crackpot ideas to find one good one, it was still worthwhile. Musselman's tire was not too good, but it was a nucleus from which something might come.

He had built a tire of extremely large cross section, fitted to a wheel of extremely small diameter. Darrow, development manager, long ex-

perienced in tire design, saw its short-comings, but he also saw possibilities in it. He gave the inventor quarters in the department, assigned
some of his best design men to work with him, and soon a curious pair
of tires went rolling across Akron Airport. They were like none ever
before seen. The principle of oversizing, of small rim diameters and
greater air space, had been carried to the extreme. In fact, there was no
wheel at all. The tire was practically built on the axle.

The company bought two airplanes to test out the tire. The pilots
found that the plane could be "ground-looped" without breaking a
wheel and turning over; could make a hard landing without going over
on its back; could be landed in fields impossible to high-pressure tires,
and landed safely in fields highly hazardous to high pressures. With
its great ground contact it could take off from fields where the high-
pressure tire would have bogged down. It flattened out ruts made by
conventional tires which had been towed out by tractor.

What would happen if so large a tire blew out? They cut a gash six
inches long in the tire, took off. The plane lurched a bit at first with
the flabby tire flapping on the ground, but gained momentum and took
the air. Immediately the centrifugal force of the spinning wheel
rounded the flat tire to normal shape. The pilot came in cautiously for
a landing. Nothing happened. The plane made a normal landing, showing only a list toward the slashed tire after it had run a short distance,
and not settling down on the hub until it was almost at a full stop.
Any high-pressure tire would go flat instantly under those circumstances. The Army and Navy, private pilots, and the transport lines,
just getting under way, became interested. They needed just such a tire
if the airplane itself was to go ahead.

Then the brake situation arose. Up to then the pilot would land on
one side of the field, count on rolling to a stop before he reached the
other side. With bigger planes and higher landing speeds he was apt
to overrun the field and get into trouble. With planes carrying passengers, brakes were necessary as a safety factor.

But the makers of brakes looked askance at the new tire. It meant a
complete new design of the wheel assembly. It was a freak thing at best,
probably would not last. With the wheel cut down to the proportion of
the hub, it left little braking surface. No wheel manufacturer was interested in changing over his equipment to build it.

So Goodyear was forced to design its own brakes, then build the
wheels for it, in order to market a new tire. Before it knew it the company was in the wheel and brake business, although it farmed out their
manufacture until World War II.

Once the brakes were perfected, Pilot Hudson worked out a series
of spectacular evolutions and toured the country to demonstrate the tire,
landing on one wheel, pulling the plane to so abrupt a stop that the tail
rose to a horizontal position, racing his motor with the brakes set till
the tail rose and the plane seemed poised for flight, startled old time
pilots by ground loops.

The Airwheel-type tire became standard in aeronautics.

One thing leads to another. As soon as the tests were completed, the
bugs worked out and the tire put on the market, the tire designers set
out to see if the principle could not be applied elsewhere.

The farm tire came first, in 1930. The following year the Airwheel
began to be used on graders and dump trucks, the beginning of the
Off-the-Road tire. The Coast Guard tried them out in 1931, on its life
boats as well as its amphibian planes, found both easier to pull through
wet sand—and continues to use them to this day. The British Army
picked up the idea for its Desert Command in 1931, using them first in
India. The Airwheel went on passenger cars and trucks in 1932.

These last, however, did not need the extreme low pressure of the
airplane tire, nor the extremely small size of wheel, settled on wheel
diameters of 15 and 16 inches for passenger tires which would be
standard until 1948.

Mounted on cars and trucks the Airwheel absorbed road shocks much
better than the balloon, made higher speeds over bad roads possible and
safe, was still harder to puncture.

Airplane tires took a new turn as World War II approached.

Farm Tires

The farm tire, as the first application of the Airwheel principle outside of aeronautics, started in Florida in 1930.

An orange grower was having trouble cultivating his grove. Loose
dry sand would slip and slide under his tractor. The lugs had nothing
to brace against. The wheels would spin and presently the tire was
buried up to the rear axle.

"You can't get enough traction to pull your hat off," he told a Goodyear salesman. They decided on a home-made experiment. Some Airwheel tires had just been delivered to the Jacksonville branch. Couldn't
they install these on the orange grower's tractor, try them out?

The large rear tires were inflated to five pounds pressure and the

Typical of the improvements the rubber-tired tractor brought into farming is this Iowa scene, as a load of baled hay is hauled away by tractor.

Rubber gave new mobility to combines harvesting oats in Nebraska (above), and (below) Illinois farmers could plant many acres of corn in a day.

Setting the brakes and taking a power take-off, the versatile tractor does a host of farm chores, like running a hammermill to grind up feed for cattle.

On this rich bottom land farm in Missouri, the hay is raked, baled and delivered to the tractor-hauled farm wagon. A girl can drive a modern tractor.

Rugged Sure-Grip tire is widely used by tractors whether pulling a plow in Michigan, harvesting oats in Kansas, cultivating corn in Indiana, or (below) pulling three-bottom plow in farming section of Central Michigan.

front ones to fifteen. It worked. The large soft tires rolled over the rough ground, climbed out of holes, even pulled out a stalled tractor.

The experiment was not a complete success, but it pointed the way. Manufacturers of tractors became very much interested, worked closely with the development men at Goodyear on the design of vehicles and tires for this huge new market. The tractors used large low-pressure tires on the rear wheels to give traction, could use smaller ones in front to steer. A new tread was needed to give extra traction across plowed fields and rolling ground. One was designed, called the Sure Grip, with heavy bars extending from the side to center, over-lapping bars, with valleys in between so that the mud would not pile up there.

The next year rubber-tired tractors were demonstrated at the National Corn Husking Contest, made a deep impression. The farmer, an observing man, noticed that rubber-tired tractors needed less power to drive, used less fuel, covered more acreage, did not chew up the ground or tamp it down like steel did. He noticed, too, that they took a lot of the jolts and jars out of his day's work, lessened fatigue.

Thinking of the growing complaints of road commissioners and legislatures to steel shod tractors on the highway, he concluded that rubber would remove that objection. Already there were signs along new roads, "No tractors with steel lugs permitted," and boards had to be laid across the highway before a tractor would even be permitted to cross over from one farm to another. The revolution in agriculture was on its way.

That revolution had started with the gasoline engine, 20 or 30 years before. Once taken to the farm, it gradually drove out the old steam engine, which moved from farm to farm, a picturesque part of the harvest season.

The gasoline-driven tractor gave further stimulus to mechanization. It furnished the power for the swaying belts used for threshers and home sawmills; it took the place of the horse to draw plows, reapers, harrowing and discing machines—or the combine, which did several threshing operations at one time. It had released thousands of boys from the farm to work in industry, enabled a smaller number of men to feed the nation.

Then came rubber, greatly increasing the usefulness of the tractor. The farmer was quick to see this.

He usually left his steel-shod tractor out in the weather. With a rubber-tired tractor he could drive it up to the house faster than he could walk in, so he put it away in a closed shed, saving maintenance and repair costs. He could drive it into the barn without damaging the floors.

Riding on rubber the tractor need not be limited to low speeds, might be driven at 25 miles an hour. By hooking on a trailer or farm wagon it could haul products to market.

Also there was no reason why rubber tires should not be applied to other farm machinery. The company had an ideal testing laboratory in the 46 square miles of irrigated land in Arizona. The engineers hurried out there, and in another two years the threshing machine, the separator, the binder, the corn husker and sheller, the mower, the potato digger, the ensilage cutter, the silo filler, and the manure spreader all began riding on rubber.

No change in transportation has ever moved faster than the swing to rubber on the farm. In 1932 there were 160,000 tractors in use in America, 3 per cent of them on rubber. But by 1941, with 95 per cent of the nation's tractors on rubber, there were 360,000 of them in service.

Off-the-road Tires

The 1930 depression, making its usual call on men's resourcefulness, saw another huge field opened up—for tires which could leave the paved highways, go out across country to mining, logging and construction camps, travel over temporary roads through snow, mud, shifting sand or abrasive rock.

These tires were variously called off-the-road tires, snow-mud tires, sand tires, construction tires and earth movers. This last name was particularly appropriate, for the earth-moving tires grew large enough in time to move, if not the earth itself, at least freight-car loads of it.

High-pressure tires, traveling over relatively firm ground, and low-pressure ones, alike proved useful. We will look at the high-pressure tire first.

There was a need for vehicles able to carry larger loads of sand, gravel or crushed rock than the commercial truck, plenty of use for them in open pit (strip) mining in coal, iron or copper—if pneumatic tires were strong enough to take the load, and durable enough to withstand the heavy punishment the treads must encounter.

Tires *could* be built strong enough. That was largely a matter of building enough plies of rubberized fabric—or later rayon. The tread presented problems, had to resist chipping, cutting, snagging and abrasion to an unusual extent. A new tread design came in, with massive

The crane came into full usefulness only when it went on rubber. Here an Arizona rancher picks up a 300 year old cactus in the desert, transplants it.

rounded grooves or lugs running at an angle across the face of the tire. The lug tread had fewer vulnerable points of attack than the diamond buttons of the All-Weather Tread, and traction was not too important, since the tires usually rode on a hard surface.

The new tire, called the Hard Rock, quickly proved its usefulness throughout the mining industry, grew to cross sections of 21 inches (which compares to the six-inch cross section of a 6.00-16 passenger tire), stood five feet high, was inflated to 70-80 pounds air pressure.

It moved next into the logging industry, particularly in the Pacific Northwest. Here conditions were different, and truck makers and tire designers again had to tailor their vehicles to that need.

The terrain in the Northwest is not a flat plain, but a series of mountains and valleys. Logging roads pretty well drained themselves, were not too muddy but that the trucks could go well back into the woods, at least as far as loading points where the logs were snaked out by cables and donkey engines, or dragged out by caterpillar tractors.

The great Douglas fir and the Washington spruce produces logs 60, 80 and 100 feet long. The load was not concentrated, as it was in an ore-carrying truck, could be distributed over a larger number of somewhat smaller tires. The practice grew up of dividing the load between the powered front section and the trailered rear section, each with tandem axles riding on eight tires, often with as many as 20 tires to the vehicle. These great logging trucks hauled freight-car loads of timber to the railroad, the river or the mill. Tire sizes grew from a seven and a half-inch cross section to 12 inches. Rubber gave important help to the great logging and mining industries.

The low-pressure, Airwheel-type tire, called the Earth Mover, had a different history. It went into the construction field where the ground was too soft for a high-pressure tire.

Most construction jobs call for moving earth from one place to somewhere else. Men used a shovel and wheelbarrow at first, but that was slow work. Then came a man and a mule and a scraper, the mule pulling the scraper, the man steering it, and dumping it when it was full.

The steam shovel came in, seemed like a big improvement. For it could scoop up huge bucketfuls of earth at a time, then swing around and dump its load into a horse-drawn wagon to be hauled away.

This, too, was slow and tedious. It took men months to move a small section of hill which the original cooling of the earth's crust had thrown up in seconds. It was expensive as well. There were hundreds of construction jobs needing to be done, dams, highways, waterways, railways, particularly in sections of the country where mountains and valleys made communication difficult. Important new fields could be opened up if the job of moving dirt and sand and gravel could be done faster, more easily, less expensively.

A contractor in California, dissatisfied with the construction equipment on the market, tried making his own—and eventually found himself in that business. LeTourneau's first step in 1928 was to mount an earth-carrying scraper on wheels. It was not too successful since he had to use steel. The Airwheel brought the answer.

Rubber tires went on the dump wagons—not that the dirt minded being jostled, but because the wagons were easier to pull on pneumatic tires. A caterpillar or tractor could tow a whole string of them, where a single wagon on steel wheels was a stout load for a pair of mules. Euclid and LeTourneau got into this, and rubber-tired wagons were used on a Mississippi levee job in 1932, worked perfectly.

Other construction machinery began to ride on rubber tires, concrete mixers, steam shovels, now called power shovels, road rollers. They used the conventional All-Weather Tread design, since they were "free rolling"—that is they were towed from one place to another by caterpillars or tractors, usually Diesel-driven.

A word might be inserted here. The name "caterpillar" came from the Caterpillar Tractor Company, but was so apt a term that it caught the public imagination, and all caterpillar-type tractors were called "cats" regardless of who made them. Consequently that nomenclature is followed in this narrative for easier understanding.

The caterpillar could pull greater loads than anything man had devised, and would be the progenitor of the great armored tanks which played so important a part in the late war. However, construction men noted that a tractor could travel at 15 to 18 miles an hour in bad terrain, and at 25 to 30 elsewhere, as against the caterpillar's four to eight miles an hour under similar conditions. Designers of construction machinery began to wonder, around 1940, if it were not possible to build power plants into their machines, let them travel under their own power.

That meant a new and tougher job for the tires. The Sure-Grip tread design was adapted from the farm tractors, since tires now must do the pulling, needed maximum traction over rough surfaces.

An exciting five years followed. The implement makers built tractors into their machines, and the caterpillar makers went into tractor-drawn vehicles. There was room for both, and need for both. Construction jobs were calling for bigger and better machinery for building dams, waterways, highways in rough country. Earth Mover tires were designed for power shovels, for concrete mixers, for grading machinery, for the "bulldozers," tough, hard-hitting vehicles which plowed into the sides of mountains and ripped them out of their path. Contractors needed larger wagons and dump trucks to carry rock and dirt and sand to balance their cuts and fills. The field grew to huge proportions.

The off-the-road tire development was well under way when World War II came on—and just in time. The nation needed hundreds of airports, big ones with mile-long runways, needed cantonments, training fields, highways like the Pennsylvania Turnpike to eliminate bottlenecks. Railroad grades and curves had to be eased for stream-lined Diesel freight trains of 100 cars, travelling at 70 miles per hour—and passenger trains at 95—with quadruple tracks and widened tunnels to speed up the transport of war equipment.

Transportation had to match up with America's tremendous war production and Earth Mover tires grew to the 30.00-33 size, standing more than seven feet high, weighing nearly a ton, inflated to 35-45 pounds, slightly more than a passenger car tire, but capable of carrying a load of 35,000 pounds.

To measure the improvement in tires in the short space of 15 years, we will compare the big Earth Mover with the 6.00-16 passenger car tire, which up to the introduction of the Super Cushion in 1947, was used on more cars than any other size.

The 6.00-16 is 28 inches high; the 30.00-33 stands as high as a man's head, almost six feet high. The one tire is six inches in cross section; the other is two feet and nine inches. The one is built in four plies; the other has the strength equivalent to 60 plies. The 6.00-16 carries 25-30 pounds air pressure, while the standard 30.00-33 Earth Mover has around 35 pounds.

The 6.00-16 carries a carload of people or, mounted on a truck, has a rated capacity of half to three quarters of a ton. The four tires on the compactor can carry a load of 400,000 pounds. The standard 30.00-33 uses more than half a ton of rubber and 125 miles of rayon cord.

Some airplane tires, such as those for the B-36 bomber, were built in still larger sizes, 36 inches in cross section and standing more than nine feet high. Earth Movers and big airplane tires, however, are not interchangeable. They have different kinds of jobs to do. The Earth Mover runs at low speed for hours at a time; the bomber tire at very high speed for a short time, and must absorb terrific impact forces unknown to the earth mover. Consequently, each type is tailored to its exact needs.

A high pressure tire was also developed in the 30.00-33 size after the war, the Soil Compactor, a tire not used to *tow* steel rollers, but to

Spectacular Earth Movers met the need for huge flying fields during the war. Above a self-propelled wagon which can carry 100,000 pounds of earth at a load, and below a six wheel tractor-scraper unit.

Four-wheel powered scraper helps build levee in Louisiana. Crawler-type Diesel (below) uses four 18.00-24 tires at Billy Mitchell Airport.

Tough going even for a prime mover on construction job in Wisconsin, but the bulldozer in back is ready to give it a shove if necessary.

act as the roller itself, tamping down the earth on new airports and highways. Four tires, carrying a gross weight of 200 tons, towed by a caterpillar, could press the earth down so compactly that the layers of crushed rock and other sub-base materials were not needed, saving millions of dollars in airport construction costs. These tires were inflated to 120 to 150 pounds pressure and each sustained a load of 10,000 pounds.

Another compaction tire was developed, a lighter one, with hammering shock loads applied to it 500 to 1500 times a minute. It utilized heavy counter-weights and an eccentric shaft to deliver the blows to the moving tire with such rapidity that the tire had no time to deflect too far but passed the impact on to the ground.

The off-the-road tire became an important part of the company's operations. Lee, Moss and Case did the development work. Fox and Calloway pioneered the sales effort, the latter in charge of sales to the manufacturers.

Calloway was made Assistant to the Vice President in 1945, the same year in which the American Road Builders Association elected him president of the manufacturers' division. He was made president of the entire association in 1947, reelected in 1948, directed the huge exhibition that summer at Soldier's Field, Chicago.

THE MARSH BUGGY TIRE

A different use for large tires came up in 1936. The Gulf Refining Company wanted a vehicle built which it could use in searching for oil in the Louisiana swamps, asked whether tires could be designed at such low pressure that the whole vehicle would float, be amphibian.

What they wanted was something which could travel through the swamp, and when it came to a river, roll down the bank, "paddle" across, propelled by its engines, climb up the far side and keep on going.

Again vehicle builders and Goodyear designers put their heads together, as they had throughout this entire development, worked out the answer. The tires were ten feet high, carried an air pressure of four pounds, worked perfectly, lasted long. More of them were built after the war for similar explorations in South America.

The Marsh Buggy tire, as it was called, came in handy in 1939 when Dr. Poulter of Armour Tech needed tires for his Snow Cruiser in exploring the South Pole area. They had to be strong enough to carry a weight of 37 tons, and so compounded as to stand up under temperatures of 75 degrees below zero.

Gulf gave permission to use its molds, the tires were built and that summer the Snow Cruiser, carrying a pair of spares in back, wheeled across the country on the 1000-mile trip from Chicago to Boston, rolled down the ramp in the Antarctic six weeks later, worked satisfactorily.

The approach of war and the lapse in government appropriations made it necessary to discontinue the explorations, and the Snow Cruiser was left in the Antarctic, with tarpaulin covering the tires to protect them from the rays of the sun until the snow drifted over them.

The Polar regions aroused the interest of several nations during the war as a shorter route between continents, and territorial claims were set up. Admiral Byrd led a Navy training expedition to the site of his old camp in 1946, was particularly curious as to what had happened to the Snow Cruiser.

The snow had drifted even with the top of it. *The tires had lost little air pressure during the six years,* and from the previous experience of the scientists as to the performance of rubber under extremely cold conditions, it was estimated that they should be good for another ten years.

The development men designed small tires as well as large during this period, industrial tires for low-slung trucks which carry materials or goods-in-process from one factory department to another; got back into the bicycle tire field; built tires for the baggage trucks at the railway station; for lawn mowers and wheel barrows; for baby buggies, and the youngsters' scooters, for practically everything which rolls on wheels —all on pneumatics.

The story of the tire totals up a rather impressive amount of work, has had no little part in the development of America.

This chapter started with the Development Department, might well close on that theme.

The department has come a long way in the 40 years, grown to a staff of more than 1250 people, and without counting the men in the test fleet, experimental workshop and clerical, has nearly 600 technically trained men—and a dozen girls. Thirty members of the department have doctor's degrees.

Few men have come into the department from other companies. For the most part it has been built up around young men straight from college, from Massachusetts Tech, California Tech, Georgia Tech, Purdue, from Michigan, Ohio State, Southern California, Alabama, Notre Dame, from more than 100 schools in all, including a few from abroad, England, Canada, Scotland, Argentina.

Although the factory looked askance at college men in 1910, many of the development men have gone far in production, including De-

Young from Akron U. who became vice president of all manufacturing, Wolfe from M.I.T. in charge of production of all the domestic plants, and Hinshaw from Illinois Wesleyan with similar responsibilities in the foreign factories.

Development furnished the company with a dozen superintendents. England has had three, Flannery of Cornell who later took charge of all engineering, Brittain of Toronto who served through the war, and Ginaven from Ohio Wesleyan. St. Marys had had three, Patterson of Michigan, Belknap of Stevens Institute, and Teissher of Ohio State. Michaels, O.S.U., went to Gadsden, Warden of Cornell to Kelly-Springfield, Cattran of Penzance School, England, to Bowmanville; two M.I.T. men went to South America, Coffin to Brazil and Gagnon to Peru. Hoesly of Wisconsin served in Sweden during the war, Rudder of Alabama went to Topeka, Spoonamore of Ohio State to Cuba, Perren of Hiram College to Mexico, Smith of Dennison to the Houston synthetic plant.

Dinsmore of M.I.T. who started as a compounder, and was largely responsible for the synthetic development, became a vice president, with three divisions reporting to him—Research, now increasingly important with the first research laboratory in the industry, Development, now divided into Tire and Chemical under Vogt of Oberlin, and Mechanical Goods under the veteran Morse of M.I.T. who had headed this work since 1915. Sebrell of Mount Union with a doctor's degree from Ohio State headed the new division as research director, with Osterhoff of Michigan head of the department.

Development personnel included Shively from Webb Institute, chief of tire design, who developed the Super Cushion tire, Brown from Georgia Tech who served in Canada and England, and headed up military production in War II, Shoaff from Southern California who ran the rubber plantations, then synthetic rubber production, McCarty, Catholic University of Washington, who went to Kelly-Springfield, came back in 1940 to take charge of all truck and passenger tire design, Dugan of Rensselaer Polytechnic who became chief compounder.

7. Industrial Rubber Goods

Belting and Hose

MECHANICAL goods, later called Industrial Rubber Goods, a field Goodyear went into rather incidentally in Canada in 1910 and in full scale in Akron in 1913, is radically different from tires.

Tires are sold chiefly to individuals, while mechanical goods—hose, belting and molded goods—are sold principally to industry, and became highly important with the growth of industry in this country.

Entry into the field represented a change in company policy. At the outset Goodyear took the position that it should not scatter its slender resources of men and money over the whole field of rubber goods. Older companies like Goodrich and U. S. Rubber might make everything in rubber, but Goodyear, the newcomer, would select one major product, concentrate everything on that, try to make the best tire in the world, tie all of its business fortunes to that.

The reasons for the change in policy in 1913 were just as fundamen-

241

tal, though unusual in business. For with 25 to 30 per cent of the tire market in its hands, Goodyear concluded that that was as large a share as was healthy for any one company to have. Rather than try to get a still larger percentage of the tire market, it should divert its excess energies into a new field. Mechanical goods as it was then called was interesting. There was much to be done there.

Mechanical goods was a much older line of the rubber business, going back to Charles Goodyear and the discovery of vulcanization, and perhaps for that reason was, if not a backward industry, at least a conservative one. It had had little benefit in the past from research, and was getting less then, due to the industry's increasing absorption in tires. The possibilities in that field were attractive. The characteristics which were inherent to rubber, and others which could be compounded into it, might give it uses to society which had not been dreamed of.

RUBBER HOSE

The biggest mechanical goods item was rubber hose, but that went far beyond garden hose and fire hose. The structural iron worker building a skyscraper used air hose to drive home his rivets. Dredges and sand suckers deepening harbors or filling in tidal flats used a series of sluice pipes resting on pontoons connecting the pipes with flexible hydraulic hose, resistant to salt water, indifferent to the rise and fall of the tide, or the movement of the pontoons in the wind.

Pile drivers lifting large weights needed rubber hose to carry the steam from the boiler to the gooseneck on top. Oil tankers landing at the wharf could connect six-inch hose lines ashore, unload the boat by suction pumps. Deep in the mines rubber hose could be dragged over abrasive rocks and ore, carry power for pneumatic drills.

The railroads needed rubber for their air brakes, machine shops needed rubber hose for acetylene gas and oxygen in welding, foundries in sand blasting castings, paving contractors in compressed air drills to break up concrete roadways. A steamship could bring in steam to warm up the hold, the food industry could use it widely in creameries, packing houses, for cleansing, sterilizing.

A Maryland city, caught in a typhoid epidemic, once ran a line of Goodyear hose to a safe water supply, carried pure water in shallow trenches underground, across marshes and a river to its people. And London fire fighters during two wars, whenever a section of the city water main was destroyed by bombs, would run a line of hose around the damaged section and carry on. A modern bombing plane uses as much as 300 feet of hose for its gasoline, oil, air and hydraulic lines.

Even the great virtue of rubber, that it could be dissolved in gasoline and used in liquid form, which barred any use for it in contact with gasoline, was overcome in the end by synthetic rubber. The petroleum industry today is the largest user of rubber hose for all petroleum products, from heavy crude oil to high octane gasoline, and for gases like butane and propane.

Pipe lines of cast iron or clay carry fluids and gases over long hauls, but for short distances rubber, in the form of hose, is the major carrier for industrial liquids and gases—and solids as well, in the case of sand blast hose and hose carrying corrosive, abrasive, salt and acid materials.

BEGINNINGS OF MECHANICAL GOODS

The typical mechanical goods factory when Goodyear started was small, usually a family affair, located in New England or New Jersey, had a good reputation for its mill hose, fire hose, transmission belts, corrugated matting, valves and gaskets—or platens for the typewriter. It concentrated on one or two items, had little overhead, did no advertising, sold the same customers year after year, usually jobbers, who might take the entire output—and made good money.

When Goodyear started up in Canada, it took over an existing factory rather than build a new one. That plant was making mechanical goods. Sales were small but profitable and Goodyear carried it on. With the merger of Goodrich and Diamond in 1912, Goodyear got a chance to pick up a ready-made organization in manufacturing and sales. Goodrich men were in the saddle and a number of Diamond people moved down as assistants. Most men do not relish working for their old competitors. Bailey, the sales manager, had already decided to leave, was going into business for himself with Burr, the Chicago manager. Both were glad to come to Goodyear instead, and in the next several months brought in a number of Diamond salesmen, and a few from Goodrich, including Foster, who became manager of the department in 1947, and Post, head of footwear.

On the factory side, William Metzler, in charge of Diamond production, brought several of his best foremen with him, as well as Hal Campbell, who later succeeded him as superintendent. Metzler was still on the job in 1949 in a consulting capacity, after more than 60 years in rubber manufacture, the longest record of any man in the industry.

In coming to a new company Bailey was on his mettle to build a bigger business than the one he had left. Perhaps the Diamond situation still rankled. He would have a freer hand than he had across town, because Goodyear was new to the business, would have to lean on his experience and that of his associates. He studied long on the matter of making the company a real factor in the business. He thought he had the answer.

Mechanical goods were largely sold on the basis of price. Jobbers and customers would pit the different manufacturers against each other to get the lowest price. There was no point in Goodyear, the newcomer, getting into that kind of cut-throat competition. Bailey proposed that they take the opposite course.

"Let's forget all about price," he said. "Let's build the best product we know how, and sell it for what it is worth. We'll lose a lot of orders, but we will be ahead in the long run if we can build up a reputation for quality. It means getting business the hard way, but the department will be on solid ground, and what progress we make we will hold."

This counsel coincided exactly with Goodyear's own thinking. Litchfield took immediate steps to assure the quality which the program demanded, drawing on the practical experience of Metzler, Campbell and the rest, but giving the young department full technical support as well. Kilborn, Number Two man in the Experimental Department, was assigned to mechanical goods, and when Hall's death in 1916 called him back to tires, another young Massachusetts Tech man moved in, Herman Morse, who has headed up the work ever since. Mechanical Rubber Goods grew to large size, and the department had to supply men for St. Mary's, Windsor, and Lincoln, and the plants in foreign countries.

There may be some significance in the fact that as other rubber companies began to call in technical men they hired chemical engineers almost exclusively for mechanical goods, while Goodyear from the outset used mechanical engineers as well, sensing the relationship of the department with industry generally. Morse himself was a mechanical engineer.

Even with a good product, however, progress was slow during the first years. Sales for the first full year amounted to only $600,000. The building of Plant II in 1916 helped, gave the department room to stretch its legs.

But in deciding to sell to industry direct, rather than leave this to the jobber, Goodyear had an uphill job. There were comparatively few customers and these not easy to sell—purchasing agents, plant engineers, mining superintendents, machine shop foremen, practical men who knew what they wanted. Belting and hose last a long time, are not bought every day. The reputation of the firm is particularly important and Goodyear was new in the field.

To meet this situation, Burr devised the famous GTM (Goodyear Technical Men) program. Under that plan, salesmen with engineering or shop experience went around to industrial plants, told the engineer or plant superintendent they wanted to look over his equipment with him.

"We want to combine your knowledge of your plant with our experience in rubber," they said, in effect. "We may find after going through that there are no improvements we can suggest. In that case we'll tell you so. If we do recommend changes, it will be because we believe they will save you money."

This approach to a selling problem, new in the industry, proved highly effective. The Goodyear men went out not to sell *a* belt, but *the* belt best fitted to the particular installation. They found places where the belt was larger than necessary, others where it was too light to carry the load. In some places pulleys were wrongly placed to give most effective results, or a different hook-up of the power transmission would improve operations. Through visiting hundreds of plants, they picked up ideas in one place which could be applied elsewhere.

This was not merely a sales technique to break into a new field, but the beginning of what we now call sales engineering. The GTM man was looking for new places where rubber could be used in industry, step up its effectiveness, create new markets for the department. And, incidentally, he came to know the industries of the country vastly better than would have been possible otherwise.

No car owner has to be sold on buying a tire. He *has* to have it. But the mechanical goods salesman often had to persuade a factory to use rubber where it had not been used before. And when he took such pioneering orders he had to know exactly what stresses and abrasion and wear the product would encounter, so that Production and Development could build that promised performance into it. Much of industrial rubber goods production is tailored to exact uses, and a unique partnership grew up between the three divisions of the business. Neither the Factory nor Development could know what new possibilities there might be in 10,000 industries scattered over all America. That had to come from Sales, living with the wide ramifications of American industry, knowing its problems, and eternally bringing in new problems to Akron.

In the case of hose, once the pioneering job had been done by GTM men, the company could go back to the jobbers, let them make the contact with the thousands of users. Hose has the advantage that it can be rolled up on a reel and cut to the desired length.

Belting, the second great division of mechanical goods, was somewhat different, for ordinarily it was not something the jobber could take down from his shelf and hand across the counter, or drag in from the stockroom and load on a truck. Much of it was built to specific uses and pioneering had to be done here as well as in hose.

Belting comes in two different classes. Transmission belting *transmits power* from the drive shaft to a machine, or to twenty machines. Conveyor belting *carries goods.*

Transmission belting is the older and originally the larger of the two, running two to one in sales over conveyor belting in industry generally, although that ratio changed at Goodyear after sensational developments which we shall encounter later.

Transmission belting was familiar to the public on threshing machines over many years, or in a maze of belts in a factory. Rubber's chief competitor in transmission belts was leather, but rubber had four inherent advantages.

Rubber belts stretch less than leather, and hence need to be taken up and shortened less frequently. Second, rubber does not need periodic dressing to keep it soft and pliable. Third, rubber belts can be made in one continuous piece, whereas the length of any section of leather belting is determined by the length of a steer's back. No laboratory has yet invented longer steers, so most leather belts must necessarily be made from many sections glued together. Fourth, rubber belts can be made more uniform, whereas a steer's hide will vary in quality, texture and strength as one progresses from the backbone down the flanks and around to the belly—and, of course, quality will vary from steer to steer.

Although transmission belting was an old and established field, two important developments were introduced in the late twenties, the V-belt and the Goodyear Compass belt. Another company had been working on the V-belt idea independently of Goodyear and without its knowledge until a patent was issued. Goodyear's own part, however, was so important that only a token royalty was paid.

The conventional transmission belt was flat, ran horizontally. The V-belt ran in a vertical position, was somewhat wedge-shaped, shorter, a more compact unit. Once put on the market, it became very popular, threatened to take over the entire field. Goodyear's Compass belt held flat belting in the picture. Cost was the determining factor. The V-belt was better in some installations. The Compass belt could compete effectively in others.

The Compass belt adapted the Cord tire principle to this field. The cords were much heavier than those in tires, perhaps an eighth of an inch in size, as against a 1/32 inch cord in tire fabric, but like it had great

ibber belt carries limestone five miles up and down through mountains to Kaiser ment plant near San Jose, California. Below belt overpass crosses a major highway.

flexibility and long wear when encased in rubber.

More spectacular developments, however, came in with the conveyor belt, which is often the least expensive way to move goods from one place to another. The principle was simple. Install a length of endless belting over a string of idlers like a ribbon over two spools, and you have a surface which will carry anything you load aboard it, coal, ore, wheat or whatever. The belt will take it to the end of the line, dump it into a bin, the hold of a ship, a line of trucks, a railroad car, a coal tipple—or surrender its load to another length of belt, or several others in line, to carry on. It is transportation simplified to the utmost degree.

Most factories are forever moving materials and goods-in-process from one department to the next. Rather than load these on a truck and have someone haul them to another point and unload them, it was much simpler to drop them on a slowly moving belt—and often further work can be done on them enroute.

For example, there are several things to be done to an inner tube after it has been vulcanized—punch a hole in it, insert the valve stem, cement the valve reinforcement in place, inflate the tube and test it for leaks. So at Goodyear the overhead conveyors carry a continuous string of tubes past the finishing table. An operator picks them off one at a time, lays them on the moving belt where the various operations are performed as they pass down the line, then through a tank of water at the end, where inspectors watch for any tell-tale bubble which indicates a leak, yanks the offender out for rework.

Conveyor belts came gradually into wide use in ship-to-shore transfer of merchandise, or vice versa, or in carrying coal and ore out of mines to the tipple or through processing departments. Goodyear engineers travelled over the world installing such belts, in the nitrate mines of Chile, the gold mines of South Africa, the silver mines of Colorado, the iron ore country of the Mesabi Range, the gold dredging regions of Alaska, the mining country of Canada and wherever else rubber could be used.

But a situation arose in 1920 which threatened to limit further progress. The finished belts were rolled up on a drum and shipped out, lashed securely to the floor of a flat car. But with increasing demands, from the mining industry in particular, the rolls grew to a size too large to pass through railroad tunnels. This came up first when a mining company near Duluth ordered a belt which was too big to ship. Would it be possible to build it in sections, then splice it together and vulcanize it in the field? Kimmich from Morse's staff set to work to develop a portable vulcanizing unit, and his crew spent much of the winter under tents in sub-zero weather. But they emerged successful, having vulcanized in the field the sections of a belt 750 feet long on centers (or 1500 feet of endless belt including the return run), a world's record for that time. This opened the way to exciting new possibilities. Kimmich put out a handbook explaining the operation in detail, and field vulcanizing became standard in such applications.

One of the most significant of these was the belt built for the Frick Coal Company in Pennsylvania in 1924.

Frick was supplying large quantities of coal to United States Steel from its mines along the Monongahela River. The steel company wanted an additional 50,000 tons a week. That meant opening up other mines lying farther back from the river, with a difficult problem of transportation. The coal would have to be hauled five miles to reach the river barges. Using a railroad would require 100 two-ton pit cars, making 40 trips a day with a 12-minute headway between trains—which would be subject to occasional derailments and consequent tieups.

Frick had been moving coal on rubber conveyor belts in some of its operations, wondered if the whole job could not be conveyorized, carry the entire 50,000 tons a week through the intervening mountains on rubber. After an extensive engineering study, this was decided upon.

The belt was four feet wide and being endless, was ten miles long, made up into 19 sections, each powered by a drive pulley, carrying it over idlers along each section to the next transfer point. Goodyear got two thirds of the order, and its sections outwore the others.

The system was still in operation 24 years later, though the belting had been replaced two and a half times, for even rubber belting will not last forever. But in that time it had carried 60,000,000 tons of coal—and without even an accident calling for hospitalization.

RAILROADS OF RUBBER

But another new concept, almost revolutionary, came into the picture in the 1930's. That was to use conveyor belting not only within a plant, or between adjacent plants, but to take it outdoors and use it to convey materials over terrain not adapted to the railroad or the truck. A three per cent grade is a tough one for the railroad and ten per cent is uneconomical for the truck, particularly on a long climb. But a belt could take a 32 per cent grade with ease.

This new use for belting came in largely through the efforts of E. W. Stephens, one of three Goodyear brothers who came up from Columbus over a nine-year period, Edward the latest, in 1928. He had worked as a salesman in Grand Rapids and Chicago, was called into Akron in 1934 as manager of the belting department.

It was a few years, however, before he had a chance to test his ideas out on two great dam projects, Grand Coulee in 1938 and Shasta in 1940, the former using more cubic yards of material than any dam ever built, including Hoover Dam and Shasta, although the latter was higher than either of the others.

Grand Coulee, one of the huge reclamation jobs of the 1930's was projected to develop power, and to furnish water for irrigation of the waste lands in the Big Bend of the Columbia River in eastern Washington.

There was plenty of sand and gravel less than a mile away from the point selected as the dam site, but the gravel pit lay at 178 feet higher elevation, and the intervening topography made conventional hauling by train or truck extremely difficult.

Stephens got wind of it, went out to see the government and contractor's engineers, reviewed the story of the Frick belt and the improvements that had followed. The idea sounded feasible.

"It might be done with three sections of belt," the engineers concluded. "Put in your power pulleys at this point, and at this, and over here, with idlers in between. It might work."

"We can drape the belt up and down over those hills and do it with a single belt without any intermediate drive pulleys," said Stephens.

"But that would mean a belt two miles long, including the returning half," the engineer exclaimed. "No one has ever done anything like that."

"The Goodyear belt can do it," Stephens insisted.

Competitors were skeptical, predicted dire things for the installation. But it was completed within a month, worked perfectly. Moving at a rate better than five miles an hour, the belt, four feet wide, made of eight plies of stout rubberized fabric, carried 2000 tons of aggregate every hour to the cement mixing plant, delivered a total of 11 million tons. The belt required 150 horsepower to start it, but generated 40 horsepower itself once it got under way with its load. The savings against any other method of transportation paid for itself during the three years the dam was under construction.

Shasta came next, in northern California, the most spectacular job ever assigned to a conveyor belt.

Created by a hundred mountain streams, rushing tumultuously down the high Sierras on one side and the Coast Range on the other, the

Sacramento River, starting near the Oregon border, drives half way down the state to meet the San Joaquin, proceeding more tranquilly up from the south, and the two discharge into San Francisco Bay.

These rivers created a great inland empire almost the full 1000 mile length of California. But with each spring's thaws the Sacramento grew turbulent and unruly, overran its banks, sometimes inundating hundreds of thousands of acres of orchards and ranch land. By August the mighty stream of water had dwindled to a trickle, and the alluvial soil it had spread along both banks reaching back many miles grew brick-hard under midsummer suns, dried and cracked in great crevasses.

Too much water in the spring, too little in summer. If a dam could be built somewhere toward the source, and only as much water allowed to pass as the land needed from month to month, it would be worth millions.

A perfect site for a dam was at hand some miles below the Oregon border near a town called Coram, where the river narrowed down to pass through a deeply-carved channel. High rock walls on each side offered secure anchorage for the dam. There was plenty of sand and gravel near the larger town of Redding, ten miles down the river as the crow flies.

However, a bird was the only creature that could make that trip in a straight line. The Sacramento makes a big "C" turn between the two towns, and the intervening topography was forbidding. A railroad and a highway ran parallel to the river.

Henry J. Kaiser's Columbia Construction Company, contractors on the Grand Coulee job, took the contract to supply the cement and aggregate for Shasta Dam. The cement was no problem. Kaiser built a huge cement plant near San Diego, California, used the Coulee belting to carry the sand and gravel down from the mountains to it, could ship the cement to Coram by railroad.

The gravel plant at Redding, however, lay a mile and a half from the railroad, so he asked Goodyear to figure on a short belt line connecting the two. A dispute arose, however, as to whether the railroad or the contractor should pay for that haul.

Stephens stepped into the middle of the argument.

"We'll take over the whole job," he said. "We'll pick up the materials at the gravel pit, and deliver them directly to the dam site."

That was quite a contract. The gravel pit lay at an elevation of 490 feet and the dam site at 650, but five miles of desert and a ridge rising to 1450 feet lay between. The rubber railroad would have to cross the river, the desert, climb nearly 1000 feet, come downhill 800 feet more, then cross the river again. It would have to haul 12 million tons of material between the two points—and on schedule.

Stephens and his engineers had figured the job carefully, showed the contractor that his aggregate could be carried more cheaply by rubber than by rail. It would take 26 separate belts to cover the 9.6 miles distance, required a total of nearly 20 miles of belting to do the job.

Washington had to be consulted, because this was a government job, but the Secretary of the Interior, after studying the cost figures, cancelled the railroad plan in favor of rubber.

The contractors, under pressure by now from competitors, suggested that Goodyear take 80 per cent of the job, two other firms getting the remaining ten per cent each. Stephens objected.

"A belt is no stronger than its weakest link," he said. "No Goodyear belt has ever failed prematurely. If we get the entire job we will be responsible for a successful operation."

He got the contract. One setback came, however, shortly after the belt went into service. To maintain uniform tension in the belts counterweights were used. On one flight the counterweight was a two ton "car" mounted on a track at a 45 degree angle.

"What would happen if enough sand blew over to cover the track and derailed the car?" Stephens asked the engineers. The contractor got the point, and made plans to put in screens to keep the sand off and a guard rail to anchor the car firmly to the track. But before that was done the anticipated happened.

Stephens got a call on a Saturday afternoon at his home in Akron. The counterweight had jumped the track, carrying the belt with it, damaged 3300 feet of line.

Could it be repaired or what should they do? They had 17 days of materials on hand, but after that the whole project would be stopped and 5000 men thrown out of work.

Chester Smith, now Stephens' assistant, took the plane that night for Spokane where a Goodyear salesman met him and drove him 90 miles across country to the Kaiser headquarters. He looked the belt over. There were tears in it every few feet.

"It might take six months to repair it," he said.

"How soon can you build an entire new section then?" they asked. He called Akron back, and early Monday morning there was an important meeting at Plant II.

It would take two weeks to build a new belt section, ten days if they were lucky. But it was an emergency and the factory worked day and night around the four shifts, completed the job in seven days.

Traffic Director Carroll had talked to the operating vice president of the Great Northern. "The belt will take up two carloads," he told him. "We are shipping it by express. We want these cars hooked on to your fastest passenger train."

The cars were attached at St. Paul to the Empire Builder, the Great Northern's crack train, and every few hours the railroad wired Carroll and the Kaiser people: "Your shipment has just passed White Cloud," or whatever the station was. It reached its destination in 70 hours, was quickly installed and the dam building went on without an hour's interruption.

The Shasta belt was made of pre-war rubber and long-staple Peeler cotton, travelled six miles an hour. The longest flight over the desert was 3400 feet, the others varying with the topography, climbing over the mountain and down again, the shortest being 800 feet. On the down grade the belt furnished enough power for all the lights needed at the dam.

The belt was not thrown away after the job was finished, but cut in thousand-foot lengths and sold. A small section of each length was sent to Akron for test, found to be from 90 to 95 per cent as good as ever, despite the huge job done. About 75,000 feet of the belt went to South Africa, the balance sold to mining companies, sand and gravel concerns and lumber companies. One long section was used to build an airport in California.

Shasta Dam was 555 feet high, three times as high as Niagara Falls, and the water had a drop of 350 feet when the dam overflowed, to create a falls higher than Niagara.

Stephens got the Litchfield Medal in 1940 for his part in the Shasta Dam job. But he was not through building rubber railroads.

The greatest wear on the belt came at transfer points. To cushion this impact, the Goodyear men hit on the device of installing a battery of pneumatic wheelbarrow tires under the pulleys. This was first installed at Grand Coulee where rocks a yard in diameter were encountered, and used again at Shasta where 520 of the tires were installed, 20 at each transfer point.

ANDERSON RANCH DAM

The next big job was the Anderson Ranch Dam across the south fork of the Boise River in Idaho, started in 1940, the highest earth dam ever built in the world, rising 444 feet above the river bed.

Like the others it had the three-fold purpose of preventing floods, creating power and providing irrigation water for the desert country in that area.

From the standpoint of terrain, the Anderson Ranch Dam was terrific. Not far from the river a plateau rose 1000 feet. From the plateau to the river bed was a canyon wall with a sheer vertical descent for one-third of the way, and a 60 degree slope the rest. Smaller canyons and crevasses marked the rest of the route. Tunnels and bridges had to be built, and bulldozers blazed a path along the side of the mountain. Certain points had to be avoided as snow slides came down there every winter wiping out everything in their way. On top of the plateau was a wealth of impervious clay which could be packed hard like a snowball, and there was plenty of pervious material and rock near the dam site itself.

Other Goodyear products came into use on this job. Power shovels scooped out the clay and dropped it into a hopper riding on huge tires. At the dam site other shovels scooped it up again from the pile where the belt had deposited it and loaded it into large, rubber-tired trucks which travelled across the dam site dropping their loads to form great windrows of clay. The bulldozers levelled it off, then tractors hauling great sheeps-foot rollers tamped it down.

THE MESABI IRON RANGE

We move next to the Mesabi Range in Minnesota, one of the richest holes-in-the-ground in the world. Originally ore was hauled out of the open pits by rail, which followed a long, circuitous route around the sides of the pit. As the pits deepened, and grades grew sharper, the traffic problem became acute.

Trains had to travel miles to gain the few hundred feet from the bottom of the pit to the top level. Trucks replaced rails because they could negotiate a steeper grade, shorten the haul. But finally the pits grew too deep for economic escape by truck, as they had to spend too much time in low gear climbing up the winding roadways with their loads.

Would it be possible for a conveyor belt to transport the ore direct from the bottom to the top of the pit?

This was a new problem. The weight of the ore would produce terrific tension in the belt. On the longest belt that grew out of these experiments, the job was equivalent to carrying 1000 tons to the top of the Cleveland Terminal Tower (715 feet high) from the curbstone in front of the Hanna Theatre, half a mile away.

The load was carried at a 32 per cent grade by belt, a climb of 32 feet in a 100 foot distance. Belts having a cotton carcass could not possibly take the tensions resulting from these extreme lifts.

But back in the laboratory in Akron, Suloff of Morse's Development staff, who had gone to Akron University, joined the company at Wingfoot Lake, taken blimp pilot training, worked on the Akron-Macon, and joined Mechanical Goods in 1934, had already been experimenting with other materials to use in building belts, in case increasing demands made that necessary. He had worked with rayon, with fibre glass and steel cables. This new assignment dropped in his lap.

Intricate stress studies were necessary, test samples made up. In the end the factory came up with a belt made of 600 fine cables of airplane steel, each one brass-plated to give better adhesion, the cables then being encased in envelopes of fabric, and rubber over that. It worked. The Oliver Iron Mining Company installed the first steel cable belt in 1942.

The Oliver people ordered a second belt identical to the first, in 1945, a third one in 1947 with a lift of 387 feet. In the same year a coal and coke company in West Virginia ordered one to carry refuse to a height of 460 feet. This called for a belt 1412 feet long or twice that, being endless. In 1948 the Tennessee Coal and Iron Company ordered one for installation near Birmingham, which would have to lift to a height of 734 feet in half a mile of distance. Each of these was a world record, and by 1948 mechanical goods men were confident that they could build a steel-rubber belt to carry a load to the top of the Empire State Building (1490 feet high) from a point a mile away.

The sloping shafts at Mesabi suggested a new way of getting coal out from the mines. Ordinarily the shaft is sunk vertically, and the coal carried to the surface in hoists. However, this called for a peak load of power when the hoist was being raised, and none at all between loads. Deliveries were irregular and maintenance costs high.

Instead of sinking the shafts vertically, why not drive them at an angle such that a rubber belt could carry the coal directly from the mine to the surface? The shafts would have to be a little longer, but this system would save power and maintenance, and permit a steady flow of coal to the waiting railroad cars.

Walters, chief engineer at Goodyear's Adena mine, a Lehigh graduate with practical experience in coal mining, joined the belting sales staff to work on these problems.

Two other big belting jobs came up in 1948, the Bull Shoals Dam across the White River in Arkansas, seven miles long, next in size to Shasta, and the highest coal mine belt in the world, in southern Illinois, which carried its loads to an elevation of 862 feet, was 3167 feet long between pulleys.

MOLDED GOODS

While belting and hose comprise the big divisions of Industrial Rubber Goods at Goodyear, there are many smaller items, such as matting, printer's blankets, and others. Third in importance is Molded Goods, another of the early uses for rubber. This includes the hundreds of small items which utilize the fact that rubber is air-tight, gas-tight, water-tight, and will take any shape desired, includes such things as washers and gaskets, and the rubber ring for the housewife's mason jar.

In the early engines a great source of lost steam—and lost energy—resulted from the fact that it was impossible to fit metal parts together with such precision as to avoid leaks. Or if an engine started out in perfect condition, friction and vibration would quickly reduce its efficiency. But put a little rubber gasket at every point where metal touches metal and the leaks stop.

The automobile came to use more and more rubber elsewhere than in tires—in engine mounts to dampen vibration and noise, sealing strips to keep out rain and cold air, seat cushions, step treads, gaskets and grommets—which led to the building of a small plant at St. Marys, Ohio, in 1939, to manufacture these items for the automobile.

TANK LINING

A new division started in 1936, Tank Lining, which grew out of processes which enabled rubber to adhere tightly to metal.

One word in this connection. Goodyear has originated so many things in the rubber industry that this narrative has probably slurred over developments which originated elsewhere. Flat-built tires started with U. S. Rubber, and Goodrich developed the first successful process of joining rubber to metal.

When Goodyear got into the field, however, it went far. Many acids have a corrosive effect on steel. Republic Steel at Cleveland placed a big contract with the company in 1937 to line with one-quarter inch of rubber, great pickling tanks 80 feet long, to keep in the sulphuric acid fumes. Tank lining came into extensive use in the chemical, paper and pulp industries, and in sewer pipe. The largest vulcanizer ever used by the company was ordered, 55 feet long and 15 feet in diameter. It made quite a caravan as it was moved from the Adamson shop in Akron to Plant III in 1938.

Not a tunnel entrance, but a press, 45 feet long, 15 feet high, where tank lining is cured. Below is a section of conveyor belt ready to ship out.

Rubber took another unusual assignment in World War II—that of stamping out parts for airplanes. As the war drew near the airplane industry was called on for large scale output, looked around for every possible production short cut. It found one in the automotive industry, where great strides had been made in stamping out parts in hydraulic presses, even to complete bodies. Steel dies, cut to precision measurements, were locked up in the press, after which it was a simple matter to feed in sheet metal and stamp it into any form desired. Such presses could stamp out plane parts from aluminum sheeting as well.

But the cutting of these dies was an intricate and time-consuming job, particularly as the contour of any airplane part is always a curving one, and the male and female dies must fit exactly. So someone at the Douglas plant came up with a suggestion. Instead of cutting two steel dies, make up only one, and use a slab of rubber as the lower half. Rubber will take any desired shape, and being incompressible, always exerts a uniform pressure.

Goodyear development men studied this idea, found it feasible, worked it out. The plan came into wide use, and rubber again helped speed up the nation's war production.

A word should be said about Goodyear's mechanical goods advertising, utilizing the blue print copy which, in technical journals and later in magazines of general circulation, showed actual installations, reproduced in color, gave facts, costs, savings. Advertising and Goodyear Technical Men both talked to their customers in language they understood.

Burr, father of the GTM plan, who had succeeded Bailey as head of the department in 1921, retired ten years later, and was followed by Winings, who had joined the company in 1916, flown blimps during the first war, came in to Akron from the Indianapolis branch. On Winings' death in 1947, Foster, who had joined the company in 1913, became manager, with the veteran Bressler and DuPree from St. Marys as assistants. Stafford took charge of production after Campbell retired in 1938, Morse remaining head of Development.

Goodyear industrial goods were early introduced into export, starting during the first world war in Australia, where German manufacturers had previously shared the business with Dunlop and two small Australian companies. Similar outlets were established after that in England and several South American countries.

The business grew to such size in time that manufacturing units went in, in Australia in 1930, Argentina and England in 1938, Mexico and Brazil during the late war, and after the war in South Africa.

By 1948 these outside plants had almost as much vulcanizing capacity as Akron, and Goodyear hose, belting, and the rest were being used world wide.

The real growth of the department came in the depressed 1930's, as industry came to utilize the manufacturing economies of rubber in increasing measure. Sales, accounting, and other functions at Akron moved out to the factory at Plant II alongside production and development in 1938, and Industrial Rubber Goods became almost a separate operation, contact with the parent company being largely at top level.

By this time, Goodyear industrial rubber goods taken alone ranked with the ten largest industries in Ohio.

OTHER GOODYEAR PRODUCTS

In addition to tires and industrial goods, five other lines of merchandise were being manufactured when the second world war broke out. Two of these went well back into the company's history, the others started in the 1930's, with depression to give stimulus to effort.

The new products were Pliofilm, Pliolite and Airfoam, the first two coming directly out of the Goodyear laboratories.

Early in that decade, Sebrell of Research went back to studies he had made and discarded ten years earlier, since there seemed no immediate use for his findings. Renewing the effort vigorously, his men came out with a process which enabled rubber to be converted through chemical action into new materials, highly resistant to water and chemicals.

One form of these was a film, light in weight and having many of the properties of rubber, being water tight, air tight, moisture proof, flexible, strong. It was named Pliofilm.

The research men undertook to find a market for the new product themselves, with Maider heading up the effort, got results so encouraging that by the fall of 1935 a small department was organized under Mechanical Goods Sales to merchandise it, leaving Sebrell and Maider free to direct manufacturing and further research. Landefeld, Litchfield Medal winner of that year, among general line salesmen, took the assignment.

It happened that Marshall Field's big Chicago store decided about that time to close its wholesale business. Three of the men displaced as a result, Richards, Boggs, and King, had become interested in Pliofilm, were about to order it for the store, so they decided to organize their own company, try to market the new product themselves. They opened a small factory, making various articles of Pliofilm, raincoats, umbrellas, shower curtains, garment bags. The goods were colorful, attractive, the men were good merchandisers with a wide acquaintance among the department stores, the enterprise was a conspicuous success.

Other manufacturers became interested. Protex in Jersey City, who had been making shoulder coverings for women's dresses to keep them clean while hanging in the store, hurried to Akron to arrange to make these of Pliofilm, later went into card table covers and other products.

Siegel at Newark developed a process of making Pliofilm into "food savers" in various sizes which could be snapped over a dish of left-overs, keep them fresh in the ice box. Ingenious manufacturers of cosmetics and other specialties came into the field. Smart designers and stylists saw its possibilities, widened the market. Other companies developed inexpensive sealing irons so that women could make Pliofilm garments at home. The product was put on the market as yard goods and was well on its way to being a staple, when the war came in to upset plans.

In the meantime Jerosch, former export executive, had opened two Pliofilm factories in France, gave a touch of French styling to his goods, was developing important European markets. Export sent Hanson to South America to open up that market. Domestic sales expanded and substantial advertising was put behind the product.

It was felt from the beginning however that the largest potential market for Pliofilm was in the packaging field, particularly for such things as coffee, cheese, tobacco, fruits, and other food products which it would seal and keep fresh indefinitely. The initial arrangement with Richards, Boggs and King proved the perfect approach to that market.

They sold Pliofilm products in smart styles and striking colors to the women of the country, who wore and carried Pliofilm accessories to football games, boat races and out-of-doors assemblages, where practically everybody in America could see it. And those among the spectators who had any interest in packaging foods saw its possibilities and came in to buy. It would have taken much longer to break into the field under any other circumstances.

Clunan, expert in the packaging field, came on in 1936 and by 1939 Pliofilm packaging was winning prizes at national exhibits, repeating in 1940 and 1941. The pilot plant at Akron was expanded into four complete manufacturing units in 1940, then a wing was added to the new St. Marys factory for Pliofilm manufacture, and this had to be doubled and trebled within a year. Pliofilm in five months went from an output of 300 pounds a day to a couple thousand a day, and at the outbreak of the war was an important factor in the transparent packaging field, which now absorbed three-fourths of its production.

The second rubber derivative, Pliolite, set out on a less spectacular but highly useful career as a base for paints, enamels and varnishes, or as a waterproof coating for materials as widely different as wood, steel and concrete, or as a moistureproof paper coating. Pliolite, too, was well on its way when the war started, under Thies of Research, who also handled sales, since the technical men from paint, paper, and other industries were the chief buyers.

AIRFOAM

The manufacture of rubber products from latex, as it comes from the trees, grew into such substantial proportions during the 1930's that it was shipped in tank steamers directly from the Far East to the Goodyear warehouse at Baltimore and from there in tank cars to the Akron factory.

Its main use at Goodyear was in Airfoam. The latex is beaten to a froth, in machines similar to the mechanical egg beater used in the household, and by the addition of air can be increased to nine times its original volume. When it reaches the proper density it is poured into molds and vulcanized through immersing the molds in boiling water.

Airfoam was molded into mattresses, seat cushions and padding for upholstery, gave a comfort which the world had not known before, and the new product was soon being widely marketed to steamship companies, railroads, bus lines, air lines, automobile manufacturers, and to furniture houses, was well launched toward an important business future when war restrictions came in.

FLOORING OF RUBBER

Goodyear had long had the idea that rubber would make excellent flooring material. It was comfortable to walk on and would not wear out easily. An inter-locking rubber tile was brought out in 1905, came into rather wide use. After 35 years some of it is still in place in older hotels and clubs, court houses and banks, and some private homes. A section laid in the hall at the General Office at Akron appeared to be good for another 35 years.

However, the first World War, like the second one, brought restrictions on the use of rubber for all but military purposes, and rubber flooring was dropped in 1917.

Manufacture was resumed in 1922 with a new type of flooring. Mr. Litchfield returning from a trip abroad, was impressed with the activities of English and continental manufacturers in producing a rubber flooring in sheet form similar to smooth surface matting. The company was just emerging from the difficulties of depression, was looking for opportunities to improve its sales volume. Rubber was low-priced. Goodyear got into the matter anew, developed a sheet rubber which would take various colors and could be cut up and laid in blocks to form an endless variety of patterns.

Attractive in appearance, comfortable to walk on, easy to clean, rubber flooring came into wide use in luxury steamers, clubs, banks, public offices, railroad cars, buses and even occasionally in passenger airplanes.

An improved flooring brought out in 1934, which could be laid like linoleum, was opening the field of private homes when World War II broke out.

The new war would have closed down the department entirely if it had not been for the development of a special type of flooring which was resistant to sparks and the accumulation of static electricity, which was installed in many munition plants and arsenals. Another war product was a non-slip, water-proof flooring—which used no rubber and which came into wide use on the decks of naval and merchant ships.

8. Goodyear in Aeronautics

Birth of the Balloon

IN 1783, the year America won its independence, two Frenchmen,
brothers, sat before a bonfire watching the smoke curl lazily upward.

"I wonder what makes the smoke go up?" one of them said.

"Perhaps warm air is lighter and the cold air pushes it up," said the
other.

"Then if we filled a bag with hot air it would fly!" said the first.

So they built a 35 foot bag of waxed paper, attached a brazier of
charcoal underneath, released it—and watched it mount into the air.

Aeronautics was born.

Word of this feat spread fast and far across France, reached the
court, the Army, scientific men. They must stage another flight, in Paris.
So the Montgolier's next balloon took off from the courtyard at Ver-
sailles. Everyone in France who could get close enough saw it with his
own eyes. But a young dandy attached to the court took a pinch of snuff.

"After all, though," he said, "what good is it?"

The American ambassador caught it up, with a reply that has come down through history.

"Of what use is a baby?" said Benjamin Franklin.

One hundred and twenty years later another pair of brothers, Americans this time, took off from a lonesome sand dune near Kitty Hawk, North Carolina, with a kite-shaped contrivance they called the aeroplane.

Out of these two episodes came the B-29's, the great Zeppelins and the sub-hunting blimps of World War II.

The Goodyear company has played a fairly important part in the development of the airplane, but is better known for its work in the field of lighter-than-air. That started with a memorable trip to Paris in 1910.

With an ancestry of Clipper ship captains and ship builders, and vacations divided between sailboats and shipyards, P. W. Litchfield grew up with salt water in his veins. He had hesitated quite a bit in 1900 about moving as far inland as Akron, but would make up for it by taking an ocean voyage whenever he could. The business he went into would permit that if it grew big enough, became international.

He had made his first trip abroad in 1900, working his passage on a cattle boat as many adventure-seeking young men did then, had gone over again in 1906. The company was in better shape by 1910, could afford a modest expense account, and there were business reasons for going.

The French and English had contributed important ideas to the early automobile—and tires—and it was well for an American company to keep in touch with what went on. One idea Litchfield got on his first trip, that of flexibility in tires, to absorb stresses rather than fight them, was worth to the company many times the cost of the trip. He had brought other ideas and processes back on the later trips.

He was 35 by now, had the title of factory manager. William Stephens, a seasoned production man by this time and his successor as superintendent, went along. One thing he particularly wanted to look into was aeronautics. He had brought out an airplane tire the year before but wanted to see what ideas they had in Europe.

Though America had been the birth place of the airplane, the Wright brothers and Glenn Curtiss had had more encouragement- abroad than at home. In France particularly, aeronautics had appealed to men's imagination. The two stopped over at a small air meet in Wolverhampton, England, where Goodyear would build a factory 18 years later. The planes had to wait until the wind died down at sunset before daring to take off. They went on from there to a much bigger meet at Paris.

Aviation interested Litchfield for a different reason than perhaps any other man in the world. Looking at it as an engineer, he realized that the airplane was destined to achieve great things for the reason that the air offered less resistance to a plane (so could get along on less horse power) than the water did to a steamship, or broken terrain did to anything which had to be dragged over the ground.

The 1910 airplane was a pretty crude thing, but engines and structures can always be improved. This was something his company should look into.

There was no dearth of interest in France. Farman, Bleriot, Paulhan, and Graham-White, an Englishman, were already famous names, and Santos-Dumont, wealthy young Brazilian who had gone to Paris to build dirigibles, was now building airplanes as well. Count Zeppelin in Germany had organized a passenger Zeppelin line to carry passengers over Central Europe. Two dirigible companies had been organized in France, and a third in Germany. A plane and an airship had flown the English Channel, breaching waters that had resisted invasion since William the Conqueror.

The young American watched everything, took notes, saw possibilities for a rubber company—wings and tires for the planes, the great bags for airships. He made inquiries, learned that the North British Rubber Company at Edinburgh had developed an excellent process of spreading rubber over fabric, made his way there.

European manufacturers were generally close-mouthed, discouraged visitors—though were less secretive in the case of Americans, whom they did not regard as competitors. The doors at Edinburgh were thrown open to Litchfield and Stephens. They had something the British very much wanted, the sensational new Straight Side tire.

Litchfield spent much of his time in the spreader room, finally went to the manager.

"I would like to buy that machine," he said.

"Very well," said the manager. "We will order one for you today and ask them to expedite it."

"No," said Litchfield. "I want that machine itself. I would like it torn down, packed and shipped to Akron on the first boat. How much would it cost?"

"It will cost you nothing," said the manager, "except the full specifications for the Straight Side tire."

"Come into the office," said Litchfield. "We will draw up the papers."
Then he stopped.

"Another thing," he said, "I want those two men who are running
the machine also."

The manager smiled. "They are not for sale," he said, "but you may
talk to them."

The two operators, Ferguson and Aikman, Scotsmen, were startled to
have the visitor walk over, ask them if they would like to go to America. They talked it over between themselves, then with their families,
accepted.

Aikman retired last year at Akron after more than 50 years in the
industry, and Ferguson remained in the spreader room until his death
in the same year.

This was Goodyear's entry into aeronautics.

In going into the field Litchfield followed the same course as he did
with the Development Department. There were no aeronautical engineers, so he picked two promising young men, Preston from M.I.T. and
Upson from Stephens Tech, turned them loose to find out everything
they could about it. Stadelman assigned his most promising salesman,
Rockhill, to this field.

Airplane wings at that time used rubberized fabric to cover the framework, and the new spreading machine quickly paid for itself, because
it produced a taut fabric which would not flutter in the wind, cut down
air resistance, increased speed.

The Wright brothers adopted the Goodyear fabric that same summer,
gave the company an order the following year for 18,000 square yards.
Atwood and Rogers used it in setting flight records, and nine out of the
ten entries in a national meet in Chicago in 1911 used it. In a letter to
the field that year, Rockhill made quite a point of the fact that an Army
plane, making a forced landing in a river in the Southwest, had been
fished out and put back in commission, the Goodyear wings being as
good as ever after they dried out. In 1913 it was specified as standard
equipment for all Army and Navy planes. A doped fabric came in later
however to supplant rubberized fabric and after that metal wings.

Much more spectacular, however, were the activities in lighter-than-
air. Upson and Preston built a balloon, arranged to use the rather heavy
artificial gas from the gas company's plant in the valley below the
North Hill Viaduct, made a number of flights, picked up what information they could get—which was precious little.

There were airship companies in France, Germany and England, but
none in America. What development there was, was done by individuals.

Roy Knabenshue and Horace Wild gave flying exhibitions at state fairs. Major Tom Baldwin, who had made balloon ascensions all over the United States and Europe, built his first dirigible in 1904 to fly at the St. Louis Fair, built an airship for the Army. Walter Wellman, an American journalist, had tried to reach the North Pole with a free balloon and to cross the Atlantic by dirigible in 1910.

Vaniman, Wellman's engineer, carried on, gave Goodyear an order in 1911 for a 400,000 cubic foot balloon section, the largest ever built up to that time. The balloon room was expanded and Upson and his staff were soon making minute calculations, drawing curious mathematical curves for the patterns of the balloon.

After the fabric had been rubberized and cut to shape, there was no little speculation as to whether the patterns would fit. Visitors saw a great mass of cloth on the floor being cemented together and double-taped at the seams. When this was inflated, would it have wrinkles where the pattern did not quite fit, or an overlap at the end, or a great gap? The bag when completed and inflated however, did fit, and represented no small achievement for the young department.

Vaniman built a hangar at Atlantic City, assembled the ship there, made his first test flight in November, and several flights in the area in the next few months. But he delayed his departure for Europe. The public grew skeptical and began to ask whether he ever intended to cross the Atlantic. There are indications that Vaniman had discovered design weaknesses in his ship during the test flights, and was working on a new design, but that public opinion forced him to attempt a crossing anyway.

Finally, however, on July 2, 1912, he started. The flight lasted less than 15 minutes. While still plainly visible to thousands of spectators, the ship burst into flames at 500 feet and fell into the ocean, killing Vaniman and four of his men. While the cause of the accident was never definitely ascertained, it is believed that leaking hydrogen gas was set fire by sparks from the engine. Fortunately Preston, who had supervised the assembly of the balloon section and taken part in the test flights, was not aboard when the final flight was made.

This inauspicious beginning was to be counteracted to some degree in the following year, when Upson and Preston entered a Goodyear balloon in the James Gordon Bennett cup race. A brief story of that then classic international contest will be appropriate.

James Gordon Bennett, publisher of The New York Herald, spending his later years in Paris, had noted a growing interest in ballooning. Using inexpensive coal gas from manufacturing plants, many sportsmen went for a week-end trip in their own balloons, much as a later generation might go for a motor trip.

So Bennett in 1906 proposed an international race, put up a silver trophy and substantial money prizes. France, Belgium, Germany, Switzerland sent in one or more entries. America had no entry, as little ballooning was done in this country. About two months before the race, however, F. S. Lahm, retired American business man from Canton, Ohio, was having lunch with friends in Paris. He had been European manager for an American typewriter company, had a winter home in Paris, spent his summers at Turkeyfoot Lake, near Akron. He was upwards of 60.

At the lunch the subject of the race came up, and someone bantered the American because his country was not taking part. That nettled the older man. He left the table, filed an entry for America that same day, purchased a balloon and hired a man to teach him to fly it. The word got back to the States and his son, Lt. Frank P. Lahm, a young Army officer, heard about it, got leave of absence, hurried to Paris, persuaded his father to let him take the balloon, went out and won the race, over sixteen rivals. Lt. Lahm later became a major general and assistant chief of the Air Corps.

The victory over the more experienced European pilots was unexpected and created great enthusiasm in this country. The second race was held in the United States. After that the cup went to Germany, to Switzerland, back to America, to Germany, then to France. The 1913 race, in which the Goodyear men were entered, started from the Tuilleries Gardens in Paris, with half a million people attending.

The Goodyear men, experts in gas-tight fabrics by now, had built their balloon with great care. They had also been studying meteorology, particularly the weather conditions over France.

The race started with an easterly wind that carried all the balloons across France toward the ocean. As the coast line loomed up ahead, one balloon after another landed, but the Americans went on out over the Atlantic, convinced that they would encounter a wind shift that would carry them back over land. Their analysis of the weather proved correct. They landed in England and won the race.

The outbreak of war in Europe, however, postponed further international competition, and set military men to planning as to how aircraft could be utilized as new weapons of warfare.

Though the American government had shown little interest in lighter-than-air, and not too much in heavier-than-air, the Germans had gone a long way with their big Zeppelins, as had the French and British with the smaller blimps, which could cross the English Channel.

With war under way, Germany sent the Zeppelins on raids over London, and the Allied nations used the smaller blimps to battle the submarines—since they could fly low and slowly, see deep under the water, hover over suspect areas—and both sides began furiously building observation balloons, sausage-shaped affairs, anchored them to long cables, used them to direct artillery fire and to observe enemy movements.

Upson and the others at Akron watched these developments with great interest. Cooper, an ingenious West Virginian, who was a member of the first Flying Squadron, was assigned to the balloon room, and quickly developed a knack of cutting, stitching and taping odd patterns of rubberized fabric and coming out with a perfectly shaped balloon.

The United States Army ordered a few observation balloons in 1916, and Goodyear, as the only company with any experience in this field, went to work. Glenn Martin had a small flying field on the Cleveland lake front, and coal gas could be had from factories in the neighborhood, so the first balloons were tested there. This arrangement was inconvenient and Goodyear, in acquiring property at Wingfoot Lake, 12 miles from the plant, to get an additional water supply, bought 720 acres of land alongside to provide room for a flying field.

The Navy, too, had been watching the developments overseas and as early as 1915, Comdr. J. C. Hunsaker, chief aircraft constructor, and Donald Douglas, his assistant, were instructed to develop a design for a dirigible. Lieut. (later Admiral) J. H. Towers, Naval attache in Europe, brought in considerable information in 1916, and a design was completed for an airship similar to the British type B.

But relations with Germany were becoming strained, and on February 3, 1917, before the design had left the drafting board, Josephus Daniels, Secretary of the Navy, ordered construction started immediately on 16 blimps.

The Navy, though taken by surprise, wasted no time, called in men from several industries. The early blimps were not too complicated a job. It was merely a matter of suspending a car and engine under the gas bag, well under it to keep sparks away from the lifting gas, hydrogen, which was highly inflammable. An airplane fuselage would do, so Curtiss built the early ones, open cockpit cars with a windshield in front. There were no landing wheels, just a pneumatic bumper bag underneath to take the shock of landing.

The important job was the gas bag, and only Goodyear and a company in Connecticut had had any experience with this.

Plans laid, the Navy told Goodyear not to wait for official word but to start at once on an assembly hangar, shops and a plant to manufacture hydrogen.

To build a hangar larger than any previously erected was no small task, but State's men were equal to the job, and ground was broken late in 1917—though that was an unusually severe winter. The formal order came through on March 14th, Goodyear to build nine ships, Goodrich five, the Connecticut company two.

The first Goodyear ship was finished before the hangar was ready, so late in May it was assembled in a large shed in a Chicago amusement park. Kraft, former motorcycle racer with a gift for mechanics, had charge of assembly.

The trial flights were successful, so he and Upson set off for Akron at midnight on May 29th, landed in a meadow ten miles from Akron at noon the next day, the oil having run out. The Navy issued a letter of commendation:

"The flight (it stated) was one of the longest made by a small non-rigid, and remarkable as a maiden flight of a new airship designed by a designer of absolutely no airship experience, and built in two months by a firm without previous modern airship experience. What is still more remarkable is that Upson was not an airship pilot, there being no one in the country to teach him. He was, however, an experienced balloonist, winner of the James Gordon Bennett Cup race, and had a thorough engineering appreciation of how the ship was to function."

The Navy started building airship stations along the coast, at Chatham, Mass., Montauk Point and Rockaway Beach, New York, Cape May, New Jersey, Hampton Roads, Virginia, and at Pensacola and Key West, Florida. The company's flying field at Wingfoot Lake was taken over as a Naval training station.

Now Army and Navy cadets in olive drab and forest green began pouring into Akron from ground schools at Cornell and M.I.T. to take flying instructions, with Goodyear men acting as instructors. Akron, far in the interior, was now a Navy base.

We might take out time for a story. Comdr. Maxfield, first commanding officer, made a good impression at Wingfoot Lake, except for two things. He wore a wrist watch and he smoked cigarets. Mechanics and riggers shook their heads. Wrist watches were worn by women, and cigarets belonged in the pool room. Men smoked cigars or pipes—or chewed tobacco. But on his first Sunday morning the new skipper came out of his quarters in bathrobe and slippers, though it was sub-zero weather, walked to the end of the dock, dived into the icy water, took

Kite balloons and sharp-pointed blimps of World War I, and (below) a closeup of a primitive blimp fuselage, suspended well below the bag for safety against hydrogen.

a rubdown and returned to his quarters. The Lake revised its opinion.

Maxfield, a gallant officer, was killed in the British dirigible ZR-2 after the war. A plaque in Memorial Rock near the pier carries his name and that of other Wingfoot-trained Naval officers who lost their lives in aviation.

Practically all of the Navy's early lighter-than-air men took their training at Wingfoot, McCrary, Hoyt, Coil, Landsdowne, Weyerbacher, Pennoyer, Norfleet, Peck, Barnaby, Anderson and Hancock. Among the cadets were a number who returned after the war to work for Goodyear, Lohmann of the sales manager's office, Post of Export, Coe of manufactures' sales, Winings of mechanical goods, Collins of Kelly-Springfield. Lange and Sewell, later to pilot Goodyear blimps, joined the Navy during this period, saw anti-submarine service at Atlantic stations.

Upson and Kraft acted as the first instructors, broke in other men and returned to the drafting room. Boettner, all-American football player, became chief instructor, with Brannigan and Maranville, natural flyers with a mechanical bent, Van Orman, later winner of many James Gordon Bennett balloon races, Wollam, ingenious mechanic, and others. Yolton, a test car driver, was at Indianapolis installing the first set of Straight Side cords ever used in a 500-mile race on Ralph de Palma's Packard when he got orders to report at Wingfoot Lake. Eddie Rickenbacher, who was entered in the race, got word the same hour to report for war duty.

Wingfoot Lake saw plenty of action in World War I.

The airships cruised lazily through the air like great silver fish; the balloons left at dawn or at sunset, quickly becoming a speck in the sky, then disappearing; the "kites" swayed at the end of a half mile of cable, or churned in high winds, or writhed on the ground during deflation like wounded elephants.

Wingfoot Lake became the Kitty Hawk of lighter-than-air. There were fast flights ahead of gathering storms, dodging the lightning; balloon flights with the drag rope trailing over the mountains like a giant snake, now catching on a tree, snapping like a great whip, sometimes pulling down a farmer's chimney or turning over an outhouse. There were hand landings, with a quick tug at the rip panel in the nick of time. There were landings in water. There were night flights, moonlight flights under an opal sky, flights where men became becalmed and floated in one spot for hours. Plenty of mishaps, ships wrecked in trees or damaged in landing as was to be expected with scores of men to be trained quickly. But in all war time flying at Wingfoot, there was never a serious accident, not a single casualty.

Goodyear engineers and the Navy worked to lessen wind resistance to the dirigible, increase the stability of the anchored kite balloons. As a new type was ordered, the ingenious Cooper had a trick of building the first one in a secret room somewhere, working day and night to complete it before the engineers had their blue prints out—again the rivalry between the practical men and the technical men which contributed much to Goodyear progress.

By the time Goodyear had delivered the last of its Type B airships in June, 1918, the Navy had developed the new Type C, of 170,000 cubic feet, large enough to carry depth charges and additional fuel to increase its range. Two engines mounted on outriggers, drove it at 60 miles per hour, faster than any airship except the Zeppelin. Goodyear shared with Goodrich a contract for 30 of the new ships, and both were well under way on this when the Armistice came. Then the order was cut from 30 to 10, and Wingfoot Lake was turned back to the company.

The C-5, one of the ships Goodyear built under this final contract, might, with a little luck, have been the first aircraft to cross the Atlantic. For out of a suggestion, shortly after the war ended, from Wollam of Goodyear and Lt. Bauch of the Navy (though they were not permitted to carry out the plan themselves), this ship made the 1400 mile flight from Montauk Point, New York, to St. John's, Newfoundland, in 24 hours, and was ready to set off on the second leg of the trip to Ireland, 1800 miles off, when a "nor'easter" carried it out of the hands of the ground crew, and out over the Atlantic. With a modern mooring mast, the feat should have been fairly easy, and a non-rigid airship have beaten all its rivals. Blimps would have to wait until the next war before crossing the ocean.

None of the Goodyear-built airships saw foreign service, were used in coastal defense. Even so there were not nearly enough of them. The program of building ships, bases, and training crews had started too late to do even that job adequately over our long coast line.

Fortunately the U-boats found the fishing better closer at home in the early part of the war, and their range was too short to make an overseas operation practical until the spring of 1918. Then six of them invaded American and Canadian waters, laying mines and launching torpedos and, despite the efforts of destroyers, seaplanes and the relatively few blimps, sank 100 ships, mostly merchantmen, in six months.

The British and French had started building non-rigid airships long before, and these put up a stout defense against German undersea boats, covered 1,500,000 miles of patrol—almost as many as the big Zeppelins—sighted 49 submarines and sank 27 of them. Admiral Moffett told Congress that no surface ship escorted by a blimp was ever successfully attacked by submarine during the entire war.

American airship pilots, of whom 170 took their training at Wing-foot Lake, saw more action than their ships. Maxfield took command of the big station at Pamboeuf, France, and his men took over French-built ships, put in more air hours than any other airship squadron.

Goodyear built more than 900 balloons during the war, and these were shipped abroad in large numbers. The balloon room built up to a force of 2800 men and girls and at the peak was turning out more balloons in a month than France, the birthplace of the balloon, did in four years.

The Edinburgh spreader machine paid off.

Balloon Racing

Balloon racing was resumed in 1919, with Goodyear going back in, though this might seem a far cry from usual business activities. It was the only rubber company to go into it.

However, the company felt that by building and flying balloons it might pick up some ideas it could adapt to the dirigible—and that this would furnish a useful training as well to the pilots who would be needed. After all, the airship is merely a balloon with engines and steering gear on it, a large vessel whose lift varies with temperature, barometric pressure and altitude. Men must learn to handle such craft in the air, and ballooning has long been the indispensable primary training for airship pilots. If an airship's engines fail, it can still be flown as a free balloon, as Lt. Comdr. (later Admiral) C. E. Rosendahl did at the time of the Shenandoah disaster. Moreover the balloon furnishes a perfect mirror of meteorological conditions aloft, of wind directions and velocities. No one had realized the full force of vertical air currents prior to the 1928 balloon race.

With balloon racing resumed in 1920, Upson, the 1913 James Gordon Bennett winner, won the first national race, with Van Orman as his aide, one of six flights which covered more than 1000 miles distance, travelling from St. Louis deep into Quebec. Upson won again in 1921, then Van Orman, who succeeded Upson as chief balloon pilot after the latter left the company, went out to win four national and three international races in this country and Europe in the next several years.

While there were a number of sportsmen pilots in the early races, the competition narrowed down finally to Army, Navy and Goodyear. A private company had some advantage in continuity of personnel, for the Army was trying to spread balloon and blimp training among a large number of officers, and Navy men had to alternate sea duty with that ashore. Consequently in the national races after the war, Goodyear scored eight victories in 16 years, the Army four, Navy three and Honeywell, an independent, one in 1920. The Litchfield Cup put up as the American trophy in 1924 came back to Akron with three successive victories, and a second cup had to be offered. Goodyear built most of the balloons used in the national races.

A balloon race is an adventure to appeal to high spirited men, and ballooning furnished four major generals and one rear admiral to the armed forces. The army pilots included the then Major O. O. Westover, who won the 1922 race and later became chief of the Air Services, Major W. E. Kepner who succeeded Doolittle in command of the 8th Air Force in Europe, Captain O. A. Anderson who made the record stratosphere flight in 1925, and was Doolittle's Chief of Staff, and Lt. U. G. Ent, who led the Ploesti raid. The leading Navy balloonist was Lt. Comdr., later Admiral, T. G. W. Settle who also made a record stratosphere flight. It was a distinguished company of men who came into Akron during the balloon racing years.

Ballooning was an older and more popular sport in Europe than in this country, and England, France, Germany, Italy, Belgium usually entered teams. But in the 15 international races after 1920, America won six, Van Orman taking three, Kepner, Settle and Hill, an independent, one each.

Balloon racing furnished many thrilling stories, as no pilot when he set out had more than a very general idea as to where he was to land or what perils might wait along the way. He matched his wits against the unseen forces of the wind. A few of the adventures encountered by Goodyear pilots should be included in this narrative.

In the international race of 1925 out of Brussels, Van Orman lost out by a peculiar turn of fate. The balloon has no motive power. It goes with the wind. No balloon pilot can control the direction of his flight. He can only drop ballast when he wants to rise, release gas when he wants to come down. However, ballooning is still not a matter of chance. The trick is to diagnose the weather conditions, and maneuver, with minimum loss of ballast, to altitudes where wind directions and velocities are most favorable. A skillful balloonist will stall for time when a storm is ahead, get out his oxygen tank and ride at 25,000 feet for hours if favorable winds lie at that level. Success in ballooning is based on good equipment, knowledge of weather, endurance, and luck. Van Orman and C. K. Wollam, his aide that year, had three of these four requisites.

The wind that afternoon was NNW, carrying the balloon south along the coast of France. Most of the contestants sat down as they came to the ocean. The Belgium Demuyter, who had won the previous year's race, landed at Brest. There was one more peninsula ahead, but Van Orman and Wollam calculating their course carefully, decided that they could make it. However, just before they reached the cape the wind shifted slightly seaward and they missed it. There was still a chance that they could make an island off the coast, but the wind continued to swing offshore and they missed it by half a mile. The Bay of Biscay was in front of them, the next land ahead was Brazil.

"Get out your radio set," suggested Wollam. "We might get some dance music from the Savoy Hotel in London."

They were passing out of the steamer lane by now and no chance of being carried back toward Spain. Night came on.

"No use both of us staying awake," suggested Wollam. "You take a nap. I'll stand the first watch."

Van Orman made himself as comfortable as he could in the bottom of the basket, was awakened at midnight.

"Lights ahead," shouted Wollam.

Sure enough a freighter lay below heading directly for them.

Van Orman caught up his flashlight, began signalling a message in Morse code. Fortunately the lookout was awake and on the alert, though doubtless puzzled. Almost immediately the ship's lights blinked off and on in reply.

Van Orman signalled asking the ship to continue on course but at reduced speed, valved the balloon down almost to the water, threw a sea anchor out to check its speed. The sea was a bit choppy, and as the balloon approached the ship the deck alternately rose above and fell below the level of the basket. By good luck and nice timing the two pilots sent their basket across the ship's rail, landed squarely on deck, pulled the rip cord releasing the gas, stepped out safe and dry shod in mid-ocean. The boat, a slow freighter loaded with onions, landed the men days later at Rotterdam. Since the rules made no provision for landing on a boat, Van Orman lost out.

Two Goodyear teams took part in the 1926 race out of Antwerp, but a curious accident put one out of the race. The balloons took off in a storm, and one piloted by Boettner and Maxson, heavy with sleet and rain, was caught in a down gust, struck the ground near the Dutch border just as Maxson was leaning over to dump ballast. He was catapulted out, but landed unhurt, while the balloon, relieved of his weight, skyrocketed, with Boettner hanging on the valve rope to check its ascent. Since the rules require that both pilot and aide remain aboard throughout the race, Boettner landed soon after.

Van Orman and Morton were more fortunate that year. They had to sacrifice considerable ballast to counteract the rain and sleet on their bag, could not see the ground, had little idea where they were. Van Orman got out his radio, picked up two stations, Madrid and Hamburg. Fixing his direction from each city, he made a rough projection on the map, concluded he must be near Bremen. Next he picked up Bremen, found he was almost over it. This gave him his speed and the direction in which he was travelling, so he decided to take a chance and cross the North Sea. Morning found him over Sweden, the winner of the race. None of the other contestants had attempted to cross the water. Radio found a place for itself that day in aeronautics.

The national race of 1928 started from Pittsburgh and brought Goodyear its first casualty—and offered striking testimony to the service the free balloon can offer to the safety of flight.

An electrical storm had been threatening during the afternoon, and broke within a half hour after the contestants took off, resulting in violent vertical currents which tossed the bags up and down like a juggler might, sending them to great heights and down again. Three balloons were struck by lightning.

Cooper of the balloon room was flying with Wollam, and their balloon was caught in a vertical up-current, raced skyward, the gas expanding with the altitude, roaring out of the appendix above their heads. At 8000 feet lightning struck the bag and set it afire. It also passed down the rigging through Cooper's body, left him disabled but conscious.

Wollam pulled the rip cord, releasing all the gas and the fire went out. But the balloon did not drop like a plumb bob. In building the bag, Cooper, who was always experimenting, had attached rings around it at the equator, attached the net to them. In this emergency the net held and the fabric partially parachuted within, checking their descent.

Wollam got out the parachutes, tried to fasten one on Cooper and hoist him over the side. But Cooper was 40 pounds heavier, and one arm and both legs were disabled.

"Take your chute and get out," Cooper suggested. "That will lighten the load and give me a better chance when we hit."

The balloon was then at 2500 feet. Wollam took a half hitch of the parachute around his chest, shook hands with Cooper, climbed overboard. The balloon fell faster than the parachute, and Cooper from the basket saw his companion rise upward in slow circles over his head. Fortunately, in landing, the balloon struck the slanting roof of a barn and skidded down the row of poles which were leaning against it. It hit the ground with such force that the pneumatic pontoons on the bottom split from end to end and the radio, by a quirk, bounded high in the air and landed on Cooper's chest, cracking four ribs and breaking his one good arm. Nevertheless, he was alive and still conscious, and directed the efforts of the rescue party, sent a car out to find Wollam, who had landed two miles away, spent a few months in the hospital, recovered in time to build the world's largest stratosphere balloon and all the gas cells for the Akron and Macon.

Two other balloons were hit. One piloted by Van Orman and Morton had twice been driven skyward to 12,000 feet, started up a third time, had reached an altitude of 3000 feet when the lightning struck. It caused an explosion which destroyed most of the fabric, did not leave enough to act as a parachute. In any event Morton had been instantly killed and Van Orman knocked unconscious. The wrecked balloon dropped at a terrific speed. Despite all this, Van Orman came to six hours later, tangled in the rigging of the balloon, unhurt except for a broken ankle. His pontoons, too, had split from end to end, which probably saved his life. He had to watch the International Race that fall from the side lines, but was back in the field the following year.

An Army balloon piloted by Lieut. (later General) Ent, was hit by lightning at 1800 feet, the aide being killed and the balloon set on fire. By quick action on Ent's part the balloon was landed without further damage.

Three pilots, Kepner of the Army, Settle of the Navy and Palmer of Goodyear fought their way out of the storm, crossed the mountains during the night, landed drenched and shivering on the Atlantic coast at daybreak.

Kepner, the winner, had one final thrilling experience as he emerged from the storm area. His balloon was being driven down a valley at the speed of an express train when high tension wires loomed up ahead with no chance to get over or under. The wires caught the balloon just above the load ring, a few feet below the hydrogen gas. For a moment the balloon remained poised, then a second blast broke the lines and freed the craft, and they emerged shortly into calmer weather.

Stratosphere balloon which ascended to record height of 14 miles (left), and (below) Van Orman taking off in racing balloon. Pontoons were forerunners of the life raft.

Wingfoot Lake, Kitty Hawk of lighter-than-air, was training field for men and experimental station for ships in two wars. Hangar was doubled in size for War II.

The 1933 International Race, starting from Chicago in connection with the World's Fair, demonstrated anew the vagaries of the wind.

Van Orman and Trotter for Goodyear, Settle and Kendall for the Navy constituted the American team. The race got away ahead of a storm which forced most of the contestants down. The three remaining ones sought to maneuver around it, followed divergent courses. Settle kept to the south, trailing his dragrope the length of Lake Ontario to check his speed, let the storm pass him, then caught a wind that carried him across New England, landing near New Haven, after a 52 hour flight for a new duration record. A Polish balloon took a middle course, made a fast flight ahead of the storm, landed within 24 hours northeast of Quebec, the winner by nearly 100 miles margin.

Van Orman and Trotter were not heard from until a week later. They had swung north of the storm, landed deep in the Canadian north woods. After travelling on foot for days, they came to a telephone line. Knowing that with a break in the service repair men would be sent out, they chopped down a pole, and in time met the repair crew and made their way back safely, their experience paralleling that of two other American balloonists, Hawley and Post, 20 years earlier.

The victory of the Polish team took the 1934 International Race to that country, whose flyers proceeded to repeat for three years in succession—and wrote finis to international balloon racing.

Mr. Bennett had long since died and his newspaper had been merged into the Herald Tribune. European flyers found it hard to finance the trip to the United States, and the races in Europe ran into difficulties as the balloons crossed national boundary lines. Competition in this country had narrowed to the Navy and Goodyear, as the Army discontinued ballooning with its airship program. The final national race was held out of Denver in 1936, the Goodyear team, Trotter and Smith, winning.

Stratosphere Balloons

Balloons invaded the stratosphere during this period. Planes had reached an altitude of 40,000 feet. World War Zeppelins had flown at 25,000 feet to get out of the range of anti-aircraft guns and searchlights—and British airplanes. Captain Hawthorne Gray, Army flier, made new altitude records in 1927 using a conventional racing balloon and open basket, depending on oxygen for respiration. On his first flight he became unconscious at 37,000 feet, coming to just before landing. On his second he reached an altitude of 42,470 feet, but too rapid a descent forced him to jump in a parachute. Undeterred he made a third attempt, reached a similar altitude, but this time the failure of his oxygen supply cost him his life.

In 1932 August Piccard, a Belgian scientist, startled the world by ascending into the stratosphere from Switzerland, using a sealed metal ball as the gondola for his balloon.

An American flight was organized in Chicago the following year, and Goodyear was given a contract to build a 600,000 cubic foot balloon, substantially larger than Piccard's. Lt. Comdr. T. G. W. Settle, U. S. Navy, was the pilot. The first attempt failed due to a valve sticking open, but Settle made a successful landing, salvaged his balloon, tried again that fall at Akron, and this time rose to a height of 61,237 feet, a new official world's record. Settle's plans had aroused the interest of the scientific world and he carried many scientific instruments with him.

The stratosphere, which begins at an altitude of 35,000 feet in the latitude of Ohio, being lower at the poles and higher at the equator, is uninfluenced by conditions on the earth, an area without thunder storms or clouds, with temperatures of 60 degrees below zero and lower. Airplane men were interested in the possibility of flying sealed ships through the stratosphere at speeds previously impossible, taking advantage of the diminished air resistance. The scientists had many questions to ask, particularly in the field of cosmic rays.

A second expedition was organized under the auspices of the U. S. Army and The National Geographic Society, ordered a balloon from Goodyear five times as large as Settle's, with a gas capacity of 3,000,000 feet. Major Kepner and Captains A. W. Stevens and O. A. Anderson were assigned to flight. Dr. Arnstein, chief airship designer, turned his staff loose on a project involving many new factors. Cooper's men spent a busy three months cutting acres of rubberized fabric, cementing and taping it into a huge ball.

The army fliers tried three times before success crowned their efforts. A word about the first mishap is appropriate. At 60,000 feet gas expands to 15 times its sea level volume, consequently the balloon was inflated only to 1/15 of its capacity at the outset and would round out completely only when it reached pressure height. During inflation the gas went to the top of the balloon, being lighter than the air, leaving the lower part of the bag sucked in and crumpled against itself. Apparently adhesions formed in that section and the expansion of the gas as the balloon neared the 60,000-foot mark ripped a great rent in the

bag. Kepner gave immediate orders to descend, but as the balloon was
within 5000 feet of the ground enough air had become mixed with the
hydrogen as to bring about an explosion, and the metal ball losing the
lifting force of the balloon, sped toward the earth. The army officers
took off in parachutes, landing without injury.

A second balloon, The Explorer II, also built by Goodyear, was somewhat larger, in fact almost exactly the size of the Graf Zeppelin, which
was 3,700,000 cubic feet. It had valves at the top, and since the pilot was
100 yards below in the gondola, compressed air was used to force them
open. It had two catenary bands around its middle, one toward the top
where the handling lines were attached while the balloon was being
inflated, the other toward the bottom, to hold the car.

Every balloon has an appendix at the bottom, an open neck through
which the gas can escape as its volume expands, the heavier air acting
as a cork. The Explorer II would not need an appendix until the balloon
was completely filled, but needed three thereafter, each seven feet in
diameter. Captain Stevens, who was in command on the second flight,
described afterward the sensation he got when the central appendix
opened at 65,000 feet and, through the porthole atop the gondola he
could see clear to the top of the balloon. The sun was shining brightly,
lighting up the inside of the great ball, which only he and Anderson, of
all the people in the world, would ever see as a complete sphere. From
Stevens' position the reinforcing tapes at the seams seemed like the lines
of longitude and latitude on the globe. There was a circular thermome-
ter suspended near the top to enable the pilot to know the temperature
of the gas, but Anderson had to use his binoculars to read it. The temperature was four degrees below zero. Due to the sun's rays, it was 74
degrees warmer inside the balloon than outside.

The balloon could lift a load of nine tons, of which one full ton was
scientific instruments. The ballast was largely carried outside, but it
could be released from inside, could in emergency be shot out with
dynamite. This was fortunate, for as the balloon rose on the morning
of November 11, 1935, from a great natural bowl in South Dakota, a
down current caught it as it cleared the rim, pushed it over toward the
cliff. Anderson, experienced in handling lighter-than-aircraft, cut a
switch, tripped 750 pounds of lead shot in three seconds, spraying it
harmlessly over the crowd below, sent the balloon into ascent again.

Every balloon has a rip panel, a section of cloth which can be ripped
out in emergency, releasing all the gas at one time. But the ordinary
racing balloon is only about one-fiftieth the size of the Explorer II, and
a new type panel had to be designed for it. This was a flexible steel

wire around the top so that Anderson could virtually tear the top off the balloon as one does with a soft-boiled egg.

This too turned out to be advantageous, for as he brought the huge bag in for its landing, under as perfect control as one would drive an automobile, he let out his drag rope, and moving along within a few feet of the ground, called out to the spectators who were following him in automobiles to take hold of it. If 20 men had taken hold, they could have held the balloon for normal deflation through the valves. One man did seize the rope but quickly let go. Everyone seemed to be afraid of this snake-like hemp moving across the Dakota prairie. Anderson finally had to pull the rip cord, practically decapitating his balloon, otherwise the gondola would have been dragged along the ground, perhaps have damaged some of the instruments. As it was, the gondola merely rolled over on its side and lay still, the entire balloon emptying itself of gas and falling inert to the ground in less than five seconds.

The flight was an entire success, reaching an official elevation of 72,395 feet, the highest point ever reached by man, and bringing back enough scientific data to keep the government and university laboratories busy for months.

The several stratosphere flights add a real chapter to the story of adventure and scientific exploration, and Arnstein's designers and those of the Army, together with the scientists from the Bureau of Standards and the National Geographic Society and Cooper's men in the balloon room, shared the credit.

Military Airships Between Wars

World War I left the various nations well impressed with the military and commercial possibilities of aircraft.

The exploits of Rickenbacher, Luke, Guynemer, Fonck, Bishop, Richthofen and the Lafayette Escadrille had intrigued the imagination of the public.

The awesome Zeppelins lost some of their effectiveness toward the end of the war as the crude anti-aircraft guns and higher-ranging planes forced them to less effective higher altitudes, but they had kept large areas over England blacked out for hours during the period of the raids, paralyzing production and transportation, and had kept troops in England for home defense who were badly needed in France.

Also the little blimps, operating over the English Channel had given good account of themselves against submarines.

England began building dirigibles while the war was still on, and its R-34 was the first aircraft to cross the Atlantic in both directions. America started off with the Shenandoah in 1919, ordered a ship from England, and acquired a third, the Los Angeles, from Germany. This country also continued to build the smaller airships.

Lighter-than-aircraft fell into three classes:

One. Non-rigids, developed largely by the British and French. These had no internal framework, kept their shape only through the pressure of the lifting gas. The British, apt at nicknames, gave them the name "blimps," since non-rigids were called "limp type" as distinguished from the German *rigid* airships, and the Type B, limp, made quite a reputation. The United States Navy accepted the word officially in World War II.

Two. Semi-rigids, largely developed by Italy, larger in size and with a metal keel extending the length of the envelope, with attachment points at the stern for fins and rudders, and in front for a metal nose cone.

Three. Rigid or Zeppelin type, often called dirigibles (though all airships are dirigible or directable, as distinguished from the free balloon which merely floats with the wind), which has a complete metal framework, the lifting gas being carried in a dozen or more separate cells inside the hull.

The Joint Board of the two services turned the development of non-rigids and semi-rigids over to the Army, rigid ships to the Navy.

Goodyear's first big assignment after the war was the 16 big gas cells for the Shenandoah, America's first rigid airship, completed in 1923.

The Shenandoah was designed by the Navy, the metal framework constructed at the Philadelphia Navy Yard, and assembly made at the Navy's new airship base at Lakehurst, N. J. It was a large ship for that period, 2,115,000 cubic foot gas capacity, almost as large as the Germans' wartime Zeppelins, though small as compared to the later Graf Zeppelin's 3,700,000 cubic feet, or the Akron-Macon's 6,500,000 cubic feet.

The Germans had held construction details about their Zeppelins as a top military secret, but the Allies got a windfall during the war when the L-49 settled down to earth in a fog, thinking it was behind its own lines. Captured by the French before the crew had time to destroy it, the big Zeppelin, meticulously measured and sketched, furnished considerable engineering data to England and America. It was not a modern type, being built in 1916, had the extremely slender shape of wartime

Zeppelins, being virtually a cylinder with pointed ends. A shorter, plumper contour would give greater strength, but this design was well adapted to mass output. The Shenandoah was lengthened by an extra bay in mid-section to add to its lift, making it 8.3 times as long as it was in diameter. The Akron and Macon had a 7 to one slenderness ratio.

Although the L-49 was an obsolete type, it was a good starting point, and Commander Hunsaker and his staff made extensive studies of their own, came up with a well-built ship, which utilized all the engineering information then available except in Germany.

In building the gas cells, Cooper's men in the balloon room tackled a job ten times as large as the biggest blimps they had built. The huge gas containers had to be as completely gas-tight as possible. The Germans had cemented goldbeater's skin to the fabric for that purpose, and this construction was specified for the Shenandoah. Goldbeater's skin is a section of the lining of a steer's intestines, a material extremely light in weight, and so tough that goldsmiths used it in the Middle Ages to hammer out gold leaf. These small sections had to be treated specially, and cemented in place piece by piece, under controlled temperature and humidity conditions. Barrels of intestines packed in brine came rolling into the factory from the packing houses at Chicago, Kansas City and as far away as Argentina.

The non-inflammable helium gas had come in in time to be used in the Shenandoah. This is a natural gas, almost as light as hydrogen, and with the great safety advantage that it will not burn. Observed in the rays of the sun in 1868 and named for helios, the Greek word for sun, it was first found on the earth, in Kansas in 1907. However, helium had remained a scientific curiosity until World War I, when the British inquired whether this country could not procure enough of this non-inflammable gas to inflate some of its blimps and observation balloons.

United States Navy Engineers developed a process of separating the helium from the natural gas, built a plant at Fort Worth and were loading the first steamship at New Orleans when the Armistice came.

The Shenandoah demonstrated its sturdiness early in its career when the nose cone pulled away from the mooring mast, ripping the three forward gas cells. Despite the injury, which would have been fatal to an airplane, the crippled Shenandoah made its way around the storm, made an eight hour flight, returned to base. Later it made the longest trip yet carried out by an airship, around the perimeter of the United States to Seattle and back.

No one in America knew much about flying big airships, though Comdr. Landsdowne, its first captain, did a little flying in England, and made the round-trip crossing to the United States in the British R34. He had to teach himself, then pass the information on to others.

The ship might have had a long and successful career if men had had in 1925 a fraction of the information about weather they have come into since, particularly about the terrific vertical forces sometimes encountered in the storm we now know as a "cold front." The Shenandoah encountered just such a storm in Southern Ohio, was caught between vertical currents moving in opposite directions, and the lead-pencil-shaped ship was broken in two, much as a man breaks a stick over his knee.

Helium confined the loss of life to the men in the control car and one engine car, which following the German practice, were suspended well below the hull to prevent any sparks from reaching the hydrogen gas. Lt. Comdr. Rosendahl, the senior survivor, who became the Navy's Number One airship advocate, was awarded the Navy Cross thirty years later for his resourcefulness at that time in maneuvering his half-ship until he could land it safely in a clearing 14 miles away.

A second airship, the Los Angeles, was at hand by then and America, had come into full construction data from Germany. The Navy carried on.

We will go back now, however, to the smaller non-rigid airships. Though the Navy came out of the war with a number of ships, the major steps for the next 15 years after 1918 were carried on, under the Joint Board's directive, by the Army.

Under the energetic direction of General Billy Mitchell, Assistant Chief of the Army Air Services, a wholehearted believer in airships as he was in airplanes, and in position to put his ideas into effect, the Army went vigorously to work.

A hangar went up at Scott Field, Illinois, near St. Louis, large enough to house a rigid airship, which many army men felt had military as well as Navy use. Wright Field was at hand to do the engineering, operating bases were set up at Langley Field, Virginia, and Aberdeen, Maryland, on the East coast, and at Arcadia, California, on the west. A training and experimental program was instituted.

In its first five years the Army ordered 30 airships of different sizes and types, ranging up to the 200,000 TC type in 1923. The Navy's C-7, in 1921, had been the first airship to use helium, but the Army switched over the next year with the AC-1, and took the further step of building the car flush against the envelope rather than suspending it below, helium making this procedure safe.

The need for greater speed in the Navy C ships during the war had brought in dual engines which were mounted on outriggers outside the control car. To moor its non-rigids in the open, the Army borrowed the British procedure of building a bull ring into the nose, with cables attached in three-point suspension to "dead men" sunk into the ground, a plan used successfully when an Army ship made the first cross-country trip ever made by a non-rigid airship.

Observation balloons were built which could pick up car and engine and travel under its own power to a new location. Two big ships were built for long range coastal patrol, the TC-13 and TC-14 of 350,000 cubic feet in 1931 and 1933, with enclosed cars as contrasted to the earlier open cockpit fuselages, quarters for a dozen men, extensive radio equipment, heavier engines—and an observation car.

This last, adapted from the wartime Zeppelins could be lowered 1000 feet below the ship in flight, with an observer to direct navigation or bombing operations, while the ship itself remained concealed in the fog overhead.

The Army entered the semi-rigid field in 1922. With little information available in this country, it ordered the first one from Italy, where this type had been extensively used. The Roma was test-flown there and shipped to Langley Field for reassembly, but on one of its first flights a control cable gave way just after the take-off, and the ship was thrown into one of the high-tension lines which then seemed to surround every airport—and caught fire.

The Roma disaster turned public opinion against hydrogen, stepped up the helium procurement program, and chilled interest in semi-rigids. Interest was revived, however, by Nobile's flight over the North Pole in the Italia, a flight largely obscured by later events, but still one of the most remarkable journeys ever made by a small airship.

Taking off from Rome the ship flew to Spitzbergen by way of East Prussia, Leningrad and Oslo, and was ready for the final dash to the Pole itself when word came in that Byrd had reached that goal by plane the day before. Nobile, on his mettle, took off anyhow, flew over the Pole and on to Point Barrow, Alaska, for a total distance of 6820 miles in five hops. Then he dismantled the ship and sent it back to Italy.

So the Army ordered another semi-rigid, the RS-1, in 1925, to be built by Goodyear. A size of 720,000 cubic feet was stipulated, as compared to the 200,000 Army TC, the largest American non-rigid built up to then, in fact the envelope when crated was too large to go through the balloon room doors, so a section of the wall was knocked out and the crate lowered by cranes. Zimmerman of Goodyear's engineering staff spent several months in Italy studying design details, brought Nobile back with him to check stress calculations. A huge cradle was built at Scott Field for assembly and Major Kepner, the Army's best airship pilot, was assigned to it after the launching. The ship was flown successfully around the middle west for several years, by which time the Army had decided that the non-rigids, which needed smaller landing crews, or the big rigids which had a much larger range, were preferable types. By this time, too, the Army was feeling pinched for funds to carry on both airplane and airship development.

Billy Mitchell was no longer around to fight for aeronautics. General Westover, Chief of the Air Services, and an airship man himself, carried on a losing battle for funds to do an effective job.

"There is no point in doing a half-way job with airships," he finally told Congress. "We should do this right or not at all." Congress took the latter alternative, and in 1935 the Army got out of lighter-than-air. The two new TC's were turned over to the Navy, the bases at Scott and Langley Fields became airplane fields, the California station was disposed of—with a quickly famous race track arising in its place—and the airship officers learned to fly planes.

Absorbed in its work with the Zeppelin-type airships during these years, the Navy had carried on a minimum program with blimps and balloons, chiefly to train officers and crews for the big ships. It still had the 1922 J-3 and J-4 when the second world war broke out, open cockpit ships, with the car slung below the bag. Lacking funds for more modern vessels, Lakehurst had thriftily built windshields to give pilots some protection from the weather, ordered larger envelopes to add to the lift.

The Navy, however, had carried what development work was possible within appropriation limitations. It had a metal-clad ship built in 1929 by a Detroit group, and took the first step toward a modern airship in 1931 with the K-1. That ship, slightly smaller than the Army TC's, had an enclosed car to add to crew efficiency in the longer cruises its greater flying radius made possible, carried on experiments in the use of the Blau gas. That gas, developed by the Germans for the Graf Zeppelin, was a fuel in gas form rather than liquid, had the same weight as air, so did not change the weight of the ship as it was consumed in the engines.

That was its last new ship for seven years, except for the TC's turned over by the Army and the Goodyear's 180,000 cubic foot Defender which was converted into a large-size training ship in 1935. The Navy bought envelopes instead. An airship envelope should be good for five years unless a training mishap shortens its life, which of course happened many times. Cars last longer. Goodyear built a total of 101 envelopes between Armistice Day and Pearl Harbor, 54 for the Army, 47 for the Navy.

It was not until 1938 that Lakehurst ordered further airships, the 400,000 cubic foot K-2, the largest yet, though still an experimental ship, and the 123,000 cubic foot L-1, which might be called a proved type, since it was practically a duplicate of the Goodyear passenger blimps which had covered several hundred thousand miles of voyaging, much of it in operations away from base.

In October, 1940, when the first preparedness program was started, the Navy blimp fleet consisted of the two 1922 J's and the ex-Army TC's, all obsolete in type, the two K's, both experimental, the 1929 Defender, now the G-1, and two modern "L" ships, which were the smallest in the lot. None of these ships had ever dropped a bomb or fired a machine gun.

A great nation which wished no ill toward others could not get too much exercised over the possibility of war, since we would never start one, nor would any other nation dare attack us.

The Airship Fleet

Goodyear blimps have long been a familiar part of the skyline of Washington, New York, Los Angeles and Miami, and during carnival season or expositions at Chicago, Cleveland, San Francisco, Dallas, New Orleans and Memphis.

People expected to see them over the Rose Bowl, the Mardi Gras, the Indianapolis Speedway; at the International Yacht Races, big football games and wherever crowds gathered for major public events. They operated in 42 of the 48 states in the Union, missing only the six mountain states, crossed the Canadian border at Toronto and Vancouver, went to Havana, the Bahamas and Mexico.

They landed on buildings, delivered mail at sea, lowered newspapers to the Empire State Building tower, once picked Litchfield off the deck of an incoming liner in New York's outer harbor. They carried camera men over the Shasta Dam and the Mesabi Range, rescued families from the Mississippi during flood times, patrolled the river and radioed the engineers as they found levees weakening. They rescued stranded fishermen in the Gulf of Mexico, dropped food and supplies to an ice-bound boat in the Chesapeake Bay. They reported forest fires in the Sierras and helped chase bandits. They made wild life studies in Florida and traffic studies in a score of cities. They carried Red Cross and Community Chest trailing banners and neon signs over a hundred cities, circled a thousand schoolhouses.

From 1928 to 1948 except during the war years, Goodyear blimps carried upwards of half a million passengers without a single passenger accident, gave an impressive demonstration of the usefulness, versatility and safety of lighter-than-air travel.

The primary purpose of these operations was to interest the public in the big passenger-carrying airships, the company's real objective. The smaller blimps also made important contributions to construction and operating technique—and turned in a vast deal of information about the still incompletely known science of weather.

The company's own operations started in a small way in California after the first war, when a small wooden hangar was built alongside the new Los Angeles factory as a base for the Pony Blimp. This was a 37,000 cubic foot ship inflated with hydrogen gas, helium not then being available. It opened the first passenger line in the country, flying between Los Angeles and the Catalina Islands, went shark fishing, explored the surrounding country, finally went into the movies. For after the depression hit, the ship was sold to Marshall Neilan, a producer, who took it on location to Montana and Arizona on a picture, "Custer's Last Fight." As there were no airship hangars around, the tiny blimp was shipped to Montana, reassembled in the open, parked at night in a convenient canyon, operated for weeks without any other shelter.

Blimp operations were resumed in 1925 with the Pilgrim, a 50,000 cubic foot ship, a little larger than the Pony Blimp, and flown with helium. Things were picking up. The Los Angeles had crossed the ocean the previous year, and Comdr. C. E. Rosendahl, its captain, with the strong backing of Admiral Moffett, chief of the Bureau of Aeronautics, was building up an operating force. The Navy helium plant at Fort Worth had brought the price of helium down to within striking distance of that of inflammable hydrogen. Goodyear took over the Zeppelin patents that year.

In the case of the Straight Side tire or the pneumatic truck tire Goodyear had not waited for the customer to come in to demand improvements but had initiated its own experimental program, finding goods the public could use to better advantage. The same principle might apply to aeronautics. So the Pilgrim was a pioneering ship, whose contributions to airship design were recognized by Smithsonian when the ship wore out, and it was installed at the Institute in Washington as marking as a milestone in aviation progress.

The Pilgrim was the first commercial non-rigid to use helium, was the first to have the car suspended flush against the bag by internal cables, was the first to use a landing wheel replacing the old bumper bag used up to that time. Wartime airships learned to taxi across the airport on the landing wheel till they got flying speed, take off with an extra load of fuel.

The Goodyear fleet however really started in 1928 when the Puritan was built to the size of 86,000 cubic feet, later enlarged to 96,000, with the Volunteer, Vigilant and Mayflower, and the larger Defender of 178,000 cubic feet added the following year.

The ships were named after the America Cup defenders in international yachting, and as the early ones encountered mishaps, their replacements were given new names, the Columbia and Reliance in 1931, the Resolute in 1934, the Enterprise, Ranger and Rainbow later.

Ship sizes were stepped up as experience showed this desirable, reaching a size of 150 feet length and a gas capacity of 123,000 cubic feet, which would give it wide range and yet not demand too large a ground crew. From that time up to World War II, Goodyear had five or six ships continuously in operation.

At the outset the ships operated from fixed bases, had a hangar to come back to at night. But the Goodyear fleet could not influence public opinion by merely flying around Akron, had to get out over the country. The company built a larger hangar at Los Angeles as a base for the Volunteer, another alongside the Gadsden factory as an overnight stop for ships bound for Florida. St. Petersburg built a hangar along the water front in Florida, and Miami took over a wartime hangar at Key West, brought it in by barge and re-erected it on the Causeway. Col. E. H. R. Green, son of Hetty Green, became interested in radio research work under way at M.I.T., built a hangar on his estate at New Bedford as a base for ship-to-shore radio operations. Navy hangars at Cape May, Lakehurst, New Jersey, Chatham, Mass., and Pensacola, Florida, and Army bases at Scott Field, Ill., Aberdeen, Md., San Antonio and El Paso, Texas, were used for overnight stops. The blimps covered more territory —but still not enough to suit Litchfield.

He set up a competition in 1930 for the design of portable mooring equipment which could be set up quickly for cross-country operations, make the ships independent of hangars.

The first step was the low mast, which could be anchored to the ship half way between the car and the nose, called "belly mooring." It could be set up quickly, with guy wires to hold it, but had the defect that in a storm the bag might be twisted around and torn. So the next step was the high mast, anchoring the ship to the nose, so that it would swing easily in all directions like a weathervane. By making this mast telescopic, it could be carried around on the ground crew's bus. Eventually the ships carried both types along, the low mast for short stops in good weather, the high mast for longer visits, reaching the point in time where the ship need not go in to the hangar at all except for overhaul, could operate all winter from the mast.

With the masting technique worked out the ships could go anywhere, stop overnight at any cow pasture and go on the next day, opened the way for them to visit hundreds of cities, cover the whole country.

An organization grew up. The first pilots were men who had learned to fly at Wingfoot Lake during the first war, Boettner, Wollam, Yolton and men who worked in the balloon room or the aeronautical shops, like Smith, Sheppard, Crosier, Massic and O'Neil. Sewell and Lange had flown airships during the war from Massachusetts to Panama and had taken rigid airship training at Lakehurst, Sewell on the Shenandoah, Lange on the Los Angeles. Fickes left the Efficiency Department to go in, would eventually have charge of all blimp operations. Brannigan and Blair came in from the Army after the RS-1 job. Adventurous young college and technical school men signed up. Trotter had gone to the Naval Academy and Furculow to West Point. Stacey, an M.I.T. student, signed up at New Bedford for the summer, never went back to school. Hobensack came in from the University of West Virginia and Crum from Ohio State.

Dixon, Merchant Marine officer born in a lighthouse at Martha's Vineyard, had two Goodyear passengers aboard, Litchfield and Tomkinson, on one trip back from Argentina. They used to stand night watches with him on the bridge, talking navigation—and presently airships. Dixon switched from sea to air.

A pilot training course was organized, covering ground handling, power plants, radio, flight operations, meteorology, rigging and maintenance, aerostatics and aerodynamics. Some 50 men were qualified as balloon pilots, 31 were licensed as airship pilots by the Federation Aeronautique Internationale and 24 by the U. S. Department of Commerce.

Many of the pilots were commissioned in the Naval Reserve and six of them took active duty at Lakehurst on rigid airships. Many of them flew on the Graf Zeppelin, the Los Angeles, the Akron and the Macon.

Interesting characters joined the ground crew. It was customary in moving to an outside base, to send only a nucleus crew along, recruit the rest locally, so that the ground organization came to include men from

Note contrast between the 1925 Pilgrim, now installed at Smithsonian Institute as pioneer aircraft, and modern cross-country blimp with its portable mooring mast.

the East Side of New York and from Hollywood Hills, boys who had left the fishing docks of New Bedford and those who had grown up in the Everglades. Many of them stayed year after year, with some of the men who signed up at the first outside operation at New Bedford still on the job 20 years later.

The fleet saw plenty of adventures, called for skill and resourcefulness on the part of the pilots, and built up operating technique.

Boettner, attempting a non-stop flight from Akron to Miami in the Defender in 1930, ran into ice and snow in the Tennessee mountains, and the oil lines froze. His mechanic climbed out on the outrigger and made emergency repairs, but the ship lost most of its oil. Reaching Knoxville by morning, he flew over the airport, dropped a note and lowered a line, hauled up additional oil, went on to the Gadsden hangar to complete repairs.

Lange snagged a dead tree in the fog over the Alabama mountains, and Smith sideswiped another while flying through a pass in Tennessee. The ships settled easily to the ground in each case, and farmers came in with stone boats, carried car and bag to town for repairs. A thoughtless passenger threw his straw hat overboard in Pennsylvania, and the propeller whipped it back into the bag, tearing a hole in it. The top of a flashlight fell off during a night landing with a similar result, in each case holding the ship up for a day for repairs. Sewell had the experience of seeing a propeller fly off while crossing San Francisco Bay, but went on to the nearest airport on one motor, mounted his spare. Fickes, near Akron, lost his fuel supply due to a leak in the tank, free-ballooned the ship over a farm house, had the farmer call Wingfoot Lake, waited in the air until crewmen came out with a five gallon can. An airplane would have had to land.

Boettner ran short of gas one night due to persistent head winds while returning from Canada, throttled down and flew low alongside a traveled highway, let his mechanic slide down the rope to the ground. There he flagged down some automobiles, whose drivers, entering into the spirit of the thing, formed a landing circle in a field with their headlights blazing while the ship took on a fresh supply of fuel.

Most of the Goodyear ships have been fired on by thoughtless hunters. Trotter, on his way back from the Dallas Fair, found the ship sluggish after three days on the mast in Oklahoma waiting for weather, discovered that his helium had been pouring out through 14 holes in the bag all that time. He had just enough lift for himself and a minimum amount of fuel, managed to fly on to Scott Field 300 miles away where repairs were made.

Aircraft which can stand still in the air are the delight of cameramen, who can get just the right angle and lighting for pictures of Niagara Falls or the Rose Bowl.

Brannigan was caught in a storm at Washington, D. C., which broke up an air meet, overturned several planes and sent the rest scattering. He took off, floated over the capitol for several hours with his engines throttled back, waited till the storm passed, then went on to Langley Field. Smith flew the Volunteer cross-country from Los Angeles in 1932 to get a new envelope and purify his helium, encountered head winds most of the way, spent ten nights on the mast, made the first round trip by non-rigid. Sewell made the same trip five years later, but mooring-out procedure had been improved in the meantime, and he had an easier time of it.

Two blimps were in the path of the 1938 hurricane which swept across New England. Lange, with the Enterprise, was at New Brunswick, New Jersey, 50 miles off the direct course of the storm. He put the ship on the mast, doubled the number of screw stakes holding the guy wires, used the bus as additional reinforcement, put extra men on the handling lines, held the ship during winds that rose as high as 73 m.p.h. Boettner, with the Puritan at Springfield, Mass., was directly in the path of the storm. With the wind roaring up to 100 m.p.h., gusts uprooted stately old trees, picked a sheet iron roof off a hangar and sent it sailing across the field like a flat stone. He attached steel chains to the mast cables but finally these gave way, threw the mast into the side of the ship cutting a hole in the fabric. He pulled the rip panel, deflated the bag to prevent further damage and after the storm passed rolled up the envelope and shipped it into Akron. The ship was back in service in a week.

It is no wonder that Goodyear pilots came to have great faith in the staunchness of their craft and its ability to keep out of trouble. Goodyear ships flew through hundreds of storms, and none was ever even damaged in the air, with the result that the pilots came to feel that once aloft away from hangars, masts and obstructions, they were safe, could fly out anything.

This conviction had something to do with the only pilot casualty over the years. The high-spirited Brannigan who had come to Goodyear from the Army where he had already distinguished himself by making repairs in mid-air when the semi-rigid Roma was ripped by a splintered propeller, saving a comrade as incident to the job. He was flying at Kansas City in 1932 when a Kansas twister headed for the airport. Brannigan took on additional gas, ordered his mechanic off, planned to fly around the storm. But before the ship could get away the storm struck, pulled the mast anchorage out, threw the ship, mast and all, against a nearby hangar.

Brannigan could have jumped. The door had been propped open for a photographer's camera, but the bag was undamaged and he had one motor left. He decided to stay with his ship. Another five seconds would have put it into the clear—but the storm struck again, carried the ship into high tension wires, and Brannigan was fatally burned.

Traditions grew up out of these experiences, and the accumulation of operating experience would be helpful in World War II to the U. S. Navy, which was able to cover thousands of miles in anti submarine patrol, operating from mooring masts only, for months on end.

The Big Zeppelins

Goodyear's primary objective in its whole lighter-than-air program was to create a new form of over-ocean transportation, faster than the steamship, more comfortable and less expensive than the airplane.

America's geographical location was a natural. It was flanked by oceans which protected it from enemy nations, handicapped trade with friendly ones. The large-size Zeppelins could bridge those oceans with ease, indeed were fully effective only over long ranges, where no fueling points lay between. No other nation could get as much benefit from the big ships as the United States.

Also America had helium gas, a safe gas, in all but inexhaustible quantities, and was the only country in the world to have any important supply of it—and had pipe lines everywhere to carry it from the natural gas fields to processing plants.

The matter of utilizing these great natural advantages to his company's advantage and his country's, had long lain deep in Litchfield's mind.

From a business standpoint, Goodyear as the ship builder (other people who knew that business might operate them) would add to corporation income, and give employment to a larger number of highly skilled men. From the national standpoint the advantages were still greater.

There were several factors following the first World War which favored consummation of the project. The company had had a useful construction experience in building the gas cells for the Shenandoah, and spare cells and an outer cover for the Los Angeles, as well as the smaller non-rigids. The acquiring of the Zeppelin patents brought virtually the world's entire experience in this business into American hands. Important operating experience was built up on its own airships by pilots and crews who would be needed to fly the big ships.

The spectacular operations of the Graf Zeppelin and the Hindenburg in the next years offered impressive proof that a craft that large could be operated with a high degree of safety, economy, comfort and regularity of schedule.

At this point perhaps, many readers will think of the disasters encountered by dirigibles. One could stop here and set down in detail, on the basis of scientific reports, what happened in the case of the Shenandoah, Akron and Macon. No explanation is needed for the Los Angeles or the Graf Zeppelin, each of which lived a long and useful life, nor the Hindenburg, since that disaster would never have happened if we had made helium available out of our vast supply.

Readers interested in the causes of these setbacks can find that completely told in government reports.

In any case, each new machine man has built has encountered mechanical difficulties, and the setbacks of the airship were no different from those of the automobile, the railroad or the steamship, were similarly understandable, and correctable.

The 158 successful ocean crossings made by the Zeppelins cannot be dismissed lightly—and the ablest scientists in America could find no reason after exhaustive study into the disasters to conclude that America could not successfully build and fly them.

Somewhere in this situation, in the case of our own ships, is the fact that America, a capable, courageous, and impatient people are prone to underestimate difficulties. Perhaps Admiral Craven was right in 1920 in thinking that we should start with small dirigibles and build up. The Germans had been flying them since 1906, and Zeppelin construction and flight crews had a continuity of experience which we were denied.

But let us return to the narrative.

In the first years after World War I the Allies, determined to prevent Germany from ever starting another war, arrived one day at the item, Zeppelins. Those on hand at the time of the Armistice had been scuttled by their crews, along with German warships, and figures representing the value of the lost dirigibles were added to the reparations total.

"But perhaps America would rather have a German-built airship in place of the money," Lloyd George, so the legend says, suggested, perhaps only half seriously.

The American representative thought his government might be interested—and found that it was. The Allies agreed, but stipulated that the reparations dirigible not be a military ship, and that after it was completed the Zeppelin works should be dismantled. This is the little known story of how this country got the Los Angeles for the U. S. Navy.

However, it seemed too bad to throw away all the accumulation of Germany's design and construction experience. A United States government official talked to someone in Goodyear.

"The Zeppelin company is a private organization," he pointed out. "Our government cannot deal with it. But Goodyear, as another private company, might do something about securing its patents and processing information."

The tip was enough. Dr. Hugo Eckener, head of the Zeppelin company, was more than amenable to the idea. The airship art must not die. Airship operations were essentially long range ones, need not merely fly between Berlin and Munich, like an airplane. Eckener, like Count Zeppelin, who had died during the war, believed that the airship, being international, might be an instrument of understanding and peace between the nations it served. America was a logical ship's run. This country had money, brains, technical competence and pilot resourcefulness. The old count had served as a volunteer officer in the Union Army during the Civil War, in fact, first became interested in lighter-than-air through flying a captive balloon over the Potomac. Airship secrets would be safe in American hands.

Transfer of the Zeppelin patents to Goodyear was effected in 1924; the Los Angeles was completed the following year; Eckener got permission from the Allies to build another ship, which he named for the old Count, and Dr. Arnstein, the chief engineer, sailed for America with a dozen of his principal assistants, to become American citizens and contribute their accumulation of technical experience and their loyalty to the United States.

American interest in airships could not but be stimulated by the first flight of the Graf Zeppelin to this country in 1928. It was not the first Atlantic crossing by air. Hawkes and Grieve had flown from Newfoundland, the U. S. Navy's NC boats by easy stages from Baltimore, and the British dirigible R-34 had made a round trip in 1929. Eckener had delivered the Los Angeles in 1925 and the Lindbergh flight was on everyone's tongue.

But the Graf Zeppelin flight was different. This was not a daring adventure achieved by high courage and a couple of sandwiches. This was a full-rigged ship of the air, with standard crew and 20 passengers, with staterooms, dining rooms, passenger comfort. It was transportation.

And in the following year Eckener took his ship clear around the world, again with a full load of passengers, with stops only at Tokyo, Los Angeles and Lakehurst, and thereafter travelled to North and South

America on regular schedule for the next several years.

The U. S. Navy co-operated thoroughly, made landing crews and fuel available at Lakehurst, getting in return not only a proper rental and service charge, but more important, a first hand contact by naval officers and men with every phase of Zeppelin operating technique. Naval observers, and presently Goodyear pilots, were carried on each ocean crossing, with free gangway throughout the ship.

The Navy's interest grew out of Admiral Moffett's realization that an American passenger airship line, once in existence, meant bases and trained crews, would be a second line of defense against war emergency, like the Merchant Marine—except that conversion of airships to war use would be easier and faster than in the case of steamships.

Eckener's willingness to throw the book wide open grew out of his discussions with Litchfield on an American airship line, dovetailing schedules and each using the other's terminals. By now he had a second ship in service, the Hindenburg, of 7,000,000 cubic feet, twice as big as the Graf Zeppelin, running on regular schedule between Europe, Buenos Aires, Rio, and North America. He had been converted to the use of the U. S. Navy-type mooring mast instead of hangars for landings, not only at Lakehurst, but in Brazil, at Seville, Spain, and at his new passenger base at Frankfurt. The Brazilian government built a big hangar near Rio de Janeiro for craft which brought it so much closer to Europe.

Zeppelin operations seemed well-established, and American capital, including steamship, airline and banking money was definitely interested in setting up an American line when the Hindenburg was lost.

Had the Secretary of Interior not refused to make helium available— for security reasons, though Army and Navy, responsible for security, had OK'd it—Eckener would have gone on and the American project got under way.

However, while the German operations built up interest in this country, Congress had not waited for that demonstration to be made. In 1926, two years before the first Graf Zeppelin crossing, it had authorized the construction of two big airships for the Navy. These were not to be combat ships, but fast, long-range reconnaissance craft, with their own airplanes to extend the scouting range still further.

Admiral Moffett wanted the Navy to have the finest airships in the world. The Navy had an expert staff, headed by Commanders Fulton, Weyerbacher, Kraus, and the civilian engineer, Burgess, all of whom had worked on airships since the first war, Fulton and Kraus acting as technical observers at Friedrichshafen during the building of the Los Angeles.

America's first dirigible, Shenandoah (above), taking off from a mast erected on a ship's deck, and (below) USS Macon anchored to a more modern mast at Akron.

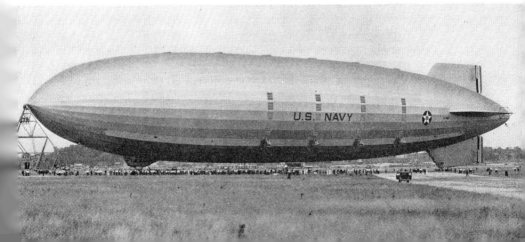

Five new features were decided upon for the new ships. These were a new type of main frame, inherently strong, so that it did not necessarily depend for strength on the cross-bracing wires required in previous ships; three longitudinal keels, extending from end to end of the ship, in place of one; the utilization of this greater strength to place the engine cars within the ship's structure rather than suspending them from outriggers outside, helium gas making this safe from a fire standpoint; the building of an airplane hangar in the bowels of the ship, with housing for five planes; a new type of gas cells.

Competitive designs were called for. Designs were submitted by 37 individuals or groups. Some of these came from scientists having past experience in airships; many were theoretical, some even freakish. An American company had taken over the rights of Schuette-Lanz, another German airship company, submitted plans based on that experience. Goodyear put in two alternative designs. The Navy studied the various designs, awarded first and second place to Goodyear. A contract approximating $8,000,000 for building two airships was signed in 1928 by Secretary of the Navy Curtis Wilbur, the year the Graf Zeppelin made its first trip to America.

The first thing was to erect an assembly hangar—lighter-than-air people call them docks—and Arnstein's staff had already made extensive studies into that.

The building would have to be very large, in fact it was the largest building ever built in the world without interior supports. The ships were to have a capacity of 6,500,000 cubic feet of helium, as contrasted with the 2,500,000 cubic foot Los Angeles or the 3,700,000 cubic foot Graf Zeppelin.

The dock was 1200 feet long, 325 feet wide and 200 feet high. A smaller building would have served for the two Navy ships, but Litchfield ordered it built large enough to house the 10,000,000 cubic foot passenger and cargo airships he visioned for the future.

The Akron airship dock was one of the most unusual structures ever built, and the most fully streamlined. Previous hangars used the conventional rectangular type, which took on a T-shape when the doors were opened, creating eddies and gusts, accentuating the turbulence at the critical point of ship entrances and departures. Arnstein's staff conceived a turtleback structure, with orange peel doors which fitted into the contour of the building as they were opened and closed. Catwalks were put in along the sides at different elevations, overhead cranes to move materials, and an elevator which would carry the workmen like flies, up and down the curving sides of the building to the top.

Navy airship Akron ready to be walked out of Goodyear Air Dock (above), while (below) the Hindenburg circles for a landing after an ocean crossing.

With the general design of the building set, Dr. Arnstein's staff moved to the ship itself. Chief Engineer State called in Wilbur Watson and Associates, Cleveland engineering company, to work on the vast amount of intricate detail design of the dock, too large a job for his own staff, then looked around for a construction contractor, found no one eager to tackle the job. To erect the arches 325 feet wide and 200 feet high offered structural challenges, but finally the American Bridge Company took it on, building the arches in three sections on the ground, hoisting the two curving sides, then the center section into place, securing these until a second arch went up to tie to—suspending cables in the meantime to discourage reckless aviators from trying to fly through. Work on the building was started in the spring of 1929, completed by December. Ship assembly started at one end of the building while the rest of it was under way.

Construction of the ships called for some 800 men, for the most part engineers and skilled workmen. The engineering staff had to include men with experience in metallurgy, including the new aluminum alloys, as well as stainless steel, brass and copper—in corrosion resistance, heat treating and welding; in aerodynamics, stress calculations, physical testing, power plants, transmission. There were three groups of engineers, Everhart, Leatherman, Zimmerman and the other Goodyear men who had been working on airships since War I; Arnstein's group; and a considerable number of young technical school graduates—who were alternated from department to department like the Flying Squadron to broaden their experience, even taking flight training in Goodyear blimps, to get the feel of the craft they worked on.

A few men came in from the outside, with experience which a rubber company had not previously needed—Collins from Bethlehem Shipbuilding, who had built the carrier Saratoga, became construction superintendent; Lt. Comdr. Wicks, who had whipped the Navy's helium plant at Ft. Worth into shape and been engineering officer at Lakehurst, was assistant chief engineer; and Coffelt, who had built bridges and skyscrapers over the world, diverted his talents to new fields.

The Navy assigned two experienced constructors, Lts. Knox and Whittle, to the resident staff, and two with operating experience. Lt. Comdr. Settle, in charge, had stood number one man in his class at Annapolis and qualified as a pilot of rigid and non-rigid ships, balloons, gliders and airplanes. The fourth officer, Lt. Mayer, had served on the Shenandoah and, like Rosendahl, distinguished himself on its final flight. From Washington, Admiral Moffett and Comdr. Fulton watched each stage of the job carefully.

Commander J. C. Hunsaker, who had designed airships and airplanes for the Navy during the first war, joined the company as vice president, began working on a passenger airship line. Harry Vissering, who had aroused President Harding's interest in airships in 1923 and so given impetus to the acquiring of the Los Angeles, was a director. F. M. Harpham, Akron businessman, distinguished for his common sense, became a vice president, coordinating relations between the airship and tire divisions of Goodyear.

The British were building two airships, and friendly relations grew up with leaders of that group—Scott, Richmond, Burney, Booth, Boothby, Lord Thompson, Lord Trenchard, the last named, a former British Air Marshal, becoming a Goodyear director.

Since new features never before built into a rigid airship were specified for the Akron and Macon, a vast amount of stress calculations were called for, something in which Arnstein's men had fuller experience than any group in the world, and which would be utilized later in airplanes. Strength of materials must be adequate, with full factors of safety, down to the last girder connection and wire cable, but could not be guessed at, since any unnecessary strength, multiplied as it was in so large a structure, would be costly in weight and performance.

These calculations must be checked by actual tests under compression, tensile, torsion, painstakingly one after another, over every last section of hull and control surfaces—and the entire structure when completed was given "hogging-sagging" tests, where tremendous weights were attached first to bow and stern, then to the mid section, as though trying to break the ship in two.

Huge crowds gathered at one end of the airship dock day after day to watch the ships take form and to marvel at the great building itself, every cross-country traveller routing himself through Akron. The great rings of the Macon were laid out on the floor while the final work was being done on the Akron, and the test flights conducted.

Goodyear engineers worked closely with those of the Aluminum Company, to increase the strength of aluminum alloys, with surprising weight reductions—which other industries could utilize—developed improved methods of treating and processing and a score of ingenious new tools.

Fabrication of the Akron started in June 1929, and the first test flight was made in September 1931. The Macon was started in July 1931, test-flown in April 1933. The Akron was christened before a quarter million people by Mrs. Herbert Hoover, and the Macon before a similar crowd by Mrs. William A. Moffett.

Captain Rosendahl test-flew the Akron, command being later turned over to Comdr. Dressel, then to Comdr. McCord. Dressel test-flew the Macon, turned command over to Lieut. Comdr. Wiley.

The Akron operated out of Lakehurst, the Macon from the new station at Sunnyvale, California (later called Moffett Field). Both ships showed high speed and endurance, vindicated the new features built into them, demonstrated the soundness of their construction. The Akron showed its essential ruggedness when it rode easily for hours up the Atlantic seaboard through a sleet storm which piled up tons of ice on its back. The Macon flew from California to the Caribbean Seas in 1934, took part in the fleet maneuvers, operated intensively thereafter with the Pacific fleet.

Airplane launchings and pick-ups, tried out on the Akron, were carried still further with the Macon. More than 3000 such contacts were made even under adverse conditions of visibility and at night, without difficulty.

The loss of the two ships in April 1934 and February 1935, followed by the Hindenburg in 1937, was a hard blow to the airship cause. Official investigations were made in each case by the Navy, Congress, scientists, administrative departments of the government. One of the most thorough of these was made in 1936, after the loss of the Macon. The Secretary of the Navy asked the President's Science Advisory Board to name a group of outstanding scientists and engineers who would make a complete study of the subject. Headed by Dr. W. F. Durand, the committee included Kettering of General Motors, Jewett of the American Telephone & Telegraph's research laboratories, Dr. Millikin of California Institute of Technology, and experts from Massachusetts Institute of Technology and the University of Michigan.

Their report agreed with the others. Technical advances had been made even since the Akron-Macon design, the report pointed out, and this with a fuller knowledge of meteorology indicated that the chance of repetition of past casualties would be reduced almost to the vanishing point. The committee recommended that the government go ahead with the construction of both rigid and non-rigid ships, determine their full usefulness to the national defense.

The causes of the Akron disaster were fairly clear. The ship was flying through a storm at a much lower altitude than the barometric altimeter indicated (and which the present radio altimeter would have given correctly) and in depressing the stern to drive the ship upward, the tail caught in the water, a mass of 200 tons flying at 100 miles an hour. No vehicle could have withstood such an impact.

A quarter-million people gathered at the huge airship dock to watch the Navy dirigible Akron christened by Mrs. Herbert Hoover.

The Macon story was different. Here one of the supports attaching the control surfaces to the main structure, began to pull loose while the ship was being flown at high speed through a storm in Texas. The ship was slowed down, continued on to Miami where temporary reinforcements were made, went on to take part in maneuvers in the Caribbean, then returned to California.

Investigation showed that the ship had been subjected, during the high speed in turbulent air, to higher stresses than it had been designed to meet. To prevent recurrence, reinforcing members were built at Akron and sent to Sunnyvale where they were installed as opportunity offered between flights. Hindsight showed that the ship should have been grounded, as is customary in such cases with a new type of aircraft until it was certain everything was all right. However, the matter did not seem serious, and the airship men were having their first chance that summer to work out with the fleet. The reinforcements had all been installed except the top fin, when that pulled loose in flight as a sharp gust struck the ship. Three gas cells were ripped and eventually the Macon set down in the ocean, with only two casualties out of the 92 people aboard.

Even while official inquiries were under way, however, Arnstein's men had set out on an exhaustive series of experiments to measure the exact effect of wind forces on every part of the structure. This involved the use of scale models, a technique which was being applied with highly accurate results in surface ship design. Wind tunnel and water tunnel testing apparatus was set up at Guggenheim Airship Institute at Akron, in the latter case jets of water being thrust against the submerged model at various angles and velocities, with instruments and still and motion picture cameras to register the effects. Other tests were conducted on a large-scale model of a ship section, with mirrors to measure deflection as various forces were brought to bear. The engineers came out of long studies knowing more about the exact strength needed in each part of an airship, and as a whole, than men had ever known before—including information which would be useful in airplane construction as well when Goodyear got into that in the second world war.

The government again became interested in airships for passenger and naval use.

Charles Edison, then assistant secretary of the Navy, wrote in 1938:

"Since 1903 something like 250,000 airplanes have been built, flown and lost or destroyed through one cause or another. In the United States alone some 25,000 airplanes have been destroyed with a loss of life of about 8000.

"In the same period less than 400 airships of all sizes have been built, including about 140 dirigibles of the large rigid type. In the United States only four such large airships have been operated. Three of these have been destroyed with a loss of less than 100 lives. The total expenditure on airship development has been only a very small percentage— say 2 per cent—of the expenditure for airplanes.

"It is only natural that the evolution of the airship has been slow. I feel, however, that a majority of fair minded people who take the time and trouble to study airship history inevitably come in some degree to the conclusion that airships are of value to us as a nation. They are a challenge. I want to see large airships proven out."

With the outbreak of war in Europe, airship proponents in the Navy saw several uses for the ships in the event the war spread to the States.

First was reconnaissance with its own planes ranging alongside and ahead to widen the range, covering vast areas much more quickly than could be done in any other way, around Honolulu, the Panama Canal, the Aleutians. Operating with the fleet they might do critical utility tasks, getting planes, materiel and weapons to crucial localities when other carriers could not get in, "vertically evading" enemy submarine blockades, carrying wounded men back from forward areas, able to function in areas of low visibility.

Beyond all else Navy airship men saw a new use for dirigibles as airplane carriers. Recalling the 59 hour flight of the Graf Zeppelin from Tokyo to San Francisco in 1929, they visioned the airship a much faster carrier than anything on the surface, one which might act also as a "mother ship," to carry fuel for many more planes than it had room to stow aboard, act as a flying gasoline station.

A squadron of such airships carrying the same number of planes as one surface carrier would appear to cost less to build, in time, critical materials, money and plant facilities than the "flat top"; would require fewer officers and men to man them, for an airship needs fewer men than a destroyer; would require far smaller base facilities; would not be vulnerable to torpedoes, mines, or surface gun fire; and would be less vulnerable to air attack considering the multiplicity of units, as against the "eggs all in one basket" situation of the surface carrier.

Design of a 10,000,000 cubic foot ship, half again as large as the Akron-Macon, with quarters for ten medium bombers, a top speed of 84 nautical miles per hour, a cruising speed of 50 and a projected range without refueling up to 10,000 miles, went on the drafting board.

A committee from Navy, Commerce and Interior brought in concrete proposals and Congress provided funds to be spent at the discretion of the president for experimental work in various fields, including a training airship. The Navy wanted a 3,000,000 cubic foot ship, large enough to develop its naval use, even on small scale, but the president thought a 1,000,000 cubic foot size would be large enough, and in the end nothing came of it.

Then war came. Too late now to build ships, train men, set up bases. The Navy needed battleships, cruisers, destroyers, submarines, carriers —particularly after Pearl Harbor so badly crippled our Pacific fleet— needed vast numbers of bombing, fighting and reconnaissance airplanes, which could be built and sent into action more quickly.

Every new naval vessel had to go through a period of skepticism and doubt. That has been the history of the submarine, the airplane carrier and the airplane itself as a naval weapon. The final possibilities of any craft can only be proved out in actual warfare—and the ships of one war may not be adequate against new weapons of the next.

So there were no airships to cover the miles of ocean around Pearl Harbor. They might have prevented that catastrophe.

9. The Sales Story

The Boom Years (1906-1920)

GOODS, no matter how well made, still have to be sold. The world may beat a track to someone's door, but that takes too long. Time is saved if one goes out after business. And time was extremely important to the Goodyear company in its first years, particularly after 1908, when the automobile industry really began to drive ahead. Whoever kept abreast of that terrific upsurge would go far.

The Goodyear company had what it took to do that.

Here was the factory coming out every few years with something new and exciting, something that would better serve the growing automobile industry than anything its competitors had—the perfected Straight Side tire in 1904, the first airplane tire in 1909, the SV solid tire for trucks in 1911, the revolutionary cord tire in 1913, and the pneumatic truck tire in 1916.

To match that opportunity, a strong selling organization grew up behind the far-sighted Stadelman, the sound and thorough Shilts, the analytical Rockhill, and the dynamic Seiberling, a hand-picked force of hard-hitting salesmen who knew they had the best tire in the world, and utilized to the last letter of aggressiveness every opportunity to build sales, the Glidden tours, Barney Oldfield, automobile shows and spectacular, hard-written, reason-giving advertising in the most widely-read publications in the country.

The story of Goodyear sales really starts with 1906, when G. M. Stadelman moved up to be general sales manager. It was high time for sales to be put on a well-organized basis. The 100,000 cars registered in America would go to a million in six years. Goodyear had, in the Straight Side, the best tire for them to ride on, and its spectacular battle to displace the clincher would bring it widespread public attention, and its victory carry it from the bottom of the list to rank with the leaders— and a still better tire ahead to carry it over the top.

The sales program had been rather hit-and-miss up to then. There were sales managers for carriage, bicycle and auto tires, and for sundries, there were branches in five cities, New York, Boston, Chicago and Cincinnati and St. Louis, and seven salesmen in other key cities

In fact everybody was selling at first. The Seiberlings overlooked no opportunity to make a sale. Litchfield and State worked closely with the Sales Department, in fact Litchfield went to Cleveland by street car in 1901 to talk to the White company, who were changing over from sewing machines to the soon-famous White Steamer, about the new Straight Side tire he had slung over his shoulder.

Litchfield had already suggested putting all sales under one head, and Osterloh, aggressive branch manager at Chicago, backed him up.

"Four sales managers and four conflicting sets of instructions!" he told Seiberling. "Why not put Stadelman in charge, have him tell us how much time to spend on each department?"

Seiberling thought it over on his way to the west coast, announced the appointment on his return.

The new sales chief studied the situation carefully. Goodyear was the leader in his own field of carriage tires, the company's biggest line, though some carriage makers were changing over to gas-driven automobiles and electrics, sometimes retaining the high wheels, the curving dashboard, the open top and the whip socket.

But as long as carriage tires remained profitable, that field would be canvassed, and Stadelman continued to call personally on some of his old accounts like the Lebzelter Company at Lancaster, Pennsylvania— which changed with the times to auto tires, was still an important Goodyear account nearly half a century later.

This 1908 picture shows the Seiberlings,
Rockhill, in front; Litchfield, Falor, State,
center; Hazlett, Shilts, Stadelman, back.

Early advertising took the form of booklets,
showing carriage tires, or (right) blacksmith
and helper prying old clincher-type tire off rim.

Carriage tires remained in the line, partially as a matter of sentiment perhaps, into the 1930's. Other companies dropped out and Goodyear took over the business until it had practically all of it, though by that time carriage tires were sold chiefly in isolated areas in this country and as rickshaw tires in the Orient. The last carriage tire machinery was shipped to the Java factory in 1934.

Bicycle tires were losing ground but would be good for several years. Horseshoe pads were fading out. Rubber bands lasted longer, boasted customers who bought as high as 15 tons at a time. Woolworth's five and ten cent stores had come into the field, ordered rubber bands by the gross, in handsome green boxes marked for bankers, accountants and housewives. Every so often someone would suggest throwing out rubber bands, but it remained into the 1920's, also as a matter of sentiment, perhaps—for rubber bands had brought in a dependable revenue when the company needed it. Flooring started in 1905 with a rather expensive but highly durable type. Other products came in. There was a pneumatic golf ball, with a practice course across the street beside the cemetery. A pneumatic baseball looked good for a while. There were novelties like rubber billfolds, cigar holders, poker chips, exercisers, too many lines, in fact, to suit Litchfield.

"Maybe we have to make these things for a while till we get on our feet," he said, "but as soon as we can, let's throw them all out and concentrate on building the best automobile tire in the world."

There was another item, more practical for the era, which the company went into a few years later. This was the air bottle. There were few places for the car owner to inflate his tires, "free air" signs marking such progressive establishments being few and far between. Usually the motorist had to pump up his tires with a hand pump. Goodyear installed compressors at its branches to encourage people to drive automobiles, sold air bottles big enough for five fillings for a Ford-size tire or three for the larger cars, even advertised them in the Saturday Evening Post.

Stadelman would nurse these smaller departments along just as long as they were needed and paid their way. But from the outset he gave his major attention to automobile tires, specifically to putting the new Straight Side over.

The company continued to make clinchers, particularly for smaller cars, scrupulously carrying out its agreement with the Association as long as that lasted, with Stadelman sending out word at times to slow up, as the company was going over its quota and would have to rebate the surplus. Considerable headway was being made with the Straight Side.

Major sales effort was to the car manufacturer, there were few dealers.

It was a big event when Reo and Buick changed over in 1906, Reo ordering 1639 sets and Buick 489. Other manufacturers became interested, Studebaker ordering 48 sets, Stephens Duryea 20, Stanley 12 for its steam-driven car, Peerless seven, Packard and Franklin six each, and Rauch and Lang two sets for its electrics that year.

Goodyear got a big order from Ford in 1907, the year he brought out his Model T—1200 sets in 28 x 3 and 30 x 3 clincher sizes. To celebrate this big achievement the company shipped the tires to Detroit in cars carrying huge banners along the sides.

Companies who were just getting started and were short of working capital, depended largely in this period on the distributor, who was given exclusive sales for a territory which might cover several states. He handled several lines of merchandise so could easily take on an additional line. This saved the manufacturer the expense of setting up his own branches.

The trouble with this system was that the distributor might or might not put any particular effort behind tires—and he might change without notice.

The Detroit distributor did just that in 1907. Michelin, the French company which had an excellent reputation, put in an American factory. The Detroit man threw out Goodyear, took on Michelin—and took the two big accounts, Buick and Reo, with him.

Stadelman moved fast. He rented a four-story building as the Detroit branch, hired Earl Jackson, Morgan & Wright's crack salesman, as branch manager. Jackson, widely known, a former bicycle racing champion and an aggressive salesman, would have much to do with establishing Goodyear's leadership in the Motor City. It would take them two years, however, to get Reo and Buick back into the fold.

Stadelman wanted to put in other branches, but a minor depression struck in 1907 and employees were paid in script for a time. Director Manton and Byron Robinson of the clay products company had to loan Goodyear $300,000 to tide it over.

He began to build up his sales force. A few college-trained men came in, as industry began to switch over from the old story-telling "drummer" type of salesman. Shilts, whose organizing ability and thoroughness had impressed Stadelman, brought in two men from his school, Mount Union College in nearby Alliance, Hazlett in 1906 (he would later be managing director in England) and in 1907, Rockhill, who moved up from repair materials and aeronautical sales to become sales manager in later years. Seasoned men like Osterloh in Chicago, and Teagan in Boston were on the job. Hamlen, who came in in 1905 would shortly have charge of solid tires, and Martin, who signed up in 1908 would take over sales through the south.

Stadelman could not afford a large sales force, but it had to be good. He knew most of the salesmen in the industry, hand-picked his men. He could not offer them more money than the big companies. He did not offer anyone an easy job. Men who went to work for the company then knew they were going into an uphill battle—to put over a new and unknown tire which cost 20 per cent more than the established clincher tires.

But if they succeeded, Goodyear would go far and they would ride along with it, buying stock if they cared to, but in any case being assured of good money if they did the sales job the situation called for—which was a challenge to the right type of men.

One of Stadelman's first steps was to send out general letters to the field, a practice continued to this day. The letters did not crack the whip over the salesman's head. They kept everybody informed as to how the business was going, what competitors were doing, what market conditions were, pointed out where sales were lagging, where new opportunities lay. Stadelman took the salesmen into his confidence, asked for comments, suggestions, made them a part of the team.

One letter early in the series throws light on his character and code of ethics. A competitor was having serious product trouble and Stadelman told the field about it. "However," he added, "don't pass this information on. If your dealers have had this experience with the tire, it avails you nothing to speak of it. If they have not, that knowledge will come to them from other sources. We strongly urge that you merely explain the good points of your own tire."

The automobile industry was beginning to grow in 1908. Car registration doubled that year. Tires for the big expensive cars like Winton, Peerless, Packard, White, Pierce Arrow, Stevens Duryea, Locomobile, Marmon, Pope, and the Thomas Flyer were largely supplied by the big rubber companies—who smiled to themselves when Stadelman went after the little fellows—Ford, Reo, Buick, Jeffrey, Oakland, Olds, Jackson and Overland, trying to pick out those which seemed most likely, through good management and sound engineering, to succeed.

He made quite a bit of headway. More manufacturers changed to Straight Sides and Goodyear got a good share of their business. Prices were cut as sales increased, cutting the margin between it and the clincher, making the new tire more attractive.

There was need for haste. Other tire companies were building Straight Sides now, since the tire was not patented, and were able in time to reproduce Nip Scott's braided wire satisfactorily.

Seiberling, with a flair for the spectacular, hired Barney Oldfield to demonstrate the tire, publicized it widely when Oldfield covered a mile in 51 4/5 seconds in 1907, made a speed run from San Francisco to Los Angeles in 17 hours and 17 minutes.

When the Glidden tours started, Goodyear salesmen got into that, sought to get their tires on the largest number of cars in that caravan.

Stadelman kept the heat on. One letter offering a new sales argument throws light on the industry of that era. Early automobiles were stripped down to little more than a chassis, engine and wheels. Tops, windshields and lights for night driving were extra equipment. But people were buying these "accessories" for their cars, even at an extra cost and Stadelman pointed out that this added to the load on the tires.

"The Straight Side design gives it 15 per cent more air space than the clincher," he wrote. "It will carry the extra weight."

The year 1908 saw four branches added, in Philadelphia, Cleveland, Boston and Denver. Sales doubled, went from two million dollars to four. Seiberling decided to go into advertising in a big way. Up to now the company had depended principally on booklets.

C. C. Hopkins of the Chicago advertising agency of Lord and Thomas was the crack advertising writer of the country, reported to get the huge salary of $50,000 a year. He was called in that fall to lay out a real advertising campaign, the first in the history of the tire industry.

"How much money can you put into this?" was his first question. No use going into it on a small scale. Even if Goodyear had to borrow the money, its first campaign must be striking enough to attract everyone's attention.

The company had made $125,000 profit in the fiscal year ending in October. Maybe it could dig up enough money to double that, make it a quarter million dollar campaign. This was a small sum by today's standards, but would serve.

The first advertisement in February, 1909, took a full page in the Saturday Evening Post, the first in the history of the tire industry. Hopkins had an inspiring theme, the story of a little company with its back to the wall, fighting the entire industry, and winning its battle because it had something better than had been produced before.

He used "reasons why" copy, explained the principle of the tire, the advantages, then as the proof of the pudding, listed important automobile manufacturers who would use the Straight Side in 1909 as standard equipment. Month after month throughout the year, he hammered

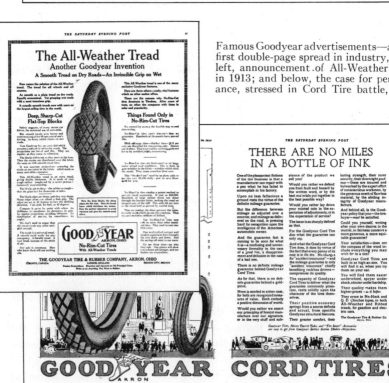

Famous Goodyear advertisements—above, first double-page spread in industry, 1910; left, announcement of All-Weather tread in 1913; and below, the case for performance, stressed in Cord Tire battle, 1917.

away in the Post, Collier's, Life (not the present one), Literary Digest, Leslie's.

Goodyear did this advertising on borrowed money. If it did not bring in enough extra business to pay for itself the company would be in trouble. But dynamic advertising, a good product, and aggressive sales-manship more than doubled sales volume. Sales went from four million to nine and a half in 1909. New branches were set up, in Pittsburgh, Washington and Atlanta.

Strike while the iron was hot, this was Goodyear's philosophy. Sales margins were cut again, and the Straight Side cost only five per cent more than the clincher. A second advertising campaign was launched in 1910, started with a double spread in the Post, also the first in the industry.

The first advertisement in this series, on January 1, 1910, listed more than 60 car manufacturers who had swung over to the Straight Side, including such companies as Cadillac, Buick, Oldsmobile, Willys-Over-land, Oakland, Hupp, Kissel, Apperson, Columbus Buggy (electrics) and 50 others, many of whose names have been forgotten in the years since.

Thirty-six per cent of the nation's cars would leave the factories on Goodyear tires. The remaining 22 tire manufacturers of the country would divide the rest of the business. To manufacture these tires the company would use nearly 4,000,000 pounds of rubber and a million and a quarter yards of Sea Island cotton.

Sales went to 13 million dollars in 1910. Goodyear, the upstart, moved from a lowly position of less than 2 per cent of the nation's tire business to one of the half-dozen leaders. Branches were installed in Los Angeles, San Francisco and Minneapolis.

The sales force was further expanded in 1910. Shilts, now manager of the Salesmen's Department, was instructed to make it the most ef-ficient selling machine in the industry.

He added 50 men the first year, going from 35 salesmen to 86— rather to the dismay of some of the men who felt that the company was moving too fast, that the new men would cut down their share of business. By the end of the year, however, Shilts reported that while the 35 men had averaged sales of $2600 a month the year before, the 86 men that year had averaged $2700 a month.

"And we're going to add 50 to 75 more salesmen next year," he said. "There are 3000 towns in the United States having ten or more automobiles where we have no distribution."

He wrote the branch managers: "You should be able to get junior salesmen at $65 a month and up, and experienced men at $1000 a year. Get Akron's approval before you offer any more money."

The men hired in 1909 included Ammon at Grand Rapids who had started out as Litchfield's office boy back in 1903, Greene of Chicago, and Moyer of Minneapolis. Telford started at Buffalo in 1910, later joining Jackson at Detroit; Burnham of Manufacturers' Sales came in 1911; Sears of Chicago, Shick of Philadelphia and Davidson of Export in 1912; Post of Soles and Heels in 1913. Cameron, tall Indianian, changed from whole-sale groceries to solid tires in 1913 in St. Louis, not dreaming that this would lead him to a territory world-wide in size, as vice president of Export.

College graduates were coming in now, and the 1912 group included R. S. Wilson, a minister's son from Wooster, Ohio, who had graduated from Princeton and spent a year teaching Latin at the famous Lawrence-ville Prep School. Wilson started in as adjuster, would become vice president in charge of sales 16 years later.

Other names well known in the company began to appear in the general letters as contest winners—Carroll in San Francisco, Mont-gomery at Denver, Zimmerman and Holcker at Detroit, Gemmill at Baltimore, the Zieglers at Chicago, Starnes and P. G. Smith (first ex-port salesman) at Atlanta, Russon, Hertzig, Senour, Richey, and Winings.

No less than 17 branches were opened in 1911, at Providence, Springfield, Mass., Baltimore, Jacksonville, Indianapolis, Grand Rapids, Toledo, Columbus, Memphis, Oklahoma City, Houston, Fort Worth, Dallas, New Orleans, Portland, Ore., Seattle and San Antonio. Part of this expansion came at the instance of car manufacturers. Cadil-lac told Osterloh in 1911 that its Seattle dealer was objecting to getting cars on Goodyears because there was no place near at hand where his customers could buy new tires as they were needed. Osterloh, now Stadelman's first assistant, put a man on the train that night to open up a branch at Seattle. The boom was on.

"Goodyear has the most branches, the most salesmen and the best salesmen," Stadelman reported in 1912. "Our advertising has made Goodyear as well known in three years as Ivory Soap, Hart, Schaffner and Marx or Steinblock clothes, Heinz 57 varieties or Eastman Kodak, who have been advertising for years."

Sales almost doubled again in 1911, from $13 millions to $25, but leveled off around the $30 million mark for the next three years with the uncertain finances preceding World War I.

There was no let-up in effort, however. Twenty more branches were added in 1912, at Portland, Me., Hartford, Worcester, Albany, Rochester, Syracuse, Newark, Brooklyn, Dayton, Louisville, Charlotte, Birmingham, Milwaukee, Des Moines, Omaha, Kansas City, Salt Lake City and Spokane. The distributor was largely out of the picture after 1910, although Johnson Brothers at Montgomery and John Kirkwood at Wichita, energetic and aggressive merchandisers, held on for many years, until 1923 in the former case and 1932 in the latter.

The automobile market continued to expand and find improvements. Kettering's self-starter in 1911 gave the gas-driven car a big edge over the "electric." He added a lighting system two years later. Cadillac and Buick brought out the first closed cars, which with non-skid tires, popularized all-year driving. Most people had laid up their cars previously, jacked up the wheels, put tires and battery in the cellar.

By 1913 there were some 200 automobile manufacturers, the largest being Ford, Willys-Overland, Studebaker, Buick, Cadillac, Olds, Oakland, Stevens Duryea, Chalmers, Reo, Hupp, Mitchell, Hudson, Packard, Paige-Detroit, Pierce Arrow and White. A few foreign cars as well, Rolls Royce, Renault, Mercedes, Fiat, Benz, Panhard, seeking to tap the rich American market. The list also included many other forgotten names which once rode proudly over the highways and through the stock markets; Locomobile, Lozier, Peerless, Stearns, Stutz, Velie, Winton, the Apperson "Jack Rabbit," Cole, Kissel, Marmon, Moon, whose passing gave mute testimony to the great gamble which is business.

Each manufacturer had its own ideas as to wheel sizes, and a tire company had to build tires to meet each set of ideas if he wanted the business. It was not safe to neglect even a small company, for with the incredible growth of the automobile, the small producer of 1913 might be a million-dollar account a few years later.

By 1915 Goodyear's volume of original equipment business had become so large that a separate department was organized to handle it under Jackson in Detroit. Today four charter members are still active, Telford and Lawrence in Detroit, Brunt in Milwaukee and Burnham in Akron.

Fast-shifting prices of crude rubber brought many headaches during this period, and in 1910 when speculators were running prices up to three dollars a pound, Seiberling, Stadelman and Durant of General Motors drew up the first cost-plus contract in the industry, which was then extended to other customers.

Manufacturers' prices on the 36 x 5 would be $178 a set if made of one-dollar rubber, $375 on three-dollar rubber, with graduations in between at 25 cent steps. A set of 28 x 3's, used by Ford and Brush

Electric, cost $63 on one-dollar rubber, $118 on three-dollar rubber.

The Automobile Shows had become colorful events as the car manufacturers brought out their new models in January at New York and Chicago. There were two shows at first, while the Selden patent litigation was on, the companies who had taken out licenses holding theirs at Madison Square Garden, and those fighting the patent at Grand Central Palace. Later automobile shows spread all over the country, until there were few points in the hundred largest American cities without one.

Goodyear salesmen tried to get their tires on as many as possible of the show cars, and lively battles were staged even on the showroom floor, with tires changed the night before the show opened. The car manufacturers sensed a public interest in the latest type of tire, favored Goodyear. The trade journals kept score, and Goodyear general letters carried dozens of reports on the results, with Goodyear leading in virtually all of them.

Stadelman did not let the concentration on automobile tires lessen efforts on other lines. The SV solid tire for trucks started an era in transport which the pneumatic truck tire would carry on. Carriage tires was still a good field, and as late as 1911 Goodyear signed up 141 carriage manufacturers, increased this to 148 in 1912, with orders for 135,000 sets.

The bicycle tire business had dwindled, with Hartford and Morgan & Wright having most of what was left, but the motorcycle came in for an exciting career. It would take an important place on the sport pages and the highways, as motorcycle racing champions supplanted bicycle riders as heroes to young America.

One of the leading carriage manufacturers, at Elkhart, Indiana, who built a hundred carriages a day, advertised its Musselman coaster brake and Goodyear 28 x 2½ white-studded tires on a motorcycle selling at $188 and $235, went on to say:

"We have been in the horse-driven and harness business 28 years, several years in automobiles and motorcycles, and we expect to be in business as long as automobiles, motorcycles and harness are made."

Goodyear went into the motorcycle tire field aggressively in 1910. Seiberling had come back from the New York automobile show impressed with the possibilities of the new vehicles on display there, called in Shelby Falor of bicycle tires, instructed him to get into it. Litchfield put Ernie Brunswick of the factory in charge of production. The two men talked to many motorcycle racers getting their ideas. They wanted something more than a large bicycle tire. U. S. Rubber Company had most of the business and Goodyear would have to do something better. Drawing on its accumulated experience, the factory did come up with a better tire. But that was not enough.

There seems always to have been a dramatic instinct at Goodyear, the impulse to do something out of the ordinary. The new tire had white sidewalls.

"Now how about putting a narrow streak of blue rubber around the center of the tire?" said Falor.

"What for?" asked Brunswick.

"Just to be different. People will notice it," answered Falor.

That brought in the Blue Streak racing tire, which became famous in racing meets and hill-climbing contests. De Rosier, one of the leading racers, came into Akron looking for Goodrich, but landed at the wrong factory. Falor hired him on the spot, sent him out to demonstrate the tire. De Rosier proceeded to smash all American records. A team of ten racers was hired to travel the racing circuits, won race after race, until every youthful motorcyclist was demanding Blue Streak tires.

Goodyear built up a million dollar business in this field in two years, had a production of nearly 1500 tires a day, as compared to 5000 automobile tires. Motorcycling began to decline about 1916 with the onsweep of the automobile, and thereafter was relegated to a less colorful but still useful career in the nation's transportation system, continuing up to the present day.

An important development in the history of the company—and the industry—came when the dealer program was set up under Rockhill in 1911.

Rockhill, former newspaper man, a student and analyst, had come into a good idea of the viewpoint of the consumer, was ready for bigger things. He went in to see Stadelman to ask for a tougher job, like selling to the big companies, the car manufacturers. Tire retailing had not attracted well-financed merchandisers and most tire dealers were small accounts with hole-in-the-wall locations, many of them former vulcanizers and bicycle repair men.

Stadelman had the situation analyzed and his man measured. The company had been fortunate in getting a gratifying percentage of the original equipment business of the country, he said, and must maintain its position there. It would be worth much to Goodyear when more new cars rolled out of the factories on Goodyear tires than on any other kind.

However a bigger potential market lay in the increasing number of individual car owners over the country. If Goodyear tires were popular with the public its position with its manufacturer customers would be strengthened. A company which based its program on selling a few large accounts was in a less stable position than one well entrenched in the confidence of the people who use cars.

"Eventually 60 per cent of the tire business will be with the car owner, and the manufacturer's business which now overshadows it, will not be over 40 per cent," said Stadelman. "We must be strong in both fields. I'm assigning you to the dealer field. You have what is potentially the most important job of any of us."

Tire distribution in America with the independent dealer as the keystone, came out of this conversation.

Rockhill's first step was to nail up the sign "Wholesale Only" on the door of each branch. All replacement sales would be diverted to the dealer. The company would not compete with him. Other tire manufacturers were rather scornful of this at first, but within a year most of them had followed suit.

The second step was what he called Selective Distribution. Not everyone could handle Goodyear tires. Goodyear must pick its dealers carefully, allot them as much territory as they could handle adequately, give them the fullest possible advertising and merchandising support, put the Goodyear franchise on so high a scale the dealers would want to get it and, once they had it, would want to hold it. The Goodyear franchise would become in time the most highly valued in the industry.

Third, Goodyear salesmen must be partners in all of the problems of their dealers—selling, advertising, accounting and management. Rockhill had the gift of graphic expression. Persistently and dramatically he reminded the field that "no salesman's job was completed when he had sold his dealer a bill of goods—that his responsibility continued until the goods had been delivered to a customer"—"that the salesman could not push any more tires into the back door of a dealer's place than the dealer could roll out through the front door"—that "if the salesman could keep the dealer's stock moving, reorders would be automatic."

Fourth, Goodyear salesmen must preach, day in and day out, the gospel of service. Service was written into the Service Station contract, and no dealer could continue to hold his franchise who did not help his customers "get out of Goodyear tires all the mileage the factory had built into them."

Rockhill believed that "whatever benefited the customer, would benefit the dealer, and would benefit the company." He made that his creed. The dealer became an extremely important factor in the industry from then on.

Typical of the beginning years is an incident at Pittsburgh in 1910.

Shortly after Hazlett went there as branch manager, L. K. Smith, a Packard service man who knew many car owners and chauffeurs, set up a vulcanizing shop across the street. He had $300 in cash, sold two U. S. tires for another $300, giving him $600 in working capital. Hazlett got the company to grant him a $50 credit limit, helped him with his books at night, steered him along. He built up a good business, and was able to sell out in 1920 for half a million dollars, retired to live in Los Angeles. Roger O'Brien in Philadelphia started a small place back of the branch there, built up a big business. Other success stories came to light as tires enabled men to become independent.

A new type of salesman was coming in. He would not spend a lot of time on trains and in hotel lobbies, did not have to know a lot of stories. He would have a limited territory and work it intensively, become acquainted with every phase of his dealer's business. He was a less spectacular type of salesman, but he did not mind getting his shoes muddy, would not hesitate to take off his coat and help out a dealer in the rush hours, might even sweep out and wash the windows as a quiet hint to a dealer to spruce up.

Sales conferences were held annually, but up to 1913 only the branch managers were called into Akron. But that year saw the first slump in sales since the big drive had begun, receding from $32 millions to $31. So Seiberling had everybody in at two big meetings, the eastern men at New York, the western men at Chicago. Both were held during the Automobile Shows to give the men a conception of the size of the industry and the size of the organization. Litchfield got back from a trip to Europe and South America in time for the Chicago meeting.

Seiberling made a fighting speech. There must be no retreat. He asked for sales of $40 million the following year. They did write up $36 million.

The next year he brought everyone into Akron. The situation was changed. The new Cord tire was on the market, a chance to repeat the spectacular advance of the Straight Side.

The salesmen formed a parade line at the Portage Hotel, marched the two miles out to the factory, the California delegation bringing a cub bear along to add to the excitement.

The Akron executives all sat on the platform, the modest Stadelman as usual merely taking a bow. The dynamic Seiberling told the story of the Cord tire, threw a challenge to his audience—a sales quota of $60 million.

That was a tough quota, from $36 million to $60, but the men went back to their territory with the bit in their teeth. No one had the slightest doubt but that the new Goodyear cord tire was the best in the world. Month by month sales totals mounted.

In July Stadelman sent out the word, "August is the harvest month. We must do $8,000,000 that month to make quota."

The men hit the $8 million mark, and made the $60 million quota for the year with three millions to spare.

The outbreak of World War I cut sales of civilian goods as production was diverted to military purposes, and Goodyear dealers had to get part of their tires elsewhere. But when that struggle ended, the company plunged in again to regain its lost markets, signed up several thousand new dealers, began hiring men again.

Hough, later to be Advertising Director, came in 1914 and Harry Blythe the following year—his hiring throwing light on Rockhill's methods.

An All-Ohio football star at Mount Union, Blythe coached the team and taught English at Canton High for a couple of years, with his eye on the coaching job at his alma mater. He was not particularly interested when Rockhill, back for an alumni meeting, suggested his taking an unglamorous job with a rubber company.

But when Rockhill repeated the invitation a year later Blythe thought it over. Why not? With a friend high up in the company he would probably go ahead fast. He reported for work.

Rockhill greeted him warmly, assigned him to a new department, Sales Promotion—then apparently forgot all about him. The manager of the department was taken ill. The other men were all new too, no one knew what to do. Rockhill did not do anything about it, so Blythe took over.

"Well, let's run it ourselves till someone comes in and stops us. There are four of us and four sales divisions. We'll each take one."

And before anyone knew it he was unofficially running the department. There was still no sign from Rockhill, and Blythe, somewhat miffed, drove in all the harder. He got his first sign of company interest several months later. That was when a man was called in from the field to be manager of the department.

It was a blow in the face. Blythe knew he had done a good job. So this was what business was like. He was ready to quit. However, his football training came back to him. You did not quit in football when you lost a game. There was another season ahead. He came in as usual next morning, found a note on his desk. Rockhill wanted to see him.

"I intended to call you yesterday but didn't get to it," said the sales manager. "You've done a good job so we're sending you out to Denver as assistant branch manager. You'll leave tomorrow."

It was Blythe's first lesson in handling men, and one he did not forget. Rockhill had not forgotten him, knew everything he was doing, but Blythe would have to get ahead on his own, not as a friend of the sales manager. He made a record in the field, switched to production, succeeded Slusser as superintendent in California, went back to sales, became vice president of tires, getting two-fold training which fitted him to direct the big war job at Goodyear Aircraft in World War II.

The story may throw some light, too, on the reason for the company's long interest in athletics. Football teaches men determination, alertness, team work, highly useful qualities if men can apply them to business. Many have over the years.

The end of World War I brought in its GI's to Goodyear, mostly blimp and observation balloon pilots who had taken their training at Wingfoot Lake, among them Coe of manufacturers sales, Winings of mechanical goods, Post of export and Lohmann of sales administration.

Another Navy man came in from the fleet, J. M. Linforth, who would go on to a vice presidency. Litchfield and Slusser had made a trip to Europe on a government mission shortly after the hostilities ended, fell into conversation with a young officer on the way back, liked his looks.

"Are you staying on in the Navy?" Litchfield asked. Linforth smiled.

"I imagine the Navy will have more reserve officers than it needs," he said. "I'll be out before long looking for a job, preferably in sales."

"Look me up when you get out," said Litchfield. "We might have something for you at Akron."

The sales curve continued upward, passed the hundred million mark when America got into war in 1917, hit a peak of $168,000,000 in 1919.

Then depression struck.

The Era of Competition (1920-1940)

After a series of lush years when with mounting production of automobiles, World War I and post-war expansion, the tire industry had had a waiting market for every tire it could turn out, it found itself from 1920 on in a severe competitive situation which lasted through to the beginning of World War II. The tire dealer was affected as well, though for somewhat different reasons. The situation was a fairly simple and illuminating example of the working out of competitive forces under Free Enterprise, might be called a textbook case.

The formula can be simply stated:

One, large demand and easy profits in any field invite competitors to rush in, until in time the field becomes overcrowded.

Two, when there are more companies in any field than the business will support, a battle for survival ensues and the less efficient ones are forced out.

Three, when competition is free, that is where no one takes unfair advantage—and it is the government's job to see to that—this battle becomes a life and death matter, and a company can survive only as it marshals full ingenuity, resourcefulness and invention, furnishes better products, prices and service—which is greatly to the public's benefit, though hard on the companies who fall behind.

Tire companies had sprung up by the score during the boom years, to share in the new business bonanza until, when the bubble burst, there were some 300 tire manufacturers in the country. But business went to pot after October, 1920, and tire companies died like flies, particularly the new ones, those underfinanced, inexperienced and inexpertly managed. The 300 manufacturers shrank to 125, which was what one might expect. However, difficulties continued in the tire industry even as general business revived under the warming sun of Coolidge prosperity, and smaller companies merged or were taken over, while even the long-established U. S. Rubber, the giant of the industry, passed its dividend in the boom year of 1928, for the first time in a quarter century. And another depression was coming, one more severe and longer-lasting than the first.

In this new competitive era Goodyear fared better than most of its competitors. It had come out of the financial reorganization with a heavy load of debt, but it at least had ample working capital, and used it to strengthen its sales position, was one of the first companies in the industry to resume large-scale advertising.

Taking vigorous advantage of the transition from high-pressure tires to balloons, the increasing use of pneumatic truck tires, the comeback in mechanical goods, soles and heels and other products, together with improved business conditions over the nation, Goodyear soon built up its sales to a point higher than ever, passed the $200,000,000 mark in 1925, retained its leadership.

Two important personnel changes came in 1928. Espenhain, vice president of sales, left to take over the management at Fisk, and Rockhill to join Miller. Bob Wilson moved up to sales manager, was elected vice president the same year.

J. E. MAYL, 1924
Vice Pres't Tire Sales

J. K. HOUGH, 1914
Director Advertising

J. T. CALLOWAY, 1918
Assistant to Vice Pres't

I. D. FOSTER, 1913
Mechanical Goods Sales

W. F. BLOOR, 1919
Statistician

L. E. JUDD, 1932
Director Public Relations

H. BROOKS, 1909
Director Purchasing

H. W. HILLMAN, 1934
Ass't Treasurer

H. D. HOSKINS, (1899) 1907
Ass't Comptroller

If Rockhill had great analytical gifts, Wilson who had been manager in succession of the Service and Truck Tire Sales Departments, then the Western Sales Division, then of Advertising, had shown the capacity to synthesize many factors into an organized program. There were other changes, Shilts became secretary of the company, Linforth took over Manufacturers' Sales, Mayl took Dealers' Sales, and Blythe came back from production in California to take over retail store operations.

Difficulties within the tire industry grew worse in the 1930's and in the bleak year of 1932 there were only 31 tire companies still in operation. Nine out of ten had folded, although a number found new financing, picked up and carried on as business improved.

The primary reason for the long difficulties of the industry was that tires were giving continually greater mileage, so that car owners needed fewer of them. The technicians had done too good a job—tires were too good. In 1916 the industry could figure that every car running on the highway meant a business of eight tires per year. Ten years later car owners on the average bought only one and two-tenths new tires a year. More people bought cars but tire sales lagged behind the productive capacity of the industry. The factories operating in 1925 had a capacity of between 50 and 60 million tires per year. But in the peak of 1928 (for sales volume turned downward before 1929), the public bought only 49,000,000 tires.

Prices went down as well. Taking a weighted average of all renewal tires built, the price fell from $20.66 a tire in 1923 to $10.82 in 1933. The industry not only sold fewer tires but got only half as much for each tire it did sell.

Also far-reaching changes came in distribution which would affect the manufacturer. The number of outlets more than doubled, which meant that each dealer's share was lessened, resulting in disastrous price wars, from which the manufacturer got the backlash.

Further to snarl up the situation was the Stevenson Act. Rubber, already highly erratic among raw materials, executed the most cataclysmic price changes in its entire history, went from 23 cents a pound to $1.12 and back to 30 cents in five years. When you place this alongside the fact that normally the change of one cent a pound means a difference of a million and a half dollars in inventory to a company like Goodyear, you may measure some of the explosive effects of these price fluctuations.

The depression of 1929 climaxed these difficulties but did not create them. With this introduction, let us examine some of the factors in this situation at closer range. What was the situation after 1920?

There were five large companies, a dozen middle-sized ones, and a host of small companies some of whose names have long been forgotten. The "Big Five" were Goodyear, U. S., Goodrich, Firestone, and Fisk. The medium-sized companies included Miller, Hood, Pennsylvania, Federal, General, Ajax, Mason, Mohawk, McClaren, Kelly Springfield and later Seiberling, who started a new company.

Oldest of the five companies in its component parts, though not in name, was The United States Rubber Company. It had never been primarily a tire company, tires being around half its business. In the early days of the century, it merged a number of small companies, particularly in footwear, and in 1910 took over a number of tire companies, including the well-known Morgan & Wright in Detroit and G. & J. in Indianapolis. A rubber company started by Charles Goodyear, after changing hands several times, was among those gathered in by U. S. Rubber. For many years, U. S. was the largest of all rubber companies, manufactured a wide variety of goods, clothing, footwear, belting, hose, mechanical goods. Goodyear passed U. S. in tire sales in 1916 but so large was its business in other lines that it was not until 1926 that Goodyear took first place in total sales.

U. S. Rubber was the first American company to go into the Far East to set out rubber plantations, became one of the largest estate owners. It had shown considerable resourcefulness and invention. It had an enviable reputation among American corporations of unbroken dividend payments on its 8 per cent preferred stock, maintained a dignified type of advertising and held an entrenched position in the original equipment field.

Second oldest was Goodrich, started in Akron in 1870 by an army surgeon with a gift for business who, in the comparatively few years of life remaining to him, had the satisfaction of seeing his little company well under way. At the outset he persuaded ten Akron men to buy $5000 or $10,000 worth of stock apiece, forming the original capital. Eight of these men in the next several years went to him and asked him to buy their stock back. The Goodrich company also manufactured a wide range of articles, using the slogan, "Everything in Rubber," and long before the automobile started had made rich men out of the Raymonds, Tews, the Works, the Goodrich family, Shaw, Mason. They became the first families of Akron.

O. C. Barber, founder of the Diamond Match Company, able but dictatorial, had built his business up to national proportions, but after a quarrel with the city over taxes had moved out of town and started the new community of Barberton nearby. He tried to trade his empty factory in Akron for an interest in Goodrich, which was next door, but Goodrich was not interested. Barber had the reputation of being hard to get along with. So he started his own tire company in the empty plant, calling it the Diamond Rubber. The plant did not do so well for several years, so in 1898 Barber put in new management headed by A. H. Marks, a chemical engineer who utilized technological improvements, built it up in the next ten years to be a formidable competitor of Goodrich. And when Diamond alertly grabbed the Silvertown Cord rights, Goodrich bought it out for $40,000,000. However, the financial

From over America and abroad salesmen, production, eng

load entailed by the purchase price proved burdensome and in 1913 Goodrich passed its dividend and the stock fell to low levels. It was several years before Goodrich returned to a prosperous position—and Goodyear had passed it during that time.

Youngest of the Big Five was a company started by Harvey Firestone, a shrewd, aggressive carriage salesman who felt that there was more money in manufacturing goods than in selling them.

In many respects the careers of Goodyear and Firestone parallel. They started in the same era, Firestone just two years after Goodyear.

and operating men gather at Akron for 50th Anniversary Homecoming.

The rising curve of sales was to run parallel, Goodyear always keeping about the same distance ahead. Like Goodyear, Firestone concentrated on a single line of goods, to get the advantages of mass production rather than a diversified line such as U. S. and Goodrich had. And as Goodyear later went into mechanical goods and soles and heels, Firestone later made rims and took over a footwear plant in New England.

To a greater extent than the others, Firestone was a one-man concern, the founder holding sufficient financial control that he largely selected his directors, rather than being selected by them, although the

Seiberlings as a group, similarly held financial control at Goodyear up to 1920.

Last of the "Big Five" was Fisk, an old conservative New England company, well-established, particularly in the original equipment field.

Competition was exceedingly active among the big companies but there was a parallel competitive battle between them and the smaller companies. The latter had some advantages growing out of their size.

When rubber was rising in price the big companies had the advantage. To assure uninterrupted production, they had to carry large in-

ventories, usually a four month supply, and these grew more valuable
as the price rose. On a falling price market, however, the advantage
went to the smaller companies, who were buying spot rubber, while
their larger competitors were suffering inventory losses.

The large companies had facilities for research and improvement,
and research was particularly active during this period, the three and a
half inch tire of 1923 growing to a six inch cross section in ten years,
with mileage increasing from an average of 11,000 miles to 23,000.
However, the smaller companies followed closely on the heels of their

big competitors in the matter of new size and types—and did not have to maintain laboratories and a big technical staff.

Tires for new cars were chiefly built by the big companies, for several reasons. The car manufacturer did not want to send his cars out on off-brand tires, wanted tires that were well known and accepted by the public. Also, only the larger tire manufacturers had the facilities and finances to ensure deliveries of any quantities which might be needed. Quality was more uniform, too, than if a car maker divided his business among several companies.

However, if the big companies got most of the original business, the replacement field was wide open and a free field—with some advantages to the smaller companies.

The "Big Five" had to pretty well blanket the country with dealers, to service the tires they placed on the nation's cars. The small companies had no such responsibility, could concentrate on major markets in the big cities, go after the cream of the business—and so needed fewer salesmen, branches and warehouses.

In many cities the Goodyear dealer was the leading tire merchant, doing a business of $100,000 a year and more. But in cities of 100,000 population and up, his chief competitor was apt to be the Hood dealer or Lee's, or Racine, McClaren, General, Seiberling—a different one in each town, but each one an aggressive trader, having an exclusive distribution deal.

The smaller companies were particularly active in the lower price field, often listing their tires at the same price as the large companies, which permitted their dealers to offer long discounts and so appeal to the bargain instinct of their customers. Their tires, too, often found their way into the hands of stores specializing in cut-price, bargain tires, picked up at distress prices and sold to owners of second-hand cars or those who were hard up.

This is a fair picture of the tire business in the middle '20's, when new factors began to come into the retailing field.

The public had long criticized the high cost of distribution. The farmer who raised a crop found after it had passed through the hands of the commission man, the food manufacturer, the wholesaler, retailer and back to the public, with each intermediary taking his profit out of it, that it retailed to his neighbor in town for several times what he got for it. Salaries of brokers and factory foremen, charges by the railroad and truck operators, rent and light and clerical hire, taxes and factory overhead had gone into the cost of the farmer's beans between the time he harvested them and they reached the kitchen of his neighbor in town.

This situation offered substantial reward to anyone who could effect some plan of mass merchandising to match the economies found in mass manufacturing. That brought in the chain store, first in groceries and drugs, and gradually into automotive accessories, including tires. The chains, buying in quantities, priced their goods a little below the independent dealers, sold for cash, made no deliveries, made a place for themselves. They became a controversial issue in every community, but brought a challenge to the independent dealer to improve his merchandising methods—which the aggressive ones promptly did, to the public's advantage.

Changes began to make themselves felt throughout the whole field of merchandising. Main Street was changing. Up to then the drug store, the grocery, the harness shop, the blacksmith had each stuck to his knitting. With the chains coming, the pharmacist took off his skull cap, threw his mortar and pestle away, put in a soda fountain, sold cameras, cigarets, tennis rackets, phonograph records. The tire business saw the advent of company stores, of mail order houses turning retailers, and gasoline filling stations selling tires and tubes.

The two big mail order houses, Sears, Roebuck and Montgomery Ward began to put in retail stores in 1926. The automobile had come in and the farmer did not have to order goods by mail, could drive to town and see what he was getting.

The two companies got a real welcome from American consumers. They had an excellent reputation, were almost an institution, particularly in the west. Thousands of farmers, ranchers and prospectors swore by them, regarded their familiar catalogue as their economic bible, bought most of their requirements from its pages, visualized them as benevolent old gentlemen from Chicago, from whom they got their canned goods and winter flannels, their kegs of nails, and needles and thread.

The legend is typical if not true of the Montana rancher who had long dealt with Sears, Roebuck and who one fall included in his order the item, one wife, and that the mail order house, after satisfying itself as to the customer's standing and seriousness, passed the word around, the challenge being caught up by a high-spirited girl clerk, tired of the city, who accompanied the shipment out to Montana—and the couple continued to do business with Sears, Roebuck.

So when business houses of such standing opened their own stores, they would naturally get a substantial volume of business.

Montgomery Ward went chiefly into the middle size and smaller towns, Sears into the big cities, selecting strategic locations, built large size and spectacular plants. The public, intrigued by the acres of merchandise, popularly priced, welcomed the innovation. By 1930 Montgomery Ward had some 400 stores, Sears somewhat fewer.

But while Sears was a third larger than its rival in total sales, Montgomery Ward was doing three times as much tire business, when Gen. R. E. Wood came into the presidency of Sears. He set out to improve sales in this field, arranged for Sears tires to be made under its own brand name, advertised them widely, went vigorously after business.

The program succeeded. In 1925, selling almost entirely by mail, Montgomery Ward had marketed 2,000,000 tires, Sears 700,000. The Sears advertising campaign doubled its mail sales in three years, but Sears added another 3,000,000 tires sold through its stores by 1928.

Sears' excursion into this field led to a notable lawsuit, in which Goodyear was affected a few years later. Sears decided in 1927 to buy all of its tires from one dependable supplier, rather than several, to get better uniformity and a better volume price, as it did with its other merchandise. The contract went to Goodyear. In the so-called Sears, Roebuck case, filed by the Federal Trade Commission, the government did not question the integrity of either Goodyear or Sears, as its attorneys specifically stated, nor did it quarrel with the long-established principle that a volume buyer is entitled to a better price than a small buyer.

It is cheaper to sell 100,000 tires to one customer than to 1000 separate customers scattered over the country. The latter requires many salesmen to get the business and keep it. It means setting up thousands of ledger accounts with many entries of small orders. It means credit investigations and involves credit losses. It means warehousing stock at the company's expense since the small buyers have neither storage space nor finances to carry a large inventory, and would buy only a few tires at a time.

The Clayton Anti-Trust Act, under which the suit was brought, recognized the validity of lower prices paid by mass purchasers due to those economies. But never before had anyone attempted to see exactly what those economies were, in a specific case, and determine from that the price the large buyer should pay. So the case went into extremely complicated accounting matters on which experts disagreed widely.

The Robinson-Patman Act was passed in 1936, while the suit was in progress, defining these discounts more specifically, and the Sears contract was cancelled. Sears bought an interest in a factory in the south, and contracted with two smaller companies for the balance of its requirements, went ahead.

The litigation, however, which started in 1933, lasted three years longer, as the Federal Trade Commission (in an era when the administration at Washington was none too friendly toward business, nor too preoccupied with business recovery) still sought to make a ruling against the company stick. Twice the Commission carried the matter up to the U. S. Supreme Court, but both times unsuccessfully. The case ended in 1939 with a victory for the Goodyear company.

The chain stores, including Montgomery Ward, Western Auto Supply and others, largely drove out the gyp dealers and fly-by-night bargain shops, furnished hard-up customers with dependable low price merchandise, but did not put the independent tire dealer out of business. Tire sales by Sears and Montgomery Ward had a considerable growth in the first years, but leveled off as the oil stations got into the business, having a thousand outlets to Sears' and Ward's one.

The only tangible result the Sears, Roebuck suit had was to take 3000 tire-building jobs out of Akron, at a time when jobs were hard to get, as Sears' business went to other communities.

The second new development in tire distribution during this period was the company store, which started in a small way in 1925. Tire manufacturers had often given financial assistance to their dealers, and occasionally had had to take one over. Goodyear, however, had put in its own stores only if it could not get adequate distribution in an important trading center from an independent dealer. But, when Firestone announced an investment of $25,000,000 in company-owned stores in 1930 and other manufacturers followed suit, another new factor had come into tire retailing.

The increasing use of trucks had a part in this. While there were thousands of individual truck owners, the big market was in fleets of trucks, operated by business, construction and supply houses. The fleet owners expected prices based on quantity purchases, preferred to have their tires serviced by a single responsible company and one having many and easily accessible outlets. Outside of the manufacturer himself, only the larger independent dealers had the finances and facilities to furnish this kind of service.

The company stores also served as experiment stations to find improved methods which could be passed on to the independent dealer.

The third factor affecting distribution was the decision of the oil companies to go into the tire business. This started with a Standard Oil subsidiary in 1929, and gradually expanded. The oil companies had thousands of stations on strategic corners. Tires could be sold by the same men who pumped gasoline and would add substantially to the total volume of business even though the sales of any single station were small. Standard contracted for tires from two of the leading manufacturers. Other oil companies watched the experiment and presently went in too, and particularly in the smaller towns got an increasing share of the total business.

So the public was not buying tires in 1934 from the same merchants it patronized in 1926. It liked the low-priced department stores the mail order houses had set up. Truck owners came to depend on the repair and upkeep service they could get from large dealers and company stores, and it was convenient to buy emergency tires at gasoline stations, have one put on the car while gas and water were being replenished, and the owner got a sandwich next door.

Mainly, however, the public still gots its tires from the independent dealer. He had the advantage that he made deliveries and extended credit; his methods and practices were more flexible, to meet exact conditions of his neighborhood, rather than standardized practices designed for the average of the country; he carried a wider selection of goods; he had a more intimate contact with his customers, and in the case of the tire dealer, a more frequent one, since he saw his customers more often than the manager of the tire department in a chain store did.

Finally he had the great incentive that the business was his own, and what he made was his. He was not a hired manager who might be moved from town to town. He was a citizen and his roots sank in. He was not easy to dislodge.

The public got better goods, better prices and better service out of this situation, but out of this competitive situation came price wars, which hit the manufacturer as well as the merchant.

In 1933 the public owned 26,000,000 cars, not counting trucks and buses. To serve these car owners were the following: 84,000 dealers; 40,000 filling stations, owned by 25 oil companies; 1350 "company stores"; 900 retail stores operated by Sears, Roebuck and Montgomery Ward; 375 stores operated by Western Auto Supply Company; 20,000 miscellaneous stores, dealing through jobbers, a total of 183,000 outlets. There were only 75,000 tire retailers in 1926.

Let us follow through and see just what may and did happen in so complicated a distribution system. Tire buying in City X inexplicably falls off in any given September, let us say. The reason is hard to state. Purchasing power is not a unit but represents the total needs of the owners of 26,000,000 cars and trucks. All of them need tires from time to time. It might happen however that relatively few of these car owners needed tires that September. More likely is it that something happened then which made those who did need tires try to delay buying them. It might be a speech in Congress, seasonal buying habits, an editorial, factory layoffs, rumors of a falling off in other lines of business. Something created a general lack in confidence. So this car owner and that, and this or that truck owner, put in a blowout patch, or had a sectional repair made, or re-grooved his tires, or just took the chance that they would last. And the lusty stream of buying diminished, fell to a trickle of orders.

Business is a sensitive thing, and in depression years a nervous one.

In community X there was an honest desire on the part of every tire distributor to keep prices at a level at which everyone could survive. But business was bad. A chain store saw itself going into the winter with an overstock, a dealer saw bills coming due for merchandise, for rent and wages and not enough money in the cash register to meet them; so someone, usually the hardest-pressed, cut prices, announced a bargain sale. He cut deeply enough and announced it widely enough to draw a stream of buyers in. Better sell at no profit or even a loss, than slowly starve to death and have the sheriff sell him out. The effect of his move was lost on no one in the retailing business in town. He reaped an advantage, but it was short lived, for as his competitors saw business getting away, saw their customers loading up, each was compelled to meet the new price. Someone added another 10 per cent cut—or rumors to that effect got around and met easy credence. Presently truck owners in the neighboring towns of Y and Z, and even as far away as Towns A, B and C heard about it, saw the chance to buy their requirements for months ahead at special prices, went to their dealer, demanded that he meet the price else they would order tires from City X. The thing spread like a conflagration.

No one made money on it—except the public.

Price wars were particularly difficult for the dealer. If he met the price cuts, he might go broke. If he did not, he would get no business —till the flood of buying was over. And his bills were falling due at once. He turned to the manufacturer whose tires he handled.

Now the manufacturer did not want to see three months' business in Towns X and the rest go to other companies. More important, he did not want to see his good dealer forced to the wall. He must and did stand behind him. And he had no assurance that price wars would not break out at any time, at any place. Anywhere from Portland to Portland a tire distributor under pressure might pull down the house of cards.

In addition to the price-cutting flurries among the tire dealers were graver ones originating with hard-pressed manufacturers, trying to stay in the business. As early as 1928, a good year for business generally, manufacturers organized an Industry Institute in the effort to stabilize conditions.

U. S. Rubber passed its dividend. Ajax and McClaren merged, Mason closed its doors, Goodrich took over Hood, which had a valuable footwear business, and later Miller, which had an excellent trade in drug sundries as well as tires. United States took over Samson, but partially to give it a production unit on the Pacific coast, as Firestone and Goodrich had created in 1927 by building their own factories, and Goodyear had done in 1920. With Fisk falling behind, the Big Five had become the Big Four by 1930 and the New England company became a part of U. S. Rubber in 1939.

Kelly-Springfield, somewhat older than Goodyear, a thorn in Goodyear's side in the early days of patent suits, had abandoned its Akron plant in 1920 and moved to Cumberland, Md., where a free site had been provided. It continued as an active figure in the business, particularly in truck tires but later ran into financial difficulties and was purchased by Goodyear in 1935 from the trustee in bankruptcy. Dunlop's American plant in Buffalo, started just ahead of the 1920 depression, never became a big factor in this country. Michelin's American plant closed. In the Akron area, Swinehart, Marathon, Star and Portage, and in other parts of the country, such companies as Federal and Racine had been absorbed by other companies or closed up. Among the Akron plants General, Seiberling, India and Mohawk remained as factors in the business.

While the public ordinarily is not particularly interested in the success or setbacks of any business, the difficulties of the tire industry during these years did attract considerable attention. Thousands of stockholders were caught in a pinch of reduced dividends and no dividends. Members of Congress began to talk about modifying the Patman and Clayton Acts in order to permit companies to make a fair profit. A Fact Finding Committee appointed by the Labor Department inquired why the tire companies did not stop price wars instead of cutting wages.

Business houses in other countries could get together and reasonably agree on price levels, people began to recall. Maybe our laws were too strict. Competition was all right, but maybe now there was too much of it—a line of thinking which eventually led to the passage of the well-meaning but short-lived National Industrial Recovery Act.

To show how far this thinking ran, the question was frequently asked during those days in the locker room of the golf clubs, the classroom of the universities, and the editorial room of the newspapers: "Why don't the tire manufacturers get together? The three large Akron companies control 60 per cent of the tire business. They should be able to reach an understanding."

But Litchfield, Firestone and Tew could not sit down in a quiet room at the City Club and divide the tire world into three parts—or any number of parts. That was contrary to both economic and statute laws. In any event they had only 60 per cent of the business, and the 40 per cent remained to be dealt with. The 60-40 ratio would not have lasted

Model tire store at Merchandising Laboratory is studied by hundreds of dealers over the country in the effort to improve their display and marketing technique.

Attractive stores of Goodyear dealers brighten up Automobile Row in many cities—and even give a modern touch to airport supply houses.

long if they had attempted to hold their own prices up to more profit-able levels. Each of the other companies was a free agent, could sell his tires at whatever price he chose. He could give them away if he wanted. Any agreement as to prices would be effective only if everyone went in, and if everyone stuck. A single manufacturer could knock over the applecart.

Manufacturer and retailer alike were in the grip of economic forces which would have to work themselves out in their own way and their own time.

If the difficulties of the tire industry seemed more acute than those of other industries, it was a difference in degree, not in kind. All American business houses were passing through similar difficulties, with results which would affect all business.

The primary reason for the troubles in the tire industry was that there were too many companies, too much production capacity, and the public would have to decide which ones would be used, and which ones would survive.

As a result of that struggle, business houses were forced to give their utmost in value as the price of survival, tires which were sturdier, safer, longer lived, which cost less, and could be obtained more conveniently from better merchants.

For the public was saying:

"I am not unmoved by sentiment, I am appreciative of courtesy, I am open to friendship, I am motivated at times by caprice. But in the long run and over the long swing, I buy on quality, because I want my money's worth; I buy on service, because I want to get full return from my purchases; I buy on convenience, for I would rather go next door than have to drive across town; and I buy on price. Whoever best meets those several requirements will get my trade.

"If more people are engaged in making or selling merchandise than I need during depression times it is no fault of mine, I didn't ask any of you to go into business. I feel no obligation to keep you in business. I didn't promise you a living. The law of the survival of the fittest applies as truly in business as in biology. Commerce is a free field."

If this seems like a ruthless philosophy, it is one which no man nor government wrote, and no man nor government can change. It was evolved by society itself through the thousands of years in which men have traded with each other for the necessities of life.

Gadsden factory

10. Later U. S. Expansion

The Reasons for Gadsden

GOODYEAR, hard hit by the 1920 depression, came back so fast that within seven years it had to expand its manufacturing facilities, at home and overseas.

Any major expansion in Akron, however, was out of the question. The thirsty rubber industry was using up most of the city's supply of water, even though the factories put in cooling systems, and used the same water over and over. The Coolidge prosperity era had created a shortage of manpower throughout the Buffalo-Pittsburgh-Cleveland-Detroit sector. In any case, the company's big customers were reluctant to give all their business to one tire company, lest an emergency of fire, flood or Act of God leave them short of tires for new cars ready to take the road.

Goodyear countered this last point with the suggestion: Did it make any difference to the car manufacturer whether he got the rest of his tires from a Goodyear competitor, or from another Goodyear plant out-

347

side Akron, unlikely to encounter emergency conditions at the same time? That sounded reasonable, and the company looked around for a place to build the new factory.

It decided to go south. Except for steel in Birmingham, and cotton and tobacco mills at various places, all of which used materials from the section, there was little of general manufacturing anywhere south of the Mason-Dixon line, such as was common in the north.

Litchfield, a New Englander, had long thought of extending manufacturing operations into that section, feeling that there should be a more balanced economy between the agricultural south and the industrial north.

He had made a trip through the foothills of the Appalachians a few years earlier which may have had more to do than he himself realized in decisions which led to Goodyear investing millions of dollars in the South, manufacturing all of its fabric there, and building a tire factory which became the company's largest production unit except Akron.

Twenty miles north of the city of Gadsden, Alabama, is Sand Mountain, a broad fertile plateau dotted with small farms. Driving across it Litchfield was struck by the circumstance of large families of good American stock living on farms which might not turn in more than $200 a year in actual cash, too little to do more than provide a living, with no chance for an ambitious youngster to think of college—with the result that hundreds of them set off for the nearest big city or the north when they reached eighteen.

Goodyear had hired thousands of southerners, found them excellent workmen. A breakdown by states of birthplaces of Goodyear employees in 1929 showed these figures:

OHIO	3973	KENTUCKY	860
WEST VIRGINIA	2986	INDIANA	492
PENNSYLVANIA	2075	GEORGIA	438
TENNESSEE	1277	ILLINOIS	320
IOWA	965	NORTH CAROLINA	271

(As a matter of fact the South was still furnishing men to the rubber industry in 1948, for a spot check at the employment office that year showed that out of every 100 new men hiring in, 36 were born in Ohio, 20 in West Virginia, 11 in Alabama, seven in Tennessee and six in Kentucky, 44 out of every 100 still coming from south of the Ohio River, and the personnel men recognized many familiar names among those registering as Ohioans, second generation southerners who, like their fathers, thought of Goodyear as a good place to work.)

The thought which stuck in Litchfield's mind was: Why not take industry to labor rather than the other way around, build a factory in the south, leave wages and purchasing power there, not force young men to leave home in order to find a job and larger opportunity?

The decision to build a factory large enough to turn out 5000 tires a day, was reached in the summer of 1928. Slusser sent his engineers out to look over various cities, check power, fuel, water supply, labor supply, shipping facilities.

Gadsden was one of the first cities built in the old Cherokee Indian country when the red men were moved west 100 years earlier.

It was the fourth largest city in Alabama, with ample labor supply there and in the surrounding country. The Coosa River furnished plenty of power and water, two railroads passed through the town. A large tract of nearly 400 acres was available along the river, across the bridge from the city proper. Furthermore, lying in the coal and iron ore region, Gadsden already had a branch plant of the Republic Steel Company, a big textile mill and smaller industries, was a community which realized the importance of manufacturing.

When the word got around that one of the large northern tire factories was looking for a location, everyone in Gadsden was interested. A Citizen's Committee raised funds to provide a large number of houses for workers alongside the projected site.

Slusser went over the engineers' reports, checked the various sites personally, talked to Litchfield on his return.

"Gadsden is my first choice," he said.

Litchfield walked over to the window, stared out unseeingly for several minutes. His mind went back to Sand Mountain. He could see square-shouldered farm boys taking jobs at the factory, going on the Squadron, finding outlet for the wide range of talents which the expanding rubber industry presented, some of them going away to college and returning to take more important jobs.

One Sand Mountain boy did just that, became a plant superintendent for Goodyear fifteen years later.

Litchfield turned back to Slusser.

"Gadsden suits me," he said.

There was quite a celebration when the news got back to Gadsden. The newspaper got out an extra. The town band turned out, paraded through the business district, its ranks augmented by scores of boys and men using dishpans as drums and tin horns as wind instruments. There was a big dinner that night. Goodyear's coming meant additional employment and purchasing power, more business for the stores, a larger city, money to be made in real estate.

Ground was broken in February, 1929, and the job rushed. The factory took advantage of all new improvements in layout and machinery, was the most modern tire plant built in America. It had an impressive facade along the main highway from town, with wings reaching back, and switch tracks alongside and behind it. The fenced-in area comprised
There was, of course, a clock tower on top.

The first tire was built June 22nd and the formal opening held in July, with the governor and leading citizens of the state present. Thousands of people came in from all over the section to go through the

President Hoover at Washington pressed a button on his desk, and an electrical impulse travelled over the telegraph wires to Gadsden, releasing the Goodyear house flag on the tower to formally upen the plant.

The production organization had already been picked, Stephens-trained men headed by Steele of California as superintendent and the long-experienced Neiger, Follo, Goodall, Rearick and others. Bloom from the University of Mississippi took Division C, Zieske, who built the factory, stayed on in charge of engineering, Frye took development, Niederhouser, tech service, Craigmile of California, personnel.

The factory paid the same hiring-in wages as the steel mills, but had some advantage as a place to work, since 90 per cent of the labor at the steel mills was unskilled, while at the tire plant only 10 per cent was unskilled, 80 per cent semi-skilled, and 10 per cent skilled. Employees could look forward to better money as they became proficient, which brought in an excellent type of workmen.

Nowhere did the athletic traditions of Goodyear find warmer reception, particularly under the incentive given by Michaels, crack golfer, and all-American footballer from Ohio State, who succeeded Steele as superintendent in 1935. An eighteen-hole golf course was built by employees in the field adjoining the plant, the company built the clubhouse. A swamp back of the factory was reclaimed by the employees, who spent their off time during most of one summer constructing a dam and creating a large lake, which was stocked with fish.

An airship dock went up alongside the plant the following year as a half-way stop for Goodyear blimps headed for Florida. A reclaiming plant was added that fall.

The building of a factory in Alabama had farther-reaching results than if the company had gone to Pittsburgh or Passaic. While Goodyear was one of the first general manufacturers to locate in the south, its example was soon followed by others, including tire companies. The money put out in wages was plowed back into the community, in good roads, the wider use of automobiles, trucks, modern farm implements, electric power, schools—and more boys going to college.

The city got an increasingly wide range of industry, built a two million dollar airport, increased in size from 15,000 people to 50,000 with 75,000 in the Greater Gadsden area.

The Southern Cotton Mills

Goodyear started manufacturing its own tire fabric in 1913, when it was up to its neck in the Cord tire battle.

It needed an experimental plant where it could make up fabric in different weaves and gauges, build each into a tire, find out which was best. The textile industry did not have time to bother with this. Rubber was a small customer.

Looking around New England, the company acquired a picturesque 100-year old stone mill at Killingly, Connecticut, which drew its power from a water wheel thrown across a tributary of the Thames River. It was a small mill, only 22,000 spindles, as compared with the later 67,000 spindle mill at Rockmart, Georgia. It had an isolated location, 30 miles from Providence, was two miles off the railroad, apt to be snowbound in the winter. But it would serve the purpose.

In taking over the property Goodyear retained the old management, sending only two men out from Akron, Coulter as treasurer, and Hunter as manager of the labor department. Killingly was the company's first experience with the mill village, typical of the industry. Many of the employees were second and third generation Englishmen, whose people had been spinners and weavers for generations. There was a smaller group of Portuguese who had come up from New Bedford and Frenchmen from Quebec.

Killingly furnished considerable information about costs, and the data from which specifications could be written to meet changing tire requirements. Its size and location prevented it from being a volume producer, but it continued to be useful as an experimental station, was the birthplace of Supertwist, and a workshop for further improvements. Its mission accomplished it was finally closed down in 1933 after 20 years operation.

The company's first full-scale operation, on a production basis, came in 1920 in Los Angeles, with a cotton mill large enough to supply the requirements of the new tire factory alongside. An experienced organization of 30 men was picked, all new Englanders, headed by S. A.

Steere, later to become vice president of fabric production and development. Modern machinery was installed, and the California mill went on to prove that there were no mysteries in carding, spinning and weaving that men anywhere could not learn.

The plant met schedules, did a satisfactory job until rising wages on the coast in the 1930's put its manufacturing costs out of line with those of the South and New England.

The breaking point in California arose when the unions came in to demand that wages in the textile mill be comparable to those paid in the more skilled processes in the tire factory. Unionism was new then, had had quick successes, was feeling its oats. Its leadership was in no mood to listen to economic arguments. It must have what it asked, or else.

So the California mill was finally closed down in 1938 and the machinery disposed of, Beggs, the superintendent, taking part of it to the new factory he was to head in Brazil.

Goodyear's next cotton mill venture was at New Bedford, Massachusetts, in 1924. The story has been told of how Goodyear took over this property in order to absorb fabric commitments made in the boom days of 1920. The Fisk Company, in a similar position, took the other half of a fairly large mill, each having 57,000 spindles. Steere, now back in Akron, brought on Hall, his second man from the coast, put him in charge.

New Bedford was to have a checkered career in the Goodyear history. It was one of the colorful cities of New England. Settled originally by the Quakers in the days of King Philip and Massasoit, it was a sizable and flourishing community during the Revolutionary War, indeed American privateers used the Acushnet River as a base for raids on British shipping, which did so much damage that the British in 1778 landed in large force and shelled the town.

After that, in the days of Moby Dick, it became the great whaling center of the country, even passing Nantucket, with more than 300 whalers calling it home port. Those activities brought in a large Portuguese element, since the ships frequently stopped at Lisbon and the Azores to shanghai, or let us say hire, Portuguese sailors to fill up their crews. Some of these men jumped ship at New Bedford, starting a stream of immigration from that country which continued to the present day, made the city a better known name in Portugal than is New York. The population today is about 65 per cent Portuguese, with five Portuguese churches and the only daily newspaper in the United States printed in that language.

The discovery of petroleum in this country, which reduced the demand for whale oil, and the finding of substitutes for whalebone, sent that industry on the decline after the Civil War, and the textile mills moved down from the inland streams where they had originally located, and the city next became one of the important textile centers of the country.

"The earth has got to be very shifty to get out of the grasp of a people equally at home on land or water," said Thomas B. Reed, then speaker of the House of Representatives in a speech there in 1897.

The textile business boomed after World War I until there were 28 great mills along the water front. When Goodyear moved in it found itself with a working force mainly Portuguese, many employees speaking no English. With the language as a barrier, it was particularly difficult for employees to understand the difficulties of their employers with the competition from the south, and Goodyear had hardly more than gotten into operation when strikes were called in practically all of the mills in town, except Goodyear.

Slusser and Hall talked it over. The company's industrial relations program of good wages and good working conditions should work in New Bedford if employer and employee understood each other's viewpoint. So a new deal was called for in 1925. The mill must be Americanized. To work there one must be an American citizen or become one. Other manufacturers were skeptical, said it would not be possible to get enough men to run the mill. But Americanization courses were set up in the factory and in the city schools, and New Bedford went on as a successful operation until 1936.

Labor troubles broke out anew during the depression, with the organization of a union affiliated neither with AFL or CIO.

The mills already had problems beyond the immediate one of depression, the foremost being the increasing competition of the southern mills which had cheaper power and paid lower wages than industrialized New England. It was the one time when management and labor should have got together to get costs down and quality up to stay in the field, but more radical views prevailed, and all the mills were closed down.

Many of the mill owners let the city take over their properties for the taxes, and some plants were torn down and the materials sold for what they would bring. Those which survived were for the most part, fine goods manufacturers, with specialized machinery and long established outlets for their goods.

The Goodyear mill lay idle for two years after 1936, was reopened for a year, then closed for good in 1938, the machinery, like that from

Georgia cotton mills, at Cartersville (with attractive mill village adjoining), and at Cedartown and Rockmart, furnish much of the fabric for Goodyear plants.

Decatur cotton mill (above), with war-built additions for making rayon fabric, and (below) Plant III, Akron, used as a warehouse and the home of the Rim Plant.

California, being shipped to Brazil. Goodyear did not get back to New Bedford until World War II,. and then with other manufacturing lines.

The Canadian factory bought its own cotton mill in 1926, going into the textile milling country in French Quebec, took over a factory in the thriving city of St. Hyacinthe, thereafter made all the fabric needed by the tire factory at Toronto and mechanical goods plant at Bowmanville.

The fifth Goodyear mill at Passaic, New Jersey, was taken over for the same reason as that in New Bedford—commitments. But the company did not operate this plant. Passaic, in the heart of the Greater New York industrial area, had many busy factories which were looking for men, since business was booming, could pay much higher wages than the cotton industry could live with. Goodyear headed south.

A Philadelphia lawyer, Colonel Adamson, serving in the Northern Army during the Civil War, impressed with business opportunities in the south, had gone back there after hostilities ceased, built a cotton mill at Cedartown, Georgia. He operated it successfully for a number of years, but was ready to retire, so Goodyear bought the plant in 1926, enlarged it, shipped the Passaic machinery down.

Operations in the South proved so successful that a second property was purchased in 1929 at nearby Cartersville, and an entirely new plant, larger than any of the others, was built at Rockmart. The three mills lay in a triangle about 50 miles apart, convenient for administration, particularly as good roads came in.

In expanding textile production, the plan was to produce about 70 per cent of its requirements in its own plants, buy the rest outside. This would put the plants in competition with each other, compel each one to remain an efficient producer—and also permit them all to run fairly full during slack times, outside purchases being curtailed.

However, as one of the steps in the New Deal's program of Planned Economy, the National Recovery Administration ruled in 1933 that a cotton mill must not run more than 80 hours a week, this on the theory that that would spread production around more widely. This directive cut off third shift operation at the Georgia mills, threw men out of work and Goodyear's textile production out of balance, brought in a fourth mill at Decatur, Georgia.

Tire fabric did not have the wide range of changes that rubber manufacture did, but the test laboratory at Akron had more to do than test the strength and elasticity of incoming fabric. Changing requirements in tires over the years brought a tighter twist; rayon came in for special uses, calling for a large amount of development work, as we have seen, and nylon after that.

A rough measure of the size of a cotton mill is the number of spindles it contains, so the following table will indicate the relative size of the various Goodyear mills:

*KILLINGLY, CONNECTICUT	1913	22,000
*LOS ANGELES, CALIFORNIA	1920	28,000
*NEW BEDFORD, MASSACHUSETTS	1924	57,000
CEDARTOWN, GEORGIA	1926	51,000
ST. HYACINTHE, QUEBEC	1926	40,000
CARTERSVILLE, GEORGIA	1929	56,000
ROCKMART, GEORGIA	1929	67,000
DECATUR, ALABAMA	1932	38,000
SAO PAULO, BRAZIL	1940	7,500

* Operations discontinued.

Steere soon ran out of his original California-trained superintendents, had to bring in new men from the textile schools and train them. He went back to New England for Parmenter to become superintendent first at Cedartown, then Cartersville. Hall went down from New Bedford to head the big Rockmart mill. Stewart, who died in 1939, took Cedartown. Young, who ran the old Killingly mill from 1922 until it was closed, took over Decatur. A small-scale Flying Squadron produced its first superintendent when Ostrander, who graduated from Cornell in 1922, took charge at Cedartown. On Hall's retirement, Powell, who had been assistant superintendent at Cartersville when Goodyear took over the property, succeeded. Behind these Number One men were assistants building up their experience, ready to move ahead as opportunities arose.

Though Goodyear mills in the south had to compete cost-wise with the industry generally, a modern labor relations program was installed at each one, similar to that in Akron. Experienced personnel men were assigned to each plant, men who realized the importance of getting good men, keeping wages fair, and employment records straight, and who sensed the importance of wholesome personal relations between management and employees.

Dean of the personnel men was Hunter, who had started at Killingly and later went to Decatur. Next in service was Murphy, who started at New Bedford, took charge at Rockmart afterward, while Powell at Cedartown and Parker at Cartersville came on later.

Cafeterias and hospitals were set up, sports and recreation programs laid out, a Wingfoot Clan printed in each plant and encouragement given to education. Rockmart, located in a town of 1400 people, had room for a golf course alongside the mill, built by employees. Baseball leagues were started, largely at the instance of Matthews from the Akron personnel department, who spent a few years there, uncovered major league baseball talent in the mill villages. The company inherited mill villages at Cedartown and Cartersville.

The village at Cartersville had an interdenominational church, a school house, park, playground and a general store. The store was privately owned, with employees free to trade there or in the city proper, a mile away. The "company store" or commissary system had been subject to abuse in many places, was something Goodyear preferred to avoid. Cedartown had none, as it lay immediately adjoining town. Goodyear had to build a mill village at Rockmart, because of the size of the community, but Decatur, a larger city, had ample housing.

The company pioneered the eight hour day in the section. All southern factories worked at least ten-hour shifts when Goodyear went south, while the cotton mills had five eleven-hour shifts a week for the night crew, and five and one-half ten-hour shifts for the day crew, making a total in each case of 55 hours a week.

The Goodyear mills followed this custom at first, but changed over in 1933 to three eight-hour shifts, wages being moved up so that the employees would earn the same amount in 48 hours as they had previously in 55. The new schedule kept the mill running until midnight Saturday night, and a few of the mill people parted a bit reluctantly with their cherished Saturday afternoons off, though they worked only eight hours a day rather than ten and eleven.

The Goodyear mill towns grew in population and wealth with steady payrolls. Decatur, the largest town, had grown from 17,000 to 23,500 by 1940; Cedartown went from 7500 to 11,500; Cartersville from 500 to 7500; and little Rockmart from a village of 1400 to a town of 5000. Goodyear was the largest employer in each town and a wholesome community and employee relationship grew up.

Kelly-Springfield

The distressed 1930's saw further substantial addition to Goodyear's facilities including the acquisition of the Kelly-Springfield Tire Company of Cumberland, Maryland. Kelly-Springfield was an old established tire manufacturer—older even than Goodyear, and its adversary in the early days when litigation over Kelly patents on carriage tires threatened the success of the young and struggling Goodyear company.

Previous additions to Goodyear's plant facilities in the United States had been to increase production. The plant organizations had no responsibility for advertising and selling. Kelly-Springfield was acquired as a complete business organization. It had its own management, engineering and production personnel, its own sales force, a strong dealer organization—and an excellent reputation with the motoring public.

The Kelly-Springfield Tire Company had its beginnings back in 1894, when Edward Kelly and Arthur Grant of Springfield, Ohio, were granted patents on the first practical method of applying solid rubber to carriage wheels. So successful was their invention that, before the turn of the century, Kelly carriage tires were known and sold all over the world—and the company was recognized as one of the leading manufacturers of quality rubber products.

Kelly started building pneumatic tires as the infant auto industry progressed, and pioneered in the early development of solid cushion tires for motor trucks. The company grew and prospered with the growth of the automotive industry, and occupied a strong position in the renewal tire field. It never seriously participated in the original equipment field, relying mainly on the renewal tire market for its sales, through its own dealers.

During the thirties, however, it gradually fell a victim to the reduced consumption and extremely competitive conditions then prevalent. After several years of unprofitable operation, stockholder dissension resulted in changes in management, eventually ending in a receivership petition, calling for reorganization under the new National Bankruptcy Act.

The conclusion was finally reached in 1935 that the best solution for the company's difficulties was to merge it with some organization, strong in finances and managerial efficiency. Goodyear looked the situation over, decided there was nothing wrong with the Kelly company which a sound management and proper financial backing could not cure. Accordingly, in August, 1935, the name, good will and all assets of Kelly-Springfield were acquired on terms relatively favorable to both institutions.

It was decided that Kelly would best continue to operate under its own management, and with its own manufacturing and sales organization. Edmund S. Burke, who had been brought in to do a reorganizing job, just prior to the receivership, remained as president, and retained the key personnel of the old Kelly company, strengthened where necessary by technical and financial men trained in Goodyear methods.

A modernization program quickly brought production methods and product up to date. Aggressive sales and advertising started to rebuild the distributing organization, which had gradually been losing out in the keen competition of the period.

Among the key personnel working with President Burke at Kelly were Swearingen, vice president and general sales manager, who had grown up in the Kelly sales organization, serving in various sales capacities in the field since 1917; Eggleston, treasurer, who had been with Goodyear during the Wilmer regime and later with Dodge and Fisk; McCarty, development manager, who later was transferred to Akron to head up tire design; Warden, factory superintendent, drafted from Goodyear development, with experience in California and England; Porter Collins, formerly with Goodyear, Akron, sales staff, and manager for several years at San Francisco, who took over as manager of advertising. Carter and Hudak, now back with Goodyear in Akron, and John Hoesly, later head of the Goodyear plant at Norrkoping, Sweden, also served for some years at Kelly, the first two as personnel directors and the latter as chief compounder. Bete, an M.I.T. alumnus, who assisted McCarty in development activities, took over the responsibility for this department when McCarty was transferred to Akron. A few Goodyear salesmen joined the organization.

Kelly, well established when the war broke out in 1941, would have an interesting career.

The Jackson Plant

The thinking behind Jackson was to have a tire factory close to the automobile industry, and one which would concentrate on a few sizes, and so achieve the full economies of mass production. Jackson would build several sizes of truck tires up to ten inches and only one passenger size, the 6.00-16, which made up the greater part of the market.

With Gadsden and California serving the South and the West, Akron had remained the catch-all for all sizes and types of tires, had to build not only current sizes but many which had been obsolete for years. The 30 x 3½ went out with the balloon tire, but was still being widely used by sturdy automobiles of older make, stayed in the line until the second World War. This, with many specialized sizes and types, not only for cars but the widening truck and farm market, had the result that Akron had accumulated molds to make hundreds of sizes. Jackson's job would

Kelly-Springfield plant at Cumberland, Maryland, greatly expanded its floor space and made two complete conversions of manufacturing operations during War II.

The Jackson, Michigan, plant, built to supply original equipment tires for the automobile manufacturers, changed over to making guns during the war—then back again.

be much simpler in the fewer sizes it would build.

An unused factory having plenty of space for expansion was purchased from the Kelsey-Hayes Wheel Company in December, 1936, a
staff of Akron-trained engineers headed by LaDue was rushed in, went
so vigorously to work that on the first day of the following June, the
first tire was produced in what was called the most modern and efficient
tire factory in America.

Jackson laid out an assembly line which started at the back door
where the crude rubber was delivered, continued in unbroken sequence
to finished tires and the shipping room in front, with freight cars rolling in alongside. Banbury mixers were used everywhere except the few
needed for warm-up, scales on wheels brought in the compounds; carbon black, now furnished in pellets, was drawn by conveyors from incoming cars into mixing tanks, doing away with the soot; conveyors
were everywhere, carrying the various tire parts to their destination and
on again; watchcase molds for individual curing of tires completely replaced the old pits, and a "merry-go-round" built, with a crew of men
working simultaneously on the various parts which constitute a tire.

As in the case of other new factories, key personnel was drawn from
the older plants, and piece workers were recruited from the surrounding
country. A Flying Squadron was set up, a factory paper started, and the
usual sports and recreation program put in effect.

Sheahan, who had started in Akron as a supervisor in 1916, gone to
California as a foreman, to England as a division superintendent, and to
Australia as general superintendent, having worked in more Goodyear
plants than any other individual, came back from Sydney to head up the
plant, but having had to wait till Condon could get out from England
to relieve him, got to Jackson only after the fast-growing plant was in
operation. Clayton, Squad leader, was acting superintendent till operations were under way. Sheahan returned to Akron in 1940 as Plant I
superintendent, was succeeded first by Lee of Argentina, then Ruffner
of Java.

The other two new plants, at Windsor and St. Marys are tied in with
the war chapter and will be described later.

11. The Rise of Unionism

The Akron Strike

THE depression which started in 1929 saw the advent of a new movement in industrial relations which would sweep the country in a few years.

This was the penetration by unionism into a new field, the mass production industries of America, whose workers up to then had largely been indifferent to it.

It was a new type of unionism. Up to then labor organizations were active chiefly in the skilled trades, transportation, and a few industries where wages were low and working conditions adverse. The new movement was no revolt against such conditions. It was carried into a field where wages were the highest in the world, where men worked in clean, well lighted, well ventilated factories, where machinery for hearing and settling grievances was easily at hand.

Goodyear was not only affected by this movement, but circumstances made that company, long known as a good employer, the proving

363

ground for it. Here notably the sitdown was first effectively employed
to close down a factory and start a strike, and here was worked out a
technique which the new unions could use successfully to break into
mass production industry generally.

Union leaders had long studied this field. Here were not only large
numbers of men, but large groups concentrated under one roof, easily
accessible if argument could be found to appeal to them. One obstacle
was the fact that these employees had done fairly well for themselves
in the vital matters of hours, wages and working conditions, perhaps
better than other workmen had done under unionism.

Attempts had been made to break into this field, notably by the Industrial Workers of the World, who had indeed gone into Akron in 1913
to organize the rubber industry, and had been not only defeated, but in
the end discredited, and had finally disappeared from the labor picture.

But new ideas and new formulas were thrashing around in the mind
of a veteran labor leader in Washington. This was to organize workmen
not on the basis of crafts and trades, but to take in everyone, men of all
trades and of no trades. After all, that plan had succeeded among the
coal miners he led. Conditions were favorable to the experiment. And
when John L. Lewis failed to convert his A. F. of L. associates to his
ideas he set up his own organization, led a revolt. All these forces were
milling around confusedly when, rather by chance, circumstances at
Akron led to the crystallization of ideas and the formulation of a
program.

Underlying in the situation was the basic factor of depression, and
the distress psychology which it created. America had had depressions
before, and had come out of them, after hardship and loss, through the
working out of economic laws. But this one seemed to have no bottom
to it. Discouraged men were ready to believe that there was no way out,
that this was the end of the industrial world they had known, that things
would never be better.

At Goodyear business dropped off at the rate of $50,000,000 a year
for three years in succession and sales by 1933 were only two-fifths of
what they were in 1929. Demand for goods, need for production, and
money to pay wages, go together.

The company instituted a work-sharing program, sought to keep as
many employees as possible in some sort of earning position, but times
were hard all over America. Millions of men were walking the streets.
Conditions in Akron were typical. Distress psychology swept the land.
Men were ready to grasp at any straw which offered relief. The time
might be ripe to launch a drive to unionize all industry.

The program would have the blessing of a national administration which was friendly to labor; it should have the support of everyone without jobs, since they had nothing to lose; it should be able as well to count on men unsure of their jobs, either because they were less competent than their mates, or had had short service, and would be next to be laid off. *Unionism might help them hold their jobs, prevent their employer from letting them go.*

The National Industrial Recovery Act gave the first impetus to the unionization movement. The long chain of CIO events goes back to the year 1933. The Roosevelt Administration had tackled the matter of depression with vigor and confidence. Past depressions had settled themselves in time, but that process was too slow. Planned thinking would achieve the end more quickly. So NIRA started with the premise that if every manufacturer and merchant got a fair price for his goods, if price cutting and chiseling were curbed, business and employment would pick up, and presently all would be well.

And lest the employer grow too strong in the process, labor should be protected also, through Section 7a, which provided that employees should have the right to bargain collectively through representatives of their choice.

NIRA did not end the depression, and long before the Supreme Court had invalidated it, NIRA had become NRA, by popular consent. Industrial Recovery was overshadowed by Section 7a, which was interpreted to mean that everybody should join a union.

Everyone was at least free to do so without hindrance from his employer—and this principle was quickly re-affirmed through the Wagner Act after NRA passed off the statute books. The effort to promote recovery by law ended and the new era of unionism was under way. The American Federation of Labor of which Mr. Lewis was still a member, albeit a somewhat disgruntled one, swung into action.

For to the leaders of Organized Labor the benefits of unionism were so obvious that certainly men everywhere would swarm to join, once they were assured of protection and organization work could be done in the open, no longer in secret behind closed doors.

Once a nucleus of men was established in each plant, the others would fall in line. The all-clear signal had been given.

Five great fields lay open—steel, textiles, the electrical industry, automobiles and rubber.

The Federation mapped out its campaign, selected organizers and staff. Coleman Claherty, well seasoned organizer, formerly of the blacksmith's union, and a friend of William Green, head of the A.F. of L., drew the rubber portfolio, hurried to Akron, went to work.

Men did flock in at the outset in the rubber plants. But as nothing much happened in 1934 and 1935, and the first enthusiasm wore off they began to flock out again. Unionism reached its lowest ebb in the winter of 1935-36. A dramatic issue was needed and Akron would furnish it. A few dates will help keep the picture clear.

1933—Passage of NIRA—small unions organized in major rubber factories in Akron.

1934—Membership drive and agitation continue. Strike in India Rubber Company succeeds in placing union label on company's goods, though India afterward went out of business. Four weeks strike at General Tire Company ends indecisively.

1935—Organization efforts continue, with less success at Goodyear than at other large plants—Union groups demand sole bargaining rights at Goodyear on pain of strike—Strike vote taken in plant, loses decisively, but union calls the vote propaganda, threatens to call a strike anyhow—Washington intervenes, resulting in "Perkins Settlement," which binds company to deal with employees.

NIRA declared unconstitutional. United Rubber Workers Union given charter by American Federation of Labor. National convention of union at Akron throws out Claherty and other Green-picked officers, discards AFL plan to divide union into smaller units, swings to Lewis program, will be first important addition to newly organized Council of Industrial Organizations set up within AFL.

Controversy over wages and hours carried to Washington, with Fact-Finding Committee reporting adversely to company.

1936—John L. Lewis addresses mass meeting at Akron Armory, castigates employers. Strike called at Goodyear, lasts five weeks—Settlement gives "representatives of the employees" more specific recognition—Decline in influence of Industrial Assembly.

CIO unions suspended by AFL convention—Wagner Act passed—Beginning of sitdown era in factory, some 600 disturbances reported, most of them inside the plant, against non-union employees or those who refuse to "slow down."

1937—Wagner Act declared constitutional—Industrial Assembly dissolved—Continued sit-downs bring suggestion of union contract as means of restoring order—Negotiations begin—Union wins election at two major plants, with 8,464 at Goodyear voting for, 3,193 against union as bargaining agency—Firestone bargains without election, which comes a year later.

Business takes new nose-dive bringing short hours and need for lay-offs, which union opposes with sit-down, holding possession of factory for several days—Public sentiment turns against excesses, and sit-downers evacuate plant as state and city officials prepare to take action—Lay-offs put into effect.

1938—Lay-offs continue, affect a total of 4,200 men—Agitation over seniority brings May riot—Public sentiment now active and rioters dispersed by city police—End of period of violence and intimidation—Negotiations resumed covering seniority rules and other controversial items—Negotiations stalemated over issue of freezing hours and wages —Citation by National Labor Relations Board.

1939—Hearings start in April.

1940—Hearings recessed in May.

1941—Contract terms agreed on in October and contract signed.

With this outline in mind, let us look at conditions just before the strike. Business was picking up that summer of 1935. The public felt more hopeful, was buying goods again, was needing tires and ready to purchase them. If Akron was to get its share of this increasing demand, it would have to get its costs, always higher than outside, somewhat closer in line with competition. Such a move would help the company in getting business, help the men by creating more work.

Piece work rates were to be cut about 8 per cent but earnings would not be affected since the men would get more hours of work per week. Some men would be laid off at the outset (though vastly fewer than had to be laid off later) but if the plan worked and production did pick up as a result of lower costs, they could soon be recalled and all would go forward.

The six hour day which the company had instituted in 1930 as a means of spreading work, was not to be discarded but made more flexible. If business continued to increase as the result of this plan, the men would be given more hours, so that they would share fully in the business upswing, after months of slim payrolls, rather than new men.

It seemed reasonable as a long range program, beneficial to both company and men, and could have been "sold" to the employees in normal times.

But the plan played into the hands of the men trying to get unionism established, gave them an issue they could carry to Washington as a violation of the "Perkins Settlement."

A "Fact-Finding Committee," union-minded, was named by the U. S. Department of Labor. Its report, though largely an expression of opinions, rather than statement of facts, was widely read by a public which was still blaming employers because men did not have jobs.

The committee concluded: (a) that Goodyear's example would probably be followed by the other Akron companies (which if the program
was sound, should be helpful to all Akron tire builders); (b) that it
would increase unemployment—which opinion considered only the immediate effect, waved aside the thinking of experienced business leaders
that it would put all Akron employees in a stronger competitive position;
(c) that the committee saw no reason for lengthening hours; (d) that
the company had violated the "Perkins Agreement" by making this
proposal without consulting the union.

This last point is significant in that it came to be used widely in labor
disputes thereafter. The company had agreed to meet with employees to
adjust grievances. The Committee interpreted this to mean that it could
take no steps of its own without consulting its employees. In later Labor
Relations Board cases the argument would be made that a company
would take no new steps without the consent of employees.

(e) That a better way to increase company income would be to eliminate price cutting.

Comment is perhaps superfluous on this final point. Any manufacturer hard up and needing money, was free to sell his goods at any price
he saw fit, free to dump his goods on the market at distress prices for
whatever he could get. This situation had long plagued the industry,
which had to meet the new prices in order to hold its customers, leading to price wars in which all suffered.

Still there was nothing the other companies could do about it except
through a hard-and-fast price agreement—which had been declared
illegal as long ago as the Sherman Anti-Trust Act.

The report of the Fact-Finding Committee, though it had no legal
binding force, was accepted as a victory for unionism, and helped create
the atmosphere for the outbreak of hostilities.

The incidents leading up to the strike were in themselves insignifi-
cant. The usual winter lay-offs were at hand. These grow out of the
fact that car-owners buy two-thirds of their tires during the five summer
months, and despite all merchandising devices to level off production,
the rubber industry remained more seasonal than most.

The winter of 1935-36 was the coldest in years. Sales were falling
off, inventories of finished tires accumulating, lay-offs, delayed as long
as possible, became necessary.

The custom in the industry in the matter of lay-offs was to start with
men having the shortest service. These automatically were on the fourth
shift. Notices were posted Thursday afternoon, February 15, listing 69
men, giving them the customary three days' notice.

However a blizzard struck the section that afternoon. Many third shift men, due in at 6:00 P.M., were unable to reach the plant. The shift fell behind, was unable to make the ticket. This meant that when the midnight shift came on, men in related departments would have to be sent home for lack of work. The foremen asked third shift men who were willing to, to work overtime till the ticket was reached.

The fourth shift came in, read the lay-off notices, saw some of the third shift still working, jumped to conclusions, sat down.

Meetings and conferences in the next few days seemed to clear up the misunderstanding; transfers were arranged for the men scheduled for lay-offs, and trouble seemed to have been averted. But a meeting was called at union headquarters Monday evening and a fiery oration by a downtown labor leader closed with the injunction, "Let's close her down." A standing vote was ordered, the motion passed, picketing began at the midnight shift, spread to Plant I and the offices Wednesday, and the strike was on.

If union leadership had preferred to start elsewhere to test out its program rather than at Goodyear, which had a good record as to wages and working conditions, it lost no time in moving in once the issue was joined. If the battle could be won there it could be won anywhere. Every resource must be put into winning the strike. Into Akron hurried seasoned leaders, veterans of many strikes, most of them Lewis followers—Brophy and Germer from the mine workers, Kryzski from the clothing workers, Rose Pesotta from the garment workers, Powers Hapgood, stormy petrel of many disturbances, McAllister Coleman, leftist writer, who prepared strike bulletins and radio speeches. Allan Haywood, already on his way to high place in CIO counsels, came on later.

The part which outside leadership played in directing the strategy of the strike may be disputed. Every man's part seems to him important. Even the Communist group in Akron claimed part of the credit, somewhat to the union's annoyance—not as a party, but as astute individuals acting on committees, furnishing orators to keep the strikers stirred up.

The leaders elected by the new union were amateurs, not only in the business of running a strike, but in unionism itself. Sherman Dalrymple, national president, had been a tire builder at Goodrich for 22 years. John House, president of the Goodyear local, had had 15 years service, had graduated from the Production Squadron, was working in the mill room at the time. Both were sincere earnest men, but without organization experience, and lacking the gift for fire-eating oratory for which the situation seemed to call.

Administration of the strike, manning of picket lines, feeding and housing the pickets and directing their movements, together with the public relations policies of speeches, mass meetings, parades, press statements, all indicated a professional job. And though the rubberworkers in time developed capable speakers and organizers from their own ranks, the bulk of the speech-making was done by outside talent.

The strike differed in some ways from other strikes.

It was not a strike for higher wages or better working conditions, but to establish a union as the bargaining agency for all employees. Grievances were aired during the strike, the piece work system was denounced as "a speed up" device, but the settlement reached at the end concerned itself chiefly with details under which representatives of the employees (the union not being specifically mentioned) could take greater part in shop affairs.

The strike demonstrated, and this was the most significant part about it from the standpoint of the new movement, that it was not necessary for a union to win over a majority of employees, that a small militant minority could not only call a strike, but could close any mass production shop and keep it closed if it could muster up enough pickets, and police and the law kept hands off.

Just what per cent of employees took part in the strike can only be guessed at. Estimates at the time that not more than 700 men out of 14,000 employees attended the meeting at which the strike was called. Several times that many non-strikers marched in protest to the City Hall, remained opposed to the strike.

The union gained members during the shutdown, but events at the time and afterward indicate that a fairly large group was out of sympathy with the movement. The very bitterness of the battle for many months within the factory afterward would seem to prove this. Perhaps a still larger number of men were uncertain which way to swing.

But the plant remained closed, with thousands of men picketing the gates, and entrance possible only by force. To help man the picket lines came union sympathizers from other rubber plants, WPA workers and the unemployed. Union speakers proclaimed that they could get all the coal miners they wanted to help out. Appeal was made to the law.

A man's right to strike, to refuse to work, is well established. His right to work is not as clear. If a plant is surrounded by angry strikers, he may waive for practical reasons whatever rights he has to enter the plant and go to work. In this case men were being restrained by force from entering the plant. The six common pleas judges in the county, sitting as a body, did not rule on their right to go in, but did limit picketing to six men at each entrance.

The strikers flaunted the injunction, tore down the notices, made no remote pretense to obeying it, kept as many pickets at the gates as they chose. At times the pickets filled the streets from side to side, and traffic had to be detoured around. They took over the streets, built picket shacks there.

The law was not enforced because public sentiment at the time prevented enforcement. The public was scared. Householders quaked in their beds, saw a new French Revolution in the making as hundreds and thousands of men filled the streets. Merchants looked uneasily at their plate glass windows, made donations of money and goods.

Appeals went to police, sheriffs, prosecutors, even the governor, to shut their eyes to the situation, not to do anything which might provoke open conflict. Militant non-strikers, out of work and angry, likewise felt the impack of a public opinion which thought in terms of appeasement, were urged not to attempt to crash the picket lines by force, but let events take their course.

The law kept its hands off.

Efforts were made by third parties, including the Assistant Secretary of Labor, to settle the strike. The settlement, when finally reached after five weeks in March, 1936, was not on the face of it, a victory for the union. It permitted "representatives of the employees," the union not being specifically named, to go into factory departments to discuss employee grievances. But the camel was inside the tent. Once in the factory the union moved to complete the unionization of employees, by force if necessary.

The next 14 months saw almost a reign of terror within the factory. Non-union men were harrassed, beaten and driven out of the plant—with immunity. The company could do nothing, the law would not. No union man could be convicted in court.

The defiance of the courts had left a feeling of irresponsibility in its train. Workmen might tell the foreman or superintendent to go to the devil. Men could make their own rules. On one occasion two men staged a sit-down which closed up whole departments.

This breakdown of discipline was to plague the union itself, a new union, not quite sure of itself, hesitant to crack down on the groups of "hatchet men" who roamed the plant at will, pulling switches, closing down departments, driving out men who refused to sign up.

Union leaders hurried out to the plant again and again to try to persuade overzealous followers to be reasonable and go back to work. But they themselves must not bear down too hard, must make compromises, make a show of radicalism or risk revolt.

Within a year the union felt strong enough to call for an election to select a bargaining agency for all employees. There was just one name on the ballot. The Industrial Assembly had been dissolved. Whatever opposition there was, was unorganized. Employees were weary of strife. The National Labor Relations Board was backing up unions everywhere. Many employees felt that further opposition was useless. CIO won by an eight to three margin. The union was in the saddle.

The company had always dealt with its employees, but had a different set of representatives to deal with now. The chief difference between the two groups was one of attitude.

The Industrial Assembly's viewpoint was chiefly internal to the plant. It had become convinced during the 17 years of bargaining that the progress of the men was bound up with the progress of the company. It could accept a long-range program, even though it entailed some sacrifices at the outset. The union was skeptical of anything other than immediate advantages.

Unionism established seniority, rather than merit, as the basis of holding a job. A company could no longer pick and choose among its workmen. It was all but impossible to let a man go on any other basis than lack of service.

Under unionism a company could no longer talk directly to its employees, but only through an intermediary. And management and men moved farther apart.

Other results came out of the Akron strike. The sit-down had proved, particularly in the 14 months after the strike, a highly useful device for unionism to break into the great mass production field.

Mass production methods as developed in this country had as their basis the simplication of manufacturing into many separate operations, easy to learn, quickly permitting volume output. The piece work system, which was part of it, employed the principle of paying a man not for the hours he put in, but for the product he produced, offered a dollar and cents incentive to put his fullest effort and skill into the job.

Akron disclosed the vulnerable point in the system. It depended for its success on a smoothly working organization throughout a factory. With manufacturing broken up into hundreds of separate processes, a complex dispatching system was needed to keep operations in balance, all producing in exact relation to the rest. Even a few absentees could throw the system temporarily off balance. The Flying Squadron at Goodyear had been devised originally to meet just this situation.

So the sitdown was a very simple monkey-wrench to throw into this manufacturing cycle. You need not convert an entire plant to your cause. All you needed was one key department, somewhere midway in the cycle—it did not need even to be a large department—and presently production was dammed up behind, slacked off and stopped ahead.

This principle could be carried to Detroit, to Flint, to Cleveland, to Toledo, to Pittsburgh, to Rochester—and would work.

Second, the chaotic conditions in the era of shutdowns forced the dispersion of the rubber industry over the country. Akron companies had no alternative but to push production outside the city if they were to fill orders and hold their trade.

Akron had had two-thirds of the rubber business of America in 1929 and one-third was done elsewhere, but a few years later saw those figures all but reversed.

Employment was affected. Men who had jobs got higher wages, but some 15,000 Akron tire workers were thrown out of work, and it was not until the impact of defense contracts was felt, in the spring of 1941, four years later, that the last of them could be offered jobs again.

A potent factor in the unionization movement during the whole period was the National Labor Relations Board.

That Board, which later came in for widespread criticism from Congress, the press and the public as being over-zealous, built up its staff at Washington and in regional offices over the country from well-meaning young men with limited legal or business experience, crusaders who would replace the system of private enterprise with one better to their liking; included some professional unionists, who would leave the Board, become labor organizers or vice versa, wherever their services were most needed; had men on their staff who were definitely left-wing.

In the hands of such a group, the Wagner Act became a useful weapon. Under the broad provisions defining "unfair labor practices," any employer who did not immediately make his peace and sign up with whatever union group offered itself, or was indicated by the Board, lived in constant jeopardy of prosecution.

Many of the smaller companies did not argue the matter. They could not afford the expense of long drawn out litigation, made such terms as they could and signed up.

The Wagner Act, while prescribing that employers should bargain with employees, did not stipulate that they had to agree with them. It did provide that bargaining should be in good faith, but that point is rather hard to establish in court, except perhaps by the test of whether in the end an agreement is reached.

So, in the case of the Goodyear citation, this came immediately on the heels of a break-off in contract negotiations, after months of discussion which had reached agreement on all points except that of freezing wages and hours, and a few lesser issues. It is possible to conclude that had a contract been signed no charges would ever have been filed—indeed the suggestion was made, after the trial got under way, that the case might be dropped if the company would sign up.

The charges were made under four out of the five classifications of "unfair labor practices." Of the 26 allegations under Section 8-I, (interfering with formation of a union) many were of "scatter shot" order, and six of them were dropped before the trial started, at the request of the Board's attorney, and 14 more were stricken out later. The other charges alleged domination of an independent union which had challenged the CIO union and asked for a new election; discrimination against some 80 employees; and refusal to bargain.

Testimony was taken during the 14 months of trial on three groups of charges, with the fourth, discrimination, remaining to be dealt with. Board attorneys then demanded certain company records, including payroll list for all employees in 230 different factory departments on 42 separate dates in 1937 and 1938, also a list of all employees hired in or transferred to 159 listed departments after January 1, 1937, with complete service records of each one.

This demand was resisted as unreasonable, if not physically impossible to comply with. Seniority lists were kept posted in all departments so that everyone knew where he stood, would know immediately if discriminations were made. The question of whether the company would still have to compile the records was taken to Federal Court, and the hearing was recessed after May, 1940. The U. S. Circuit Court of Appeals ruled in late 1941 that the Labor Board's request for some of the documents was well made, but in other cases was unreasonable and therefore not maintainable. In the meantime a contract had been signed with the union in October 1941, and the case was dropped.

Wartime Developments

With the advent of World War II, the government moved promptly to limit war profits and keep wages from skyrocketing. With thousands of men being drafted into the Army, a shortage of labor was inevitable.

The War Labor Board was set up in January, 1942, largely overshadowed the National Labor Relations Board during the war. For while NLRB had largely concerned itself with strengthening the position of labor in the United States, this objective had now become less important than that of winning the war.

To keep wages from getting out of hand, the War Labor Board set up the "Little Steel" formula, under which wages were to be held at not more than 15 per cent above the January, 1941, level. However, the standard work week would be 48 hours, with time and a half for overtime beyond 40 hours, and double pay for work done on the seventh consecutive day.

Larger take-home pay should be an incentive for maximum war production. Other incentives were held out to the unions. Under certain circumstances, WLB would order "maintenance of membership" and the "check-off."

Maintenance of membership meant that anyone who joined the union must remain as a dues-paying member during the life of the union contract, though a 15 day "escape period" was provided when the contract was signed. The check-off meant that the employer must deduct union dues from the pay envelope and turn them over to the union.

Both of these were highly important in the early days of unionism, with men free to drop out, and dues collection always difficult, since it had to be done in most places outside the factory, and at times with a picket line around the entrances on payday to enforce it.

A "no strike" pledge was obtained from the principal unions for the duration.

Machinery was set up to adjust grievances through regional boards with right of appeal to the national board, rulings being made retroactive back to the filing day.

However, all of these carefully prepared plans did not bring peace or good labor relations. Grievances poured into regional and appeal boards in such volume as to clog up the machinery. There were major strikes which closed down whole plants, and thousands of minor ones to plague the war effort.

The great drive for war production brought a manpower shortage. Employers in all sections of the country were competing for a limited supply of labor, and the Akron area was particularly short.

Labor difficulties are usually more acute in large industrial communities because of the concentration of workmen there, easily influenced by mass action. Next, perhaps to Detroit, Akron was one of the greatest centers of disorder, slowdowns, and work stoppages during the war, though there was plenty of work at good wages, with record take-home pay due to overtime, and tires were vital to success in the air and war on the ground, and rubber boats, life vests, and bullet-proof fuel tanks for airplanes were saving the lives of American soldiers.

Eighty-five per cent of the strikes and stoppages arose over wages, mostly affecting relatively few people. New weapons, improved weapons, and constantly changing specifications to meet changing war needs required time studies to be taken in each case to determine a fair piece work rate. With new products coming in, these studies often had little information to work from, and starting rates had to be high before the union would accept them, with the result that as the work became familiar, and employees got the knack of the job, earnings mounted. A green girl, nimble-fingered, might find herself earning as high as two dollars an hour.

The union claimed that the high earnings grew out of the effort and efficiency of the workers. There were indications, however, that this was not the sole reason, for whenever word got around that a given operation was to be discontinued, employees in the department really went to work to get maximum benefits out of the situation while it lasted, and earnings for these few days mounted fantastically.

Even under ordinary conditions employees in some departments found themselves making not merely more than their foreman, but more than the old line workers, long experienced tire builders, whose pay, like that of the foremen, was frozen.

But instead of working with the management to bring piecework rates for all positions reasonably in line with the skill, intelligence and effort required, the union opposed each proposed adjustment. Even when jobs were changed, and an operation simplified, the piecework rate could not be cut without a fight, probably a work stoppage and the possibility of a complete shutdown of the plant.

John House, the first president of the Goodyear local, had been defeated in 1940 and, except for one year, Wheeler of Mechanical Goods headed the union during the war years.

How much vital war production was lost by the accumulation of slowdowns and scores of work stoppages during the war is beyond determination. The government made every effort to impress on the union leaders the importance of rubber production to the armed forces, even sent a group of them to France to see first-hand how badly Eisenhower needed tires in the great break-through into France then under way. New pledges were made by the unions, but disorders continued.

In addition to the hundreds of minor stoppages, there were two major ones.

A demand was made early in 1942 for a blanket wage increase averaging around 11 per cent, despite the Little Steel formula. The company had no authority to act on this and it went to the WLB.

The Board was in an awkward position. To deny the increase would mean trouble, bad feeling and probably a strike. To grant it would crack the Little Steel formula wide open. The greatest increase possible, even using an industry-wide application of the formula, would hardly be more than 3¢ an hour.

The Board delayed making a decision for nearly a year but finally did so in June, 1943. It was for 3¢ an hour, which the Board made retroactive to July 1, 1942, and granted the union the maintenance of membership and the check-off.

All of the Akron rubber unions promptly went out on a five-day strike over the small amount of the increase. Maintenance of membership included an "escape period" when members might withdraw, but the union staged a membership drive during the period, gained members rather than losing them.

The second strike, starting in June, 1945, was much more serious, for it closed the factory for 18 days, despite the utmost efforts of many government agencies.

This started with seemingly unimportant arguments in the rim plant and the pit, affecting only a handful of men.

The Smith-Connally law provided for a "cooling off" period of thirty days before a strike could be voted. The union asked the National Labor Relations Board for authority to call a vote, and the board prepared the ballots and supervised the election. No specific grievances were cited, but only generalities like "evasion of WLB directives," "stalling on negotiations" and "not living up to contract."

Two arguments were presented to members as to why the strike vote should be passed: first, that the union did not intend to call a strike, but needed this vote as a club over management; second, that this was a fight between Labor and Management, and that anyone who voted against a strike was letting the union down, was willing to let the company run things. Working men must stick together.

The strike vote carried by a vote of 8561 to 3039, out of the 17,000 employees. The authority given the union officers to call a strike was promptly exercised, though negotiations were still under way. The plant was completely shut down, including the offices, in a surprise move over a weekend. It lasted from June 17th to July 5th.

Perhaps no single labor disturbance in the whole troubled era came in for such universal condemnation from the government, the public, the press and even other unions. War needs were still critical in the Pacific. Airplane tires were being flown out to desperately-held fronts and the biggest tire company remained closed. Soldiers wrote in bitterly: "Would the strikers like to trade jobs?"

The international union disavowed the strike, the War Labor Board subpoenaed the union leaders, heard their story, ordered them back to work, even the union members of the Board voting against them. The union defied the order and the Board suspended the night bonus and liberalized vacations, threatened to take away the cherished "maintenance of membership" and the "check-off." Union heads remained obdurate, announced that if that were done the men would stay out until those privileges were restored.

The Secretary of War, the Secretary of the Navy and the governor of the state all urged the men to return to work—without effect. The Selective Service Board took steps to send into the army any strikers who had previously been exempted as essential war workers. Reminders of the "no strike" pledge made by the international union brought the rejoinder that the Akron union had not joined in that pledge, but had opposed it in the convention. The strike vote constituted a directive from the members of the union to call the strike, and his action was entirely legal, the president of the union reiterated.

The government could compel Management to bargain with the union, but it could not compel the union to accept a decision it did not like. Moral suasion having failed, government had no recourse except to send in troops. President Roosevelt ordered the Navy to take over the plant and the men went back to work.

The shop quieted down after the Navy came in. It needed only a little show of firmness to indicate that they meant business. The second day after the Navy took charge, two maintenance men refused to repair a break in a steam pipe, on the ground that that was a plumber's job. They promptly found themselves in custody of the Shore Patrol, and the word went around that the Navy was not fooling. Production proceeded satisfactorily after that as long as the Navy remained.

One instrumentality which had worked well elsewhere was set up during this period, the naming of an "Impartial Umpire," to whom union or company might appeal for a ruling on those cases which involved the interpretation of the union contracts or of government directives. Hundreds of such cases had been carried to WLB, took a long time to be tried and a decision made. The Impartial Umpire could give a prompt answer and his rulings would be final. He was to be selected jointly by the union and the company, or in case they could not agree, by the War Labor Board.

The Umpire system had been installed in many companies at the suggestion of the union, and over the objections of management. At Goodyear, however, the company proposed it and the union opposed it. After considerable delay it was ordered by the War Labor Board—which also had to pick the Umpire as well, since company and union could not agree on a selection. The post went to W. E. Simkin of Philadelphia, who had had considerable experience in labor relations, particularly in the shipbuilding industry.

The Navy turned the plant back after VJ-Day, and trouble promptly broke out again. The union came in to demand the immediate restoration of the six-hour day. That had been relaxed during the war emergency by agreement between the company and the union. The agreement, however, had defined the "emergency," bound the company to go back to the shorter work day "when sufficient qualified manpower was available."

But the manpower was nowhere in sight. There was a tremendous dammed-up need for civilian tires. A cutback to six hours would reduce production 25 per cent or compel the hiring in of 25 per cent more people. There were thousands of Goodyear employees in uniform, who might be months getting back, and would be entitled to their old jobs when they did return. The union, however, insisted on immediate action.

The employment men went out recruiting workers over the state and even into adjoining states. Men were not particularly anxious to come to Akron, knowing that the job might be temporary, that the veterans would have preference when they came back. The union finally set October 1st as the deadline.

The matter went to the Impartial Umpire. He canvassed the labor situation, looked over the agreement. There was only one possible ruling he could make. Sufficient qualified labor was not available. The company must continue on an eight-hour day until February 1st, unless the situation cleared up in the meantime.

The union refused to accept the ruling, made plans to picket the plant. Umpire Simkin resigned. If the company or the union could decide which of his rulings they would accept and which they would reject, there was no point in his continuing in office.

Pressure began to build up against the union position, from the International Union and within Wheeler's own organization. His own board finally over-ruled him and the union agreed to go along, invited Simkin to return, which he did after a five-week interim. The labor shortage had adjusted itself by the February 1st date he had set, and the six-hour day went into effect in the Akron plants.

Only in the rubber industry, and only in Akron in that industry (except for one plant in Detroit and two in Los Angeles) does the six-hour day, which Goodyear itself had instituted in 1932 to share the work among employees, remain in effect. Only in rubber does society pay men a day's wages for six hours work. And Akron rubber workers make more money in six hours than rubber workers elsewhere do in eight.

With the end of the war the "Little Steel" formula went out the window, and wage demands were made in hundreds of industries, in motors, steel, coal mining, railroads, utilities and, of course, rubber.

The Akron unions demanded an increase of 30¢ an hour and over-time pay for work beyond six hours in a given day, or 30 in a given week. Action on this waited on the results of demands elsewhere, particularly at General Motors, which was shut down by strike for four months. Strikes broke out in other industries, affecting more than a million men.

The General Motors settlement, granting a basic increase of 18½¢ an hour (with certain union concessions as to plant security, meaning un-interrupted production), set the pattern for the rubber industry.

Then, for the first time, the four large companies agreed to negotiate jointly for their 41 plants, which by then accounted for 50 per cent of the nation's tire production. The settlement reached provided a pay in-crease of 18½¢, with overtime for Sundays and six holidays.

Conversion from war to peacetime operations was slowed down by these developments. A steel strike and later one in soft coal had a para-lyzing effect throughout industry, strikes in parts manufacturers slowed down production in plants they supplied; output of building ma-terials dragged, despite the gravest housing shortage in history; manu-facturers were hesitant to go ahead on products where profit margins were narrow; and when industry hesitates men fail to get jobs which otherwise would have been open. Twelve months after Japan quit, pro-duction was still lagging, war savings dwindling, war bonds being cashed in, millions of unproductive dollars were being paid out in un-employment insurance, despite the tremendous dammed-up demand for consumer goods which should have created jobs for millions of men.

The next three years saw three rounds of wage increases throughout industry with rising prices and living costs, but with labor conditions in Akron gradually stabilizing.

Climer, who had been in personnel work ever since he came up from Miami University in 1917 (except for four years as superintendent in Argentina), became a vice president. He was convinced that one reason for the difficulties in the plant was that relatively few employees took part in union activities, even though they belonged to the union.

Not more than ten per cent of them even bothered to vote, the elections bringing out from 1400 to 1800 voters—in contrast to the Industrial Assembly where as high as 90 per cent took part in the annual elections. He pointed out this situation to the supervision, who passed it on in discussions with employees in their department. It sounded like good sense to the workmen, and the 1946 election brought out a vote of 5600, and incidentally defeated Wheeler, bringing in as president Milliron from the Power House, who had campaigned on a "stop the sitdowns" platform. When Wheeler attempted a comeback unsuccessfully in 1948, 8200 votes were cast.

The second step was a labor column in the Wingfoot Clan, started in August, 1945, which reported on all grievances carried up to the Impartial Umpire and his decisions on them. These reports were kept unbiased, were merely statements of fact, whether the report hit the company or the union. The column came to be widely read—and was copied by other companies, had a good influence.

The third step was to insist the union live up to its "no strike" agreement. Under the contract a strike could not be called unless the grievance which occasioned it had been threshed out between the company and the union, and if not settled carried up to the Impartial Umpire.

Penalties were provided for violation of this part of the agreement, offenders to get a week's layoff and in case of a second offense, discharged. But this had been a dead letter. Any attempt to discipline men merely brought on a new strike and the company had to shut its eyes to scores of contract violations.

So the next wildcat strike brought prompt suspension of the offenders. The plant was closed down in protest, but the company stood by the language of the agreement, and the men presently came back. The second unauthorized work stoppage brought another suspension, but this time the strike only closed one plant. The third one saw the union leaders going into action to get their men back to work, and the week's suspension was modified to four days. In no case had there been a second offender.

The first company-wide contract was signed in March, 1947. It set forth the principles of company security and union security, the responsibility of management to run the plant and enforce discipline; the right of the union to the check-off, seniority, vacations, and a standard procedure for layoffs and transfers. The principles being set forth, each plant worked out its own local agreement in accord with them.

The forced return to the six-hour day after the war had added a 25 per cent overload in personnel. For 10,000 men working six hours a day turned out no more tires than 8000 men working eight hours a day—in fact somewhat fewer, with four interruptions at shift change in place of three.

The industry could absorb this surplus manpower as long as the postwar shortage of tires lasted, but once supply and demand came in balance in the spring of 1948, inventories began to accumulate, and production had to be cut back. The work week went down to 24 hours, and after that layoffs started. Summer driving helped temporarily but it appeared that the six-hour day had brought in more manpower than the industry needed, except under emergency conditions.

DEVELOPMENTS IN OTHER PLANTS

Labor relations in Canada followed the general pattern of that in the States, but more slowly. The CIO set out in 1936 to organize the Canadian automobile, steel and rubber industries, but it was not until March, 1944, that a contract was signed at Bowmanville, and the following month at New Toronto. There were no major work stoppages in either plant during the war, but trouble broke out shortly after VJ-Day.

The international started a drive for higher wages, shorter hours and more liberal overtime and holiday pay. Goodyear had just signed contracts covering these points for a year's time, and the union made little headway with other companies, with the result that a general strike was called in May, 1946, lasting until the end of October. The agreement reached at the end of the strike provided for a general increase of 13¢ an hour with a bonus for second and third shifts.

The National Catholic Syndicate of the textile industry organized the St. Hyacinthe cotton mill, got a contract in June, 1945. There were no work stoppages at the mill.

The other American plants encountered some difficulties. These will be reported in the chapters dealing with them.

12. Operations Abroad

The Beginnings of Export

ONE of the most important phases of the Goodyear history is its invasion of foreign markets.

From a tiny business started in the earliest years, when one man could handle what orders trickled in and many of the tires went on horse-drawn vehicles, Export grew to become one of the major divisions of the company, with factories on five continents, and prior to World War II, distributors in every country in the world except Russia and Abyssinia.

Canada played an exceedingly important role in the development, but not as a market for Akron-made goods. Goodyear did not export goods *to* Canada except incidentally, but did export in great volume *from* Canada, whose position in the British empire made it a stepping stone into many markets.

There were many things to learn when the company went into export. America, having a great home market, had not been an important exporting nation, except in raw materials like wheat, cotton and lumber. Europe had made a business of it. There was a lot of mystery about export, strange languages, habits of mind, business customs, much to be learned even about the mechanics of the business, foreign exchange, customs, duties, clearance papers, plenty to find out even about packing goods which had to be carried half-way around the globe in steamship holds and sent ashore on lighters.

Goodyear's first export orders came from Great Britain, through Davis & Allen, importing firm who had arranged to distribute Goodyear's first Straight Side tires there in 1901, though this connection was short lived. For a few years, S. S. Leonard, a clerk in the Auto Tire department who knew several foreign languages, was practically the entire export department.

Four men, F. A. Seiberling, Stadelman, Litchfield and Shilts, early visualized the possibilities of export. It was not until 1912, however, that the company was in a position to go ahead aggressively. The Canadian factory helped.

England was the largest user of automobiles next to the United States, the most attractive export market. British manufacturers had a good product and were aided by tariff duties which gave them an advantage in the colonies. Canada was in a position to get into that field and began in 1911 to solicit business from importing agencies abroad, largely handled by correspondence.

In 1912 Goodyear decided to open its own factory branch in London and Van Bever of the Canadian company was given that job. He, like Macfadyean who joined the company about this time, was the aggressive, optimistic type needed at the moment to give impetus to the uphill job of invading foreign territory.

The London branch got under way quickly. The first English sale after the branch started was made by W. Fogin, a traveller in the Midlands district, who sold two 815 x 105's his first day out. London under way, Van Bever set off over Europe, establishing agencies at St. Petersburg, Moscow, Kiev and Odessa; at Berlin, Dresden and Hamburg; The Hague and Amsterdam, Vienna, Stockholm, Christiania, Helsingfors; not to mention agencies set up by long range in Johannesburg, in Capetown and in Durban, South Africa. Negotiations were on for outlets in Italy, Spain, Portugal, Australia, Belgium, France and the East Indies.

The non-skid All Weather tread helped. Leather treads and steel-studded rubber tires were still in use and European manufacturers were doubtful about an all-rubber tire. Goodyear proved that its new non-skid

King Edward VII

Goodyear tires early invaded British Isles, with King Edward VII (left) as an early patron— While elsewhere over the world, as in India (below), men found larger loads could be pulled on rubber.

tread would outwear one of leather and steel, that the steel-studded tire would be completely worn out when the Goodyear tire had merely been worn smooth.

A victory was won in Rumania where Goodyear tires were adopted as standard equipment for all government cars—over the competition of European companies.

Macfadyean travelled over Europe, recommended a plant in France, went on to South America, recommended one in Rio de Janeiro.

Litchfield made the trip over the same territory, taking Kilborn of Development along, felt the French plant premature, but was interested in Brazil. The government there, faced with the loss of its rubber trade to the East, was interested in seeing factories set up to use the rubber locally, was willing to issue franchises for plants in Rio, Pernambuco, Bahia and Manaos, with a creping plant also in the Amazon valley.

Shipping and water considerations pointed to Rio and a site was purchased, but the outbreak of World War I prevented the plan being carried out—and other events later would delay it almost up to the time of the Second World War.

In the same year 1912, P. G. Smith, truck tire salesman at Atlanta, went to Cuba to locate a tire dealer, and to show his men how to sell Goodyear tires. The Cuban market had been largely overlooked by American car manufacturers, despite its proximity to this country, two-thirds of the cars being of European make, and the tire market largely in the control of Michelin, French, and Continental, German. Smith found an agent willing to take up the battle for Goodyear, went on to Jamaica, a strong British market where Dunlop was well established, again made an advantageous connection. Panama was the next stop. There were only a few automobiles there, but Smith, looking ahead to the future, established an outlet.

Goodyear had been represented in Puerto Rico for some time, but unsatisfactorily, in fact the agent was ready to give up. Smith diagnosed his trouble, put his business on a sound basis, sent orders in quadrupling his stock. Venezuela was less fruitful. There were only 70 automobiles in the republic, and these in the two towns of Maracaibo and Caracas. Gasoline sold at 75 cents a gallon. He moved on to Trinidad, to British Guiana and the Barbados. Here he found Goodyear favorably known through the solid tires sold by New York export houses.

Returning from the missionary jaunt, Smith was made manager of what was called the foreign department. Saylor of Canada succeeded Van Bever in 1913 in Europe, Macfadyean remaining in South America. Carl Davidson, who was to be perhaps the most prodigious traveller among the export pioneers, went to New York to work with exporting houses.

The year 1914, which saw war break out over the world, was important also to Goodyear export. The year opened normally. Davidson left for the West Indies, following up the work established by Smith, visiting Puerto Rico, Jamaica, Haiti, Santo Domingo. Smith left in May to see what business could be dug up in Australia and New Zealand.

His trip across the Pacific proved unexpectedly difficult. Instead of the scheduled four days' stop in Honolulu, the ship stayed 10, and when it did arrive in Japan, the owners disposed of the vessel to Japanese buyers who were making large purchases of foreign ships. Another week's delay was incurred until a sailing could be obtained for Shanghai and Manila.

At Manila, Smith transferred to a North German Lloyd steamer and was in mid-Pacific when the European war broke out. The ship carried no wireless, and the passengers knew nothing of the conflict until they arrived at Brisbane, where the ship was boarded and seized as a prize of war. Smith, the only American aboard, was treated with courtesy but business was at a standstill.

He found, however, urgent cables from President Seiberling, who had dispatched several messages to the Orient trying to locate him. Rubber shipments from the Far East had been halted by the outbreak of hostilities, and Goodyear faced a shortage. Odell of the crude rubber department had sailed for Singapore in August, but Seiberling wanted Smith to hurry over and handle the situation until Odell could get there. They managed to buy several hundred tons of plantation rubber and were assured shipment to San Francisco. Seiberling had also cabled Macfadyean in Rio ordering him to Para to buy rubber there for immediate shipment. Other cables went to London, the great rubber market, so by prompt action in three continents Goodyear not only secured ample supply but at favorable prices.

The outbreak of the World War created tremendous dislocations in the business of every firm engaged in export trade. In the long run Goodyear was to benefit by the circumstance that European manufacturers had virtually to give up their outside markets and concentrate on manufacture for government use. The immediate effect was a partial paralysis of export shipments. Goodyear had excellent representation in Germany and Australia, but the government there stepped in, took over the stock and ordered more, which could not be delivered. Shipments to South Africa and India were disrupted by the mobilization of troops. Van Rossum, able agent in Holland, was left for a time with little or no stock. Agents in Spain and Portugal were in the same position. One Goodyear story came out of this period.

Business had grown panicky in London even before the declaration of war. Banks were closed, gold was almost not to be had. With the declaration the government took over British industries to assure itself of full production. No one knew what the next move would be.

Many companies, including English tire manufacturers, contracted a bad case of nerves. Tires were generally sold on consignment basis. The first act of competitive companies was to withdraw all credits, insist on immediate payments of all accounts, and order all consignment tires returned immediately.

Barker & Company, the most prominent coach builder in the city, London agent as well for Rolls-Royce cars, was refused a set of four tires unless the money was paid in cash on delivery.

Learning what his competitors were doing, Saylor wired all his salesmen to come in immediately, determined on a bold stroke. If he won, Goodyear would come through the crisis with renewed prestige and business. If he lost, Goodyear-England would probably take on a new managing director.

Goodyear dealers' credit was still good, he announced to his men. With a stock shortage at many points, extraordinary efforts must be made to get tires delivered at the earliest possible moment. One set of tires ordered by a Liverpool firm was shipped by passenger train within the hour. Goodyear men must stand ready even to the point of going out to sell tires, to help garages who were embarrassed by the emergency conditions. Many proprietors were enlisting, leaving the business in the hands of subordinates.

Saylor sent assurances to the government that its requirements would be fully supplied. He advertised throughout Great Britain the message, "Goodyear stands by the Trade."

Saylor's action had electrical effect. The Dealers' Association in Sheffield passed a resolution approving Goodyear's action. The Motor Trader, principal trade paper, commented editorially on Goodyear's steadiness in time of panic.

Naturally competitors quickly came to their senses, wired their agents to disregard former instructions. But the damage had been done, and in many cases, the business lost did not come back. Goodyear greatly strengthened its position by Saylor's resourcefulness. The London branch went ahead. By the end of the year it was able to supplement American shipments of tires to Spain, Portugal, and Holland from its own stocks—even to Reykjavik, Iceland.

Saylor did not lose his job. He made such a reputation that when Dunlop, the big English company, built a plant at Buffalo to get into the American business, he was picked to head up its sales—and later made a spectacular success in building up Canada Dry Ginger Ale.

At home and in the field Goodyear export men sought to take full advantage of the widening markets created by the war. In 1915, with Smith still in the Far East Macfadyean was called in from South America as export manager, with Ralph Daniels, Kansas City salesman as assistant. Hunter of Canada was sent to Australia to open a sales branch there, Ross White, Chicago branch manager, to start operations in Argentina, and Frank Daniels, in Cape Town, South Africa.

Despite difficulties of war travel, Avery, assistant manager of the English branch and Ball, secretary of the English company, travelled widely through the warring and neutral nations, France, Spain, Switzerland, Italy, strengthening the distribution system.

In Spain, Ball found Goodyear already well known, and developing a steady acceptance. In one town, Valladolid, there were only 107 motor cars, but each of them had at least one Goodyear tire. In Alicante he found a similar condition, 24 cars, each having at least one Goodyear.

Davidson set out on a long swing through Central America, Panama, Colombia, Venezuela, and Puerto Rico, made a special investigation of Cuba, recommended a branch there, which was opened the following year.

The year 1916 was a busy and fruitful year for Export. Australia was doing well, with three sub-branches opened. Chatfield joined the company as the first employee, the second being Kither, another Australian, who was to move up to managing director, guide the company's activities long and wisely. Rurode from Denver went out to set up mechanical goods sales.

South America got its second branch in Brazil, Goodyear's sixth, and Daniels and Davidson left for the Far East, surveying conditions in China, Japan, the Philippine Islands. Davidson stayed over to open the Java branch with Nason of Buffalo, as secretary-treasurer, married Nason's daughter. New Zealand took on branch status. Croke went to Puerto Rico.

Let's pause for a progress survey. Export, the ragged Cinderella of a few years earlier, had become the fairy princess. Sales were mounting into the millions, the entire organization became fully conscious of the importance of foreign trade. Stadelman made his first export trip, to South America. The Akron staff had increased from ten men to 22. Goodyear now had branches in seven foreign countries, many of them with sub-branches, located at strategic distribution centers.

The Canadian factory, under Carlisle's guidance, had grown with the growth of export. As many Canadians then laid up their cars during the winter, export business largely levelled off the seasonal surpluses, kept the Dominion factory operating at full efficiency. Canada's sales in 1916 were bigger than those of the parent company eight years before.

Then came 1917 and America's entrance into the World War. Daniels became export manager. The war brought some recession in business but in no wise diminished the work to be done. Rather, the difficulties increased. If Goodyear and other American tire companies which followed it into export had held an advantage over European tire companies prior to America's entry into the war, they now found themselves in a similar position—government requirements taking priority over normal business needs. It became more and more difficult to get materials. The government limited civilian requirements in order fully to meet military necessities.

Export lost its favorite son status. Domestic customers were crying for goods. Export took what was left. Not only did it have to fight for tires, but its difficulties were not over when these were shipped out. Cargo space on merchant ships was commandeered by the government. Many ships were sunk by submarines. On one occasion a $150,000 shipment of Goodyear tires bound for Brazil was sunk en route by a delayed fuse bomb, placed in the ship's hold before departure. Goodyear lost thousands of dollars worth of goods, and while this was covered by insurance, was much more concerned in maintaining its distribution, preferred to get its money from car owners rather than the insurance companies.

Three carloads of tires for Buenos Aires had to be shipped to Los Angeles by train, to Santiago, Chile, by boat, and then hauled over the Andes. The delivery took almost six months.

Despite all the difficulties of war time, the company's foreign trade increased, going from $3,500,000 in 1916 to $17,500,000 in 1919.

The war over, Goodyear drove ahead anew. Foreign companies, released from war necessities, went out to regain their lost markets. A post-war conflict began. There were rich prizes at stake. Again men were needed.

Daniels turned to the domestic organization, picking men trained in Goodyear ways. Two of them would go far in Export, and markedly to affect its development—A. G. Cameron and A. E. Patterson. They had joined Goodyear in the same year, 1913, Cameron as a truck tire salesman in St. Louis, Patterson as general line salesman at Seattle. Cameron had made an excellent record, was promoted to district truck tire manager before he had been with Goodyear a year, became branch manager at Dallas, then St. Louis. Patterson had become manager of the Tacoma branch.

Daniels established four sales divisions, with Cameron given charge of Australasia. Shipping conditions between North and South America were still unsettled, so a large warehouse was opened at Panama. C. N. Gates, later advertising manager, got his first Goodyear experience there. A young man just discharged from the Navy hired in as a salesman. This was F. T. Magennis, later to be manager in Brazil, then Argentina, then vice president of all Export.

Davidson packed up again in 1919, went to the Philippines to open a branch warehouse, later taking charge of sales in the Far East, Japan, China, Singapore.

Nicholson, Philadelphia salesman, went to Australia to sell truck tires; Delling, Minneapolis to Sweden, Norway and Finland; Hadley, Minneapolis, to Japan; Steiner, Chicago to China. Hilgers came into export operating, joined Orr in the New York office.

Another addition in early 1920, important to Export, was P. E. H. Leroy, later to become vice president in charge of finance. The fluctuating exchange in many countries made many difficulties and Leroy came in from New York as an expert in that field.

The matter of a factory in Brazil came up again but was held up by the 1920 depression, which brought other changes to Export.

Export Comes of Age

Though Export was hard hit in 1920 by depression it came back faster than most divisions of Goodyear.

President Wilmer brought in a new Export manager, Frank K. Espenhain, who had had extensive merchandising experience, domestic and foreign. He had just come out of the Army, where he had had charge of procuring and operating warehouses for its vast stores of war materiel. Daniels, his health affected by six strenuous years, went back to domestic, after a rest, as manager in San Francisco.

Espenhain, a dynamic personality, saw that Goodyear might take a dominant position in foreign trade, if it moved fast enough. Other companies were still hard up but Goodyear, thanks to the refinancing, had money to spend in expansion, personnel, advertising. One thing in its favor was that it had not closed its foreign offices when times grew hard, as many other companies had, had carried on in reduced scale, kept its foot in the door.

Export was divorced from Domestic after Espenhain came in, just as Manufacturers' Sales had been separated from Dealers' Sales years before, and for the same reason. The field was big enough and important enough to demand full concentration by a skilled staff having no other responsibilities. A new subsidiary was set up in 1922, The Goodyear Tire and Rubber Export Company.

Cameron was made manager of Export, with Patterson and Gleichauf as assistants. Things happened fast. Sales offices were opened in India, Nicholson started a branch in Singapore. Mexico, which had been served from the San Antonio branch, was transferred to Export under Blakeny, who had travelled the territory for Domestic. Three other Texans came in, Bauman, who went to Central America, and the Riveire twins, starting on a trail which would take them into many countries. Jacobs signed up in 1919, went to Jamaica.

Three men from the operating section came in, Bollinger of the Treasury Department, who started with Goodyear at 17, would spend years in South America, became vice president of the Argentine company; Long, who started work at 15, would also spend years south of the Rio Grande, become managing director of Brazil, and P. B. Prentice who would make many trips as export auditor.

Faltin, a native of Czechoslovakia, who had become an American citizen, had been working in the factory, but spoke five languages, was sent to the Balkan States. Brazil-born Andrews went to work in Rio.

Espenhain and Cameron set off for Europe in 1922, found things going badly in France and Spain. They hired C. G. Jerosch, who had had extensive experience in the automotive field, left him to straighten things out in Paris, pulled Croke out of Cuba, where he had reorganized the business, sent him to Spain.

During this trip Cameron negotiated the sale of a 21-car train load of tires to a single European customer, the largest single order ever received in Export or Domestic.

Jerosch found the Paris office housed in a stable, a very elaborate stable, it is true, with steam-heated stalls, a building 165 years old where Napoleon had kept his horses. Later it became a famous riding school, one which Edward VII always visited when he went to Paris to replenish the royal stables.

Less interested in tradition than in efficient quarters, Jerosch soon had Goodyear more appropriately housed, built up the business, became manager for all Europe, then assistant manager of Export.

Croke, took on his second assignment as a "trouble shooter," in Spain. He had learned that useful trade through nine years with telephone companies, first in his native Colorado then in the Philippine Islands. Joining Export in 1916 he was in Puerto Rico when War I broke out, went into the Army, came out a captain, returned to Export, was sent to Cuba. He would go on to India, then spend many years in Latin America, become assistant to the general manager of Goodyear Export Company in 1948.

With all this pressure, Export moved ahead, and in September, 1922, did 20 per cent more business than it had ever done in a single month in its history. Canada, which manufactured the lion's share of its goods, increased its business by 684 per cent in 1922 over 1921, twice the country average. All this on the heels of depression!

It was not long before Graham, handling Export shipments out of Canada, could report that more than 100 million dollars worth of Goodyear merchandise had been sent out from the factories at Toronto and Bowmanville.

The drive for men went on.

Personnel is the vital division of business, and nowhere is this more true than in Export. Special characteristics were required. The Export salesman must be flexible-minded, able sympathetically to understand the temperament of other races and work effectively with them, yet preserve his independence and American viewpoint. Export is no job for a stay-at-home. Its territories are much larger than those in domestic and a great deal of travel is necessary. Always there is the possibility of territorial changes. About the time a man feels himself well settled in a given country he may be needed elsewhere.

Men transferred from domestic did not always live up to expectations. Travelling in this country, with the branch manager a few hours' drive away, easily available for consultation—and with Akron at the other end of the telephone or telegraph line—is different from handling sales on the other side of the world, with problems coming up requiring decision, and the home office available quickly only by cable. So a lot of men went into Export and out again. A few left, missed the lure of foreign lands, returned. But the inoculation did not take with everyone. There might be children to be educated, or the climate was unfavorable, or the men themselves not adaptable. The men who went into Export and stayed were a marked group.

Quite a bit of travel was made necessary, too, by the vacation system. A policy grew up of bringing key men into Akron every three years for extended leave. There were health reasons for this, in the case of tropical countries, but more important, the industry was growing and conditions were changing, so that they should return at intervals in order to keep up to date on product and policy. Furthermore a fresh infusion of American thinking at intervals is advisable.

When Stadelman became president, Espenhain took over his work with the automobile manufacturers, though retaining contact with Export, and Cameron became the active head of overseas sales.

Competition for foreign business grew keener as general business improved in the mid 1920's, but Goodyear was well entrenched by then in the major markets.

A school was started in 1922 to teach Goodyear policy to men familiar with export, and export technique to Goodyear men. Some men came straight from college, like House, who had attended the Universities of California and Pennsylvania. A student with a different background was a Swedish youngster named Melander, who came in speaking little English and not at all interested in what salary he would get, but extremely ambitious to learn the business and go back to his own country for Goodyear.

Something came up one day about foreign exchange, an intricate matter that had everybody stopped. Melander was referred to for some minor facts, and had the full information. If this had grown out of an interest in exchange, an intricate subject that does not interest most people, he might have made a job for himself in handling such things. But he was not specially interested in that. He just had the habit of thoroughness. In a few years Melander had charge of sales for Denmark, Sweden, Norway, Finland and Iceland, became vice president of the Swedish company when a factory was opened there in 1939.

Magennis, who started in Panama in 1919 and travelled in the next seven years over Venezuela, Colombia, Ecuador, Peru, Bolivia, Chile, Central America and the West Indies, went to Cuba as manager in 1926.

Crittenden, fresh out of Yale, set off in 1925 for the Canary Islands and Casablanca, continued on around the perimeter of Africa on a trip that took two years, set up distributorships over a continent where Goodyear had previously been represented only in South Africa and Egypt.

Export was so far removed, however, from any immediate contact with Akron that Espenhain and Cameron sometimes found it hard to stir up much interest in its problems elsewhere in the company. They made some headway when they persuaded Supt. Stephens to make a trip around the world, visiting dealers and branches at every stop. He

. T. MAGENNIS, 1917
Vice President Export

W. A. HAZLETT, 1906
Managing Director England

A. G. PARTRIDGE, 1925
President Canada

I. J. STEINER, 1915
aging Director Australia

R. C. BERKINSHAW, 1920
Gen'l Manager Canada

A. E. PATTERSON, 1913
Ass't Manager, Export

M. HASTINGS, 1920
ging Director Argentina

E. E. LONG, 1917
Managing Director Brazil

THURE MELANDER, 1922
Managing Director Sweden

came back with a new conception of Export's importance, issued instructions that overseas was to get all new products immediately, and in every case only the highest quality merchandise. Slusser took his cue from that, and once Litchfield came into the presidency in 1926, Export was assured of entire management support for its needs, since Litchfield, an indefatigable traveller, who for many years spent at least half of his time away from Akron, personally following up outside operations, had made a dozen trips to Europe by 1929 and two to South America, and in 1935 went clear around the world. Leroy continued an active interest in Export.

Branches were added in Germany and Chile and in 1926 there were 20 sales companies in 20 countries, and special representatives covering practically the rest of the world.

The Export map continued to be a chess board. Men were shifted from one country to another to fill gaps resulting from promotions. Wallace Riveire went to Mexico, Venezuela, New Zealand, Havana, Mexico City, Puerto Rico in a single decade. George Riveire, his brother, filled key posts at Puerto Rico, Mexico, Brazil, Spain, the Philippines, Argentina, Washington. Magennis went to the important post of manager in Brazil in 1930.

A truck and bus tire department was instituted under Linforth, with Hastings, Hartford salesman, as assistant. When Linforth took charge of manufacturers' sales out of Akron, Hastings moved up, later headed the Argentine company.

Mechanical goods were growing in importance in the export field, as it was in this country. D. R. Burr had gone to Australia in 1918, spent a year organizing a sales force, established the plant analysis system. Rurode followed up, and Australia furnished many large mechanical goods orders and became the seat of Goodyear's first manufacturing plant overseas for mechanicals.

Argentina ranchers were having difficulty with farm belting due to the high winds. Ordinary thresher belts would not hold to the pulleys. Akron developed a belt to meet the requirements, and took over most of the business there. Word of the performance of Goodyear mechanical goods travelled far, and the plant analysis system brought business from textile mills, coal mines and large industries in many countries.

Business in Mexico, Central America and South America came largely from mining, oil companies and sugar centrals. Goodyear representatives penetrated deep into Latin America, visited isolated mining sections to analyze installations. Some of Goodyear's biggest belting orders came from South America.

Plant analysis paved the way for sales in Africa. A field representative visited the mining districts of the Belgian Congo near the Equator. This is one of the hottest places in the world, the miners themselves being unable to stand the strain for more than a few months at a time. But the Goodyear man made his analysis, got a trial order and later by mail an exceptionally large order. A similar thing happened in South Africa, where a 1500-foot conveyor belt was sold to one of the largest gold mining concerns in the world, after an analysis had been made and satisfactory service delivered by a trial belt.

Mechanical goods grew to such size that in 1927 Herman Post was drafted from domestic to head up the department in export.

Partridge went into Export in 1928. A long-time Firestone executive, he had resigned as sales manager in 1921, but after a few years grew restless, wanted to get back in harness. Goodyear had no job appropriate to his experience but something might turn up. He was given a desk in the sales manager's office, busied himself with small town distribution, then took over two domestic branches, had been with Goodyear about a year when Wilson moved over to advertising manager. By that time Partridge knew the organization, had learned its ways of doing business, became manager of the western division. From there he went to take charge of the biggest overseas territory in England, later went to Toronto, became president of the Canadian company.

However, new factors had come in well before that time.

Building Foreign Plants

Further expansion of export ran into a snag after 1926—import duties set up in many countries, which would put American-made tires at a serious price disadvantage as against tires made in those countries which paid no duty. Out of this came new Goodyear plants abroad.

In the evolution of world trade, certain nations, like those of South America and the Orient had largely furnished raw materials while others, particularly the United States and Europe, did most of the manufacturing.

But World War I had interrupted this friendly exchange, left a new spirit of nationalism in its wake. Nations which had depended on other countries for materials or supplies found these curtailed or cut off by the war, resolved not to be caught again, sought to be self-contained.

Manufacturing began to spring up in countries which previously had

done little of it. Tires had been made up to the war in but six countries
—Great Britain, France, Germany, Italy, Belgium and the United
States. Another decade would find tire factories in 28 countries, usually
with strong government support in the shape of tariff duties, even in
England, long an advocate of free trade.

This situation first became serious in Australia and England, then
Argentina, three countries in which Goodyear had long been entrenched,
since 1913 in the case of the first two, and in Argentina since 1916.

The duty in Australia was 150 per cent, and though smaller in the
other countries was still difficult, if not impossible, to meet, unless
Goodyear moved in behind the tariff walls with a factory of its own. It
must do that or abandon important markets.

In almost each case where Goodyear did build abroad, it was the first
American tire company to do so, pioneering in fields where there was
little previous experience to go on.

AUSTRALIA

Australia was first. Vice President Stillman set out for Sydney in
1926 with Urquhart of Engineering, met Kither, the managing director,
went over the situation with government and banking groups. Goodyear merchandise had an excellent reputation in the Antipodes, and the
men found everyone cordial to the idea of a Goodyear factory which
would provide high-quality, low-cost tires—and good wages and opportunity for Australian workmen.

James Kell, who had formerly been the governor of the Common-
wealth Bank, which was comparable to the Federal Reserve Bank of
the United States, accepted the chairmanship of the board. The Goodyear Tyre and Rubber Company (Australia) Ltd. was organized, capi-
talized at 1,200,000 shares, each having a par value of one pound, then
about $4.86 in American money. Goodyear took up 500,000 shares of
ordinary stock (comparable to common stock in the United States).
The stock offered to the public was over-subscribed two and a half times.

Urquhart found a satisfactory site at Granville, 15 miles from Sydney, on the Parramatta River. There was plenty of room, so instead of
building a factory several stories high, he laid it out all on one floor,
with a saw-tooth roof which gave good lighting, a plant easy to enlarge,
which quickly became necessary.

Ground was broken February 14, 1927, with orders to push ahead
vigorously. Goodyear would lose money or lose sales every day until
the plant was built and turning out tires. With the decision that

Urquhart was to stay on as superintendent, Moorhead took charge of construction and installing machinery, his staff moving all the faster with the news that Goodyear had decided to build in England also, another rush job.

LaDue's men in England merely had to remodel an existing building, so keen rivalry developed between the engineering crews on the opposite sides of the world to see which would be ready first. Australia, with its earlier start, won, building its first tire on October 12th, two months before the first British tire left the molds.

The formal opening of he Australian plant was attended by leading government and business officials of the country, and the factory started under favorable auspices.

Starting its foreign plants, Goodyear realized it would be dealing with men of different habits and customs, and later with those speaking a different language. But while any plan must be fitted into its environment, the company felt sure that men everywhere would respond to fair treatment, react to good wages, rise to opportunity—and might well catch the spirit of teamwork and comradeship which marked its industrial relations program, if that was set up with sincerity and good judgment.

As a matter of fact, Urquhart and his men had no trouble recruiting competent workmen and finding men of foreman and staff capacities, with Australians on the Squadron presently furnishing men for all but a few key jobs.

Akron furnished production men who knew methods, machinery and materials, were thoroughly grounded in the principles of mass production, since in countries new to the business there had been no opportunity for men to acquire this experience. The technical and compounding phases were special to the rubber industry. The personnel men must know the wage payment plans, must have adaptability and horse sense, and if they liked sports, as most of them did, so much the better.

Australia had strict laws as to hours, wages, working conditions. However, the government's desire to protect its wage workers and Goodyear's traditional policy ran along parallel lines. The company was quite willing to establish a minimum wage, and to pay men beyond that as they proved themselves. Safety regulations were deeply imbedded in the Goodyear code.

One thing, however, that impressed the Australians was the tendency of the Americans to disregard class distinctions. Lines between the boss and the workmen were traditionally drawn in most industries there, the employer or foreman on one side of the line and the employee on the other. But the Americans stepped over the line freely, came to know their men on a first-name basis, took part in athletics and social gatherings. Employee organizations came into existence, directed at first by the Americans, but soon taken over by the sports-loving Australians. There was room on the factory grounds for baseball and cricket fields. The Americans quickly decided that they liked Australia and its people, and the feeling was mutual.

Goodyear sales grew fast after the factory went up, and three additional units had to be built, bringing the factory from a capacity of 1000 tires a day to 1500, to 2500, then to 3500 in the first two years of its existence. Floor space was practically quadrupled. Manufacture of mechanical goods under Maxwell was added in 1930 to meet the demand for hose and belting.

The original group included men from Canada and California as well as Akron—and Riggs, tech service man from California would meet and marry in Sydney the daughter of Bliley, production man from Canada—so do corporate movements affect men's lives.

Changes came with the years. Sheahan, who had served in Akron, California and England, succeeded to the superintendency, was followed by Condon who had been division superintendent in England.

Kither, managing director for many years, Jaffray, manager of mechanical goods, Chatfield in New South Wales and Firth in Victoria were natives of Australia. Steiner, who had gone from Chicago to China and Japan in the early days and had the longest continuous export service of any Goodyearite, became Kither's assistant, later succeeded him.

ENGLAND

· The conditions that dictated a factory in Australia held also in England. With the increase of unemployment, the movement to get people to buy British-made goods and so to give more work to English workers was intensified. Advertising campaigns were laid out, speeches made, meetings held. The injunction "Buy British" faced people everywhere, in their newspapers, on the billboards, the public platform.

Goodyear had been a big factor in the English tire market since 1913, having a considerable investment in stock, property and good will, was one of the three leading distributors in the country, and its two principal rivals, Dunlop, English and Michelin, French, already had factories in Great Britain. Goodyear would have to build a plant if it wanted to continue to sell tires, and must move fast.

English factory (above) was added to again and again, and Australian plant (below) had to be enlarged four different times, and again during War II.

Argentina factory was erected well away from business center, close to deep water harbor, with attractive British settlement close at hand.

Zieske, engineer, and Linnane of Production, one of Stephens' men, went over to look for a site. Stillman, just back from Australia, followed to work with the lawyers, bankers, government people, and Litchfield and Slusser, a little later, to make the final decisions.

A favorable site had been found at Wolverhampton, an industrial city of 140,000 people in the Midland district near Birmingham, 76 acres of ground with a factory formerly used for making enamelware which could be remodeled quickly. The engineers went to work.

The corporate structure had been worked out. Goodyear put up 800,-000 pounds, taking the entire issue of Share Capital of The Goodyear Tyre and Rubber Company of Great Britain, Ltd., while 800,000 pounds in 6½ per cent shares of Debenture Stock was offered to the public, the two securities corresponding roughly to the common and preferred stocks in the United States.

Influential British capital became interested. Baring Bros. acted as registrars and Barclay's Bank took stock applications. Sir James Alexander Cooper and Sir Arthur Dickenson, distinguished business leaders, accepted directorates and Lord Trenchard, chief of the British Air Forces during the war and at that time Air Marshal of Great Britain, became a director later. Under those auspices the stock, like that in Australia, was over-subscribed.

Linnane stayed on as superintendent and LaDue as chief engineer. R. T. Brown went over from Canada on development, Patterson from Akron was chief chemist, Sheahan from California as division superintendent. Walker, a versatile Englishman, became personnel manager.

Tire fabric could be bought in England, as could zinc oxide, sulphur, and other compounding materials.

To get into production quickly 51 men from the Squadron and 20 production men from Akron were sent over to train employees, most of whom had had no previous experience in the rubber plants, many of them being unemployed coal miners, who proved good workers.

While the Australian factory got its first tire out ahead of England, no other Goodyear factory had ever gotten into production as quickly as Wolverhampton. The first public announcement about the factory was made in July, 1927, and the first tire came out of the mold on December 15th.

An initial force of 1000 men was employed, and Goodyear's long interest in sport proved a leavening factor in employee relations. Soccer and rugby fields went up alongside the factory with a recreation building and dance hall added later. The sports-loving British employees organized an all-year athletic program and Goodyear teams contributed to health and morale. A relief association was set up and a Squadron. The American Squadron and production men went back to Akron as soon as new employees had learned the processes and men had been trained for foremen and staff positions.

The factory soon had to be enlarged to twice its original size, floor space growing from 190,000 square feet to 440,000, with a capacity of 3750 tires and tubes a day. A sole and heel department was added with a capacity of 34,000 pairs of heels and 7500 soles. Mechanical goods was added in 1938, with new buildings for warehousing and raw material storage already provided.

Flannery of Engineering, Steele of California, Brittain and Ginaven of Development, became superintendents in turn. Patterson, assistant manager of Export, Partridge, head of Goodyear Canada, Thomas who became president of Goodyear, Hough, head of Advertising and the veteran Hazlett, served as managing directors, Bishop, an Englishman, being general sales manager. Sullivan from California served as treasurer for many years.

Goodyear England would have quite an experience in World War II.

ARGENTINA

The starting of each new Goodyear factory is a separate story since conditions in no two localities are the same. In Argentina Goodyear was not merely entering a country which spoke a foreign language, but also one primarily agricultural and commercial. Argentina is almost a third of the size of the United States, a country rich in cattle and wheat, its broad pampas extending almost to the door of its chief city, Buenos Aires, which is the cultural and commercial, as well as political, center of the nation.

Buenos Aires, where Goodyear decided to build its factory, is larger than any city in the United States except New York and Chicago, having a population now of around two and a half million, an area almost as great as that of Los Angeles, and a climate not unlike that favored city. It has broad avenues, parks, magnificent public buildings and its people call it the "Paris of the New World."

Racially Spanish, Argentina's population includes 900,000 Italians, 80,000 French, 28,000 English, 27,000 Germans, and about 4000 Americans.

The Germans held many technical and engineering positions, controlled many hotels and department stores, were active in the power companies. The British controlled the railroads, were active in the banks, remained staunchly British, brought their polo and rugby with them, established little British communities, the principal one being Hurlingham, where the Goodyear factory was located.

The tariff arose as an obstacle to Goodyear's further program in the country in late 1928, for the same reasons as in Australia and England, created an identical problem at Akron.

Argentina was the seventh country in the world in car registration and long had been an important market for Goodyear tires. Michelin had had the tire business pretty well sewed up when Goodyear opened up a sales branch there in 1916, in fact, was advertising that it controlled 75 per cent of the nation's tire business. In a few years, however, Goodyear had taken the lead and held it.

With the passage of the tariff, Michelin, French, and Pirelli, Italian, purchased sites, made plans to build factories. Stillman packed his bag again, set off in April, 1929, taking LaDue, construction engineer, and Gould, industrial engineer, with him.

Selection of a location and the setting up of the Argentine company took some time but a decision was reached in the latter part of the year, and Kroeger and Sivaslian went down to build the plant.

After picking men at Akron (and the outside plants) to handle key responsibilities in new factories at Australia, England and Gadsden, it might be expected that Goodyear would be getting toward the bottom of the barrel. It was a test of Litchfield's program of always having trained men at hand to meet any emergency. This was Goodyear's first entry into any country speaking a language other than English (except St. Hyacinthe where the personnel were recruited locally). Latin America was an important market and one not easy to enter because of the difference in national habits and customs.

The Goodyear system, however, proved equal to the test. How carefully the men were selected may be indicated by their later careers.

Climer, personnel manager at Akron who became the first superintendent, would late become vice president of Goodyear and no less than five of his men would move later to superintendencies of Goodyear plants. Lee, his assistant, succeeded him at Buenos Aires, then went to Jackson. Carter of personnel and Coffin of tech service became superintendents in Brazil. Hochberg, who headed the Squadron, went to Java and Gagnon of Development went to Peru.

West, California Squadron graduate, went out as a foreman, became division superintendent. Batson, one of Hochberg's Squadron men, became development manager at Brazil and another, Novick, became assistant superintendent at the Charlestown powder plant and later

Goodyear introduced spectacular American advertising abroad, as in Buenos Aires (above left), and in Sao Paulo (below)—while bus lines in Algeria and over the world call for rubber tires, as do other vehicles down to this Brahmin-drawn garbage wagon in Java.

division superintendent at South Africa. The imprint of the Argentina organization will be felt throughout Latin America in the company's later expansion on that continent.

South America had long been an important source of raw materials for the world and, consequently, an important market for manufactured goods from other countries. However some business houses which sought to do business there made little effort to adjust themselves to Latin American thinking or even to learn the language.

White, who had long been in Buenos Aires and was a leading figure in the American colony there, and Magennis, one of the promising later-comers, had urged on Akron the importance of a different viewpoint in this extension of manufacturing to that part of the world. As a result classes in Spanish were set up in Goodyear Hall for the men picked to go to Argentina, including Hochberg's 29 Squadron men.

The Squadron men sailed from New York on Thanksgiving Day, 1930, arrived in Buenos Aires 17 days later to find the factory again a building all on one floor, with saw-tooth roof, well on its way to completion, but the machinery which had just been unloaded almost buried in mud and silt from a flood which had struck the area. Buenos Aires is only a few feet above sea level. Consequently, a busy three weeks cleaning machinery and moving it into position was the Squadron men's initiation to the new job.

The first tire was built January 2, 1931, and three weeks later, with the plant in running order, the formal opening was set, one that people would long remember.

President Uriburu, colorful fighting man who had upset the long rule of President Irigoyen, drove out the 24 miles to the factory in person to open the plant, marched into the building between lines of plumed soldiers, the Latin flare for color and ceremony giving impressive significance to the opening. White, Vice President Slusser and Cameron, head of Export, who had gone to Buenos Aires to be present for the ceremony, greeted the Argentine executive. A long-distance telephone connection had been arranged between the speaker's stand at the factory and Litchfield's office at Akron, one of the first to be made between the two continents, and at the appointed hour President Uriburu formally declared the plant open, then speaking over the telephone to Mr. Litchfield welcomed Goodyear to Argentina. Mr. Litchfield's reply, amplified by loud speaker, was heard by thousands of spectators.

Although Buenos Aires was not an industrial city, there were a number of smaller factories there so that the matter of getting men was not too difficult. American packing houses had large plants, and General Motors and Ford had assembly plants there. The government built roads, encouraged the building of grain elevators, industrial plants. The Argentinians proved good workers, quick to learn, conscientious, ambitious, responsive to good treatment.

The factory, once it was filled up, presented a curious appearance. The workmen, German, Spanish, Italian, or other nationals, all wore pantaloons tied in at the ankles, broad bright-colored sashes around their middle, and caps like the French beret on their heads.

While the plant was being built, many of the workmen came by train from a considerable distance. Most of them brought their lunch in the form of a huge roll of bread, a segment of cheese, and a bottle of wine. They were surprised to find a rule against bringing liquor into the factory. Little wine shops, however, soon sprang up nearby.

As the plant was well away from the center of the city, and housing not available for factory executives, a number of company houses were built, in Latin American architecture, with high walls around courts and patios.

Production once under way the usual Goodyear activities started. Tennis courts and a rugby field were laid out on the company property. There was a polo field not far away, for the Argentinians, natural horsemen, had picked up polo from the British, and developed many excellent players.

An Argentina Wingfoot Clan, printed in Spanish, was received with enthusiasm, as nothing like that had been seen in the country. The plant paper served a useful role in getting the management and men acquainted with each other's ideas and habits of thought.

A unique arrangement was made with Dunlop, the English company, when Goodyear went to Argentina. Dunlop had plants in the principal British territories, was considering an Argentinan factory when the question was raised: "Why should two big companies like Dunlop and Goodyear duplicate manufacturing facilities in the various markets? One big plant could operate more economically than two small ones."

So Goodyear agreed to build Dunlop tires to its specifications in Dunlop molds in Argentina, and later in Java, Sweden, Brazil and Peru, while Dunlop built Goodyear tires to its specifications in Goodyear molds in South Africa, India, Eire, and later in New Zealand.

Climer returned to the States in 1934, was succeeded by Lee, then by Patrick, head of the Akron reclaim plant, who served during World War II. Croke, Magennis and Hastings followed White as managing director, with the veteran, Bollinger, acting as secretary-treasurer, and later financial vice president.

The first three outside plants had turned out well, so with the first signs of business upturn in 1933, the company studied the world map to see whether further expansion might be desirable.

Europe was canvassed, and the decision was made *not* to go into certain countries, including Germany, where political conditions might imperil a long-time investment. Sweden looked all right and a factory went up there in 1938. Brazil came back in the picture. But the most promising immediate location for a plant was in Java.

Goodyear had been in the Netherlands Indies since 1916, with a sales branch in Java and a rubber plantation in Sumatra. Hadley, Goodyear manager, had urged a factory to serve that market. The government was friendly, for there were no industries except oil and sugar refineries, and this would furnish employment. Also it would get quality tires at lower prices than through importing them. The Japanese were invading every possible market with manufactured goods, including tires. The Goodyear factory would be the only one in the whole area.

The rubber situation was favorable. Restrictions were on again, but Goodyear could buy rubber in its front yard well under the market price, make further savings through manufacturing them in Java than by shipping rubber half way across the world to the States or Canada, fabricating it and sending it back.

Flannery, then superintendent of England, and Uhrich, Goodyear engineer, were sent out to make a survey. They recommended a site in the city of Buitenzorg, 30 miles inland and high enough up to have plenty of cold water for the mixing mills and a favorable temperature.

The factory would be the smallest one yet built, with a capacity of 600 tires a day, though with machinery enough at first for 300. LaDue went out to build the plant, with instructions to have it in operation by May 1, 1935—though the first ground was broken on the preceding November 8.

The building of the factory was unique among Goodyear construction jobs. Most of the machinery and part of the materials had to be shipped in from the United States. No wheelbarrows, picks or shovels were used. The natives carried the materials on their heads, used primitive tools.

When the factory was half finished, they came in and requested a Slametan to ward off evil spirits. There had been one or two minor accidents. On the advice of the Hollanders, LaDue agreed. The following day there was a big procession around and through the plant, the medicine men bearing the heads of a water buffalo and two goats on a sort of sedan chair. Dancing girls headed the procession to the tune of native music. The procession stopped at each point which they felt was dangerous, while the priests chanted and the natives screamed to frighten the evil spirits from the spot. At the end of the ceremonies the buffalo head was buried alongside the shipping room and the goat heads before the front and rear entrances, while the medicine men explained to the spirits why this was being done and promised that further ceremonies would be held if that was not sufficient. Afterwards the goats and the buffalo were barbecued and served at a great feast on the floor of the factory building.

It happened two weeks later a workman fell from the roof, landing on his head, but was not seriously hurt, so the natives felt that the Slametan had been a complete success.

Even without modern construction equipment, and with shipping delays which handicapped progress, the six-month deadline was met. Fires were started in the boiler on April 25th and the first tire built four days later, two days ahead of schedule.

Mr. Litchfield had long wanted to visit the rubber plantations where $12,000,000 of the company's money was invested, but there were no airlines then spanning the Pacific and each year something arose which made it impossible for him to find the necessary four months in his business calendar for the journey. However, in 1935 he made it, the opening of the Java factory being the immediate occasion, but affording opportunity as well to make his first visit to the Australian factory and the Sumatra plantations.

The formal opening in June was a colorful sight. Chinese merchants from Java and neighboring islands attended with their wives, many in native costume. Dutch officials were present. Goodyear was formally welcomed to the Far East. Mr. Litchfield pressed a button, the machinery started up with a roar, and another Goodyear factory was added.

The venture proved fully successful. Production quickly built up to the 600 tire-a-day capacity and additional machinery was shipped out to produce 9000 bicycle tires a day, and later for carriage and rickshaw tires.

Like other outside factories, Java provided a useful training for men. Belknap, development man, the first superintendent, was superintendent at Aircraft during World War II, and later of the big Chemical Products Division. He was succeeded by Ruffner, later head of the Jackson plant, then Hochberg who had been manager of the Squadron.

The Squadron men who went out to start production also had a useful experience, four of them later becoming division superintendents, Rosenberger at Topeka, Reece in Peru, Rinke at Java. DeYoung found Java his first stepping stone toward the vice presidency. Hadley, who succeeded Nason in charge of Export Sales, became managing director. We shall hear from these men later.

Two other overseas plants were opened in 1938, in Sweden and Brazil, but that story is part of the war chapter.

Approach of World War

Export was well-entrenched in the English-speaking nations of the British Empire when World War II drew near; in the Scandinavian nations; Latin America; the Philippines; Holland and the Netherland Indies; the Balkan nations; China and the Far East; as well as the Near East and Africa.

There were 18 foreign subsidiaries, 37 branches, 28 depots, 10 warehouses, several hundred distributors. Its advertising was printed in Greek, Turkish, Arabic, Hebrew, Persian, Chinese, Japanese, Malay, Hindu, Spanish, Portuguese. Even in isolated outposts like Madagascar, Mauritius, the Belgian Congo, the Gold Coast, Borneo, the South Seas, Iceland, the Faroe Islands—the Goodyear name, the All-Weather Tread and its dealer signs were as familiar sights as they are in most cities in the United States.

The three countries where it had no business were those with which America would find itself at war. It had never operated in Russia.

In Japan, the well-known Mitsubishi Company acted as its distributor until 1932, when Japan set up prohibitive duties. Mussolini drove foreign interests out of Italy when he came to power. The company had had a flourishing business in Germany under Crittenden with sub-offices over the country, but when the Hitler regime came in, things tightened up. Foreigners might see too much of the secret military preparations under way. Things came to a head suddenly in 1932 with a ruling that outside companies could take no money at all out of Germany, except in trade, at state-set prices, which might be twice as much as the goods were worth.

Goodyear had about $250,000 tied up in Germany, including tire stocks, office furniture, cars and bank deposits, which it could not get out. Cameron, head of Export, unwilling to lose this money, pondered long as to what he could buy in Germany that the company could use. Then he had an idea.

Construction of the big airships, Akron and Macon, was under way and he recalled that the Navy had specified German Maybach engines similar to those on the Graf Zeppelin, since no American engines had been developed for this purpose. He called Dr. Arnstein to see whether the purchase had gone through. The deal had been closed but the money had not been paid.

"All right," said Cameron, "Export will buy those for you."

This reduced the bank deposits to around $16,000. Cameron, making a trip to Europe shortly afterward, discussed the matter further with Crittenden. The export company was expanding its advertising program and at the moment was working on dealer identification using big metal signs. Such signs could be made in Germany and shipped out through the free port of Copenhagen. So they bought enough of them to reduce the money to $1600.

Neither man was staying long enough in Germany to use up even this amount in hotel expenses and meals. However, Cameron had been passing the plant of the Faber Pencil Company on his way from the hotel to the branch. That would do it. They bought $1600 worth of lead pencils, sold them to dealers over the world to be given out as souvenirs, cleared out the account.

In 1939 Goodyear's various activities outside the United States, factories, sales companies and the rubber plantations, were brought together under a new subsidiary, Goodyear Foreign Operations, Inc. Litchfield became president, Thomas and Leroy vice presidents, Cameron vice president and general manager, Hinshaw vice president in charge of production, with Oseland as treasurer, Shilts as secretary and Riddle as comptroller.

Goodyear Canada, oldest of Goodyear's operations abroad, had always been a separate activity and so remained.

Export alone was doing a larger volume of business than the total business of any American rubber company outside the "Big Four." In many countries, Goodyear was relatively a more important business house than it was in the United States, got a larger per cent of the total rubber business.

Goodyear men were leaders in the American colony in many countries, and men like Hazlett in England, Hastings and Bollinger in Argentina, Long in Brazil, Melander in Sweden, Partridge and Berkinshaw in Canada, Steiner in Australia, ranked with the leading business men of these nations.

.   .   .

It was the long-time policy of Goodyear Overseas to make itself an integral part of the economy of the countries it served, to speak their language, to furnish quality goods at economic prices, offer larger scale employment to individuals, and opportunities as in the States to men of talent.

Finally, Goodyear Foreign Operations sought to make what contribution a group of men might, to international understanding and friendship.

For the overall Goodyear organization, Export cushioned financial difficulties as these struck the United States, averaged the risks of business on a world-wide scale, often afforded help at home when that was needed, added to the stability and soundness of the House of Goodyear.

The overseas organization would have a man-sized job waiting for it when the war came—and would be willing and ready.

BOOK

2

Goodyear's Part in World War II

Typifying the Value of a Strong Industry
in a National Emergency

Using assault boats, quickly inflated and deflated, Marines wrote a new chapter in amphibious operations and ship-to-shore movements.

GOODYEAR encountered its third war in 1941. It had scarcely been conscious as a corporation of the Spanish-American War. The Rough Riders rode horses, bought no tires. The second war found it in position to make considerable contribution to making the armed forces more mobile. The third war found all American industry a critical factor in victory.

The art of war had gone a long way since Julius Caesar and George Washington—or John J. Pershing for that matter. This was a war between machines—heavily armored, fast-moving, hard-hitting machines, which travelled over land and water, high in the sky and below the sea, supporting and supplying the man with the gun.

America had to meet the challenge of mechanized war, with a war going on. That it did so, in such amazing volume, called for performance on the part of industry, whose importance to life in these United States today is still imperfectly realized.

Except perhaps that it covered a wider range than some, Goodyear's part in all this was merely as example of what went on in a thousand factories from Bangor to San Diego.

The company, of course, built tires during the war. That was its business—endless carloads of tires to meet the diverse and exacting requirements of battle on the African desert, the Alcan highway, the Pacific islands, the Burma Road and mountain roads in Italy. New and different tires, huge ones higher than a man's head for earth movers; tires for gun carriages and mobile machine shops; low-pressure tires for bombers taking off from improvised landing fields, high-pressure tires for landing on carrier decks; tough tires for the hill-climbing jeeps, tires that would keep on going after they were riddled with shrapnel—and at home, farm tires to supply the army with food, and truck and tractor tires to keep industry and transportation moving.

It developed and manufactured in tremendous quantities the bullet-sealing fuel tank which kept America's fliers from going down in flames; pneumatic boats in case engines failed and they fell into the sea; huge assault boats for the Marines to use at Tarawa and elsewhere; pneumatic pontoons to bridge the raging rivers of Germany.

It built blimps and barrage balloons, gas masks, "Mae West" life vests, heavy-lugged soles for the ski troopers and bevel-heeled ones for the paratroopers; its Pliofilm enabled airplane engines to go into service immediately on arrival 10,000 miles away; it turned out pinhead-size sealing rings to lock in the lubricants for delicate but vital instruments.

Air power became all-important in World War II. Army and Navy could not do a fighting job without air cover.

Few companies in America had been so long and thoroughly convinced of the importance of aviation as Goodyear, and from 1910 on it had made every contribution to its advancement that a single company could, short of building airplanes. In this war it found itself even doing that.

For it not only turned out a huge volume of airplane tires, and the wheels and brakes for more than half of the nation's fighting planes, but getting completely out of character, a rubber company became one of the ten largest plane manufacturers in the United States, building parts for Superfortresses, P-38's, and 20 other combat planes—and 4000 complete Corsair fighters for the Navy, some of which saw action in the Pacific 48 hours after they left the assembly line at Akron.

Finally the company did its full part in the development of synthetic rubber, which was basic to the entire effort, and manufactured that synthetic in mounting tonnages.

Up to Pearl Harbor most of the civilian population thought the possibility of war as remote as Chamberlain hoped it was when he set out on his fateful journey to Munich. But Army and Navy, charged with the nation's protection, set to work to strengthen those defenses. Litchfield put out a letter to the organization in the summer of 1940:

"The needs for our country's defense will receive the first consideration of Goodyear's facilities, its research and personnel."

So the company was knee-deep in what was then called Defense Production when the Japs struck, was already building blimps, barrage balloons, life rafts, fuel tanks, gas masks, rubber tracks for tanks, had opened a powder-loading plant near Louisville and had 3500 men building parts for airplanes.

The outbreak of war saw immediate action taken by the government to throw the fullest possible weight of the nation's productive forces into the manufacture of goods directly connected with the war effort. The automotive industry was one of the hardest hit, since passenger cars and the tires for them became "non-essential."

November, 1941, saw a production of 3,100,000 passenger car tires in America. Restrictions took effect in December, cut that to 1,900,000. By January it was down to 230,000—and in July to 61,000.

Sixty per cent of Goodyear's business was tires, and it had three and a half million of them frozen in warehouses under government order. But it did not become a ghost plant, nor were its 60,000 employees thrown out of work. Like the automobile makers it threw its vast resources into the manufacture of war materiel, much of it foreign to its previous experience, and number of employees and tonnage of output climbed to record heights.

It was ironical that the war should catch Litchfield just at the time he was planning to give up part of the increasing load he had carried in his 45 years in industry.

He was only 65 and in vigorous health when he relinquished the presidency in 1940 to E. J. Thomas, though retaining executive responsibility as chairman of the board. The world-wide Goodyear organization was strongly manned at every key point, production, sales, finance, engineering, research. The Army and Navy retire their generals and admirals at age 64, unless an emergency has come up. But emergency had arisen and Litchfield, like Marshall and King, would remain in the harness, finding himself working harder than ever.

On the Monday morning after Pearl Harbor he called a meeting of all the company officers, told them that Goodyear's main job from then on was war. There would be no separate department of military production. That was everyone's job, everyone's main job. Development would work on the design of military products; Engineering would furnish the machinery needed; Purchasing would bring in military mate-

rials; Industrial Engineering would develop layouts and processes for
the most efficient operations; Production would turn out goods for war
instead of goods for peace. He followed this up with a letter:

"As we enter the most trying and crucial period of our national life,
I want to impress upon everyone that everything this company has is
dedicated to the cause of America's fight for freedom.

"A sacrifice has been asked of us by the government in the matter of
tire production. We accept it cheerfully because we know that individual
or commercial discomfort must be subordinated when every pound of
available rubber must be conserved for defense.

"We have been asked to step up the rate of production of various
defense materials we are making. This, too, we will do to the very
limit of our ability, because these materials are the weapons used by
the men of our armed forces who are offering their lives in the fight
for freedom. These materials must be where they are needed when they
are needed. There can be no failure on our part."

The wide range of Goodyear's war production makes it difficult to
pigeonhole the various activities in any orderly fashion. There were
things like tires and mechanicals which the company had always made,
new products foreign to its experience but having something to do with
rubber, and new products having nothing to do with either rubber or
its past experience.

Some products were made both at Akron and the outside plants, and
some only at Akron, or at an outside plant. Goodyear Tire and Goodyear Aircraft had different fields, but the tire company loaned manufacturing space to Aircraft and built the envelopes for its blimps. There
was no set rule as to where a given job should be done. Wherever it
could be turned out fastest and best, that was where it went.

It is not accurate to say Goodyear almost quadrupled its peacetime
production during the war, since labor and material costs went up, but
sales volume gives some measure of the war job. And this went from
$200 million in 1939, to $217, to $330, to $451, to 726, to $786 in
1944, reached $716 in 1945 as war contracts were cancelled. The five
war years, 1941-1945, saw a total volume of more than three billion
dollars.

13. Organize for War

Plants and Personnel

IF the war brought supreme test of the resourcefulness of an industrial nation, and the effectiveness of its production machine, it brought also a test in Goodyear's case of its long personnel program, since fast growing factories must be competently manned at every point.

The company had quite an accumulation of facilities by 1940. Count ing Akron as one (though there were two tire factories, and plants making mechanical goods, airships and synthetic rubber in Akron), the company had five tire factories, four cotton mills and two special goods plants in this country. It converted two plants from rubber to Ordnance and opened a third one, reactivated a closed factory, added two synthetic plants, created a major airplane factory, with four subsidiaries to handle the overflow, and had two more factories under way when the war ended.

Outside this country it had three factories in Canada and six elsewhere (England, Argentina, Australia, Brazil and Sweden), would lose one and add two (Mexico and Peru), and start three more during the war. Production had to be organized to make maximum use of these facilities. That included development and research, engineering and traffic, industrial engineering, personnel, purchasing. Accounting and finance had their hands full keeping track of costs on a wide variety of contracts, and the payrolls for a peak of 60,000 men in Akron alone.

And someone had to maintain continuous contact with government requirements. Brown of Development, who had come in from Georgia Tech 25 years earlier, was assigned to coordinate the various phases of military production. Sales came into new and special duties.

Sales-minded engineers and technically-minded salesmen had to sit down across the desk from the customer, who was now the U. S. government, find out from week to week what was wanted, in what changing quantities and schedules, so that Akron could determine how and where its manufacturing facilities could be most effectively employed.

But the government was no longer Washington. It was Army, Navy, the War Production Board, Ordnance, the Bureau of Aeronautics, the Bureau of Ships. It was Lend Lease and many foreign missions, 78 at the peak. It was Somerville, Knudsen, Campbell and Donald Nelson. Needed were a wide range of products, with unvarying insistence on precision and workmanship and on difficult delivery schedules.

Wright Field took over the huge airplane procurement job, specifications, testing and acceptance. Ordnance worked directly with the builders of tanks, trucks and jeeps, as well as guns, and Aberdeen Proving Ground, and a new one in the Imperial Valley of California, took on new assignments in mobilized warfare.

Most of the equipment for Army aircraft was GFE (government-furnished equipment) which was Wright Field. Many Naval aircraft jobs were CFE (contractor-furnished equipment) with the prime contractors selecting their own suppliers, under Navy supervision and approval.

So sales must maintain contact not only with Washington, Dayton and Akron, but with Santa Monica, Burbank, Wichita, Dallas, Baltimore, Seattle, Hartford, Buffalo, and every point where planes were built. Manufacturers Sales must continue in close touch with Detroit, since the automobile companies, blocked from building passenger cars, threw their great resources into building planes, tanks and other war products.

Contact must be continuous and understanding and subject always to revision as war needs changed with new requirements growing out of things happening in Africa, the Pacific, Sicily and Normandy. Footwork must be lightning fast to keep up with those changes, regardless of what hours designers, tooling, scheduling, purchasing and sub-contracting had to put in.

Immediate responsibility for this far-ranging contact lay with J. M. Linforth, who had gone quite a way with the company since he came out of the Navy after World War I, was now vice president in charge of sales to the manufacturers and the government.

The company had long had a one-man office in Washington, under the veteran Ammann, to keep in touch with the various government departments. Jacobs was manager of the department in Akron. Kernochan was in Los Angeles, in touch with the airplane industry on the West coast.

This little organization had to be expanded. Linforth talked things over with Litchfield and Thomas, began to pick men to meet fast-growing, constantly-changing problems. It was a flexible organization, built to meet needs as they arose.

Mefford, district manager at New York, picked to head up the enlarged Washington office, was a strong figure. He had built up his own business in Lima, Ohio, sold out and joined the company, shown administrative ability as district manager at Columbus, then Cleveland before going to New York.

Export sent George Riveire who had got out of Manila just ahead of the invasion, on to Washington to maintain contact with foreign nations, and get priorities and shipping space for carbon black, bead wire and other critical items needed by Goodyear's overseas plants to carry on their part of the overall war job. At Detroit, Telford, in charge, worked with Ford's Willow Run operation, Coe with Chrysler's war jobs, as well as Hudson and Nash, Lawrence with Willys on the jeeps.

Jacob's group kept track of all contracts, particularly airplane tires, wheels and brakes, automotive tires and lighter-than-air, while Knowles at Aircraft worked on the wide ramifications of airplane parts manufacture.

A third group was set up at Akron under Davis of Commercial Research, who was widely acquainted with products and markets, to handle the field work with the airplane factories over the country. Mefford and Davis took the title of Assistant to Vice President.

Both the Washington office and the field group out of Akron had to be strongly staffed. The Washington group included veterans like Ammann, Wilson of Tire Sales, Summers of Mechanical Goods and younger men like Shiner from Cleveland, Dunkle and McLaughlin from Baltimore. Brown of Military Production had engineers in Washington most of the time. Mason of Tax-Insurance took over the headaches of priorities—since the wide range of Goodyear's war products brought continuous conflicting demands for equipment and materials.

In the field organization, Richardson of Mechanical Goods went to Wright Field, built up a staff to work with Army engineers, Williams went to Buffalo to deal with Curtiss and Bell; Bruns to Kansas City with the Wichita and Texas plants; J. H. Stephens to Baltimore with Glenn Martin; Rainey to Seattle with Boeing; Critchfield went to New York; Kernochan and his staff carried on at Los Angeles with the coast plane makers, Douglass, Lockheed, Consolidated, Northrup.

These men had to know everyone, from the policeman at the gate to the chairman of the board, keep in touch with new aviation developments, became a sort of Flying Squadron working on tires, wheels, brakes, fuel tanks, life vests, reported to various departments in Akron, and acted as well as field representatives for Goodyear Aircraft.

Riveire took over at Washington when Mefford's health failed (he died during the war), Richardson became head of the new Aviation Products division. Williams succeeding him at Wright Field. Most of the men went to more important duties after the war, in Manufacturers Sales and the new Aviation Products Division, now grown to important proportions.

In Sales, as elsewhere, the war brought a real test of personnel. Other companies with lesser war responsibilities fell down on important war assignments because they did not have enough competent men to go around. Goodyear had sought since 1908 to spread experience and training widely enough that competent men would always be at hand to meet any requirement of expanding business.

The program proved adequate. Men rise to emergency, particularly if they have been schooled to show initiative, to accept responsibility, to plan their work and coordinate it with that of others.

Production Personnel

Personnel was the key to Production as well. Rubber is a comparatively young industry, and Goodyear, reaching age 50 in 1948, is still a young company, with quite a few men around who had joined it in its first generation, had a seasoned organization.

Akron always had to supply men for the outside factories—and have men ready to fill their places at home. This grew more difficult during the war, when the demand for men increased sharply.

The company had always been training-minded, and every foreman and general foreman had to be on the lookout to find promising young men and develop them—and were backed up by formal training programs almost from the first days, carried on under the immediate attention of top management.

E. R. Wolfe (1915) who had started on the Squadron, gone up through production to assistant superintendent of Plant II, was detached in 1937 to head up all supervisional training. He had not only to intensify that training during the war, to provide men for bigger responsibilities, but must continually study the organization to see where men could be spared, as needs grew apace. The supply of experienced men stretched thin at times but never broke. There were always men ready to move ahead.

Plant II had all the smaller size passenger tires under the veteran Denny (1908) and industrial rubber goods under Stafford (1918) who had trained under Metzler and Campbell. Plant I had truck and tractor tires, earth movers, airplane tires and all miscellaneous passenger sizes. Beckwith (1916), who had come on from University of Nebraska, had tire building; Appleby (1909), member of a large Goodyear family, had stock preparation; Ritter (1912) had the pit, where the tires were vulcanized; Chassagne (1907), who had fought with Dewey at Manila Bay, had the tube room, retired after the war; Sowers (1918), big West Virginian, who had gone through the Squadron, served in England and Jackson, was the second man in tire building, and took charge as Beckwith moved up to be assistant plant superintendent.

As passenger tires all but went off the ticket, Plant II going from 25,000 tires a day down to 700, and demand for truck and military tires went up, part of this was diverted to Plant II, which in the 9.00-16 combat tires built up a production of 3000 a day.

In Mechanical Goods, Stafford found himself compelled to give practically full time to the fuel cell job and Tidyman (1912), who had started in building bicycle tires when he was 16, fought as a Marine Corps officer in World War I, divided up the regular work of the department with Leo Smith (1914).

Maney (1929), University of Kansas graduate, was superintendent of Plant I, and Sheahan (1916), who had served in California, England, Australia and Jackson, had Plant II. Ruffner (1917), unable to return to his post in Java because of the outbreak of war, took over the Balloon Room when Braden left, became superintendent at Plant I when Maney went to Gadsden in 1943.

General superintendent at Akron was Tomkinson (1918), who had been a football star at Akron U. and had served as superintendent of California. Factory manager under Slusser, in charge of all production in domestic plants was W. S. Wolfe, who had helped start the development department in 1912, and later headed it.

Truck tire production under Beckwith, with Young (1920) who had served in Australia joining the department after a period in fuel cells when he returned from Sweden in 1942, built up fast, reaching a total of 6500 a day, including the big earth movers which weighed as much as 2000 pounds, took two or three days to build.

The solid rubber bogie tires for tanks, and the steel and rubber tracks for the speedy "half-tracs" to run on, dropped into Ritter's lap in the Vulcanizing Department, was immediately under Brewer. These were produced by the thousands with a negligible per cent of discards, although Goodyear manufactured about half of the Army's total requirements in both items. The half tracs poured out of Plant I at the rate of 180 a day, with virtually none scrapped, and bogie tires hit a thousand a day.

Reclaimed rubber became extremely important as every possible pound of rubber must be put into use, and this plant under Fisher (1914) who took over when Patrick went to Argentina, operated seven days a week throughout the war.

The rim plant, now called Steel Products, came under Pierce (1926), Purdue graduate, who had been manager of the Efficiency Division. It made rims for military tires, and the spacer bands for the run-flat tires which kept them from pulling off the rim when deflated by bullets.

These were the key men on Akron production, responsible for the fullest coordination of men, materials and machines. They had behind them hundreds of division and department foremen, and supervisors, who also could not forget about things and go home when the whistle blew.

Other departments were just as essential if production was to meet its responsibilities. Engineering, of course, which had to provide, build and maintain an increasing volume of machines and equipment in Akron and outside. The department grew from 1200 men to almost twice that by the end of the war, under Flannery as chief engineer, with large staff sections covering every division of engineering, plus the huge machine shop under Clark and Patterson.

Production Control, Purchasing and Materials Divisions were also undecorated soldiers in the nation's defense in this emergency.

Purchasing is as old as business itself, but took on highly important new duties. To a greater extent than ever it became procurement rather than purchasing, something different from a buyer sitting at his desk listening to salesmen, saying yes to this one and no to that one.

There was a time when the purchasing agent got only a nominal salary, was expected to collect his pay out of tips from the people he bought from. But that was long before Goodyear's day, and purchasing had become a highly-skilled profession, and at Goodyear bought and allocated rubber and fabric—and critical compounds like carbon black for all the factories. During the war Purchasing had not only to watch the inventories of a thousand hard-to-get items, manage to have enough always to meet changing needs, but also had to go out and find materials and equipment, or persuade companies to produce them—and perhaps teach them how—and have expeditors follow through to make sure of deliveries.

Brooks (1909), who started the department which had originally been headed directly by C. W. Seiberling, had long had the responsibility also of supplying Akron-trained purchasing agents to the outside plants, felt the pinch during the war when, with the work at Akron greatly increased, he still must spare personnel for new war factories. Price (1922), his second man, was requisitioned by the Quartermaster General to serve in England in preparation for the invasion of France. Chittenden (1920), veteran assistant purchasing agent, was assigned exclusively to war materials procurement. Key men Murphy and Laibe were drafted for the huge job at Aircraft. After the war and Price's death, Chittenden, Laibe and Murphy became division managers of the Purchasing Department.

Production Control had become an extremely important phase of the business.

Since the Mass Production system provided, in theory at least, that no workman need ever waste time going to the storeroom for materials, but have them always in arm's reach, and that each department in the production cycle would have an adequate supply of goods-in-process ready for it, the industrial engineers had started before World War I to create a smooth running system to achieve this. The first department, called Schedule and Dispatch, set up bulletin boards in each department (the men presently named them ouiji boards), designed to show the foreman at a glance where he was on schedule on the various items and where falling behind.

The peacetime system started with Merchandise Distribution, which took the long list of customer's orders, broke them down into size and types, preferencing those reported urgent, scheduled the day's production—so many tires of such types and sizes, so much conveyor belting, garden hose, soles and heels and so on.

This went to Production Control, who broke it down into pounds of rubber, fabric and compounds which each factory would need to turn out the product assigned to it.

Tied up with this were the Materials Division, Stores, Receiving, Shipping and Internal Transportation, which came to be grouped into Division C, reported to a division superintendent. Gillen and Braden had held that post, Child took it when he returned from Charlestown, Hudak of Kelly took it when Child went to Chemical Products.

The ramifications did not stop at Akron, for a similar system must be set up on a smaller scale in each outside plant—and an overall system created, under Fleming for all plants, covering inventory control, warehousing, and traffic, with Lee coming in after the war on machines and methods, world-wide.

To keep 100,000 men and thousands of machines in 30 factories continuously supplied with hundreds of separate items, including engineering requirements, without shortages here and excess there, which would make men idle or tie up millions of unnecessary dollars in inventory, was a continuous and vital requirement on the back of American industry, and played its part through huge production of military goods created in winning the war.

Many Production Control men used their experience to go ahead in production proper. Condon of Australia, Spencer of Topeka, Stafford of Mechanical Goods, Follo of South Africa, Evans of Windsor and others became plant superintendents.

14. The Battle for Rubber

A Story in Three Phases

WITHOUT rubber we might well have lost the war.
The Baruch Committee bluntly summarized the situation when it said in 1942:
"Of all critical and strategic materials, rubber is the one which presents the greatest threat to the safety of the nation and the success of the Allied cause . . . if we fail to secure quickly a large new rubber supply our war effort and our domestic economy both will collapse."

Three things saved the situation.

One was that America had a year's supply of rubber on hand when the war broke out, an enormous stockpile, relatively speaking, acquired beforehand by what now seems a master stroke of foresight. This would have to last ourselves and our Allies through until an additional supply could be somehow procured—if that miracle were possible. It was estimated that 100,000 tons of rubber was the minimum amount the world could get down to and still carry on, the critical point below which we dared not go. But before synthetic began to come in in any volume, we got down to 60,000 tons—so narrow was the margin.

Second was the heroic effort to get additional natural rubber from distant and all but inaccessible parts of the world where rubber still grew wild.

Third, of course, was the development of synthetic rubber.

In each of these phases the United States took a leading role, and in each one Goodyear men took part.

The Rubber Stockpile

The stockpile story can be told briefly.

With war clouds rolling over Europe, Mr. Litchfield, the world's largest buyer of rubber, early became concerned over the supply situation. Half of the rubber grown in the East was being held off the market under the 1934 restriction plan to force a better price. America had only 125,000 tons on hand when war started in Europe, a little more than a month's supply.

Litchfield went to Washington early in 1939 with an important suggestion. The government had millions of bales of cotton held against crop loans, much of it surplus, and Britain, a big cotton user, had more rubber than it needed. A shrewd Yankee trade would give this country a reserve supply of rubber, and help stabilize cotton prices—be highly advantageous to both countries.

Washington saw the logic of this, and in June, 1939, three months before the war broke out in Europe, effected an arrangement under which 600,000 bales of cotton, f.o.b. New Orleans, were exchanged for an equal dollar value of rubber, f.o.b. Singapore. This country got 90,000 tons of rubber without a dollar changing hands. The rubber, though held as a reserve, was not left to deteriorate in warehouses. American manufacturers could draw on it and replace it with new rubber, keep the supply rotating.

Then Germany invaded Poland and the war was on. A still larger stockpile would be useful. The Rubber Reserve Company was set up in June, 1940 under the Reconstruction Finance Corporation, and authorized to buy 100 to 150 thousand tons of additional rubber. The buying committee included men from the five leading rubber companies, Ingle being the Goodyear member. Further funds appropriated by Congress in 1941 brought the stockpile up to around 600,000 tons by the end of that year. This, with the rubber in the hands of private industry, gave the country about a million tons, approximately a year's supply.

It was not enough to run a war on, but would help tremendously in the emergency. America was the only nation to have a substantial amount of rubber on hand when the Japs made their way down through Malaya and the Netherlands Indies early in 1942.

Once over the shock of the loss of rubber growing areas, the nation moved vigorously. Conservation came first. We must make our present tires last as long as possible. Driving slowed down to 35 miles an hour, since higher speeds shorten the life of the tire. Gasoline rationing was ordered, not so much to save gasoline as to save rubber. Forty million tires were commandeered from manufacturers and dealers, and another four million from private owners. These latter were sorted and classified, and those worn smooth must be recapped or retreaded to get the last mile out of the carcass, and worn-out tires reclaimed and the rubber put back to work.

Wild Rubber Procurement

One of the exciting but little known stories of the war was the procurement of wild rubber from South America.

The Japs swept down through the rubber-growing areas of the Malay Peninsula immediately after Pearl Harbor, took Singapore in mid February and crossed the straits into the Dutch Indies.

But growing public concern over the possibility of a rubber shortage changed to enthusiasm with the news on March 2, 1942, that 17 South American nations would make their full resources in wild rubber available to the Allied cause.

Brazil alone had turned out 50,000 tons of rubber a year at the peak, could easily double that with a little help from the States—to say nothing of the rubber available elsewhere in Latin America.

Under the Washington Agreement, the United States was to supply technical help and transportation and would pay a fixed price for every pound of rubber the various nations could spare, and each nation agreed to cut its own consumption to the bone, the rest of it going into the pool for the war effort.

Valentin Boucas, a director of Goodyear-Brazil, and unofficial economic advisor to the Brazilian government, was chairman of the negotiating committee for his country.

The rubber taken from the jungle during the next three years did prove important, and with the huge synthetic output, saved the day for the Allies. However, Brazil would not be able to turn out 100,000 tons of rubber overnight. It had produced only 5000 tons in 1939 and all the other countries combined had added only another 5000 tons—and that figure included 2200 tons of Mexican guayule. Heroic effort would be required to get out even 100,000 tons—and America alone was consuming upwards of a million tons a year in peacetime.

Someone had to be more realistic. One thing, however, which proved vitally important in America's entire war effort was that in the emergency the nation turned to practical hard-headed business men, familiar with large-scale operations, put the tough jobs up to them.

It was assigned to Rubber Reserve, the stockpile agency, under the direction of Reconstruction Finance Corporation, then headed by two dynamic Texans, Jesse Jones, operator in lumber and other commodities, and Will Clayton, the world's largest textile broker, both of whom later landed in the cabinet. These men knew nothing about the problem involved in getting wild rubber out of the jungle, looked around for men who did.

One of the men called in was Bogardus of Goodyear, who had had more than 20 years experience in plantation rubber in Sumatra, and had also an up-to-date picture of wild rubber procurement, since he had made a trip through the entire Amazon region just two years before to arrange a supply of rubber for the Sao Paulo factory. Bogardus' report to Jones was not reassuring.

"I don't think we should fool ourselves," he stated. "It will be a tremendous job to get any substantial increase in production from the Amazon Valley."

He went on to tell why. A large organization had been built up in the old days, when rubber was worth a dollar a pound and Brazil's 50,000 tons a year supplied most of the world's needs, when ocean ships travelled a thousand miles up the river from Belem to carry out this liquid gold, when thousands of seringuiros (tappers) with their accumulation of rubber poured into Manaos, a fabulous city with great warehouses and docks—and an ornate theatre where the great opera stars were summoned from Europe.

But a third of a century had passed, and the Amazon furnished less than one per cent of the world's needs. The wharves had fallen to pieces, jungle insects had bored a million holes in the theatre walls, the fleet of ships had dwindled to a few old wood-burners, some of them 40 years old, the army of seringuiros was down to little more than a corporal's guard. The situation was a precarious one.

He pointed out that rubber trees were scattered, perhaps one or two to the acre, over a territory larger than the continental area of the United States; could be reached only by trails cut afresh almost every day as the turbulent jungle growth sprang up overnight; that each tree produced only a cupful of latex at a tapping, of which one-third was rubber—and that the best growing areas were the most remote, so that rubber from there could be shipped out only during the rainy season, when boats could penetrate deep into the interior. On the other hand tapping had to be done during the dry season, for at other times the Amazon over-flowed its banks to create great inland seas, covering the tree trunks with water—while torrential rains would wash the latex out of the cups anyhow.

He emphasized the matter of distances. From the headwaters of the Amazon and its tributaries in Bolivia and Peru to the Atlantic was far-ther than from the United States to Europe.

"We should face the facts," he concluded. "This will not be an easy job."

The audience sat silent for a full minute. Then big Jesse Jones ham-mered on the desk.

"But it has to be done," he said. "Take a plane immediately for Brazil, and bring in your recommendations as to how to do it. Remem-ber this is not a matter of getting 300 tons a month for your Sao Paulo factory. We need every pound of rubber we can get. Take your time to do the job thoroughly. But be back here in a month."

Bogardus outlined his recommendations on his return. Hundreds of boats, launches and barges would be needed, Diesel-powered, gasoline-propelled and outboard-motored, with airplanes and radio to maintain contact; with the seringuiros as the nucleus, draw on Brazil's vast pop-ulation for the thousands of additional men, and pay enough wages to get them; hire technicians and administrators and assign them to terri-tories, with the responsibility of training workers in tapping and coagu-lating procedure—and of finding new areas; build docks, warehouses, camps, hospitals, tool stores; set up a financial, inspection and account-ing system.

There was just one rubber plantation in all Latin America, the Ford company's, which had battled with the leaf disease for years, finally abandoned its original site for a new one lying on high ground where the breeze from the river apparently cleaned out the blight.

But the year before had seen unusual heavy rainfall and high winds, and the blight had struck again, spread over the new plantation. There was little hope of getting much rubber there. America would have to go back to the jungle.

Bogardus' report was so complete and comprehensive that he was drafted by Rubber Reserve for the duration, became assistant to the president. When a new agency, The Rubber Development Company, took over after 1943, leaving Rubber Reserve to concentrate on synthetic, Bogardus went along, remained in Washington throughout the war.

An organization was put together. Jones looked around for men who knew rubber, men familiar with Latin America, business men and engineers who knew transportation, construction, warehousing, shipping, accounting, finance. He took men from the rubber companies, the oil companies, packing houses, banks, steamship lines. He demanded top-bracket men who could get a job done. The situation required it. If any company objected to losing a key man, he or Clayton would get the president of that company on the telephone, tell him, "We need him. You'll have to get along without him."

Jones assured these men of a freer hand than was usual in government. In the pulling and hauling inevitable in democracy, there was certain to be clashes with other departments, having different ideas of what should be done, and issuing conflicting directives. Congress would want to check every step of so vital a program, as was its duty. The press might be critical. To move fast, which was necessary, would probably mean stepping on other people's toes.

"I'll keep these people off your neck," he told his men. "You don't need to worry about anything except getting on with the job."

Rubber Reserve went to work in Washington, Rio, Belem, Manaos, Iquitos, and Bolivia, with wider powers than any United States government agency had ever been given in a foreign country, but an arrangement which worked, because the governments in North and South America worked with the common purpose of maximum production.

Another Goodyear man was drafted to organize the actual procurement in Brazil. This was Akron-born E. E. Long, who had started in at 15 as an office boy, become office manager in Puerto Rico at 22, served in Chile and Spain, had been Goodyear's treasury representative in Brazil since 1929. He moved up in July, 1942, to equator-hot Belem, a city of 300,000 people, to set up shipping, warehousing, purchasing, financial arrangements. The Rubber Bank was organized, 60 per cent of the capital being Brazilian, 40 per cent American, two of the five directors, including Long, being American. It would buy all the rubber brought in, allocate the agreed amount to the various countries.

Work got under way on docks, warehousing and barracks. Airports were built for land planes at Manaos and Iquitos, Peru, and emergency fields elsewhere. Long had hardly reached Belem before he found himself running an airline. A dozen flying boats which could land on water reported for duty, old Pan-American Clippers and Navy PBY's.

The little fleet brought in its radio operators and mechanics, set up radio stations at every strategic point over thousands of miles, kept contact with the entire job, flew in personnel, medicine, emergency supplies, had two forced landings but suffered no casualties.

Washington recruited a force of 50 technicians headed by Manifold, Goodyear technical man from Sumatra, most of them with rubber experience there or in Liberia. Stalder of the Akron staff took charge of a station in Bolivia. Each man had a territory larger than Texas to cover, and without Texas' miles of highway. They were assigned a launch with two-way radio, but did much travelling by small boat, canoe and on foot, living for weeks at a time on the food rations they carried with them, directed the vast field effort. They uncovered thousands of acres of new rubber-growing areas, some of which may be useful in the future. Also they mapped the entire Amazon region with a thoroughness never done before, their surveys being filed after the war with the Library of Congress for whatever future use they might have in the development of Brazil. Several of these technicians lost their lives in the service.

The Brazilian government instituted a wide-spread recruiting campaign in the densely populated cities along the coast, sending men at times 3500 miles from home. Some 10,000 men took their families into the jungle with them. The U. S. government, which had the most at stake, paid so much a head to every workman landed in the rubber-growing areas. Slowly and painstakingly the force was built up to more than 100,000 men.

Long's group at Belem had to maintain contact with this far-flung native army, see that boats left on schedule carrying fresh supplies and food, and picking up the rubber, paid for the rubber, saw to its shipment.

The Rubber Bank took steps to improve quality and uniformity by inspecting and grading the rubber in the field. The seringuiros were often careless about curing the center of the rubber ball properly, and it was an old custom to leave rocks and other foreign matter in to add to the weight and payment price—which might not be discovered until the rubber reached a factory in America. Now every ball was cut in two and inspected before shipping, and those loaded with stones or with improperly smoked center sections, which might spoil in shipping, were given a penalty grading to discourage these practices.

A considerable amount of rubber was flown in to the States. The early years of the war saw a well-defined air highway grow up across the Atlantic over the relatively narrow channel between Recife at the hump of Brazil, and Dakar in Africa. Many of the returning planes came in light, most of the traffic being eastbound, so Long's men stopped every one, inquired how much room it had to carry rubber on to Miami, loaded it up. Some of the big planes carried as high as 40 to 50 bales.

Quite a bit of rubber, too, was salvaged from the ocean, as German ships running the blockade were intercepted and sunk, or Allied ships were sunk by German subs—until Goodyear-built Navy blimps, operating from bases from Trinidad to Rio, chased them out of South American waters.

The results achieved by the program were, under the circumstances, remarkable. Brazilian rubber production went from 5000 tons in 1939 to 30,000 tons in 1945, of which it retained only 10,000 tons a year for itself, and a quarter of that was built into tires and other goods to supply the needs of the other South American nations. So Brazil produced 106,000 tons of rubber in the three-year battle, contributed a net of 60,000 tons—which was just the size of the world's stockpile at its lowest mark.

The procurement program extended into Bolivia, Peru, Venezuela, Colombia and Ecuador, all served by the mighty Amazon. Castilloa rubber came into use. It was not as good as that from the Hevea Braziliensis, but every pound was needed. The castilloa trees were tapped only twice a year but poured out a bucketfull of latex at a time. Except in Ecuador the practice had been to chop the trees down to get the latex, so that most of the other areas were pretty well cleaned out. Ecuador became important.

Peru has special interest in that a Goodyear factory was built in Lima during the war to use Peruvian rubber. Of all the Latin countries where rubber grows, Peru was farthest from the Atlantic seaboard. The rubber producing area extended to within 250 miles of the Pacific, but the Andes lay between. Peruvian rubber could be flown into Lima from Iquitos in 3½ hours, or shipped down the Amazon to the Atlantic through the Panama Canal and back up the coast on a 10,000 mile trip which took 30 days. A third route could be used in the dry season by small boats to the headwaters, by truck over the mountains, by boat to Lima.

With the physical difficulties of getting rubber out, Peru's pre-war production had dwindled to almost nothing, only 65 tons being produced in 1941. But the Peruvian government recruited thousands of Indian workmen, built up to a production of 3000 tons a year. Of this nearly 90 per cent was used directly in the war effort, Peru retaining only 428 tons a year for her own needs. The government of Peru built a highway across the Andes during the war, effecting the first connection between the Atlantic and Pacific, and while it was completed too late to contribute much to the rubber procurement, it did remain as a permanent asset to the economy of the country.

Many other Goodyear men worked on rubber production. Losa of Export's Havana office had charge in Peru. Golz of Sumatra was stationed at Belem. He was on his way to Singapore when Pearl Harbor was attacked. The ship turned back and he joined Rubber Reserve. Northrup of Export, who had been stationed in Trinidad, went to Mexico City, worked on conservation and allocation of rubber, and Klippert, head of Goodyear's Costa Rica plantation headed the work in Central America.

The possibilities were much smaller in Central America, but some rubber was being produced, most of it used locally in footwear and clothing. There must be more. In the smaller countries, it should be possible to locate a larger per cent of the producing trees than in the vast Amazon region if the search was thoroughly organized, which was done.

Instead of setting up new agencies Klippert worked with the private companies already engaged in getting out natural resources. They knew the territory, had men, camps, fleets of trucks and motor boats, accounting systems, were glad to make a contribution to the rubber program.

Central American rubber, like that of Ecuador, came chiefly from the castilloa tree. The latex was coagulated by an alkali solution instead of acid, as was needed in latex from the Hevea, the juice from a native vine being used. Tapping procedures were radically different. Instead of tapping the trunk four or five feet from the ground the Central American tappers threw a noose over high-up limbs, climbed the tree, using spurs like a telephone lineman (or in Mexico going up barefoot), used a machete or sometimes a special cutting knife to tap a deep V into the side of the tree, waited while a gallon or more of the latex spurted out.

Nicaragua, which had by far the largest number of trees but had produced only 450 tons of rubber in its biggest year (1900), and was down to 27 tons in 1939, reached a peak of 2000 tons annually under the stimulus of war. Costa Rica had turned in 80 tons in 1910 when rubber was selling at $2 a pound, but brought in 500 tons a year during the war, retained only 30 tons for its own use. And it was an occasion to hoist the flag when little Salvador, which had been entirely off the market, reached a peak of 15 tons a month.

Some extravagant stores were circulated during the war as to the cost of the rubber produced under these conditions—that it ran to $5 and $10 a pound. Rubber smuggled out of Bolivia and some parts of Brazil did command as high as $5 and $7.50 a pound on the black market. But authoritative Rubber Development figures show that of all the rubber brought in from Latin America during the war, the cost averaged only 69¢ a pound, even with assets like tools and supplies written off and left in Brazil rather than being sold or brought back. And rubber had reached 75¢ a pound in the first world war, when every producing field was open.

Synthetic Rubber

By all odds the most important contribution made to the war effort by the rubber industry was rubber itself.

That was basic in peace and war. If within ten weeks of Pearl Harbor our enemies had taken over 90 per cent of the world's steel, the result would hardly have been more disastrous. It is difficult to realize six years later, now that the danger is past, just how devastating was the effect of the loss of rubber.

World War II was a war of movement, fast, powerful, heavy-laden, world-wide. Planes could not fly without rubber, guns and tanks would be immobilized, supplies would move snail-like over the land, and ship movements be seriously handicapped.

That America was able to start making synthetic rubber in the same calendar year in which the Japanese overran British Malaya and the Netherlands Indies, and within 48 months be turning out as much synthetic as we ever used of natural rubber is a measure of industry achievement.

But it was touch-and-go for a long while. We had a stockpile to start with, of rubber and tires, perhaps a year's supply which we had to make last until we could build a huge, highly complex industrial machine, starting from scratch, and bring it up to full momentum. War demands mounted as the struggle went on. It seemed impossible at times that synthetic would ever catch up. The stockpile of natural rubber kept going down, and production of new rubber grew with painful slowness.

Research came into its own during War II, with a great rubber laboratory, where scientists had facilities to develope synthetic rubber and find new plastics. Dr. Sebrell, Research Director, in conference with his staff (center, below) with Dr. Osterhof, manager of the department, at his right.

There was not a single plant in America to make synthetic on a production basis when the war started. We had to build 51 separate factories with the war under way, throw three-quarters of a billion dollars into the project—and find people able to operate them.

The thing that saved the day was that America did know how to make synthetic rubber, in the laboratory, or in small pilot plants. The scientists had demonstrated some years before that synthetic rubber could be manufactured, at a price. But that price was too high. The mysterious bio-chemical forces of nature, working in the veins of a million trees growing wild in the tropics, would produce better rubber, in unlimited quantities, at a fraction of the cost. Synthetic rubber had no practical value, was an adventure in pure research.

Necessity, however, is a great prod to men's ingenuity, and Germany, shut off from its rubber supply in the first World War by the British blockade, had tackled the synthetic enigma in grim earnest. Rubber was the most vital of all supplies its armies needed and could not otherwise get. Its scientists succeeded in producing an ersatz rubber, of a sort, used it to make tires for trucks and field guns. But with the Armistice and the collapse of German currency the matter lapsed.

It was not until the Nazi regime came into power at Berlin that the search for synthetic was actively resumed. Ambitions of world power were stirring the German leaders, and plans were made so that this time they should not fail. Rubber again would be cut off in all likelihood at the beginning of the war.

German scientists went to work, found a Buna-type rubber which they felt was really practical. With the military program in mind the government gave them fullest support. An import duty was laid on rubber and the money put into research. Hitler cracked the whip, factories were built and a substantial supply of synthetic rubber was accumulated.

America had no such incentive. This country could get all the rubber it wanted, saw no need to bother with more expensive and less satisfactory substitutes. However, the high-priced rubber brought by the Stevenson Act sent Goodyear's research men into the laboratory in 1924 to look at synthetic again. They had some success and Dinsmore, the chief chemist, patented a process to make synthetic in 1927. It was still high-priced, however, and the Stevenson Act had collapsed. The project was shelved.

But as early as 1933, long before the war clouds began to gather over Munich, Litchfield called Dinsmore in.

"We have done some work on synthetic rubber, but more urgent things have always come up to interfere with it," he said. "I want you to put somebody on it full time, make it a major assignment, bring us fully up to date. It isn't important commercially now, but we have to keep looking ahead."

Dinsmore raised the question of German patent angles which they might run into.

"Damn the patents," said Litchfield, in effect. "We'll cross that bridge when we come to it. Our job now is to find out everything we can and go on from there."

German chemists had developed two types of synthetic. One, called Buna N, had oil-resistant properties which might be sufficiently useful in specialized fields like gasoline hose, to justify the higher cost. The other, Buna S, was more workable, more elastic, had been tried on tire treads, and the Germans claimed it was better for that purpose than any other synthetic at least. That was of some interest to Goodyear, as a tire manufacturer, even though the possibility was remote of having to make tires out of synthetic rubber. The company was more interested in the oil-resistant Buna N.

The Germans had indicated that they might put their synthetic on the market or license its manufacture. Dinsmore made a trip over in 1935, thinking to learn something from the German experience.

Then and thereafter he and other American chemists got little help from the Germans. Sebrell, his assistant in charge of research, made a trip over in 1937, and Dinsmore made a second trip in 1938. The Germans were quite willing to show samples of goods made from their synthetic but would give out no information as to how it was made. Even Standard Oil which was dickering for the American rights, got precious little information.

Dinsmore and Sebrell picked up a few hints, however, found that the German synthetic was tough, hard to process. They learned of processing difficulties, of trouble getting characteristics they wanted. The reaction period took 40 hours. The Goodyear men were able to cut the reaction time to 15 hours, even before the war.

The most important thing they learned, however, was that if they wanted to make synthetic rubber, they would have to work it out themselves. The biggest thing American chemists accomplished was to duplicate the German rubber in a remarkably short time through their own research.

Dinsmore and Sebrell got out their notes on the experiments of the previous decade, including emulsification (the use of soap and water)

Manufacture of synthetic is largely done out of sight in a maze of inter-connected tanks and reactors, with gauges everywhere to check progress.

Rubber Director Jeffers looks over operations at Goodyear's plant at Akron

Operator checks temperatures as synthetic travels through driers.

Tanks and building of government-built synthetic plant operated by Goodyear at Akron, one of the first to be erected as rubber crisis neared.

Synthetic rubber is coagulated into crumb-like form.

In final operation synthetic is pressed into 100-pound bales.

to induce the polymerization of the molecules, which became standard in American-made synthetics.

Setting up a five gallon kettle in the laboratory they produced a rubber in 1937 which seemed fairly satisfactory, built their first synthetic tire. The next step was the installation of a 75 gallon kettle in 1938, duplicating results on a larger scale, then a "pilot plant" of one ton daily capacity in 1939. This went up alongside the chemical plant. They named their synthetic "Chemigum." The plant was designed to produce either the oil-resistant Buna N, or the all-purpose Buna S. Let us look at the technical phases involved.

Rubber is still a mysterious substance. Its elastic properties seem to be determined not so much by the chemical elements which compose it as by a chain arrangement of its molecules. Rubber is a hydro-carbon, member of a large and useful family. Perhaps some other hydro-carbons could be persuaded to rearrange their molecular structure into similar chains.

An ingredient called styrene had been useful in upsetting molecular structures elsewhere, was worth trying. It worked. Scientists found it possible to get the molecules in an ingredient called butadiene to link themselves together in a great ring-around-the-rosy chain, four or five thousand of them, forming a larger molecule (though these resultant larger molecules would be still too tiny to be seen under the most powerful microscope), in quite similar fashion to that of natural rubber. This linking together was called polymerization. It produced a milk-colored "synthetic latex," which could be coagulated much as natural rubber was.

Butadiene could be made from petroleum, coal, limestone, natural gas or alcohol. The Germans used coal and lignite. American chemists preferred petroleum, another hydro-carbon. They knew perhaps more about petroleum than scientists in other countries because they had had more occasion to study it. America has greater petroleum resources than others, and greater use for it in its millions of automobiles. Its research chemists had done a lot of work in the field of special purpose gasolines and fuel oil for cars and planes. The "cracking" process which produced the high octane gasoline used in aircraft left a residue to the extent of about two and one-half per cent by volume, which was the same butadiene the Germans were using. Here was a ready, and immediate, and less expensive source of supply.

Styrene, the other ingredient, had been developed commercially because it had other uses, was readily derived from ethylene, a petroleum product and benzine, a coal tar product.

We have quoted Litchfield as saying in June, 1940, that the national defense must have first priority in all the company's planning. So in August he went before his directors and asked for a quarter million dollars, later increased to $400,000, to build a larger Chemigum plant, capable of producing 2000 tons a year. He admitted that this still was too small for commercial production, except for the oil-resistant Buna N, and might become obsolete as further improvements were found.

This was a year and a half before the fall of Singapore, but already he felt the need for haste.

The U. S. government, too, was watching the situation, and in August, 1940, Rubber Reserve, set up primarily to accumulate a stock-pile of natural rubber, called in an advisory committee from the four rubber companies, and in the following March recommended that each one build a plant with a capacity of 10,000 tons a year, although with equipment for only 2500. Government and industry were still reluctant to make large commitments in plants they might never need.

But the tension grew and in May, 1941, the Office of Production Management recommended that the four companies put in the rest of the equipment, bring manufacturing capacity up to 40,000 tons a year. Then Pearl Harbor was attacked and Rubber Reserve directed that the 40,000 ton program be increased to 400,000, and when Singapore fell the 400,000 was upped again to 800,000.

For the fall of Malaya and the Netherlands Indies took rubber out of the laboratory and put it on the front page of the nation's newspapers. It was no longer an academic question. America had plenty of incentive now to produce rubber synthetically. The need was immediate and urgent for a nation which used more rubber than the rest of the world combined. Thanks to research in the rubber, chemical and petroleum industries, started long ahead of any apparent need, this country was not caught flat-footed.

The first thing was to decide on a standard type of synthetic, which every factory could use, put all the nation's energies behind that, whether it was perfect or not. Improvements could come later. Rubber Reserve set up a committee from the top men in each company, Dins-more being the Goodyear member. All secrets were pooled, and a cross-licensing arrangement set to cover patents. The committee studied everyone's ideas, sought to determine what ones, or what combination of ideas would produce the most practical synthetic rubber, one easiest and quickest to manufacture and most readily adapted to processing.

The standard decided on was a composite and was called GRS, mean-ing Government Rubber, Styrene, to distinguish it from the special

Some 40 plants went up in huge synthetic project, including those for butadiene and stryene. This one operated by Goodyear at Los Angeles.

Copolymer plant at Houston, Texas, operated by Goodyear; beyond is foundation for wartime tire factory (later cancelled) scheduled for Kelly-Springfield.

Synthetic plants, government and company, sprung up beyond Plant III, became center of Chemical Products division after the war.

Butadiene is mixed with styrene, emulsifying agent and other ingredients in large reactors, then warmed for several hours: result, synthetic rubber

purpose rubbers which did not use styrene. These included GRA, the oil-resistant Buna N; GRM, which was Dupont's Neoprene, already on the market; and GRI, which was Standard Oil's Butyl rubber. The big need, of course, was for the all-purpose GRS.

The next thing was to get manufacturing under way—factories to produce butadiene, both from petroleum and alcohol, plants to produce styrene and other chemicals needed, and on top of that the copolymerization plants which would actually produce synthetic. Ingle of Goodyear was in the midst of all this planning.

Where would the plants be built? Since the butadiene and styrene could be shipped in tank cars it seemed better at the outset to put them alongside the rubber factories, which could use their output immediately without further transportation. But a shortage of tank cars developed, and synthetic manufacture had to go to the oil fields after all, get its butadiene and styrene in Texas, Louisiana and California, pump it into the copolymer plants alongside by pipe lines.

The nation's great chemical industries, Monsanto, Dow, Koppers, Carbon and Carbide, were assigned to produce styrene. Oil companies like Standard, Shell, Sinclair, Sun, Cities Service, Phillips and Humble, would produce the butadiene. The four big rubber companies would operate two or more copolymerization plants each, and two new corporations were organized among the smaller companies, one including General, Lee, Hewitt, and Inland, a subsidiary of the Minnesota Mining and Manufacturing Company, the other including Armstrong, Dayton, Gates, Mansfield, Lake Shore, Pennsylvania and Sears, Roebuck.

Goodyear got a 30,000 ton plant at Akron and 60,000 ton plants at Los Angeles and Houston. Construction got under way.

But time was passing. Plants must be designed to permit the most efficient results, construction materials found, the work organized. Many government agencies were involved—the Office of Production Management, Office of Price Administration, the Chemicals Bureau, Agriculture (since alcohol was derived from grain, which had other uses), Army, Navy and the Munitions Board.

We were well into the summer. Congress and the public became impatient. So in August, 1942, the president appointed a committee of three of America's ablest men to make a complete study of the situation —Bernard Baruch, President James B. Conant of Harvard and President Karl T. Compton of Massachusetts Tech. The committee reported in five weeks, on September 10, 1942, threw a bombshell into the situation.

Production of 200,000 tons of synthetic in 1943 and 800,000 in 1944 was imperative, it stated. Action must be taken promptly and vigorously.

The committee recommended that the entire program be centered in a single individual, with extraordinary powers, a free hand and top priorities to get whatever was needed, regardless of all other war necessities. Rubber was the paramount need.

The president acted on the recommendation, picked a hard-boiled railroader, Jeffers of the Union Pacific, who if he knew nothing about rubber, knew how to get a job done. Jeffers took office September 17th, looked over the program Rubber Reserve had laid out, moved fast to energize it, put it in effect in buildings and equipment—and keep it in balance. The Rubber Director must see that production of alcohol, of styrene and butadiene and copolymerizing facilities kept in step, and that carbon black, cotton, rayon, nylon—and manpower—and tire manufacturing facilities were available.

He moved with a vigorous hand and "bulled it through." Only a few smaller plants were completed in 1942, but 1943 saw most of the 51 factories in operation, and output beginning to climb. But the situation remained critical.

The total production of synthetic rubber in 1942 was only 3500 tons, about one-third of it being neoprene, not the urgently needed GRS. But 1943 began to see results, with a production of 200,000 tons, though a tenth of it was neoprene.

Five million tires were built from synthetic rubber in 1943, which with the remaining prewar tires, and those taken over from private owners, made a total equivalent to twelve million good tires put into service during the year. America had bought 50 million tires the year before the war.

The year 1944 saw the 800,000 ton mark set by the Baruch Committee reached and passed. With the synthetic program in good shape Jeffers went back to his railroading, and synthetic production was returned to Rubber Reserve.

The technical men were not through when they set the GRS specifications and methods. They were just well started. Dr. Dinsmore, who had been chairman of the Industry Committee, was made Assistant Deputy Rubber Director, to direct and coordinate all research and technical phases. There was much to be done in perfecting and improving processes, in compounding, in adapting synthetic to a wide range of products and uses—and since synthetic was harder to work with, took longer to process, a long program to improve this situation, save time.

Synthetic was not as elastic and lively as natural, tended to be stickier when hot and stiffer when cold. It had a shiny dry surface, not soft and sticky like rubber. A tire builder was accustomed to slop a little gasoline to each ply to make it adhere better to the next, but synthetic was likely to run all over the place under that treatment. Splices in inner tubes did not hold as well. Butyl would hold the air well in tubes, but did not vulcanize well with other rubber. Synthetic needed more carbon black, the tread needed more cement. A saving was made later by using a thin layer of natural rubber on the tread in contact with the road, since it wore better and had better nonskid qualities. A complete revision of temperature controls in the factory was necessary. Dr. Dinsmore organized committees from the rubber and chemical industries and the universities, set them to work on various phases of the job. He did not spare his own men, and a total of 125 members of Goodyear's Development Department served at one time or another on committees. *Men worked as a team, compressed 30 years of intensive research work into four.*

Dinsmore had the technical phases well organized by May, 1943, and could return to important duties in Akron. The big Research Laboratory was finished, and he had been made vice president of the company in charge of research. Further recognition of his work in synthetic came in 1948 when the Colwyn Gold Medal was presented to him in London, England, by the Institution of the Rubber Industry.

Germany, Russia and Italy all made synthetic during the war, but not in large quantities. The Germans were handicapped by the shortage of petroleum, and German rayon stretched too much and cracked the rubber. Russian production was said to be 80,000 to 125,000 tons a year, but the rubber was harder to process. The Italian synthetic was not too satisfactory. Canada, the only other country to make synthetic, working closely with the Americans, did an excellent job, with Berkinshaw of Goodyear heading the program. The two nations began shipping synthetic to England in 1943, to Sweden and South America in the following year.

15. Standard Production

The Need for Tires

TIRE manufacture, Goodyear's largest department, took a nose
dive after Pearl Harbor, with passenger tires all but crossed off
the production ticket.

But that situation changed before the struggle was many months old.
The automotive industry swung over to production of mechanized mobilized equipment as the Army put much of its striking force on wheels,
with the result that by 1943 Goodyear was building more rubber into
tires than it had ever done.

We will look first at tires for land vehicles. The great tanks, Shermans,
Grants, Pershings, spearheaded the land attack, and the rest of the army
had to keep up with it. Guns rode on tires, anti aircraft guns, six pounders, 25 pounders, howitzers. There were flame throwers, armored cars,
weapon carriers, personnel carriers, ambulances, amored fighting vehicles,
fire engines, tank cars, reconnaissance cars. There were mobile repair
shops, tire retreading units, medical and dental units, bakeries, laundries,

bath units, wheeled landing craft. Cars with man-high tires carried mobile cranes which could pick up an airplane or disabled tank, load it on a trailer, haul it back to a repair depot.

On top of this was an increasing need for tires at home, truck tires linking up war production plants, farm tires to increase the food supply, earth movers on construction jobs.

Military needs, growing with the expansion of our own mobilized forces and the requirements of Russia and other allies, were climaxed as the greatest land armada in history was assembled for the invasion of Europe.

The entire supply of prewar tires was used up by 1943, and existing factories could not turn out new tires fast enough. So Jeffers called on RFC in August, 1943, for $70 millions to build new factories, the operation of which would land on the shoulders of the five big companies, which were used to dealing in big units and could move fast.

Goodyear as the largest got four separate assignments. The Jackson and Kelly-Springfield plants were to be converted back from Ordnance to tires, Gadsden got an addition half as large as the original plant, and an entire new factory was started at Topeka, Kansas. Other plants got under way, for Goodrich in Oklahoma, for Firestone in Iowa, for General in Texas, and U. S. Rubber in Wisconsin.

The new plants got into production none too soon. Patton's tanks got under way across France, outflanking whole armies, and all of the supplies needed for his forces must keep up with that terrific pace. The retreating army blew up bridges, roads were pitted with shell holes, tires gave out after 5,000 miles, repair crews worked all night, fresh tires were flown in. That did not matter. No time to spare the horses.

Needs grew greater as the enemy fell back toward the Rhine, the famous "Red Ball" express truck line had to carry supplies on rubber from the harbor towns hundreds of miles into the interior. It was extremely severe service beyond any previously known. Eisenhower called for 20,000 more truck tires a day.

The production program had to be expanded again after the breakthrough of December 1944, and $100,000,000 was authorized to erect still more plants, mostly for truck tires, for Goodyear at Nashville, with a capacity of 1,800 tires a day, for Kelly at Houston, for Goodrich in Alabama, Mohawk in Chattanooga. The war was nearer its end now than anyone knew, and the second expansion program was canceled when Germany threw in the sponge.

Goodyear had many problems of design and construction as well as those involved in attaining all but impossible production schedules.

Vulnerability, which had handicapped the use of pneumatic tires in the first world war, had been corrected by the time the second one broke out. Armor plate could protect the vital mechanical parts of a wheeled vehicle, but the tire was its Achilles' heel. A single machine gun bullet or a stray chunk of shrapnel could put a truck out of action, unless the tire could be changed under fire.

The British got into this with the outbreak of war in Europe, developed what they called the Run-Flat tire. America followed up quickly with a similar, though not parallel, development, since uses were different, got into production in 1940 with the Combat Tire—one which would keep on for another 50 to 100 miles after being hit. The tire might be ruined, but the men and the truck would be safe, and ready to fight another day, which was the big thing.

The Combat Tire had a heavy reinforcement of rubber inside the casing to keep it from going entirely flat and out of control. It also had a "beadlock," a Goodyear development which soon became standard. This was a set of steel rings placed between the beads, holding the bead in place after the tire was hit, prevented it from twisting to pieces or tearing off the rim. The Goodyear rim plant at Akron built thousands of these.

Combat Tires, built into many sizes, and used on a wide range of army vehicles, saved lives and equipment in thousands of cases.

The army early decided to standardize on a single tread design for all military tires, since tires must be repaired in the field by soldiers, and molds for sectional repairs could not very well be stocked for different designs. A competition was set up among the companies. Goodyear brought in what it called a non-directional tire, a design it had developed and turned over to Kelly-Springfield. This did not have the familiar diamond tread design, was a compromise among the several characteristics of strength, traction, resistance to skid and ruggedness needed under a wide range of driving conditions. The Goodyear tread averaged out better than the others and became standard, company names largely disappearing from war tires.

The solid rubber "bogie" tires for tanks became an important and difficult manufacturing item. Large masses of solid rubber heat up faster than in pneumatic tires, and the bogie tires had to stand up under heavy punishment of long, fast sweeps over rough terrain. The larger tanks used as high as 24 of these tires to support the huge weight and Goodyear built thousands of them.

Synthetic rubber brought special difficulties in the larger size tires, because it heated up faster. Some of the first ones blew out almost before they got around the corner. Satisfactory results could be had by mixing natural rubber with synthetic, but that called for a prohibitive amount of it in the big tires.

Recalling their experience with rayon truck tires, Goodyear engineers suggested substituting rayon for cotton. Everyone pooh-poohed the idea. The rayon factories could produce only 18 million pounds a year and the country would need ten times that much if rayon were used in tires.

"Then you'd better expand your rayon facilities," the Goodyear men said.

Washington was finally convinced and gave the green light of top priorities in equipment and personnel to the rayon industry. Production was accelerated, was increased more than ten-fold by the end of the war, reached an output of 200 million pounds annually, which would be highly useful in peacetime.

Reclaiming of used rubber became extremely important to put every pound of rubber into use until synthetic production reached full scale, and get the last possible mile out of each present tire. Both were familiar fields. Goodyear had reclaim plants at Akron and Gadsden, and had developed retreading technique, materials and equipment for its dealers for years. Retreading plants went up over the country and in many war areas.

Goodyear technicians acted as trouble shooters in every war theater, watched for changes in the war picture which would bring new demands on rubber, and passed the word back.

This program started before the war, in the maneuvers held during the winter of 1940-1941 across half a dozen southern states, as the Army tried out full-scale a practice game in the mass movement of men and supplies, preparing itself for the new era of mobile warfare.

The Army suggested that the rubber companies might want to send technical observers along to see what tire problems might be encountered. Goodyear accepted the invitation, and its men lived with the Red and Blue armies, got a first-hand picture of tire wear and tire needs under service conditions.

Tire conservation to get maximum wear, maintenance, and inspection to prevent premature wear, and field repair stations operated by trained Army personnel, grew out of the maneuvers—and helped keep the Army rolling later in Africa and Europe.

Gaylord was flown out to Pearl Harbor by Navy plane early in January, 1942, the first of Goodyear's field service men. Wright went to the China-Burma-India theater, started the manufacture of airplane tires in Dunlop's plant in India, then in South Africa. Other men went to

Tobruk, to Guadalcanal, Trinidad, Saarbrucken, Dutch Harbor, and all points in between (and served the Royal Flying Corps as well), working not merely on tires, but on fuel cells, life rafts, life vests, wheels and brakes, assault boats, Pliofilm, and all other equipment having to do with rubber—men who might be summoned day or night to be flown by Army plane 1000 miles to some point where trouble had arisen, and technical advice was needed.

AIRPLANE TIRES

Donald Douglas built his first airplane in Goodyear's backyard at Los Angeles in 1920, using the contractor's shed for its assembly—and his first order for ten tires for Douglas planes went to his landlord.

Goodyear built the tires for the Army's Round-the-World flight in 1924, for Lindbergh's Spirit of St. Louis which flew the Atlantic in 1928, and for most of the prototype planes through the pioneering years of aviation.

About all the company got out of it, however, was experience. There was little money in it, little manufacturing volume. The field remained small almost up to the time of the second war, when it burgeoned to large proportions, bringing many problems, but problems a little easier for a company who had followed aviation from the beginning.

When we left the airplane tire story some pages back, the flotation principle of the low-pressure Airwheel was fully established. Through exceptional efforts in applied research, something which had been just an idea had been translated into a practical, and outstanding product.

But new conditions began to come in in the mid 1930's to affect its use in aeronautics. Just as the change from dirt roads to concrete 20 years earlier had affected transportation, so now cow pasture airports were being improved with concrete aprons and runways—and the original values of the Airwheel in pulling a plane out of the mud, grew less important. The Navy preferred high-pressure tires for its carrier-borne planes. Retraction gear was coming in, to pull the landing gear up into the wings or nacelle after the take-off in order to cut down wind resistance. The big low-pressure tires took up a lot of room and the plane designers begrudged every cubic foot of space.

The landing gear was his great bane anyhow. It contributed nothing to the strength of the plane or its flying characteristics, was just dead weight—and he had to add still more weight to put in the hydraulic retraction gear to haul it aboard. All he wanted was enough tire and wheel to take off and set the plane down safely. Smaller tires inflated at higher pressures would help. The trend toward high and intermediate pressures got under way before the war, and rayon came in for airplane tires as it had on truck tires, this starting in 1939.

Rayon was stronger than cotton, which meant that tires could be built in smaller dimensions with the same strength. Rayon was also lighter in weight, and while this was not too important to the truck, it was very much so to the airplane, where each saving in weight could be utilized in fuel to increase the range, or enable it to carry additional armament and payload.

The cords in rayon being smaller than in cotton, can be laid closer together, need less rubber to impregnate and insulate them, might save a pound of rubber for every five pounds of fabric. Rayon truck tires stood up better than cotton ones under the punishment of high speed and heavy loads.

Goodyear brought out its first rayon tire for airplanes in April, 1939. Other companies were working along the same line, and the industry quickly changed over.

Planes and tires continued to grow larger, carried heavier loads, called for reinforced strength in the tread and at the beads, as well as in the rayon carcass. Construction changed from a single bead to a double, but Akron was beginning to wonder if even this was enough when an incident occurred at an Army Air Show at Bolling Field, Washington, in April, 1940, which settled that.

That was when a crack new Boeing plane, built for Pan American's South American service, blew a tire the day before it was to make its debut in front of dignitaries of the government, industry and the diplomatic corps who had been invited out for rides.

The big new Boeing 307, weighing 45,000 pounds, had a landing speed of 75-80 mph., was mounted on 19.00-23 tires, standing five feet high, the largest ever built for planes up to then. The pilot made one short hop late in the afternoon to test out the newly constructed landing strip. The tires threw off a blue smoke as they made contact with the rough surface of the new concrete, and the bead pulled out. The plane skidded off into the muddy field alongside without damage.

Shiner of the Washington office called Akron, and Keller of Development set off immediately with a new tire. They mounted it during the night, and applied a chromate paint to the rim to keep the beads from slipping. Test flights the next morning showed everything in order and the show went on without incident. But the triple-bead construction was pushed night and day after that, and within the month Keller was able to scrap the few double-bead tires in that size, replace them

Largest airplane tire ever built, used on Consolidated XB-36. Tire has 36 plies of nylon, is 100 inches in diameter. Tire, tube, wheel and multiple disc brake weigh a total of 4000 pounds. (Left), Goodyear's Richardson and Bell inspect tire, wheel, brake installation on new Douglas transport, DC-6.

with the new type. Another difficulty had been met and overcome.

But the planes continued to grow still larger and heavier, and Good-year began experimenting in 1941 with another man-made fabric, ny-lon, which had some advantages over rayon in the vital strength and weight factors.

Nylon was more expensive, so was not practical at that time for truck tires, but cost was less important in military tires than the matter of the most efficient planes possible. War was under way in Europe.

The tire designers did not have the long battle that the truck tire men had had in the cotton-rayon switch, for they could adapt that ex-perience and some of the adhesives to the airplane tire. There was a shortage of nylon, but enough was procured to build one experimental tire, a relatively small, low-pressure tire, with an eight-inch cross sec-tion, to be used on a 7000 pound fighter plane. It was built in six plies, had a smooth tread, as most early airplane tires did. The first tire was completed and put on test early in February, shortly after Pearl Harbor.

They got more nylon, built a second tire in March, this time a big one for a 26,000 pound transport airplane, a 17.00-16 built in ten plies, also a low-pressure tire. The Army liked it. It was superior to rayon in the identical way that rayon was better than cotton. It was stronger, lighter, could be built in smaller overall dimensions, take up less room.

Before the end of the year all the tires for combat planes, and even the big transports used overseas, were built with nylon.

Heavier guns, cannon and armor plate were added to fighting planes as the war went on, more fuel tanks, bullet-seal tanks. Weights kept climbing. The B-29 Superfortress went to 135,000 pounds, and that was not the top.

The story of tire progress under the pressure of war might be shown by comparing an airplane tire with a truck tire of the same size—for example, the B-17 Flying Fortress, riding on 56 inch nylon tires, 16 ply, with a big truck using 16 ply, 14.00-24 cotton tires. The airplane tire carried 100 pounds air pressure and the truck 80, the truck tire with inner tube weighed 321 pounds and the airplane tire 250 pounds. But the truck had a maximum load rating of 9150 pounds, less than five tons, while the airplane tire could carry a 35,000 pound load.

Or take another comparison—a six-ply 7.50-16 rayon truck tire with the eight-ply 30 x 7.7 nylon tire on a fighter airplane. The weight of tire and tube was 41.2 pounds for the truck tire, 35 pounds for the air-plane tire. The truck tire carried 36 pounds air pressure, the airplane 135. But the truck could carry a maximum load of only 1560 pounds, while the airplane could take off with an 8250 pound load.

The development of inner tubes for the larger airplane tires followed that of the casing, but one new element came in. That was to adapt the principle of the Goodyear Lifeguard to those planes using tricycle landing gear.

These had a small wheel under the nose. If that front tire blew out under the impact of a hard landing, a heavily loaded plane would tend to nose over, might possibly go out of control.

The airplane Lifeguard—the Army called it the Dual-Seal—was different in one respect. The tube-inside-the-tube was sealed off, had no connection with the outer tube. The reason is apparent. The airplane is traveling faster when it touches the ground than most automobiles ever do, and in case of a blowout, the airplane pilot does not drive on down the road to the next filling station. The plane stops as quickly as the brakes permit, and the Dual-Seal tube gives instantaneous protection.

One other development came in toward the end of the war. On huge planes like the B-29 and the later P-80 and P-84, the inner tube was taking heavy concentrated loads as it was forced against the bead. That could be corrected in the conventional way by adding another fabric flap around the bead. But a nylon fabric base built into the tube itself would accomplish the same purpose, and save weight.

OTHER GOODYEAR PRODUCTS

While tires remained, in the war as in peace, Goodyear's largest production item, every department played a part in the war.

Industrial Rubber Goods were highly important in keeping war industries producing a large volume and often at new peaks. The need for hose of all types (everything except garden hose) was almost insatiable, since fire hose, gasoline hose, air hose, fuel hose and the rest were used on warships, carriers, submarines, airplanes, tanks and the other war vehicles, and in a thousand war factories at home. The department grew from a peace time force of 2200 employees to more than 3000, worked seven days a week. Conveyor belting stepped up the production of iron ore and coal, and transmission belting served a thousand industries and V-belts went on cars, trucks and tanks.

Pliofilm was shipped out by the ton, for packaging articles, from foodstuffs to airplane motors. Prior to its advent, airplane engines were shipped out with a heavy coating of oil to keep precision parts from rusting in humid climates, and keep dirt out of the delicate parts of the mechanism. It took some time to clean them off after they arrived at their destination in Europe or the Pacific. But by wrapping them in

Pliofilm, they arrived at the fighting front in perfect condition, ready to go on the plane immediately.

Airfoam went out of use for furniture and automobile seats, but had a number of specialized war uses. Bombs were packed in Airfoam to prevent premature explosion, and airplane cameras were mounted on it to prevent vibration, give the reconnaissance forces sharp photographs of war targets to be bombed the next day.

Flooring made of rubber, highly conductive of electricity, with wires cured into it to lead off electrical charges, was used in critical areas like munition plants before the war, but the shortage of rubber after that brought first reclaim, then the development of synthetic compound using no critical materials. This came into wide use on board ships, as it was resistant to oil and gasoline, and sailors could hold their footing better in bad weather.

Balloons and Pneumatic Boats

No manufacturing department in Goodyear, or perhaps in all American industry, has more drama packed into it than the Balloon Room.

After doing an outstanding job in the first world war, it fell on evil days between wars, but was a department that Litchfield would not let die—for it contained practically all of the processing experience in its field in America.

That decision was justified in World War II. From 60 people working six hours a day, four days a week in 1932, it had to expand to 4000 men and girls working in all the floor space available in Akron and overflowed to branch factories in Massachusetts on the Atlantic coast and Los Angeles on the Pacific, came up with a fabulous production total.

The Balloon Room was the birthplace of two developments most important in saving the lives of our flying men, the fuel tank no enemy could send down into flames, and the famous "raft," the pneumatic rubber boat, to which hundreds of fliers who fell into the sea owe their lives—not to mention the assault boats which the Marines used so effectively at Tarawa, Iwo Jima and Okinawa; it built practically all of the envelopes for 154 Navy blimps; more barrage balloons than the rest of the industry combined; carloads of the "Mae West" life vests, and a fleet of dummy planes, guns, tanks and landing craft, a hush-hush secret during the war, which plagued the enemy and upset quite

A lot of room, acres of fabric and scores of people are needed to lay out the balloon section of a sea-going Navy blimp, or even a barrage balloon.

a bit of his planning at the time of the Normandy landing.

The story of the Balloon Room is one of feast or famine. There would be a whale of a big contract, like the 14 gas cells for the Shenandoah which would take a year, or an envelope for an Army or Navy airship which would keep the place busy for a few months, then maybe nothing at all between times except odds and ends, and transferring people out with a string attached to get them back when needed.

The department boomed in the early 1930's, with the Akron-Macon outer covers and gas cells, a dozen cells for each ship not counting spares, the largest as big as a Navy K-type dirigible—then things grew slack again.

Jacobs in Sales and Cooper in the factory racked their brains in the down periods for things they could make and sell to hold the organization together. Every time Cooper transferred men out he lost some of them for good.

So they dreamed out, built and sold waterproof tarpaulins for football fields and baseball diamonds; salvage covers which underwriters rushed out to burning stores and warehouses to protect goods from water and chemicals; "breather bags" which, housed alongside gasoline storage tanks, breathed in the fumes as these vaporized in the sun, condensed them and poured them back in again as the tanks cooled off at nightfall; built "nurse bags" for the balloon and airship men to store helium in as the gas was purified or condensed; built swimming pool linings, advertising balloons, wrestling mat covers, anything to make an honest living.

Their most spectacular job was the great figure balloons first used by New York's R. H. Macy Company in its annual Thanksgiving morning parade in 1928, and later by carnival men as far away as Australia. Artist Tony Sarg would make a rough sketch of the figure on cardboard —it might be Pinnochio of the fairy tales, or the Katzenjammers of the comic strips—then Cooper and his crew would make up intricate patterns, cement them together, assemble the grotesque figures, some of them ten stories tall, inflate them with helium gas, start them on their march down Broadway.

The rubber "rafts" started in the spring of 1918, with the first war on. Van Orman was on a training flight with some Navy cadets, landed in the lake at Milton Dam, near Youngstown, expecting the balloon to bounce up. But it sank into the icy waters and the men had to swim ashore. He talked to Cooper, and they built some L-shaped pneumatic pontoons along the bottom and one side of the basket, later joined two pontoons to make a rectangular rubber raft, the granddaddy of the

200,000 Goodyear would build in World War II.

Back in 1919 Upson took one of these boats along in the national race out of St. Louis, built a better one in 1923 for the Indianapolis race. If the balloon were forced down over the Great Lakes the pilots could paddle ashore. The boats attracted little attention until Goodyear pilots in 1929 inflated them before starting, hung them in the rigging overhead, finding it no easy job to pump one up with a bicycle pump in the small space of a balloon basket. Army, Navy and foreign pilots took notice, asked for boats.

The L-shaped pontoons stayed in, since a balloon which landed in the water would not sink but skid along before the wind, with its drag rope as a rudder, might take off again if conditions improved, or at least continue until it reached shore. Boettner and Cooper had exactly this experience in the 1927 race out of Akron, rode halfway across Lake Ontario, came out in the sunlight at the mouth of the St. Lawrence, when the balloon lifted and continued on into Canada. Pontoons also saved the life of both Cooper and Van Orman in the Pittsburgh race the following year, cushioning their landing when their balloons were struck down by lightning.

There did not seem to be any large market for the boats which grew out of this but the balloon men continued to experiment, took the boats along on hunting and fishing trips, put outboard motors on them, built them in compartments so that a puncture would not send them to the bottom. They were easy to carry, could be rolled up and put in the car, inflated at a gasoline station or with a cartridge of CO_2 gas. They sold a few of these boats to sportsmen.

The department hit bottom in 1932 in the worst of the depression. The Macon job was finished and the Army, short of funds for aviation, turned its lighter-than-air work over to the Navy. The department got down to 60 people.

But they were important people.

Cooper himself, first of all, the West Virginian mountain boy who directed the fabrication of 98 per cent of all the lighter-than-aircraft in the United States. He now had an experienced second man in Rodgers, Ann Arbor trained, and a promising third man in Evans. Hardacre ran the cutting tables and Nave, a painstaking Pennsylvania Dutchman had directed seaming, taping and assembly from the first war days. There was Davis, a Kentuckian of 30 years service, Estright whom Hank Gillen had brought in as a youngster, Kelly and Humphreys who inflated the balloons on the flight field and set them up, Abbot who painted all the Macy figures, McCune who became second man at New

Bedford, then Akron. Several women, too, like Sophie Burkhammer, Bessie Parks, Edna Baker, Mary Thompson who helped build Rickenbacker's boat, Flossie Anson who set up a department at Woonsocket— these were irreplaceable people. A lot of esprit de corps in the department, too, and former workers thronging back when needed—like Laura Truman who was in Honolulu on Pearl Harbor Day with her husband, a master sergeant in the Army, and her soldier son. Thinking her experience in the balloon room might be useful, she headed for Akron like a homing pigeon, stayed till the Japs surrendered.

A number of interesting developments were under way in 1932, but no actual orders.

Litchfield put his foot down. "Depression or no depression, the Balloon Room has been cut back as far as it is going to go," he said. "We must keep this nucleus of trained people for the future. We'll need them some day."

How right he was, events later proved.

One time during that period the cupboard was absolutely bare of orders. Not one thing for the department to do.

Cooper took off his coat. "We've got to keep going," he said, "so today we'll scrub the floors and walls, and tomorrow we'll start painting the place."

It may again be pointed out that certain business activities which cannot justify themselves on the profit and loss sheets of any corporation sometimes do pay off in amazing measure if they are honest and sincere.

Goodyear made no money out of balloon racing, for example, though that would furnish invaluable experience in manufacture and operation —and add to the world's store of information about the still little-known field of weather. Also it made Akron an air center, one which drew flying men in from Wright Field, Selfridge, Chanute, Scott, whenever even a remote occasion permitted, if only because there they could find men there who were also interested in aeronautics, and who at least knew the difference between a biplane and a kite balloon. Doolittle, Kepner, Anderson, Hunter and many others who became two and three-star generals in World War II, were frequently in Akron during the dog days of aeronautics, and being alert young officers, kept their eyes open.

Some of them saw wider possibilities for the pneumatic boats, men like Lieut., later Admiral, Settle of the Navy, whom we have met before in lighter-than-air, and Captain, later Major General, St. Clair Streett, then chief of the flight test section at Wright Field, who laid out the

Army's first Round the World Flight back in 1924.

Streett was particularly interested in the idea of carrying inflatable boats on Army planes which had to do any flying over water, pushed the matter at Washington. From 1935 on Goodyear began to get orders from the services, small orders of half a dozen boats.

Then Lt. Col. Walter Farrell of the Marine Corps (he retired as a Major General) came in in 1938 with an idea which the boats had suggested, that of building them large enough to carry a dozen Marines with full equipment ashore from a destroyer on landing operations. A rubber boat would draw less, be better able to cross shallow reefs. It was flexible (the old cushioning so important in tires), would give and come back, not be smashed to pieces if it hit a hidden rock or got wedged between a pair of them. The floor would have to be solid enough to ride smoothly through the water, sturdy enough to carry the weight of men, guns, ammunition, and to support an outboard motor in back.

It was just an idea on the part of Col. Farrell. Goodyear might never get an order—in fact Jacobs had to go clear up to President Thomas to get an OK for spending time and material on something which might not pan out. But it was an idea which intrigued the imagination of Cooper and his group.

They experimented, tested, sat up many nights until after midnight working on it, finally came up with a boat that they thought would do the trick. After that it was a matter of getting Washington's approval. The Marine Corps was ready to try anything that looked promising. No one in the Corps had any remote comprehension of the vast extent of amphibious operations which World War II would bring, but landing men from ship to shore had been in the Marine tradition since the beginning. A dozen boats were ordered and arrangements made with the Navy to try them out at the next fleet exercises at Guantanamo, Cuba.

That turned out to be quite an operation.

The conventional wooden shore boats were used, also the old whale boats, and the steel Higgens boats. But the rubber boats stood up so well that the Marines adopted them, and as the war grew nearer, began to place large orders.

There were two other developments, the spray tube which kept the water from splashing over the gunwales, and a quick-release attachment—the latter item not difficult for the Balloon Room to figure out from its aeronautical practice. A destroyer towing several assault boats, as they were called, could dash up at full speed as close to shore as it dared, and on signal each boat could cut loose instantly and head for its objective.

Colonel Farrell and Cooper talked over another idea, that of camouflaging an airport by spotting pneumatic barns, houses, haystacks and cows, with green tarpaulins to simulate a pasture. He was ahead of his time with this idea, however, and it was not until the war was under way and Farrell on combat duty in Europe and the Pacific, that Goodyear would find itself making the dummy planes, guns and boats which he and Cooper had envisioned.

The fuel tank story is told elsewhere, but it started in the Balloon Room two years before the war, and 250 men were building tanks when the avalanche of orders came. Fuel cells moved out after that, became a separate department. The Balloon Room's experience was more vitally needed for work which only it was equipped to do.

BARRAGE BALLOONS

The barrage balloon was familiar territory.

Goodyear had built the observation or "sausage" balloons in large quantities in the first war, but now small planes could do that job better, being much more mobile. However, a new type of balloon had come in.

The barrage balloons were developed in England, for the defense of London and other strategic points against air raids. They were like the observation balloons in that they were anchored, were sent up on long cables and pulled down by a winch. But these carried no observers. They were sent up perhaps a mile apart, in irregular pattern, to form a veritable forest of steel cables through which any enemy plane could pass only at great peril of becoming entangled and brought down. The effect was to force raiders to fly at much greater altitude, with a corresponding sacrifice of accurate bombing, and the virtual blocking off of ground strafing attack. The balloons, generally flown at around 2000 feet, might easily escape notice and their slender cables were invisible at a distance.

When the Army indicated an interest in barrage balloons, Goodyear's airship men were given data on the British type, but instead of making Chinese copies of them, drew on their experience in design, streamlining and weather phenomena to build balloons which could be flown higher, would ride more stably, do a better job. Far different in appearance from the sausage balloons of the first war the new balloons were shaped like shorter and stubbier blimps, some of them with six stabi-

Observation balloons being towed behind warships, and (below) barrage balloons of more modern, starfish-shaped design are tested at Wingfoot Lake.

lizers, giving them a starfish appearance from the back. They were tested out in various types all one summer at Wingfoot Lake, then went into production—on a large scale. Helium gas was available for American barrage balloons, to prevent their being set on fire by incendiary bullets.

Two ways were developed to take care of the expansion of gas due to altitude. One was a sort of accordion pleating along the side, held by flexible cord, the other was to build in four or six lobes such that at the ceiling the balloon would round fully out, revert to its lobe shape as it was drawn down.

The most striking of these balloons was the big Strato Sentinel, which had a ceiling of 15,000 feet. During the tests at Wingfoot Lake these monsters carried small anenometers and radios, with receiving sets on the ground to measure wind velocity, and degree of yaw and pitch.

The manufacture of the balloons was the first job pushed out of Akron. The war had not even started, but many departments were already clamoring for floor space. Someone thought of the New Bedford textile mill, which had been closed for several years. The long rooms formerly occupied by batteries of spindles and looms might be adapted to laying out large balloon patterns. Slusser, Braden and Cooper made a trip down, decided it would do, and operations started in June, 1941, the veterans Kelly and Humphreys going down in charge of manufacturing.

COVERS FOR BIG GUNS

Cooper stopped over at the Philadelphia Navy Yard on the way back to talk over another job the Navy had asked about—gun bucklers.

The barrels of the big guns recoil into the turret in firing, then return to position, creating first a vacuum, then extreme compression. Rust-creating spray splashed into the opening, affected the precision of the guns. Leather coverings were used to cover them, but were not standing up as guns grew larger. Would rubber?

Cooper studied it. The bucklers, as they were called, would have to be extremely strong to withstand the terrific effect of first sucking in, then ballooning out. He would need heavy canvas, perhaps nylon. He would have to use synthetic rubber because of the grease and oil.

"Can do," he finally announced. He was a "can-do" guy like the Sea Bees. He built more than six hundred of these, largely tailor-made for each gun, including replacements as they were damaged in action.

This was Cooper's last assignment with the company. His health was definitely failing by now. Rodgers took over active management of the

Balloon Room, Cooper carrying on as long as he could, but he died in October of that year.

Navy lighter-than-air men from up and down the Pacific coast gathered in Long Beach, California, in the following year, to be present at the christening of the Liberty ship, "J. F. Cooper," paying the tribute of the Service to a civilian who had served the Navy long and exceedingly well.

Barrage balloons stayed in, mostly at New Bedford, as an important production job until 1943, by which time the Allies had taken the offensive, and other military needs had higher priority.

RUBBER LIFE RAFTS

The rubber boats or "rafts" also became important before the war started. Airplane carriers came into use in this war, and every carrier-based plane must have a two or five-man boat stowed away in a hatch where the pilot could yank it out instantly by pulling a lever, to be inflated automatically with CO_2 gas. The planes themselves would sink in a few seconds, but the crew would escape.

Probably no one in the Balloon Room noticed a newspaper item of January 16, 1942, five weeks after Pearl Harbor—a Navy chief petty officer and two sailors flying a Navy bomber reported missing after a reconnaissance flight from a carrier in the Pacific.

The old-timers in the Balloon Room took a personal interest in the airships they built, but hundreds of new people were hiring in, to whom the department was merely a tedious job of cutting and seaming and taping rubberized cloth, sometimes on their knees on the floor, sometimes bending over a long table.

But the war moved into the room alongside all of them 34 days later, when the news crackled over the radio around the whole world that Chief Dixon and his two men had landed safely on an island 1000 miles away from where they crashed—in a rubber boat. *Particularly after it was learned that this boat they had lived in for five weeks was Goodyear-built, one made in the experimental days five years earlier.*

In the book, "The Raft," by Robert Trumbull, Dixon relates how he saw the name and the date of manufacture stenciled on the boat, wondered if it would survive the battering given it, made a mental note, "I'll have to write the Goodyear people about this if I ever get back."

The boat eventually landed in the Navy museum, but not before it had been sent to Akron for everyone to see. Men and women alike squared their chins as they looked at it. After all their job was more than

Wingfoot Lake was testing ground for life rafts long before war approached.

Hundreds of airplane pilots shot down over water owed their lives to rafts

Dixon and his Navy shipmates with the Goodyear-built life raft in which they lived for 34 days in 1000 mile epic voyage over the Pacific.

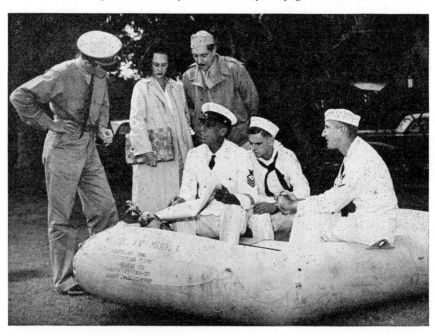

Life rafts became big production item in the factory—and led to development of ship-to-shore assault boats used by Marines in landing operations.

cutting and seaming fabric. They were saving men's lives.

Army and Navy noted this, too, and orders for boats were stepped up. Every plane which flew over water must carry a rubber boat aboard.

Then on October 21, 1942, a Flying Fortress out of Honolulu over-shot its mark, ran out of gas, plunged into the sea. Aboard was Ricken-backer, ace flyer of World War I, making an inspection trip of Pacific air bases. The B-17 had a crew of seven, carried two five-man boats and one two-man boat stowed away in back—all Goodyear-built. With this small caravan the men travelled for 21 days, were finally rescued off Australia.

Captain Rickenbacker came to the Akron Balloon Room on his first opportunity after his return, had his picture taken with Mary Thompson, Flossie Anson and Elmer Brown, who, the records disclosed, had built his boat. He was also emphatic in telling the War Department of the importance of the boats.

"However," he said in an aside, "whoever called it a five-man boat was exaggerating a bit."

He was right. The boat would support 20 men, or as many as could find hand-hold, but it was not devised as living quarters for a period of weeks. Captain Cherry, the pilot, went to Wright Field to devise equip-ment to make the boat as habitable as possible in case men again were lost over long periods—as many would be.

Moving around in the early boats was something like walking on a feather bed. The floors must be stiffened. Oars must be secured so they would not be lost as Dixon's were. A waterproof kit was devised to carry condensed food, signal flares, a sea-water distilling set, first aid, compass, pliers, a Boy Scout knife, a flashlight—and a Bible.

Other things were added later, and a one-man boat was designed for fighter pilots, to be attached to their parachutes.

One of many pilots to owe his life to the one-man boat, a Goodyear man, Frank Baldwin (Capt. Baldwin, Marine Corps ace), had first caught the company's attention as a high school boy in Michigan by win-ning a farm essay contest. After writing a distinguished combat record he had been assigned to training work in 1944 at a camp near Santa Barbara. A plane flown by one of his students collided one day in the air with his Goodyear-built Corsair, and Baldwin parachuted into the sea. He inflated his Goodyear-built raft, and was rescued by the crew of a Goodyear-built blimp—in water so rough that flying boats could not land.

Elsewhere is told the story of the blimps built by Goodyear Aircraft. The Balloon Room built the envelopes, and those for the M-type ships were as large as some of the Zeppelins of a score of years before. An M-ship, 325 feet long, 72 feet high, might be compared to a row of five to seven story buildings more than a block long.

MAE WEST VESTS

Another big job was the "Mae West" life vest, not much larger than a necktie, which a pilot would hang around his neck, and in case he went overboard could pull a cord, release the compressed gas and have a life preserver—one so designed that even if he were unconscious he would still float with his head high above the waves. These cut the loss of life tremendously as carriers were knocked out and crews had to abandon ship.

This was not a Goodyear development, but its engineers did make a contribution in the latter part of the war when the government set up a contest among the rubber companies to see what ideas might be found to make it more efficient. Goodyear came up with the winning design, one which would hold a man in vertical position, rather than on his back, so that he could see the next big wave coming and have time to duck, rather than be submerged. A three-compartment system was included to give greater buoyancy.

A contract for 25,000 of these vests was issued in June, 1945, and was continued after the war ended.

RUBBER PONTOON BRIDGES

The assault boats led to another development initiated by the Corps of Engineers, that of pneumatic pontoons to be carried by the mechanized army across Europe, quickly inflated and strung across a river. These were shaped roughly like boats except that they had a removable log-shaped center section, so that when lashed together side by side, they would make a sort of corduroy road on which metal tracks could be laid. They had to be tough enough that tanks and gun carriages could roar across over them, after which the engineers would deflate them and carry on. Or they could take out the center section and use them as boats. They were called "pontons," to distinguish them from the conventional pontoons.

One unique assignment has been omitted, the building of pneumatic replicas of ships, guns, tanks and trucks, something that almost drove German fliers and Hitler's GHQ out of their minds in the tense weeks before Normandy.

The Germans knew, of course, that Eisenhower was planning to carry the war across the Channel, but where would he strike? That was one of the most highly guarded secrets of the war. Nazi reconnaissance planes were everywhere looking for clues. From time to time they would spot large concentrations of Allied planes, tanks, trucks and field pieces at a secluded spot along the coast, with landing craft waiting in the bay, some with their ramps down.

Back would go the reconnaissance planes to summon the bombers. As soon as they were out of sight, Allied soldiers would deflate these Goodyear-built dummy ships and shore installations, bait the trap elsewhere miles up the coast—while English Spitfires waited high overhead for the enemy bombers to come in.

General Farrell should have been around then to see how well his ideas worked out.

The Army was well advised in asking the Balloon Room to construct these curious craft. The men who made the towering figures for the Macy parades from a Tony Sarg sketch on a single sheet of letterhead, would have no trouble executing such an assignment—even to an imitation 155 mm. gun, riding on eight or ten-wheel carriages, with a gun barrel 15 feet long.

It can easily be imagined that with boats, balloons, pontons and the rest, all breaking into large proportions at the same time, and for the most part before the war ever started, that the Balloon Room would outgrow its modest prewar space.

EXPANSION OF PRODUCTION

As a matter of fact, it spread out all over the place—until it encountered other departments, equally under pressure for production. It filled up two entire floors of Building 29 and Building 41, a large section of Plant III, took over the big gymnasium at Goodyear Hall and the top floor of the club house.

New Bedford got much of the overflow, taking on boats when barrage balloons were cut back, added life vests—and bullet-seal fuel tanks —had 2000 people at the peak, was larger than the Akron Balloon Room. Business men and housewives, working in shifts, helped the plant to achieve maximum production on schedule.

Windsor, Vermont, the sole and heel plant, took on life vest manufacture, and the California and Kelly-Springfield plant at Cumberland, Maryland, took on part of the boat job.

An unused textile factory in Woonsocket, Rhode Island, was taken

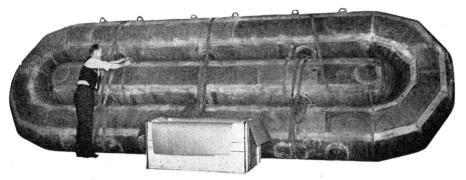

Rubber pontons were lashed together to make a bridge for tanks to cross over rivers in invasion of Germany—or with center section removed were used as boats.

Deflatable rubber ships, guns and tanks set up on English coast before D Day, confused enemy reconnaissance planes—and laid ambush for Nazi bombers.

over as New Bedford overflowed, opening in January, 1944, to build pontons and Army life rafts, later took a million dollar order for 100,-000 life vests at $9.99 apiece, built up a force of 800 people.

Akron did all the development work on these various jobs, only pushed a job out when the "bugs" were all out, and it had become strictly a production job—with Akron still furnishing the rubberized fabric in most cases, and contributing part of its diminishing supply of skilled personnel. Kramer succeeded Kelly as superintendent, then Hochberg who had got out of Java just ahead of the Japs.

All of the big rubber companies, and many of the smaller ones as well, got contracts to build the new military weapons Akron had helped bring into existence. A tent and awning company in Cleveland lent a hand in cutting and stitching fabric, with Akron sending out what people it could spare to help them over the beginning difficulties. Exact specifications can be written and rigorously enforced, and were, but a vital factor still was the long experience of the old-timers who could sense when a cement, for instance, had lost just a trace of its required stickiness, was too dry or too moist. Men's lives depended on each part of the job being done right.

Fortunately, since the Army was combing the country for men, a considerable part of the work could be done by women. It was always a picturesque sight when a blimp envelope was to be tested for gas leaks, to see a line of 50 women in colorful slacks and moccasins walk straight into a half-inflated bag to drive the air forward bellying up in the far end, so as to permit detailed inspection of each square yard of it—and girls crawling inside, into the dark cave-like labyrinth, where a tiny pinhole of light would shine like a Klieg light at a movie studio.

Few, if any, departments had a better labor record. Only one sit-down occurred during the entire war, and that for a few hours only—and the girl who started it later went into the WAC's.

The Balloon Room, including outside Goodyear plants, turned out nearly 200,000 rubber boats during the war, 125,000 life vests—including the 25,000 on which work was continued after the war—4880 barrage balloons, 160 blimp envelopes.

End-of-the-war cutbacks saw New Bedford shrink from 2000 employees to 100, who would lay the foundation for post-war work, and Woonsocket from 800 to none. Some transfers were made at Akron, but there were no layoffs, for there was a big job to be done in other lines.

Some of the women who had now notched up the second war on their records, retired after VJ-Day, went back to their families. Rodgers who had taken over the manufacturing load when Cooper retired, was making plans for a long-deferred fishing trip to northern Michigan when Factory Manager Wolfe changed his mind for him.

"New Bedford has worked out so well as a manufacturing center that it will be continued," Wolfe said. "It will be one of our first reconversions. Hochberg is to go back to Java as soon as the Japs clear out. Evans can take over the Balloon Room at Akron. You have been selected to head up the new factory at New Bedford."

Rodgers put his fishing plans out of his mind, but not so far but that he could get to them again. There was good hunting and fishing in New England. He could get into that once things were running smoothly on the new job.

Soles and Heels

Although rubber soles and heels go back to the earliest days of the company, the story of the department is told here because of the outstanding war job it did in World War II, when rubber supplanted the hobnailed boots of previous wars, and the Army, Navy and Marine Corps demanded it for their millions of fighting men. There is quite a bit of history behind that result.

Rubber heel manufacture had started in the United States in 1898, the same year Goodyear opened its doors, and the little company got into the field in 1901 with heels, and in 1905 with soles, mostly on a jobber and special-brand basis.

Progress was slow in the first years. The public had always worn leather heels. The product was none too good. Finally, in 1914 Litchfield called a meeting, reviewed the history of the department, and said that Goodyear should either get in or get out. By getting in, he meant that the company should make a better heel than anyone else, identify it with the Goodyear name, and sell it on the basis of quality—not price.

Things began to happen after that. Bailey, who had come over from Diamond to head up Mechanical Goods—which now included Soles and Heels—caught up the challenge. Morse, who had come on in charge of Mechanical Goods Development, sought and found better compounds. The famous Wingfoot heel was born that same year. A vigorous sales and advertising support was put behind it, the business began to grow, and fast.

The Wingfoot heel went far to sell the American public on the use of rubber for this purpose. People tried rubber heels, liked them, put them on as their leather ones wore out. The shoe manufacturers, watching the buying habits of the public, decided to make up part of their shoes with rubber heels, but ran into difficulties because of the amount of hand labor involved. So Morse got into that, worked with the United Shoe Machinery Corporation to develop a method by which this could be done in a single nailing operation. Things really boomed after that, and Goodyear built up to a production of 500,000 pairs of heels a day.

They tried rubber soles next, with the outbreak of World War I to create a shortage of leather and give incentive to their efforts. In 1915 came Neolin, a rubber-fabric sole. It was developed, tested extensively by crews of Squadron men and mail carriers, launched on the market. For a time it promised to match the sensational success of the Wingfoot heel. But difficulties arose. Other companies went into the field with a similar product, and these did not stand up, so presently the whole business got a black eye with the public. Goodyear kept on with rubber soles, in a small way, but heels had to carry 95 per cent of the department load. Soles must wait for a later generation.

Goodyear heels quickly took a leading position in the industry, and continued to hold that leadership, but fell on evil days in the 1930's. Wages had to be kept reasonably in line with those in the tire division, and Akron had become one of the highest wage centers in the United States. It became increasingly difficult to compete with companies located in lower wage communities. The 1936 strike was the final blow. Goodyear would have to move the department out of town or close up shop.

A new location was sought, one closer to the New England shoe industry, and with ample labor supply. They found such a place at Windsor, Vermont, a town of some 4000 people on the Connecticut River, where a factory with a power plant and railroad facilities could be bought at a favorable price.

Windsor was the birthplace of the machine tool industry, and the National Acme Company of Cleveland had a branch plant there which had closed down during the depression. Another machine tool company was running along with a few hundred men. The little town had felt the effect of hard times. An ambitious apartment house project, with 72 apartments, was occupied only by the caretaker. Goodyear was made welcome.

An organization was picked, largely from mechanical goods. Cox was superintendent, with Hall and Speer in Production. Kavenagh, who had come out from Chelsea, Massachusetts, with Litchfield, had headed the Canadian plant at one time but had left the company, was back, took over Development. Edsall had Compounding, Joel, Engineering, and Evans, Production Service. Goodyear took over in November, 1936.

Cox and his men knew that it was a sink-or-swim matter. They would have to put the business over or Goodyear would get out of it for good. It was up to them. They would follow company policy as to quality, sales practices and labor relations, but beyond that it was their battle to win or lose—with not too much help from Akron unless they asked for it.

Things began to happen almost at once, growing out of a situation no one had fully realized previously. The little department had been so overshadowed at Akron by tires and mechanical goods that its specialized needs were often lost sight of.

A shoe manufacturer might want a different color heel. The great mill room was too busy to change over for so small an order.

"You can have black or brown," said the mill room.

Another manufacturer wanted to increase his order of one size of heel, reduce it on another—or change the delivery date. He would call the Goodyear salesman, who called Akron, and the inquiry would finally reach Evans in Production Control, who had soles and heels, along with some other mechanical goods scheduling. Evans had never been inside a shoe factory.

As one of its first steps, Windsor set out to find out more about the shoe industry itself—what its problems and specialized requirements were. Cox took the shoe factories, Evans the repairmen, with Kavenagh visiting both groups. They made trips around the New England industry with Blake and the other salesmen, studying these things, and soon coming to know everybody in the business. Things went better after that.

Now when a shoe manufacturer wanted to make a change in his order, he would call the factory directly. Again the inquiry came to Evans. There was no delay. If necessary, he could talk to Production— that was Cox and Hall across the table—or to Development, that was Kavenagh, next door. He did not have to talk to Shipping because he himself was Shipping.

Teamwork, flexibility, and a continuous understanding of customers' needs quickly became more important than wage differentials in putting the plant on a paying basis.

The other factor was Development. Kavenagh did not have to go upstairs, explain his problem to people who had larger concerns on their minds. He would just walk out into the plant, experiment to his heart's content, without having to get Akron's permission.

The isolated position of Windsor helped. Everyone had a new sense of freedom. As long as they turned out a good product and made money, Akron would let them alone.

Production and Development, working with Joel of Engineering and getting effective help when they asked for it from Kilborn and Snyder in Machine Design at Akron, set out on a program of mechanization and conveyorization to reduce hand labor and manual hauling.

Riding on conveyors the compounded rubber went from the warm-up mill to the calender, which sheeted it out like biscuit dough (though to exact gauge), then on to the cutting machines, which stamped out the heels, again like the housewife cutting out biscuits. The conveyor took the raw heels on to the presses, then carried the remaining stock back to the warm-up mills to start over again. The program was climaxed by what was called the Windsor "Merry-Go-Round" a six-deck press, with a conveyor running completely around it.

The process is difficult to describe, since it is continuous,—hard to say where it starts or stops. But we might start as the mold, carrying 24 or more cured heels (the number depending on the size) slides out on the conveyor. There the top half opens up automatically, turns over on its back, starts around the conveyor to the right. It is glistening with steel points, eight to thirteen of them in each of the 24 or more curing cavities. This half of the mold moves past two girls, one of whom cleans it with compressed air, while the other places a tiny washer on each bristling point. She does not do this by hand. An ingenious machine sweeps over the surface, dropping the washers accurately in place. Then the plate continues on to the back of the press where it meets its fellow, which has gone around the other side. Two operators are enough to remove the cured heels, clean it, put in uncured ones.

As the two plates meet, the one carrying the 200 or more washers turns over on its face, magnets holding the washers in place, and heels and washers move into the press, where the latter are embedded securely and accurately in place during the vulcanizing process.

Improvements in compounding brought the curing time down to eight or ten minutes, and this one press can turn out 25,000 pairs of heels a day. Every heel, after being cured and trimmed, is carried on conveyor belt through an X-ray booth where a girl operator can immediately see if any of the hidden washers are askew or missing, push it off the belt.

Perfecting of this process was accomplished during the early war years, as was the development of another ingenious process for soles.

Originally, soles were stamped out like heels, but it was a little harder

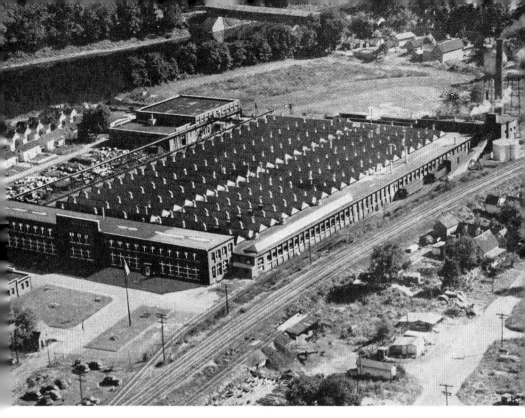

Windsor Factory, above, on the banks of the picturesque Connecticut river, did a big war job, was the birthplace of Neolite.

Testing crews hiked hundreds of miles through Vermont mountains to try out wearing qualities of new types of footwear developed at Windsor plant.

with anything as big as a sole to do this with complete accuracy of gauge and contour. But why bother to shape the soles at all? Put in the exact amount of compounded rubber and the mold will give it the desired shape. Why not simply calender it to a given gauge, slit it into thick ribbons and cut it off into slabs?

You need not even weigh the slabs. That would take too much time. Edsall's men, knowing the weight of the rubber and the compounds in it, could compute the length needed for a given weight. So it would be a simple matter to set the cutting knives at the proper point, and as the bands of rubber were carried past on the conveyor, chop it into specified lengths.

With all these things, Windsor got its costs down and sales volume up, was ready to take over a mass production assignment when the war broke out.

That started slowly. The government allocated the relatively small supply of natural rubber to vital uses, and rubber heels for civilians were not one of these at first. Windsor made "Mae West" life vests, molded parts for gas masks. But soles and heels quickly came back for the Armed Forces—and the civilian population. People working in war plants needed sturdy, waterproof foot protection, which rubber could give—and the nation's supply of leather was running short.

American people were using more shoes than formerly, as a glance into the clothes closet will show. Back in 1900 a man needed only a pair of work shoes and a pair for Sunday. But from 1900 on he usually owned several pairs—and his wife had a still larger shoe inventory.

The population of the United States increased 80 per cent between 1900 and 1941, but production of shoes increased 120 per cent, and the production of sole leather went up less than 35 per cent. Rubber had been a life saver, and in the years immediately before the war, 50,000,-000 to 75,000,000 pairs of shoes were made each year with heels other than leather. And Europe was starving for leather.

Military needs boomed. Rubber-soled Army shoes were waterproof, and lessened the fatigue of long infantry marches. Hobnailed boots might strike sparks on metal parts of planes and trucks, or a gravel road, reveal the presence of a scouting party or parked planes. Rubber soles and heels could be more easily repaired in the field—not be thrown away. Army and Marine Corps went over to rubber, particularly in the combat zones. The Navy used rubber heels, but not soles at the outset.

Now Windsor's mass production technique began to pay off. And also the specialized experience of its personnel. Kavenagh found himself drafted on industry committees, was soon spending half of his time in Washington. One day there he saw a heavy shoe on an officer's desk, a leather shoe dotted with steel lugs.

"What are you doing with that?" he inquired.

The officer explained. "This is a shoe used by mountain climbers in the Swiss Alps. We are trying to find out if soles like these can be made of rubber, with the lugs molded into them."

"Why didn't we get in on that?" Kavenagh asked.

"We didn't think you'd be interested," was the reply. "Another company has been working on it for three months. It's too late for you to start now."

"Can we try?" Kavenagh asked.

"Go ahead," said the officer.

Kavenagh hurried back to Windsor that night, turned out a wooden sole in the carpenter shop, had a mold made up, and in 48 hours was back in Washington with a rubber lug sole—and had attached to it a shoe—one which was so successful that it was adopted and came into wide use for all troops operating in mountain regions throughout the war—and incidentally, was the progenitor of the sports sole which became popular after the war.

Windsor took part in another wartime development—shoes for parachute troopers, with a beveled heel which would not catch on a rock or other obstruction in landing, break an ankle.

As military and civilian production increased, Windsor ran into a labor shortage. It is the smallest town in which any Goodyear plant is located. The draft had cut down the supply of manpower; the machine tool plant nearby had increased its working force from 350 to 2200, and another company in town was making chemicals for the Army, both having higher labor priorities. The company built up its force from 600 prewar to 1000 men, but it was hard going. Mechanized processes increased output with a minimum working force, but military requirements were insatiable.

Sub-contracting was resorted to on a wide scale, and with great ingenuity. Factories were canvassed throughout the entire country. One in Brooklyn had curing presses but no mixing and compounding equipment. One in Maine could cure and trim. Windsor took whatever processing it could get. Part of the increasing requirements, however, finally had to go to other Goodyear plants, in Akron, Los Angeles, St. Marys and Muncie. Then Goodyear erected an entire new factory at Gadsden, Alabama, to make soles and heels. This was a permanent production unit, with greater capacity than that of Windsor.

Synthetic rubber brought its problems when it came in, but once these were solved, soles and heels could be made completely of synthetic rubber—something not possible with tires.

The dramatic Neolite story began before the war. Up to then no one had ever made a completely satisfactory sole for people's shoes, from leather, rubber or anything else.

As early as 1937 Post asked the factory to build a rubber sole regardless of price, see if the company could not take a really superior product into the market. He even had a name for it, Neolite. Edsall and Kavenagh worked over it for a long time, came out with a sole in 1941 which was definitely better than any rubber sole yet made.

But it was not good enough. It could not be something which was merely better than others on the market. It must do adequately everything expected from the sole of a shoe.

The ideal sole should be waterproof, comfortable, look well and be something which could be stitched onto a shoe. Rubber could meet these requirements.

But also it must be firm and stiff, give a solid platform to the foot, protect it from the irregularities of the ground, hold the shoe in shape. And it must be as light as leather. That was the rub. Once you built a sole stiff enough to protect the foot, it was too thick and too heavy. The difficulty was inherent. Rubber was essentially flexible, pliable.

However, the development men kept on, under Post's prodding, even after the war came on with heavy production demands. The Army too wanted something as stiff as leather for its foot soldiers. But by 1943 Development was ready to state bluntly that Post's requirements could not be met with rubber, natural or synthetic. If the company wanted something better, it would have to find a new material.

The problem went to Research, who tried to develope a plastic sole, without success. Other companies experimented with a composition sole, but the public turned up its nose at that, since it marked up the floors.

However, at a meeting in June, 1944, R. S. Wilson, vice president in charge of sales raised the question again. "Have you made any headway at all on it?" he asked.

"We haven't got to first base," said Post.

"You might try Research again," Wilson suggested. "Plastics isn't the answer, but there might be something else. This matter is important. People have been using rubber soles during the war, but they have not been too satisfactory, and everyone will want to get back to leather when the war is over. But if we could find the right thing *now*, something that is better, get them used to it while the war is on, they'll never go back to leather. If it's right, it'll stay in the picture."

So the problem went back to the Laboratory, and George Gates, a young research chemist who had been working on plastic soles, took the assignment, started all over—with the heat on to get results.

Painstakingly, as only research scientists can, Gates went to work. Every previous research project was reexamined. One of them, a rubber resin, looked promising.

Gates made some up, tested it, and ran into one extremely interesting fact. It was stiff but it had some *give* to it. It could be flexed indefinitely without cracking. This might be just what the doctor—or R. S. Wilson —ordered.

It was a new material, something that did not previously exist. The years of research had paid off in an unexpected quarter. Gates ran it through a full cycle of tests, shipped off a quantity to Windsor with full information.

It was not, of course, Neolite. Other compounds must be used with it, and Windsor must call on its fullest experience to determine what compounds, and in what quantities and under what pressures and temperatures. However, that did not take too long. Windsor quickly became excited about the new material, put in long hours overtime trying all kinds of expedients. In the end Kavenagh called Akron:

"This is it," he said. "It isn't rubber, it isn't plastic. It's the new material we've been looking for. We've built soles from it and put them through the hardest tests we know and they stand up perfectly. I'm sending you some tonight air express."

Akron ran further tests and the initial skepticism was quickly replaced by something as near to enthusiasm as scientists permit themselves. They reported to the management OK.

Things began to move. It was late in 1944 by now. No time to be lost. Dinsmore started production of the resin on a large scale at the useful Chemigum plant. Neolite went into production.

With something as important as this on its hands, the launching of the product must be as dramatic as that of its discovery. So Goodyear put $600,000 in advertising behind a brand-new, unknown product, the first advertising appearing in February.

The rest of the story is better known. Neolite made merchandising history. By the time the war ended it was fully established, and by 1948 two hundred shoe manufacturers were using it and 25,000,000 people were walking on Neolite soles and heels.

So peace brought no cutback in employment at Windsor, it remained at the war peak of 1000. The foreign market continued to grow and production had to be increased. Heel manufacture abroad started in Argentina in 1931, was followed in England in 1932, in Brazil in 1939, Sweden in 1940, and postwar plants were set up in Australia, Mexico, Cuba, Peru and Colombia. Canada, which had been making soles and heels at Bowmanville, put in a new plant at Quebec primarily for these two articles.

With soles and heels now more important in the company picture, the Shoe Products Division was reorganized under Post as general manager. Evans moved up to production manager, Kerr to sales manager, Edsall to assistant development manager. Production continued at Gadsden.

Some 1600 men were earning good wages in an industry which had utilized the inherent characteristics of rubber to create a product which millions of people found they could use to their own advantage—offering a new example of the relationship between research and enterprise on the one side, and employment and standards of living on the other.

16. New War Goods

Bullet Sealing Fuel Tanks

NEXT to synthetic rubber, the most important single contribution to the national defense made by the rubber industry during the war was the bullet-sealing fuel tank for airplanes.

This is the concensus of top military opinion.

It was one of Goodyear's biggest, as well as most important, wartime assignments. Fuel tanks in all shapes and sizes, from those big enough for a grand piano to some no larger than a lady's hatbox were built in every square foot of floor space that could be spared at Akron, and overflowed from there to five of its outside plants—and half a dozen smaller rubber companies acting as sub-contractors.

California, having an empty cotton mill on its hands, built up an output even greater than Akron; Gadsden built an entire new wing for fuel cells; New Bedford changed over from life rafts; Jackson, released from the gun contract for more urgent truck tire production, still had to make room for a fuel tank department; and an empty factory was converted to their manufacture at Lincoln, Nebraska. At the peak Goodyear had 5000 men working on bullet-seal tanks.

This was not an exclusive Goodyear assignment. With every combat plane in America demanding rubber tanks, not to mention our allies, this was too big a job for any one company.

However, the Goodyear design became standard; its research men found the solution when the entire program appeared to be blocked; it built more fuel tanks than any other company—and the original idea came out of its laboratory back in World War I.

We will start with that first war. In the final months of 1918, 75 per cent of the planes lost in action were shot down in flames. Combat tactics revolved around the skill of individual pilots, each trying to maneuver into position to send a burst of machine gun fire into his enemy's fuel tank. If incendiary bullets did not do the work, sparks or a short circuit was likely to as the gasoline gushed out over the structures.

Goodyear Development men conceived a plan at that time to avert these casualties, by utilizing another of the characteristics of rubber itself.

One thing to which rubber was vulnerable was gasoline. It would swell up at once and could be entirely dissolved if there was enough gasoline—in fact that is the way rubber cement is made.

Someone raised the question: Could this shortcoming of rubber be turned into an advantage? Rubber tends to close up around a hole and seal it anyhow, and would do so more quickly with gasoline present. So why not line the outside of the fuel tanks with rubber? Then as the gasoline poured out through a bullet hole, the rubber would close it.

By the time this was worked out, however, the war was over. It was interesting but not important, since there would be no more wars. The Army approved the idea, and allotted the company $20,000 to complete the experiment. After that it went into dead storage and was fairly well forgotten until 1938, when war again threatened in Europe.

Grumman, Boeing and other manufacturers building planes for the British, recalled Goodyear's earlier experiments, came in to see whether some such protection could not be provided for the fuel tanks of the new planes. Wright Field got into it, set the other rubber companies to work.

Dinsmore and Sebrell of Research handed the assignment to a serious young Akronite, James Merrill, a few years out of Cornell and M.I.T., gave him a group of young engineers, most of them from the Flying Squadron, men who had been out of college less than a year.

They started out on a different course from that of World War I. Synthetic rubber had come in, and the Buna N type was resistant to gasoline, could be used as an inner lining in the tank, with natural rubber on the outside to seal up the hole.

Perhaps they could get away from metal entirely, use other materials. Metal was in demand elsewhere, and was not too satisfactory anyhow, since it flared out widely when hit, left a big hole. And the U. S. Army was changing over from 30 cal. guns to the more destructive 50 cal., and doubtless the enemy would also. With a rubber-covered tank, even the larger bullets would merely make a sharp hole like an ice pick.

Other materials were studied. The Army suggested cowhide, which was stiff and would prevent scuffing and abrasion. Plywood was a possibility, since it would not splinter but spring back into place after the bullet passed through. The Balloon Room and the Experimental Work Shop built forms of wood, of plaster, of papier mache, hand-built several types of tanks.

A firing range was set up at Wingfoot Lake and Slusser and Rodgers tested the tanks out with the 30-06 hunting rifles, until the Army loaned the company a 30 calibre machine gun.

Then another idea came in which was extremely interesting to the airplane designers. That was to discard the leather and plywood, make a flexible tank out of rubber and fabric only. Such a tank could be doubled and squeezed into unused corners of wings and fuselage, enable the plane to carry more fuel, increase its range. Now they were getting somewhere.

The use of rayon in place of cotton solved the remaining difficulties. The plan arrived at was to build the tanks in sandwich layers of rubber and rayon like plywood. A .04 inch layer of the Buna N synthetic went on the inside next to the gasoline, then two layers of natural rubber .11 inch thick with rayon between them as a binder, then two layers of rayon cord fabric on the outside as the cover.

The flexible tank was approved and from then on Goodyear built both rigid and flexible types, its prewar Pliolite coming into use as a stiffener for the latter, and a layer of Airfoam improving it further.

Production was slow at first. The tanks were built around a form, the first ones being of metal. After completing the tank, they sawed it in two, then cemented it together again after taking it off the form. Wooden forms followed, which could be collapsed by pulling one board out. Plaster forms came next and finally papier mache, either of which could be dissolved and cleared out more easily.

Other troubles arose. More benzol was used than in any other product, and the accumulation of fumes had a toxic effect. Employees became ill, had to be sent home. The Goodyear hospital found what was wrong. Slusser closed the department down, ordered everyone examined, and those whose blood count was low were sent home on pay for a week or as much longer as necessary. The department remained closed until a ventilating system could be built in to make working conditions safe.

By 1940 the development was pretty well in hand. Production got up to 80 or 90 tanks a week. The Air Forces' needs were increasing. The Goodyear tanks were tested at Wright Field and Dahlgren, Virginia, with 50 calibre bullets and even cannon fire, tried out at 20 degrees below zero to simulate high altitude flying.

Production soon grew to the point that a separate department was created in Mechanical Goods under Stafford, with Joslyn of the Sales Department coming in as coordinator between the factory, the plane manufacturers and the armed forces.

But trouble arose the month the war started, in December, 1941. An aromatic content was being added to the gasoline to give the engines better performance on take-off, and much of the gas in the Dutch East Indies was already high in aromatics.

The Army and the rubber chemists knew that Buna N would not offer as effective resistance as before to a gasoline having a high aromatic content, and took steps to meet that situation. A resistant solution was put into every tank in the field and shaken up thoroughly before the fuel was put in. Despite this, things quickly became very serious.

The gasoline began to work through the synthetic, penetrate into the natural rubber. Plies began to separate, the tanks grew heavier as the rubber swelled, soon were carrying less fuel without realizing it. In long distance flying, the pilots compute their range on the basis of the fuel carried. A bomber plane could run out of gas over the ocean when it should have ample supply to get back to base.

There were hectic times for the next sixty days. Army and Navy issued imperative instructions. Instead of fuel tanks being merely filled, the gasoline was metered as carefully as at an automobile filling station, and any tank which could not carry its approximate stated capacity was promptly yanked out and a new one put in.

At the Goodyear laboratories, the research men tried first to improve the synthetic, make it more resistant. The resultant product, however, tended to become brittle in the low temperatures of high altitude and Arctic flying. They could not tell the Army to fly low in a time of war, or to keep out of Alaska. They looked for some kind of a barrier, thin and light in weight, to protect the rubber completely from any contact

Merrill of Research gets citation from his Commander-in-Chief for his
work on bullet-proof fuel cells; (below) typical manufacturing scene.

with gasoline. Another emergency they must meet—and fast.

Several things were tried, including metal foil, but nylon proved to be the solution. A special grade nylon would effectively bar any penetration of gasoline into the tank, even up to 40 per cent aromatics. Two thousandths of an inch in thickness, it caused no increase in weight, would perform well at low temperatures, adhere well to the synthetic. Also the nylon could be sprayed or brushed on, or inserted in film form, did not slow up production.

The trouble arose in December, was cured by February.

It is often difficult in any scientific development to single out any one individual for credit, as many men usually have had a hand in it, but Merrill came into unique recognition for this job.

The War Production Board broadcast an invitation to Labor-Management committees throughout industry, to nominate men in their plants who had made significant contribution to the war effort, either through individual performance, or by devising new tools, methods, products, or ways to speed up output. The board was particularly interested in ideas which had been applied in other industries, affected the war production generally.

Nominations poured into the board from everywhere, nearly 400,000 in all. A large force of men was needed to appraise them. In the end the board awarded certificates to 26,000 individual workers, 55 to men who had made important contributions, and singled out six for special citation. One of the six was Merrill.

If he had not won recognition for his part in developing the bulletproof tank originally, he certainly had done so when he turned back the threat which aromatics offered to its continued usefulness.

Merrill was called to Washington in December, 1942, and President Roosevelt presented the citation to him personally at the White House.

Back home Goodyear gave him merited promotion, and he became assistant director of all the company's research work.

Up to the time the war started, each rubber company built tanks for its plane manufacturer customers—under Wright Field approval. But it seemed advisable to standardize on one type since production was increasing fast, and the tanks would have to be serviced in the field. An Industry Committee, set up to work with the Army, selected the Goodyear tank as standard, and all specifications thereafter were written around that.

Tank production was a difficult job because of the wide range of shapes and sizes. The B-17 had some 30 in all, was designed so that the rigid tanks could be installed in the fuselage and wings. Many of these were big enough for a girl to work inside. The Curtiss Warhawk also used rigid tanks. The Superfortress, the Liberator and the Billy Mitchell used flexible tanks, but they carried some of the rigid ones along as well in the bomb bay to get added range.

The flexible cells were a boon to the plane designers, since they could be forced into place between struts, anywhere there was room. Famous combat planes like the Mustang, P-38, the PBY flying boats, the Aerocobra, and the Grumman Hellcat all used flexible cells. The range of shapes and sizes widened.

To complicate things further every fuel tank had to have a number of metal fittings built into it. There must be openings to put in the gasoline, to carry it to the carburetor, to indicate on the pilot's gauge how much fuel there was in each tank, inter-connectors to enable the transfer of fuel from one tank to another, breather fittings to avoid creating a vacuum as the gasoline was used. Fittings must be strongly built to withstand a surge of gas when a plane flew upside down or did an Immelman turn or other violent maneuvers. And each tank was different, called for a different set of fittings.

Because of the multitude of sizes and types, and the fact that soldiers and sailors out in the field would have to remove them for inspection and repair, and put them back in in the least amount of time, Gaylord was flown out to Pearl Harbor immediately after the war began, worked up a manual showing where each tank was in each plane—a manual which had to be changed from time to time. Schools were set up in Akron to teach maintenance and repair to officers and men from both services.

Army and Navy decided soon that every plane in the combat zone must carry bullet-seal tanks. Production increased in astronomical proportions.

Equipment was installed in Goodyear's outside plants and sub-contracts given to smaller companies. Akron had to send men out to train men in the other plants. The English factory even sent a man over in the midst of the war to study manufacture and repair.

Despite the size of the job, however, it was one war assignment on which there was no serious production trouble. In fact other companies who got into difficulties sent men to Goodyear to study its operations.

Natural rubber, scarce as it was, was still used as a sealing medium until 1944 when, after a long series of experiments, the factory was able to adapt a GRS synthetic to this purpose.

Early in the war Goodyear engineers wondered whether the bullet-seal tanks might not be used on the PT boat. A new weapon in World

War II, the PT boat, small, fast, maneuverable—and expendable—could dart in under cover of fog or darkness and launch its torpedos against armored men-of-war—and might or might not get away.

The PT boats had to be made of plywood which would absorb rather than resist the vibration from its three 2500 h.p. Packard engines. In so small a craft the vibration might buckle a metal hull or break a weld.

They had armor plate around the gun turret on deck, but boat captains usually ripped this off and threw it away once they were at sea. If their men had no protection, they would ask none.

Carrying 3100 gallons of gas, as well as ammunition for the 50 calibre machine guns, these deadly craft were especially vulnerable. So Goodyear designed a 1350 gallon belly tank and two 875 gallon wing tanks, suggested their use. The boat builders were skeptical at first, since their fuel tanks had always been made of metal, but the Navy, seeing the protection rubber was giving its flying men, wanted it extended to its sailors as well. The Goodyear tanks became standard equipment.

Another step was to extend bullet-seal tanks to scout cars. Self-sealing tanks were built as well for oil, using somewhat different compounds, since the reactions are not identical, and along with that fuel and oil hose to replace aluminum tubing. The hose had to withstand the impact of 50 calibre bullets and cannot fire, and stand up at low temperatures.

Tank manufacture was cut back radically after the war but not closed down. There were too many new planes coming in, including jet propelled, which offered a different set of problems, and tank designs could not wait until a war broke out again.

One interesting commercial development came out of all this after the war, nylon tanks, called Pliocel, weighing only a fraction as much as metal or rubber cells. A 100-gallon Pliocel can be folded to the size of a woman's handbag, slipped in place through small access doors, and then filled. Weighing .08 pounds to the square foot as against half a pound to the square foot of a metal tank, Pliocel offers important savings in weight, and has no seams to loosen up in hard landings.

Tank Tracks

A small plant in a small town, started a few years before the war to make up a miscellaneous line of molded goods, grew to great size and usefulness during that struggle, turned out at the peak nearly one-tenth

A big production item was the building of rubber tracks for tanks and half-tracs to ride on, and the rubber-tired bogie wheels which carried the load.

of the company's entire military production. This was at St. Marys, Ohio, another plant which manufactured goods having to do with rubber but not previously made by the company on large scale.

Molded goods is one of the oldest lines of rubber manufacture, going back to Charles Goodyear. It utilizes another of rubber's useful traits, namely that if you drop a piece of compounded rubber into a mold and subject it to heat and pressure, it will take the exact shape of the mold, and after vulcanization will hold that shape indefinitely. All the little odds and ends of rubber goods, rubber horseshoe pads, door stops, nubbin ends of a billiard cue, plugs for sinks and bathtubs, gaskets (washers), and on through a long line of products, are molded.

Goodyear had had such a department from the beginning, and in the early years it was a good money maker. But it became relatively less important as industrial rubber goods and tires grew to large size, fell in the general category of rubber bands, carriage tires, flooring, matting, soles and heels, small departments which the mill room in a volume production industry found something of nuisance. The factory liked to run one compound for several days at a time, not be changing over all the time for the varying requirements of the minor departments.

Molded goods were relatively inexpensive to make. Competition was, to a considerable degree, what was called "alley shops," usually a two-story brick building somewhere in back, with a small mixing mill, a few tested formulas, a line of molds and a few regular customers, mostly jobbers, who might take all of its output, relieving the plant of advertising, sales, overhead or warehousing expense.

What may have saved Molded Goods from being thrown out entirely, as carriage tires and rubber bands finally were, was that Rubber's big customer, the automotive industry, came to use rubber more and more —as did the airplane. Motor mounts, to absorb vibration from the engines rather than transmit it to the frame, came in, was called "floating power." Weather stripping for the car windows added to driving comfort.

And the new customer wanted quality goods, even if they were only small items. Individual attention must be given by the compounders to each item, which made more grief for the mill room, small runs of a larger number of formulas and each with meticulously accurate requirements as to curing time and temperatures.

The needs of Molded Goods were apt to be slighted in a mass production plant, and could not be, for important customers.

The situation was fairly parallel to that of soles and heels, which began to improve almost immediately after moving to Windsor, where a small group of men could concentrate on its problems and could relate production directly to the market. So a new plant was decided on for molded goods, but it was still thought of as a small operation, another "alley plant" with its face clean.

The plant should be somewhere in the Detroit area, close to the car manufacturers and not too far from Akron. St. Marys was a town of 5000 people, a farming community, with some manufacturing. The larger town of Lima was only a few miles away. There was plenty of water from a big reservoir built before the Civil War, to keep up the water level on a canal running from Toledo to Dayton, the largest body of water in Ohio. There was good rail transportation, good highways for the trucks. It was 165 miles from Detroit, 180 from Akron. Men from the Development department acted as superintendent, first Patterson, who had served in England, then Belknap, who had started the Java plant, then Teisher of Mechanical Goods.

Pliofilm was added. The flexible, water-proof, smart-looking, new film was going great guns. The food packaging industry was becoming interested. Processers were taking every pound Akron could turn out, and space there was becoming congested in the late 1930's. A wing was added for Pliofilm.

St. Marys was a success from the start. The thinking had been correct. Almost before it got into production, enlargement was necessary, and another addition after that.

Then defense production started, and Goodyear got an order for parts for tank tracks, and needing space at Akron, sent that to St. Marys.

Tanks played as big a part in the war in North Africa and Europe as bombing planes did in the Pacific, huge land battleships, carrying armor plate like ships and big guns like ships, able to travel fast and irresistibly over broken terrain, could be stopped only by greater tanks with heavier or longer-range guns. The production facilities of the great automobile companies were called on, with results dismaying to the enemy, first with the General Grants, then the 65-ton Shermans, and the 90-ton Pershings toward the end.

And someone had realized, well before the war started, that rubber might be largely used instead of steel, in the wide tracks the tanks unrolled ahead of them, and picked up behind—that this would cut down maintenance and save steel. Whether the tanks drove along a concrete highway with their steel plates striking sparks, or plunged off into open country, climbing hills, diving into ditches, crossing streams, smashing through woods and underbrush and brick walls, the track took plenty of punishment, which rubber, through its great virtue of giving way and coming back, could resist better than steel could do.

Also rubber would hold the road better than steel over ice and frozen snow—in fact the 2nd Armored Division, finding itself slowed down by the slippery Belgian roads as it roared into the Battle of the Bulge in the fateful Christmas week of 1944, pulled its tanks off the highway, two or three at a time, took off the steel tracks and replaced them with rubber—with the battle going on.

Men had learned to make rubber adhere to metal in automobile motor mounts, so it was a simple matter to encase the steel framework of the track in rubber, give it complete protection from destructive terrain.

This job St. Marys took in its teeth, evolved conveyors which would embed the metal framework in vulcanized rubber, by mass production. Output built up, took all the available space, and a second plant opened at Muncie, Indiana, 70 miles away, to take care of the overflow. At the peak the two plants were turning out $7,000,000 worth of vital war work every month. St. Marys grew to a force of 1650 employees, and Muncie to 700.

Other things beside tank tracks were made at St. Marys. The second largest item was sealing rings or gaskets. There might be 40 or 50 of these in the hydraulic cylinders of a single airplane or armored car. They were used as well in all machinery where rubber performed its useful function of making metal joints completely air, water and gas tight.

The O-rings for hydraulic ran as large as 12 inches in diameter, and from there went down to sizes hardly bigger than a pinhead. St. Marys produced as high as 100,000 rings a day.

Another interesting item was a flexible coupling gasket, which enabled fuel to be pumped through steel pipes on top of the ground, up and down hill over broken terrain, to supply the ravenous appetites of tanks and planes in highly mobilized warfare.

There was no time to dig ditches and lay pipes in the conventional way, but with these flexible couplings two men could lay a mile of pipe a day. The rubber had to be able to withstand a temperature of 60 degrees below zero. At one time it was proposed to run a fuel line over the Burma Road but war conditions interfered.

Molded goods retained many prewar uses as well, in motor mounts for the trucks and Army vehicles, to dampen vibration and so cut down repairs and simplify maintenance.

Pliofilm for parasols and shower curtains went out with the war, but there was a real need for it in encasing airplane engines to be shipped overseas. The remaining Pliofilm equipment was converted to processing fabric into waterproof and mildew-proof duck for tents.

The end of the war found St. Marys five times as big a factory as it was in the beginning. War contracts were cancelled, but the Sales department went to work to fill up the empty floor space—and so successfully that presently Muncie, too, which was closed down at the end of the war, had to be reopened as a branch plant.

St. Marys saw an increasing interest on the part of engineers and designers in making new uses of the versatility of molded rubber. New jobs came in at the rate of three a day, each of which had to be specially compounded and tailor-made, to meet customer specifications.

Teisher, superintendent, and Dupree, the development manager, made it clear that they were not too much interested in making stoppers for bathtubs or anything in which quality and workmanship and design were not important. They were interested only in products which called for scientific engineering.

Within two years St. Marys had almost as many employees as it had at the war peak, was the largest molded goods plant in the world.

Gas Masks

Goodyear's first war job was making gas masks, something it had done in the previous war as well.

This started as early as 1938. It was not the same gas mask it had built before. The Chemical Warfare Service had continued experimental work during peacetime on protection against gas attack, had developed a new type in 1926 which became standard. Now, with war clouds gathering over Europe, it asked Goodyear and two other rubber companies to study the production methods needed. That landed in Morse's division of mechanical goods development.

Teisher, later superintendent of St. Marys, Dupree and Sturtevant went to work, developed a molded face mask which could be vulcanized in mass production. The mold could be built fairly flat, so save metal, and the face pieces be cured in presses like rubber heels. They later developed an ingenious system of using platens to retain the heat between cures—somewhat like a hot plate in a restaurant—which with improvements in compounding, eventually reduced the curing time from 18 minutes to six.

This was important because it trebled the capacity of the presses and increased output without adding machines or floor space.

The masks had to be so made as to fit practically every shape and size of face, and the first ones were taken to Edgewood Arsenal and tried out on 100 soldiers. Chemical Warfare stated that they would have to fit 98 per cent of the men, but they hit 100 per cent of them.

Then came an educational order in April, 1939, for assembling the several parts of the mask—in addition to producing certain molded parts—to develop a system that would work large-scale. The finished mask comprised five main parts, the face piece with inlet and outlet valves, the hose tube, the head harness, the carrying case and the canister. The company had also to work out a program of filling the canisters with the charcoal and gas resistant compounds and filters.

Sturtevant took 15 people out to Plant III warehouse, cleared out two bays, set up an assembly line, worked out the program and began training employees, for this job would use more than 2000 people before it was over.

Before the educational order had been completed, however, or the molds for the face pieces OK'd, Goodyear was asked to build up an assembly of 200,000 masks a month. This was just before the Nazis marched into Poland to precipitate the war in Europe.

Other contracts followed, to manufacture the face pieces, the accordion-shaped rubber tubing, which was assigned to Windsor, the carrying cases, a sewing machine job done at Plant III, the nosecups, in Akron and Los Angeles, and various types of valves. Several companies were working on gas masks now and Goodyear found itself shipping parts it had manufactured to other companies, and assembling parts made elsewhere, all parts being pooled and distributed among the various companies, so as to build up total production as fast as possible.

There were changes as in all war products. The hose tubing was eliminated and the canister fastened directly to the mask. Morse's men had to work on the design of special-purpose masks—Navy masks which would not interfere with the use of binoculars, even gas masks for horses and gas-resistant leggings for them, in the event that cavalry would be used in some war theaters.

While the assembly work was done in Plant III, eventually taking up an entire floor of that 200 x 600 foot building, the manufacture of face pieces was a molded goods item which Stafford's men carried on in the Mechanical Goods Department at Plant II, now tooled up to full production. Experimental masks were made up in the plaster shop, cast in bronze and templates made from them, and 250 molds and two two-deck presses were built by Akron machine shops. Goodyear also had to

Production of gas masks for the Army moved so fast that this assignment was closed out early in war, won Goodyear one of its first Army-Navy "E" Awards.

arrange for production of the metal eye pieces, valves and canisters which was done by other companies.

Martin headed production until the fuel tank job grew to large dimensions when Richardson took over. Wendt set up a testing laboratory at Plant III. So excellent a job was done that that plant got the first Army-Navy "E" Award of any Goodyear factory in September, 1942.

Production of gas masks, one of the first war jobs started, was also one of the first completed. Through its foresight and aggressiveness, Chemical Warfare had five million gas masks on hand by the time of Pearl Harbor, was able to slow down on military masks a little later, build up a supply of simpler civilian masks, of which Goodyear made large quantities in Gadsden. By the end of 1944 it could practically close out this job as finished.

Contrary to the experience in the first war no gas masks were used in World War II. The enemy knew that America had a huge supply on hand, as well as noxious gas of its own, realized that if it started gas warfare retribution would be prompt and deadly. Huge production was good insurance, acted as an effective deterrent to the use of gas against American troops in this war.

17. Airships and Airplanes

Goodyear Aircraft

ANOTHER major chapter in the story of Goodyear's war work was the construction of airplanes and airplane parts.

Here was a rubber company turned plane maker, a company which knew little at the outset about the intricate business it went into, but became one of the ten largest airplane manufacturers in the country; which went from a working force of 30 people to 35,000 in two and a half years, dwarfing the parent company; which filled up the great airship dock, then built a quadrangle of plants around it with seven times the floor space the dock itself had comprised, rivalling Willow Run in size—and with another plant in Arizona nearly a third as large.

Most plane manufacturers built a single airplane, albeit in two or more models, lived with it, specialized on it. Goodyear made major components for 12 different airplanes, 56 components in all, each a separate tooling, materiel, layout and production job. No other company took on so wide a range of airplane assignments.

Each job was important and urgent, for the list included many of America's most famous war planes. Here are the principal ones:

Boeing B-29 Superfortress, greatest of all the Army's long range bombers, which delivered the final punch before the atom bomb —Aircraft built fuselages as large as a farmer's silo, also the high-vaulting dorsal fins, the stabilizers, elevators and rudders.

Consolidated B-24 Liberator, long-range Army bomber, brother of the Flying Fortress—outer wings, and modification into Navy PB4Y's.

Consolidated PB2Y Coronado, Navy flying dreadnaughts—flight decks, outer wing sections, wing floats and complete empennage.

Curtiss P-40 Warhawk, Army fighter—stabilizers.

Grumman TBF Avenger, Navy torpedo bomber—complete empennage, fins, stabilizers, rudders and elevators.

Grumman F6F Hellcat, Navy fighter, a comrade of the Corsair—wings, ailerons, elevators.

Grumman F8F Tigercat, a big brother of the Wildcat—control surfaces.

Lockheed P-38 Lightning, great Army fighter in all war theaters—stabilizers, fins, rudders and elevators for its great twin-tailed empennage.

Lockheed PV-2 Ventura, offspring of the British "Hudson," medium bomber—wings and complete tail surfaces.

Martin B-26 Marauder, Army medium bomber—ailerons, fins, stabilizers, rudders, elevators, engine nacelles and 71 foot wings.

Martin PBM Navy flying boat—flaps, inboard and outboard, complete control surfaces.

Northrup P-61 Black Widow, Army night fighter—wings and the complete twin-tail section.

Sikorsky Helicopter—tail cones.

Vought Corsair, Navy fighter—complete planes.

Wheels and Brakes—for more than half of all America's combat planes.

Navy Blimps—113 type K, 10 type L, 7 type G, and 4 type M.

There are several reasons for this unusual production record. One was general, the application of America's Mass Production System to the job. By providing tools, fixtures and machines, and breaking down a highly complex job into simple sections, a green girl from the country could turn out parts for airplanes as perfectly as a highly-skilled artisan, and a hundred times as quickly.

A second reason, also general in industry, was the creation of hundreds of sub-contractors, each producing special parts, and who by coordinated truck, plane and train transportation, became practically a department of the plant, though located 500 miles away.

Other reasons were specific to Goodyear.

Its work in lighter-than-air, particularly in the big Navy airships, had given it wider experience than most companies in the use of light metals, in heat-treating, fabricating and developing special tools for them. Included in this was extensive research work carried on before the war with the Aluminum Company of America which brought the 24-S alloy into wide use in airplane construction. It had the strength of steel at half the weight.

Second, its airship work had compelled Goodyear to go into the matter of stress calculations more intricate than were needed elsewhere. Strength must be adequate, with an ample factor of safety, but anything beyond that was dead weight, and in a vehicle as large as a rigid airship, this would run into large figures, cut performance.

Third, the company had operated large machine shops for years, built much of its own machinery, had equipment, technique and machine design background which would be extremely helpful in building jigs, fixtures and even some machine tools, which became a critical shortage during the war.

Fourth was personnel. There was still a small but highly experienced aeronautical group, rather there were three—those who had built airships in the first war, those who came in with Arnstein in 1924, and the young technical men who came in for the Akron-Macon job. Some men had drifted away or were on other work but there was a substantial nucleus of men around. They had utilized their experience to build a train for the New Haven Railroad, built a few blimps cars for the Navy or Goodyear, carried on extensive research work. The airship dock had been used for rubber storage, its walls echoing occasionally to the roar of switch engines or of test cars engaged in LifeGuard experiments. But plant and men were available when needed.

The big dock had been built on the far side of Akron Airport, five miles from Plant I. The land acquired by the company there was exactly —and imperceptibly—bisected, as it happened, by the Continental Divide, so that rain falling on the dock and the adjoining Plant B flowed north to the Great Lakes and the St. Lawrence, while that falling on the later Plants C and D made its way to the Ohio River and the Mississippi.

The company's work on airplanes started in a small way in Decem-

Goodyear Aircraft (left) became larger than the parent plant. Below are the Arizona aircraft factory and the enlarged airship dock at Wingfoot Lake.

ber, 1939, shortly after the war broke out in Europe. Glenn Martin got a big order for B-26 medium bombers, and being familiar with Goodyear's experience in light metals, asked the company to build the tail sections and even do some of the detail design, in order to meet deliveries.

A new subsidiary, Goodyear Aircraft Corporation, was set up the same month to handle this and any other airplane business which came along. The airship men formed the nucleus of the organization, under Arnstein and Wicks, not over 20 men in all. Litchfield himself took the presidency, with Russell DeYoung, promising young production executive, as his follow-up man, soon came to spend fully half of his time at Aircraft.

This was something new for a rubber company, but a field in which Litchfield had always been intensely interested, and the company must not fall down. Its engineering, workmanship and volume of production must stand comparison with that of airplane manufacturers who had been in the business for years.

The Martin surfaces were built in the big airship dock, showed excellent workmanship and got well under the weight specifications, something of immediate interest to airplane manufacturers. Other companies came in with work. Grumman in September, 1940, sublet the complete empennage section of its TBF torpedo bomber, and Curtiss placed an order in October for the Warhawk stabilizers.

The company had always farmed out its wheel and brake business to a Cleveland company but the demand was growing, and it set up a small department at the end of the machine shop to make some itself, a department which soon expanded out on the floor of the dock and kept on growing.

The empennage sections of any plane are tricky to build. They are small as compared to wings and fuselage, but involve high stress concentrations on relatively small areas, must be built to high precision— and were subject to many design changes in the effort to match the maneuverability of the Jap Zeros. Also the empennage was a separate job, convenient for sub-contracting, but too important to be entrusted to a manufacturer without aeronautical experience. Goodyear had made a reputation in this field, seemed always to get the tail surfaces on each new job.

Consolidated came in in December, 1940, wanted the company to build not only the empennage section for its PBY flying boats, but also the big wing floats. The airship dock was filling up.

A second order came in from Martin in February, 1941, surfaces for the PBM flying boat. Spring brought another huge job, the biggest yet.

The Army needed bombers, all it could get, turned to the automobile industry, which was used to large scale undertakings. Automotive teams were organized to supplement the output of the original producers. The four-engined B-24 Liberator would be built by Ford as well as Consolidated, the B-25 Billy Mitchell by General Motors and North American, the Martin B-26, for which Aircraft was already building tail surfaces, by Goodyear, Chrysler and Hudson.

Chrysler was to build the front and center section of the fuselage, Hudson the aft section, Goodyear the wings and engine nacelles, while Martin would erect an assembly plant at Omaha, well away from enemy bomber threats. The Army wanted to get up to a production of 100 complete planes a month as fast as possible.

Goodyear's part of the job, it was estimated, would require 7000 employees and more than 400,000 square feet of floor space, larger than the entire floor space in the airship dock. A new building was planned, Plant C, to be 1000 feet long by 400 feet wide, later increased by 350 feet, with messanine floors on each side, and a section 32 feet high through the center. With a heating plant, a drop hammer building, railroad sidings and parking lot, Plant C would occupy nearly 25 acres.

Bulldozers and earth movers started in to raze the hills and fill in the low areas. Tons of steel, cement, sand and gravel rolled in, and more than a million feet of lumber. Construction started April 15, 1941, two weeks after the Army gave the green light.

Things hit a snag in September when it was decided that the wings, Goodyear's part of the job, should be lengthened from 65 feet to 71. That meant marking time until Martin engineers could completely redesign them.

The first drawings came in November, as the building was nearing completion, but complete designs were not released until January. The first wings were scheduled for delivery in March. Men worked day and night. There were difficulties finding vendors to produce sub-assemblies and machine parts fast enough to meet schedule, and Plant C had to build many of them itself. It took several months for Aircraft to catch up, but once on schedule it remained so.

Plant B was started alongside the dock in May, 1940, to take care of the overflow from there, with an addition under way before it was ready, and a new plant started in Arizona to build flight decks for Consolidated PBY's. December brought a job from Northrup, to build outer wings and tail assemblies for its twin-tailed Black Widow night fighter.

So by the time the world war started Goodyear was under way on half a dozen huge contracts, had three new plants under construction and 3500 people on the payroll. And February 1942 brought in the Corsair contract, a complete plane this time, necessitating a fourth plant bigger than any of the rest, a high-bay plant, 450 feet wide and 1450 feet long.

Pearl Harbor brought the threat of a Japanese invasion of our West coast, with heavy concentration of airplane factories. Goodyear's Arizona plant lay well inland beyond the mountains, away from bombing raids. Consolidated, an overnight truck distance away at San Diego, threw additional work to the new plant. It, too, had to be enlarged.

The next two years were hectic ones, with production booming on the various plane contracts, together with a growing blimp program.

The payroll went to a peak of 35,000 people in 1943. Aircraft took a contract for Grumman's Hellcat fighter, and a huge reconversion job. The automotive team had done such a good job on the B-26 that it was changed over in July 1943 to a larger one, the Superfortress, Goodyear getting one-fourth of the job. This threw a bombshell into the plant. It called for clearing out half of Plant C to start the new job while finishing up the Martin contract across the aisle. But the first B-29 wing was shipped just five weeks after the last one for Martin. The only major change after that was to cut back the blimp program to make room for parts for the P-38 Lightning, again stabilizers, fins, rudders and elevators.

Well before the war started, Aircraft's need for personnel had outgrown the old airship group. With tire production cut back so sharply after the war started, Aircraft thought it could get all the men it needed there, but the tire plant took on war jobs, began to grow too. It could spare only a few men, usually the Number Two or Number Three men in a department. Goulding and Carter came in from Brazil on plant engineering and personnel. Murphy came over in purchasing, Martin in traffic, Weyrick in materials, Knowles on sales, which largely meant Army-Navy contracts, and Sherry, the trouble-shooter, on the difficult industrial engineering phases. These men had to find their own assistants, build up their staff, train men. Virtually no experienced men in any field came in from outside.

Once the war broke out the organization was further expanded. Blythe, with wide sales and production experience, came on as vice president and general manager, DeYoung and Arnstein were made vice presidents of production and engineering and Knowles later of sales. Wicks took Plants A and B; Stout, industrial engineer, and later Belknap of Java, became superintendent of Plant C; Michaels came up

Section of Plant C where wings for the Martin bomber were built, and later the fuselages for the Superfortresses, each as large as a farmer's silo.

from Gadsden with Follo and half a dozen of his key production men to take over the Corsair job. Hudson, who like Knowles had been on the engineering phases of the Akron-Macon job, took charge in Arizona, was followed later by Titus from Sumatra.

There was an acute need for engineering and technical men in a field so foreign to the company's experience, but aeronautical engineers were not to be had. No one had any to spare.

Starting with nine engineers Aircraft built up to a staff of 1200, of whom 400 were technically trained. The men in the small original group had to divide their time between their own work and training new men, who must hand that training on to still others. They got a few mechanical and electrical engineers from the tire plant, not many, hired in civil engineers, highway engineers, even architects, adapted their experience to aeronautics. Aircraft got some men fresh from college, although Army and Navy took most of them, upgraded machinists from the Engineering Squadron, set up training courses at the Universities of Akron and Cincinnati, hired in women who had had some technical education and put them to work on the drawing board.

Tooling, something new in Goodyear's experience, became and remained large due to the wide range of contracts, and the engineering changes which combat requirements were forever bringing in. Outside engineering companies sprang up, and were brought in. However, they did not do so well, and in January, 1943, Sherry was put in charge, reorganized the department, cut it from 2600 men to 1000, did a better job.

The tire plant had few foremen or supervisors to spare, but Squadron men filled part of that gap, and Worthington, Wicks' Number Two man on the Akron-Macon job, organized training classes, made supervisors out of domestic and export tire salesmen, rubber planters, salesmen of automobiles, vacuum sweepers, refrigerators and other mechanical appliances.

Procurement of materials and organization of a huge sub-contracting system began a large scale job under Murphy, the purchasing agent. Salesmen became buyers and expeditors of deliveries. Companies must be found who could manufacture parts, and Aircraft hurried men out to factories whose normal business was upset by the war, gave contracts to manufacturers of stoves, linoleum, metal furniture, tin cans, glassware, brassware, wrapping paper, fishing tackle, hosiery, ambulances, caskets —and sent men out to help them organize production and get equipment and materials. Makers of thermometers changed over to building valves, washing machine companies to making hydraulic cylinders and actuating control rods. An outdoor advertising company made wheel sub-assemblies. The M. O-Neil Company, an Akron department store, used its knowledge of fabrics and sewing machines to make wing covering, map covers, head rests, using its storage warehouse as a factory.

Machine shops were a critical part of the program and nearly 400 of them scattered through the Middle West were canvassed by the Purchasing Department. A manufacturer of golf clubs at Newark, Ohio, leased his plant to the company to machine forgings and castings, a glove factory at Uhrichsville and a bus maker's plant in Millersburg, Ohio, taken over for the same purpose. Garages made their service departments into factories, and retired machinists set up shops at home.

Martin's staff in traffic kept parts and materials moving into the plant and shipped out complete units to prime contractors.

However, one of the most difficult jobs was that of recruiting a working force, in a nation where most of the young able-bodied men were in uniform.

To go from 3500 men at the time of Pearl Harbor to 35,000 men 18 months later, at a time when manpower was as critically short as steel, called for prodigious effort, first under Pope, then Carter as personnel director, with Clayton having a similar problem in Arizona.

Housing, transportation and training were included in the job. The company combed the surrounding states—until the War Manpower Administration and the U. S. Employment Service got into that picture— brought in men by the thousands. Women were hired and trained, made up more than 50 per cent of the total force.

Skilled men were particularly needed, and one of Blythe's first acts in 1942 was to send out a letter to 2500 tire dealers over the country, outlining the situation and enclosing application blanks. This brought in machinists from as far off as Texas and California.

Machines and jigs went up into each section of new building as soon as it was under roof, and hiring offices and cafeterias moved out of doors under circus tents. One tent was picked up by a high wind on a chilly afternoon, carried across the field and draped over a barn.

Retired machinists, insurance men, politicians, part-time ministers, athletic coaches, musicians, actors, acrobats, war brides, housewives, high school boys and teen age girls came in, learned to operate drills and rivet guns, and even heavy machines, played an exceedingly important part in meeting diversified and exacting delivery schedules. A couple of midgets came in and were promptly hired, since they could crawl inside an airplane wing, hold the rivets in position to be driven home.

The story of Goodyear Aircraft furnishes an example of the response of the American people to the war emergency, and the value of the nation's industrial and transportation systems in the maximum production of war materiel.

A FLEET OF BLIMPS

Responsibility for building blimps for the Navy, and testing and delivering them, naturally went to Aircraft, even though the balloon room at the tire plant built the fabric envelopes for the lifting gas. For Aircraft was an outgrowth of the company's work in lighter-than-air, which had brought into existence not only specialized engineering experience, and equipment, but the only buildings in the country large enough to erect the big blimps of War II.

The non-rigid K-ship is only one-fifteenth the size of the big Zeppelins, but called for a clear space 300 feet long, 100 feet wide, with 100 foot headroom for its assembly. The big airship dock and Wingfoot Lake were the only privately-owned structures in the country big enough for that purpose.

So while Goodyear shared production with other companies on every other war weapon, this one it did alone, and so effectively that by the spring of 1944 the Navy had all it needed, and the floor space could be diverted to other war work.

It was true, too, that no other company in America knew much about the reactions of a large volume of enclosed gas under changing barometric and temperature conditions on the ground or at the mast, much less as to what could be expected as it battled with the forces of storm, wind, rain and lightning aloft. A company which had flown airships all over America twelve months out of the year should be able to do a better job than one which merely followed specifications furnished it.

The procurement program started before the war. In February, 1940, Admiral King recommended building up the nation's lighter-than-air defenses, with additional ships, men and bases. Congress took action in June. In approving the 10,000 airplane program, it authorized the construction of 48 non-rigid airships, with facilities to match. The first contract was issued in October for six K-type blimps, with an option for two more.

The Navy had one aircraft base at Lakehurst, New Jersey (Moffett Field, California, having been turned over to the Army), and a total of nine airships. Most of the ships were of obsolete type, old Army TC's and Navy J's—the latter even having open cars suspended below the bag like those of World War I—two experimental K-type ships and three training ships. The former Goodyear Defender was one of these, and the other two were type-L, the size of the Goodyear cross-country blimps. None carried guns or bombs.

While work was under way on the new ships, the General Board of the Navy, in January 1941, recommended the construction of five airship bases along the Atlantic coast and three on the Pacific.

Construction of the first K ships was a large-size order. They were larger than any blimps previously built in the world, with a helium capacity of 412,000 cubic feet, as compared to the 350,000 of the Army TC's. They were 253 feet long, stood 80 feet high on their landing wheels and the fins and rudders were larger in area than the wings of a B-29. Five of the six, however, had been delivered by the time of Pearl Harbor, the sixth being finished ten days later. The Navy had taken up its option for the other two ships by then, and that was under way.

Once the war drums sounded, however, procurement took a new tempo. German U-boats moved in to attack our vulnerable coast-wise shipping from Newfoundland to Panama, looked particularly for tankers bringing gasoline up from Texas. The Japs struck along the Pacific, got their first victim, the U. S. Medio in December off Eureka, California, bombed the oil derricks near Santa Barbara in February. By spring ships were being sunk in the Atlantic at the rate of one a day, faster than new ones could be built. Destroyers and flying boats were able to do little against this unseen enemy, which struck hard and without warning.

The Goodyear blimp in California became the first privateer in the Navy service since the War of 1812, when Sea Frontier Defense at San Diego asked the Ranger, based at Los Angeles, to lend a hand, ten days after Pearl Harbor. The Navy had to defend the coast from Mexico to Vancouver with only a handful of planes and surface ships.

Would the blimp run down clues, protect the mine-laying crews, do what patrol work its cruising radius permitted? San Diego explained that until the ship was officially taken over by the Navy it would have to operate under privateer status, which meant that if captured, its crew could be shot under the rules of war.

However, that sounded like a lark to Pilots Sewell and Hobensack and the crew, and they operated until mid-February with Sewell's hunting rifle as the only armament. Then ship, pilots and most of the crew went into the Naval service formally the same day in a single ceremony.

Goodyear's other five ships were taken over and sent out on patrol until bigger blimps could be built. Passenger accommodations were ripped out to make room for a machine gun and bomb rack. Work was rushed on hangars, each large enough to house half a dozen blimps, near Boston, Norfolk, Savannah, Miami, Los Angeles, San Francisco and Portland, others being added later on the Gulf coast. The Navy ordered 24 more K ships in June and the first Type-M.

The U-boats continued to raise havoc with shipping, the oil shortage became serious. The Big Inch pipe line was started and dredging began on the inner channel up the coast from Florida. Despite all the defense efforts, however, 454 American ships went to the bottom during 1942.

In a press interview in Sweden Admiral Doenitz, chief of the German submarine service, boasted that his U-boats had proved more than a match for all the enemy forces sent against them except the "little Zeppelins."

Goodyear set to work immediately after Pearl Harbor, to expand its manufacturing facilities. Wingfoot Lake hangar was doubled in length, and the supporting girders outside the building covered over to give additional room for shops and stores. The gymnasium in Goodyear Hall had a 43 foot ceiling, became an assembly shop for the great rudders and fins. The peacetime hangars at Chicago and New York were torn down and reerected in Akron to furnish more assembly space. This was not nearly enough, and a large addition to Plant II went up at the Airport.

As fast as the cars were finished they were hauled out to the Lake by truck, with police escort before and behind, since the great outriggers took up most of the highway.

Most of the Goodyear pilots were in the Naval Reserve and were called to active duty even before the war started. The rest quickly followed, their experience being highly useful to the Navy, which was trying to train several hundred pilots against time. Navy bases earmarked Wingfoot Lake machinists, riggers, fabric men, made petty officers and chiefs out of them. Army sergeants and Navy chiefs are the backbone of the armed forces.

Fickes, in charge at Wingfoot Lake, had to stay behind to direct assembly, test flights and deliveries, had only three of his experienced pilots left, filled in the gaps with junior pilots whose training, fortunately, had started the year before.

In June, 1942, Congress authorized an increase in the strength of the airship fleet to 200. The Navy ordered 24 more in October to be delivered at the rate of three a month, called for 14 more the following January and 48 more in June, 1943, this time at the rate of 14 a month. Still another addition was built at Plant B, 1100 feet long, and the first

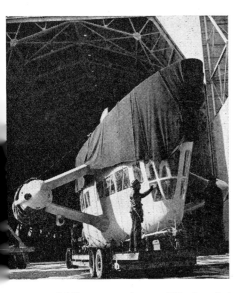

A blimp car arrives at Wingfoot Lake where the bag is attached; below, first airship assembly line in the world where 30 cars could be worked on at a time.

airship assembly line in the world was opened, with room for 30 cars, these being turned upside down half way down the line to permit work to be done from the floor on the upper section.

The ships grew in size from 416,000 cubic feet to 456,000 cubic feet, the 30 calibre machine guns were replaced by 50 calibres, racks were built to carry 300 pound depth charges, additional radio and radar equipment was built in.

Some airship envelopes were sub-contracted and Moffett Field, California, now back in the Navy's hands, acted as an additional assembly point, some 40 cars and envelopes being shipped out from Akron.

Goodyear delivered 154 complete ships during the war. Those assembled at Akron were flown over the mountains to Lakehurst by Goodyear crews who picked the weather to catch a tail wind, often made the 400 mile flight in four hours, at a rate of 100 miles an hour. Pilots and crews went back by plane to start on the next ship.

Despite the size of the program and the speed at which it was executed, the delivery flights did not have a single mishap.

Fickes got a citation from the Navy after the war for his work in procurement and delivery.

Goodyear built four types of ships, the L's and G's being used for training and the K's and the still larger M's for patrol.

The M ship had started as a Navy project in 1937. Extensive calculations and water tunnel tests showed that ships could be built half again as large as the 400,000 cubic feet size which was then considered the limit. A prototype M ship was included in the contract of October, 1941, to be built to a size of 625,000 cubic feet. The Navy ordered 22 more M's the following year, though the cutbacks of 1944 reduced this to four.

The first M called for extensive research, marked an important step forward in non-rigid airship design—and performance.

The car was 115 feet long, spreading the load over 40 per cent of the length of the envelope, and was articulated in three sections, like a Pullman train, to give greater flexibility. The forward section was the control car with quarters for pilot, machine gunner, observer, navigator, flight engineer, and for radio, radar and detection gear, well away from the noise and vibration of the engines. These were mounted on outriggers on the middle car—which also had a turret below for a second machine gunner and the bombardier. The after car carried fuel, cargo and a lookout.

The ship had a forward landing wheel like the tricycle gear of the airplane, a semi-rigid type of bow mooring, hydraulic power for the bomb bay doors, electrically operated propellers with controllable and reversible pitch, enabling the ship to land in a short space by reversing the props and using them as brakes. The M ship handled more like a rigid airship, developed great range and efficiency, had a useful load of 7½ tons. Later M ships had additional panels built in to increase its helium capacity to 725,000 cubic feet, and preliminary designs were made on a Type O, to have a million and a half cubic feet.

It was an M-type ship which made a non-stop flight from Lakehurst into the Caribbean and Gulf of Mexico in 1946, flew for a period of 170 hours, the longest sustained flight made by any aircraft of any type.

AIRSHIPS IN WAR

The blimps were sent to Navy bases as fast as they were completed, and proceeded to justify the faith that Moffett, King and Rosendahl had in their ability to turn back the submarine threat. By 1943 they were patrolling a 5000 mile frontier which extended from Newfoundland to Rio de Janeiro, covered the Gulf of Mexico and the West Coast.

Once the fleet attained any size, the blimps were coordinated with planes and surface ships into an anti-submarine defense which quickly cleared the enemy out of American waters. As the subs retreated to Florida and the Gulf of Mexico, the airships followed, then into the Caribbean, and on down to the coast of South America to Rio de Janeiro.

Sinking of American ships dropped off rapidly once United States' defenses became effective. Though there were 454 ships sunk by enemy action on the Atlantic in 1942, only eight were lost in 1944. Enemy submarines wanted no contact with craft which could approach silently out of the night and overcast, out of range of their own radar—"One problem not yet completely solved," as Admiral Doenitz, the German submarine chief, said. The very presence of blimps in any area was apt to send the U-boats scurrying off to safer waters.

The airships took over night patrol from the airplane, operated around the clock, proved their ability to carry on when other craft were grounded. More than once fog-bound planes on shore radioed out over the ocean to the blimps to inquire what the weather was like there. Was there enough visibility for the planes to operate if they could get through the fog that blanketed the coast?

The blimps did an extensive job of escorting merchant ships as well, could organize convoys expeditiously by voice and blinker lights without breaking radio silence, whip stragglers into line. *Nearly 90,000 American ships were escorted by blimps during the war, ships carrying mil-*

Majestic M-ship has flown non-stop for a week at a time. Typical scenes of K-ship coming in for landing, aboard ship and on submarine patrol are shown below.

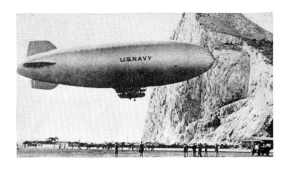

Akron-made blimps guard coasts of both Americas and the Mediterranean;
Aircraft workers watch christening of 73rd K-ship on Navy Day.

lions of troops and billions of dollars worth of military equipment and lend lease supplies—without the loss of a single vessel.

The sturdiness and dependability claimed for the airship was demonstrated in the fact of all the ships assigned to the fleet, 87 per cent were "on the line" at all times, in operation or in readiness—an outstanding record for aircraft. Only one blimp was lost by enemy action.

The blimps did an excellent job, too, in air-sea rescue, searching for survivors of torpedoed ships and crashed planes, directing ships to their air or even picking up survivors themselves.

They went overseas to operate in the Mediterranean in 1944, a Squadron of six ships making the transatlantic crossing to Africa by way of Newfoundland and the Azores. There they bottled up the Straits of Gibraltar against the passage of enemy submarines, and basing at mooring masts at Port Lyautey, Bizerte, Toulon, Rome, Venice, Pisa and Malta, carried on mine sweeping operations as well. A second fleet left for Europe the following summer, taking a 3500 mile route from Norfolk, by way of Bermuda, the longest mass flight of non-rigid airships.

The appearance of the schnorkel-type submarine in the English Channel in the spring of 1945 brought a call for more blimps. The schnorkel had a long tube extending to the surface so that it could pump in fresh air and remain under the surface for weeks at a time, was a dangerous new weapon.

A base was set up in England and the fleet was ready to sail from Lakehurst when the Germans surrendered.

One of the less publicized operations of the war, the blimp fleet, so quickly assembled, did its full bit in the emergency, saved hundreds of merchant ships and warships from torpedo attack, demonstrated surprising weather worthiness under a wide range of temperature and aerological conditions, gave new demonstration of what could be expected from the larger rigid airships in passenger use. It also trained hundreds of pilots and crews who might find a place in that program, and huge new hangars came into existence at strategic points, big enough to be used by the Zeppelin-type passenger airships.

GOODYEAR CONTRIBUTIONS

The airship story is unique in the Goodyear history. Not only did the company build all of the ships and supply trained personnel, but its experience enabled it to render other important services.

Its personnel was highly useful in the training of 5000 Navy pilots and flight crews. Lange reached the rank of Captain, Rieker, Stacy,

Smith, Boettner, Hobensack, Sewell, Furculow and Dixon became commanders, and a number of the junior pilots reached lieutenant commander rank. Lange became commanding officer at Tillamook, then Chief of Staff to Admiral Rosendahl, Rieker became second in command at Moffett Field and Stacy at Lakehurst. Goodyear's airship mechanics, riggers, fabric men serving at many bases, had a part in the amazing "on station" figure attained by the blimps as a result of experienced maintenance and expedited repair.

Two pre-war developments were also highly important, the taxi wheel and the mooring mast.

The taxi take-off which the Goodyear blimp pilots inaugurated a dozen years earlier, in which the blimps taxi'd across the airport like a plane until they got flying speed, became standard practice in Naval operations, enabling ships to take off with a much heavier fuel load, extend their range of operations. The M ships could carry 6000 pounds of additional fuel through this device.

The use of mooring masts as operating bases, which the Goodyear fleet had worked out, since the Navy had had little occasion to travel over the country, came into wide use during the war, as blimps could be refueled and reserviced in the open. Between each major base around the perimeter of the country were two or three mast bases, where ships returning from 20 hour patrol could tie up in case of head winds, or leave from to get more quickly on station. There was no time to build hangars in the Caribbean or South America, except for a small one-ship hangar in Trinidad. The Navy airships had to operate in the open for months at a time from mooring masts, which were set up in Canada, Cuba, Puerto Rico, Panama, the Guianas, and a long string of them around the hump of Brazil.

Except for Trinidad the only shelter south of Miami was the big airship dock built near Rio de Janeiro for the Hindenburg, which was now shared as an overhaul base by American blimps and Brazilian airplanes. Maintenance and servicing was done out of doors.

There was only one airship hangar on the Mediterranean, one the French had taken over from Germany as reparations after World War I and reerected at Toulon, France. It had largely escaped damage during the second war, but the little American squadron saw little of it. When the transatlantic flights were planned it was an easy matter to ship masts ahead of time to Newfoundland, the Azores, Bermuda and Morocco, and to send additional ones along as needed in Italy and North Africa. Similarly on the Pacific coast, masts extended the efficiency of airship patrol from the Mexican border to Canada.

Since Aircraft was building complete airships, Litchfield was anxious to build complete airplanes as well, round out the production picture. He discussed the matter with the Aircraft Procurement Board at Washington. His audience was friendly. The company had built parts for planes, could do the whole job. The need was urgent.

Army and Navy were both in need of a large number of fighter planes, had given contracts to Curtiss and Chance Vought. Curtiss decided to erect an additional plant to meet its schedule, but Vought was glad to get help on the production end.

The Vought Corsair was the first one to carry a 2000 h.p. engine. It had a range of 1000 miles, a ceiling of 35,000 feet, a top speed of close to 400 mph., and a landing speed of 85 mph. It carried six powerful 50 calibre machine guns in the wings, which the pilot could fire singly or in salvos. It was to be a carrier-based ship, and must not be taller than 17 feet with the wings folded, to fit in the hangar deck (the wings had to be squared off and shortened by two feet for Corsairs turned over to the British where headroom was less). The various requirements had resulted in an inverted gull wing design which kept the wing hinges low.

The Vought company was already starting production and a contract had been given to Brewster. Goodyear got its Letter of Intent in February, 1942. The Vought-built Corsair was the F4U and the ones Goodyear built would be called the FG1, F for fighter, G for Goodyear and 1 meaning the first of its type.

Goodyear would have to build a complete new plant, the largest one yet, before it could even start, and later build a huge flight hangar, 800 x 300 feet, big enough to house 70 planes at a time with the wings folded, also a great concrete apron and a gun range. Runways must be extended to connect with those of the municipal airport, a test crew must be recruited if enough men could be found whom the Army and Navy had not taken, a control tower built on top of the airship dock, radio communication organized, and 10,000 new men, skilled and unskilled, hired in—and the company was already nearing the bottom of the barrel in manpower.

Goodyear had never built an airplane—and this was a complex job calling for hundreds of jigs and fixtures, thousands of drawings and templates, for models of parts and complete planes. To meet the schedules stipulated, it must find hundreds of sub-contractors—and must lay out an assembly line before it built the plant.

The assembly line, when completed, was nearly a mile long, making three trips up and down the great building, with switch tracks to pick

Gull-wing Corsairs and Grumman fighters, flown by Marine and Navy pilots from flattops and island bases, wrote new chapter in aviation history.

up engines and sub-assemblies. The line was flanked with bins, so that the workman would find each screw and bolt almost in arm's reach as the plane-in-process moved at imperceptibly slow speed past his station, at first hung from the ceiling and in the later stages moving on its own landing gear. Also there must be room for a huge shop to make parts, with dies and presses, a paint shop and a section where the curving main beam, the keystone of the plane which gave it the gull wing shape, was fabricated.

However, the building of something as mysterious as an airplane can be just another production job, albeit in tremendous volume and precisions unknown in tires, calling for great patience, endless work and the use of every manufacturing shortcut.

There are 10,000 separate parts, let us say, in the plane, each one of which must be made in precisions of one ten-thousandth of an inch. What parts can we find some other company to turn out, and what is the fastest, most efficient way of turning out those we ourselves build? Then devise and build tools and fixtures, train employees and set up a Production Control system which will keep half a million parts moving up to pre-assembly, sub-assembly, final assembly.

A small group of skilled workmen could build a complete plane in less than half the time it took Mass Production to get out its first one, but once that mighty production machine got under way it could turn out planes at the rate of 100 a month, or twice that.

This was the whole secret of America's Mass Production system, which quickly drove the country's enemies out of the air by sheer weight of numbers and fighting power.

Despite the large number of things to be done, the first Corsair was ready for test flight in February, 1943, just one year after the company started. Given the Navy OK after exhaustive tests of speed, rate of climb, ceiling, and fire power, Aircraft plunged into production under a schedule that rose almost as sharply over the months as the climbing angle of the plane itself, reaching a peak of 200 a month.

By February, 1944, a year after the first plane was flown, a thousand Corsairs had been delivered. The 2000 mark was reached in September, and if weather delayed flight-testing for a few days, a hundred planes piled up on the apron. By February, 1945, 3000 planes had been built and the total by VJ-Day was 4008.

Brewster had become involved in labor difficulties early in the war and dropped out of the Corsair picture, and Aircraft and Vought had to take up the slack.

The Corsairs got into action in the Pacific early in 1943, and with

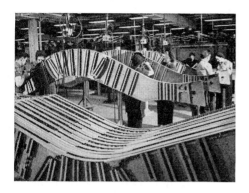

Building the curving main frame; joining center and forward sections; Marine planes warming up for strike against the Japs; carrier pilots moving in to man their planes (Navy photos). Below, completed planes at Akron awaiting flight tests.

the Grumman Wildcat, in which Goodyear also had a part, proceeded to write a new chapter in the history of air combat.

These two became the Navy's greatest single-seater fighters, the Grumman being assigned to carriers and the Corsairs, at first, to the Marine Corps as land-based planes.

The first reports were released in May that year. The Corsairs had tasted blood at Guadalcanal, a great Allied bastion which the Marines had seized and stubbornly held against everything the Japs could throw at them from land, sea and air.

On May 16, 1943, a squadron of 25 Japanese Zeros flew over the island and the Corsairs rose to meet them. They not only knocked them out of the sky, but demonstrated that this was a plane the Zeros could neither outmaneuver, out-fight, nor even run away from. The Navy called the Corsair a better plane than any Zero.

Naturally there were many engineering changes, to improve visibility, to increase speed, range, rate of climb and fire power, each of which brought headaches in the factory. Bombs, eight five-inch rockets, and cannon were built in, giving the Corsair a fire power matching that of a destroyer. Speed moved up to 425 mph.

The Corsair continued in succeeding months to roll up one-sided scores against the enemy. One squadron, equipped with 20 mm. cannon, shot down 50 Kamikazi. A Marine squadron got 90 planes in 30 days, sending down 24 Jap planes in 25 minutes one memorable day in April, 1945, went on to a total score of 124 to nothing. It was a Corsair which delivered the final blow of a thousand-pound bomb to the Yamoto, last of Japan's heavy battleships.

News of each victory was promptly sent back to Akron and went up on the bulletin boards. The men and women buckled down harder to their tasks. This was their plane.

In the fall of 1943 the Navy pondered the matter of putting even more power into the Corsair. With the load of armament it now carried, the plane had about reached the limit of possibilities with a 2000 h.p. engine. Pratt and Whitney was building a 3000 h.p. Wasp Major. Goodyear Aircraft got the assignment on December 1, 1944 to build the new engine into the plane. It was called the F2G, meaning fighter, type two, Goodyear-built.

The assignment was not merely to take out one engine and put in a different one but called for extensive redesign of cockpit and control surfaces. However, the first F2G was ready for testing in May, 1945, showed amazing performance, climbed at the rate of 7000 feet a minute to 12,000 feet, turning over as it climbed, dived at the speed of better than 500 miles an hour, had an official rating of "better than 450 mph."

The Navy ordered 400 of the F2G's but only a few of them were ready when the Japs threw in the sponge—and the emergence about that time of jet-propelled planes shortened a promising Navy career for the new fighter.

Wheels and Brakes

Two of the most important products manufactured at Aircraft—and products the organization generally knew little about—were wheels and brakes for military airplanes.

That department would be about the last place one would expect to find any drama, but it is there, notably in two instances.

The first lies in how the company happened to go into this field at all, since it was so foreign to the rest of its manufacturing experience. That story has been told. It had to build wheels for the 1929 Airwheel tire, since no one else would bother with something that was little more than an axle, and too small to build brakes into. Goodyear had to go in or else give up a tire it thought important—even though for a number of years the principle in that tire was more widely used on farm tractors and earth movers than on airplanes.

There is even more drama, however, in the fact that the company remained in this field through the years. A company building tires for automobiles could easily spare the time to keep up to date in what was, during the 1930's, the very much smaller field of airplane tires—just as a company making wheels and brakes for automobiles could carry on a department to take care of the more difficult needs of the airplane.

But for a tire company to make wheels and brakes for the tiny airplane market would seem, on the face of it, as far-fetched as for Bendix or Hayes to set up mills, calenders and compounding laboratories to go after the relatively small airplane tire business.

What is difficult to appreciate fully now is the fact that the airplane industry was still fairly small up to 1940 when the nation started its preparedness program. Military production was limited. The air lines were still struggling to get on their feet. Goodyear's total sales in wheels and brakes in 1936 were $81,000, and the department lost $35,000 that year. From that point sales crawled slowly upward to $158,000, to $328,000, losing money each year, passed the million mark only in 1940, when the first profit appeared.

Three men carried on an unusual pioneering job through these years, Guinther in charge of sales of airplane tires, wheels and brakes (he died in 1940 just as the business he had fought for began to break big), Bell, Ohio farm-born pilot (he has CAA license 127, though he was flying before the U. S. Department of Commerce started issuing licenses), who hired in as a pilot-service man in 1929, and Jacobs, manager of government and aeronautical sales, who fought the department's battle as red ink succeeded red ink in the year's ledgers.

A business house less deeply convinced of the ultimate importance of aeronautics would have closed up the department long before the war. But aeronautics would have lost something if that had happened.

Aviation in this era was a small and rather clannish group, Army and Navy men who carried on the Billy Mitchell tradition; the men running airlines; the fixed-base operators; the designers of airplanes, and those who built its engines, landing gear, hydraulic gear or developed high octane gas. Everybody knew everyone else, and one man's problem was every man's, for whatever helped aeronautics was their business. The annual air races, designed to attract the public's interest in aviation, were alumni reunions for these men.

Guinther was one of the leaders in this group, and had a perfect counterpart in Bell, who did not look like a salesman and did not call himself one though he won the Litchfield medal later as the salesman of the year. Also Bell was a practical engineer who came to know a lot about mechanical features of airplanes—and did not talk.

Airplane designers had no hesitancy in showing him the features of a new plane they were working on, even though they knew he would be talking to their competitor the next day. Character is as important in business as technical knowledge.

Bell was the kind of a salesman who would go out in the shop and work over mechanical features with the mechanics and engineers—or take a trouble-shooting job on a lonely airport without lights or heat or repair facilities.

This kind of selling did not pay off at once. Any new plane is likely to take two years or longer to travel from the drafting room to the point where orders are placed. There were years when the total sales were less than the operating budget for the department.

Even the company airplane was a luxury from the standpoint of expense-to-sales, and Guinther and Bell were among the first flying salesmen in the industry. However, their customers were widely scattered over the country and when they wanted something, it was usually in a hurry. And Bell's opinions as a pilot with a wide range of flight

Forced into the manufacture of wheels and brakes to fit a radical new type of airplane tire, Goodyear was able in World War II to furnish these for more than half the nation's combat planes.

experience, carried added weight with men who built planes.

However, as a result of this pioneering work, World War II found Bell with an intimate first-hand acquaintance with the wheel and brake mechanism and the tire requirements of every important airplane in America.

A plane manufacturer, planning an improved plane, was apt to go over the entire landing gear problem with Bell, and their joint conclusions were incorporated into the formal proposal to the government.

Goodyear did not get all the business it helped create, of course. Once the specifications were decided on everybody could bid on it, but Goodyear at least when it got a job knew all about it, which helped to meet schedules.

At one time in the war, the two services were working on 46 different experimental planes and the great majority of them carried Goodyear equipment. If Goodyear had any advantage it might be that tires, wheels and brakes fit together logically in the landing gear of the airplane, and the company had built a considerable volume of experience in all three.

As we will recall, Chief Engineer State and Snyder of Machine Design developed the first airplane brakes for the Airwheel tire, mechanical brakes, air brakes, hydraulic, and then the multiple disc brake.

Bell as a practical machinist had largely to carry on from that point, with the help of a small department at Akron. It was not until the war loomed and the volume of business began to grow to large proportions that a full-scale department was created under Zimmerman, another of the company's useful group of airship builders, and Gunsaulus, both of whom had worked on this at the tire plant.

If Keller in Tire Design had to grapple with constantly growing problems of tire strength, shock absorption and heat, heat was an immediate and pressing factor to the designers of wheels and brakes. A 50 ton airplane, landing at 100 miles an hour, generates terrific heat as the brakes are applied, and metal grows cherry-red with the absorption of kinetic energy. The department had to call on the research men and the metallurgists, go into the characteristics of metal itself.

Magnesium came in for the wheels, and special steel developed to meet mounting requirements for brakes. At times the steel plates improved to where they outwore their brake linings, and the department had to concentrate on that, only to find presently that the brake linings outwore the steel, go back into that field. All of this was far removed from the field of rubber but the company must follow through.

Though Goodyear had developed the multiple disc brake, it went over

to the single disc during the war for reasons of weight, easier maintenance, heat resistance, and better cooling properties, although the single
disc brake remained on some planes.

In starting in wheels and brakes the company farmed out the manufacture to the National Acme Company in Cleveland, but with the
organization of Goodyear Aircraft set up a small manufacturing department of its own in a corner of the airship dock. The Cleveland people
were somewhat disturbed about this at first, but Goodyear was sure
there would soon be need for the facilities of both companies, which
proved to be the case. Orders came in from everywhere and *Aircraft
found itself building more than half of all the wheels and brakes used
on America's expanding fleet of combat planes.*

The wheel and brake department was less effected than others at
Aircraft by the cutbacks that came after VE-Day, and the department
went vigorously into the commercial field as well as continuing in the
military—with the jet-propelled planes bringing in new problems.
Goodyear landing gear was specified for the great DC-4's, DC-6's, the
Constellations and other modern civilian planes, along with the P-80's,
P-82's and the P-84's.

As was the case in automobile tires more planes, military and commercial, land on Goodyear tires and wheels, and are stopped by Goodyear brakes than any other kind.

Summary of Aircraft Work

It is hard to convey much of an idea of the magnitude of the job
done at Aircraft during the war.

That 4008 FG1 Corsairs, ten of the F2G fighters, and 154 blimps
were built completely and flown away is easy to understand, but the entire job, including component manufacture for other prime contractors
is harder to visualize.

Only another aircraft manufacturer can appreciate the fact that production increased from 11,000 pounds of airframe in 1940 to 18,000,-
000 in 1944—not counting spares or government-furnished equipment
—and was smashing ahead at the rate of 21,500,000 pounds a year
when the first cutback came in July, 1945.

Seven million dollars a month paid out in wages at the peak of July,
1943, is impressive—and tax payers, who paid all the bills of war production might be interested in the fact that while wages rose to an aver-

age of $2550 per man the total monthly payroll was 15 per cent less by the end of the war, though production had increased by 60 per cent.

The pictures of the great buildings totalling 4,750,000 square feet of floor space—1,250,000 square feet Goodyear-owned—give some notion of the size of the job, but the work involved in producing thousands of complicated and important airplane components, wings, flight decks, stabilizers, ailerons, rudders, elevators, complete fuselage and complete empennage is still hard to grasp.

We might visualize it by conceiving a great armada setting out with one or several of the major components in each plane built by Aircraft.

Not counting the tremendous volume of wheels and brakes supplied to a long list of war planes and its own production of Corsairs and blimps, there would be some 575 of Boeing's great Superfortresses, 165 Liberators (including the Navy version PB4Y2), 5800 Martin bombers, nearly 3000 Grumman Torpedo bombers, 1400 Martin Flying Boats, nearly 900 Lockheed Lightnings, 300 Curtiss Warhawks, 900 Northrup Black Widows, 3000 Grumman Hellcats, 600 Grumman Tigercats, 235 Consolidated Coronados, 125 Helicopters and more than 600 Venturas to which Aircraft contributed vital parts.

18. Production for Ordnance

Bag Loading at Charlestown

PART of Goodyear's war production had nothing to do with rubber, merely called on the company to use its facilities or manufacturing experience to make other products for which there was imperative military need.

When field guns were changed over so that they would turn in 360 degrees radius and fire in any direction, tracks were needed for them to turn on, and the Goodyear rim plant built a large number of these in its machine shops.

The major Ordnance assignments, however, were a bag-loading plant at Charlestown, Indiana, across the river from Louisville, which started in 1941 (and a second one in Mississippi in 1945) the manufacture of high explosive shells and 50 cal. machine gun cartridges at Kelly-Springfield, and 90 mm. cannon for tank and anti-tank warfare at Jackson.

The Charlestown job came out of the blue. President E. J. Thomas got a long distance call from St. Louis one Sunday morning at his home. This was in October, 1940. A Colonel Miles was on the wire.

"I'd like someone from your company to meet my train at Cincinnati tonight at 8:30," he said.

"What is this all about?" Thomas inquired.

"Sorry, I can't tell you that," said the colonel.

"But I should have some idea, so I'll know whom to send," Thomas pointed out.

"That's true," the colonel agreed. "We want your company to take on a bag-loading operation. It will probably call for a $35,000,000 plant, and is extremely important to the Army."

The term "bag-loading" alone, with no explanation, was not completely familiar to Thomas. However, he promised that a proper Goodyear representative would be on hand as requested, and called Vice President Linforth, who had served in the Navy in the first war. Linforth had loaded plenty of charges into the big guns, recalled that the powder bags were made of fabric, mostly silk.

"Better take Braden along," Thomas suggested. Braden was superintendent of the balloon room, knew fabrics. The two men took a plane for Cincinnati. At the station they found themselves paged, then escorted to a private car filled with Army officers.

Miles explained the situation. The Army planned to build two huge plants along the Ohio River, one for Dupont to make smokeless powder, and another alongside for Goodyear to make powder bags and do the loading. The train pulled out while they were still talking, but by the time they got to Pittsburgh Linforth had arranged for a visit to the government arsenal at Picatinny, New Jersey, to see what the operation was like.

Flannery, engineering manager, went with them. They were taken aback when they were first searched for matches, then had adhesive tape placed on their shoes. Their nervousness quickly wore off, however, as they went through the arsenal.

"It's like putting sugar in a bag," said Flannery, "except you have to be more careful. It's just another manufacturing operation, which we can learn."

Akron, too, was a little nervous when the men reported back, but agreed to accept the responsibility. Linforth continued to stay on the assignment. Leroy, vice president of finance, and Hyde, general counsel, worked out complicated arrangements with General Campbell, chief of Army Ordnance.

Cutting out pieces of cloth, sewing them into bags, and loading them with powder did not sound like a difficult production job, such as making automobiles or airplanes, or tires for that matter.

They found out quite differently after they got into it.

Goodyear was to make up the charges for some 60 different guns, including new ones which came in during the war. There were two major types. The smaller ones were for the howitzers, guns which could be fired from one side of a hill at unseen targets on the other side, comprised the mobile field artillery, like the French 75's of World War I, except that the larger 105's were in wider use in this war. The smaller guns were carried also on armored cars, on tanks and even on the big airplanes later on.

The big guns, ranging from eight inches up to 16, for which Goodyear was also to make charges, were those which moved up to the front on railroad cars (or a large number of pneumatic tires), were used also on Navy battleships and carriers, could send an armor-piercing projectile weighing more than a ton through space to a target miles away which it might never see.

The bags Goodyear was to load ranged in size from those no larger than a tobacco pouch weighing perhaps three pounds, to some larger than an oil drum, and weighing 800 pounds. The "charges," as an assembly of loaded bags was called, were shipped to shell-loading plants in this country. The big ones were apt to go directly to the fighting front in Europe or the Pacific. In either case tolerances were exceedingly close, had to fit exactly into the shell or gun barrel, to 1/100 of an ounce in the smaller charges.

Many of the men assigned to Charlestown thought of powder as being in granulated form like coarse sugar, but actually it came in pellets, shaped like a cigaret butt, except not that large for the smaller guns, and more than two inches long and an inch in diameter for the big ones—which must be stacked rather than poured into the bag, a special machine being devised for that.

Also they did not realize that these pellets were really plastics, and consequently varied in size and weight, if ever so slightly, with the atmospheric conditions at the time of manufacture. Charlestown must compensate for that in loading the bags, and even take into account the fact that the fabric in the bag also varies with humidity—and bag-loading plants are not air conditioned.

A given weight of propellant will carry its projectile a certain mathematical distance. Too much powder would mean over-shooting the target, and too little under-shooting it—and the howitzer often fired over the heads of its own troops. Within .001 of an inch in length or width they might vary the size of the loading bag for the small howitzers, but each charge for the big guns must be virtually tailor-made—

even though this job must be done on mass-production scale.

Moreover the assignment was tremendously important, for men's lives and the fate of battles might rest with them. It was a job where there could be no mistakes, a factory which could have no "seconds." Above all it was a whale of a big job, to be done against time, and with regard for safety such as Goodyear had never known. Charlestown would handle a million pounds of powder a day and there was dynamite in every ounce of it.

Engineer Flannery had seen only a part of it in a small pilot plant using hand methods. Bag-loading was more than weighing sugar into a sack, but Goodyear accepted the responsibility.

The formal contract was signed December 31, 1940. It was a cost-plus-fixed-fee contract, that is the government paid all the bills of wages and materials provided under the contract and the company got a fixed fee for its work. Actually, of course, Goodyear made up all the payrolls, did the buying, inspecting, checking, paying invoices and was reimbursed.

In many respects this was the most unusual of all of Goodyear's war contracts. Ordnance said, in effect:

"Here's what the job is like. We can get people to design the buildings and contractors to erect them. What we want you to do is to draw on your manufacturing experience to lay out a plant that will permit the largest possible production, then take it over and operate it.

"Ordnance will furnish the schedules. It will be your responsibility from then on. We want all the production we can get. We don't know how tough this war will be, nor how long it will last, but we intend to make sure that the fighting forces never run short of ammunition."

Any job, no matter how big, can be broken down into component parts, and this was the Goodyear men's training. They must see in detail just what was to be done. It grew more complex the further they got into it.

An organization was picked to match the assignment. H. W. Hillman, assistant treasurer of Goodyear, became vice president of the Goodyear Engineering Corporation, the subsidiary formed to handle the job. His training was in finance, but an investment house with which he had been associated had had to go into the affairs of many business firms, and Hillman had made himself something of a reputation as a doctor to sick companies, getting them back on their feet. R. H. Gray, New England textile man, then treasurer of Goodyear's cotton mill at Decatur, Alabama, became resident manager. Production called for a large-scale and detailed organization of materials, machines, manpower and transportation, and H. R. Child, who started with the company in 1913, was picked as superintendent. Norway-born Soderstrom, later succeeded by Hoch, was chief engineer, with the veteran Urquhart as consultant. They would have the job of laying out highways, railroad lines, and 400 separate buildings spaced at explosive distance apart over 5000 acres of rolling Indiana countryside—and have as well the continuous responsibility of devising machines, conveyors and equipment to increase output.

Charlestown would handle two kinds of powder, smokeless powder making up the bulk of it. That gave distance and hitting power, was the propellant force which hurled the projectile through space. Black powder was the igniter, the force which set off the charge, fired the gun. It was the more dangerous of the two, had to be handled in a separate, more isolated area.

A gun "charge" is made up of several bags of powder fastened together, often as high as seven. These are called "increments" and marked "Zone One," "Zone Two," etc. In the "semi-fixed" charges for the smaller howitzers, the gunners could use all of the increments, to get maximum distance or the destructive effect of point-blank range, or as Fire Direction gave the word, "Fire Three" or "Fire Five," would open up the shell case, remove some of the bags, reduce the range.

The charges for the big guns were "fixed," not to be opened. The howitzers up to 155 mm. used a primer to ignite the charge, like a blank rifle cartridge, so the Zone One bag was made somewhat kidney-shaped and Zone Two doughnut-shaped to leave room for it.

For the big guns, Goodyear had to manufacture the igniter as well. That is where the black powder came in. It had first to be treated in a separate building, including drying, to get all the moisture out of it, being spread on trays and put in an oven under extremely rigid control of time and temperature. Only one person was permitted in the drying room at a time, and he had to know his job, for it was a place where there could be no mistakes.

The black powder igniter was loaded into flat, pancake containers which were quilted up and down or across before loading, to distribute the powder evenly. These deadly pancakes might be placed between the large bags for the big guns, or shipped separately, to be placed later in the powder chamber of the gun. In either case the charge had to be packed tightly, then spiral-taped like a puttee to make a rigid structure. It was shipped out in an air-tight metal case.

Silk is preferable for propellant charges since it is completely consumed by fire, while cotton may leave embers which might set off the next charge prematurely. This was not too important in smaller charges which were loaded into a cartridge for firing, and cotton could be safely used there, the silk shortage making this desirable. But shortage or no shortage, silk must be used for the black powder igniter. This was not the silk used in a lady's dress but a raw silk looking much like burlap.

With this further light on the problem the Goodyear men sat down with men with explosives know-how, Colonel Holmes of Ordnance and men from Hercules Powder Company, who were also to operate a bag-loading plant, to figure out how to change over from a laboratory operation to mass production. Let's see what kind of a plant was laid out.

The site selected ran for three miles along the Ohio River, extending the same distance back into the interior, with a small jog to leave a church and burying ground intact, totalled nine square miles. It was called the Hoosier Ordnance Plant.

The reservation was divided into two areas, the "explosive area" making up about three-fourths of the property, and the "inert area." Since no hazards are involved in making bags, a conventional factory building could be constructed there, equipped with 1500 power-driven sewing machines, with slitting machines, conveyors and the rest.

In the inert area, too, went a huge laundry, for everyone working in the explosive area must wear a uniform, furnished by the plant, and those worn in the smokeless powder area must be laundered three times

a week or oftener, and in the black powder area were washed every day, and in some places had to be changed three times a day. The black powder workers wore white uniforms so that any bit of powder dust could be instantly seen. The others wore blue.

Each one of the billion and a half bags which Goodyear produced must have its zone number printed on it, also the firing load number to identify it in firing ballistics. So Charlestown had the equivalent of a full-rigged printing plant, though the actual equipment was not concentrated at one place but placed wherever was most convenient. There was also a dye house, as the igniter charge bags were dyed red, to make sure the gunners would get the right end into the gun first, and certain propellant charge bags were dyed green for proper identification.

The administration buildings went up in the inert area and 26 warehouses for non-explosive material. Thirty residences were built at the back of the property along the river bluff for Goodyear and Dupont executives and Army officers who had to live on the reservation, be on call day and night.

This part of the job presented no difficulties. The big assignment was to lay out the buildings in the explosive area. No conventional factory building would do there. Only so much powder could be present in any building, only so many people could work in a room, and each

World's biggest sewing circle—making bags for gun charges.

structure must be well separated from the next one. The explosive distance was around 400 feet, although that could be reduced if an earth barricade, natural or artificial, separated any two of them.

In the explosive area Goodyear engineers worked closely with Ordnance, followed its practices, leaned on the experience to Colonel R. E. Hardy, first commanding officer (he was later elevated to brigadier and made chief of the whole Ammunition Division of Ordnance), and Colonel Kelly Lewis, his successor.

The key parts of a bag-loading plant are the loading lines, where the powder is put in the bags, and the "igloos," where it is stored, before and after loading.

The loading line was a group of well-separated buildings, with connecting walks covered over from the weather, and the magazines for the powder and the finished charges.

The loading building had hoppers for the powder on the second floor and gravity feed down to a series of loading booths on the first floor. None of these loading booths connected with any other, and the bags when loaded were carried on a transfer chute to a center aisle through double doors, only one of which could be opened at a time so that air could not go from one to the other.

Each loading line had its own cafeteria, so that no one would have

Camera swings around to show rest of the room.

to walk far for his lunch—there were 16 cafeterias in all in the reservation—which was also a refuge in case an electrical storm threatened.

The loading lines were designed so that several different types of charges could be made in each one, keeping the loading system flexible to meet changing requirements created by action at the front.

There were eight loading lines for the smokeless powder, and four for black powder, and since each was double, this gave the equivalent of 24 separate factories.

There were 177 igloos for powder storage, curious concrete buildings with rounded roofs like a quonset hut, which were covered with four feet of earth and sown to grass, looked from the air like a mound builders' burying ground—or monster gopher holes. Three of these igloos, with a capacity of 50,000 pounds each, were for the black powder. The rest, for smokeless, could store half a million pounds of powder apiece. From the middle of the war on they were usually filled to capacity.

The rest of the organization was carefully picked, got to work as soon as the contract was signed. Shaw, Lyons, Moon and Novick were Child's chief aides in production. Coultrap took on technical phases including ballistics. Jordan as works accountant, and Finney as cashier took on a wide range of new responsibilities.

Transportation was highly important because of the great distance to be covered, with thousands of employees to be taken from the plant entrance to their place of work, which might be three miles away, brought back at the end of the shift. Coburn, head of Inside Transportation at Akron, took this post, had 34 buses and 100 passenger cars, working on staggered schedules—and tighter ones than any city bus line. Every operation must be continuously manned without interruption around the 24 hours, and the incoming man must be ready to take over as the outgoing one finished. Employees were paid for eight and a quarter hours a day, and Coburn's men must see to it that each man was at his post within seven minutes after he left the "change house," which will be described later.

Coburn had to run a railroad and a trucking company, too. Scores of freight carloads of materials and finished goods must be hauled in and out every day. He had four locomotives equipped with two-way radios, 20 box cars, 400 trucks and trailers at his disposal. There were 100 miles of highway and 17 miles of railway within the reservation. Coburn did so good a job that Ordnance borrowed him for two months to study the transportation systems at other ammunition plants. His recommendations saved the government the expense of buying many additional vehicles.

Fire prevention was of major importance, so Foran, chief of the Goodyear fire department at Akron, was sent to Charlestown. Walker, young engineer whose father had come over from England and become assistant master mechanic, took charge of safety, with unusual authority. Plant protection was imperative against sabotage, and a cyclone fence ran around the entire property and a second one around the explosive area, which must be patrolled day and night. Gandee, Number Two man in the police department at Goodyear Akron, took on that assignment. Procurement of all the things needed for Charlestown would be difficult, and Bloom was called back from Brazil as purchasing agent. Tittle from Jackson took charge of the storage and shipping of explosives in the igloo section, and Carper of the warehouses in the inert area. Puckett had production control, which was especially important.

Even Maintenance, which was Purnell's job, had phases unusual in a production plant. Highways, railroad right-of-way and 400 buildings had to be kept up, calling for handcars, tractors, cranes and earth movers. But there was a lot of land not built on, rich Indiana farm land, with plots planted to supply fresh vegetables for the 16 cafeterias, and other areas which must be sowed to grass to prevent erosion and keep down the dust, which would affect powder weight—and grass which had to be cut to prevent fires. Well-kept Charlestown became almost a beauty spot.

Personnel would have plenty to do, and Wrobleski, University of Pittsburgh basketballer, and at the outset, Charles Blythe, tackled the big hiring job—and were loaned to the contractor erecting the plant (as was Chief Gandee), hired 17,000 men for him before starting their own job.

Charlestown was a busy place once construction got under way on the two huge plants, for the Dupont powder plant was built at the same time. The railroad ran special trains in bringing in one group and taking out another. The state built a four-lane highway past the plants. Payroll men travelled in armored trucks taking the pay envelopes out to the men. Trailer camps sprang up, though mostly for the construction workers who, in that era, often travelled from one big job to another.

Well before construction was finished Wrobleski and Blythe were assembling the permanent organization. Every new employee had to be investigated to avoid any possibility of sabotage. Each had to be trained in advance, key employees spending six to eight weeks in intensive work at government arsenals, then breaking in the production workers. Those who were to load powder practiced with kernels of corn.

There were no trailer camps for the permanent employees, no "ghost towns" to be left behind when the job was finished. Men came to work in buses, or their own cars on a share-the-ride plan, from Louisville and 30 other cities in the two states, some from as far as 70 miles away.

Operations started on Labor Day, 1941, three weeks ahead of schedule and three months before Pearl Harbor, with a few hundred employees on hand, built up fast as new loading lines were completed. Charlestown was under way.

Safety was everywhere pervasive, starting with the original layout. The loading booths had but one door which opened outward. There was no communication between booths, and escape chutes were installed on the second floor so that employees could slide down to safety. The roofs of all buildings were almost tacked on. Powder explodes upward, and the roof must offer no resistance. Conductive shoes were issued to everyone who entered the explosive area, so that any static which built up in his body was dissipated into the soles, and from there into the ground by conductive flooring. Employees loading black powder wore transparent, shatter-proof, plastic shields to protect their faces.

To guard against electrical storms, Goodyear engineers made up a storm indicator which showed the direction, intensity and imminence of lightning, checking their conclusions with a barometer. If a storm threatened or a dangerous amount of static had accumulated in the atmosphere, a gong sounded on the loading lines in that area, and everyone took shelter in the cafeteria until the danger was past. Atmospheric conditions were not always uniform over the nine square miles, so that at times half of the plant was working in bright sunlight while the rest waited for the static to disperse.

The ground around Charlestown is largely of chalk formation, so that all lightning and static arresters in the plant were eventually grounded below the Ohio River. The fire department had the latest and best equipment and fire crews were fully acquainted with the hazards and thoroughly drilled in their duties.

Safety lay, too, in the control of powder. Just so much powder could be in the magazines and the hoppers at any time and no more. There would always be enough so production would not be delayed, but no surplus. If a storm stopped operations temporarily, the powder went back to the igloo.

The most spectacular step in safety, however, was the "change house," which was unique in this business. Every person who went into the explosive area had to pass through it. Workmen had two lockers, one on the "inert" side of the building, and one on the "explosive" side. He took off his clothes on one side, passed over to the other, found his uniform waiting there. There were no pockets in it, no chance to hide a match or cigaret. Women employees had the same arrangement on their side of the building.

A person might carry his lunch, but he could not take it through the change house. The guards would inspect it, and deliver it to him on the job later.

The change house was no respecter of persons. No matter how much gold braid of Army or Navy rank a visitor wore, or how high he might be in industry, he had to take off his street clothes and change into uniform before entering the explosive area. A smaller change house was provided for these visitors, but everybody went through. Charlestown took no chance that anyone would inadvertently carry any contraband into the danger zone.

As a result of careful advance planning and stringent safety regulations, the plant went through the entire five years safely.

The Dupont plant alongside made only about half the powder loaded at Charlestown, the rest coming from various plants over the country. Samples from each lot were fired by Ordnance at its proving grounds, and the ballistics men reported back to Charlestown. Coultrap's men in the laboratory made the correction, and the bags for that lot might be just a trifle larger or smaller. For the smaller charges these could be made

Plane's eye view of Charlestown plant, "change house", bag manufacturing and storage buildings in foreground, storage igloos in far distance. Below, closeup of one of the twelve "loading lines", six well-separated buildings where the powder was actually loaded, then trucked off to the igloos.

in three standard sizes and still fit the shell. The bags must be made to order for the larger charges.

It was to be expected that men experienced in mass production would find improved methods. The men at Charlestown were cautious at first about suggesting any changes in a job having to do with explosives. But they found ways to modify equipment for explosive use, and the impulse to find improvements had to find outlet. Hundreds of shortcuts were found, and, with the consent of Ordnance, installed.

One change was unusual, and paid off well. Powder bags had always been round and would have to be in the big sizes. But why not make them square for the 105 mm. bags, the largest production item? Circular sewing takes longer and wastes materials. With square bags all of the machines in one line could be connected as a continuous process, all sewed up at a time, then cut off.

It was a startling innovation but Washington, after studying it, found that square bags could be packed in just as tightly as round ones. Charlestown got the "go ahead." *That was one of some 150 improvements that the Goodyear men developed in the five years, which were recorded completely in the government files in Washington to be drawn on in case of another emergency, if one comes.* The improvement made a huge saving in cloth and also balanced the shortage of manpower, enabled it to hit schedules with fewer men.

In the first world war ten plants were set up to manufacture shells and guns, not one of which was in production when the Armistice came. Ordnance would take no chances of running short this time, determined to make sure that depots and bases were amply stocked around the world, and no gun crew on land or sea would ever run short. It could always cut back if it got too much.

So the Ordnance program called for 60 government-owned ammunition plants. The big problem of General Campbell, Chief of Ordnance, was to find companies to operate these plants after the powder companies had already exhausted their supply of experienced personnel. He decided wherever possible to assign the loading of shells, bombs, small arms and bag-loading to companies who, even though they had no former experience in explosives, were mass producers and could get a big job done fast. He assembled on his "industry team" automobile, rubber, oil, chemical and engineering companies, and corporations like Quaker Oats, Coca-Cola, Procter & Gamble, and Sherwin-Williams.

There were four bag-loading plants, Charlestown being the largest.

With this concentration of effort, there were times when Ordnance had more powder and shells than it needed. No one can ever tell in advance how much ammunition the artillery, tanks, planes and ships will need, particularly in stubbornly contested battle, nor what type. More ammunition might be needed at one time for the big guns and at another for the 105's. And world events like the North African invasion or that at Normandy would upset all calculations. Also munition ships were torpedoed and their cargo must be quickly replaced.

On top of this, Army, Navy and Air Corps were constantly calling for bigger, longer-range, more devastating weapons. New ones came in like the bazooka. The 100 pound bomb gave way to 10,000 pound block busters. The 75's all but went out, the 105's taking their place, and toward the end the still more powerful 155's threatened to replace them. These things disrupted schedules at Charlestown and elsewhere—with an occasional dramatic incident.

Most Americans will recall the bitter fighting at Mount Cassino in Italy, the famous monastery on top of a hill which the Nazis fortified with long-range guns, kept the Allies at a distance. Ordnance had just brought out a new howitzer, the 240 mm., the largest mobile gun yet built. It was made to order for this situation. However, tests showed that none of the ammunition on hand would work effectively with it. So Ordnance got Charlestown on the phone, explained the situation. The proving ground provided the ballistic specifications, and the plant went to work. Men and women volunteers worked day and night for 36 hours over a holiday to get out the order. A special high priority train was waiting. When the job was finished, the charges were rushed to the seaboard, and gun and Charlestown powder flown to Italy, went into action immediately.

Charlestown, like all war plants, encountered cutbacks, the first one coming in 1943 after it had built up to a force of 6500 people. Supervision took pains to explain to employees the reasons which made it necessary. Everyone took it in good spirit. The men and women who had been furloughed went in to shake hands with their foremen before leaving. One large group even gave a dinner for its foreman—an incident which got back to General Hardy's office and impressed Ordnance with the high morale at the plant.

In any case schedules were soon restored, and increased. The plant went to 9000 employees and that was not enough, so a bag-loading plant in Mississippi, about half the size of Charlestown, was reactivated in 1945 and Hoch went there as superintendent. It got into production the day the war ended in Europe, continued on until the Japs quit.

Each increase in Charlestown's schedules sent the personnel men out looking for manpower—which was not easy to find in a section already well combed over. Caravans went out over many counties in Indiana and Kentucky, carrying an interviewer, an investigator, a doctor and a man from the U. S. Employment Service—and sometimes one from the Farm Bureau to see that the need for foodstuffs was not jeopardized.

Across the river in Louisville were a Curtiss airplane plant, a Reynolds aluminum plant, Bowman Field and Naval Ordnance. There was a huge quartermaster's depot in the next town of Jeffersonville, and Chrysler had a small arms plant farther down the river at Evansville. Charlestown was classified as a textile industry and even Dupont was permitted to pay higher wages because it manufactured the powder.

The employment men had to sell the plant, show its importance to the war effort. They had to take what they could get, took farmers who could work only during the growing season, school teachers who could work only during the summer, editors of country newspapers who could spare three days a week, business men and housewives who could work half a day. The fact that a high percentage of women were used helped, as the bag manufacturing division made up about a third of the employees. The personnel men hired in a total of 30,000 people during the war.

Morale remained high throughout. Incentive pay and upgrading of promising employees helped hold people. Incidents like that at Mount Cassino kept them close to the battle front. It was a common and thrilling thing to hear a hundred men and women on the night shift loading line singing at their work, sometimes a hymn, sometimes a popular song. *There was not a single work stoppage during the entire period.*

Charlestown proved a willing and efficient producer, taking on more and more work as mass production economies were effected. The man hours per thousand charges averaged 500 in 1941, dropped to 330 in 1942, to 175 in 1943, to 120 in 1944, and was hitting 100 hours per thousand charges and better when the war ended. *Without this increased production it would have been necessary to build a second loading plant as large as Charlestown.*

Outgoing shipments gave another measure of the work done. The plant averaged 16 freight carloads of finished ammunition a day in 1943, went to 35 the next year, to 62 in 1945. That does not include 700,000 pounds going out daily by truck and trailer, to make a total of more than 75 carloads a day. In 105 mm. production, the biggest single item, it was able to produce six times the capacity of the original contract.

It is not surprising that Charlestown won the Army-Navy "E" in October, 1942, won it each succeeding year for a total of five, the only

Goodyear plant to get this 100 per cent recognition.

Every Goodyear man assigned to the operation benefited by the experience and many went on to better jobs. Gray returned to the cotton mills as vice president. Child became superintendent of Chemical Products' big plant at Aircraft Plant C, Purnell joining him there. Shaw became plant manager at Lincoln, with Wrobleski as personnel manager; Novick became division superintendent in South Africa, and Walker plant engineer in Mexico; Gandee and Foran, once they had their work organized at Charlestown took over plant protection at Aircraft for the rest of the war. Soderstrom became engineering manager at Topeka.

Operators of the 60 government-owned ammunition plants soon discovered their job to be different in many ways than if they had been producing for themselves.

General Hardy, however, believed that with whole-hearted cooperation between industry and Ordnance a smoothly functioning organization could be created, capable of getting things done, and within the framework of Army's somewhat unusual (to industry) requirements.

The Hoosier Plant was one of the first to get its operations on such a basis, streamlining both contractor and government procedures and organization. Application of this plan to all plants seemed desirable, and Hillman found himself drafted to help General Hardy set up industry committees which would capitalize on the best features of each plant's operating methods. He later acted as advisor to the Field Director of Ammunition Plants on a part-time basis.

Operating flexibility as well as manufacturing efficiency proved useful to the war effort.

Kelly-Springfield Changes Over

The Kelly-Springfield Tire Company, located on the Potomac River at Cumberland, an industrial city of 40,000 people in western Maryland, a few miles from the Pennsylvania and West Virginia state lines, was a prosperous and successful company when the war broke out.

The cutback in passenger tire production ordered by the government when the war started would hit a factory which made only tires and tubes harder than one like Goodyear Akron, which had a wider variety of products—and already had several war contracts.

Tires were Kelly's bread and butter, its entire business. But with a war on, certainly there must be many places where a big factory, with its own power plant and 1100 experienced workmen, would be needed. President Burke went to Washington.

He did not have to wait long for an order. Ordnance looked over the plant facilities, was well impressed, and gave the company a contract on January 31, 1942, to build eight-inch High Explosive shells. This would utilize only part of the floor space, however, would need only 400 employees, so a second much larger assignment was given the company in April, the large-scale production of machine gun bullets. We will follow the two contracts separately.

HIGH EXPLOSIVE SHELLS

The big shell was originally planned for Navy use on heavy cruisers, proved ideal later on for bombarding Jap shore installations on the Pacific islands, since it burst into countless pieces when it hit. So the Army quickly called for large numbers of them as well, firing them from howitzers and mortars against fortifications and pillboxes. This shell stood 28 inches high, was eight inches in diameter. Kelly was to take forgings, machine them into complete shells, ready to be loaded with TNT and the detonating fuze screwed in.

The eight-inch High Explosive shell had previously been made only in laborious hand fashion in government arsenals. It was a job entirely foreign to anything in the company's experience. Its men had first to find out what a High Explosive shell was. After that they must learn how it was built, what equipment would be needed, in what plant layout, and what methods used to produce it in large quantities, then estimate what the whole thing would cost and put in its bid in two weeks.

From the time Washington asked Kelly to bid on the job, on December 27, 1941, it was practically a night and day job for engineering, production, purchasing and everyone else, but the figures were turned in in time and the company got the contract.

Kelly had its own machine shop, was familiar with shop practice, but the shells called for specialized equipment. There was room enough in the basement of one building for an assembly line to carry the shells continuously past the machines, each one doing its specialized job, then on to the heat-treating furnace which was housed in a separate building erected for it. Two long-time Kelly men, Schleif from Sales, and Smith, division superintendent of mills and calenders, headed this up, and although neither had any experience in the field previously, did an outstanding job. Schleif died suddenly just before the war ended.

There were two parts to be made, the shell itself, tapered down to

Machine gun bullets being placed in shell case by automatic machinery at Cumberland (above); being drawn out to length (below left); final inspection (right).

extremely exact dimensions, inside and out, and a band which was shrunk onto it to fit the gun barrel. The shells came in as rough-turned forgings, and after the series of machining operations, went on to the nosing furnace.

Here one end was heated white hot and placed under a hydraulic press which exerted tons of pressure on it to form the tapered nose shape. Heat-treated in another series of furnaces, cooled in oil quench, tested for hardness by microscopic devices, the shell moved down the conveyor line to its next operation, which was to bore the hole in the nose for the detonating fuse, and cut the threads so that it could be screwed into place.

The band, which also came in as a rough forging was machined to fit over the shell, then heated, placed in position and shrunk as it cooled, to fit tightly in place. Then it passed down the conveyor to lathes which machined in the band to fit the gun or howitzer barrel, and cut the special grooves required. The shells when completed were shipped to loading plants.

While Kelly's other war job, the manufacture of machine gun bullets, was discontinued in 1943, the big shell job continued through the war, on larger scale and increased floor space.

MACHINE GUN BULLETS

The machine gun job had quite a different history.

The original contract called for the plant to build up as fast as possible to an output of 2¾ million 30 calibre bullets a day. However, while the 30 calibre was the standard size in World War I, the Army early decided to use the heavier 50 calibre bullets in the second war. Kelly, busy getting set for the 30 calibre job, got word to change over to the armor-piercing 50 calibre bullets, primarily to be used in airplanes. By moving fast they still got into production only five weeks later than planned.

Kelly knew nothing about munitions, and as in the case of Aircraft and Charlestown, there were no experts to be hired. They would have to learn how the job was done and adapt their past experience to meet it.

Some 140 tire foremen were sent to the small arms plant in St. Louis for four to eight weeks training period, 325 men went to Frankford Arsenal to be trained as machine adjusters, and 75 men as inspectors. These constituted the nucleus force. As machines arrived and were set up, employees were trained on them, using scrap materials.

In laying out the manufacturing program Kelly made one important decision. It would take a lot of time to move out all of the tire equipment. The vulcanizing pits extended deep into the ground and could not be moved, the mills, calenders and Banburys were extremely heavy, so Kelly simply covered over the big equipment, built around and on top of it, moved out only the smaller machines. As Kelly-Springfield was allocated a certain amount of tire manufacture, some molds and other equipment were shipped to Akron and Gadsden to take care of that.

There were only two "Akron" men at the Kelly factory, Superintendent Warden, Cornell-trained development man who came on from the California plant before the war, and Hudak, O.S.U. graduate in industrial engineering, who came on as personnel manager in 1939, after ten years in the Efficiency Department at Akron.

Four separate departments were set up, one to make the cartridges, another to make jackets for the bullets, a third to make the primers, and an assembly plant where shell, primer and bullet met. The plant also had to set up and operate a 200-acre powder farm across the state line in West Virginia, seven miles away, where all the powder would be stored, and the deadly primers loaded with explosives, which must be kept under water at a constant temperature until used.

The Kelly plant was well adapted to carrying on these several operations without interfering with each other. It consisted of one long main building, with five wings leading off from it, separated by wide courts. The equipment was placed so that production could reach the greatest possible volume as quickly as possible.

It will not be necessary here to go too much into manufacturing details, further than to show the versatility of the organization. The materials for the cartridges arrived at the plant in the form of small cup-shaped brass forgings, which were drawn and tempered in a series of operations until they reached an almost microscopic degree of thinness. They then were trimmed to length, the open end crimped down to fit the bullet, and the bottom punched for the primer cap.

The bullet jacket also started as a cup-shaped forging, must also be drawn and shaped to the exact dimension of the hardened steel bullet core, given a copper jacket over the end.

The small deadly primers were made in the factory and shipped out to the farm to be loaded. They were fitted into place in the cartridge before it reached final assembly. That was done in the loading room, well-separated from the main plant. Here the powder was brought in from the farm, in just the quantities needed, and loaded into the cartridges in quantities exact down to the last grain. Then the jacketed bullet was inserted into the tapered end and the cratridge was ready to go back to the main plant for final inspection, packaging and shipping.

Cartridges from each day's run were taken out to the farm to be test-fired on the range, with velocity and accuracy carefully checked.

The factory force grew to large size, over 5500 people being employed at the peak, nearly half of them being women. Fortunately, there was plenty of labor available in the area immediately surrounding Cumberland.

The factory was in full swing as a shell and small arms plant, was meeting schedule on the big shells and spitting out a million machine gun bullets a day when the change order came. While guns and ammunition were more critically needed than tires when the war started, that situation changed within 18 months and Kelly was authorized to go back to the tire business, and to get out as much production as possible.

BACK TO TIRES

To change over its facilities completely twice, without too much loss of time, called for all the ingenuity of Superintendent Warden and the rest of his factory organization. But Kelly built its last tire in April, 1942, turned out its first machine gun bullets in September, and was in full production well before the change order arrived in the following June. Again the production men moved fast. Kelly made its last bullets at the end of September, 1943, and got out its first tire on November 15, though complete reconversion took longer.

Some 3500 employees were furloughed but were not long out of work. Employment men from other war industries and the U. S. Employment Service hurried in, and within a week everyone who wanted a job had one. Many of the 2000 women workers, however, who had responded to a war emergency went back to their homes.

The wisdom of the decision to cover over the tire building machinery, rather than dismantle and store it, became clear when the plant turned back to tires. However, reconversion was not merely a matter of restoring the old layout. Many changes had come into tire manufacture since the plant was built in 1920—actually it was designed in 1916, although operations had been halted by World War I. Automatic machinery, conveyors, watchcase molds, straight line assembly, almost every major operation in fact had been changed. The layout which fitted the requirements of the earlier years was none too efficient by 1943, and the building did not lend itself to modern assembly-line methods.

The Army wanted maximum tire production so Kelly had to do four jobs at once. It had to dismantle the munitions plant, to enlarge HE shell output, get into production on tires quickly, and enlarge tire building facilities to increase ultimate output. Engineers from Goodyear Akron were sent over to lend a hand.

The courts between wings were covered over and paved, with walls cut through to provide communication for conveyor lines without backtracking, modern equipment was procured. Production and construction were going on at once. Tube manufacture, accessories and inspection went on the upper floor, leaving the ground floor free for tires.

Still further expansion of the nation's tire production was needed the following year, and a plant was started by the government at Houston, Texas, for the company to operate. Hudak, the personnel man, who had moved up to assistant to the president, was picked as superintendent. This factory, however, was cancelled when the war ended, did not get into production.

The end of the war brought a large demand for civilian tires, and Kelly having a modern plant, 50 per cent larger in floor space than before, and with twice the production capacity, became one of the important tire producers in the country.

Gun Making at Jackson

Goodyear, already having a part in tank warfare by building tracks at St. Marys, got into another part of it by building guns at Jackson to be fired from tanks against tanks.

The three-year seesaw battle across North Africa was largely a war between tanks, and the army which had the biggest, fastest, hardest-hitting armored force won.

Wavell defeated a much larger Italian force at Sidi Barrani in 1940 when 40 U.S.-made tanks made a long, closely-timed sweep to attack the enemy from the rear just as the battle got under way. Rommel sent the British reeling back toward Alexandria in 1942 when his heavier Tigers knocked out the General Grants. America was already working on the 32 ton General Shermans, carrying 75 mm. guns, and making plans for the 65 ton Pershings to carry 90 mm. guns. Goodyear got in on the 90 mm. gun job early in the war, was later assigned to the slightly smaller three-inch gun, also to be used in tank warfare.

"General Campbell needs guns more than he does tires," the word came out from Washington. "With tire production cut back, could

Goodyear use some of its surplus floor space and manpower to build guns?"

Goodyear looked over its facilities. There was no room at Akron. Jackson was the only plant built all on one floor, with foundations strong enough to take the weight of the great presses and other heavy machinery. That was a brand new plant, the most modern tire factory in the world. Still it was wartime. If the government wanted Goodyear to make guns, that was it.

Goodyear knew as little about making guns at it did about the manufacture of High Explosive shells, machine gun bullets or loading powder bags, but here as at Kelly and Charlestown, it was demonstrated that a company with a competent engineering and production staff could tackle almost anything.

Jackson was to make the three main parts of the gun, which as any hunter knows are the barrel, the breech ring and the breech block, some 60 smaller parts being assigned to other companies. But the businesslike way in which it tackled the job led to a second contract, to be carried on simultaneously, that of assembling guns from parts manufactured elsewhere.

The manufacture of barrel, ring and block was a machine shop job, a matter of taking rough castings and forgings, sending them through milling machines, drills, presses, broaching machines, more than 100 separate operations in all, taking out more than half of the original metal during the process—and with tolerances unheard of in the tire industry.

But Goodyear had had a machine shop almost as long as it had built tires, had 1200 men in the engineering department. Vice President Slusser and Superintendent Lee had a wealth of specialized talent to draw on. Patterson, assistant master mechanic of the company, was assigned to the job, with his chief, the veteran Elmer Clark, spending much of his time there, too, until things got in running order. Soderstrom came up from Charlestown.

The Goodyear men studied the technique at the Watervliet Arsenal, and once they knew exactly what was to be done, specified the equipment they wanted, laid out the plant for expedited production, made up estimates of time and materials needed to meet schedules.

Watervliet raised its eyebrows over some procedures, which were radically different from those at the arsenal where guns were handmade, but there as elsewhere Ordnance and Industry worked hand in hand to adapt mass production methods to meet the situation.

Planning started in December, 1941, just as the war broke out. The

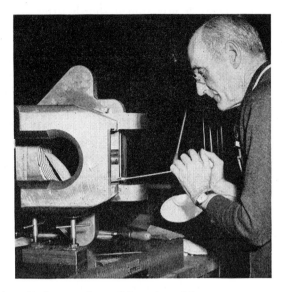

Final work on breech block at Jackson and a striking view of inside of spiralled barrel; below big guns arrive at final assembly stage.

contract was signed shortly after and procurement of gun equipment started. The last tire was cured April 27, 1942, after which the tire building equipment was moved out and stored. So fast was the work pushed that the first guns were completed in September, just six months later, and were test-fired at Aberdeen Proving Ground in November.

The gun barrels were delivered as large log-shaped forgings, 14 feet long, with a small hole through the center. These had to be machined down inside and out to exact size down to the tapered end. Bringing the inside of the long barrel to a polished curving wall with the exactness of .0005 inches called for a high degree of craftsmanship. After the inside of the barrel had been honed to a highly polished surface, a series of circular broaches began to cut the spiral rifling, removing from .0015 to .003 of an inch in each pass. Forty-three passes were required to complete the rifling.

Next the barrel was sprayed with zinc chromate paint and dried in ovens lined with infra-red lights, after which it was ready for assembly in the gun. After assembly and inspection the complete gun was dipped in a tank of oil at 120° F. before being boxed for shipping.

The tire building force of 750 employees grew to a thousand gun builders and output mounted, reaching 300 guns a month by January, 1943 and 500 a month by March. But by the summer of 1943 the increasing need for truck tires became even graver than that for guns, and Jackson went back to its old trade. Goodyear had built 2200 guns, assembled more than 2800 more from parts made elsewhere.

The last gun was shipped October 27, tire equipment taken out of storage, reinstalled early in 1944 and put to work.

The plant was enlarged, came out of the war with the capacity of 11,500 tires a day, as compared with the prewar capacity of 8750. The force of employees grew to 1400 people, almost twice as many as in 1941.

Superintendent Lee was called back to Akron after the war to head up a new department called Planning and Methods, having to do with the materials and machinery for the growing list of Goodyear plants at home and abroad, and Ruffner came in from the new Topeka plant to be Superintendent at Jackson.

19. Other U. S. Production

Big Job at Gadsden

GOODYEAR'S five southern plants made an effective contribution to the war effort. The tire factory at Gadsden took on so many jobs that it came out of the war two-and-a-half times as large as when it went in, and the cotton mills in Georgia and Alabama handled every demand for fabric, including rayon and nylon.

Gadsden was set to do a good job. It was a young plant, and one kept young by the character of its personnel, and by the immediate adoption of every new process found in tire manufacture during the fruitful 1930's. The word obsolescence was not in its book.

The personnel situation was favorable. Farm boys from a 30 mile radius, used to hard work, quick to learn, handy with tools and machinery, held key engineering and technical jobs, as well as production.

When Supt. Michaels was called to Aircraft to head the Corsair plant, he took 30 men with him, but only one man came in from Akron as replacement. That was Maney, who became superintendent. Gadsden-

559

trained men filled the other gaps in the factory organization.

Unionism had not come in, despite several attempts, did not get established until half way through the war. There was no resistance to improvement, but welcome to it. Management could talk directly to the employees, did not go through a third party.

Manpower was plentiful as well as cooperative. While Akron and Jackson had to recruit men over a wide area during the war to meet their schedules, men still came into the employment office at Gadsden looking for work.

There was plenty of latent power to be had at Gadsden, which was especially important, since a tire plant needs a great deal of steam for vulcanization. The power plant itself was trebled in size as the factory expanded during the war.

With all these factors the Dixie plant was in a position to give vigorous support to the nation's critical war needs.

Gas masks and fuel tanks came in first, before the war. In the former case it was an educational contract to train 500 employees, was set up on the top floor so as not to interfere with other production, continued for six months, then was shut down but kept in standby status for the rest of the war.

Fuel tanks lasted longer and grew to great size, brought an addition to the plant in 1940, a large room extending one-third the length of the main building.

"Better run it the entire distance," Litchfield suggested. "That will round out the building—and we'll need the space."

Tire production picked up with Army demands, mostly tractor tires, truck tires and those for the jeeps, and when major expansion became necessary in 1943, Gadsden got a big addition, a building as large as the original plant.

Sole and heel production was added in 1945 to take some of the pressure off of the Windsor factory, a $750,000 addition being built, Gadsden remaining in this business after the war, since that market enlarged with the improvements found in Windsor.

A third major expansion, a big one, costing $4,000,000, a building about half the size of the original plant, was started during the last year of the war, was converted later, built inner tubes only, the equipment being located to get a straight-line assembly, resulted in the largest production capacity for truck, tractor and passenger tire tubes in the United States.

Taking the inner tubes out of the main plant gave opportunity for further improvements in layouts in tire manufacture.

The original Gadsden plant had a floor space of 600,000 square feet, including the blimp hangar and the reclaim plant, ended with 1,460-000 square feet. By 1948 it had a capacity of 16,000 passenger tires a day, 1200 farm tires, 200 giant truck tires and 30,000 inner tubes.

Employment, which had gone down to 700 during the worst of the 1930 depression, stood around 1200 when the war started, went to 2750 in 1943, to 3350 in 1944, reached a peak of more than 4000. A housing addition, built nearby at the outset, became overcrowded during the war, and the city had a housing shortage—despite the fact that 30 to 40 per cent of the employees still lived on farms outside town, drove back and forth to work.

The city of Gadsden built a boulevard across the river past the front of the factory, naming it Goodyear Boulevard, extending it well past it into the surrounding territory. The plant, with its broad facade, was not only Goodyear's second largest tire factory, but one of the largest manufacturing establishments in the south.

The company's investment in southern manufacturing, including the cotton mills, was close to $40,000,000.

Cotton Mills Busy

All of Goodyear's fabric manufacture had been concentrated in the south by the time the war began, in factories at Cedartown, Cartersville and Rockmart, Georgia, and at Decatur, Alabama.

With a continuous shortage of manpower brought about by the draft and the competition from high-pay war industries—Cartersville had to hire in 2000 people a year to maintain a working force of 1400, and Decatur 3000 to have 1500 people on the payroll—the southern mills labored valiantly 24 hours a day, seven days a week from 1942 to the end of the war, met every requirement for cotton, rayon and nylon for the Goodyear factories in this country and many of those abroad.

Looms, carding and spinning machines will turn out just so much fabric a day, but the mills got out every pound possible, and without any additions to the plants except a rayon mill at Decatur, reached a peak production of 100,000,000 pounds a year, 50 per cent greater than ever before.

Rayon manufacture had been carried on experimentally at Cedartown in 1935 and 1936, and was installed on a production basis before the war at Rockmart, the largest mill. With tremendously increased demands during the war for military tires and fuel cells, Rockmart expanded output to a peak of 30 million pounds of rayon, as well as ten million pounds of cotton fabric—and two million of nylon.

Rayon manufacture was reestablished at Cedartown in 1943, making up about one-tenth of its output, and on larger scale at Decatur with a new Goodyear-built factory, going from two million pounds to 30 million in two years. The other mills remained on cotton.

As the dipping process came into tire manufacture with synthetic rubber, Decatur put in its own dipping unit, shipped pre-dipped fabric to the American plants which did not have dipping equipment of their own, and to most of the foreign factories. Many of the overseas plants could get cotton fabric locally, but pre-dipped rayon fabric was shipped to the Goodyear plants in England, Australia, Brazil, Argentina, Peru and elsewhere.

The rayon was delivered to the mills in the form of yarn, did not have to be carded or spun but only twisted and woven, making a shorter process. Also it had no seeds or linters to be combed out, making for a cleaner factory and better working conditions. The Decatur mill, with a government-built addition started in 1945, and taken over later by Goodyear, was a model factory in this respect.

The plant additions at Decatur made this the largest of Goodyear's cotton mills in poundage, as the old measurement of number of spindles did not apply in a factory which did not do the spinning.

Cedartown started a new cotton milling unit in the basement in 1945, got into full operation only after the war, but proved highly useful in meeting the big civilian demand for tires after VJ-Day.

The cutback in tire production of the beginning of the war slowed down operations only temporarily, as the mills turned to making yarns for the heavy duck needed for duffle bags, cartridge belts, tents and other war supplies. They produced 40 million pounds of this in 1942, could spare equipment only for 20 million in 1943, eked out five million pounds in busy 1944.

Each of the four mills won the coveted Army-Navy E Award for outstanding production, and each was able to add a star denoting continued excellence, Decatur being cited three times, the others twice each.

The manpower shortage made itself felt as soon as production began to pick up in 1943 with the growing need for tires. Men from the labor department, going out to recruit employees, found it harder to get people and to hold them than it had ever been before.

The draft took its toll there as everywhere, but more important was the appeal of glamorous and better paying jobs in the great war plants in the area. Bell's big bomber plant at Marietta, turning out Flying Fortresses, employing 25,000 men, was only a few miles down the highway from Cartersville. There were big posters everywhere urging workers to support the nation's need for airpower. Decatur had a shipyard which grew to a payroll of 2000 men, sent its ships down the Tennessee River to the Gulf. There were shipyards, too, at Brunswick, Savannah and Mobile. Coca Cola had a powder bag-loading plant at Talladega. Training camps and flying fields went up over the area, at Camp Seibert, just outside Gadsden, at Camp Oglethorpe, Forts Benning, McPherson, McClellan, Wheeler, Gordon, all calling for civilian help. Men slipped away one or two at a time, not noticed at first, but with adverse cumulative effect. Other men travelled still farther to Detroit, St. Louis, even to San Diego and Seattle.

Textiles was a low-pay industry compared to the war plants, and the mills went to the War Manpower Board seeking permission to raise wages in order to get people to man their looms and spinning frames. Half a dozen such increases were granted, with the result that wages at the end of the war, with overtime, were twice prewar levels.

Turnover was never an important problem in the cotton mills before the war. It was a stable industry, with many employees staying on year after year. The 20-30 per cent annual turnover represented girls who left the mill to get married, people who moved away, men who grew old. But in the war, turnover loomed to large dimensions, went to 50 per cent, 100 per cent to 200 per cent. The older established employees stuck by their guns, but many of the new people hired in did not stay too long.

The mills had been on three eight-hour shifts before the war, most of them working five days a week, but stepped up to six and seven days a week to meet production needs—which was a factor in the heavy turnover.

The recruiting men had to go further afield, 20 or 30 miles away, which brought up the matter of transportation. The mills got temporary permits from the state and borrowed school buses and Army buses to help set operators up in business. At Cartersville the industries chipped in a few hundred dollars apiece, ran their own bus line on a break-even basis. This was liquidated after the war, but some of the other bus lines which came into existence remained as permanent additions to the transportation system of the state.

The percentage of women workers, always fairly high in a textile plant, went up from 35 per cent to 50 per cent and in some places as high as 65 per cent. Nursery schools were set up close to the mills, where mothers could leave their children for the day.

In recruiting women the mills encountered competition from an un-expected source, the chenille bedspread industry, largely a household occupation. This business, starting a few years before the war, was booming. Some large-size plants went up, but much of the work was done in the home, and the saying was that a person could find his way from Atlanta to Chattanooga by following the lines of bedspreads hung up for sale along the two sides of the road. As the mills went out to hire women, they met the understandable situation that a woman who could make as much money working at home, and still keep up her housework, was not too much interested in driving ten or 20 miles in order to work in a mill all day.

Farmers were hired, though schedules were snarled up at planting time and when the cotton was ready to be picked, with 50 or 100 men leaving their posts.

Cotton milling had low priority for manpower until the war was well along. It was only when the invasion of Europe brought a sharply increasing demand for motorized equipment and new tire factories sprang up over the country, that Washington recognized that tires could not be made without fabric. After that cotton went up from the bottom of the priority list almost to the top, with only the Atomic Bomb Project ranking ahead of it. But the horse was out of the barn by then, and the mills still had great difficulty building up their working force, and still greater difficulty in increasing production, since most of the replace-ment labor they managed to get was comparatively inexperienced. At that the mills grew from 4500 employees to 6500.

Both CIO and AFL sought to unionize the cotton mills. Decatur went AFL in the spring of 1945 by a three to two vote, with organ-izers capitalizing on the fact that inexperienced construction workers were getting $1.25 an hour on the government rayon plant alongside, while experienced textile workers were getting much less. Rockmart went AFL later in the year by an eight to five vote. Cedartown was tackled next in April, 1946, this time by the CIO. It proved more dif-ficult, employees turning down the union issue six to five. In October, however, the National Labor Relations Board suddenly called for a second election. Organization work had been going on quietly, and this time the union won by a margin of 35 votes. Cartersville employees turned down the union in the fall of 1946 by a three to one vote.

Morale remained high through the war, even though employee activi-ties were curtailed by the seven day week. Cartersville staged its first postwar picnic in 1946, and Cedartown celebrated its 20th anniversary, giving out pins to employees who had been at the plant since the beginning. Competing with every other Goodyear plant around the world, the southern mills twice won the Slusser Cup for the best safety record, Cedartown in 1941 and Decatur in 1945.

Employees contributed thousands of dollars to War Bonds, Red Cross and USO drives. Cedartown took great pride in the fact that the fabric for the famous Rickenbacker life raft was made there.

The new conditions of better wages and higher standards of living in the industry which grew out of the war, seemed likely to affect the "company house" system, the last vestige of the paternalistic relationship which had plagued the industry since its establishment in England. That system, carried from Old England to New and from there south, provided low-rent company houses for employees as an offset to the low wage levels characteristic of the industry.

Goodyear had inherited villages from the previous owners at Cedartown and Cartersville, had to build one at Rockmart, because of the small size of the town and the lack of housing. Decatur, a larger city, had adequate housing.

Since the wage levels in the industry had increased with the war, comparable to those elsewhere, there was no longer economic justification for low rents as offset to wages, and in any event there were enough houses only for a third to a half of the employees, the rest having to buy or rent outside, so it seemed likely that the system would in time be abandoned.

Rayon, which ran 40-60 to cotton during the war, seemed certain to remain in the rubber industry, though the decline in the production of military tires cut the rayon ratio to one-third. The industry, however, was still one of the smaller users of cotton, only four or five per cent of the nation's cotton being used in tires.

California in the War

California was one plant which did an outstanding war job without expanding its floor space.

It was laid out with a capacity of 5000 tires a day, but with the many improvements in processing in the next 20 years could turn out 10,000 tires a day in the same space, and outside of warehousing, the factory designed in 1920 was still large enough two decades later. With the depression of the 1930's, however, production was running around 5000 tires daily.

Still more space which it did not need became available in the summer of 1938 with the closing down of the textile mill, which occupied one of the three wings of the building, made up about a third of the plant. Unionism had come in, and was demanding the same wages for textile workers as for the' tire builders, despite the difference in the operations, and the fact that many of them were performed by women. There were only 13 women in the tire factory against hundreds in the textile mill.

It was pointed out that fabric costs in California were already out of line with those of the south; that the two groups had worked alongside each other at different wage levels for 18 years; that the company would be placed at a serious competitive disadvantage with other tire manufacturers—which would affect the tire builders as well—if it paid machine tenders in the one wing the same money it paid tire builders in the other. Fabric manufacture in California was barely hanging on as it was. An extra cost load would drive it out. No one else was making tire fabric in Los Angeles.

Perhaps if the issue had come up a decade or two later, when union leaders had come to recognize that economic forces were stronger than men's wishes, the outcome might have been different. But unionism was new, and feeling its new-found power, brushed these considerations aside. It was that or else. So the mill was closed, part of the machinery being shipped to the new factory just opening in Brazil.

Ironically enough this surplus floor space enabled California to make a larger contribution to the war effort two years later than would otherwise have been possible.

Passenger tire manufacture went down from 5000 to 1200, but other products came in. The west coast became the largest center of airplane manufacture in the world, with the great Douglas, Lockheed, Consolidated and North American plants ringing Los Angeles, and Boeing at Seattle not far away. California had not built any airplane tires until a year or so before the war. Akron's facilities had been adequate up to then. Now California got into airplane tires in a big way.

Fuel tank production came in early and grew fast, built up to a production of 500 and 600 cells a day, ranging from some no larger than a suitcase to others almost as large as a locomotive boiler. This department at the peak took almost a third of the total manufacturing space.

Barrage balloons, 30 feet high by 70 feet long, came in early, were air-inflated for test outdoors between two wings of the building.

Supt. Steele, who had come to Goodyear from Case School, Cleveland, in 1912, been superintendent in Gadsden and England and returned to the coast in 1938, had a seasoned tire organization headed by Wilson and Braley who had come out with the opening of the plant, but no one who knew anything about barrage balloons. He picked a young California shift foreman named Cota who had shown aptitude and resourcefulness, sent him to Akron and New Bedford to learn the business, went to work building balloons with new people who had never seen one before.

Life rafts and pontoons came on next. Cota made another trip east, brought back specifications and know-how, soon had a force of 1200 people turning out these imperative war products.

Gas masks came in as Akron ran out of labor, built up to a schedule of 7000 a day.

California by now was feeling the manpower pinch, too, with the huge expansion of the airplane plants. Women came in in larger numbers, one department of 75 employees being manned entirely by women, having an average age of 65, most of them with sons or grandsons in the service.

Tire manufacture sloughed off at first, but came back strong. Unlike Jackson and Kelly-Springfield, California did not have to move out its mills and calenders to get into war work, but in the end had to borrow equipment from Kelly to meet its quota.

Goodyear California had 1300 employees at the time of Pearl Harbor, but within a year the number had passed 4000 and was over 5000 in 1943. Men worked 24 hours a day, seven days a week through the emergency, with 3000 women employed at the peak—including one 88 year old great-great-grandmother.

· · ·

The end of the war saw the Coast plant in a position to start vigorously to work on reconversion, building up fast to a production of 10,-000 tires a day to meet postwar demand, expanding truck tire manufacture, continuing in the airplane tire field, and going for the first time into industrial rubber goods, in the former textile mill.

Starting with compass belts, V-belts, the rugged rotary hose used in oil drilling, including that done under water, the plant expanded into tank linings, car mats and a growing range of industrial goods, diversifying its production. Fuel tank manufacture was continued for a number of months, with the new light-weight tanks coming in.

Southern California, one of the world's great playgrounds, played an important part in automotive, electrical, aluminum and synthetic rubber manufacture during the war, with the oil companies as important contributors. Los Angeles grew from 1,900,000 population to more than 3,000,000, with 40 per cent of the population of California living in Los Angeles County.

The tire factory which Goodyear built east of town on the old Teague Ranch in 1920, which gave stimulus to manufacture in the area, can claim a small part at least of the credit for pioneering an industrial development which helped win the war.

Arizona Did Its Part

The experiments in mechanized farming at Litchfield Park and the use of machines and conveyors to transport and process farm products enabled the ranch to continue to produce foodstuffs on a large scale, even though much of its manpower was drawn off.

The huge Goodyear Aircraft plant alongside the property had 7500 employees at the peak. An aluminum plant was nearby, an air research operation in Phoenix employed 1000 men, and there were many civilian jobs at Luke Field, an advanced training base for single-seater Army fighters, built within sight of the ranch.

Replacement help came from two sources different from anything else in Goodyear's war work. One was Mexican labor brought across the border under an arrangement with the Mexican government for the emergency. The other was war prisoners.

A large POW camp was set up nearby and German and Italian prisoners worked the fields and harvested the crops. The first ones were the surly submarine crewmen, then arrogant members of Rommel's Afrika Korps, but after the invasion of Normandy the prisoners were more docile, no longer sure that Germany would win the war.

The Wigwam was closed as a resort hotel and facilities and cottages utilized by Army personnel from Luke Field.

The war brought in a much larger use of the sorghum, hegari, with Goodyear going into this aggressively for use as cattle feed, relieving the demand for corn, the sorghum being ground and processed in the mills on the property.

The Wingfoot Homes pilot plant alongside the airport relieved housing shortage in the war industries and elsewhere over the valley, with the cement balloon houses offering additional housing and warehousing space.

New Plant at Lincoln

With bullet-seal fuel tanks in full production at Akron, California, Gadsden and New Bedford, and Army and Navy calling for more to meet seemingly insatiable demands, Goodyear looked around during 1943 for an empty factory which could be put into use quickly. It should be somewhere in the Middle West, perhaps near Omaha and Wichita, major centers of airplane manufacture.

A site was found at Lincoln, Nebraska, a plant which had been used in turn for truck and airplane manufacture, as a storage depot for grain under AAA, and by the Air Corps for the storage of B-29 parts. It lay five miles southeast of the city on the Burlington Railroad, with a good truck highway alongside.

The property was bought and equipped with company money, not RFC funds, was so well adapted to the job that while remodeling and getting in equipment started in December, 1943, the first fuel cell was built February 26 and the first carload shipped out March 26. The plant swung into operation fast, moving up to an output of 125 complete fuel tanks a day.

These were built for such famous fighting planes as the Mitchell B-25, the Curtiss C-87, Consolidated's B-82, Boeing's B-17 and B-29, the B-24 Liberator, the P-47 Thunderbolt, AT-10 trainers and some for the P-51 Mustangs.

Gadsden-born Walter Rudder, who had gone to Alabama Tech before joining the company a dozen years before, worked in Tech Service and production, and was then in charge of the fuel tank division at Gadsden, was made superintendent. Personnel was hired locally, 75 per cent being women. The plant ran at full momentum up to the end of the war, had a peak payroll of 1000 people.

Production continued briefly after that to complete some cells for the B-29, then the plant was closed. Rudder went back to Gadsden, by then a much larger plant than the one he had left, became second man to Michaels. Materials and machinery not needed were disposed of, retaining only mills and calenders, power house and office equipment, until the company decided the next move.

What to do with the Lincoln plant? How could its location and personnel be used most advantageously? The city of Lincoln was anxious to have the company stay on, offered to buy adjoining property and move some houses off to provide room for expansion and recreation facilities.

With Jackson and Kelly back in the field, a new plant at Topeka, and larger floor space at Gadsden, the company did not particularly need the space for tires. How about mechanical goods?

That division, now called Industrial Rubber Goods, had grown to large proportions. The V-belt, which started during the 1920's, to transmit power over short distances, had come into increasing usefulness as the nation grew more and more mechanized. The fan belt on an automobile is a V-belt, and these belts were used in washing machines, air conditioning units, refrigerators, deep freeze units, motorized grass cutters, hand-steered tractors, air compressors and scores of other places. Demand was increasing too for the older transmission belt, used to transmit power over longer distances, as in the farm harvesters, combines, hay balers, corn pickers, ensilage cutters, to operate pumps; in lumber mills, machine shops, in oil fields, stone quarries, creameries and packing houses.

Lincoln would be an excellent distribution point for both types of belting, so became Goodyear's first Industrial Rubber Goods plant outside Akron—except those in foreign countries. The plant took over all V-belt production in sizes of 22 inches up to 120 inches circumference, all fan belts for cars, trucks and farm vehicles, and all transmission belting from two inches to six in width, up to 500 feet in length. This was the big market. The new plant could take advantage of mass production principles.

Two other farm products were added, frictionized fabric aprons for use in harvesters, and hay baler belts which carried the hay up on the wagon. Equipment to give a capacity of 25,000 feet of radiator hose a day, and 45,000 V-belts was set up. That would make a large size plant, with a payroll of 1,000 people—of whom 35 per cent might be women. Lincoln started up on the new basis in March, 1946.

Fred Shaw, who had headed production in the "explosive area" at the Charlestown bag loading plant, became superintendent, was succeeded later by Richard Jay, an Iowan, who had gone through the State College in chemical engineering, joined Goodyear in Jackson, on the Squadron.

Like Windsor and St. Marys, Lincoln would be as autonomous and self-sufficient as possible, doing its own research, testing, scheduling, ordering, shipping and machine shop operations, calling on Akron for technical help only if it got into difficulties, but with the personnel quickly developing a pride in solving their own problems as far as possible. It was given the most efficient equipment in the field.

Lincoln installed an incentive program of wage payment similar to that at Charlestown. An employee might progress from learner to beginner, to qualified, to experienced, to expert, to master in his department, in fairly rapid strides. Promotion to new status was based not only on how many pieces a workman turned out, but also on quality, safety and waste reduction—which included mistakes which bring rejection of goods that other departments had worked on.

Pay was based on weekly, rather than daily output, so if an employee came to work not feeling well, and did not make the expected production, he might make it up later in the week. If he was falling behind, the foreman or supervisor might stop at his machine to see if he could help—and even if only a situation at home was bothering him, it helped to have someone to talk it over with.

A company not interested in seeing how little wages it must pay, but in how much well-built, low-cost product it can take into the market and sell, may experiment with other factors of production than compounds and machines.

Topeka is Added

The Topeka plant throws light on another contribution made by industry to the war effort, the organization technique required for large scale production.

While Rubber Reserve and Rubber Director Jeffers had to bend every effort to get synthetic production under way fast, they must also dole out the remaining natural rubber from the stockpile for urgent military needs, making sure that it lasted until synthetic arrived in volume. That called for an intricate and complicated task of balancing stocks against expectations.

As between the various war goods which used rubber, combat tires, airplane tires, fuel tanks, fire hose, life rafts, life vests, blimps, barrage balloons, gas masks, tank tracks, rubber foot wear and clothing, and the rest, the joint chiefs-of-staff must determine which were the most important and in what order and volume. Then Jeffers' men had to see how much more rubber was imperative to keep the big production machinery going in this country—truck tires, insulated wire, industrial belting, hose, molded goods, and the rest.

Someone must know at all times just where we stood in the supply of natural and synthetic rubber now, next month, and a year from now, so as not to run short. And beyond this, must take all these items, military and industrial, hundreds of thousands of them, break them down by size and type, determine how much rubber would be needed in their manufacture—and how much cotton, rayon, nylon, carbon black, zinc oxide, sulphur, etc.,—then set up priorities and allocations to see that just that amount of materials and not a pound more was turned over to industry.

But industry was not a single factory. It was 36 tire companies, some of them having several plants, and 1200 other companies making rubber goods other than tires.

So Jeffers had to know the capacity of each of these 1236 plants, how many Banburys, molds, machines, vulcanizers, presses and other equipment each one had, so that contracts could be given them which would keep them completely busy, and after that help them get new equipment and floor space to expand their output.

Scheduling had to be flexible enough to meet changing requirements at the front, or changes in construction which called for different materials or in different amounts. For example, when it became necessary to use rayon in large size synthetic tires, production of that fabric had to be expanded from 18 million pounds a year to 200 million.

To continually vision more than 1,000 factories scattered over the country as if they were a single plant under one roof, and keep materials pouring in in so exact a balance that production would not be interrupted anywhere due to shortage of any item, nor inventory accumulate elsewhere, was a man-sized job.

The rubber story is no different from that of a score of other industries but is probably typical as showing how production of war material was accomplished—a job completely obscured by more exciting news from day to day of land and sea and sky battles, but which played a part in the outcome of those battles.

For this was no job for a Government Bureau. Government had had no experience like this. But unless war production was organized for maximum output it would fall far short of the need.

However, Big Business had had a similar problem over the years in its own plants, and since any company could lose money hand over fist unless this was organized expertly, the Production Control system had evolved over the years. Jeffers and Rubber Reserve urgently needed such a department.

And just as Washington had called in Dinsmore to direct the development of a practical synthetic, and Ingle to lay out factories to produce it, and Bogardus to gather up all the wild rubber he could find around the world, so Spencer, a Goodyear production control man, was called

Government plant at Topeka, later taken over by Goodyear (above), and (below) Lincoln plant acquired for manufacture of fuel tanks, now making V-belts.

in, along with men from other companies, to organize this phase of the war effort. For the five years previously he had headed a division controlling the inventory of materials and finished goods for all of Goodyear's domestic factories. The job was down his alley.

And as the need for tires manufacture grew Spencer's group had to see where more machinery could be put in here, and plant additions built there, to stretch out the productive capacity of the nation to the utmost—and after that to lay out huge new facilities called for in the $70,000,000 expansion program of 1943, and the $100,000,000 program of late 1944.

In planning these new plants, Spencer did not dream that he would later go out as superintendent of the one assigned to Goodyear at Topeka; nor that after operating the plant a couple of years, he would be drafted again by the government, General Clay needing his particular talents in Germany in the administration of the American Zone.

The Topeka plant was built on a 75 acre site, two miles from the city, served by the Rock Island, Missouri Pacific, Santa Fe and Union Pacific railroads, with well organized trucking lines extending in all directions. The Reconstruction Finance Corporation furnished the money. LaDue, veteran plant builder, was resident engineer.

Ruffner, who was on home leave from Java when Pearl Harbor was attacked, and had been acting as Plant One Superintendent at Akron, was picked to head the plant, took two of his men from Java along—Rosenberger, as production superintendent, and Washburn of development as technical superintendent. Soderstrom came on from Charlestown as chief engineer. Some 70 men were assigned there in all, including a force of Squadron men to get production under way fast. The plant got into operation in March 1945.

War needs had continued to grow, however, even as the factory was under construction. Originally planned as a building 900 feet long and 150 feet wide, it was widened to 250, then 350, and a large building went up for material storage.

Once the plant was in production, 36 of the Squad men went back and later employees came from the area around Topeka. The University of Kansas at Lawrence, Kansas State at Manhattan and the University of Missouri supplied graduates who quickly qualified for staff and production supervision.

Production of large size combat and tractor tires started in March, 1945 and after VE Day big flotation tires, up to 20 inches in diameter, were added, to be used in the invasion of the Chinese mainland which then seemed necessary to defeat Japan.

However, between the Navy, MacArthur, the Superfortresses, and finally the atomic bomb, the war in the Pacific came to an end in August, sooner than anyone had dared hope, and the government found itself owning a large number of factories it could not use. The Topeka plant was taken over by the company in September as a convenient location for the manufacture and distribution of large truck and farm tractor tires, which were in large demand. With passenger tires also critical, equipment for this purpose was installed in the last 100 x 900 foot addition, and an administration building added.

Topeka took a production ticket of 650 off-the-road tractor tires, 600 truck tires, 5500 passenger sizes per day. As men came back from the war and the Air Forces training camps in the area began to release men, labor conditions became easier and Topeka was able to build up quickly to a staff of more than 1000 men.

In the meantime Spencer had been released from government service, came back to run the plant he had helped build. When he went to Germany, two years later, Rudder of Gadsden, wartime superintendent at Lincoln, took over.

With the growing number of outside plants each one was given greater local autonomy. It was responsible to Akron for quantity, quality and cost, was encouraged to solve its own problems as they came up. Since the problems of a small plant are often different from those of Akron, Topeka made a practice of sending its production and staff people out to study operations in other Goodyear plants, to get ideas which might be applied to Topeka, with excellent results.

Excellent community relations grew up. Topeka is not primarily an industrial community, so the plant encouraged visits from townspeople, members of the legislature and state government, tire dealers, business groups and the schools. More than 30,000 people visited the plant during its first year of operation, and approximately 1000 continue to come in each month to see how tires are built.

Sao Paulo plant supplied large volume of wartime tires and fabric for Latin America, and (below) Swedish plant which had hard sledding during the war.

Rangoon branch set afire by Jap shells

20. Foreign Operations

Exodus from War Zones

THE outbreak of war in Europe in September, 1939, brought hardship and adventure to many Goodyear people abroad, dangers and prison walls for many of its foreign distributors.

Akron's first thought after the war broke out was to get the women and children out of the danger zone. Hazlett in England arranged passage home for the American families.

In the Swedish factory, which had just got into production in May, Superintendent Follo, coming to work the morning after war broke out, found the office practically deserted, and only 15 men out of 400 employees in the factory. Sweden had wasted no time in mobilizing, and Follo, who had taken pains to hire young men, found most of them called to the colors.

His next thought was for the Squad men who had left a couple of days before for America by way of Paris. They were right in the war zone. He managed to reach them on the telephone through the Ameri-

577

can Express offices, told them to get the next available plane for England. They asked what the urgency was, got the first news by way of Sweden that the world was at war. They had seen a lot of soldiers, a bit of excitement on the streets, but since they did not speak or read French, had not realized what had happened. Their baggage had been lost when they got to Southampton so they left without it.

Follo next arranged for the wives to return. They had to cross Europe, sailed from Genoa just before Italy got in the war. Bassler, works accountant, returning for medical treatment, was only 12 hours out of Norway when that country was invaded. When the British blockade reduced the supply of rubber and the ticket was cut 75 per cent, four of the Americans were sent home. Direct routes across the Atlantic were blocked by now, so they had to travel all the way across Siberia to Vladivostock, take a ship there for Shanghai, then on to Manila. Russia was invaded as their ship passed Japan. The trip home took nearly three months. Other men left later as production dwindled.

Deepest in the war zone was Faltin, special representative in the Balkans, a native of Czechoslovakia, but an American citizen. He had seen inflation, war and revolution close-up many times in his 20 years in export, witnessed the Bolshevik uprising in Bucharest, the Nationalists revolt in Egypt, the German invasion of Austria and Poland. He was in Akron when the Nazis moved into his homeland of Czechoslovakia, where he had left his wife, being deceived, along with statesmen and generals by the German promises at Munich. Hurrying back, he paid a Gestapo agent $300 to procure the release of his wife, moved on to Rumania.

He did not head for home after that, however. He spoke five languages, had friends in many countries, might be able to help some of his distributors. He soon had the chance.

Akron got a cable from Mrs. Medvay, wife of the distributor in Austria, asking that Faltin return immediately to Vienna. He had just been there, but Cameron sensing it might be important, sent the word on. Faltin returned, found that Medvay, who had been permitted to operate up to then, had been thrown into jail on a trumped-up charge, and his home and business siezed. The Goodyear man pulled strings, got him released and sent across the border into Switzerland with only ten shillings in his pocket. However, Medvay had some securities in the bank at Prague, so Faltin went over and got them for him, Medvay selling off enough to take him to New Zealand where he bought a garage.

But that was not all. Seeing trouble ahead, Faltin had suggested some time before that Medvay overpay his Goodyear account, have some money in the States against emergency. Once safe in New Zealand, he drew on Akron for the $25,000 he had in the Goodyear vault.

Smythe, Goodyear distributor in Yugoslavia, had used a similar plan. Some time before he sent a carefully worded letter to Akron, mailing it from Ankara, Turkey, asking that he be overcharged 10 per cent on all purchases, the money to be credited to his account. He got out of Belgrade just ahead of the Germans, his building being bombed over his head, was two years getting back to the States. His troubles were over when he got to America, as Goodyear was holding $50,000 for him.

Faltin also managed to get some money to his Polish distributor, who was able to send his family out of the country into Latvia while he followed on foot.

Other Goodyear salesmen in Europe not only got out in time, but collected the bills before closing their offices. Ogle in Finland even collected for a Goodyear electric sign shot out by the enemy. Erne, former Paris manager, who had retired to a farm in southern France, came back to the States, took a job in Domestic. Jerosch abandoned his Pliofilm factories in Paris and Marseilles, joined the army of refugees heading for Portugal, eventually got back to New York.

The invasion of Denmark came so suddenly that Steffensen, the manager there, a Dane, had no chance to get away, so continued in business selling charcoal, refrigerators, anything he could get hold of. Goodyear did not hear from him for four years, found his books in order and a net profit in the bank when his country was liberated.

Van Rossum, Goodyear distributor in Holland for 35 years, also kept going throughout the occupation years. Nauta, head of the company, cut down used automobile tires for bicycles, raised tulip bulbs, not to sell but to eat, called in sewing women, had them make up his stock of Pliofilm into baby pants which he peddled to farmers in exchange for food.

Goodyear's distributor in Brussels got a break, he and his Dunlop competitor being assigned to handle the distribution of all tires sold in the country during the war.

Only in the three neutral spots in Europe were the Americans able to carry on, Serge Wulff in Switzerland, De Francis in Portugal and Melander in Sweden, selling such goods as the British blockade permitted to meet the minimum internal needs of their countries—at least until the rubber supply was cut off. The Swedish plant could no longer export to Norway or Denmark, though shipments to Finland were permitted for a while, because of its long friendly relations with Sweden.

Scores of export salesmen, who were nationals of their countries, went into the army.

Another story before leaving that part of the world. An inner tube wrapped in a gunny sack came into Export one day. The tag had been mutilated and was illegible, so the package went to an adjustor's desk, lay on the floor for two or three days. When no letter came in, the adjustor finally opened the package, and inside the tube were hundreds of $20 bills.

A dozen people had stepped over it and the janitor had swept around it unknowingly. A letter came in later from a distributor in Iraq. He explained that he did not dare to register or insure the package, lest it be opened and its contents revealed. He recovered his money.

On the other side of the world, Goodyear men also encountered the hardships of war after 1941, with the hell of internment in Japanese prison camps for many of them, though fortunately most survived.

When Pearl Harbor was attacked, the company had a factory in Java, rubber plantations in Sumatra and the Philippines, sales offices in Manila, Singapore, Batavia and Rangoon, and rubber buying offices in Singapore, where millions of dollars worth of rubber were cleared through annually.

Although the Japs had invaded Indo-China, the chance of the war reaching any further seemed as remote to the Middle East as it did to the rest of the world. A few men sent their families home, not many. Business continued as usual. The company took an order from the Indian government shortly before the war for almost a million dollars worth of tires and tubes, 25,000 9.00-16's, the largest single order for that size tire ever taken by Export up to that time. Riveire, sales supervisor for the East, blocked one even larger by tipping Akron off that though ordered for Manchukuo, its ultimate destination was to be Japan.

The first blow fell at Manila, a Goodyear stronghold for 25 years. In charge there was Reuel Bradney, a bachelor with export service in Egypt and the Near East. Bunnell, one of the relatively few Akron-born Goodyearites, was office manager. The staff included Montana-born W. C. Waldo, big, good-looking chap who had attended the School of Foreign Service at Georgetown University, Washington, been with the company two years, was a truck tire salesman. Several salesmen had hired in Manila. Among these were Albert King, born in the Islands, and Charles Blue who had lived there for years, had taught school for a while, was near 60 when he joined the company ten months before. Two Americans also hired in, Ferrier from California and Wetzel from Ohio.

The Japs struck at the Philippines immediately after Pearl Harbor, soon took Manila, and most of the Goodyearites, with their families, were put in nearby Santo Tomas prison camp. They did not fare too badly until the Japs began to feel the pressure of McArthur's invasion, but were on the verge of starvation when they were rescued early in 1944 in a daring foray by American parachute troops and Philippine guerillas. Waldo, however, had already succumbed to disease, and Blue died three days after liberation as a result of the hardships encountered.

King was in charge of the Goodyear branch in Iloilo on the Island of Panay. When the Japs struck there in April, he took his wife and two year old son, headed for the interior, lived in the jungle for a year and a half. Then he made his way to a guerilla camp, enlisted in the Army, was ambushed and killed a little later, got a posthumous presidential citation.

In charge of the Goodyear plantation on the southernmost island of Mindanao were two men, Huber, who had started in the factory in 1918, gone on the Squadron, spent several years in Sumatra. He was in prison camp when his 25-year service pin came due. His assistant was Lundberg, Vermonter and Annapolis graduate, with three years of rubber growing experience. Lundberg was due for home leave, had sent his family on ahead of him. Huber's wife and three small children were on the Islands.

The plantation was located on an island, 80 miles from the harbor town of Zamboanga. There was no connecting railroad. Supplies were brought in and the rubber carried out by barges. The men had built a stout boat with a semi-Diesel motor to bring in the mail and tow the barges of rubber to Zamboanga, installed a short wave broadcasting tower to send messages to Manila, from which point they would be forwarded to Akron. The boat was big enough to have carried the Americans out as far as Borneo at least, from which point they might have picked up a ship or plane. Lundberg was an expert navigator.

But the faithful motor, after battling 11 years in the South Seas, was so badly worn in the fall of 1941, that it was decided to send it in to Manila for overhaul. The Japanese crisis seemed to have passed. The Japs had sent their leading officials to Washington to keep peace between the nations.

The engine was still in Manila when the Nipponese smashed into the Philippines. Lundberg and the Hubers were held in prison camp at Zamboanga until Corregidor fell, when they were transferred to Manila and eventually freed.

Over on the mainland, Focken, an Englishman, stationed at Shanghai, sent his family to Australia, moved his headquarters to Hong Kong, and when that was threatened, joined the British army as a captain, was not heard from again.

Singapore was next on the Japanese time table. In charge of sales there was Wilbur Fender, one of the most promising of Export's younger men. Graduating from Oberlin and Ohio State, he joined the company in 1928, went to Cuba, won the Master Salesman Medal in 1932 and 1934, also the Litchfield Medal the latter year as the best Export salesman. Before sailing for Singapore in 1937 he had married Patterson's secretary, Margaret Gillingham.

W. E. Thomas, Jr., whose father was personnel manager of the Squadron, was office manager. Both men had had military training, so they joined the U. S. Army, were commissioned as captains, left Singapore only as further defense was futile, went to Australia. There Fender, then a major, died of pneumonia in 1944, Thomas became a lieutenant colonel.

Mayers was in charge of the rubber buying offices at Singapore, and his escape furnished a story which the Associated Press carried over the world. His ship was torpedoed and sunk, and Mayers and his wife and daughter thrown into the water. A rescue boat came along but was taking only women and children, because of over-crowded conditions. Little Mary Ann Mayers, 12, insisted that they pick up her father, too. He was wounded, as they could see, and she would have to go back to him unless they picked him up. The sailors responded to her plea and all arrived home safely.

When the Japs moved into Burma, Allen, an Englishman who was manager at Rangoon, evacuated his European staff, joined the British army as a captain, fought in defense of the city until the enemy captured the waterfront and set many buildings afire, including the Goodyear branch. Before he left, however, Allen piled the remaining company records and furniture into the brightly-painted Goodyear truck, doused it with gasoline, set it afire, then stepped into one of the three last launches leaving for Australia.

Somewhere in the confusion he lost his cherished Master Salesman pin, but in time another was sent out, with Akron's good wishes.

Morehead in Ceylon remained at his post, the only rubber-producing area untouched by war—though control of that rubber lay with the British government.

Elsewhere in the Far East, George Riveire had had some interesting experiences just prior to the war. A Texan who had started in San Antonio, served in Mexico, Spain, Argentina, the Philippine Islands, he was then supervisor of all sales activities in the Far East.

He was the only Goodyear man to drive over the Burma Road to Chungking, arranged for the delivery of train loads of truck tires to the Chinese; had handled negotiations with the Philippine government to start the rubber plantation in Mindanao. Riveire was in Akron, however, when the war broke out.

Pleasanter is the story of Sir Maynard Hedstrom in the Fiji Islands, who had one of the most up-to-date of all Goodyear depots. He also had the leading car agency in the islands, had banking, marine insurance, and other mercantile interests. He was on a trip to the States, however, when the war broke out on the Pacific and being unable to return, settled down in California for the duration.

Retreat from Sumatra

War came to Sumatra just as the Goodyear plantations were coming into full bearing, 6,000,000 trees at Wingfoot and 1,500,000 more at the earlier plantation, Dolok Merangir, standing straight and tall, averaging 1200 pounds of rubber to the acre, the largest stand of bud-grafted stock in the whole world. The plantations represented an investment of $15,000,000, Goodyear's largest outside of the United States. They turned in 35 million pounds of rubber in 1941, expected a yield of 45 million by 1950.

But blighting shadows out of Nippon were moving steadily southward through the jungles of Malaya. Paul Shoaff, Goodyear manager in Sumatra, had thought over the possibility of Japanese occupation of the islands in the event of war, while he was on home leave in early 1941. He found few Americans who thought this likely. One person who did, however, was P. W. Litchfield, who instructed him to draw up a memo covering the evacuation of personnel and the disposition of the property if worst came to the worst. The Dutch overseers would not be permitted to leave the islands, but Shoaff must get the Americans out if the Japs did break through.

Litchfield studied the memorandum carefully, nodded. "Protect the company's property as long as it is prudent to do so," he said, "but remember always that human life is more important than property." That was in May, 1941.

Shoaff got back to the plantations to find the Dutch government working on a "scorched earth" program. Sumatra, sprawling over hundreds of miles, thinly populated, accessible by a hundred bays and coves, would have to be abandoned if the Japs took Singapore. The Dutch would fight a retreating action, fall back on Java, make their final stand there.

The trees on the plantations themselves could not easily be destroyed. There are no forest fires in a rubber grove. The leaves of the trees and the cover crops below absorbed the dense humidity of the air like a sponge, were wet with dew every morning. To chop down Goodyear's 7,500,000 trees alone would take months, to say nothing of the thousands of other acres set out in rubber. Sumatra was the largest rubber growing area in the world, with huge British and Dutch estates there.

By the calendars beyond the international date line Pearl Harbor was attacked December 8. When the radio brought the news in that morning a dozen Dutch employes were immediately called up for military duty.

Shoaff had the women and children flown to Java, where a ship was available, the day after Christmas. Weida's men at Wingfoot and Titus' at Dolok would stay as long as was prudent. Tapping was stopped, and all the rubber possible was shipped out. Demolition arrangements were made as instructed by the government.

The situation grew darker by the hour. Jap bombers were over Medan. Finally, late in January, he called a meeting, turned the management of the plantations over to DeBoer at Wingfoot; and Riedhorst at Dolok.

The Hollanders took the news calmly. "You are doing the right thing," they said. "The Japs will probably treat us fairly well, because they need our production but they have been trained for years to hate the Americans."

The Japs were already knocking at the doors of Johore, across the straits by then, would soon have all Malaya.

The demolition plans ordered by the Dutch government covered three phases. In the first phase all unused equipment was to be boxed, marked in a code known only to the government, and shipped to a secret destination. Everything which was to be demolished or made useless—including locomotives, trucks, processing machinery, machine tools, electric motors and Diesel engines were to be marked conspicuously with red paint.

In the second phase, which the government would announce by radio code when invasion became imminent, locomotives and trucks were to be brought into the Head Emplacement (plantation headquarters) and could not thereafter be moved. All finished rubber must be taken from the building and piled out of doors, with five gallon cans of gasoline convenient at hand. Latex was to be poured into the drains or the ocean.

All launches and lighters would be tied up to the dock; the engines would be soaked in oil to prevent rusting and dropped in the river. Holes must be bored in the boats so they could be sunk on short notices. Electrical connections should be made to all the equipment marked for demolition.

The third phase called merely for carrying out these plans. Shoaff reviewed them with his organization, made sure everything was set. All demolition must be done by the military; for a civilian to take part would be sabotage, punishable by death at the hands of the Japs.

The invasion of Sumatra was under way well before the final stand was made at Singapore. The little Goodyear group left in February.

They got away as planned, but it was none too soon. It took five days to make the 1200 mile trip along the coastal highway to Oosthaven. The road was none too good at the best, winding through mountain trails, narrow, twisting, full of detours, dotted with streams which must be forded, or wider streams with rickety bridges. The narrow gauge train provided little better transportation.

They were almost the last people to use the highway, for the bridges were destroyed by the Dutch military five days later, to keep the Japs from using the road.

Shoaff had planned to stay at the Goodyear factory at Buitenzorg, keep in touch with the plantations by phone, but found that Java, too, held no security. He talked to DeBoer over the radio phone on February 15, the day Singapore fell. A code phrase previously agreed on let him know that the government had ordered the third phase of demolition.

Java Factory Taken

Java was next on the Japanese timetable, brought the first casualty among Goodyear's foreign plants.

The Japs were already in Sumatra when Singapore fell on June 15, 1942, encountering little opposition. The Dutch prepared to make their stand in Java, but they had lost too heavily in men, guns, ships and planes. A hectic week followed for the little Goodyear group.

There were a dozen of them there, headed by Hadley, managing director, who had spent much of his Export service in the East, Hochberg, acting superintendent (Ruffner was on home leave), and British-born

Gow, secretary of the company, who had gone to the East Indies originally for an English firm, joining Goodyear in 1922.

They went to Batavia, the capital, discussed the situation with American Navy and consular officials, who told them that the islands could
not be defended. Dr. Foote, U. S. Consul General, made plans to evacuate the 72 Americans on the islands, employees of Goodyear, Standard
Oil, National Carbon and other companies. By the end of the week he
had located an old cattle boat formerly on the Bali run, and found a
captain willing to sail it to Australia, Captain Hoffman, whose own
ship had been torpedoed the week before. By the end of the week arrangements had been completed and the ship was to sail Monday. He
wanted all the Americans on the island to leave on it. There was no
time to lose. The enemy was moving fast.

"I can't order you to leave," he said, "but I urge it in the strongest
possible terms."

Hadley, Hochberg and the rest decided to go while there was still
time. Gow, however, felt that he should remain until the Dutch military
commander formally released the plant, then under government control.
Stevenson, the office manager, another Englishman, elected to stay also.

There was not too much margin of time. Oosthaven in Sumatra, just
across the Straits, was being occupied by the Japs when the Americans
arrived Monday morning, and Batavia itself was under preliminary
bombing attack. Captain Hoffman decided to wait until afternoon, slip
through the Straits under cover of darkness. The evacuation ship had
no guns or radio or navigating equipment except an old-fashioned compass, but reached Australia safely eleven days later.

The factory, as it happened, had ten days grace, as the Japs waited at
Oosthaven to bring up supplies before striking at Java. Gow reported in
each day's production by cable to Akron. Then the Japs struck, hard and
overwhelmingly. Two hundred planes might have saved the day, but
the Allied supply was spread too thin and the heroic defense failed.

The Dutch commander issued the demolition order on March 4th and
Gow and Stevenson went to Bandoeng, temporary seat of the government. Three days later Bandoeng surrendered, and Gow and Stevenson
spent two years in jail, the first six months in solitary confinement, then
were moved to a detention camp, from which they emerged sometime
after VJ-Day, emaciated but with unbroken spirit, made their way back.

•   •   •

The Japs were able to put the factory back into operation after five
months, ran it with limited production throughout the war. New markings in Japanese were cut into the molds.

War Story of Canada

Goodyear Canada had gone far in resources and resourcefulness in the 30 years since this narrative broke off in 1917, and as a result was able to make important contributions to the war effort in World War II.

The first outside factory had become the largest Goodyear operation outside the United States during the intervening years.

The more highly populated southern section of Canada is a narrow ribbon of land 200 or 300 miles wide and 3500 miles long—with a dip in the center following the Great Lakes—and beyond that lie great resources of timber and mineral wealth.

Canada has 500 million acres of forest land and supplies much of America's paper and some of its timber; it has 80 per cent of the world's nickel in Ontario, most of its asbestos in Quebec and its gypsum in Nova Scotia; there is gold, silver, zinc, copper, lead, coal and iron ore in Canada—and substances like uranium and pitch blende. There are also great fishing industries off the Gulf of St. Lawrence and Puget Sound, and the world's largest supply of furs.

But these resources did not lie conveniently at hand for men to get at them, and the inherent characteristics of rubber made it particularly useful in processing them and transporting them to the market place.

So Goodyear-made conveyor and elevator belting became as useful in processing ores in Ontario as it was in Chile and South Africa, carried logs through pulp and paper mills, asbestos rock to the crushers. Air drill hose, steam hose, suction hose, hydraulic were used on pile drivers, cranes, hoists, power shovels, on locomotives and donkey engines, on motor boats, diesels, fishing boats, river steamers and ocean liners moving up the St. Lawrence. Power transmission belting, both flat and V types, were used on the many and varied types of power machinery employed to extract the ores from the mines, the logs from the forests and lumber from the trees—played a most important part too in the processing of pulp to paper, raw ore to refined metal, logs to finished lumber and in thousands of other manufacturing operations.

In this land where natural resources were so well hidden, men had located an iron range matching the potentialities of the Mesabi, but which lay at the bottom of a lake,—Steep Rock Lake in Northwestern Ontario, 75 to 300 feet deep. To get at it would take four years. But with a war on and steel needed it had to be done in 18 months, with the lake to be pumped dry and a new river created, a job which would have been impossible without rubber hose connections.

When you speak of a hose connection you think of something you can pick up in your hand, but these had to be tough and strong to resist abrasion and the terrific force of the water, were 12 feet long and weighed nearly a ton apiece—and were turned out at Bowmanville at the rate of one a day.

There are 50 million acres in wheat land across the West, not spring wheat but hard wheat, one of the world's great graneries.

Perhaps nowhere in the world were Goodyear farm tires more important and useful than across the great wheat fields of Alberta, Saskatchewan and Manitoba and the vast new Peace River field north of Edmonton, southern terminus of the Alaskan-Canadian highway.

Also Goodyear elevator belting speeded up the operations of a great string of grain elevators stretching across Canada, and in one at Fort Churchill on Hudson Bay, 1000 miles north of the Great Lakes, to enable ocean going steamers to use the shorter Great Circle route to Europe.

Canada has always been a great exporting nation, shipping its surplus wealth of raw materials to other nations. It produces three times as much wheat, for example, as it consumes. Canadian banks and insurance companies operate widely over South America and elsewhere abroad. The Canadian Pacific is the name of a great steamship company sailing the two oceans, as well as the name of a trans-continental railroad.

Canadian-made automobiles and tires found their way into world markets, not stopping with those of the British empire. There have been periods when more than half of its output was shipped overseas.

Canada's war story includes Operation Muskox, a 600 mile journey taken by a fleet of snowmobiles (in the development of which Goodyear had an important part) across the uncharted wastes of northern Canada, accessible otherwise only by dog team, navigating by compass, keeping in touch with each other by radio, and being refueled by airplane.

Goodyear Canada was well established as an integral part of the economy of the Dominion when the first World War broke out, was the leading rubber company of the country. It ran into financial difficulties in 1920 but worked its way out, declined help from Wall Street, got back into the black ink in 1922, showed an average profit of better than $1,000,000 a year from 1910 to 1940, with a peak of more than $3 millions in 1929. It continued to make money during the 1930 depression, had an authorized capitalization of $8 millions by 1941.

Floor space had trebled and New Toronto, built in 1917 for a capacity of 2000 tires a day, turned out a million tires in 1940.

It had acquired a mill at St. Hyacinthe in French-speaking Quebec Province in 1926 to make fabric for its tires and mechanical goods. Mr. Carlisle became president of the company that year, was one of the recognized business leaders of Canada, subsequently taking the presidency of the great Dominion Bank and being a director in many important Canadian industries. He turned over the Goodyear reins in 1936 to Partridge, who had come back from the English plant the year before, but remained on the board of directors. The veterans Koken at New Toronto and Hardy at Bowmanville were still in the harness, but younger men were coming up.

Another interesting figure who moved into the official family after the first World War was R. C. Berkinshaw, native of Toronto, a law graduate who had served overseas as a major in the Canadian engineers. He joined the company as assistant secretary working on legal matters, handled many of the details of the 1920 reorganization, qualified himself for larger responsibilities, became secretary and general counsel in 1927, treasurer and general manager in 1933 and vice-president in 1945.

Purdue-trained A. Wallace Denny who had been in airship engineering at Akron, efficiency manager at California, then assistant superintendent at New Toronto, became superintendent in 1940, Koken moving up to vice president in charge of production for the three Canadian plants. English-born, Akron-trained Charles Cattran, long development manager at Bowmanville, was assistant superintendent.

The sales organization, always aggressively manned, was under R. W. Richards with C. B. Cooper as assistant. Canada had 6500 dealers and distributors in English-speaking Canada, 1000 in French Canada, independent merchants covering every city and town from Halifax to Vancouver and way into the north, 85 per cent of them handling only Goodyear merchandise year after year.

The organization was primarily Canadian born, with Carlisle, Koken, Richards and Cooper taking out citizenship papers.

Goodyear had been the first American rubber company to settle in Canada, though British Dunlop had come in earlier and there were two Canadian companies, largely making mechanical goods, one of which was later taken over by U. S. Rubber. The Firestone company followed in 1919, Goodrich in 1925 and Seiberling two years later.

The Goodyear organization was aggressive in bringing to Canadian markets every new development in rubber, auto tires, truck tires, farm

Canadian-made hose connections used in cross-country pipe line during war to pump out a lake 300 feet deep, uncovering iron ore deposits rivaling Mesabi.

Goodyear-Canada is proud of its crack drill outfit from World War I; views of Canada-designed Snowmobile which rubber made possible, below.

tractor tires, airplane tires, mechanical goods, as fast as these became available, was the leader in introducing and pushing new products, kept Canada on modern equipment.

Its advertising program was written in Canada and directed at the home market, though Akron's counsel was available as needed.

So Goodyear Canada was a grown-up company, strong, ready to go, when World War II broke out.

The Dominion did not find itself automatically at war with Germany when the mother country threw down the gauntlet. It was free to go in or stay out. But it lost no time in making its decision, and immediately after the invasion of Poland on September 3, 1939, Canada declared war, would supply men and materiel to the Allies in large volume.

President Partridge telegraphed Prime Minister Mackenzie King, "We offer you everything Goodyear has."

Goodyear Canada had 2600 men and women on the payroll at that time, including the three factories and the sales branches, a force that would grow to more than 4700 at the peak, though more than 1100 men went into the Armed Forces. The New Toronto factory alone increased from 1187 employees to nearly 3300.

Production of defense materials went on a 24-hour basis. Bowmanville began turning out fire hose in large quantity and at high speed to meet the emergency of the German air attack on London, produced more than two million feet of hose in 50-foot lengths during the war, of which three-fourths went to England.

After Pearl Harbor, Bowmanville began building solid rubber bogie wheels for Canadian-built tanks, turned out 25,000 of them the first year. The shortage of rubber compelled a changeover to synthetic, which brought new problems as the war center had shifted to Africa. Would synthetic stand up under those high temperatures? There was no place in all Canada where African desert conditions could be simulated, so testing grounds were set up in Southern California and Arizona. The first results were disappointing, but in the end Bowmanville technical men came up with the answer, and by the end of the war had turned out more than 90,000 bogie tires.

Bowmanville also made Bren gun clips, water-proof gaskets for boats and landing craft, fuel hose, military soles and heels, de-icing equipment, a large volume of conveyor belting for Canadian industries working on war contracts, and a long line of molded goods and extruded parts, particularly for the automotive and electrical industries.

New Toronto was called on for tires, big 16 and 20 inch tractor tires, run-flat tires, sand tires, airplane tires, to be shipped out in large quantities to England, France, Africa and elsewhere on the fighting front. Next to the United States, Canada became the principal tire supplier for the Allied forces, its production even surpassing that of Britain, which was able then to divert more of its harassed production facilities to ships, guns and planes. New Toronto also took on the manufacture of bullet-seal fuel tanks for airplanes and inflatable life rafts and life vests for use by the Air Force.

A few figures will show the changeover from civilian to military production. In January 1940, New Toronto built 250 tires for the Army as against nearly 100,000 for civilian use, and during the year built 64,000 military tires out of more than a million total. Two years later, although the rubber shortage had cut production in two, only 76,000 tires out of 540,000 went into civilian use.

With the war coming closer home in 1942, the Canadian plant blackened its windows and directed floodlights around the property to guard against sabotage. Life Guard tubes went out early and fuel cells, life rafts and life vests came in in increasing volume. Fuel cells starting in April 1943, reached an output of 1300 by December, went on up to 2000 a month. Life rafts started in March, moved up to 100 a month, and life vests a little later hit a monthly peak of 1250.

The most striking single contribution made during the war, however, was the Snowmobile, a five-ton armored tank, built to travel through deep snow and over swamps and marsh land.

Warfare slows down during the winter season and armies dig in and wait for spring. Early in 1942 British Army men fell to wondering whether there was anything in the mechanized warfare program which might be utilized to break the impasse of weather, make reconnaissance and even surprise attack possible in the wintertime. Perhaps Canada, which got a lot of snow, would have some ideas on the subject.

The Dominion did have a vehicle used for that purpose, a half-track, with a plywood station wagon body and skis in front for steering. It was being used on a small scale by doctors, mailmen and others on the back roads of Quebec during the winter. It was not big enough to do the military job in mind, but was a starting point. Canadian Army engineers got busy, presently talked to Goodyear, who had built half-track tires.

Design of the tank itself was not too difficult. Key to success lay in the caterpillar tracks on which the wheels would ride. Cattran, assistant superintendent at Bowmanville, who had long been its development engineer, and Varcoe, his successor, were intrigued with the problem. The tracks must be wider and longer, wider to distribute the load like a snowshoe, not sink in as a wheel would, and must be longer to get the fullest possible traction. Pneumatic rubber tires instead of steel wheels would reduce weight, although an armored truck is quite a heavy load to put on an air filled tire, and these were installed in tandem, four duals to a side, 16 tires in all. Run-flat tires which would continue on after being riddled with bullets were used so that the Snowmobile would not be crippled in combat.

In Goodyear's overall manufacturing picture, outside plants were not expected to do a great deal of original work in development. Full facilities had been concentrated at Akron so as not to duplicate effort, with all results made available to all plants—and the Accounting Department charging back to each plant its proportion of expense. Ideas from the outside were welcome and many had come in over the years, but each plant was expected to send any tough problems into Akron.

However, in the case of the Snowmobile, Akron had its hands full and outside plants were trying to handle their own work as far as possible. In any case the Snowmobile was to be a made-in-Canada job—and the North country had natural testing facilities, which Akron or England did not have.

Without going into too much detail, the answer when it came up, was an extremely wide track for each of the eight sets of tires to ride on, almost a yard wide in fact, the two tracks in total being 70 per cent as wide as the whole vehicle.

And the track was a rubber and canvas endless belt of extremely stout construction, with metal crossbars to furnish traction.

It was not a problem to be solved overnight, nor without many setbacks. But in the end it was solved, and Bowmanville got the contract to build 400 of these tracks—with New Toronto supplying the proportionate number of bogie tires—set up eight separate assembly lines to turn the tracks out against time.

That was no simple manufacturing operation. After the tracks were built, the factory had to punch and countersink 396 holes into each one, install metal collars, cleats, specially hardened steel crossbars, the bolts, and finally clinch the threads above the bolt heads to insure permanent union.

The tracks did the job, distributed the load to give a ground pressure of one and a half pounds per square inch, or a tenth of that of the tanks. The Snowmobile proved that it could travel through wet or dry snow, four to five feet deep, through bog and marsh land which would swallow up any truck or tank, and over country so rough that even a strongly built truck would be shaken to pieces. It could climb an incline of 43 degrees, slash its way through second growth bush, and trees four to five inches in diameter, was useful for towing heavy loads and extricating bogged-down trucks and other vehicles.

In the test run into the Arctic Circle the expedition covered the 600 miles of snow-covered wastes in nine days, making as high as 100 miles a day at times.

The development of the Snowmobile took a lot of time and did not come into full use by VE-Day, was then included in plans for overland invasion of the marsh lands of Japan, except that events of the summer of 1945 made an invasion unnecessary.

Synthetic rubber in 1943 brought in a new job for Berkinshaw. Early in the war, in February, 1941, he had been borrowed by the Canadian government as director of priorities of the Department of Munitions and Supply, and in August moved up to be Director General of the Wartime Industries Control Board, the "czar of Canadian industry"— and shortly had the duty of announcing a drastic cut in tire production and of civilian use of rubber.

With synthetic rubber coming in in 1943, he got a still tougher assignment, that of building a $60 million synthetic plant. Selecting a site at Sarnia, Ontario, with plants of the Dow Chemical and Imperial Oil companies alongside, he got this huge operation into production within a year, was able to produce enough synthetic to keep the lines of communication open at home and on Canadian battle fronts over the world.

Nicholls was called from his Goodyear post in mechanical goods to act as Deputy Rubber Controller, the office which had the allocation of all natural and synthetic rubber throughout Canada. American and Canadian governments worked as a team in the synthetic program, forgetting international boundaries and customs duties. If one country ran short of styrene or of butadiene, the other would lend a hand, pooling resources to get maximum production from the two countries.

Goodyear Canadian plants were expanded during the war, four and a half million dollars being put into this. At New Toronto where the need for space was greatest, floors were built across the light wells, half the garage was changed over to manufacturing space, new wings were added. Bowmanville enlarged its belt room to be the largest in Canada, occupying two floors of a building 280 feet long and 60 feet wide. Storage for all but the immediately needed materials went elsewhere, with warehousing leased 20 places around Ontario for rubber, zinc oxide, carbon black. A 20,000 sq. ft. freight house was leased from the Canadian Pacific railroad as far away as Fort William.

Inside the plant a new steam generating boiler to furnish high pressure steam for the turbines, an installation costing a third of a million dollars, went in early. Conveyors and monorails and additional Banbury mixers were put in, while the machine shop having to handle much of its own work added boring mills, lathes, drills and welding equipment.

Canada did an excellent job during the war, but there was no time to relax after VJ-Day. Tire production went up to a million and a quarter to meet the wartime shortage, and in 1947 the new Super Cushion was launched.

In that same year, three new modern plants were added. These included an Airfoam plant with a capacity of 100,000 pounds a year, a Pliofilm factory to produce 3000 pounds a day, these going up alongside the tire plant at New Toronto, and a new factory in Quebec for the manufacture of soles and heels and a widening range of molded goods.

There is a story of civic enterprise behind the St. Malo plant in Quebec, the company's second operation in French-speaking Canada.

The Dominion is famous for fishing, hunting and winter sports. Visitors by the thousands pour across the Peace Bridge at Buffalo throughout the summer and fall, heading for Georgian Bay, Lake Nipissing, the Trent Waterway, the Kawartha Lakes, Algonquin Park, the Rideau Lakes, Muskoka, Timagami, seeking muskellunge and small mouth bass. Others head in the fall for Northern Ontario, the Laurentians and other hunting grounds seeking moose, deer, bear and Canadian partridge. Others go for skiing and tobogganing to Banff and Lake Louise in the Rocky Mountains, the Laurentians in Quebec, and a score of Ontario resorts. Still others visit the Thousand Islands, Ste. Anne de Beaupre or go to British Columbia, the California of Canada.

The tourist industry is as important to Canada dollar-wise, as its wheat crop. However, the most famous city in all Canada is Quebec, with its Citadel, its walled city, its narrow streets reminiscent of old France, the Chateau Frontenac, the Cathedral, the Plains of Abraham where history was made.

Old Quebec, founded in 1608, was one of the best known cities in the hemisphere, but it had fallen behind lesser known cities in population and civic wealth. Montreal had come out of the war with upwards of one and a half million people in its metropolitan area. Toronto had around a million, while Vancouver, Winnipeg, Ottawa, Hamilton and others were larger than Quebec, which had around 100,000 people at the beginning of the war though adding considerably to that population during that struggle.

For while Quebec was not one of the important industrial cities, it had taken on a substantial amount of war work, particularly the St. Malo Arsenal, a small arms plant employing 10,000 people, built around the car shops of the Canadian National Railroad. The Arsenal was closed after the war, and while many employees went back to the small towns they had come from, Quebec faced an unemployment problem—and the opportunity to set up an industrial center to supplement its commercial and distribution activities.

So the city bought the entire property from the War Assets Corporation, went out looking for industries to move into the vacant buildings. It hoped it might sell off the property to recover what it paid for it, but even if it lost something it was still a good deal, as a contribution to employment and future growth. However, so aggressively was the project pushed that the city was able in a short time to fill up the entire area and make a tidy profit.

Goodyear took over the largest single unit for rubber footwear and molded goods manufacture, a sort of combination of America's Windsor and St. Marys. It also took over the power plant to sell steam to its neighbors. These included such companies as General Electric and International Harvester, also factories making plywood, auto parts, airplane parts, prefabricated houses, paper products, comprising a well-diversified industrial center. Goodyear's plant got into production in the spring of 1948.

The new plants brought opportunity for three men. English-born Art Hurst, plant manager in Quebec, had a broad production background. Joining the company at New Toronto in 1926, he had been foreman of the tube room for 15 years, then of life rafts and fuel tanks during the war, became production superintendent at Bowmanville in 1944. Sydney Fearman, superintendent of Airfoam, born in Hamilton and educated at the University of Toronto, joined Goodyear in 1934, served in Akron on the Squadron, tech service and tire design, went to Java as manager of tech service in 1937, got out ahead of the Japs, returned to Toronto, was division foreman of fuel cells during the war. W. T. Barge, superintendent of Pliofilm, joined the company in 1937, went through the Squadron, was assigned to the cement house, went to the synthetic rubber plant at Sarnia as production superintendent.

Addition of these three factories clinched Goodyear's leadership in tires, mechanical goods and allied products. It had an organization capable of meeting the problems of the future. Partridge was still at the helm, with Berkinshaw now vice president and general manager. Carlisle remained on the board of directors. Some of the veterans relinquished heavy responsibilities to younger men, but stood by as consultants.

Among these was Koken, with 52 years experience in rubber, Tipple in accounting, and Hardy and McCrea at Bowmanville, who had been with the old Durham plant before Goodyear took it over in 1910, Hardy for 11 years in production and McCrea for eight years in sales.

Denny was vice president in charge of production for all plants. Cattran had succeeded Hardy at Bowmanville and Lamontagne had followed the veteran Goudreault at St. Hyacinthe, with his second man, Rider, having personnel and manufacturing background. Cryder was still in charge of development at New Toronto, and Varcoe, who had done most of the work on the Snowmobile tracks, had moved up at Bowmanville. Shumaker was in charge of industrial relations for all plants. Allman was superintendent, with Barrett, Smith, Stannah and other Akron veterans still in the harness.

New men had come up from the ranks. D. C. Carlisle, who had studied engineering and worked in the Goodyear machine shops in the summer while attending college, found himself pitchforked into accounting instead, began as a travelling auditor in 1928, went up the line to comptroller and in 1946 succeeded to the important post of treasurer, which had been held in turn by his father, by Garry Lane, one of the earlier stalwarts, and Berkinshaw.

O. H. Barrett, whom Berkinshaw had picked out of law school, joined the company in 1924, became secretary and legal counsel eight years later, spent six years in the Army during the war, coming out as a full Colonel and Deputy Director of Supply and Transport for the Second Canadian Corps, returned to become assistant to the president.

Nicholls came back from the Rubber Controller's office to succeed McCrea in charge of mechanical goods sales. J. G. Williams, who won his spurs at Goodyear Aircraft during the war, became comptroller of Canada in 1946. Cooper moved up to be general sales manager, Richards remaining as vice president, and S. R. Skelton went from advertising manager to assistant manager of sales.

Behind these men was a well-organized production, engineering and administrative staff.

Canadians like hunting and fishing as well as do their cousins from the States, and the Canadian company purchased property on Lake Timagami near Litchfield's camping lodge where hundreds of Boy Scouts from the Goodyear plants had gone every summer for years, opened it up to Canadian Scouts generally, provided vacation facilities for employees during the fishing and hunting season.

Goodyear employees have had many champion hockey and soccer teams over the years, and one unique organization, the Overseas Veterans Club, which in 1940 won first place in all Canada as the best marching outfit at the Canadian National Exhibition, in a competition which saw 120,000 men march past the reviewing stand. Membership in this club was limited to veterans who had had overseas service in World War I, factory men who had had little opportunity to drill in peacetime. But they showed the effects of thorough basic training.

Of the 1100 Goodyear men who saw service during the war, 47 were killed in action, and a number received high military decorations, one of them, Flight Lt. David Hornell, chemist at New Toronto, being one of the six men in the Dominion to win the cherished Victoria Cross. Lt. Hornell attacked a German submarine in the North Atlantic and sent it to the bottom, at the cost of his life.

Goodyear Canada contributed a total of more than $11,800,000 through the purchase of Victory Bonds in the nine Victory Loan campaigns starting in 1939. Of this the company invested $7,500,00 and employees $4,250,000.

This rounds up the story of Goodyear in Canada, one of the colorful results growing out of Frank Seiberling's purchase in Chicago a half century earlier—for less money than Canada spent during the war for a new air compressor.

England's Heroic Effort

England stands out as a gallant chapter in the history of Goodyear, since it was the only plant directly in the combat zone.

Wolverhampton presented a cross-section of a nation fighting to survive, its towns in flames at night, its coast threatened by invasion, its lifeline and communications in peril, but one whose people forgot personal hardships and ragged nerves, continued doggedly on to "produce the tools and finish the job."

Great Britain had to build planes, guns, tanks, ships, with the war under way, something like "a man riding a bicycle while he was building it," as Sir Ronald Storrs, the Dunlop historian described it, and an organization which had made itself a part of the industrial fabric of the nation did its full share.

Men worked at their machines with their gas masks always within arm's reach, under exhausting conditions of continuous blackout, with the constant nerve-racking threat of attack from the air (the factory siren sounded its arresting alert 281 times during the war) and with the deadly V-bombs in the final months of the war.

Wolverhampton lies in the heart of England's industrial section, only 14 miles from Birmingham, the nation's second greatest city, and 25 miles from Coventry, the motor center and hardest hit city in England.

However, the Goodyear plant went through it all unscathed—though it had some close calls. Once a residential district immediately adjoining was blasted. If the pilot had pressed his release a second sooner, the plant would have been hit. More than once showers of incendiary bombs fell adjacent to the factory grounds, but were swiftly dealt with. Shell splinters often broke the glass in the blacked-out skylights, left a gleam of light to attract the attention of the next sky raider, until it could be blocked off.

One curious fact which came out after the war helps to explain why the factory led a charmed life. Enemy flyers carried maps showing targets in their assigned areas, but those found in planes shot down revealed that Nazi efficiency slipped for once. The German maps showed the Goodyear factory as an innocuous enamelware plant. British Intelligence did not bother to pass the word on to Berlin that the plant had been converted to tire manufacture back in 1929.

A more immediate explanation of the factory's immunity from attack was that the British did an excellent job of air raid protection. Wolverhampton lay in a valley surrounded by trees and was perhaps the most completely blacked-out town in England. The roofs and plant grounds were painted in ingenious camouflage design, so that a reconnaissance plane would look down on what appeared to be merely rows of houses, shops, streets and gardens.

Defense started in August, 1939, before the war broke out. The factory was closed for three days and the cement house worked day and night making black-out cement, which 400 employees used to paint out all the windows and skylights. Others built underground shelters of steel and concrete, each big enough for 50 people. Sand bags were piled nine feet high around the buildings. Walls of brick and concrete were built 14 feet high around the pump house and the electrical substation, to protect them from high explosive bombs.

A fire department of 120 men was organized and equipped; a first-aid group, who must also see to it that every employee got to shelter stations when an alarm was sounded—themselves to be the last to take shelter; a decontamination squad to get rid of poison gas.

Several hundred employees were carefully drilled for actual combat, in case of invasion. The factory defenses included machine guns, anti-tank guns, a Smith gun which would throw a 12 inch shell, and a mortar which would destroy a tank at 50 yards. Spotters were on the roof with walkie-talkies. The control station was manned day and night. Each employee knew exactly what to do in case of an air alert—shut off his machine, put on his gas mask, proceed to his designated air shelter. The frequency of air raids led to so much lost time that shelters were later built above ground adjoining each department.

The athletic field alongside the plant was set up as an emergency center, with equipment to serve 500 meals, and non-perishable food kept on hand. A factory garden raised 80 tons of peas, beans, potatoes, cabbage and parsnips.

Due to excellent precautions, Goodyear lost less time than any plant in the area.

The air raids did not break the morale of the employees. Someone always had a mouth organ, and would start a song session while the raid was in progress. After the first few months employees would gather on the roof of the air raid shelters to watch the sky battles.

When the war broke out Goodyear had a factory force of 1700 people. Fortunately, a mechanical goods division had been put in the year before, soles and heels were being made and a Pliofilm plant had been approved, though that, of course, was shelved.

The American personnel included less than a dozen men—the veteran Hazlett who had started as a salesman in 1906, was managing director, Sullivan secretary-treasurer, Hendon operating manager. Anderson and Balazs who had come over from California in charge of Development and Compounding, Pribble on Engineering, Forrest as purchasing agent, Lore on Tire Production, Newlon and Perrin on Mechanical Goods. Flinn of Production had to return in 1942 because of his health. Walker, the personnel manager, was an Englishman. Brittain, superintendent, was born in Canada, but had long been an American citizen.

Perhaps some of the Americans may have thought at times of their Goodyear associates working peacefully away in Ohio, Alabama or California, but no one complained, though the job meant separation from their families, bicycles for transportation, rationed food and clothing and unrationed danger. England was their assignment, so they tightened their belts and carried on. After all their lot was better than that of the men flying planes and parachuting down from them, or stoking boilers in destroyers on the North Sea, or slogging across the muddy fields of France.

Production encountered all the difficulties of shortages of material, equipment and labor that other factories did—and some others beside.

Picture taken at Dunkirk in June, 1940, by Goodyear salesman serving with British Army shows how tire became a foxhole in that famous action.

At right, sandbags guard the entrance to Goodyear-England plant; Below, employees take refuge in air shelter as alert is sounded.

Replacement tires had often to be rushed off at night in the blackout by skilled drivers at top speed so that immobilized transport might get going again by daybreak. Airplane tires were often taken out still steaming from the molds and hurried to an airport where planes were waiting to carry them to some hotly contested battle front. Technicians dashed out to repair damaged tires, wheels and brakes. Vital war supplies had to be removed from the docks before the Luftwaffe came—or even while the Luftwaffe was actually overhead.

Tire development generally paralleled that in the States, but the British Army called for a wider range of special purpose tires. The normal interchange of information between Akron and Wolverhampton was largely cut off and the English plant had to work out its own problems, including those concerned with synthetic, rayon and nylon. Fortunately Brittain's own experience had been in development, as one of the company's best tire designers.

Akron tried to get each of the Americans back to this country once or twice during the war, to have some time with their families—and to familiarize them with new technical developments. Most of the men used the opportunity also to take back some American clothes, since these were sharply rationed.

Synthetic brought special difficulties, and the English organization could not wait for Akron to solve them, bought a test car which ran 400 miles a day uphill and down dale over an old Roman road, tried out synthetic in various percentages to natural rubber, working closely with the government and other manufacturers to arrive at a ratio which would give satisfactory mileage.

The first synthetic tires hardly lasted out the day, but in the end did an entirely satisfactory job.

Four types of tires were built, the greatest volume being in "giant tires" used on trucks and tractors. These extended through a wide range of war operations, carrying guns, troops, fuel, wounded men, and in unusual uses on fire engines, flame throwers, searchlights, radar equipment, cranes and earth-moving equipment.

The technical facilities of all English rubber companies, like materials, were pooled, under government direction. But Goodyear engineers played an important part in the development of the Run-Flat tire which would carry on for another 50 or 100 miles after being shot through. The Cross Country tire, for use on soft ground and mud, used Goodyear's Sure-Grip tread. A special tire was needed for warfare on the North African desert, and Malmquist, tech service man in Sweden, joined Anderson, development manager for England, in a trip to that area to study the situation. Their recommendations had a part in the development of the Sand Tire, a low-pressure, Airwheel-type tire which spread out like the foot of a camel. The value of this tire was attested by Rommel, the "desert fox," for instructions found in captured tanks were:

"Only captured English trucks are to be employed in desert reconnaissance, as German trucks stick in the sand too often."

The second largest type of tires in units was for passenger cars. These were used by the services on staff cars, in the back areas overseas in essential personnel and light goods transport, and played a necessary part in Britain's wartime economy and industrial effort.

The next largest field was airplane tires, nearly two million of these being built during the war, with the Goodyear factory starting from scratch, having built none at all except experimentally up to 1940. But Wolverhampton reached a peak production of 75,000 airplane tires a year, ranging from the small ones for the tail wheel of the Spitfire to the huge tires for Lancaster bombers. Although Goodyear started late in this field, it still produced 22 per cent of all the airplane tires built in England during the war. These were chiefly for British planes.

The fourth field was land and tractor tires, used on the farm to enable the country to feed itself as far as possible, without taking up valuable shipping space needed for other supplies from overseas.

The following table will show the magnitude of tire production in England under war conditions—and Goodyear's part in it:

TYPE OF TIRE	ENGLISH PRODUCTION	GOODYEAR PRODUCTION	PERCENTAGE
Giant Tire	12,398,389	1,926,464	16
Passenger Car Tires	9,324,882	1,456,022	15
Airplane Tires	1,970,381	442,141	22
Land-Tractor Tires	823,089	102,645	12
Bogie Tires	2,627,057	56,112	2

The trail of the diamond tread was carried over every corner of the world in which the British Army fought.

The mechanical goods division also made important contributions, built hundreds of thousands of feet of fire hose—which could also be used to detour a city's water supply in any section when the water mains were destroyed by bombs; built miles of gasoline hose to fill the tanks of fighting planes, at airports and aboard carriers; manufactured tough five-inch hose for the tankers to refuel destroyers and other craft at sea—something specially useful in the Arctic convoys; built air hose and oxygen hose for airplanes; thousands of V-type fan belts for armored vehicles; and a large volume of conveyor belting, 80 per cent of it used to expedite the production of coal, though part of it was shipped to the Russian allies.

England was the springboard for American planes to carry strategic and tactical bombing deep into Germany, so Fox, English-born development man, was sent to Akron to pick up full information about the U. S.-made bullet-seal fuel tanks. This information was useful to British manufacturers, and to Wolverhampton in modifying and repair.

These tanks prevented a plane from catching fire when hit, but took considerable punishment in doing so. More than 2000 American tanks were repaired and put back in service at the British factory.

Retreading of tires came into wide use in England as elsewhere, and a big department grew up to handle this. Soles and heels were cut back with the rubber shortage, but picked up by using reclaim and later synthetic.

While the Goodyear factories in the States built a wide range of military products, Wolverhampton stuck to tires, tubes and mechanical goods, with one exception. When tire production was curtailed in 1942 by the rubber shortage, the factory utilized its big belt presses and other facilities for the next twelve months to make tons of plywood for pontoons and landing craft, most of it formerly made in a factory on the Isle of Wight, which had been heavily bombed.

With the outbreak of war in 1939 tire production increased each month until Japan took over Malaya and the Dutch Indies. But once synthetic came in and the processing difficulties were cleared up, production moved sharply upward again, breaking records month after month.

Arrival of two Banbury mixers from America helped, and the mill room was extended another 300 feet, at a 134 foot width, to increase needed output.

The English rubber growing areas in the East were cleared after the war, much more quickly than those in Dutch possessions, so the English factory was able to get back to natural rubber not too long after the war ended. No synthetic was made in quantities there, the supply coming from America. Wolverhampton was using natural rubber entirely, while Akron and America generally, was still largely on synthetic.

Despite the shortage of labor the factory payroll went from 1700 people to 2400. Nearly 750 employees went into the Armed Services—of whom 40 were killed—and the Wingfoot Clan, printed in smaller size during the war, carried a column in each issue "News from the Lads," with extracts from letters from Goodyearites in Burma, North Africa, Egypt, Italy, Iraq, Reykjavik and Murmansk. Garage men, office workers, store clerks, and men from the building trades came in to take the places of men called to the colors. Many women came in, working at a wide range of jobs, building tires, building bands and tending steam. The 175 women at the beginning of the war grew to a force of 550.

The Goodyear employees contributed a million dollars in war savings to the government.

Management and men worked closely together throughout the war, using a Works Counsel, elected by production employees, and an Engineering Counsel selected by the engineering staff to handle employee relations. In contrast to the record in the States, Goodyear England went through the entire war without a single serious work stoppage.

The British factory saw five and a half years of war, and as the struggle neared its end, the American personnel began to return to the States, Hollinger, Lore, Forrest, Balazs. Brittain became Hinshaw's assistant at Akron, overseeing production in outside factories. Girnaven, promising young production man took over. Managing Director Hazlett who had divided his 42 Goodyear years between Akron, Pittsburgh, Cleveland, New York and Los Angeles, preferred to stay in England. You grow closer to people after going through a war with them.

This rounds up the story of the work of Goodyear England from September, 1939, to August, 1945. However, a summary of its war production concludes with a tribute to the men and women who achieved it, which might well be included in any history of Goodyear!

"Before the account is closed, it might be peculiarly apt to think of the individual who went through it all at Goodyear; the neighbor in the next garden; the man in the local 'pub'; the fellow you meet every day—the man in the street—in this case, the man who worked at Goodyear side by side with his neighbors.

"What were his thoughts at Dunkirk when his son was captured or killed? When his other lad was fighting a rearguard action in the Western Desert during those last desperate days of July, 1942, when a battered Eighth Army was reeling back from El Agheila to Alamein, and the world thought the Middle East was gone.

"He just got on with his job; he stayed at his bench and shared his troubles with his workmates. They, too, had sons who were fighting for their country in other countries, and from whom the news was only too often scant and sparse.

"He got on with his job, too, when the heat was stifling through the long summer nights, but no windows could be opened because of the blackout; when his nerves were tattered with constant air raid alerts; when he was working his hardest at his job and then doing extra duty in the Home Guard or the Fire Service or in the Air Raid Protection.

"He got on with his job—the man who works for Goodyear. He did his share and did not count the cost in fatigue, nerve strain and the worry over dear ones in danger. He did his job!—and because of him and the thousands of his workmates, Goodyear-Great Britain contributed its own mighty blow against the forces of evil. Goodyear-Great Britain is proud of him."

Sweden's Difficult Position

Another unique chapter in the Goodyear war story is that of Sweden, a factory started just before the war.

Surrounded by the warring nations, Germany, Russia, England and Finland, and the occupied nations of Norway and Denmark, its only connection with the outside world was by sea way, water alive with warships and underseas boats. Sweden's battle to preserve her neutrality and maintain her internal economy was obviously fraught with difficulties.

Rubber was a part of that.

From the day of the outbreak of the European war in September, 1939, gasoline cars and trucks practically went off the streets to save gasoline. Even the military, the police and the doctors had to install charcoal burners on their cars.

Little rubber came into the country. The world had none to spare and what little the British let through the blockade was for Sweden's use only. None could be manufactured into goods bound for Germany—a proviso which the Swedish government safeguarded by barring all exports of rubber goods, since it had only a fraction of enough to take care of its own needs.

The Goodyear plant got a total of 220 tons of rubber and seven tons of pigments in 1940, and from there on the figure went down, reaching a low of 35 tons in 1943 and 30 tons in 1944.

That the factory carried on at all, reclaiming used rubber in home-made apparatus, making repair materials, building flat tread tires for cars and trucks, mostly for the army, out of what rubber it could get, plus reclaim, even screening the rubber out of floor sweepings to make heels, constitutes another story of resourcefulness and ingenuity.

The factory was just well under way when the war came.

The Scandinavian countries under Melander's leadership had long been an excellent market, and a survey had been made in 1932 as to the possibility of building a plant. The time was not ripe and it was not until 1938 that it got under way.

A site was selected at Norrkoping, not far from Stockholm, Sweden's fourth largest city and second largest textile center. A 30 acre plot was acquired on the river, accessible to ocean shipping, on ground nine feet above sea level, piling being driven to a depth of 75 feet. The plant was to have a capacity of 600 tires and tubes and 10,000 pairs of heels a day, tires to be manufactured for Dunlop, Kelly-Springfield and India as well.

V. L. Follo, Michigan-trained engineer of Scandinavian ancestry, who had been a foreman at Akron and division superintendent at Gadsden, was picked as superintendent, with Campbell who had helped start the English plant and Young from Akron as division superintendents. Hoesly had Development. Men went over to head tech service, engineering, purchasing, personnel, and a dozen Squadron men to teach factory processes to the new employees. Melander was managing director.

Construction was started in August, 1938, the first tire built the following February and production had reached 550 tires a day when Litchfield went over in May for the formal opening, which was attended by government and industrial leaders.

By September the plant had built up to capacity in tires and was turning out 8000 pairs of heels per day. Then war broke out, and the following morning Follo found office and factory practically deserted as most of the employees had been called into military service. Most of the wives and the Squadron men were sent home at once, others following later as production dwindled. Follo himself left in 1942, leaving three men in charge, Hoesly as plant manager, Campbell on production, and Gifford, engineering squadron man in charge of engineering.

The Swedish government had accumulated something of a stockpile of rubber and compounds, and took over control of all materials in the hands of the three rubber companies, doled them out from then on. But it was not to be a short war, and conditions grew worse after the invasion of Denmark and Norway in April, 1940, only 16 tons of rubber and compounds coming in during one seven-month period.

Many trucks went out of service, the tires being confiscated by the government for more urgent use elsewhere.

Goodyear production had reached 77,000 tires in the half year of 1939, but dropped off fast, reached a low of 630 in 1944. Not a single inner tube was manufactured in that year. The company built up a considerable business in repair materials, using reclaimed rubber to repair and recap tires. In 1943 it inspected and classified 20,000 passenger car tires and 2250 truck tires confiscated by the government, repaired several thousand of them for army trailers.

Sweden made a trade with Germany in 1943, got some Buna synthetic rubber and chemicals in exchange for paper, pulp and iron ore, but Germany stipulated that none of the rubber could be used in an American factory in Sweden.

Learning that Litchfield was going to London in the summer of 1943 for a rubber conference, Melander made a secret trip there by air, argued the case for Sweden to get synthetic. Litchfield said he would make every effort to get him a supply in eight months. When Melander reported this upon his return, it created quite a stir, and German-controlled newspapers in the occupied countries denounced it as Yankee propaganda.

But the synthetic got through, though delivery was delayed by the preparations for D-Day, but with the U. S. State Department lending a hand, the first shipment of 80 tons arrived the following year, earmarked for the Goodyear plant.

Some eyebrows were lifted over this but Melander pointed out that he had been allowed no German rubber, so this evened things up. Anyhow the government was glad to get rubber on any terms. More came in later from the States, was allocated by the government to the various plants.

The normal flow of technical information from Akron was all but blocked off during the war, as were materials and machines, and Hoesly, always short of carbon black and other pigments, had to work out single-handed the formulas, specifications and technique of using synthetic efficiently, a matter which had brought headaches to the other factories. None of the pre-dip and post-dip equipment used in the States was available. His experience in development was helpful in this case, as elsewhere throughout the war.

One Banbury mixer had been included in the original equipment for the plant but the rotor which activated it was broken early in 1941. Not too hopefully the factory asked Akron to try to deliver a new one, went back to the old mixing mills in the meantime. That was quite a job to put up to Hurley's men in Inter Plant, but the iron ring around Sweden had one tiny spiracle in it, the port of Petsamo in northern Finland, 1250 miles from Norrkoping, and 300 miles deep in the Arctic Circle. Inter Plant found a steamer bound that way, and that fall a cable came into the plant that the rotor had reached Petsamo. It still had to be hauled in by sled 300 miles through deep snow to the nearest railroad point, but within a month had reached Norrkoping and was installed.

Three weeks later it broke again!

However, by this time the supply of materials was so low that it did not matter too much, and what they had could be mixed on the mills. Labor supply grew shorter, but was enough for the limited production. It was 1945 before another rotor was delivered.

Though tire production was down to low levels the factory kept going. As the government got hold of a little rubber, it called for bids to make it into army tires, and the plant picked up business. It added a little revenue by machining manifolds in its machine shop for the wood-burners used in the tractors.

Fuel was long a critical item. The company had a small inventory of coal that was frozen by government order, and wood, stumps, straw and peat were used in the boilers, and tires were cured only on certain days of the week to save steam. As late as 1945 the company used 1000 tons of straw as fuel. However, the four-year-old supply of coal was released in 1946, fuel oil began to come in, and the boilers were reconverted to normal uses.

Using synthetic rubber, tube manufacture was resumed in March, 1945, for the first time in two years and truck tire output slowly increased.

Natural rubber began to come in, in 1946. With the war over the plant faced a very large demand for tires, built back fast and by the end of 1947 had the highest production in units and tonnage in its history. Truck tires went over to natural rubber in January, 1947, passenger tires in May.

The year 1948 saw the factory booming, floor space expanded, new equipment brought in and men put back to work. The payroll which had reached 260 in 1939 went down to a low of 60 in 1943, bounded back after the war to a force of 450, continued to move ahead.

Wyles went out as division superintendent in April, 1945, succeeding Campbell who went to California in the same capacity. Wyles had started in Akron as a trucker, went through the Squadron, served in Gadsden, Argentina and Java, was Goodyear's representative at Dunlop's India plant and a technical representative with the Air Forces in

the Pacific. Hoesly returned to Akron in 1948, was succeeded by Clayton who had been Squadron foreman, acting superintendent at Jackson,
personnel manager at Arizona Aircraft during the war, and started the
housing plant in East St. Louis.

Melander built up his sales and distribution force fast after the war.
There, as in the factory, were many able men of Swedish citizenship who
served loyally through the war. One American, Ogle, who had been
manager in Finland, came back. He had escaped to Sweden with no
little difficulty when the war started, returned to the United States,
worked at the Aircraft plant during the war.

Goodyear Sweden was again on its way.

Argentina's Curious Story

The story of Goodyear's war operations overseas varied with each
country, due to factors of geography, history and internal resources, and
Latin America was different from any of the rest, each country following a pattern of its own.

Goodyear had a well-established plant in Argentina, a new one in
Brazil, a third just being completed in Mexico when the war started,
with others to go up in Peru, Colombia and Cuba, as well as retreading
plants in Venezuela, Panama and elsewhere.

The Argentina story is one of the strangest in the Goodyear history.

The factory there made no *direct* contribution to winning the war,
since Argentina almost until the end of the struggle elected to remain
neutral, but *indirectly* it did an extremely important job.

For it helped trucks, railroads, mines, factories and packing houses
to keep going and so enabled Argentina to process and keep moving to
the seaports the great supplies of wheat and meat so desperately needed
by the Allies.

And Goodyear Argentina did this with the smallest amount of crude
rubber ever used in tire manufacture. It almost literally built bricks
without straw. At the low point the rubber supply in the country was
down to 250 tons a year for the three tire factories. The Goodyear factory alone normally consumed that much in three weeks.

Improvising a reclaiming plant with practically no equipment from
the States, the factory made what rubber there was in the country go
farther than was ever previously believed possible. The story went that
Goodyear could build a 32 x 6 tire out of the rubber in a pair of crepe-

soled shoes. Since the government prohibited the use of any natural rubber in the manufacture of mechanical goods, the trick was to make a conveyor belt hold together long enough to be vulcanized—after which, like the reclaimed tires of the period, it gave surprising service.

No other large nation got along with as little rubber during the war as did Argentina. What wild rubber the Allied nations were able to procure went into the war effort, except enough to meet their minimum internal needs. Both Axis and Allied powers sought to apply the great silent force of economic pressure to bring Argentina into the struggle on their side, and the strongest weapon in the hands of the Allies was rubber.

Outside of a trickle of rubber coming in after 1943 from Bolivia, Argentina got none at all until she declared war on Germany and Japan in March, 1945, after which some natural rubber from Brazil and synthetic from the United States began to arrive.

In 1941, when the war broke out, Argentina was one of the most successful of all of Goodyear's overseas operations. Starting in 1915 Ross White had built a sound foundation of public acceptance, which the building of the factory had greatly strengthened. Sales in 1941 were larger than in any previous year.

The operation was strongly manned, with Croke, then Magennis following White as managing director, Bollinger in charge of finance, George Riveire, then Huff in sales, Climer and Lee heading production. Lee left in 1939 to be superintendent of the Jackson factory, was succeeded by Patrick who had previously had charge of the reclaiming plant at Akron, a happy selection, as things turned out. Hastings became managing director in 1941 as Magennis moved up to a vice presidency.

The outbreak of war in Europe in 1939 brought some interruption of shipment and supply, but the company developed local sources, found machine shops that could make up equipment needed. Tire fabric made in Argentina ran into difficulties when low-stretch fabric came in, and Parmenter came down from Cartersville to help make the changeover.

There was trouble getting fuel. Argentina produced little coal, imported most of its needs from England and the States, and the government ordered a 30 per cent curtailment in the use of fuel. Goodyear was using fuel oil in its power plant, and the resourceful Scotch-born Hunter, plant engineer, had to change over one boiler to use corn on the cob.

These were minor difficulties, however. The plant was enlarged in 1940, a Banbury mixer and other equipment added to increase production.

Things moved fast after Pearl Harbor. Argentina had long had a large and influential German colony, and Berlin had high hopes of bringing that country into the war on the side of the Axis. Nazi cells were organized and an effort was made to bring every German into them, willing or not. Many of these men were skilled mechanics, employed in the industries. At the suggestion of the United States government in December, 1941, the American companies discharged them, Goodyear losing 28 in the vital engineering department. Acts of sabotage followed, and for many months American personnel took turns remaining at the factory at night, kept it under guard night and day.

With the cut-off of rubber supply by the Jap invasion of the East Indies, the Argentine government took control over rubber, cut truck tire production to 80 per cent, passenger tires to 40 per cent, rationed gasoline. A retreading plant started in the factory, grew to large size. The heel department was closed by government order and that rubber diverted into mechanical goods which formerly had been imported.

As weeks passed and it became evident that Argentina was not going to get any more rubber, the management began thinking of building a reclaiming plant. If the equipment was brought in from the States, it would cost upwards of a million dollars. With a shortage of machinery there, on top of shipping difficulties, it was out of the question anyhow. Maybe they could build one themselves.

Engineers, development and production men spent their time after hours scouting the junk yards of the city and surrounding country, looking for any kind of equipment which might be used. Hunter was a practical mechanic who could make anything work, and Patrick had had more experience in the intricate matter of alkali reclaiming than anyone in the Goodyear organization.

Unorthodox equipment came into the factory by truck and railroad car. There was a water wheel which had been used to create power at a sugar refinery, a bread-mixing tank from a sunken battleship, a centrifuge and some agitating tanks from a sugar refinery, differential joints from an automobile junkyard. One machine shop was able to build a tank for the devulcanizer, and so with this ill-assorted equipment they built a reclaiming plant more bizarre than anything Rube Goldberg had ever dreamed of—and which cost hardly a quarter as much as a new plant.

And it worked. Old tires and tubes, raincoats, rubber boots began to pour into the plant. Out of this assortment, plus a minimum amount of new rubber, they were able to build tires which gave unexpectedly good mileage, though at one time they got down to 1/10 of a pound of new rubber content in passenger tires and 1½ pounds in a truck tire.

There was a mechanical drier in the executives' washroom, which sent a stream of hot air on wet hands, saved towels. It disappeared one night. Scotty Hunter concluded that he could use that to dry rubber in the reclaim plant.

Other products were produced on homemade equipment. Multiple V-belts were built up over a roller carved out of quebracho wood, in place of steel, a very hard native wood, the name meaning axe-breaker.

The plant lost three men in 1942, Gagnon of Development and Miller of Production who went to Lima to start the plant there, and Delaney who returned to Akron, their duties being divided among the remaining men. Output had declined nearly 40 per cent.

The supply of natural rubber grew steadily shorter in 1943. An arrangement was made with Bolivia in February for 250 tons a year. That was a life saver, but was less than a month's normal consumption at Goodyear and had to serve the entire country. Even the supply of scrap rubber was being exhausted. Practically all of the rubber in the country was allocated to the tire companies. Contraband demanded a fantastic price, and plant protection was stepped up, for a workman could carry away under his shirt a chunk of rubber worth more than he would earn in wages in a week.

The remaining boilers were changed over to burn corn cobs, and when that supply failed, Scotty Hunter changed to linseed, and in the end fell back on wood, particularly the useful quebracho.

Other vital shortages developed—carbon black, bead wire, valves, Holland cloth and the oil used in reclaiming processes to make the reclaimed rubber more plastic, a supply of which was presently found in Chile.

Retreading became a big factor, increasing from 5000 tires in 1942 to 30,000 in 1943.

Argentina broke off diplomatic relations with Germany and Japan in 1944, but conditions remained critical. Outside the little rubber from Bolivia and what was smuggled across the border, not one pound had been brought into Argentina since December, 1941. Goodyear got down to ten tons of rubber a month as against 300 tons a month before the war.

The "third party deal" came in. All tariffs had been taken off imported rubber but Brazil, the biggest producer, was prevented by the Washington Agreement from furnishing any. However, the law could not prevent an enterprising individual from slipping across the border at some out of the way point, and once in Argentina his 60¢ rubber might be worth five or ten dollars a pound if he could find a buyer. Neither Goodyear nor any other responsible company could buy bootleg rubber, but the government asked industry to make tires for anyone who brought in his own rubber. So an emissary might come in with this story: "I have 500 pounds of rubber in my truck. I will sell it to you at the government price, and will pay you the legal price for as many tires as you can make from it."

The factory made a calculation as to how many 6.00-16's or 32 x 6's that rubber would produce, built the tires, turned them over to the agent.

The company could not charge more than the fixed figure for the tires, but an individual who had tires to sell might get $100 or $150 apiece for them.

This third party program extended also into used rubber. A man walking down the street with a pair of crepe-soled shoes might find a stranger tapping him on the shoulder, wanting to buy them.

Shoe repair men were particularly on the alert for rubber. It was all but impossible to get rubber cement, but any piece of scrap rubber could be dissolved in a solvent and used to fill the bill.

It was only after Argentina formally declared war on the Axis powers that a three-power agreement was made between Argentina, Brazil and the United States under which natural rubber came in from Brazil, with the States supplying the latter country a similar tonnage of synthetic.

Later synthetic came in in large quantities and gradually in 1946 the situation returned to normal, although there was still so large a backed-up demand for tires that Argentina permitted the import of a million tires from the States to bring its automotive equipment back to normal.

While Goodyear tires and mechanical goods made important contributions to Argentina industry and transportation in the years since White opened the branch at Buenos Aires in 1915, the experience of living in the country and being a part of it, particularly after the factory went up, did something for the company itself.

Goodyear learned much about South American habits and customs which it could use elsewhere. It tried to be a part of the country. Every American employee had to learn the language, tutors being brought in for the new men during the lunch hour, and they had to speak Spanish or go hungry. Promising Argentinans moved into key staff jobs in engineering, production and finance, and some were sent into Akron for additional training.

Argentina was a useful training school for Goodyear men, and its graduates ranged far over South America and elsewhere. Some of the production men have already been listed.

Four secretary-treasurers trained in Argentina under Bollinger— Powell of Brazil, Dunwiddie of Peru, Blackstock of Sweden and Booth who returned to Argentina from Sweden after Bollinger's death. Magennis, Croke and Hastings as managing directors, Huff, sales manager, Higginbotham, division manager, Sales Managers Davis in Brazil, Pruessman in Peru and many others gained valuable experience there.

Importance of Brazil

Goodyear Brazil, which did a highly important war job, was just getting in production when the war started in Europe, though it had been projected as early as 1912.

The company acquired a factory site in Rio de Janeiro the year it opened a sales branch there, but a series of events delayed matters for a quarter of a century.

Brazil was the largest country in South America, both in area and in population, larger in fact than the United States with another Texas thrown in. Extending 2700 miles north to south and almost as wide, its coastline was greater than the distance from New York to Liverpool, and the mighty Amazon River was navigable by ocean steamers for 1000 miles into the interior.

Rio was one of the glamorous cities of the New World, with Portuguese, French and Moorish influences shown in its architecture and culture. It had one of the great harbors of the world. Friendship and cooperation marked the relations between the two nations.

Virtually all the tropical goods the United States needed grew in Brazil, including rubber and 60 per cent of the world's coffee. It was a customer for the manufactured goods which North America produced, created a natural basis for international exchange of commodities. There were few factories, and the Brazilian government was interested in seeing plants built to use Brazilian rubber.

The Goodyear factory was delayed, however, first in 1914 by the war, then in 1920 by depression, and when the company did embark on its first expansion of overseas manufacture in the late 1920's, a new depression came on before it got to Brazil, so that it was late in the 1930 decade that the project became a reality.

During all those years, Brazil grew rubber and cotton and imported tires.

While Rio with its great harbor had been the company's first choice as a factory site, Sao Paulo, 250 miles to the southwest, was becoming the leading industrial center. It lay 40 miles inland on a plateau 2200 feet high, which gave it a temperate climate through the year, was in the center of a great farming area, had mineral wealth in the mountains to the west, plenty of labor, ample water supply, which was important in rubber manufacture, and plenty of power.

The power supply grew out of the ingenuity of American engineers, who built great reservoirs along the edge of the plateau, then poured all of the water almost straight down through half a dozen 48 inch pipes into 90,000 h.p. turbines to create a massive hydroelectric plant below. A railroad and highway connected Sao Paulo with the harbor town of Santos.

Goodyear's entry into Brazil was followed almost immediately by other manufacturing firms from the United States, Canada and Europe. The city grew to a population of 2,000,000, was called the "Detroit of South America."

The Rio site was disposed of, and an empty textile factory found in Sao Paulo, which could be changed over fairly quickly. The plant was larger than the company needed. One large wing had been used as a political prison, with bullet holes in the walls where men had faced the firing squad.

"Take that wing, too, if you can get it," Litchfield said. "We might want to add a fabric mill later."

The building had been designed in Portuguese architecture, with broad corridors, patios and the usual high walls around, and once Goodyear moved and set out tropical flowers and vegetation, it looked more like a Southern California university than a factory. It is one of the most attractive of Goodyear plants anywhere.

The project encountered delays. Except for a small plant in Rio, this was the first tire plant in the country (although another American and an Italian plant would quickly follow) and legislation was necessary to fit it into the economy of the country. Vice President Stillman and Managing Director Croke spent many months conferring with the Brazilian government over the details of starting operations.

Then in 1937, on the day that the enabling legislation was to come up for its final reading in the Senate, the Congress was dissolved, a new government came in, and negotiations had to be started all over again. And two days after production actually began, in September, 1939, World War II broke out in Europe.

The outbreak of war made a bigger impact on the consciousness of South America than North America. To the Latins, tied as they were to Europe by blood, immigration and business relationships, the war seemed closer at hand than to people in the United States, who would not become involved in the struggle until two years later.

Plans for a big formal opening were cancelled in view of this, though flag poles were going up, decorators were busy, and invitations had gone out to important government and business people. President Vargas did come out with some of his staff to see the first tires built.

A salesman for a German firm called on Goodyear the day war broke out about some equipment they had been discussing.

"You had better buy it today," he said. "This is all I have, and I don't know when there will be any more."

The factory started with a production of 500 tires a day. Once the rubber mill was in operation, orders came from Akron to go ahead with the fabric plant. Some machinery was bought new, supplementing that shipped in from New Bedford and the California plants. Except for St. Hyacinthe this was Goodyear's only cotton mill outside the United States. Beggs, last of the series of California fabric superintendents, came out to take charge, with Ross of Cartersville and McGehee of California as assistants. The new plant got under way just in time. For once the war was on there was little chance to get additional equipment, and the engineers had to improvise their own, even building a cotton loom.

The first superintendent of Brazil was F. J. Carter, Arkansas farm boy who had started in Akron as a tire builder after World War I, learned his industrial engineering in the factory, headed the personnel division in Argentina, helped lay out Sweden. Two Squadron graduates, Lamphear and Murphy, were division superintendents. Goulding, of the Squadron, took engineering. Coffin moved from Argentina to take charge of Development. Bloom from Gadsden took Purchasing, Hilliard of California, Personnel, Batson from Argentina became compounder.

Croke remained as managing director and Long, who had gone out to Brazil ten years earlier as operating manager, became secretary-treasurer. Brazil-born Andrews was sales manager.

BRAZIL WAR STORY

Having rubber and fabric and a manufacturing industry, 80 per cent by weight of her materials being "home-grown," Brazil was able to supply most of South America (except Argentina) with tires and mechanical goods throughout the war, without drawing on hard-pressed North America.

Producing the biggest supply of rubber in the hemisphere, Brazil could have driven a harder bargain, demanded that her own internal needs be amply taken care of in exchange for the raw rubber she would furnish to a rubber-hungry world. But instead, Brazil tightened her belt like her Allies, put a ban on unnecessary travel, barred gasoline-driven cars from the highway (the charcoal-equipped substitutes would travel less, and so save rubber), got along on 10,000 tons of rubber a year, one-fourth of which went into manufactured goods for the other countries in South America.

The new Goodyear plant, and two rival tire companies who followed it, were highly important to the economy of all South America.

Goodyear's fabric mill also proved important. Brazilian cotton remained fairly stable in price, tended to keep costs down despite the rising price of rubber. The fabric mill operated seven days a week, 24 hours a day, from 1943 to the end of the war, overhaul and repair being saved up for the carnival seasons. It supplied the fabric for Goodyear Brazil, some for Goodyear Peru and also supplied some to competitors, since fabric was hard to get from the States and all possible cargo space was needed for the war effort. The Peru factory almost had to shut down once when a ship loaded with fabric from Sao Paulo was sunk in going around the Horn.

Though well away from the war zone, Goodyear Brazil still felt the effects of war. The country had a large Japanese population. With huge areas of undeveloped territory in the interior, the government had made arrangements with Japan 15 years earlier to encourage emigration into the country, with the result that there were upwards of 300,000 Japs in Brazil when World War II broke out. They owned thousands of acres of farm land, particularly in the Sao Paulo district, supplied most of the food crops there, as they did in Southern California.

There was a large German colony too, started generations before, particularly in the south. In many places the natives spoke German rather than Portuguese. In the cities Germans had important technical positions, controlled many important business enterprises.

In the overall Nazi strategy the enemy made no secret of the plan that once Europe was overrun, they would turn on the United States, striking first at South America, with the large resources of Brazil only 2200 miles from Dakar as the most immediate and tempting target.

It is fairly well-established that large stores of arms and military supplies were smuggled into Brazil, found their way into the hands of Jap farmers, and that great quantities of oil and other war necessities were landed from submarines and buried along jungle coves up and down the coast.

The Brazilian government was fully conscious of this situation but not quite sure how to meet it. The United States was too fully occupied in building up its own forces to offer much help. For more than a year the Goodyear plant and other American factories were closely guarded, with American personnel on duty day and night.

Nazi and Jap leaders quietly boasted that they would take over the government when the word came, were waiting only for the signal from Tokyo and Berlin, presumably in conjunction with the landing of an invasion fleet.

But the Axis powers waited too long for the victory in Europe which would give them a free hand to invade South America, and in the fall of 1942, Brazil declared war on Germany, and in a carefully planned movement seized hundreds of the leaders, interned them. This decisive action settled matters.

However, outbreaks of violence occurred in the Japanese colony after the war ended, as they did among isolated groups in the Pacific, led by fanatics who refused to believe that Japan had been defeated. The government called the leaders together, read the Mikado's surrender rescript and things quieted down.

Shortly after the United States got into the war, Superintendent Carter was called to Akron to be personnel manager at the huge Aircraft plant, and Coffin of Development took over the job of getting out maximum production from the plant.

The 10,000 tons of rubber allocated to Brazil were divided among the four tire factories and upwards of 100 smaller plants making other rubber products. Under its allotment, Goodyear was able to increase production from 500 tires a day to 800, most of these being truck tires. Rubber Reserve, working closely with the Brazilian government, purchased all the tires, allocated them to Chile, Venezuela, Colombia and the other countries, with each section of Brazil getting its quota. So good a job was done that a substantial surplus of tires were shipped to the United States for Army, Navy and Lend-Lease.

Goodyear Interplant Relations watched the supply situation so carefully that when a ship sailing out of New York with the vital zinc oxide was sunk by enemy action, it had a second shipment under way within the week.

In addition to tires Brazil needed fire hose, air hose, transmission belts, and V-belts to keep the railroads and factories operating. Goodyear got a belt press delivered which had been ordered before Pearl Harbor, and industrial rubber goods became a permanent part of the business.

Also airplane tires came in, though the volume was not large and

Goodyear was the only company to put in equipment to build them. However, aviation grew to considerable size, and the company had another important manufacturing division to serve future needs.

Tire production increased from 800 to 1350 tires a day after the war got under way and the factory which seemed too large at first became over-crowded, even the corridors being covered over and used for warehousing and manufacturing. The plant emerged into an important position in the company's operations, as Brazil, now becoming more extensively industrialized, attained new stature.

The payroll grew to 2000, including 500 men and women in the fabric mill, 99 per cent of the working force being natives of Brazil.

Goulding went to Aircraft early in the war and Derhammer, Apprentice Machinist graduate, who had helped start the Java plant and been master mechanic at Jackson, succeeded him. The Squadron was well represented elsewhere in Brazil. Batson, one of the original Argentina group, moved up from chief chemist to succeed Coffin as development manager. Dunn, another Sand Mountain boy from Gadsden, joined the Squadron there, was one of the original group at Sao Paulo, moved back to Gadsden, to Aircraft, to Peru, then back to Brazil as division superintendent. Smith, the other division superintendent, had helped start the English plant, worked at Aircraft, then Gadsden. Ryan, Indianian who had attended the University of California, was another of the original Squad group at Sao Paulo, returned to Akron to work in compounding, then back to Brazil as division superintendent, started the Goodyear plant in Cuba, became plant manager in Brazil after the war, Coffin returning to Akron as assistant to Hinshaw.

Davis, OSU graduate from Texas, who went to South America originally on a commercial research assignment, liked the country, returned later to be assistant sales manager in Argentina, became sales manager at Sao Paulo after the war. Croke, whom we met while he was on a trouble-shooting job in Spain in 1923, served as managing director through the war, having been in India, New Zealand, Cuba, Puerto Rico and Mexico in the meantime and vice president of Goodyear Argentina. He returned to Akron as assistant to Cameron, and Long's outstanding work in rubber procurement brought him promotion to managing director of Brazil.

Long had hired in at 15 (his brother, John, manager of General Accounting, Akron, signed up at 14), was office manager in Puerto Rico at 22, went to Chile, then Spain, became operating manager in Brazil in 1929, had an intimate knowledge of Latin America. Powell, with 15 years' experience in Argentina and Peru succeeded him as treasurer.

Brazil-born men, too, had come into important places in the organization. Among them was Fred Andrews, commercial manager of the company, who joined Goodyear in 1920, was manager at Rio for years. His son, Luiz, won a Pan-American industrial scholarship during the war, asked for assignment to Goodyear Akron, and being on his mettle to prove that youngsters from Brazil could take their full part in industry, not only won the Litchfield Medal but made one of the highest grades on the Flying Squadron ever made since it started in 1914.

He returned to the Brazil factory on staff work before graduation, but on the night that his class received their diplomas at Akron, the organization was called together at Sao Paulo and as a surprise to both men, Fred Andrews presented the medal and diploma to his son. He became a division superintendent at Sao Paulo in 1948.

Other Brazilians held key posts in sales, factory and operating.

A Plant in Mexico

Manufacturing started in Mexico City right after Pearl Harbor. The reasons went well back.

Goodyear had sold tires in Mexico since 1917, at first with salesmen travelling from the States, then with a branch in Mexico City. It had an excellent business there for years and its products had a good reputation.

But the depression of the 1930's hit other countries as well as the United States. In Chile, long an important market, the depression coincided with the shrinking of the country's great nitrate market. Harrington, the manager, was called into Akron, and when restrictions were put on money leaving the country in 1932, Manning, the office manager, who had carried on, closed up the branch, went to Mexico City.

Conditions were no better there. Competition had grown extremely difficult. German and Japanese companies were active. One American company had arranged with a Mexican factory to build tires under its name in exchange for technical counsel. Two other American companies made manufacturing arrangements, and these got the principal share of what business there was, since Goodyear had to pay duty on goods it imported into Mexico.

Seals Morgan, the manager, came into Akron in 1936 and again Manning, the office manager, took over, found himself running virtually a two-man branch. The other man was George Olbert, born in

Mexico City, his father being an engineer with Cannanea Copper Company in the north. For some time the branch kept its head above water chiefly on what mechanical goods could be sold, with Manning getting the hint from Akron that any time the business went into the red he was to turn the key in the door and close up shop.

The two men divided up office work as well as sales, made up balance sheets and monthly statements, did everything but sweep out. They held things together, but it was a tight squeak. One month saw a profit of only $200.

Conditions began to pick up with defense production. Olbert went to Chile, was succeeded by McNair, a Texan, who had spent most of his life in Mexico. Then McNair moved to Chile, as Olbert came into Akron, and Hart became the salesman.

Conditions continued to improve. Other American industries were coming in. The city was growing. Mexico and Canada were America's two next door neighbors, and the great republic to the south had important resources in minerals, cattle, oil, sugar and coffee, a great potential market, where Goodyear products had stood well in the past. It was time for the company to do something if it was to recover its position—probably a factory.

There were four tire factories in Mexico, three of them with American connections. The country had a "saturation law," under which the government could limit the number of companies in any field, to prevent wasteful competition. One company, Mexican owned, might provide entryway.

That company, called Oxo, had been started a dozen years before to make tires and heels. It was a struggling concern, short of capital and modern equipment. The superintendent, Mexican-born Henry Schmid, had spent five years at the Goodyear factory at Los Angeles, and picked up further ideas from technical salesmen who called on him.

Negotiations for the purchase of Oxo were instituted by Vice President Leroy, and in January, 1942, Goodyear took over.

Things moved fast after that. Tube manufacturing was added, with molds and vulcanizing equipment brought in from the States. No extruding machines were available, so the factory went back to the older process of rolling the tubes on mandrels, built locally under its direction.

With business picking up, the mining companies found a need for high-pressure air drill hose, industrial water hose, conveyor and transmission belting. Government controls went in, due to the rubber shortage, and equipment from the States became hard to get because of the mounting war effort across the border. Production of heels was discon-

New plants built during the war in Mexico City, above, and Lima, Peru, below, helped maintain internal economy of those countries.

ational interest in razil's first tire fac- ry shown by Presi- ent Vargas' visit to ant, where Manag- g Director Long ex- ains manufacturing ocesses.

tinued, and that equipment changed over to mechanical goods, the hose now being rolled on a mandrel like tubes, other equipment being improvised locally. Tire production was stepped up from the initial 50-60 tires a day to better than 100. Realizing the importance of the little company's contribution to its needs the Mexican government allowed three tire molds and a belt press to come in.

Mexico, like other nations in the hemisphere, was seeking to conserve its rubber and keep its cars and trucks in operation. Rubber Reserve established an office there to get in natural rubber and presently synthetic.

The Oxo plant outgrew its facilities and a new site was found in Lecheria, 19 miles out in the country on an old cattle ranch. Production was continued in town while the new factory was going up. It got in full production shortly before the war ended.

Mexico City was booming, would become one of the great cities of the hemisphere, with two and a half million people. The new location was in the dairy country (the word "Lecheria" means dairy) with ample labor supply at hand. The old ranch house with its high wall and bullet-scarred watch tower (for revolutions had been fought in the area), its patio and quarters for cattle and poultry within the enclosure, was cut up into apartments for factory men. Two railroads paralleled the property. There was ample water supply at 300 feet for cooling purposes. The power company built a sub-station nearby, ran a line out to the plant, under an arrangement by which the company would pay the cost of putting it in, and get credit in its power bills. Other manufacturing industries—steel, aluminum, electrical, automotive—followed the power line out, created a flourishing industrial settlement.

A few of the best workmen and supervisors went along to the new plant. Schmid went to Akron to study manufacturing operations in the States. The new plant opened July 25, 1945, with a capacity of 450 tires a day, but soon had to increase this to 800, with a wide range of sizes, opened a complete line of mechanical goods, soles and heels.

Mexico provided opportunity for several individuals. Speakman, development man from Jackson, who had gone there as a technical consultant, died suddenly and his replacement, Perren, also from Jackson, became superintendent. Schmid and Ruston, of the Squadron, became assistant superintendents.

Manning became president of Goodyear Mexico, brought in Olbert and MacNair, his assistants in the lean years, as sales manager and assistant for mechanical goods. Hart took the Monterey branch, and Aguilar, who started as a company truck driver and knew his city intimately, became manager of the Mexico City branch. Raymond, secretary-treasurer, had long experience in Latin America, particularly in the Caribbean.

With the new Lecheria plant in full operation, the company was turning out five times as much product by 1948 as it had the first year. Branches were set up at six strategic points over the country, and Goodyear-Mexico, manned by young, hard-hitting executives who had gone through hard times together, drove ahead fast.

Mexico City had become a great metropolis. Its manufacturing industries were marked by two contrasting elements, that of the small shops and stores around the public squares, some dating back to the Aztec or early Indian days, alongside the huge developments of large-scale business. Modernistic buildings went up as business houses, banking and importing sought a foothold in this important commercial center.

Goodyear in Peru

Like scores of factories built during the war in the United States, Goodyear's fourth Latin American plant, opened at Lima, Peru, late in 1942, was a war plant.

World War II was a struggle of economic resources as well as men. Peru had a wealth of minerals important to the war effort, needed rubber tires, belting and hose, which up to this it had imported largely from the States. But now the nation was moving to procure rubber from its vast jungle territory beyond the Andes. Why not build tires in Peru, save that much shipping?

Goodyear, as the leading American rubber company operating in South America, was glad to take on this responsibility. It had done business in Peru for years. Its tires carried cars and trucks over the tortuous roads into the Andes. Its conveyor belting was used in many mining operations. Its distributor in Peru, Eduardo Dibos, was an important figure in business and the government, had been Mayor of Lima and a leader in the Trans-American Highway movement. He had long urged the building of a factory, and now war needs gave new weight to his arguments.

Under the Washington Agreement, Peru agreed to limit its own rubber needs to 428 tons a year, turn the rest over to the general war effort. Careful calculations were made. The country could get along on 10,000 new passenger tires a year, put the rest of the rubber into truck tires.

That would make 16,000 truck tires a year. Building and equipment were planned on that basis.

A location was found just outside the city, on the highway built by the Incas to the harbor town of Callao. Uhrich went out from the Engineering Department at Akron to construct the building. It was designed in the typical architecture of the country, with a high wall around it. Enough land was acquired to take care of expansion if that proved necessary. Ground was broken in September, 1942, for a building 300 feet long by 75 feet deep.

There were the usual difficulties in getting in machinery and equipment, despite the aid of American and Peruvian governments, and a complete stoppage occurred in September—due, as they learned later, to the diverting of all possible shipping to the North African invasion.

However, the rest of the machinery arrived in the spring of 1943, the first tire was built in June and a big ceremonial opening took place in July. Litchfield, Hinshaw and Oseland came on from Akron. President Prado with his cabinet attended the opening as did many members of the diplomatic corps and the business and industrial leaders of the country. The Archbishop of Lima gave his blessing to the enterprise.

Dibos became managing director of the Peruvian company, and Argentina furnished most of the key men—Gagnon, the superintendent, who had spent eight years in Canada and 12 in Buenos Aires; Pruessman, the sales manager, a UCLA graduate who joined Goodyear in California, spent seven years in Argentina; Dunwiddie, the secretary-treasurer, who had gone to Buenos Aires in 1934 after banking and industrial experience in Akron.

Peru gave Joe Reece a chance to settle down after many miles of Goodyear travel. A North Carolinian who had joined the company in 1920 and gone on the Engineering Squadron, he had helped start production in England, Gadsden, Java, Jackson and Sweden. He served as a foreman at Aircraft, went to Brazil as a foreman, became production superintendent in Lima.

The factory quickly built up to capacity, and when synthetic became available in 1944, was enlarged to permit truck tire production to be doubled, without going beyond the allotment of 428 tons of crude rubber. Further additions were made after the war, building capacity up to nearly 300 tires a day, treble the original output. The factory gave steady employment to labor, put Peruvian rubber to good use.

The decoration of the Order of the Sun was bestowed on Mr. Litchfield in 1948, in recognition of his contribution to the economic life of the nation, through setting up the Lima factory. This order was created by General San Martin, the Latin-American liberator, in 1821.

In becoming part of the industrial life of Peru, Goodyear found itself in a new and interesting environment. Peru and Mexico had much in common, great mineral wealth in gold and silver and important agricultural resources. Well before the discovery of America, the two countries had the largest population in the hemisphere, with the Mayas, Aztecs and Incas building up a high level of civilization. The wealth in these sections attracted the interest of the Spanish, and Cortez and Pizarro founded great colonial empires.

Lima was a great city before any other in North or South America, was the gateway to Argentina. For Spanish colonial policy continued to send traffic across the Isthmus of Panama, and goods must be carried by mules and llamas and on men's backs over the Andes to Argentina. Lima's churches, haciendas and its San Marco University are among the oldest in the Americas.

"O Lima!" . . . exclaimed a contemporary writer. "How many shape gold and silver in the shops of Milan and Sevilla, how many work linen in France, how many loads of wool are carded in England and Ireland; how many weave labyrinthine rolls of gold cloth and Flanders lace; how much delicate glass from Barcelona and Venice; how many Belgian and Roman engravers work metal sheets and presses; how many carpets are designed in Cairo and filigrees in China—tributes you garner in the universal fair of Portobello."

In Lima, now a city of 600,000 people, as in Buenos Aires, Rio de Janeiro, Sao Paulo, Mexico City and other great Latin American cities, the various governments spent millions of dollars after World War I in building stately plazas, broad avenues and Army, Navy and government buildings, often cutting a great boulevard through the business districts, ripping out the narrow streets of the early years, sometimes turning three narrow streets into one very wide one, sometimes having to jog around a cathedral or historical building. Modern business blocks went up as American, Canadian and European industry showed increasing interest in the South American markets, giving a modern touch to the Spanish and Portuguese atmosphere.

Lima offers a good example of this, a modern city built against the background of old ruins "like tombs smothered with roses, jasmine and daisies."

The topography of Peru divides the country into three sections, each radically different from the others. Paralleling the ocean the length of the country is a flat shelf, 60 to 100 miles wide crossed by rivers leading from the mountains and producing long-staple cotton, sugar, cattle and orchard crops in the valleys. Lima lies along one of those rivers, and the Humboldt current off the Pacific gives the city a cool, comfortable climate despite its nearness to the Equator.

Beyond the lowlands lie the Andes, where 60 per cent of the population of the country still lives and makes its living, with a few highways and a railroad out of Lima scaling the heights through tortuous passes and tunnels—and a new highway to the interior built during the war.

Beyond the mountains lies the tropical jungle of the upper Amazon.

Events in Australia

Goodyear Australia had an uphill job throughout the war, mostly as a result of its location on the world map, and its strategic position in the war itself.

After the Japs swung through the Netherlands Indies in early 1942, it looked as if Australia would be their next objective. New Guinea, across the channel to the north, was overrun that summer, except the key city of Port Moresby—and when the situation was most critical, the Allied forces could do least about it. The Americans had lost the Philippines, Britain had lost Singapore, and Australia itself had lost most of its fleet in the gallant retreating naval warfare off the northern coast.

But Japan waited until it could fortify the islands it had taken, and the danger passed. MacArthur built up his land and air forces, struck back into New Guinea in September, drove the enemy back across the Owen Stanley range by the end of the year. Australian troops saw service in many theaters of the war, but their homeland was safe.

Some Jap reconnaissance planes flew over Sydney, shells were thrown into the city from a large submarine, and four small two-man subs attacked a naval base and a munitions ship in Sydney Harbor—but were destroyed when the U. S. cruiser Chicago and Australian patrol boats dropped depth charges. That was all that the country saw of the war first hand. Army headquarters were moved north to Brisbane in late 1942 as the Allies took the offensive.

If the Allied forces could not spare much military equipment to Australia when that nation was threatened, its defense grew less important once the danger of invasion passed. It was on its own after that, must take care of its own needs. And the very remoteness of its geographical location, and the shortage of shipping to bring in goods and machinery it normally imported from England or the States, proved a continuous challenge to the ingenuity of the country. Goodyear was a part of that.

Australia raised wheat, cattle, sheep, could feed itself, but clothing was rationed and gasoline very strictly. The Allied nations (Australia like Canada was a full partner in the Empire, made its own separate declaration of war) would pool all their resources, with top emphasis on military requirements.

Australia got some natural rubber during the war from Ceylon, the only remaining source in the British Empire, had to make that do. Synthetic rubber from Canada and the United States did not appear until 1944 because of shipping difficulties. Other materials remained hard to get. Carbon black and other compounds were a continuous headache. The Royal Australian Air Forces, the British Royal Flying Corps and the U. S. Air Forces all wanted rayon, then nylon for airplane tires and fuel tanks, and these were even harder to get in Australia than in the States. The Goodyear factory which pioneered the manufacture in Australia of both vital items, also made wheels and brakes there—but encountered shortages of magnesium for the wheels and steel for the single disc brakes.

Labor was always in short supply, with a high percentage of men going into the armed services, and with communistic influences infiltrating into labor unions in Australia as in the States. Until they were thrown out, the communists managed to prevent the most effective use of what labor supply there was, through slowdowns and work stoppages—and blocked the seven-day work week even when things were at their grimmest.

But the biggest single obstacle was the fact that this war was so highly mechanized, and the intricate machines and machine tools which had been developed elsewhere over the world had to be shipped to Australia over thousands of miles of danger-infested waters. The loss of a single vital machine part in a ship torpedoed enroute could disrupt carefully-laid production plans.

Even technical information took long to get through. It took six weeks to two months to get drawings and specifications across the Pacific, and by the time the information reached Sydney things might have changed widely. New types of tires came in, new processes were found, new materials used. Even Akron, with all its facilities, encountered grave difficulties in the use of synthetic. Australian industries had to use their fullest resourcefulness to substitute, to improvise, build home-made equipment.

With this lag in communication the U. S. Army finally took action.

Why take Ceylon rubber for instance half way around the world to Ohio to be made into bullet-seal tanks, then ship those tanks back to Australia? Why not build them there? Goodyear was the only American company with a factory in that country and was the leader in the fuel tank field.

Wright Field talked to Akron, and presently Harold Martin, foreman of the department, was flown out to Australia to start fuel tank production. After that quite a bit of technical information on tires, and on synthetic rubber was flown out by Wright Field in packets addressed to the Commanding General, who relayed it on to the factory.

In view of all these difficulties the Australian plant did an outstanding production job, almost doubled its prewar output, proved highly useful to the country, and to the American forces stationed there.

It did not turn out as many tires as Akron, of course, but had practically as many types and sizes to handle. It built the run-flat combat tires, airplane tires, mud-snow tires, added twelve new sizes of truck tires up to the big 18-inch size.

The fact that Goodyear had built an industrial rubber goods plant in Australia ten years before proved fortunate as well, for that division turned out a large quantity of armored hose, oil hose, V-belts, tank linings, made all the bogie tires for the tanks, took over the fuel tank job after Martin set it up, built thousands of feet of stirrup pump hose for the Australians to pump water, in case the city was bombed and fires broke out.

Industrial Rubber Goods got one unusual assignment early in the war. Garden Island in Sydney Harbor, half a mile from shore, had long been a naval workshop, and a huge dry dock to extend from there to the shore was projected when the war came. Could rubber hose, resistant to sea water, be built quickly and inexpensively and used instead of steel pipe, to carry water out to the island during the two or three years it would take to build the dock? Maxwell's men came up with a six-inch pipe, 2700 feet long, that would do the job, covering the metal parts with rubber to prevent corrosion.

A small reclaim plant had been built before the war, came in very handy with the critical rubber shortage, had to be doubled in size.

Despite the labor shortage, Goodyear Australia grew from a prewar force of 800 or 900 people to 1500. This included some 350 women, mostly in the fuel tank division, working under special license from the government, which gave the company high priority in labor and material because of the importance of its work. Not more than 35 women had worked in the factory previously.

Reconversion after the war ended came on more slowly than in other parts of the world because of the losses of shipping. It was late in 1946 before natural rubber came in in adequate supply. With a big demand for tires as gasoline became available to civilians, the factory built up production in 1947 to a point 76 per cent higher than its biggest prewar year, and further additions had to be made to the plant, giving 40,000 more square feet of floor space.

Many of the American personnel returned to the States in the next few years after the war, including Starrett and Mears of Production, and Slay of Purchasing. Mears had returned in 1937 but went back in 1940 to relieve Reynolds on home leave and had to stay there, since Reynolds could not get back. Moorhead was the only one of the original group still in Australia in 1948.

Other men who had gone out later and served during the war, returned afterward, including Meiser of Personnel, Maxwell of Mechanical Goods and McGrath of Development. But for the six Americans who came back, only three men went out as replacements. Reese, who had gone to Gadsden in 1929 with the Squadron to help start production and stayed on, went to Sydney in late 1945 as production superintendent. Rossiter, another Squad man, went out a little later as division superintendent, and Gharki from the Swedish plant became purchasing agent.

Australia experience helped everyone who served there and the "alumni" are still loyal to that country. Reynolds went to Aircraft as a division foreman on his return to Akron, headed the Akron synthetic rubber plant, then became a superintendent in Chemical Products. Bennett, the treasurer, came back to be assistant treasurer of Aircraft, then the parent company. Meiser became manager of Efficiency, Starrett and Mears went into Production, Reed of Advertising became assistant manager of all Export Advertising. Blank, one of the original group, took an important post in Development.

Steiner became managing director of Goodyear Australia when the veteran Kither died in 1944.

Wartime Summary

Measure of Goodyear's war production may be seen in the annual sales figures. A business of 217 million in 1940 went to 330 million in 1941, to 451 million in 1942, to 726 million in 1943, to 786 million in 1944, dropped with cancellations to 716 million in 1945.

War taxes held the net earnings, however, to 3.9 per cent in 1941, 3.2 per cent in 1942, 2 per cent in 1943, 1.9 per cent in 1944, 2.1 per cent in 1945, and refinancing was necessary after the war to provide working capital for a larger volume of business done at higher cost for labor and materials.

Employment, world-wide, went to 107,000 during the war peak of 1944, leveled off to 75,000 in 1948, of which 55,000 was domestic.

A total of 26,197 men from world-wide Goodyear served in the armed forces. Only 265 of them lost their lives. From the tire plant at Akron went 4886 employees, of whom 3087 returned to find their jobs waiting for them—and more than 6000 GI's who had not worked for the company before were given employment.

Fifteen different Goodyear plants won the Army-Navy "E" (for Excellence) out of the thousands of war plants—less than five per cent of the American industries received this award. The Charlestown powder plant was the first, in September, 1940, and repeated each year, getting five stars. Plant III got the award early for its work in gas masks. Arizona Aircraft was another of the early ones to win recognition, followed by St. Marys, Kelly-Springfield, Gadsden, all four of the cotton mills, Cedartown, Cartersville, Rockmart and Decatur. Goodyear Aircraft was given its award just after the war ended.

BOOK

3

Postwar Developments

Industry's wartime experience used to
strengthen economy in peace time

Bronze tablet in Goodyear Hall pays tribute to the thousands of employes who served in the armed forces during the war, and the 149 from Akron—including two women—who did not return.

21. The Need for Tires

Huge Building Program

GOODYEAR had to move fast after VJ-Day to close out its war contracts, move out war equipment and get back as quickly as possible to its main job of making tires—and industrial rubber goods—to meet clamorous demands from the public.

For nearly four years car owners had had to drive slowly, repair their tires as treads wore smooth, make them last. They did stretch the supply farther than anyone would have thought possible, but tires will not last forever no matter how carefully driven. Now with the war over everyone wanted new tires. And the automobile manufacturers needed five for each new car. Large tires, too, were needed everywhere, for trucks, buses, farm tractors, cargo airplanes and grading machinery.

In the next three strenuous years the company spent $100 millions in modernizing and expanding its factories, at home and abroad, used every trick in its manufacturing experience to arrive at maximum output. Business recovery, in industry, commerce, mining, agriculture, logging and construction work, was tied up directly with transportation, and in America transportation meant rubber, as well as steel and electric power.

It took some time to catch up with the accumulated demand. Old tires continued to wear out as fast as new ones were built. Early estimates as to how long it would take proved optimistic, despite the fact that war needs had already increased production facilities in America by nearly 40 per cent.

However by the spring of 1948 the industry did begin to catch up—though many other essential consumer goods were still in short supply and would remain so.

The company turned out 100 million tires between August, 1939, and December, 1946. By contrast it had taken 20 years to build its first 25 million, that total being reached in June, 1919, and eight years more to reach its first hundred million, in April, 1927, nearly 30 years after the company started in business. But the curve moved upward after that, reached 200 million in September, 1932, 300 million as the war started in Europe, 400 million after the war ended and reached the 450 million mark in September, 1948, in time for the 50th anniversary homecoming.

Tire prices remained approximately at prewar levels, despite higher labor costs. Quality continued upward. Improvements in tires for civilians, for which there was no time during the war, got under way, the most spectacular result being the Super-Cushion tire of 1947.

Industrial rubber goods, though turning out record output during the war, went up instead of down after the war ended, as hundreds of civilian items ruled as non-essential came back with public demand, and the factory started with empty shelves.

Mechanical rubber goods indeed took a new turn with a dramatic project launched in 1949—namely, to run a dual line of conveyor belting clear across Ohio from Lake Erie to the river, to carry coal north and ore south. A "rubber railroad" should result in impressive savings in transportation—and cheaper steel.

Though airplane production, too, was cut way back after VJ-Day, Goodyear was well-entrenched in aeronautics. The company continued its interest in lighter-than-air, including the big passenger and cargo carrying airships. There were other technical and business developments. It looked at new lines of business, including housing. Foreign operations came back in full swing with a glance also at the strategically important Alaskan territory. Synthetic rubber presented a problem as the plantations came back.

Some of these developments call for further discussion.

Synthetic Rubber

The question of what to do about synthetic rubber once the supply of natural rubber was back to normal, came up soon after the war.

It was no problem at first. With the dammed-up demand for tires and other rubber goods America used both natural and synthetic rubber, every pound it could get. American consumption, which stood at 651,000 long tons in 1940, went up after the war, reached the million mark in 1946, continued upward to 1,122,000 long tons in 1947. Part of this grew out of the emergency demand, but there were indications that America would continue to use more rubber than it had before.

British plantations got back into production much earlier than those in the Dutch possessions, where the political situation held things back. With conditions stabilized the plantations presumably could supply the world with all the rubber it needed. But the United States could supply a considerable part of its own needs with synthetic. The world did not need the full capacity of both the plantations and the synthetic factories, could not absorb both.

Would America make its own rubber or buy it?

Rubber, often a subject of world controversy, came up again for discussion in Congress, in the press, and in industry, here and overseas. Leaders of the industry were called to Washington to give their views.

The problem had conflicting phases. Plantation rubber was important to the economy of Britain and the Netherlands, and consequently to world recovery. On the other hand America had put upwards of a billion dollars into synthetic manufacturing facilities, and no one wanted to throw that out the window. The plants were good insurance against another emergency, and in any event their output would be needed until the plantations were fully restored.

So the government decided to keep controls on for the time being, with natural rubber still pegged at 22½ cents and synthetic at 18½. Synthetic production was cut back, some plants being closed and put in standby status. Each rubber manufacturer had to use a specified percentage of synthetic. The plants operated by Goodyear at Los Angeles and Houston were continued on somewhat reduced schedules, the smaller government plant at Akron being closed.

The country had used 781,000 tons of rubber in 1941, of which an almost negligible 6000 tons was synthetic. Consumption of natural rubber went sharply down and synthetic up after that until the end of the war, when the figures reversed themselves, albeit more gradually, as shown by the following table:

YEAR	NATURAL	SYNTHETIC	TOTAL
1945	105,000	694,000	799,000
1946	278,000	762,000	1,040,000
1947	563,000	559,000	1,122,000
1948	623,000	450,000	1,073,000

A rubber-hungry world was getting all the rubber it needed, with synthetic averaging 55 per cent of the total, ranging from 73 per cent in 1946 to 42 per cent in 1948.

Controls on natural rubber were released on April 1, 1947. What happened thereafter was significant. There was still not enough natural rubber to go around, as the table shows. It might be several years before the plantations could produce enough, since Dutch output was still retarded. The price of rubber varies with supply and demand. If synthetic had not been on hand to fill the gap, the price of rubber would have skyrocketed to a dollar a pound and over—and with black market operations on top of that. This country had paid $1.25 a pound 20 years earlier under the artificial shortage created by the Stevenson Act.

But the synthetic plants had not been closed down at the war's end. Natural rubber, left to find its own price level, fluctuated for a time, down to 14 cents, up to 25, but leveled off at around 19 cents—only slightly above the price of synthetic.

As between dollar rubber and 20 cent rubber the saving to the American buyers of tires and other rubber goods was estimated by Mr. Litchfield in a formal statement in February, 1949, at $100 millions a month, or a total of $2 billions up to that time.

Synthetic rubber was responsible for those savings. It had served the world well in a great emergency. Now it also proved to be a good investment. Moreover, the world was using more rubber than it had ever done—even after war shortages were met. Low prices invite wider public use.

Supply is flexible in the case of a manufactured product, can easily be cut down or increased—which is not true of plantation rubber. Synthetic costs, too, were coming down. These ran as high as 30 and 40 cents at first, reflecting emergency construction and the need to discover efficient methods. But costs had ranged downward even during the war, and with the less efficient plants closed afterward, got much below the pegged figure of 18½ cents.

Quality, also, had improved. The chemical engineers had stayed on the job, and the development of low-temperature polymerization, the so-called "cold rubber," brought better wearing properties, made synthetic more of a general purpose material.

The automobile tire is one of the few postwar articles still selling at prewar price levels—despite rising labor costs. One reason for that result is synthetic rubber.

Looking ahead at the beginning of 1949, it seemed likely that America would continue to produce at least 150,000 pounds of synthetic a year,— and to keep in standby status, ready for action, the capacity to produce up to 600,000 tons when and if necessary to hold the price at stabilized levels.

The Super-Cushion Tire

Passenger tires had seen a long series of improvements in prewar years, along with those in tires for trucks, tractors and airplanes, but with the war over it seemed time to take a fresh look at the whole business, just as was done in 1932. The tire developed in that year had brought the Airwheel principle into passenger tires, but it had also balanced all the factors in materials and design so carefully that the tire had stood unchanged, except for minor improvements, for years. It was time to do this again.

Shively, chief tire designer, sat down with his staff to see what might be done with a tire having still greater air volume, and inflated to still lower pressure,—carry the cushioning principle of the balloon tire and the flotation principle of the Airwheel still further.

The tire they came out with in the summer of 1947, called the Super-Cushion, made an impression on the popular mind as striking as the original balloon tire. It needed only 24 pounds of air pressure, as against the 28 to 32 pounds then used. The least technically-minded car owner could grasp that, and confirm its significance through his own experience. This affected the performance of the car itself, made it almost float over the ground, made small cars ride like big expensive ones.

In that 24 pounds air pressure can be traced the whole history of tire development. The drum-hard tire of 1921, which in the smallest size was inflated to 50 pounds pressure, rode hard, snagged and punctured easily, might blow out when it hit obstacles. Air pressures had come down gradually. Using the smaller size tires as a yardstick, these pressures were reduced to 35 pounds in 1928, to 32 in 1933, to 28 pounds in 1935. Now it was down to 24 pounds.

Other factors in tire design went along with this. The skinny high-wheeled tire of 1921, still looking more like a bicycle tire than one for the automobile, was three inches in cross section, or at most 3½ inches. The volume of air carried in a tire—and air is the real cushioning force —had increased with the larger cross sections, to 4.40 inches in the 1925 balloon tire, to 4.75 in 1929, 5.50 in 1933, six inches in the 6.00-16 of 1932, which quickly became standard on 60 per cent of all automobiles. The new tire was 6¼ inches in cross section, twice as fat as that of 1921.

Though the Super-Cushion had 12½ to 25 per cent more air volume than its predecessor, it was no taller, in fact was two inches shorter than the 1921 tire. The hole in the doughnut had shrunk. That hole in the old 30 x 3 was two feet across and the tire did not remotely suggest a doughnut in appearance. And while the 6.00-16 had an inside diameter of 16 inches, the new tire standardized on a 15 inch diameter in all sizes. Also the new tire rode on a wider rim. The 1921 rim was 1.76 inches wide, the new one was 4½ inches across.

What are the advantages of the lower-pressure, greater-air-volume principle brought out in the new tire? It cushioned the load better. The wheel did not bounce up as it hit an obstruction. The softer tire absorbed the jar, did not pass it on to the semi-stiff bead of the tire, nor to the shock absorbers or the frame of the car. There were fewer rattles, and rattles mean that a mechanical part is working loose.

The new tire lessened wear and tear on the car itself. And for the same reason it lessened wear and tear on the driver, particularly on a long cross-country trip. It had steadier, more positive steering control at all speeds, on good or bad roads, on turns—gave the driver a feeling of security—which many felt was the most important feature.

Two, a softer tire which gives and absorbs a blow rather than resisting it, is less likely to puncture, to cut or blow out. Such a tire also distributes the stresses of the flexing of rubber and fabric in the carcass over that much wider an area, makes tires last longer, since it heats up less, and internal heat due to flexing is the long enemy of any tire, shortens its normal life. The new tire would take hold and pull better on a rough highway, and the flotation principle of the early airplane tire applied here as well, improved its traction.

Throughout the development of the Super-Cushion Goodyear engineers worked closely with the automobile engineers, found rising enthusiasm as results became apparent. One car manufacturer stopped midway in his tooling-up, made changes in the design of his new car to enable it fully to utilize the advantages of the Super-Cushion.

As the principles to be embodied in the tire were fully worked out, a comprehensive testing program was set up. The tires were tried out on smooth super highways and rough country roads, over the desert, mountains and winding roads, at 35 miles per hour and at 100 miles per hour, put in millions of miles in testing before they were released to the market.

The development men must see too that the larger tires would fit present wheels, for car owners wanting them as replacements, and check its use with LifeGuards. It was well they did so, because the new tire, once announced, got an unusual reception from the public as well as from the car manufacturers.

It was formally announced in a series of newspapers advertisements in August, 1947 and followed up in the magazines, with the result that the company had to build 3½ million Super-Cushions in the next six months to meet the demand.

As had happened many times before, the rest of the industry followed, swung over to the 24 pound air pressure tire.

Postwar Sales

Passenger tires, like new cars, all but went off the market when the war broke out, bringing sharp challenge to the ingenuity of the nation's tire dealers.

Many of them closed up shop, turned their stock of tires over to the government. But there was still business to be had by men who went after it, intelligently and aggressively. The great majority of dealers stayed in business and came through in a stronger position than before.

With a devastating shortage of rubber, the supply on hand must be made to go as far as possible. The biggest supply was that on the cars of private owners, on trucks, buses, farm tractors, mining and construction vehicles. The individual car owner was not at all sure that he could get a new tire as his old ones wore out, so he must take the best possible care of them.

America's tire dealers faced a new responsibility. Tire maintenance meant driving carefully, but it also meant balancing tires, rotating them, keeping proper wheel alignment and proper brake action, and as tires wore down meant repairing, recapping, retreading. These were things alert dealers thoroughly understood, whose importance they had long preached and now were in a position to prove.

The results were amazing. Tires gave mileage greater than ever thought possible, and as a result the American people were able to drive their own cars throughout the war—something that happened in no other country—and with minimum draft on the slender stock of tires allocated to the public.

This result was a tribute to the increased sturdiness built into tires, but it was also a tribute to the service given by the tire dealers of the country, working to give the public the fullest possible mileage—a service which paid off to the public and to the dealer.

There was also a considerable volume of new tire sales, to truck and bus operators, farmers, contractors and individuals engaged in essential war work. As the necessity was shown, the government released tires to the manufacturer to be sold to the public through the dealer.

Tire dealers who recognized their responsibility to the country came through the war in good shape.

Affecting the situation, also, was a new development in merchandising, which started before the war and became exceedingly important during that period and afterward.

NEW MERCHANDISING TRENDS

To have the best merchandising program in the industry was something Stadelman, Rockhill and Wilson had sought continuously since the early years. District managers and salesmen worked closely with the growing army of dealers on matters of location, identification, store layout, advertising, display, credits, collections, and later budget selling —and always service.

Tire retailing was still a young business in 1920, compared to groceries and drug stores. Big dealers had impressive and well-operated establishments, but the typical medium-sized dealer was likely to be located in a narrow store building, often in the middle of the block. He might have a gas pump and air line at the curb, a Goodyear sign painted on his window or projecting over the sidewalk. There were long counters and tire racks inside. He tried to get a location with an alley alongside, so that his customers could drive through to the back for service, and failing that sometimes built a driveway through his store, front to back.

But as automobile registration grew and traffic increased, there was soon no room for the car owner to stop for gas or tire service. Ambitious dealers sought better quarters.

Company stores came in during the 1920's, giving the manufacturer opportunity to experiment widely on plans to improve distribution. Goodyear hired architects to design service stations which would give maximum convenience in sales and service and be inviting in appearance, since a good looking building costs little more than an ugly one—and soon pays for itself.

The new stations were not built flush with the sidewalk, but set well back, with a generous-sized service court in front, room for the car owner to drive in. The buildings were identified with blue and gold Goodyear colors, so that a man well-served by his Goodyear dealer at home would be apt to look for a Goodyear sign when he was on a trip.

Building plans were made available to dealers in some 20 different designs, covering various conditions, and men from the Engineering Department were assigned to assist dealers wanting to remodel their place, or erect a new one.

Gasoline filling stations and car dealers followed the same line, and gradually the automobile began to change the face of Main Street in hundreds of cities.

Chain stores were coming in now in every field of retail business, including tires, to challenge the position of the independent dealer. Goodyear, in a position to study the methods of hundreds of dealers and with its stores as testing laboratories, could help. The program was strengthened. The engineers developed still more attractive store fronts with better lighting, bigger windows, effective paint jobs. Porcelain enamel fronts came in. The Advertising Department created standard window displays with timely and seasonal messages, package displays which were changed regularly, it developed poster boards for the service courts, sent identification crews out over the country, wrote mailing pieces and newspaper advertising copy. Dealer meetings in every district became forums on sales, service, advertising, display, operating methods.

However a new factor was coming in and growing more important. Better tires, giving longer mileage, were a boon to the public but had the effect that people came in less frequently to buy new ones. Tire dealers had long used gas and oil sales, lubrication and tire service to keep in touch with the public and add revenue, but things took a striking new turn late in the 1930's—one in keeping with changing trends in merchandising.

Tire dealers began to take on new lines of goods—accessories for the automobile, and electrical and other supplies for the home, things they knew and could service. They put in electric washing machines and refrigerators, electric irons, fans, heaters, mixers, razors, clocks, also radios, bicycles, lawn mowers, outboard motors, golf clubs, tennis rackets, ice skates, aluminum ware and snow shovels.

Company stores pioneered this field and put Goodyear in a position to give important help to its dealers.

This brought in many new problems, and the Sales Department concluded in 1940 that it was time to take a fresh look at the whole business of mass merchandising, brought in Vernon H. Jones from Chicago, who had had broad experience in that field, to direct the study.

Department stores, handling thousands of different items, had long since found it necessary to give scientific study to arrangement and display. But a tire dealer in a town of 5000 people had no such experience to draw on, nor could he afford to hire specialists who did have it.

Could a manufacturer work out a program, applicable to large, small and medium-sized dealers which would give them the advantages found in mass merchandising?

It was definitely an innovation for a manufacturer to try to do this for independent dealers who owned their own business. The tire dealer was an individualist, his money and his future were tied up in his store. No one could tell him how to run it.

However, the dealer-manufacturer connection at Goodyear was close and of long standing, and the dealers with whom Jones and his men talked were soon convinced that the company was honestly seeking to find a formula which would improve their sales volume and profit position.

The study went into the practices of dealers who had long marketed tires successfully, and also into those of department stores and chain stores, to see what principles might be adapted to this situation. The World War came along to interrupt the program, but made the need even more urgent. The study was pretty well worked out by 1943. Associated Merchandising, covering lines other than tires, became a major division of Sales under Harper, who had been salesman, independent dealer, district manager, advertising manager and division sales manager. Store Planning and advertising were tied in to enable dealers to cash in on post war demands for tires—and consequent readjustments after immediate needs had been met.

The end of the war released some 20,000 square feet of space on the top floor of Goodyear Hall and the Visual Merchandising Laboratory, as it was called, was opened there. Model stores were laid out, a large store, a small one, a gasoline filling station, and a modern repair shop.

The Merchandising Laboratory was opened in October, 1945, and brought in marketing experts, men from the university schools of business administration, business writers and after that a steady stream of dealers and college students. An innovation in tire distribution, the laboratory continued to attract widespread attention over the country, got important recognition in 1948 by an award made to Jones by the American Marketing Association for his "contribution to the advancement of the science of merchandising—setting a pattern for coordinated merchandising efforts of manufacturers and dealers."

Goodyear dealers throughout the USA were quick to recognize the merchandising value of the program, and to put it into effect in their own stores.

THE DEALER ORGANIZATION

We might meet some of these Goodyear dealers, a cross section of tire distribution in the United States. It is a colorful group of men, in the great cities, the county seat towns and the cross roads all over America, shrewd New Englanders, hardy Middle Westerners, Texans in ten-gallon hats, men from the mining country, the big woods, the corn belt, the cotton belt and the Pacific Northwest.

Many of them built up a business of $100,000 a year in Goodyear merchandise alone, and some ran up to half a million. Thousands of them have found in tires the opportunity to establish a business of their own, become independent, leaders in their community.

Many of them have handled Goodyear tires year after year, in some cases as long as they have been in business. Every one of the 46 districts has accounts on its books which go back more than 30 years. There are 800 dealers with 25 years of association with the company, and 15,000 who have handled its goods for a decade or longer.

One of the first accounts signed up by G. M. Stadelman when he came to Goodyear in 1902 was Philip Lebzelter & Sons at Lancaster, Penna., who had started making farm wagons for that rich farming country back in 1856, built Conestoga covered wagons for westward bound pioneers. Stadelman sold them a big order for carriage tires.

Changing with the times from carriage rubber to automobile, farm and truck tires, Lebzelter is still an important Goodyear account 48 years later, an unbroken manufacturer-dealer relationship unusual in business.

Out in San Angelo, Texas, Henry Ragsdale started a trading post in 1904, went into tires five years later, converting his wagon yard into a service yard, became the largest tire dealer in west Texas, director of the big bank, and a member of the Upper Colorado River Authority.

Up in New England William A. Rowe, champion high-wheel bicycle racer, took on Goodyear tires in 1908 as the Harper Garage, and 40 years later, at 84, was still active in the business, had just modernized his four attractive places at Beverly and Salem, Massachusetts.

There are scores of success stories among these dealers, men who started as mechanics, repair men, blacksmiths, farm boys handy with tools—opening up in hole-in-the-wall shops and winding up with impressive frontages on Main Street. The growing use of truck tires and farm tires brought in opportunities in every community.

Fifty years is a long time and many of the early dealers have passed on or retired, with the business carried on by sons or nephews or employees, though usually retaining the original company name for the good will value it had in the community—and still handling Goodyear tires.

In hundreds of cities the Goodyear dealer is the principal tire dealer in his community. The Rockhill principle has paid off well, both to the tire dealers and the company, namely that Goodyear was not so much concerned about how many tires it could sell to a dealer as in seeing him succeed, grow strong. For if he did the company would benefit.

Another fundamental principle went along with that, that a dealer's success rested on service to the public. "Whatever helps the consumer would help the dealers and help Goodyear."

The company tried always to have tires for its dealers to sell which were at least as good as any on the market, and to bring out new ones from time to time which were better—the balloon tire, the LifeGuard, the farm tire and the earth mover.

The dealer picked up from there, with emphasis on service. The successful dealer was more interested in giving his customers trouble-free mileage than in getting a repair job—and ready to get up in the middle of the night and drive long miles to take care of a customer in trouble.

Many others dealers started in business in the decade after 1910, as automobile ownership began to climb. Up in New England are firms like G. F. Blake at Worcester, automotive pioneer, and Harrie J. Rowe in Marlboro, who started in the tire business when he came back from the first world war.

In the New York area are big Dick McDonough (1913) at Newark, champion shot-putter in his day, taking part in the Olympic games, Tom Lane, who started in Jersey City a little later, as did Frank Van Syckle at Perth Amboy. Bergin and Zaager at New York City also started in 1913. These are all large-volume dealers. In the same era an ambitious immigrant boy decided while enroute to this country that he would pick an American name, easier to pronounce than the one he was born with. As the boat steamed into the harbor, the Brooklyn Bridge loomed in the skyline. He asked its name.

"That's me from now on," he decided.

Abe Brooklyn, the big tire dealer of Passaic, New Jersey for 30 years, passed away in 1948.

Swing over into Pennsylvania and you will find W. F. Price & Son at Reading (1913), Kitsee at Wilkes Barre, the Automobile Supply Company at Hazeltown, and the Ellsworth Case Service at Easton, which opened up in a blacksmith shop in 1909, was operated for some years by Mrs. Case and more recently by C. C. Rice who went to work there as a repair man after World War I.

R. E. Allen & Son had been selling Goodyear tires for more than 30 years at Cortland, New York, and in the Baltimore area we meet such veterans as Kunkle at Belair and R. D. Grier & Sons at Salisbury.

Long service dealers in the south include Dan Wexler at Johnson City, Tennessee, who built up a large-size business in a relatively small town, McMillan and Cameron in Wilmington, N. C., McCracken in Raleigh and Henderson, and Thibaut & Livingston at Jacksonville, big names throughout the section. Short's Tire Service at Louisville has long been headed by Ed Altsheler, one of the leading citizens of the city.

In Lancaster, Ohio, in a rich farm country like its namesake in Pennsylvania, Herbert Huddle started in 1910, a business now being carried on by his son. One of the biggest outfits in the middle west is Al B. Maier at Chicago.

Other long service dealers in the section are Belsky at Dubuque, Iowa, the Grill Brothers at Jackson, Michigan, Ogiers at North Platte, Nebraska, Wells at Edwardsville, Illinois, Peter Anderson who started in at Lafayette, Indiana, in 1906, Holden at Superior, Wisconsin, who saw the first buses come into existence, carrying miners to the Mesabi Range, and the Stuber Brothers at Winfield, Kansas, who started with John Kirkwood at Wichita, the last of the distributors. Farther west the Schulte Hardware Company at Casper, Wyoming, in the cattle country, was started in 1918, and the Yellowstone Park Company, servicing cars and buses in the great national park, about the same time.

Travelling on west we find Paul Bennett's store at Phoenix, a show place on Automobile Row. In Los Angeles the Hollywood stars take their tire troubles to Vernon Farquhar, who was selling Goodyear tires before the company built a factory there. The big dealer in San Francisco is Kahn & Keville who started in 1913, and across the bay at Oakland, Dempsey and Sanders have long been tire headquarters for the city. Up in Seattle is the Commercial Tire Co. which Alex Gray and Frank Hawkins started years ago, built to large size.

Thousands of these dealers sold Goodyear tires exclusively, except during the late war, when they had to take what tires they could get—as did the company's own stores. The nation's supply was pooled by the government and portioned out regardless of the brand name, with the result that the display rack in a Goodyear dealer's place might have more competitor's tires on it than his own. But they swung back to Goodyear as the supply became normal, with the Super-Cushion to give added impetus to distribution.

SALES ADMINISTRATION

Sales administration continued along the dual lines of Field and Staff, as postwar volume of business fell off only slightly from war peaks of $786 millions in 1944 and $716 millions in 1945, leveled off in peacetime to $616 millions in 1946 and $670 millions in 1947—twice that of the greatest prewar year.

Consumers sales of the company's major products—Tires, Industrial Rubber Goods, Chemical (General) Products, Steel Products and Footwear—reported directly to Vice President Wilson. But tires bulked so large in the company's operations that Mayl had been called in from California to direct their sales under Wilson, taking the title of Vice President of the Goodyear Tire & Rubber Company, Inc., the sales company.

Field sales started with some 400 general line salesmen, and others specializing on truck and tractor tires, as well as warehousing and accounting personnel who worked out of 46 district offices. Two new division managers came in after the war, Fitzgerald at Chicago and Thorp at Los Angeles, to join the veterans McConky at New York, Shepherd at Atlanta, Bailey at Dallas. Sanford took Mayl's place in California. Lohmann, on special work, also reported to Wilson.

Staff functions at Akron were carried on by departments continuously studying the problems of sales to the American car owner, through independent dealers, who formed the biggest group of outlets, doing more than half the nation's business; the gasoline filling stations; car dealers, and the chain stores. Other men handled sales to fleet operators, trucking lines, bus lines, industries, the big stores, taxi companies; others studied the public's changing needs for various types of tires, passenger, farm-tractor, truck, bicycle tires—and there was always the important functions of the service department, to enable car owners to get maximum mileage out of their tires—and with retreading which became important during the war remaining so long after it ended.

So on Mayl's immediate staff were Holt on Tire Sales, Osmun and Metzger on Trade Relations, Miles on company stores, Harper on Associated Merchandise and Pippett on repair materials and camelback. The big tire field under Holt had to be broken down still further, with Zonsius having passenger tires, Fairchild, farm tractor tires, Kemmel, truck tires, Loder, mileage sales, Lewin, dealer problems, Gaylord, petroleum companies, Ammerman on service, and a long list of men in the further ramifications of an always-changing distribution system.

These staff men had come into Akron after long experience in the field, and the company's personnel program called for bringing promising men into the home office to familiarize themselves with staff phases, so as to qualify them for more important duties either at Akron or sales administrative work in the field.

ADVERTISING

Advertising continued under Hough. Goodyear had notably been advertising-minded from its earliest years, and to become a 600 million dollar company in peacetime had to utilize the fullest resources of advertising over its widening line of products. It became one of the important advertisers of the country.

Magazine advertising included not only the big-circulation, popular magazines, read by everyone who bought tires, but must include farm papers, trade papers, aeronautical, construction, petroleum, chemical, automotive, and industrial journals, more than 150 magazines, each calling for copy written directly to the consumer group in question.

Newspaper advertising became more important and called for new technique in retail copy with the broader line of car and home supplies carried by its dealers and stores. Direct mail had grown far beyond the illustrated post cards for a dealer to send out, and three pictorial magazines were developed to be sent out by dealers to farmers, truck operators and the men in the construction industry.

Sales Promotion went also into motion pictures, covering various products in various uses, put out sales training pictures, and scores of manuals. Advertising went into window display and internal point-of-sale display—the Visual Merchandising Laboratory being an outgrowth of the department—created dealer material, continued to work toward standardized fronts for dealers' stores.

Another important advertising medium had come in, the radio. Good-

year had been one of the pioneers in this, having its own station for
a time, WEAR, which later became the big Cleveland NBC outlet,
WTAM. Various types of programs were tried out over the years, but
it was not until fairly recently that it came to use the radio to maximum
advantage. Two programs were started, one a "chain-break" program,
sandwiched in between standard programs and devoted to Neolite,
which brought that sensational product immediately to the attention of
people in thousands of cities.

The other was in an entirely different category. In a strict sense the
program, "The Greatest Story Ever Told," started in 1947, was not
advertising at all. Indeed men inside the company and out questioned
the wisdom of spending three quarters of a million dollars on a program which made no effort to sell goods. Reflecting Litchfield's belief
that in the troubled postwar days America would be benefited most by
going back to the basic principles of religion, the program dramatized
stories of the Bible, and the lessons behind them. The only company
reference was the identification of the sponsor required by the Federal
Communications Commission. The programs merely stated: "The
Goodyear Tire and Rubber Company presents . . ."

This program, however, struck a new note in the field, was warmly
received by the public, the press and the church, won many citations.

With the company's continued interest in lighter-than-air, a fleet of

Navy blimps, purchased as war surplus, travelled widely over the country carrying advertising messages in electric signs along their sides.

Boedeker, Art Director, Buchanan, advertising, and Cartwright, sales promotion, were key men in the department.

Like most advertisers the company has used the services of many advertising agencies, but one connection is unusual. When the company first started advertising on a large scale in 1908, Lord and Thomas of Chicago assigned a young copy writer named C. R. Erwin to the account. Some years later Erwin established his own company, Erwin and Wasey, taking the Goodyear account along, and another young copy writer, Arthur Kudner, was assigned to it. Kudner in turn also set up for himself later on, again taking Goodyear business. The Kudner Agency, Inc., is still the company's principal advertising representative —a 40 year manufacturer-agency relationship.

Other agencies used were Young and Rubicam, N. W. Ayer and Son, and Compton on product, with Prince and Company on direct mail.

PUBLIC RELATIONS

Public Relations was not limited to sales, but covered all phases of the company's operations, continued under Judd, former Akron newspaper editor.

Goodyear was one of the first business houses to realize the importance of public contact, set up a department right after World War I. The name Public Relations had not even been coined at that time, and "publicity" was something put out by circus press agents. Today virtually every company of any size in the country has such a department —as has every department of the government, including Army and Navy.

Goodyear's approach was a *news* approach—the erratic changes in the supply and price of rubber, which were important to every consumer; the expanding usefulness of rubber to society through the transportation of men and goods; the revolution in agriculture brought in with the tractor and the tractor tire; earth-moving tires in the construction field; rubber belting which became a railroad; the growing use of hose, molded goods and other mechanical goods in industry; synthetic rubber; new fabrics like rayon and nylon; air transport which rubber helped make practical, and the colorful field of blimps and passenger airships.

This information was put out through releases to newspapers, general magazines, trade magazines; through books and pamphlets to colleges and grade schools; through motion pictures made in the company's laboratory at Akron, covering various phases of the industry and shown to millions of people each year in schools, clubs, churches, granges, business and technical meetings; and finally through public addresses by Litchfield and other executives at important business and economic gatherings.

Supporting the contour farming program of the U. S. Department of Agriculture, designed to battle erosion and bring more land under cultivation, Public Relations sponsored a contest in 1947 among farmers in eight midwest states, with awards for those who did an outstanding job. In aeronautics a light plane contest at the Cleveland Air Races, also started in 1947, stimulated the ingenuity of individual designers.

Industrial Public Relations, however, must look inward as well as outward. The Wingfoot Clan, at Akron and the outside plants, kept employees advised about developments in the business affecting them. It analyzed the annual statements, discussed simply and without preaching basic economic matters like capital, labor, profits, taxes, prices—and the relationship between the progress of the company and that of its employees.

The department also put out a monthly magazine, Goodyear News, for the thousands of dealers, and a weekly paper, The Triangle, for the men in the sales field.

22. New Postwar Manufacture

Fill Empty Floor Space

LIKE MANY war producers—and the U. S. government—Goodyear
came out of the war with manufacturing space it did not need.
And idle floor space was abhorrent to the Goodyear philosophy,
which held that buildings and machines should be kept at work producing goods and furnishing employment.

The company had six modern tire plants, including the government
plant at Topeka which it soon took over, well equipped, razor-keen
from the war drive, ready to meet the urgent need for tires. Two other
plants, in Lincoln, Nebraska, and New Bedford, Massachusetts, could
be converted to tires, but would probably not be needed once the immediate demand was met. Windsor and St. Marys offered no difficulties,
could go back to their old trades.

The two synthetic rubber plants beyond Plant III, however, including
Goodyear's Chemigum factory, would not be needed for that purpose.
There was a still bigger problem at Aircraft, five huge buildings, includ-

ing Goodyear's plant and a half, the airship dock and part of Plant B. The Government wanted to dispose of the rest, and Goodyear was welcome to buy them if it could find use for them.

And if this did not constitute enough of a corporate problem, Goodyear was already knee-deep in a new venture, housing, one which would not contribute to filling up the vacant plants, since housing had enough obstacles without taking on those involved in a location in the highest wage market in the United States.

The company looked around for production to go into the various factories, perhaps new products which would utilize the new skills developed during the war.

But if it went into new lines of manufacture, it would find that, except perhaps for finances, the problems of a large company are no different than those of a small company doing so. Size itself was no help, would in some ways be a handicap. Big company or small would still have to produce something as good and preferably better than anything on the market, must turn it out at a comparable price, then go out and find a market for it in the face of intrenched competitors.

What happened in the next three years may be illuminating to the student of business. We might start with housing, which was first in point of time to get under way.

An Adventure In Housing

No chapter in the Goodyear narrative matches that of the housing venture initiated in 1943 with the war on. This was something entirely foreign to the rubber industry. Virtually no rubber is used in building homes. But there were reasons behind it, typical of an industrialist apt to think along unconventional lines.

The building of homes was something which should pay off financially if it succeeded. But Litchfield was not thinking primarily of making money. He believed that every business house owed something to society.

Home ownership was of tremendous importance to the individual. It promoted self-reliance, thrift, stability and a normal family life, things which had business as well as social importance. And housing was in a mess in America. Thousands of families were denied a normal home life. The nation was ten years behind in the matter of homes.

People had not been able to buy homes proportionate to the increasing population in the depression of the 1930's, and when overtime war payrolls did make this possible in the 1940's, government controls of materials had come in. Veterans came back from the war to find no place to live. Government recognized the problem, but had not found the solution. Whoever could help out should try to do so. Goodyear had co-operated in a balloon housing project, in which half-balloons were inflated with helium and cement sprayed on—after which the balloons were deflated, moved to the next location.

Goodyear's second reason for going into housing was a business one. Every business house must continue to offer problems and opportunities to men if it is to attract and hold the right type of men. Long before it had exhausted the possibilities in its own field, it must somehow provide new ones big enough and tough enough for men to set their teeth in. He agreed with Henry Ford that complacency is the greatest threat to permanent success.

Housing offered problems aplenty. For Goodyear would not follow usual lines in trying to break into the oldest of all industries, not merely seek to out-quality and out-price companies long in the business. An entirely new approach was in mind.

Could mass production factory economies and those of large-scale purchasing be somehow utilized in the construction of something as tailor-made, individual and localized as a house? That was the query Litchfield threw out to the organization.

Prefabricated homes, factory-made and assembled on the owner's lot had been tried, and had made considerable progress. That was not what he had in mind. He wanted a completely built and equipped house, ready to move into and live in once light and water and gas had been connected up, one which could be delivered intact to any point within practical hauling radius. It had to be a house a man could pick up and take with him if he moved to another city, build up an equity in, not have to sell at a sacrifice.

But a house is a large thing, the biggest thing a man buys. The maximum clearance any load may take on the highway was eight feet. However, the word impossible is not in the American lexicon. And finally someone came up with an answer—an extensible house, with the bedrooms recessed in at the factory, pulled out and sealed when it was delivered, making a T-shaped building 15 feet wide at that point and 26 feet long.

That hurdle past, design work started. It was imperative to keep the finished price as low as possible, but there must be no skimping of materials or equipment. Beds, shower, toilet, closets, drawers, kitchen sink, screen doors, insulation, weather stripping would all be built in at the factory, and equipment like the gas range, water heater, kitchen cabinet and the like installed there. The purchaser need only buy bedding, drapes, table and chairs—which might cost around $250.

The house must be as strong as any other, indeed stronger, since it had to be transported, and airplane experience was drawn on to give it a box-like form and girder strength. One of the early houses got an unscheduled stress test during a delivery trip in New Mexico, when the truck driver misgauged the clearance of an overpass and the house was knocked off the truck. However, outside of some superficial damage where it hit, it was as good as ever, nothing out of plumb.

The costs arrived at a figure of $2650, and trucking operators estimated delivery charges at 45 to 50 cents a mile, including the cost of unloading and setting the house up on its waiting foundations. A radius of 500 to 700 miles seemed economical. Utilities could be connected up in 12 or 24 hours.

A subsidiary company, Wingfoot Homes, Incorporated, was organized, and an airplane hangar which the Army had ordered but decided it did not need was procured, and this was set up on company property at Litchfield Park, Arizona, as a temporary factory—with a larger plant in East St. Louis used for a while. But difficulties arose and mounted.

Any new enterprise must expect these, but the housing project was so different from others that it got more than its share. The first difficulty came from the government. Housing officials ruled that the house was too small, that the rooms should be larger.

The house was not as large as people would like, but it was the largest one that could be transported over the highway, and owners would at least be much better off than thousands of families living in a single room, in basements, or with relatives. In any event, it would seem that size would be something the individual owner could decide for himself, not ask the government to decide for him.

Although Congress appropriated millions of dollars to relieve the housing shortage, not one dollar of that went into Wingfoot Homes, and it was not until the housing group in Washington was changed and controls relaxed that materials could be bought—and later that buyers could get an FHA loan.

Building codes varied from state to state, and city to city, in any case were not devised for a house of this type. This was the greatest and continuing difficulty, handicapped sales on a nation-wide basis.

Arrangements were made with local contractors to connect up the utilities, agents to merchandise the houses, banks to handle financing.

The portable, factory-built, Goodyear house enroute over the highway;
in use in a housing unit at Litchfield Park, and a view of the interior.

Labor difficulties were minimized by hiring only trade union carpenters, plumbers and the like at the regular scale.

A house is a highly individual affair and some people wanted a different room arrangement, or more rooms. However, factory economies can be had only by standardized design, and individuality and variety could be secured with the paint trim, awnings and shrubbery. Later on the company arranged to provide additional rooms knocked down for people wanting more space.

The early houses were sold mostly in Arizona, New Mexico, Utah and California, although some were shipped out by flatcar to Montana and the Dakotas, most of these to contractors, building dams and other reclamation projects, who liked the idea of houses which could be moved away when the job was done, not left to rot.

Real estate operators could landscape a tract of ground, plant trees, shrubbery, create a new housing development quickly. The Atomic Energy Commission ordered 125 of them to be delivered at Los Alamos. Despite unusual obstacles, the project was well under way by 1948 and more than 2000 houses had been produced and were in use.

J. C. Thomas, salesman and draftsman, who at the time was developing more efficient buildings for company stores and dealers, headed up the project, had three other Litchfield Medal winners with him, Ostergren, superintendent, who had been the outstanding Squadron graduate in 1938, Crafts, sales manager, who had been the best store manager in 1924, and Chase, personnel, the Squadron winner in 1934. Thomas himself had won the Medal in 1935 for the best suggestion of the year.

New Bedford Reopens

New Bedford, closed as a textile mill in the tumultuous 1930's, and reopened as a war plant, was converted to peacetime operations in a new field after the war ended.

That city had entered on a third industrial career. It had been the whaling center of the nation, then an important textile center, but most of the cotton mills had been closed shortly before the war and a number of them had been seized for taxes and torn down. However, the remaining plants found immediate usefulness in war production, and New Bedford emerged with a diversified line of manufacture, was no longer a one-industry town.

Goodyear found a new spirit in the community. Its own mill which

Aircraft's Plant B was largely converted to chemical products manufacture; New Bedford factory, below, also took on new postwar assignments.

had been converted from textiles to barrage balloons, to rubber boats, to fuel tanks, began its fourth conversion after the war—to bicycle tires, repair materials and printers' supplies.

At New Bedford these smaller departments would no longer be over-shadowed by tires and mechanical goods, be free to work out their own problems—which might well be different from those of the company's major products.

Repair materials had become a fairly good size business. Competition was, to a considerable extent, in the hands of small companies who made nothing else, made a good living. In a large company like Goodyear, accounting people might differ as to exactly what manufacturing costs were in the case of these smaller items. Printers' supplies were also manufactured largely by companies who specialized in that field. Rubber blankets for printing presses had to be perfect. There could be no seconds.

The bicycle had its big boom in the early 1900's before the automobile and the motorcycle came in, after which America, in contrast to most other nations, gave up the bicycle for transportation, though it had remained in the American picture as a recreation vehicle.

Goodyear discontinued bicycle tire manufacture in 1916, but had resumed manufacturing in Akron on not too large a scale before World War II, and was making them in Java. The war brought the bicycle back.

Rodgers, who had directed the far-ranging activities of the expanded balloon room through the war, went to New Bedford when that was over, to finish out the wartime contracts and change over the factory for its new duties. Moyer, who had left the Army after World War I to join the company in the flooring department, returned to the Air Forces in the second war, reaching the rank of colonel. He was back at Akron, took charge of cycle sales. The New Bedford factory was not too modern, having been constructed in 1892, but was well-built, and the town had ample labor supply. It started on its third career in the company's manufacturing program.

Chemical Products

The roots of Chemical Products, a new major division in the company, extend back through 40 years of its history.

It started in 1908 with Research, a tiny section of the Development Department which sought for compounds which would make rubber

stronger, increase its resistance to sunlight, and accelerate its vulcanization. In later years Research brought out important new products, played
a major part in the development of synthetic rubber, was given great
stimulus by the building of the Research Laboratory during the war,
and found further stimulus afterward as the great Aircraft plants became idle.

The company owned the airship dock, part of Plant B and part of
Arizona Aircraft at Litchfield Park, so it took over the balance of B and
disposed of Arizona after the war, so as not to have divided ownership,
leased space temporarily in Plants D and E, and later purchased all of
Plant C, where parts for the B-29 Superfortress, the B-26 bomber, and
the Northrup Black Widow had been made.

The Navy took over Plant D, the Corsair plant, and established a
Reserve base there, so that the many years in which Akron had played
an important part in aeronautics finally got recognition in the establishment of Naval Air Station, Akron. The city got Plant E, the big flight
hangar. The space acquired by the company was divided between Aircraft and Chemical Products.

Creation of a division dealing with chemical products did not mean
that Goodyear was going into the manufacture of chemicals generally.
The new products were all related to rubber, used its derivatives or synthetics, and in some cases utilized the Banburys, calenders and warm-up
mills of the tire industry.

America as a nation was not as research-minded as some others, not
so much concerned with academic explorations as in making practical
application of new findings, a job it did exceedingly well. But the 1930
decade saw research flourishing throughout the nation. With business
hampered by well-meant efforts of Planned Government Economy, the
chemists went back to the peace of their laboratories, bent not on merely
improving present products but on finding new ones, inaugurated the
Plastic Era.

Rubber was low-priced, and Goodyear's research men went into the
study of the material itself, came up with Pliofilm and Pliolite, which
were derivatives of rubber. Airfoam, its third important new product of
the 1930's, was not a rubber derivative but rubber itself in latex form—
and was not a company development but introduced by the Dunlop
company in England.

*But world war and synthetic rubber took chemical research out of the
laboratory, made it a matter of first import to the nation. The staff grew
in size and competence as tangible results came into sight.*

The Goodyear Research Laboratory, first in the industry, was opened

Airfoam assembly line in high-ceilinged Plant C, Aircraft, looks as if it were out of doors.

Left, Goodyear chef opens oysters packed in Pliofilm, and (below) workmen lay vinyl flooring.

in May, 1943, with modern scientific equipment, complete test facilities, and elbow room for men to go to work scientifically into the matter of rubber resins. Dr. Dinsmore became vice president in charge of Research and Development, and Dr. Sebrell, Research Director. With them were Osterhof of Michigan, D'Ianni of Akron U. and Wisconsin, Clifford of Ohio Wesleyan and Ohio State, Mallory of Cornell, Gehman of Pennsylvania, Ferner of Purdue, Lichty of Iowa, and Merrill of fuel tank fame.

Research was no longer an academic matter, but an immediate and exciting undertaking. GRS rubber could be improved, and must be made more workable, the vulcanizing time reduced. Experiments must be carried on with a wide range of compounds, to fit varying needs of different rubber-made war goods.

GRS rubber used 75 per cent butadiene and 25 per cent styrene. Perhaps other ratios had possibilities, 60-40, 50-50, 25-75. The amount of soap used in emulsification might be increased or lowered. Better results might be had at different temperatures—and pressures, since butadiene is a gas at room temperature.

The research men ran thousands of experiments, brought out some 300 different rubbers which looked promising enough for further study and made some of them into products. Each was checked for a wide range of characteristics, flexibility, stiffness, brittleness, electrical properties, abrasion resistance and was carefully catalogued. Some were useless in one product but might be valuable elsewhere. Most of these polymers were discarded, but some offered promise for the future.

Pliofilm, Pliolite and Airfoam all had usefulness in the war, but used natural rubber, which could not be spared. Rubber flooring went off the market entirely. But synthetic substitutes came to light in each case. The Vinyl resins, derivatives from coke, lime and salt, proved highly useful. Goodyear research men were chiefly responsible for the development of the kind of synthetic latex necessary in Airfoam manufacture. A synthetic substitute was found for Pliofilm—and a Pliolite highly useful in stiffening fuel tanks, and in insulating wire for the Signal Corps. The spectacular Neolite which revolutionized sole manufacture came out of this research drive.

A synthetic rubber cement named Pliobond, which would adhere to metal, fabric, paper, glass, ceramics, concrete, plaster, natural and synthetic rubber, plastics, came into use in the manufacture of tracks for the armored tanks. Previously steel had to be copper-plated before rubber would adhere to it satisfactorily. Pliobond was far different from the glue made from horses hoofs and fish heads. A later product was Pliotherm, which could be heated by electrical action, used on walls and furniture.

There was no time while the war was on to attempt commercial application of these findings, but once it was over the company moved fast to start manufacturing goods from those synthetic materials which were ready to go into production, and resumed manufacture as well of pre-war products using natural rubber.

Pliofilm started up again at St. Marys and was expanded at Akron. Airfoam continued to use synthetic rubber, but got into natural rubber as fast as latex began to come in from the Far East. Pliolite went into the old Chemigum plant, which had chiefly made Buna N synthetic during the war. The flooring department started up again at Plant II.

Further expansion was needed in the next two years as the rubber supply became easier, and the company took over part of Aircraft. Natural Pliofilm and Airfoam went into Plant C, while Plant B took the new plastic film, and the flooring and garden hose made from vinyl synthetic. A million dollar laboratory went up on Archwood Avenue in 1946 alongside Chemigum and the government-owned synthetic plant, as a stepping stone between research and production.

The company had been buying its vinyl resins from other companies, but now it seemed desirable to have its own plant, to study this material first-hand and procure its own requirements. A million and a half dollar factory, the Pathfinder plant, was opened in 1946 at Niagara Falls, within pipe line distance of factories making the acetylene and hydrogenchloride gases, and with power available from the Falls.

The company was still operating synthetic plants for the government at Houston and Los Angeles. The chemical plant, started in 1915 near Plant II, and now comprising ten separate buildings, made many of the compounds used in the factory, and manufactured accelerators and anti-oxidants for the industry generally.

With this broad range of activities, widely scattered physically, steps were taken after the war to bring them all together under what was called the General Products Division, with its own manufacturing, development and sales staff. Pliolite later became a separate division called Chemical Products.

Research had largely developed the new materials, and in some cases had also directed manufacturing and even sales. Many of them, by now, however, were far enough along by now to be set up as production jobs. Still it was something Dinsmore and Sebrell could not walk off and forget about. The new products, because they were new, and must be fitted to changing markets, would still call for the immediate attention

of Research, and with full-time resident staffs set up at the new Archwood Avenue Laboratory and elsewhere to follow through. Barnes,
who had come on from M.I.T. 25 years earlier, gone into research and
been development manager on Airfoam since 1940, continued in that
capacity. DeFrance of Pittsburgh headed the Chemical Laboratory and
Gracia of M.I.T., chemical engineering at Archwood Avenue.

Manufacturing, too, was largely set up under men with a development background. Belknap, who drew the complications of the number
one job, had joined the department in 1919 after graduating from
Pratt Institute and serving as a naval officer in World War I, but had
gone into production in 1934, been superintendent in turn of the Java
plant, Airfoam, St. Marys, and Aircraft's Plant C. Maider, another
development man, who had also had Pliofilm production at Akron
from the first, and was manager of the chemical plants, became part of
the division. Maxwell, who had gone out to Australia on mechanical
goods development and later took charge of manufacturing, took over
Airfoam production.

Reynolds, who had served in Australia and Aircraft and headed the
Akron synthetic plant, took charge at Plant B, also overseeing the operations at the Pathfinder plant at Buffalo, where Manchester of Development was plant manager. Child, superintendent of the Charlestown bag-
loading plant during the war, took over at Plant C. Lyon from the
Chemical Division, who had headed Pliofilm manufacture at St. Marys
and been follow-up man to Ingle during the war, was production manager of the two synthetic manufacturing plants, with Shoaff from Sumatra in charge in California, and Forster, who had returned from
Venezuela, operating the Houston plant. The synthetic made by Goodyear remained government property, was allocated out to various manufacturers to be processed.

In the sales end of the Chemical Divisions, Joslyn, who had come up
through mechanical goods, and had headed fuel tank sales during the
war, took the top job, later becoming general manager. Ellies, his right-
hand man on fuel cells, became his assistant, in immediate charge of
Pliofilm sales, with Clunan on the packaging phases. Hogan from Los
Angeles took charge of Airfoam, with Manufacturers Sales selling to
the automobile manufacturers. Biggs took flooring. The sales organization handled both the natural and synthetic product, fitting each to its
proper use. Many interesting developments followed.

Synthetic Pliofilm is more resistant to sunlight than that made from
natural rubber so it entered fields like shower curtains and garment bags,
where Pliofilm had made its first big impression, while natural Pliofilm

moved into large possibilities in packaging.

Clunan, who had largely developed that field, was a Cornell graduate from Brooklyn who was selling Cellophane when he encountered Pliofilm in 1936 on a business trip to Akron, was so intrigued by it he virtually hired himself in and thereafter invented several automatic machines for packaging goods with Pliofilm.

Most of the goods that society uses are grown or manufactured at one point, used at a million other places, must be packed, shipped, stored in the interim. Men used barrels, wooden and cardboard boxes, jute and paper sacks, glass bottles, tin cans. Foodstuffs, fruit, vegetables, meat, fish, are vulnerable to delays in shipping, occasion vast waste due to spoilage between the farm or the fisherman's boat and the retailer's counter. Refrigeration came in, but as recently as the decade after Litchfield got out of college, adventurous young men could get a free trip to Europe by tending cattle shipped abroad on the hoof.

Pliofilm was a new packaging material, particularly adapted to foodstuffs since it was water-proof, moisture-proof, transparent, tough, flexible. Also it was thermoplastic, that is, when heated, it would take any shape, and on cooling take a permanent set. It could be heat-sealed, was adapted to automatic machine operations, could be used on any articles no matter how irregular their shape, fresh fish, pineapple, a dressed chicken.

Foodstuffs have different characteristics, which Pliofilm could meet by changes in the material or by using different plasticizers. For articles like bread the moisture must be kept out, for others like cigars it must be kept in. Oxygen must be kept away from ham and bacon. Grapefruit, tomatoes, corn on the cob breathe in oxygen, breathe out carbon dioxide like people—and must breathe out some moisture vapor as well to remain fresh and edible. Coffee must expel carbon dioxide, but oxygen must be kept out. The apple is one of the most exacting of all fruits. Pliofilm could keep moisture in or out, transmit a little moisture or much, transmit gases or hold them in.

There were different requirements too for fresh food, cooked food, dehydrated food, frozen food, vacuum-packed goods. By lining a cardboard container with Pliofilm fresh shrimp could be shipped in from the Gulf of Mexico and salmon from Alaska—or orchids from Rio. Pliofilm could be used for butter, cheese, cereals, crackers, berries, spices, cigarets, for live roots and bulbs, for drugs and pharmaceuticals, or as was found during the war, for engines, machine parts and delicate instruments which could be protected over a long journey, be ready for use on arrival.

Airfoam too had great possibilities. Demand rose immediately after the war, and for a curious reason. People did more travelling then than ever before, soldiers bound for training camps, wives journeying to see their husbands, civilians taking defense jobs. Many of them became conscious of something new in seat cushioning, for Airfoam had just come into use on trains and airplanes. People made a mental note of it. That was something they wanted for their homes after the war ended.

Goodyear, while making synthetic Airfoam, built its own latex plant at Johore in Malaya, to expedite the delivery of natural latex in this country, set up three large assembly lines at Plant C for Airfoam manufacture, two for automotive use, the third for the furniture market.

The flooring department took a new name, Builders' Supplies, since its products could be used on kitchen drainboards, enamel ware, counters, desks, and wall covering as well as flooring, and in the vinyl form, which took a wide range of colors, was stain and flame resistant. Being a thermoplastic the seams could be heat sealed. The vinyl resins could be made into film of .004 thickness with a tolerance of .0002, laminated into flooring in gauges down to 1/32 of an inch, or extruded into a garden hose which was resistant to sunlight. It used rubber machinery, was mixed in a Banbury, sheeted out on the calender, cured under heat.

Pliolite, now called Chemical Products, remained under Thies. Originally, this product, made from natural rubber, had been used in paints and in coating paper, but several synthetic Pliolites developed during the war had further uses. It gave a stiffening quality to rubber, could be used some places instead of carbon black and so open the way to a wider range of colors. Compound Pliolite and Balata and you got a golf ball cover easier to mold, more resistant to cuts. It came into use for football helmets. It could be mixed with many materials to resist abrasion and wear. It continued to be useful in insulating wire. It could be used with ink to make it dry quickly. It would be used with paint in increasing volume, since it could be varied to resist moisture, corrosion, acids, alkalis, and the effect of weather.

Thies' salesmen, headed by Aiken of Texas A. and M., were all chemical engineers, working with the technicians of many industries, coming back to the factory with detailed specifications of what characteristics were needed, with the order virtually tailor-made. Unlike the others, Pliolite was not an end-product but a material to be used with other materials to obtain a predetermined result. Pliobond sales also were turned over to Thies' division for a similar reason.

An important export market was just opening up when the war

began, particularly for Pliofilm and Airfoam, and in addition to the increased production capacity at home, plants were built at Toronto, after the war ended, to manufacture these two products, and a Pliofilm factory under way in England was completed and went into production.

Goodyear Aircraft

With Japan's surrender Aircraft cut back from 20,000 employees to 3000, nearly half of whom were on temporary work, completing some contracts and cleaning up accounting and financial details resulting from the large number of war contracts taken.

Most of the men who had gone to Aircraft from the tire plant returned there, often with better jobs growing out of their experience. The only permanent employees were those in wheels and brakes, and the engineers working on experimental and design contracts for the Army and Navy—jobs which required few production workers. The five great structures now became suddenly quiet.

Though Aircraft's future looked none too favorable, the company was of course unwilling to close up the plant and walk out. It had been in aeronautics for too many years, was familiar with its ups and downs. But how would it utilize its accumulation of technical experience? There were no more airplane subcontracts such as had filled the plants to the brim during the war. Plane manufacturers, too, had been cut way back.

It had precision machines which might be used in mechanical appliances, but no consumer goods required the high precisions of the airplane.

There was ample floor space, but floor space is a liability rather than an asset unless it is used, merely builds up overhead costs. Aircraft buildings were all of high-bay construction, with space which could not be used but had to be heated and lighted—in contrast to the less expensive, special-purpose buildings of prospective competitors.

Lastly, in whatever new manufacturing field it might pick, Goodyear would find itself competing with its tire and mechanical goods customers, for everyone was a customer for these products.

Despite all these difficulties, however, plus shortages in steel, aluminum and other materials, Aircraft not only continued on, found a place for itself, but in two years had built up from a postwar low of 2000 employees to a peak of 3500. Manufacture used all of Plant A, most of Plant B, overflowed at times into Plant D and the big flight hangar.

The postwar factory that grew out of this was unusual, a combination of extremely technical work on the one hand, employing perhaps 500 engineers, and close-to-the-ground, bread-and-butter jobs on the other, mostly in the field of consumer goods which were in short supply in the first postwar years.

Blythe resigned shortly after the war, and DeYoung moved up to be general manager, then took a second step as vice president of the parent company, Knowles succeeding him at Aircraft. Arnstein remained as vice president of engineering, Zimmerman taking charge of production and Crum becoming sales manager.

Not as a sales company but as a manufacturer of private brand goods for other companies, Aircraft adapted its wartime experience (and often used the same materials and equipment) to making ice cube bins, deep freeze units, kitchen cabinets, music boxes, storm doors and parts for washing machines—as well as caskets to bring back the war dead, and huge metal "cans" as big as a ten-room house for the storage of military planes.

Continuously, however, it sought and found work to do in aeronautics. Wheels and brakes continued to furnish a substantial volume of business. Wright Field and the Navy Bureau of Aeronautics, respecting its engineering experience, continued to assign research and design projects to it, many of them secret and highly-specialized, such as participation in the program for the development and manufacture of special weapons. It also built radar equipment and jet engine parts for General Electric and others.

Aircraft had developed plastic bubble canopies for pilot cockpits late in the war, particularly for the F2-G Corsair. These were better from an optical standpoint than any other, so Aircraft became one of the principal manufacturers of canopies, particularly for the fast new planes. Extending its work in the laminated field, it worked with the parent company in fabricating fibre-glass shells to be used with the bullet-sealing fuel tanks as a complete unit ready for installation in the airplane. The company also developed stainless steel blades for helicopters.

Aircraft had developed a plane of its own during the war, the amphibian "Duck," a project started to try out quickly, and on a small and inexpensive scale, many ideas which the engineers had brought in, but which could not be embodied in military planes until completely worked out and proved.

The "Duck," officially the GA-2, incorporated many new features, had an excellent performance, was adapted to mass production after the war, but the market was not ready for it. Experimentation continued,

Note angle of wheels to plane's course as big DC 3 taxis in on Goodyear cross-wheel landing gear. Close-up at left. Below amphibian "Ducks" at Wingfoot Lake.

however, and 15 planes were built and loaned out to fixed-base operators in 1947, under an arrangement by which the pilots using them would make regular reports back to the company, particularly on water landings and take-offs, and as to short-comings and possible improvements.

If men could find out more about airplanes by building one to their own design and working the bugs out of it, by the same token they might do a better job if they learned to fly, knew the pilot's problems first-hand. So several types of light planes were purchased during the war and arrangements made for engineers and production heads to take flight training at Akron Airport.

A big airplane hangar was erected at the airport, to house company planes, and act as a laboratory for the merchandising of aeronautic supplies.

Two hundred acres of woodland at Wingfoot Lake was sold off in 1944, bringing the holdings to 520 acres, but left ample room for blimp landings and for an airplane runway there.

Aircraft also worked with the Civil Aeronautics Board on a cross-wind landing gear, developed a castered wheel which would travel straight down the runway while the plane itself headed into the wind at an angle to the line of travel. This was tried out first in February, 1947, on a Piper Cub, and one year later was installed on a big DC-3 passenger plane, which landed successfully with a 45 mile wind blowing at a 90 degree angle to the runway.

This was hailed as one of the most important developments in airplane safety in recent years, created widespread discussion of the possibility of building one-strip airports in mountainous country or close to population centers, the latter placing terminals within minutes of downtown, and built at a fraction of the most of multiple-strip fields ten to 25 miles away.

Planes equipped with the Goodyear cross-wind wheels did not call for last-minute split-second judgment on the part of the pilot in making his landing, the wheels automatically castering into position.

Lighter-than-air still provided tasks for Aircraft, including a K-type airship sent to Wingfoot Lake for modification to incorporate improvements, including communication, for which there was no time with the war on.

The development of the long-range Snorkel-type submarine by the Germans late in the war—many of which fell to the Russians as prizes of war, along with the elaborately-equipped yards in which they had been built—brought a distinct challenge to the supply lines of other nations. They could cruise under water faster than earlier submarines could on the surface, offered an excellent means of bringing high-powered weapons and missiles close to the shores of any nation with which they were at war.

World War II, however, had shown the blimp to be one of the best methods of finding and destroying these underseas craft, so the non-rigid airship remained in the picture. And in 1948 Aircraft was working on a new type airship, one even larger than the big M's of War II, and capable of higher performance. The details of the new N-type ship were still on the secret list, but was a large-scale project which would take considerable time to complete.

So Aircraft postwar continued to use its experience in light-weight, high-strength, clean-appearing design so necessary in aeronautics, kept Goodyear an important factor in this field.

Big Commercial Airships

One of the early projects that Goodyear brought out and looked over again after the war was the big passenger airship.

This was an idea that for a third of a century had lain close to the mind of a corporation which more than most companies was impressed with need for efficient transport between nations, as being important to the growth of this nation in peace time, and to its security in time of war.

Lighter-than-air, which Goodyear believed could serve that purpose, had had more than its share of vicissitudes during that 35 year period, had its high moments of appeal to the public imagination, and its tragic setbacks.

But reviewing the whole business, Goodyear could still see no reason why the big airships could not render a service to the country which no other vehicle could do.

The time was none too propitious. The nation was busy cleaning up the debris of war. Labor troubles were everywhere. Inflation reared its ugly head. Ten million men returning from the wars must be refitted into the civilian economy, and be housed. A breach arose between this nation and one of its wartime allies. America had a hundred problems on its mind. But if a project had value it must be pursued.

More than ever in a global world, America needed the best and most completely integrated system of international transportation possible.

It was the only major nation flanked on both sides by broad stretches of ocean, and the particular forte of the airship was in long distance travel over water, where there were no intermediate or emergency landing points, since it needed none.

The airplane had made great technical advances during the war, was able to bridge either of the oceans easily. But passenger comfort had not increased with speed. If anything it was just the reverse. The slower moving steamship was sold out and had long waiting lists. Speed was not the complete answer. And the airship offered a comfort comparable to that of the steamship (but without seasickness), and twice its speed. It had far greater comfort than the airplane, much greater speed than any other transoceanic vessel except the airplane, and the record showed much less likelihood to delays in take-off occasioned by weather.

The original cost of ships and operating bases was large, but the return should be enough to carry the project once started. *There is a basic economy in lighter-than-air travel, due to the fact that while the airplane must use a considerable amount of power merely to keep aloft, the airship floats through the air through its own buoyancy, uses its engines only to push it ahead.*

Mooring masts had made it unnecessary for the airship to go into a hangar on arrival. It could load up its passengers and cargo, refuel, gas up, be fully serviced from a mast which could be erected anywhere. The airship went into the dock only for major overhaul.

Some of the blimp hangars built during the war were large enough to take a ten million cubic foot airship, and others could be modified to do so. Those bases had landing fields and complete servicing facilities which could be put to use.

High initial costs had not discouraged America from other large-scale projects.

America had accumulated extensive engineering and construction experience—if it did not wait too long to use it—in building the wartime blimps, and its research work on rigid airships after the Macon.

It still had a considerable nucleus of operating experience, with the several hundred Navy and civilian blimp pilots who had flown intensively during the war, an experience which could be converted to big ships if a training ship was included in the program—which would find many utility uses afterwards.

The big airship was not a combat vessel, but could be a highly useful auxiliary craft in the event of war as a troop carrier, a cargo carrier, or a reconnaissance ship. The existence of a commercial operation, having ships, personnel, bases and service facilities which could be immediately commandeered, would be extremely useful to the nation as a secondary line of defense, like the merchant ships on the surface.

Finally America had helium gas, a great safety factor which no other nation had, giving this country an unusual advantage.

Despite setbacks there remained the fact that the Germans had operated big passenger airships safely over a long period of years (except for the loss of the Hindenburg due to hydrogen) and these had indicated that a passenger airship line would be sound financially.

Reviewing all these considerations, Goodyear believed that commercial airships still had a definite place in our transportation scheme.

Project designs were made up of alternate types of a ten million cubic foot airship (about half again as large as the Akron-Macon) which could provide deluxe accommodations for 112 passengers, Pullman-type accommodations for 232, or tourist accommodations for 288. Such a ship used as a cargo carrier could carry 180,000 pounds payload from San Francisco to Honolulu, or 110,000 from Honolulu to Shanghai, non-stop. Used as a flying hospital, it could carry 248 casualties, with space for an operating room, dispensary, quarters for doctors, nurses and mess attendants.

The matter finally came to Washington's attention, and two committees, one named by the president, the other by Congress, made independent studies of aeronautics, including airships.

So in 1948 Congress passed a bill which called on the Maritime Commission to make a complete study on the project and report back to the next session. President Truman, however, failed to act on it after adjournment, constituting a pocket veto, so the matter was again delayed.

The big airship still remained as an unique opportunity for America to have the most complete transportation system of any nation, using the steamship, the airplane and the airship, each in the field for which it is best fitted.

Entrance to South Africa plant

23. Foreign Operations

Recovery and Expansion

THE COMPANY'S OPERATIONS abroad, harder hit by the war than any other, came back fast.

The Java plant was reopened after some delay, a new factory was built in South Africa and long-needed expansion of manufacturing space was started in England, Australia, Argentina, Brazil, Peru and Sweden—and also in Canada. The rubber plantations were reopened as soon as conditions permitted and export sales started hiring again.

By action as vigorous as that which followed the 1920 depression, Export drove ahead to meet the needs of nations long hungry for tires and mechanicals, and despite the shortage of dollar exchange in many countries, shipping delays and congested ports, got back into every market which was open, and by 1948 was doing the biggest business in its entire history.

Export alone, by this time, was a larger business enterprise than many entire rubber companies.

675

Personnel, always a vital factor in business, became particularly so in Goodyear Foreign Operations, once the war ended.

In the three divisions, sales, factories and rubber plantations, few new men had been hired in for five years. The war took jobs out from under many men. Some of them went into the armed forces, others were loaned to the government, and still others came into Akron for reassignment.

There was no trouble placing men with production and technical experience. Hochberg became superintendent at New Bedford and Woonsocket, and the others found places where their experience was exceedingly helpful. Aircraft could use all the men it could get. The plantation men did a rather surprising job, Titus becoming superintendent of Arizona Aircraft, and Figland, a division superintendent at Akron Aircraft. Others filled important places in the greatly expanded purchasing department where business background was needed.

It was a little harder to place the sales people, as the domestic sales force had also been cut back. But men are versatile and the need for war production was extremely urgent, so export salesmen like domestic, found themselves ringing clock cards and directing production, did not quarrel with the assignment since airplanes were needed to win the war.

The men loaned to the government were picked because of specialized experience in various fields now grown highly important, did an effective job, came back with an enriched experience.

We have seen the work of Dinsmore and Ingle in synthetic rubber, Bogardus, Long and others in wild rubber procurement, Berkinshaw and Nicholls in synthetic in Canada. House held a key post with the Foreign Economic Administration in Spain and Portugal, directing economic warfare against the Axis powers, came back after the war to be manager of the Near East and African division. Rich of Operating served in Washington as Chief of the Rubber Division of the same agency, came back to be manager for Europe. King, assistant sales manager in England, was Deputy Director of the Tire Administration there, controlling production and retreading, went out to Africa afterward as sales manager. Perry, district manager at Bombay, who had held a position in India similar to King's in London, became manager of export sales for England. Davis of Argentina served with the Rubber Administration, went back to Brazil as sales manager.

Unique experience was that of Buitendijk who served under four flags. Hired in at Java and trained at Akron, he was a salesman in South Africa when the European war broke out, served in succession with the South African Guard, the Netherlands Tank Corps, the British Royal

Flying Corps and the U. S. Air Force. He went to Holland as special representative after the war.

The company's first concern after the shooting stopped was to get its people back from prison camp—and after that to see what had happened to its Eastern properties during the Japanese occupation. Little information had seeped out as to what the enemy had done with the great plantations which supplied 90 per cent of the world's rubber.

THE RUBBER PLANTATIONS

The first lifting of the curtain came when Klippert and Figland arrived in the Philippines in June, 1945, while the fighting was still on. Hochberg left for Java in September, Shoaff, Arnold and Titus the following month for Sumatra, and Harrison for Singapore.

The Philippine plantation was on the southernmost island of Mindanao, fairly remote, could be reached only by boat from Zamboanga. America's supply of rubber was all but depleted, and the government sent Klippert and Figland in by Army launch, which carried a small boat aboard with an outboard motor. The launch captain was unwilling to get too close to shore lest he go aground, put the two Americans off in the motor boat at dark several miles from the plantation, armed only with .45 automatic Army pistols.

The Goodyear property lay up a river, hidden by an island. The men were not too sure of their directions, but finally reached the plantation, found no sign of life anywhere. Huber's house had been burned down and that of Lundberg stripped of everything. They hung up their insect-proof hammocks, got out their Army rations and settled down for the night. The jungle telegraph worked, and by morning the natives began to assemble, including Filipino guerillas who had carried on, on the side of the United States, through the war.

They went over the property, found the buildings and machinery useless, but the trees intact—and were led by the natives to bodegas where 43 tons of rubber, secretly tapped and coagulated, had been stored waiting for their return.

Figland stayed on for a year to put the buildings and transportation in shape, while Klippert continued on to Manila where he arranged for shipment of 600 tons of rubber the Japs had left behind. Huber and Lundberg got back in July, 1946, to pick up where they had left off.

Harrison had little difficulty getting to Singapore, although he had to wade ashore from an LST with the Marines. He found that the go-downs (warehouses) had been used by the Japs as barracks and were in bad shape, all wiring, furniture and equipment being ripped out for sale on the black market. However, he reopened a buying office, got a considerable supply of rubber which had been abandoned by the Japs in their flight, arranged with British planters to ship rubber to the States.

One lot of rubber allocated to the company by the U. S. government had been produced on the Goodyear plantations, still carried its markings. Presumably it had been seized by the Japs, and later by looters in the confusion at the end of the war.

Shoaff and the Sumatra party found the doors tightly closed to the Netherlands Indies. Only a few towns on the coast were held by the Dutch, including Belawan, a port town, and Medan 18 miles away. The Indonesians held the interior. Dolok Merangir was 70 miles from Medan, the Wingfoot plantation still more remote.

Barred from the plantations, Shoaff returned to his duties at the California synthetic plant, and Arnold, Titus and Buckley started work on a latex plant in Johore to get Goodyear back into the Airfoam field. The latex was treated with ammonia as a preservative, picked up by tank trucks and taken to Johore, where it was processed to reduce the water content, in equipment something like a cream separator, ending with 62 per cent rubber as against 32 per cent in pure latex. Latex was a promising business. Consumption reached nearly 50,000 tons in 1947 as against 30,000 tons prewar, and Goodyear had wasted no time getting into the field.

It was not until October, 1947, that Arnold and Titus got their first look at Dolok Merangir, after more than five years' absence. The Dutch government was anxious to clear out the rich estate areas on the East coast, which produced rubber, tobacco, palm oil, tea and copra. They began military operations in July, 1947, to effect this, though operations were halted on account of protests from the United Nations—but not before the way had been opened for the Goodyear men to reach the older plantation.

Within an hour former employees began to swarm in from over a wide area, each wearing the best clothes he had managed to save, and many with their Goodyear service pins. One watchman could hardly wait until Arnold noticed a decoration on his coat. It was his four service pins, including the 20 year one, made up into a badge, brought out of hiding on the occasion of his country's liberation. Gold was a forbidden possession, and he probably would have been shot if the Japs knew he had the pins. One employee brought in hundreds of feet of insulated wire which he had buried.

Rubber trees had been cut down on nearly a third of the plantation to raise foodstuffs for the Jap army, corn, sweet potatoes, rice and tapioca, but the enemy had saved the best trees. The rest were untouched, would produce more latex for the first year after tapping was resumed. The processing plants were pretty well ruined, the pondoks or native houses in bad repair. It would take considerable time to restore Dolok Merangir to its former productive status. Nothing was known about the second plantation at Wingfoot by the fall of 1948.

Not till after the war did Goodyear get any news as to the fate of its principal Dutch assistants in Sumatra. Riedhorst died in a prison camp which was ravaged by typhus and cholera. DeBoer who had gone to school in Holland and taken his master's degree at the University of California, survived the ordeal of internment, though his weight fell from 165 to 111. Oberman, field inspector, who had been educated in Canada, joined Goodyear on the Squadron in 1935 and been sent back to his home country, went into the army in Sumatra and after the Dutch capitulated was sent to a labor camp in Burma. He was eventually liberated by Mountbatten's forces and returned to Akron.

RECOVERY OF JAVA

Hochberg got back to Batavia, the capital of Java, early in November, 1945, and went out to the factory at Buitenzorg the next day with a military escort. The Indonesians had taken it over three weeks before, when the Japs left, but had not started operating it. Things were in disorder. The plant had been looted three times in that period.

He got in again five weeks later, found the Indonesians at work building 30 automobile tires and 75 bicycle tires a day, with a stock of rubber, fabric and compounds on hand.

The political situation made any thought of Goodyear's resuming manufacturing operations out of the question, and it was not until a year later that this was possible. Most of the former employees were still around and 300 of them reported for work when, on New Year's Day, 1947, Hochberg and Carroll, the personnel manager, took over.

Records in the plant showed that the Japs had changed the markings on the molds to Japanese characters, had produced a total of 350,000 bicycle tires, 70,000 truck tires, 60,000 passenger tires and 12,000 airplane tires during the occupation.

Housing had been neglected but machinery and equipment was not in too bad shape, considering the wartime shortage of parts and repair facilities.

There was a big overhauling job to be done, to get the plant into efficient shape. There was plenty of labor, however, and of the 850 prewar employees all but 12 came back to take their old jobs. Each man wanted his old machine, the usual result being that the men from the three shifts not only put their machine in perfect running condition, but polished it until it shone.

Of the American prewar organization, Rinke, who became division superintendent, was the only one outside of Hochberg to return after this lapse of time. Buckley, plant engineer, who had been in Brazil during most of the war, went out at the outset, and stayed on to build the latex plant at Johore. Nance, who took charge of engineering, had gone through the Apprentice Machinist's course and the Engineering Squadron, served at Aircraft in charge of the machine shop, the welding shop, then general foreman. The other division superintendent was Boyle, Squadron graduate, who had been a foreman in truck tires, then at Aircraft. Wiland, who took charge of purchasing, a member of a well-known Goodyear family, had been in the stores division and served as an expediter during the war.

Java brought an opportunity for Carroll, who had joined the company in 1919 as a band builder, been a supervisor there and in bicycle tires until the war, when he went into Efficiency. He was sent to the Woonsocket, Rhode Island, plant on time study in 1943, later took charge of personnel, then became superintendent under Hochberg. Picked originally to take charge of personnel and purchasing in Java, he succeeded Hochberg as plant manager in the summer of 1948, when the latter returned to Akron for a new assignment.

With the reopening of the Java plant, it was thoroughly modernized and quickly returned to its former place in overseas manufacturing, with expansion of facilities soon becoming necessary.

EXPORT SALES

Back at the home office, Cameron and his staff surveyed sales conditions at the end of the war, set out to rebuild fences.

Markets had been destroyed in half of Europe and the Far East. Germany was smashed, England had paid a heavy price for victory, Russia had never been a market for American goods except Lend Lease, the Balkans lay dangerously close to expanding Soviet ambitions. Switzerland, untouched island in a warring continent, would be affected by recovery outside. France, Italy and the Near East were question marks.

Conditions were better in the Scandinavian nations to the north and in the liberated Lowlands, where men used their native thrift and industry to put those nations back on their feet. The bright spots in the world were South America and the English-speaking nations of Australia, South Africa, New Zealand, India and of course, Canada.

There were more gaps in the Export staff than the other divisions. Kither of Australia had died during the war, and Bollinger of Argentina and Barton of Mechanical Goods at Akron afterward, Chamberlin of Akron, Morgan of Mexico and Baumann of Central America had retired. Hanson, Crittenden and Thompson had left the company, Riveire had new duties in Washington, and other men, well-located in domestic remained in the States.

However, there were strong men and long-experienced to build around, Hazlett and Bishop in England, Hastings and Huff in Argentina, Long and Andrews in Brazil, Nicholson in South Africa, Melander in Sweden, Steiner and Richards in Australia. In Akron Magennis and Croke, with years of experience in Latin America, were in key export positions, and other seasoned men were around, Patterson, Hadley and Davidson in Sales, Gleichauf in the tire division, Gates in advertising, Horne in operating.

Though Export had operated with a skeleton staff during the war, it had kept its offices open in every country where it could still get needed rubber goods to carry on the internal economy and transportation of that country.

Wetzel and Ferrier who had hired in at Manila, went back there as managing director and sales manager. Wetzel, an Ohioan, had gone to the Islands to teach school but left to join Goodyear in 1929, served later in Trinidad, Colombia and Brazil. California-born Ferrier was one of the men caught there during the war. Sullivan Kafer went to Java, Hadley having moved up to division manager for the Far Eastern Division, and his brother, Frank Kafer, became sales director in India.

Faltin, stormy petrel of the Balkans, went to Switzerland, kept an eye on changing conditions east and south. Another veteran, Serge Wulff, Russian-born French citizen, went to Portugal, covering North Africa as well.

What are called operating functions, those phases that are neither production nor sales, had become more important in Goodyear's work overseas. Akron has large departments to do the cost accounting and sales accounting, to handle the company's cash drawer, look after credits and collections, budgets, taxes, insurance, traffic, warehousing, legal and government regulations. Each outside plant had the same functions, but had additional work arising out of the fluctuations of foreign exchange, tariffs, and legislation affecting a company doing business abroad under innumerable government regulations and restrictions.

The office manager, operating manager or secretary-treasurer (the titles differed with the size of the operation) had to know at all times what it cost to make goods, to sell them, take care of overhead and have the money on hand to pay bills and wages, giving production and sales more time to work on their own problems.

Operating men developed sales and administrative aptitudes. Bollinger was a vice president as well as treasurer in Argentina at the time of his death. Long in Brazil and Meyer in India became managing directors and Manning president of the Mexican company.

Meyer had started in the Credit Department in 1927 at Akron, worked in New York and Chicago, joined Export in 1930, served in Germany, Brazil, Poland, Switzerland and New Zealand before going to India to relieve McCorkle, who went into Export's New York office as manager of the Eastern Division.

Export was faced with a big recruiting and training job immediately after the war. Foot and Van Epps, domestic salesmen who had been with Aircraft during the war, transferred to Export, the former as manager for the Australasian and Eastern Divisions, the latter as assistant sales manager in Australia. Eichman, another Aircraft alumnus, went to Export, first in charge of aeronautics, then the South American division. Failing, who had handled Export's legal phases, became assistant managing director in New Zealand.

New faces came in, men who had served in the Army and Navy air forces, who had gone far and learned much during the war. The American Institute for Foreign Trade, set up in Phoenix, Arizona, by General Yount, wartime commander of Luke Field alongside Litchfield Park, furnished a number of men.

In rebuilding its position after the war, Export continued to make the fullest use of airplane travel to maintain contact with its world-wide organization.

Goodyear, a company which had always believed in aeronautics, had been one of the first users of the airplane in the export field, where distances were great and water travel slow. There were places in Venezuela and Colombia in the early years where it took a salesman several days to get over the Andes to reach an isolated city in his territory, travelling by single gauge railroad, river boat and even on muleback. Before the airplane came and extended its network of routes, Baumann often had to wait several days for a coastal steamer to take him from one Central American country to the next. Air travel was relatively expensive at first, but so is lost time, and Export made full use of expedited travel to study markets at close range and build up sales in foreign markets.

Blandin's rubber plantations also had a recruiting-training job after the war, had lost two key men, Ingle who had retired, and Shoaff who had gone into synthetic production. But he had a nucleus of seasoned men to build around.

THREE NEW FACTORIES

Hinshaw had a similar problem in the outside factories. He found men to fill the gaps in Java and to man new factories in Colombia, Cuba, and South Africa.

The Colombia plant, first one in that country, a small-scale, foot-in-the-door operation, grew out of retreading.

With a shortage both of tires and shipping in most foreign countries during the war, Goodyear felt its biggest contribution would be to make present tires last as long as possible. Retreading equipment was added at the various outside factories and small plants set up in Cuba, Panama, Venezuela and Colombia. The Panama plant was particularly important with the large military defenses in the Canal, retreaded as many as 3000 tires a month. The plant at Cali, Colombia, a city of 200,000 people lying at 3500 feet, got a mill, a calender and a tubing machine as well.

Colombia is a large country, with great natural resources and inadequate transportation, by rail or highway—and when the Goodyear factory went up, it delivered tires to its distributors by plane, which was no more expensive than by rail.

But oil in the north, coffee, sugar cane and rice in the interior, and gold and other minerals in the mountains were creating an increasing need for automotive transport—and tires.

So the repair plant was enlarged in 1944 to permit their manufacture, with a capacity of 40 tires a day, with heels coming in shortly afterward. The project was successful and by 1948 production was upwards of 200 tires a day in eight sizes. Jacobs, Squadron graduate who had formerly headed Goodyear Industrial University was superintendent, Delaney from Panama of sales.

The Venezuela retreading plant was also expanded to build tires after the war but encountered adverse political conditions and was closed.

The new factory in Cuba got under way in 1946, with Ryan from Brazil as superintendent, though succeeded shortly by Spoonamore when Ryan took over Coffin's work at Sao Paulo. Spoonamore had previously been Goodyear's representative at the Dunlop plant in India.

The South African plant was an important one in a growing market

Toronto, Canada

Post war demands for tires brings new factories in South Africa, Cuba and Columbia, while Canadian company erects plant at Toronto to manufacture Airfoam and Pliofilm, and acquires new plant in historic Quebec.

Quebec, Canada

Port Elizabeth, South Africa

Havana, Cuba

Cali, Columbia

where Dunlop had previously manufactured tires for the company.

The factory was the most modern tire plant yet built outside the United States. It was erected at Uitenhage near Port Elizabeth, with a mechanical goods plant alongside. Steel and tire equipment was purchased as war surplus from the government after the projected Goodyear plant at Nashville, Tennessee, was cancelled.

Follo, picked as head of the new factory, had been superintendent at Sweden, then at Goodyear Aircraft's Plant D, which built Corsair planes for the Navy. Four Aircraft men went with him, Stanley in Production, Willett in Personnel, Watts who won the Litchfield Medal as an Apprentice Machinist, as purchasing agent, and Brundage as accountant. Nigosian from Gadsden, who has built several Goodyear factories, became engineer, and two other production men had had experience in outside plants, Novick in Sweden and Charleston, and Conrad in California and Woonsocket.

Nicholson remained as managing director, King and Hendon of England became sales director and secretary-treasurer respectively.

The first South African tire was built in January, 1947. Litchfield, Hinshaw, Hyde, legal counsel, and Ginaven who was to be superintendent in England, flew out in June for the opening which was attended by business and political leaders of the country.

24. Summary of 50 Years

Importance of Manpower

DURING the 50 years since Goodyear started, in 1898, the public has bought more than nine billion dollars worth of the products it turned out.

Apparently its basic manufacturing policy was sound, namely to utilize every possible resource of research and development to turn out a product which was at least as good as could be had elsewhere, and every resource of machines and engineering to get the cost down so that a maximum number of people could afford to buy.

For 32 successive years, that is in each year from 1916 on, car owners have bought more Goodyear tires than any other.

Of the million tons of rubber America consumed in 1948, Goodyear used well over one-fifth in its various factories—and including the foreign plants, used one-sixth of all the rubber consumed in the world.

The company has not made a great deal of money, as these things go, on this nine billion dollars worth of business. Averaged over the

687

years profits have run around 4 per cent, although falling off with the
war years, as did those of most companies who turned out a large volume of war production. *Goodyear made an average profit of 2½ per
cent during the war—though many people have the impression that business made huge war profits.*

For the last 20 years profits have been around 3.6 per cent, reflecting
the policy of keeping selling prices low, in order to bring goods within
the reach of as many people as possible.

*For example, of the $670 millions which the consumer spent for
Goodyear merchandise in 1947, more than half of that, or $300 mil-
lions, went into raw materials, $200 millions went into wages, $43
millions into taxes, and $11 millions went to the stockholders.*

Incidentally all of that $43 millions in taxes did not go to the various
divisions of government—federal, state, county, city—in this country.
Some of it went abroad. Other countries where Goodyear did business
have sales and property taxes, as well as customs and import duties.
The Federal government's take in this country, however, did not stop
at that. The public paid another $40 millions to Washington in excise
taxes on the Goodyear tires it bought in 1947—with foreign nations
taking another seven million dollars in the same way, to make a total
of $90 millions in taxes a year growing out of the company's operations.

Throughout the years more than half of the company's earnings have
been plowed back into the business. It needed them.

Any company which went from a two million dollar business in 1908
to $63 millions eight years later—and by 1948 had multiplied that
figure by ten—would have to spend a lot of money for buildings and
equipment. Particularly one which adopted the mass production principle, used machines, conveyors and mechanized transport wherever
possible—and a business which saw many changes in its manufacturing
technique.

The tire industry was highly competitive, and any company could
survive and go ahead only as it kept its factory costs down and maintained uniform quality—even though that meant scrapping old machines as fast as better ones were developed. The flat-built tire drove
out the State tire-building machines by the hundreds, watchcase molds
made the costly pot heaters obsolete, Banburys drove out whole lines
of mixing mills, and a single change in tire design might mean the
scrapping of a million dollars worth of molds, even though metal in-
serts were used as far as possible.

Goodyear's investment in the land, buildings and equipment in use
in June, 1941, stood at $308 millions. Actually a great deal more money

than that had been put into the plant. But as all these machines and molds wore out or were scrapped, they went off the books, as did buildings razed to make way for new ones. The property account covers only the buildings and equipment the company is currently using.

The $308 millions plus that went into the plant—actually well over $400 millions,—came in part from earnings, and in part from fresh capital furnished by the stockholders and the people who bought the company's bonds.

Moreover, every building and every machine begins to wear out the day it goes into service, and keeping on the conservative side, Goodyear consistently set aside funds (totalling $190 millions by June, 1948) to cover depreciation and amortization, bringing the book value of the property then in use down to $117 millions.

Money put back into the business creates jobs for more men. But in a highly mechanized industry like this one, a lot of money is required. The land, buildings, machines, inventories of raw materials and finished goods, and the other moneys needed to carry on the business averaged $8000 in 1948 for each employee on the payroll.

Working capital is an important requisite in business. Wages, for instance, must be paid every week, and materials paid for within 30 days if the company is to earn its discount (which is a sizable figure on $300 millions worth of material a year), and this money will come back to the treasury only after the goods made from those materials have been sold, which might be several months later. The company must have enough money on hand to finance this during that interim.

Goodyear, twice its prewar size by June, 1948, carried $250 millions in working capital. To provide this, and help pay the $85 millions spent in the three postwar years to modernize and expand its factories, and take up the last of the $36 millions in outstanding bonds, the company made an important change in its financial structure in 1947, issuing $100 million in unsecured promissory notes.

Goodyear stock is not closely held, not concentrated in any small group. There are 45,000 stockholders, living in every state of the Union and in many foreign countries, none of them very large stockholders. They represent the venture capital which started the company, or which came to its aid when it was in trouble, and investment capital as the business got on a solid basis and its securities became a sound investment for people's savings.

The growth of the company has provided jobs paying well over the industry average for 73,000 employees by 1948, 55,000 of them in this country. Their earnings, running at $200 millions as we have seen last year, created additional purchasing power, stimulated the production of every conceivable line of goods, meant cars, home ownership, and the chance of a college education in thousands of families.

As the company reached age 50, it had factories in 16 cities and towns in the United States, counting Akron as one plant, and omitting the government-owned synthetic rubber plant in Houston. It had four in Canada, and 11 in other countries. Some of these were located in great world cities like Buenos Aires, Sydney, Mexico City, Sao Paulo, Los Angeles, Toronto, Havana and Lima. Others were in small towns like Windsor, Vermont, and Buitenzorg, Java.

The 1948 Homecoming, marking the 50th anniversary of the company, took on international character, since it brought in men from every foreign plant and sales office, as well as the men from the American factories and district offices—including more than a hundred men, many with long service, who had never been in the United States before.

The Goodyear story has turned out to be a fairly long narrative. However, 50 years is a long time, and this company has had a wider range of activities than most. In a way it is also a more colorful story than some, since by design or chance it went into a business dealing not primarily with dollars or machines, but with men's daily lives, getting them to and from work, getting their groceries delivered, directly affecting their work on the farm, in the factory, the mines or the woods.

So this becomes a dozen books in one, a book on rubber, on transportation, on industry, on labor, on aeronautics, on merchandising, procurement, research—and must as well show something of the changing business and economic background in which the company carried on its work—a background which any large-scale business house must, to some degree, affect.

Many names are used. That, too, seemed necessary, for business as you get close to it turns out *not* be to something carried on by an intangible, mechanistic corporate entity, but by individuals. Modern industry must have men, hundreds of them, in every strategic spot, men able to analyze a situation and make a decision. If it is not to lose ground at this point and that, but to advance on many fronts, it must have men in every key position who can not only swing their own job, but create a bigger one.

Nor can it select these leaders by favor, any more than the Army can. Too much is at stake. It makes no difference whether they come in from the great technical schools or the "cow" colleges of the midwest, or started in overalls and came up through the ranks, as many here did.

No one can study the ramifications of a big business house like this without becoming profoundly impressed with the importance of man-power—and the opportunities which a successful business brings to the individual who can measure up, and in the doing put his full latent abilities to work.

There are scores of small departments at Goodyear which taken alone would make up a million dollar enterprise. Men must direct these.

And beyond this, industry must have thousands of men at the work bench with a pride of workmanship and the mechanical ability and in-genuity so widely present in American society to solve daily difficulties as they arise.

And so American business, if the Goodyear company is a faithful example, has not only given millions of workmen a better break than those of other countries, offered opportunities to ambitious men, and contributed to rising living standards, but industry has helped make America the greatest commercial and industrial nation on the globe, and by reason of that fact, better able to defend itself against attack.

The story of Goodyear is an unfinished story, and will continue to be as long as people *want things and bestir themselves to get them,* and those wants serve as a stimulus and challenge to business.

Goodyear's fortunes in the next 50 years rest on the shoulders of the young men coming in today, tomorrow and next year. They should know what happened during the first 50 years and why.

Which is the principal reason this book was written.

Wingfoot Clan "extra" opens Homecoming conference;
(below) officials lead march to Seiberling Field—Climer,
Thomas, Litchfield, Leroy, Cameron, Shilts, Tomkinson.

Against a stage background at Goodyear Theatre symbolizing world-wide operations, plant superintendents see 450 millionth tire built by company.

Pageantry marks Homecoming as girls in costumes of all nations greet managing directors from abroad; (below) officials and directors welcome visitors.

Homecomers in wind-up

dyear gymnasium.

List of Goodyear Plants

Akron, Ohio (Plant I)		1898
Bowmanville, Canada	Mechanical goods	1910
Killingly, Connecticut *	Textile mill	1913
Akron, Ohio (Plant II)	Tires, mechanical goods, reclaim	1916
Litchfield Park, Arizona	Cotton plantation (33,000 acres)	1916
Sumatra	First rubber plantation (20,000 acres)	1916
New Toronto, Canada	Tires	1917
Adena, Ohio	Coal mine	1917
Los Angeles, California	Tires, textile mill	1920
New Bedford, Mass.	Cotton mill (bicycle tires after 1945)	1924
St. Hyacinthe, Canada	Textile mill	1926
Cedartown, Georgia	Cotton mill	1926
Sydney, Australia	Tires, industrial rubber goods	1927
Wolverhampton, England	Tires, industrial rubber goods	1927
Sumatra	Second rubber plantation (40,000 acres)	1927
Philippine Islands	Rubber plantation (2500 acres)	1928
Gadsden, Alabama	Tires, soles and heels	1929
Rockmart, Georgia	Cotton mill	1929
Cartersville, Georgia	Cotton mill	1929
Akron Plant III	Warehouse, manufacturing	1929
Buenos Aires, Argentina	Tires, industrial rubber goods	1930
Sumatra	Third rubber plantation (33,000 acres)	1931
Decatur, Alabama	Cotton mill	1933
Buitenzorg, Java	Tires	1934
Panama *	Rubber plantation (2850 acres)	1935
Cumberland, Maryland	Tires (Kelly-Springfield)	1935
Costa Rica	Rubber plantation (2500 acres)	1936
Windsor, Vermont	Soles and heels	1936
Jackson, Michigan	Tires	1937
Sao Paulo, Brazil	Tires, textiles	1938
Norrkoping, Sweden	Tires	1938
St. Marys, Ohio	Molded goods	1939
Goodyear Aircraft	Aircraft, then chemical products	1942
Mexico City, Mexico	Tires, soles and heels, industrials	1942
Akron Research Laboratory		1942

* Discontinued operation.

Lima, Peru	Tires	1943
Muncie, Indiana	Molded goods	1943
Lincoln, Nebraska	Fuel cells, then V-belts	1944
Cali, Colombia	Tires, heels	1945
Topeka, Kansas	Tires	1945
Havana, Cuba	Tires, heels	1946
Port Elizabeth, So. Africa	Tires, industrial rubber goods	1946
Niagara Falls, New York	Chemical products	1947
Quebec City, Canada	Soles and heels, molded goods	1948

. . .

Sales by Years After 1907

1907	$ 2,189,749.49	1929	256,227,067
1908–09	4,277,067.06	1930	204,063,229
1909–10	9,560,144.92	1931	159,199,831
1910–11	13,262,265.63	1932	109,051,758
1911–12	25,232,207.03	1933	109,655,636
1912–13	32,998,827.25	1934	136,800,764
1913–14	31,056,129.31	1935	164,863,974
1914–15	36,490,651.64	1936	185,915,675
1915–16	63,950,399.52	1937	216,174,513
1916–17	111,450,643.74	1938	165,928,944
1917–18	131,347,258.48	1939	200,101,704
1918–19	168,914,982.83	1940	217,540,079
1920 and 1921 *		1941	330,599,674
1922	122,818,947	1942	451,493,034
1923	127,880,082	1943	726,569,275
1924	138,777,719	1944	786,722,287
1925	205,999,829	1945	716,176,748
1926	230,161,356	1946	616,508,162
1927	222,178,540	1947	670,772,647
1928	250,769,209	1948	704,875,941

* During time of reorganization, statements were not published. There were a few interim statements, however.

Chronology of Rubber

1498   Christopher Columbus discovers rubber, "a peculiar elastic substance."

1736   Rubber brought to Europe from Peru by a French surveyor-explorer.

1823   Charles Mackintosh manufactures first waterproof coats in England.

1832   India Rubber Company, Roxbury, Mass., starts manufacture of rubber bottles, mackintoshes and overshoes but these grew hard in winter and soft in summer.

1835   Edwin Chaffee, co-worker of Charles Goodyear, invented the calender, developed rubber mill in following year.

1836   First rubber belting manufactured in the United States.

1839   Charles Goodyear discovers vulcanization.

1856   First American solid rubber tires made by Boston Belting Company.

1870   First solid rubber bicycle tires introduced to British market.
Goodrich, Tew & Co. organized at Akron, making fire hose chiefly.

1872   Westinghouse patents the air brake, employing flexible rubber hose.

1876   Rubber plant seeds taken from Brazil to England by Wickham.

1888   First pneumatic tire built by John Boyd Dunlop of Belfast, Ireland.

1890   North British Rubber Co., Ltd., manufactures first clincher tires.

1892   Several companies combined to form the U. S. Rubber Company.

1893   Single tube bicycle tire (Tillinghast patent) brought out by Col. Albert Pope on the Columbia bicycle. Patent owned by subsidiary of U. S. Rubber Company.

1894   First experimental automobiles built by Duryea, King and Haynes.
Kelly-Springfield Tire Co. started at Springfield, Ohio.
Diamond Rubber Company established.

1895   Dunlop Pneumatic Tyre Co., Ltd., established to make bicycle tires.

1896   First practical carriage tire.

1898   The Goodyear Tire & Rubber Company incorporated August 29.

1899   R. C. Penfield succeeds D. E. Hill as president.

1900   Tillinghast bicycle tire license withdrawn from Goodyear.
P. W. Litchfield joins Goodyear.
Firestone Tire & Rubber Company organized.

1901   Goodyear develops original Straight Side tire, with braided wire bead.
First advertisement featuring Wingfoot trademark.

1902   Capital stock increased to $1,000,000.
G. M. Stadelman joins company as manager of carriage tire sales.

1903   L. C. Miles becomes president.
Silvertown Cord Tyre brought out in England.
Wright brothers make first flight at Kitty Hawk, N. C.

1904   Improved Straight Side, with side rings to make it quickly detachable.

Seiberling-Stevens patent issued for tire building machine.

1905 Goodyear becomes largest manufacturer of carriage tires.
W. D. Shilts joins company.
Five year battle begins between Straight Sides and clinchers.

1906 F. A. Seiberling becomes president. Stadelman and Litchfield directors.
Brazilian rubber pool runs price up to a dollar a pound.
Organic accelerators used by Marks and Oenslager at Diamond.

1907 First taxicab in America.
Goodyear Cord tire for electrics . . . Fisher Body Co. organized.

1908 All-Weather Tread design adopted . . . First large addition to the factory built.
Ford Model T brought out . . . General Motors Corporation formed.
First full-page advertising used by Goodyear in Saturday Evening Post.

1909 Goodyear builds first airplane tire, to replace Wrights' sled runners.
Relief Association organized.

1910 Straight Side tire wins industry battle.
Plant acquired at Bowmanville, Canada.
Labor department started.
Second Brazilian pool runs price of rubber up to $3 a pound.
Improved airplane tire gets immediate acceptance.

1911 Harry N. Atwood sets world's flight record from St. Louis to New York in 11 days, using Goodyear tires.
Rogers makes first transcontinental flight in 84 days with 63 landings.
Earl Ovington uses Goodyear tires in first airmail flight, September 23.
Slusser joins company as stenographer.
C. F. Kettering develops self-starter and car lighting system.

1912 New unit of general office built on Market Street.
Goodyear Heights and Seiberling Field Started.
R. S. Wilson joins company as service man.
Branch office opened in London.
Diamond Rubber Company merged with Goodrich.

1913 Mechanical Goods Department started.
Cotton mill acquired at Killingly, Conn.
Flying Squadron started.

1913 Vacations for factory men . . . Eight-hour day.
Goodyear Cord tire starts new industry war.
First Goodyear conveyor belt.
First specially designed solid tires, the S-V.
I.W.W. strike ties up Akron rubber plants.
Upson and Preston win International Balloon Race.

1914 World War I starts in Europe . . . First kite balloons built for British.

1915 Sales branches opened in Australia and Argentina.
Carbon black comes into rubber processing.
First clock tower.

1916   Goodyear developes pneumatic truck tire.
Plant II built.
Goodyear's first rubber plantation, 20,000 acres, started in Sumatra.
Wingfoot Lake field acquired.
Pension plan started, with insurance for employees.
E. J. Thomas joins company as stenographer.
Cotton plantation started in Arizona.
Goodyear becomes the largest tire company.

1917   New Canadian factory built in Toronto.
Cord tire battle won as Army bans rival cord construction.
Coal mine at Adena, Ohio.
First unit of factory office built on Market Street.
First blimps built for Navy.
First cross-country truck line, Wingfoot Express, Akron to Boston.

1918   Goodyear Heights bus line.
Pontoons for racing balloons, forerunner of "life rafts."
Bayer Company in Germany produced 2500 tons synthetic rubber.

1919   Industrial Assembly started . . . P. E. H. Leroy joins company.

1920   California factory opened.
Goodyear developes bullet-resistant fuel tank for airplanes.
Portable vulcanizer for conveyor belts.
Depression begins in fall.

1921   Reorganization, Seiberlings retire, E. G. Wilmer becomes president.

1922   Captax marketed.
Great Britain enacts Stevenson Act to strengthen rubber prices.

1923   Balloon tire brought out . . . Supertwist fabric developed.
G. M. Stadelman becomes president.

1924   Cotton mill acquired at New Bedford, Mass.
Goodyear acquires Zeppelin patents.
Studies begin into synthetic rubber.
Chrysler Company organized.
Rubber belt, ten miles long, built for Frick Coal Co.

1925   Rubber prices reach peak of $1.23 under Stevenson Act.
Balloon tire adapted to busses.
Dr. Karl Arnstein joins company as airship designer.
Goodyear becomes largest manufacturer of rubber heels.
Pilgrim built as first unit in the airship fleet.
Rim plant starts at Robinson Clay Products building, later Plant III.

1926   Goodyear becomes the largest company in the rubber industry.
G. M. Stadelman dies, P. W. Litchfield becomes president.
Cotton mills at Cedartown, Georgia, and St. Hyacinthe, Quebec.
Van Orman wins James Gordon Bennett Balloon race.
Refinancing effected, returns control to stockholders.

1927 Factories built in Australia and England.
      Hospital Association started.
      Wingfoot plantation started in Sumatra, 40,000 acres.
      Airwheel tire, developed for airplane, is industry milestone.
      Dinsmore takes out first synthetic rubber patent.
      Tire production total reaches 100,000,000.

1928 Rubber plantation of 2500 acres acquired in Philippines.
      Putnam balloon tire patent invalidated.
      Stevenson Act repealed.
      Goodyear given contract to build two rigid airships for the Navy.

1929 Plant III built, world's largest airship dock started.
      Blimp fleet gets under way.
      Tire factory built at Gadsden, Alabama.
      Cotton mill at Rockmart, and Cartersville, Georgia.
      Major depression begins.

1930 First use of Airwheel type tire on farm tractors in Florida.
      New factory completed in Argentina.
      Third rubber plantation, 33,000 acres, acquired in Sumatra.
      Airwheel tires go on Fords and Chevrolets.
      USS Akron completed.

1931 Spot welding developed for aluminum alloy.

1932 Rubber reaches an all-time low of 2⅞ cents a pound.
      Price wars and industrial distress.
      Total Goodyear tire production reaches 200,000,000.
      Hydraulic disc brake developed for airplanes.

1933 National Industrial Relations Act passed.
      USS Macon completed.
      Goodyear resumes synthetic rubber research.
      Cotton mill acquired at Decatur, Alabama.
      Magnesium alloy airplane wheels developed.

1934 Factory started in Java.
      New rubber restriction program adopted in East.
      Research men develop Pliofilm.

1935 LifeGuard tube brought out.
      National Recovery Act unconstitutional.
      Kelly-Springfield purchased.
      Goodyear-built "Explorer II" invades stratosphere to 72,395 feet.
      Rubber plantation in Panama—2850 acres.
      Non-directional tire, forerunner of Army combat tire, developed.

1936 Rubber plantation in Costa Rica—2500 acres.
      Akron rubber strike.
      Goodyear Sure-Grip tire for tractors, a mud-snow, go-anywhere tire.
      Airfoam manufacture starts.
      Sole and heel manufacture moves to Windsor, Vermont.

1937   Goodyear developes satisfactory synthetic rubber, Chemigum, builds
        pilot plant . . . Tire plant built at Jackson, Michigan.
        Marsh Buggy, or amphibious tire developed.

1938   LifeGuard principle adapted to nose wheel of military planes.
        Conveyor belt (a railroad of rubber) at Grand Coulee.

1939   Plant opened at Norrkoping, Sweden.
        Tire and fabric plant at Sao Paulo, Brazil, opened.
        St. Marys plant started.
        Goodyear takes contract to build plane parts for Martin.
        Goodyear Aircraft Corporation formed.
        Statue of Charles Goodyear dedicated, marking centennial of rubber.
        Begin gas mask production for Army.
        Shasta Dam belt.
        Goodyear builds 300,000,000th tire.
        World War II open in Europe.

1940   Goodyear bullet-seal fuel tank for planes adopted as standard.
        Construction starts on $400,000 Chemigum plant.
        E. J. Thomas becomes president, P. W. Litchfield chairman.
        Production under way on barrage balloons and airships.
        Goodyear selected to operate powder loading plant at Charlestown, Ind.
        Aircraft starts work on Grumman, Curtiss and Consolidated parts.

1941   New Bedford reopened as defense plant.
        Plants B and C started at Aircraft. Contract for Martin B-26 wings.
        Arizona Aircraft plant started . . . New factory in Mexico opened.
        Navy orders 21 more airships . . . Pearl Harbor, December 7.

1942   Rubber growing areas taken by Japs.
        Jackson changes over to produce guns, Kelly shells and bullets.
        Corsair contract. Plant D started.

1943   Plant opens in Peru.
        Aircraft starts work on B-29 contract.
        First M-type airship flown.
        Total tire production reaches 300,000,000 mark.

1944   Plant acquired at Lincoln, Nebraska, for fuel tank manufacture.
        Neolite developed.

1945   Production starts in Topeka, Kansas, Colombia and Venezuela.
        End of World War II.
        Chemical products work started.

1946   Total production reaches 400,000,000 tires.
        Plant in Cuba.

1947   Goodyear perfects cross-wind landing gear for planes.
        South African plant opened.
        Java plant reopened.

1948   St. Malo, Quebec, plant.
        Homecoming marks Goodyear's 50th birthday.

INDEX

Adena mine, (see Coal Mine).
Advertising, 649 et seq; Saturday Evening Post, etc., 24, 27, 39, 314, 317; radio, 649, 650; agencies, 651.
Air bottle, 314.
Airfoam, ("sponge rubber"), 144, 261, 663; in war, 458; Canada, 595.
Airplanes, tires, (see Tires); wheels and brakes, (see Wheels and Brakes); Corsairs 508.
Airships, Non-Rigid, 284; Pony blimp, 121, 290; Volunteer, 122; in War I, 48, 269; C-5, 273; Goodyear fleet, 289 et seq; Defender, 289, 291; K-type, 289; Pilgrim, 290; Puritan, 291; Navy use in War II, 434, 512 et seq; Ranger, as privateer, 513; M-type, 516; in Mediterranean, 520; N-type, 672.
Airships, Rigid, 284, 297 et seq; German, 298, 300, 308; in War I, 269; Shenandoah, 284, 298; Akron and Macon, 298, 300 et seq, 306, 307; Los Angeles, 290, 299; air plane pick ups, 306; Durand committee, 306; in postwar commerce, 672 et seq.
Airships, Semi-Rigid, 284; Roma, 287, 297; RS 1, 287.
Akron, airship, (see Airships, Rigid).
All-Weather tread, (see Tires).
Aluminum Co. of America, 306.
American Federation of Labor, 364, 564.
American Institute for Foreign Trade, 682.
Americanization classes, 187.
Apprentice Farmers, 159.
Apprentice Machinists, (see Squadron).
Archwood Avenue Laboratory, 664.
Argentina plant, 403; in war, 610 et seq; reclaiming plant, 612.
Arizona, cotton ranch, 149 et seq; in War II, 568.
Army-Navy "E" Award, 499, 548, 562, 632.
Arnstein, Dr. Karl, 299, 506, 508.
Assault boats, for Marine Corps, 463.
Australian plant, 398 et seq; war story, 628 et seq; industrial rubber goods, 630.

Bag-loading plant, (see Charlestown, Ind.).
Baker, Newton D., 69.
Baldwin, Frank, 470.
Balloons, observation or kite, 48; racing, 268, 274; stratosphere, 280-2; in World War II, 458 et seq; barrage, 464, 567.
Banbury, F. H., mills, 44, 64, 362.
Barber, Ohio C., 18, 106.
Barrage balloons, (see Balloons).
Baruch Committee, 446.
Bases, Navy, 291, 306, 512.
"Beadlock", (see Tires, combat).
Bell, Clarence, 528.
Belting, Transmission, 246; Compass, 246;

V-belts, 246, 567, 570; conveyor, 248; Frick mine, 249: Shasta and Grand Coulee Dams, 250; Anderson Ranch Dam, 253; Mesabi Range, 254.
Berkinshaw, R. C., 589, 594.
Blandin, J. J., 130.
Blimps, (see Airships, Non-Rigid).
Blue Streak racing tire, (see Tires, Motor-cycle).
Blythe, H. E., 122, 200, 326, 330, 508, 669.
Boedeker, A. E., 651.
Boeing Aircraft Company, 454, 486.
Bogardus, R. B., 430.
Bogie tires for tanks, 424, 451, 591.
Bowmanville, (see Canadian plants).
Boy Scouts, 172; in Canada, 597.
Branch offices, 320 et seq.
Brannigan, Charles, 200, 292, 296.
Brazil, rubber pool, 32, 84; rubber in War II, 429 et seq; war production, 615 et seq; cotton mill, 616, Sao Paulo plant, 616.
Brewster Aeronautical Corporation, 522.
Brook, C. H., 61.
Bud-grafting, 137.
Buick Motors, 315, 316, 319, 321.
Bullet-seal fuel tanks, (see Fuel Tanks).
Buna-type rubber, (see Rubber, Synthetic).
Burke, E. S., 359, 550.
Burr, D. R., 396.
Butadiene, (see Rubber, Synthetic).
Butyl rubber, 446.

C-5, (see Airships, Non-Rigid).
CIO, 365, 564.
Cadillac Motor Car Co., 319, 321.
California plant, 117 et seq; cotton mill, 351; in War II, 565 et seq.
Cameron, A. G., 320, 390, 394, 680.
Campbell, General L. H., Jr., 534.
Canadian plants, 49, 111 et seq, 390; Bowmanville, 114, in war, 591; Toronto, 116; labor relations, 382; war story, 587 et seq; synthetic rubber, 594; Airfoam and Plio-film, 595; St. Malo, Quebec, 596.
Capital stock, original, 54; refinancing, in 1921, 56; 1926, 68; 1936, 78; in 1938, 79, post war 688.
Captax, (see Compounds).
Carbon black, 64, 101, 362.
Carlisle, C. H., 112, 130, 589.
Carriage tires, (see Tires).
Carroll, H. J., 61, 212.
Carter, F. J., 192, 619.
Cartersville mill, (see Cotton mills).
Cedartown mill, (see Cotton Mills).
Central American Rubber plantations, (see Plantations).
Ceylon, (see Rubber, Wild).